The Business of Tourism

The Business of Tourism

FIFTH EDITION

J Christopher Holloway

LONGMAN

Pearson Education Limited
Edinburgh Gate
Harlow, Essex CM20 2JE, England
and Associated Companies throughout the world.
Published in the United States of America by Addison Wesley
Longman Publishing, New York

First published 1983
Second Edition 1985
Third Edition 1989
Fourth Edition 1994
Fifth Edition 1998
Reprinted 1999

ISBN 0 582 32881-0

Visit Addison Wesley Longman on the worldwide web at
http://www.pearsoneduc.com

British Library Cataloguing-in-Publication Data

A catalogue record for this book is available from the British
Library.

Set by 3 in Sabon and News Gothic
Produced by Pearson Education Asia (Pte) Ltd.
Printed in Singapore (COS)

Contents

Preface to the Fifth Edition

In the preface to the fourth edition of *The Business of Tourism*, published in 1994, I wrote of the enormous changes occurring in tourism generally, in the tourism industry and in tourism education since publication of the first edition a decade earlier. The pace of this change has, if anything, intensified over the past four years, necessitating further substantial rewriting for this fifth edition.

It is always a challenge to prepare a text for a subject which has to provide a set of underlying principles coupled with contemporary examples drawn from real-life industry experience, while at the same time ensuring that the material will not date too rapidly. A new challenge now emerges in attempting to ensure that the text is distinguishable from the numerous other texts on tourism which appear almost weekly on the market. When *The Business of Tourism* first appeared, it was virtually unique as a basic introductory text dealing with the subject of tourism for practitioners or those entering higher education. Today it would be possible to identify upwards of a dozen basic texts in the subject, aiming by and large to satisfy the same market. Yet this text remains, I am happy to say, the most popular in the country as introductory reading for BTEC and degree level students, while sales abroad are rapidly approaching those in Britain and translations have been made into Spanish, Polish and Slovakian since the last edition appeared.

On the principle, 'if it ain't broke don't fix it', and after a survey carried out by the publishers which has established that the format is popular without fundamental changes, the structure of this fifth edition appears very similar to that of its predecessor. However, this new edition does represent a very thorough rewrite, reflecting the changes that have occurred in tourism and the industry in the past four years. I have not tried to tamper with the underlying format apart from some minor cosmetic changes which have been suggested by some lecturers. Specifically, greater emphasis is placed on sustainable tourism, which has become an issue of growing importance. I have also attempted to give a slightly stronger emphasis to international, and particularly to European, issues and examples throughout the text, recognising that this is valuable not only for those overseas who will be reading the text, but also for those teaching tourism in the UK who are facing up to the need to internationalise their curricula to meet their students' needs and employers' expectations. I have also expanded substantially on the chapter devoted to visitor attractions and their management, an area which I feel has still not been sufficiently addressed in other texts and which represents a sector in which many students will aspire to find employment.

Nevertheless, the book's perspective remains essentially British, for which I do not apologise. The aim of this text has always been predominantly to serve the needs of students aiming to gain a thorough introductory overview of how the tourism industry in the UK and its component parts operate and interact, and how external forces moderate and influence the industry in its activities in Britain and abroad.

No one book can provide a solid grounding in all the aspects of travel and tourism, and I welcome the many specialist texts which are now appearing on the market to support this introductory text; not merely those detailing the operations of the various sectors of the industry, but also the growing numbers which examine tourism, for example, through systems theory and organisational analysis, or from a historical, geographical or anthropological perspective. Tourism cannot, in my opinion, be justified as a discipline in itself, but there are grounds for believing that the subject has now come of age as an applied multidisciplinary field of academic study. A body of knowledge exists which both academics and employers recognise as an essential grounding for the study of tourism for vocational purposes, and while my own view is that this is best allied to the study of business and management if a career is sought in the industry, a variety of approaches can also be considered appropriate for those contemplating a career in specific areas such as tourism planning, while a broad understanding of tourism is relevant for careers in many other fields, including leisure and hospitality management. The subject is also one which, because of its unique characteristics, many students of humanities may wish to follow as an option, as a topic of intrinsic interest. This book is therefore designed to give all such students an insight into the possibilities engendered by the study of tourism, not only the largest, but also the most fascinating, of industries.

As ever, a number of people have aided me in the factual evidence presented in this edition, and I am grateful in particular to Neil Taylor, Managing Director of Regent Holidays, and to Beulah Cope, Senior Lecturer in Tourism Management at Bristol Business School, for their contributions.

List of Abbreviations

AA	Automobile Association
ABTA	Association of British Travel Agents
ABTAC	Association of British Travel Agents' Certificate
ACD	Automatic Call Distribution
AIEST	Alliance Internationale d'Experts Scientifiques de Tourisme
AIT	Air Inclusive Tour
AITO	Association of Independent Tour Operators
APEX	Advance Passenger Excursion Fare
ARTAC	Association of Retail Travel Agents' Consortia
ASTA	American Society of Travel Agents
ATB	Automated Ticketing and Boarding pass
ATC	Air Traffic Control
ATOL	Air Transport Operator's Licence
ATTF	Air Travel Trust Fund
ATTT	Association of Tourism Teachers and Trainers (formerly ATT Association of Teachers of Tourism)
ATUC	Air Transport Users' Council
AVE	Alta Velocidad Espagnola (Spanish high-speed train)
BA	British Airways
BAA	Organisation operating airports, now privatised, formerly publicly-owned British Airports Authority
BABA	Book a bed ahead
B&B	Bed and breakfast
BEA	British European Airways, later merged with BOAC to form British Airways
BHA	British Hospitality Association
BHTS	British Home Tourism Survey
BITOA	British Incoming Tour Operators' Association
BITS	Bureau International de Tourisme Sociale
BNTS	British National Travel Survey
BOAC	British Overseas Airways Corporation, later merged with BEA to form British Airways
BTA	British Tourist Authority
BTEC	Business and Technology Education Council
BTS-M	British Tourism Survey Monthly
BTS-Y	British Tourism Survey Yearly

CAA	Civil Aviation Authority
CAB	Civil Aeronautics Board (USA)
CBI	Confederation of British Industry
CGLI	City and Guilds of London Institute
CIM	Chartered Institute of Marketing
CIMTIG	Chartered Institute of Marketing Travel Industry Group
CIT	Chartered Institute of Transport
CN	Canadian National
COTAC	Certificate of Travel Agency Competence
COTAM	Certificate of Travel Agency Management
COTICC	Certificate of Tourist Information Centre Competence
COTOP	Certificate of Tour Operating Practice
CRN	Countryside Recreation Network
CRS	Computer Reservations System
CTC	Certified Travel Counsellor
CTT	Council for Travel and Tourism
EC	European Commission
ETB	English Tourist Board
ETC	European Travel Commission
ETNA	English Tourist Network Automation
EU	European Union
FTO	Federation of Tour Operators
GDP	Gross Domestic Product
GDS	Global Distribution System
GIT	Group Inclusive Tour-basing fare
HCIMA	Hotel, Catering and Institutional Management Association
IAE	International Aero Engines
IATA	International Air Transport Association
ICAO	International Civil Aviation Organisation
IFAPA	International Foundation of Airline Passenger Associations
IFTO	International Federation of Tour Operators
II	Interval International
IIT	Independent Inclusive Tour
ILG	International Leisure Group
IPS	International Passenger Survey
IT	Inclusive Tour, also Information Technology
ITS	International Tourist Services
ITT	Institute of Travel and Tourism
ITX	Inclusive tour-basing excursion fare
IUOTO	International Union of Official Tourist Organisations (later WTO)
LCR	London and Continental Railway
LTT	Lufttransport-Unternehmen Touristik
LTU	Lufttransport-Unternehmen

MOMA	Museum of Modern Art, New York
MMC	Monopolies and Mergers Commission
MTAA	Multiple Travel Agents' Association
MTOW	Maximum take-off weight
NAITA	National Association of Independent Travel Agents
NBC	National Bus Company
NCVQ	National Council for Vocational Qualifications
NTB	National Tourist Board. Also the former National Training Board of ABTA
NUR	Neckermann und Reisen
NVQ	National Vocational Qualifications
OECD	Organisation for Economic Co-operation and Development
PATA	Pacific Area Travel Association
P&O	Peninsular and Oriental Steam Navigation Company
RAC	Royal Automobile Club
RCI	Resort Condominiums International
RTB	Regional tourist board
SAS	Scandinavian Airlines System
SNAT	Societé Nouvelle d'Armement Transmanche
SNCF	Societé National de Chemins de Fer
SOLAS	Safety of Life at Sea
SPR	Size to passenger ratio
SSSI	Site of Special Scientific Interest
STB	Scottish Tourist Board
STOL	Short take-off and landing
TAC	Travel Agents' Council
TDAP	Tourism Development Action Plan
TGV	Train à Grande Vitesse
TIC	Tourist Information Centre
TIM	Tourism Income Multiplier
TIP	Tourist Information Point
TIQ	Tourism Intelligence Quarterly
TOC	Tour Operators' Council
TOMS	Tour Operators' Margin Scheme
TOP	Thomson Holidays' computer reservations system
TOSG	Tour Operators' Study Group
TRIPS	Tourism Resource Information Processing System
TTC	The Travel Training Company
TUI	Touristik Union International
TWA	Trans World Airlines
UATP	Universal Air Travel Plan
UBR	Uniform Business Rate
UKTS	United Kingdom Tourism Survey

UN	United Nations
UNESCO	United Nations Educational, Scientific and Cultural Organisation
VAT	Value Added Tax
VFR	Visiting Friends and Relatives
VTOL	Vertical take-off and landing
WISE	Wing-in-surface effect
WPC	Wave-piercing catamaran
WTB	Wales Tourist Board
WTO	World Tourism Organisation
WTTC	World Travel and Tourism Council

1

An Introduction to Tourism

OBJECTIVES

After studying this chapter, you should be able to:

- define what is meant by tourism, both conceptually and technically, and distinguish it from travel, leisure and recreation;
- identify the characteristics of the tourism product;
- list the various forms of tourist destination, identifying the attraction of each;
- explain why destinations are subject to changing fortunes.

Defining tourism

In a book dealing with tourism, it is sensible to begin by trying to define exactly what we mean by the term, before we go on to examine the different forms which tourism can take. In fact, the task of defining tourism is not nearly as easy as it may appear.

While it is relatively easy to agree on technical definitions of particular categories of tourism or tourist, the wider concept is ill-defined. Firstly, it is important to recognise that tourism is just one form of recreation, along with sports activities, hobbies and pastimes, and that all of these activities are discretionary uses of our leisure time. Tourism usually involves some expenditure, although this is not *necessarily* the case: someone cycling or hiking in the countryside on a camping weekend in which they carry their own food may contribute nothing to the economy of the region. Many other examples could be cited in which tourism expenditure is minimal. We can say, then, that tourism is one aspect of leisure which usually, but not invariably, involves some expenditure by the participant.

Tourism may be further defined as the movement of people away from their normal place of residence. Here we find our first problem. Should shoppers travelling from, say, Bristol to Bath, a distance of twelve miles, be considered tourists? And is it the *purpose* or the *distance* which is the determining factor? Just how far do people have to travel before they can be counted as tourists for the purpose of official records? Clearly, our definition must be specific. In the United States, the National Resources Review Commission established in 1973 that a domestic tourist would be 'one who travels at least fifty miles (one way)', and this was confirmed by the US Census Bureau, which defended tourism eleven years later as a round trip of at least one hundred miles. However, the Canadian government defines it as a journey of at least twenty-five miles from the boundaries of the tourist's home community, while the English Tourism Council has used a distance of twenty miles and at least three hours' journey time to define leisure away from the home; so consistency has by no means yet been achieved.

One of the first attempts to define tourism was that of Professors Hunziker and Krapf of Berne University, in 1942. They held that tourism should be defined as 'the sum of the phenomena and relationships arising from the travel and stay of non-residents, in so far as they do not lead to permanent residence and are not connected to any earning activity'. This definition helps to distinguish tourism from migration, but it makes the assumption that both *travel* and *stay* are necessary for tourism, thus precluding day tours. It would also appear to exclude business travel, which is connected with earnings, even if that income is not earned in the destination country. Moreover, distinguishing between business and leisure tourism is extremely difficult, since most business trips will combine elements of leisure activity.

In 1937, the League of Nations recommended adopting the definition of a 'tourist' as one who travels for a period of at least 24 hours in a country other than that in which he usually resides. This was held to include persons travelling for pleasure, domestic reasons or health, persons travelling to meetings or otherwise on business, and persons visiting a country on a cruise vessel (even if for less than twenty-four hours). The principal weakness in this definition is that it ignores the movement of domestic tourists. Later, the United Nations Conference on International Travel and Tourism, held in 1963, considered recommendations put forward by the IUOTO (now the World Tourism Organisation), and agreed to use the term 'visitor' to describe 'any person visiting a country other than that in which he has his usual place of residence, for any reason other than following an occupation remunerated from within the country visited'. This definition was to cover two classes of visitor:

(a) Tourists, who were classified as temporary visitors staying at least 24 hours, whose purpose could be categorised as leisure (whether for recreation, health, sport, holiday, study or religion), or business, family, mission or meeting;
(b) Excursionists, who were classed as temporary visitors staying less than twenty-four hours, including cruise travellers but excluding travellers in transit.

TOWARDS AN AGREED DEFINITION

Once again, these definitions fail to take into account the domestic tourist. The inclusion of 'study' in this definition is an interesting one, since it is often excluded in later definitions, as are longer courses of education.

A working party for the proposed Institute of Tourism in Britain (which later became the Tourism Society) attempted to clarify the issue, and reported in 1976: 'Tourism is the temporary short-term movement of people to destinations outside the places where they normally live and work, and activities during their stay at these destinations; it includes movement for all purposes, as well as day visits or excursions.' This broader definition was reformulated slightly, without losing any of its simplicity, at the International Conference on Leisure–Recreation–Tourism, organised by the AIEST and the Tourism Society in Cardiff in 1981: 'Tourism may be defined in terms of particular activities selected by choice and undertaken outside the home environment. Tourism may or may not involve overnight stay away from home.'

Finally, the following definition devised by the World Tourism Organisation (WTO) was endorsed by the UN Statistical Commission in 1993 following an International Government Conference held in Ottawa, Canada in 1991:

> Tourism comprises the activities of persons travelling to and staying in places outside their usual environment for not more than one consecutive year for leisure, business or other purposes.

The above definitions have been quoted at length because they reveal how broadly the concept of tourism must be defined in order to embrace all forms of the phenomenon. Indeed, the final definition could be criticised on the grounds that, unless the activities are more clearly specified, it could equally be applied to someone involved in burglary! With this definition, we are offered neither guidance on activities undertaken, nor distance to be travelled. In fact, with the growth of second home owners, who in some cases spend considerable periods of time away from their main homes, and timeshare owners, it could be argued that a tourist is no longer necessarily 'outside the home environment'.

Figure 1.1 illustrates the guidelines produced by the WTO to classify travellers for statistical

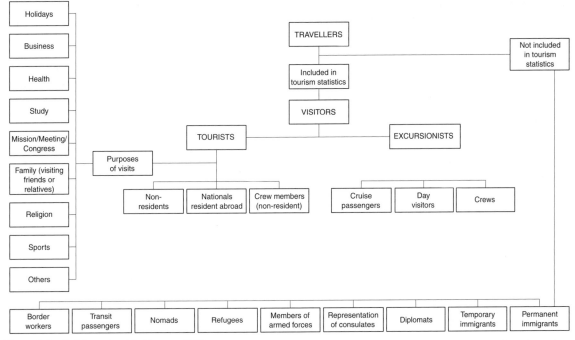

Figure 1.1 Defining a tourist. *(Source: WTO)*

purposes. Some loopholes in the definitions remain, however. Even attempts to classify tourists as those travelling for purposes unconnected with employment can be misleading if one looks at the social consequences of tourism. Ruth Pape has drawn attention to the case of nurses in the United States who, after qualifying, gravitate to California for their first jobs, since employment has been easy to find and they can thus enjoy the benefits of the sunshine and leisure pursuits for which the state is famous. They may spend a year or more in this job before moving on, but the important point is that they have been motivated to come to that area not because of the work itself, but because of the area's touristic attractions. Many other examples could be given of young people working their way around the world (a kind of twentieth-century Grand Tour?), or of workers seeking summer jobs in seaside resorts.

We must also consider the case of pensioners who choose to retire abroad in order to benefit from the lower costs of living in other countries. Many Britons have moved to southern Spain after retirement, while Americans have moved to Mexico; they may still retain their homes in their country of origin, but spend a large part of the year abroad. Canadians, known as 'snowbirds' because of their migrant behaviour, also come down in their mobile trailers to the sunshine states of the US West during the winter months, to escape the harsh winters of Canada. Once again, the motives of all of these people are not simply to lower their costs of living, but also to enjoy an improved climate and those facilities which attract tourists to the same destinations.

Conceptually, then, to define tourism precisely is an all but impossible task. To produce a technical definition for statistical reasons is less problematic. As long as it is clear what the data comprise, and one compares like with like, whether interregionally or internationally, we can leave the conceptual discussion to the academics. With the advent of twentieth-century mass tourism, perhaps the most accurate definition of a tourist is 'someone who travels to see something different, and then complains when he finds things are not the same'!

Figure 1.2 The World Travel Market, London – marketing the tourist product. *(Photographed by the author)*

The tourist product

Having attempted a definition of the tourist, we can look at the tourist product itself. The first characteristic to note is that this is a service rather than a tangible good. The intangibility poses particular difficulties for those whose job it is to market tourism. It cannot, for example, be inspected by prospective purchasers before they buy, as can a washing machine, a hi-fi or other consumer durable. The purchase of a package tour is a speculative investment, involving a high degree of trust on the part of the purchaser, the more so since holidays are one of the most expensive purchases made in the year.

It has often been said that 'selling holidays is like selling dreams', and this is to a great extent true. When tourists buy a package tour abroad, they are buying more than a simple collection of services, such as an airline seat, hotel room, three meals a day and the opportunity to sit on a sunny beach; they are also buying the temporary use of a strange environment, incorporating novel geographical features – old-world towns, tropical landscapes – plus the culture and heritage of the region and other intangible benefits such as service, atmosphere, hospitality. The planning and anticipation of the holiday may be as much a part of its enjoyment as is the trip itself; recalling the experience later, and reviewing slides, videos or photos are further extensions of the experience. These are all part of the product, which is therefore a psychological as well as a physical experience.

The challenge for the marketer of tourism is to turn the dream into the reality. The difficulty of achieving this is that tourism is not a homogeneous product; that is, it tends to vary in standard and quality over time and under different circumstances, unlike, say, a television set. A package tour, or even a flight on an aircraft, cannot be consistently uniform; a bumpy flight, or a long technical flight delay, can change an enjoyable experience into a nightmare, and a holiday at the seaside will be ruined by a prolonged rainy spell. Because a tour comprises a compendium of different products, an added difficulty in maintaining standards is that each element of the product should be broadly similar in quality. A good room and fine service at a hotel may be spoilt by poor food, or the flight may mar an otherwise enjoyable hotel stay. An element of chance is always present in the purchase of any service, and where the purchase must precede the actual consumption of the product, as with tourism, the risk for the consumer is increased.

Another characteristic of tourism is that it cannot be brought to the consumer; rather, the consumer must be brought to the product. In the short term, at least, the supply of this product is fixed; the number of hotel bedrooms available at a particular destination cannot be varied to meet the changing demands of holidaymakers during the season. The unsold hotel room or aircraft seat cannot be stored for later sale, as is the case with tangible products, but is lost forever. Hence the great efforts that must be made by those in the industry to fill empty seats or rooms by last-minute discounting or other techniques. If market demand changes, as it does frequently in the business of tourism, the supply will take time to adapt. A hotel is built to last for many years, and must remain profitable over that period. These are all problems unique to tourism, and call for considerable marketing ingenuity on the part of those in the business.

The nature of a tour

To analyse the topic of tourism systematically, it will be helpful at this point to examine more closely the characteristics of a tour under five broad categories.

THE MOTIVATION FOR TOURING

Motivation identifies firstly the purposes of a visit. There are three broad categories of purpose, these being:

1 holidays (including visits to friends and relatives, known as VFR travel)

2 business (including meetings, conferences, etc.)
3 other (to include study, religious pilgrimages, health, etc.).

It is important to distinguish between each purpose of visit, because the characteristics of each will differ. Business travel will differ from holiday travel, in that the businessperson has little discretion in their choice of destination or the timing of their trip. Business trips frequently have to be arranged at short notice, and for specific and brief periods of time. Business travellers need the convenience of frequent, regular transport, efficient service and good facilities at the destination. Because the company will be paying for all the travel arrangements, the individual traveller will be less concerned about the cost of travel than if they were paying themselves. Higher prices are unlikely seriously to deter travel, nor will lower prices encourage more frequent travel. We can say, therefore, that business travel is relatively *price inelastic*. Holiday travel, however, is highly *price elastic*; lower prices will encourage an increase in the number of travellers generally, and will encourage others to switch their destinations. Leisure travellers will be prepared to delay their travel, or will book well in advance of their travel dates, if this means that they can substantially reduce their costs.

We therefore need to identify the reasons why a specific type of holiday or resort is chosen. Different people will look for different qualities in the same destination; a ski resort, for example, may be selected because of its excellent slopes and sporting facilities, because of its healthy mountain air, or because of the social life which it offers to skiers and non-skiers alike.

THE CHARACTERISTICS OF THE TOUR

These define what kind of visit is made and to where. First, one can distinguish between *domestic* tourism and *international* tourism. The former refers to travel exclusively within the national boundaries of the traveller's country. The decision to take one's holidays within the borders of one's own country is an important one economically, since it will affect the balance of payments, and reduce the outflow of money from that country.

Next, what kind of destination is being chosen? Will travel be to a seaside resort, a mountain resort, a country town, a health spa, or a major city? Is it to be a single-centre visit, a multicentre one (involving a stopover at two or more places) or a tour which will involve extensive travel with brief overnight stays along the route? Or will a cruise be taken, in which case statisticians have to decide whether to count this as international travel if the vessel visits foreign ports.

Next, what length of time is being spent on the trip? A visit that does not involve an overnight stay is known, as we saw earlier, as an excursion, or is frequently referred to as a 'day trip'. Expenditure by day trippers is generally less than that of overnight visitors, and statistical data on these forms of tourism are often collected separately. A visitor who stops at least one night at a destination is termed a 'tourist', but can, of course, make day trips to other destinations; these could even involve an international trip. For instance, a visitor staying in Rhodes may take a trip for the day by boat to the Turkish mainland. For the purposes of Turkey's records, that visitor will be recorded as an excursionist.

Finally, for the purpose of accurate record-keeping, some maximum length of time must be established, beyond which the visitor can no longer be looked upon as a tourist. There are different approaches here, some using a low figure of three months, others six months and in some cases a full year is viewed as the maximum period.

MODE OF TOUR ORGANISATION

This further refines the form which the travel takes. A tour may be *independent* or *packaged*. A package tour, for which the official term is 'inclusive tour', or IT, is an arrangement in which transport and accommodation are purchased by the tourist at an all-inclusive price. The price of the individual elements of the tour cannot normally be determined by the purchaser. The tour operator which puts together the package will buy transport and accommodation in advance, generally at a lower price because the products are being bought in bulk, and the tours are then sold individually to holidaymakers, either direct or through travel agents. Agents and operators can also package independent tours, or even tailor-made tours, by taking advantage of special net fares and building the package around the specific needs of a client.

THE COMPOSITION OF THE TOUR

This consists of the elements comprising the visit. All tourism involves travel away from one's usual place of abode, as we have seen, and in the case of 'tourists', as opposed to 'excursionists' it will include accommodation. So we must here identify the form of travel – air, sea, road or rail – that is to be used. If air transport is involved, will this be by charter aircraft, or a scheduled flight? If an overnight stay, will this be in a hotel, guesthouse, campsite or self-catering facility? How will the passenger travel between airport and hotel – by coach, private taxi or airport limousine? A package tour will normally comprise transport, accommodation and transfers, but in some cases additional services will be provided in the programme, such as car hire at the destination, excursions by coach or theatre entertainment.

THE CHARACTERISTICS OF THE TOURIST

An analysis of tourism must also include an analysis of the tourist. We have already distinguished between the holidaymaker and the business traveller. Now we must identify the tourist in terms of their nationality, social class, sex, age and lifestyle. What stage of their life cycle are they in? What type of personality do they have?

Such information is valuable not only for the purpose of record-keeping; it will also help to shed light on the reasons why people travel and how patterns of travel differ between different groups of people. Research is now focusing much more intently on personality and lifestyle as characteristics in determining the choice of holidays, rather than looking simply at social class and occupation. The more that is known about such details, the more effectively can those in the industry produce the products that will meet the needs of their customers, and develop the appropriate strategies to bring the products to the attention of their customers.

The tourist destination

We can now examine the tourist destination itself. This is quite a complex topic, as a destination can be a particular resort or town, a region within a country, the whole of a country or even a larger area of the globe: for example, a package tour may embrace three separate countries of South America. In some cases the destination can be highly precise, as in the case of a resort hotel which provides a range of leisure facilities on site. In such cases, it may be the tourist's objective to visit the hotel purely and simply because of the facilities it provides, and the entire stay will be taken up with enjoying these facilities alone – this is a characteristic which is commonly found among certain resort hotels in the USA.

However, all destinations share certain characteristics; their success in attracting tourists will depend upon the quality of three essential benefits that they offer the tourist: attractions; amenities (or facilities); and accessibility, or ease of getting to the destination. These benefits will be discussed shortly. Here, we will first look in more detail at the nature of the destination itself.

VARIETIES OF DESTINATION

Destinations are of two kinds: they may be either 'natural' or 'man-made'. Most are 'managed' to some extent, whether they are natural or man-made; national parks, for example, are left in their natural state of beauty as far as possible, but nevertheless have to be managed, through the provision of access, parking facilities, limited accommodation, litter bins, etc.

The type of tourist destination with which we are most familiar is the *seaside resort*. The attraction of the seaside is the combination of sun, sand and sea which still appeals to the largest segment of the tourist market, either as a form of passive recreation – lying in a deckchair or on the sand and watching the sea – or a more active pastime, including swimming and other watersports, beach games, and the like. The most significant shift in the movement of tourists in the past thirty years has been that of the northern Europeans away from their own beaches to the Mediterranean beaches, as prices for air transport fell and the

Figure 1.3 Traditional tourism: sun, sea and sand. *(Courtesy Thomson Holidays)*

tourists could be assured of sunshine – something that was always a gamble when holidaying in northern Europe. Similarly, lower fares have enabled the Americans to fly to their warmer beaches in Florida or California, or even further afield to the Caribbean, abandoning the traditional northern beaches of resorts such as Atlantic City, New Jersey or the Long Island beaches of New York State.

Some seaside resorts that are not blessed with guaranteed sunshine have nevertheless managed to retain a substantial share of the remaining market for domestic holidays, with top resorts in Britain drawing over a million visitors a year, particularly the more conservative tourists who tend to be in the older age brackets. Resorts such as Blackpool, Torquay, Scarborough, Brighton, Newquay and Bournemouth have continued to attract tourists by a process of continual investment and updating of their attractions; for example, by providing more all-weather facilities, and conference centres to attract business visitors all year round. Some have also been successful by promoting the resort as a base from which to explore the surrounding countryside, rather than as a static holiday resort – important, when one realises that most tourists arrive at the seaside in their own cars today.

A second category of destination is the *town* or *city*. Urban tourism has grown steadily in recent years, fuelled by a growing interest in cultural activities such as visits to theatres, museums and art galleries, as well as interest in historical architecture and in the opportunity to undertake shopping expeditions. Britain is well placed to attract large numbers of tourists, both domestic and overseas, to these destinations, as it has a plentiful stock of towns of both architectural and historic importance. Capital cities, including of course London, have long exercised a particular draw for the tourist, and the recent growth in short-break holidays of one to three nights has fully capitalised on opportunities to visit Europe's premier cities.

As with all resorts, the urban resort with an established reputation and image attracts the tourist more readily than those towns which have no clear image. Cities like London, Paris, Rome, Venice and Amsterdam all have clearly recognised images – although it is interesting to note that in the early 1990s the London Tourist Board expressed concern that Japanese tourists were diverting to Paris rather than London; the reason was that among Japanese visitors the female tourists are in a majority, and they perceive Paris as being gentler and more feminine. Such is the power of the image to influence tourist choice.

More recently, cities such as Glasgow and Barcelona have also succeeded in creating an image of a city with many attractions to offer the visitor. Some cities, however, suffer from a lack of a clearly defined centre to provide the focus of a visit. Los Angeles, Moscow and Tokyo all have this disadvantage, which reduces their appeal to the independent traveller.

Many cities benefit from having a waterfront, or watersite, often part of a defunct working harbour. Only recently has the tourist potential of these sites been recognised and what was formerly a decaying port transformed into an area of recreation for residents and visitors alike. An outstanding example of this is the Inner Harbour of Baltimore, USA (see Chapter 11, Figure 11.2a), which, through a combination of private and public investment, has become a magnet for tourists due to the wide variety of attractions that have been developed along the harbourfront. In Australia, Sydney's Darling Harbour has similarly benefited from renewal as a leisure and marine site, while in the UK more than a dozen water-

Figure 1.4 Quintessential England: Robin Hood's Bay. *(Photographed by the author)*

fronts have been renovated, while retaining the many attractive warehouses and other features of their former port status. London's Docklands, the Albert Dock area of Liverpool (site of the Tate Gallery's first provincial art gallery), Southampton's Ocean Village development and Bristol's Historic Floating Harbour have all taken on a new lease of life as areas of leisure as well as commercial activity.

Thirdly, *the countryside* offers a very wide range of attractions to the tourist. The natural beauty of the country is a draw which was first recognised in the romantic era of the nineteenth century, but the desire to get away from the congestion of big cities has led to renewed interest in the tranquillity of the natural landscape in the second half of the twentieth century.

Mountains have strong appeal to the tourist, and offer the benefits of year-round tourism; in summer for walks and simply to admire the beauty of the peaks, and in winter, for winter sports. The Alps and Dolomites in Europe and the Rocky Mountains in North America draw millions of tourists each year. Similarly, lakes, rivers and canals – the latter form of watersite coming into favour for leisure boating – all provide opportunities for relaxation and leisure activities in addition to their natural beauty.

The lakes of Sweden, Finland, and Britain's own Lake District or the Norfolk Broads have all been well exploited for tourism. Some areas, such as the Norwegian Fjord country or Switzerland, are fortunate enough to have a combination of lakes and mountains to offer the visitor, giving them a unique appeal. Other natural draws include safari parks (especially in East and South Africa), wilderness areas like the great national parks of North America, and the more tranquil, undulating scenery of the English countryside, which, with its combination of pleasantly winding country lanes and small, picturesque villages, is the ideal basis for a touring holiday by car or coach. Some regions of the world offer natural spectacles of immense significance for tourism, such as Niagara Falls, on the US–Canada border, or the Grand Canyon in America's West.

All of these destinations can suffer from overuse. The problems this raises, and the need for careful management of city centres, beaches and natural countryside, are subjects to which we shall return in Chapters 16 and 17.

ATTRACTIONS, AMENITIES AND ACCESSIBILITY

Earlier, it was made clear that all these destinations require adequate attractions, amenities and accessibility, if they are to appeal to large numbers of tourists. Let us look at these three characteristics in turn, and in greater detail, here.

The more attractions a destination can offer, the easier it becomes to market that destination to the tourist. Listing and analysing attractions is no easy matter, especially when one recognises that what appeals to one tourist may actually deter another.

In the description of destinations given above, it will have become clear that many of the attractions of a destination will be the physical features

Figure 1.5 The appeal of mountains and water: Athabasca Falls, Banff National Park, Canada. *(Photographed by the author)*

of that destination: the beauty of mountains, the fresh air of a seaside resort and the qualities of a particular beach, the architecture and 'atmosphere' of a great city. To these can be added numerous man-made and purpose-built attractions to increase the pulling power of the destination. For example, Blackpool maintains its lead among the seaside resorts in Britain by investing in indoor entertainments, a conference centre and other features which will appeal to the tourist; cities like Paris build new museum and exhibition complexes such as the Pompidou Centre and the Musée d'Orsay, or entertainment centres such as the new Opera House in the Bastille area; rural areas offer stately homes or castles as focal points for visits by day-trippers. Sometimes, the man-made attraction becomes its own destination, as is the case with theme parks like Disneyland Paris. The success of many spa towns on the Continent

Figure 1.6 Britain's heritage attracts tourists worldwide: Ludlow Castle, Shropshire. *(Photographed by the author)*

rests on their ability to combine man-made attractions such as casinos with the presumed medical benefits of the natural springs, while the popular ski resort must provide adequate ski runs, ski lifts and après-ski entertainment to complement its combination of good weather and mountain slopes.

The operation of managed visitor attractions is dealt with in some detail in Chapter 11. At this point, it will be sufficient to draw the reader's attention to certain distinctions in the nature of attractions.

Firstly, attractions may be either *site* or *event* attractions. Site attractions are permanent by nature, while event attractions are temporary, and are often mounted in order to increase the number of tourists to a particular destination. Some events have a short time-scale, such as a Red Devils air display; others may last for many days (e.g. the Edinburgh Festival) or even months (the ten-yearly Floriade Garden Festival in Holland). A destination which may have little to commend it

to the tourist can nevertheless succeed in drawing tourists by mounting an unusual exhibition, while a site destination can extend its season by mounting an off-season festival of arts.

Secondly, destinations and their attractions can be either *nodal* or *linear* in character. A nodal destination is one in which the attractions of the area are closely grouped geographically. Seaside resorts and cities are examples of typical nodal attractions, making them ideal for packaging by tour operators. This has led to the concept of 'honeypot' tourism development, in which planners concentrate the development of tourism in a specific locality. Aviemore in Scotland is an example of a purpose-built nodal tourism resort, with its attractions and amenities closely integrated. Linear tourism, on the other hand, is that in which the attraction is spread over a wide geographical area, without any specific focus. Examples include the Shenandoah Valley region in the United States, the Highlands of Scotland or the Scandinavian lakes and countryside – all ideal for touring holidays, rather than 'stay-put' holidays. Motels, or bed-and-breakfast accommodation, have sprung up to serve the needs of the transient tourist, who may stay only one or two nights at any one destination.

Readers are reminded that much of the attraction of a destination is intangible, and depends upon the image which the potential tourist has of it. India will be seen by one group of travellers as exotic and appealing, while others will reject the destination because of its poverty or its alien culture. Images of a destination, whether favourable or unfavourable, tend to be built up over a long period of time, and once established, are difficult to change. Britain, for instance, is still seen by many as a fog-engulfed, rain-battered island with friendly but rather reserved inhabitants – an image frequently stereotyped in the media. Overcoming such stereotyping is an important task of the national tourist board of the country.

Amenities are those essential services catering for the needs of the tourist. These include accommodation and food, local transport, information centres and the necessary infrastructure to support tourism – roads, public utility services, parking facilities. Naturally, such amenities will vary according to the nature of the destination itself; it would clearly be unsuitable to provide an extensive infrastructure in an area of great scenic beauty such as a national park, and those planning to visit such a destination will recognise that the availability of hotels and restaurants must inevitably be limited. Such sites are likely to attract the camper and those seeking only limited amenities.

It should also be recognised that on occasion the amenity itself may be the attraction, as was discussed earlier in the case where a resort hotel offers a comprehensive range of *in situ* attractions. Similarly, a destination like France, which is famed for its regional foods, will encourage tourists whose motive in travelling may be largely to enjoy the food. In this case, the amenity is its own attraction.

Finally, a destination must be accessible if it is to facilitate visits from tourists. While the more intrepid travellers may be willing to put themselves to great inconvenience in order to see some of the more exotic places in the world, most tourists will not be attracted to a destination unless it is relatively easy to reach. This means, in the case of international travel, having a good airport nearby, regular and convenient air transport to the region at a price that can be afforded, and good local connections to the destination itself. Cruise ships will be attracted by good deep-water ports with moorings available at reasonable cost to the shipping line, and situated at a convenient distance from major attractions in the area. Other travellers will be drawn by good access roads or rail services, and coach links.

On the other hand, if access becomes too easy, this may result in over-demand and resultant congestion, making the destination less attractive to the tourist. The introduction of new motorways in Britain opened up the Lake District and the West Country to motorists, resulting in severe congestion during the peak summer months from day trippers.

It should be noted that the *perception* of accessibility on the part of the traveller is often as important as a destination's actual accessibility. Many people in Britain perceive Corfu as being more accessible than Cornwall, in terms of travelling time. Such perceptions will undoubtedly affect decision-making when tourists are planning their travel.

Now that we have looked at what motivates the tourist to visit certain destinations, let us look at some examples of these destinations to see how their benefits act as a magnet for large numbers of tourists.

THE SEASIDE RESORT

Bournemouth, England

Bournemouth is counted among the half-dozen top seaside resorts in Britain, with a reputation that goes back to the Victorian era. In fact, the town has built on its Victorian heritage as a central theme, highlighting the many fine buildings and splendid shopping malls of the late nineteenth century, and incorporating Victorian-style street furniture and lighting in the recently pedestrianised centre. The heritage theme is enhanced by two piers, one of which has been virtually rebuilt in recent years to bring it up to modern standards and ensure its long-term future.

Figure 1.7 Royal Crescent, Bath. *(Courtesy Bath and North East Somerset Council)*

The town has good transport links, being close to a motorway from London and having fast Intercity rail connections with London and other parts of the country. There is an international airport, and ferry services from the Continent at nearby Poole. It is well sited on Britain's warm south coast, in a sandy bay with gently shelving beaches (which are scrupulously cleaned each day). The beaches have gained Blue Flag awards, and although winter storms frequently deplete the sand, the council regularly augments the beach by adding freshly dredged sand.

The town benefits by not being entirely dependent upon tourism, with the result that shopping, from speciality shops to department stores, is on a par with the best in Britain. Good entertainment is available at all levels (Bournemouth has, for example, a symphony orchestra of international standing), and this is supplemented throughout the summer by special events such as the Bristol–Bournemouth vintage car rally, powerboat festivals and illuminations.

The town boasts mature central gardens, originally planted a century ago, and floral displays for which it has gained awards. As a base for touring it is among the best sites in the country. The older towns of Poole and Christchurch on each side offer historical and cultural interest, while the New Forest, the Isle of Purbeck and Dorset countryside are all within easy reach of the motorist. Poole harbour, said to be the second-largest natural harbour in the world, offers a magnificent setting for the boating enthusiast. Bournemouth has also been successful in drawing the business visitor, who may be willing to come out of season, through the construction of a seafront International Centre, which provides facilities for the leisure visitor and the conference visitor alike. The success of the town can be judged by the wide range of accommodation available, from five-star

Figure 1.8 The Passion Play at Oberammergau, Germany. *(Courtesy Verkehrs- und Reisebüro Gemeinde Oberammergau OHG)*

hotels to bed and breakfasts; the town's guidebook lists over 650 places to stay.

THE HISTORIC TOWN

Bath, England

This city firmly established its reputation as a spa over 200 years ago, based on springs which were recognised for their healing powers in the time of the Roman occupation. Its attraction initially lay in the supposed healing properties of its mineral springs, and it became fashionable to 'take the waters' for the sake of one's health at this and other contemporary spas in England. Patronage by royalty and other members of the establishment reinforced the success of the city as a social venue, and over a period of time the town gradually changed from being merely a fashionable resort to a fashionable place of residence. In the twentieth century, the town experienced a regeneration of tourism, as interest focused on the extensive remains of the Roman baths and the superb collection of Georgian buildings with which the city was endowed. The town has become a popular venue for both domestic and overseas tourists.

Mass tourism has been aided by Bath's proximity to London – a convenient day trip for the foreign tourist – and by the fact that it is close to the M4 and M5 motorways. Bath is noted for the quality of its entertainment and shopping and the city's success has been further boosted by a growing number of unique museums, and cultural events such as the annual Bath Festival. Complemented by a good stock of accommodation and eating places, the city is now a major tourist destination, although tourist officials are concerned that its geographical location close to London makes it difficult to encourage many overseas visitors to stay overnight.

THE SITE/EVENT DESTINATION

Oberammergau, Germany

This village resort in Bavaria manages to combine both site and event attractions. As a mountain resort in the Bavarian Alps, the village lies at the heart of Europe, accessible through Munich by air from all over the world, and with good road connections from elsewhere in Germany and from Austria. It is both a winter and summer resort, offering summer guests peace and tranquillity, healthy mountain air, outstanding alpine scenery and opportunities for hiking and mountaineering. In winter, the resort offers winter sports opportunities and the usual appeal of a snow-clad landscape. The village is picturesque, with many of its wooden or rendered houses painted with murals in the local folk idiom. There are high-quality shops for the tourist, including wood-carving shops, while the established up-market shopping centres of Munich and Garmisch-Partenkirchen are less than an hour's drive away. The town boasts excellent leisure facilities, including a modern indoor–outdoor swimming pool complex, and a good stock of accommodation at all prices. However, the fame of the resort rests principally on its famous Passion Play, which has been performed once every ten years since the Middle Ages. This event is a draw for international tourists from all over the world, and overseas tour operators vie with one another to obtain an allocation of seats for the performances in order to package a programme. In other years, the theatre where the play is staged still draws countless day trippers.

Figure 1.9 Event tourism: history and heritage – Edinburgh Military Tattoo. *(Courtesy Scottish Tourist Board)*

THE SUCCESSFUL DESTINATION

Three important points should be highlighted in relation to tourist destinations. First, the chances of their long-term success will be significantly enhanced if the benefits they offer are unique. There is only one Oberammergau Passion Play, just as there is only one Eiffel Tower, Grand Canyon or Big Ben, and these attractions can provide the focus for a destination's marketing campaign. Because of the singular properties of 'heritage' tourism, these types of destination retain their attraction even if their prices may become less competitive with other destinations, providing the increase is not exorbitant by comparison.

However, it is true to say that the majority of the mass tourism movement is directed at sun, sea and sand destinations, which the Mediterranean and Caribbean countries provide so effectively. Such destinations are seldom unique, nor do their customers require them to be so. The tourists will

be satisfied as long as the amenities are adequate, the resort remains accessible and prices are competitive. Indeed, the similarities in attraction and amenity, as well as the way these destinations are marketed, gives rise to the concept of the 'Identikit' destination. This results from the evidence produced by market research studies designed to find common denominators among the various international markets in order to develop a product with guaranteed mass demand. These Identikit destinations have been developed through the activities of multinational tourism organisations. In the development of such destinations, the emphasis changes from an attempt to distinguish the product to one which is concentrated on maintaining or improving its image, by offering good standards which reflect value for money and ensuring that the destination remains competitive with other, similar destinations. The characteristics of Identikit destinations are discussed in greater detail in Chapter 3.

The second point to stress is that the more benefits a destination can offer, the greater the attraction of the destination. Multiple attractions provide 'added value', and the concentration within a specific geographical area of a number of different products appealing to different markets (such as the City of Bath, and the region surrounding Bournemouth) will improve the chance of success.

Finally, it should be clear that resorts cannot rest on their laurels. Most destinations depend at least to some extent on the return visitor, and will need continually to update and augment their range of attractions to encourage repeat visits. This means constant investment. Destinations, like all products which depend upon consumer demand, have 'life cycles', in which they experience periods of growth, expansion and, eventually, decline. If we examine the history of any well-known resort we can see the truth of this. Along the French Riviera, Nice, Cannes, Antibes, Juan les Pins, St Tropez have all in turn enjoyed their periods as fashionable resorts; but ultimately, their visitors moved on to more fashionable resorts, often to be replaced by less fashion-conscious, less free-spending tourists.

A decline into decay, all too evident in many British seaside resorts today, can only be arrested through redevelopment and innovation. In some cases, resorts have been allowed to run down to an extent where the cost of renovation may be beyond the scope of the council, and decay becomes inevitable.

QUESTIONS AND DISCUSSION POINTS

1   What potential problems can you foresee in less developed countries turning to tourism in order to boost their economy?

2   Identify two tourism destinations known to you, one of which is attracting a growing number of tourists, the other facing a decrease in tourism. Account for the changing fortunes of each. Is either likely to experience a change in demand in the future? What would need to be done by the destination facing decline in order to increase its attractiveness?

3   Explain the differing requirements of business and leisure travellers for (a) air transport, and (b) hotel accommodation. Do the growing numbers of businesswomen have needs distinct from businessmen that should be catered for by transport companies or hotels?

ASSIGNMENT TOPICS

1   You have recently taken up the position of Assistant Tourist Officer in a county of your choice. The county has only recently created a tourism department, and your immediate superior is preparing a new plan of action to increase the number of visitors during the next five years. She asks you to produce a brief report for her which:

   (a) looks at trends over the past decade in domestic and in-coming tourism,
   (b) identifies significant trends and forecasts the future flow of tourism within Britain, and
   (c) suggests relative advantages and disadvantages of the county in attracting more visitors.

   Your report should specifically indicate the shortcomings you find in the amount and quality of the statistical data you seek, and what further research you think may be needed to guide the department in its planning.

2   As an in-coming ground handling agent serving the needs of the US market, you have been approached by a specialist tour operator, Ralph Quackenbusch of Quackenbusch Tours, Sacramento, California. He is interested in bringing groups to your area of the country, and has written to you to ask for your assessment of local towns which might be attractive to older Californian residents. Select one town you consider might be suited, and subject this to an evaluation of its attractions, amenities and accessibility for this overseas market, bearing in mind that some groups will be wanting to spend some time in London, while others will prefer to come more directly to your part of the world.

   Write a short business letter spelling out the attractiveness of the destination as you see it.

2

The History of Tourism: from its Origins to the Age of Steam

OBJECTIVES

After studying this chapter, you should be able to:

- explain the historical changes which have affected the growth and development of the tourism industry from its earliest days;
- understand why particular forms of travel and destinations were chosen by the early tourists
- identify and distinguish between enabling; conditions and motivating factors affecting tourism demand.

Introduction

A study of the history of tourism is a worthwhile occupation for any student of the tourism business, not only as a matter of academic interest, but because there are lessons to be learned which are as applicable today as in the past. One thing we learn from history is that the business of tourism three thousand years ago shared many of the characteristics of the business as we know it today. Many of the facilities and amenities demanded by modern tourists were provided – albeit in a more basic form – from the earliest days of travel, including accommodation, catering services, guides and souvenir shops.

The earliest forms of leisure tourism can be traced as far back as the Babylonian and Egyptian empires. A museum of 'historic antiquities' was open to the public in the sixth century BC in Babylon, while the Egyptians held many religious festivals attracting not only the devout, but many who came to see the famous buildings and works of art in the cities. To provide for these throngs during the festivals, services of all kinds sprang up: vendors of food and drink, guides, hawkers of souvenirs, touts and prostitutes. Some early tourists took to vandalising buildings with graffiti to record their visit and Egyptian graffiti dating back to 2000 BC have been found.

From about the same date, and notably from the third century BC, Greek tourists travelled to visit the sites of healing gods. Because the independent city-states of ancient Greece had no central authority to order the construction of roads, most of these tourists travelled by water, and since most freight also travelled in this fashion, the seaports prospered. The Greeks, too, enjoyed their religious festivals, which in time became increasingly oriented to the pursuit of pleasure and, in particular, sport. Already by the fifth century BC Athens had become an important destination for travellers visiting the major sights such as the Parthenon, and inns – often adjuncts of the temples – were established in major towns and seaports to provide for the travellers' needs. Innkeepers of this period were known to be difficult and unfriendly, and the facilities they provided very basic: a palette to sleep on, but no heating, no windows, and no toilet facilities. Courtesans, 'trained in the art of music, dance, conversation and making love' were the principal entertainment offered.

EARLY GUIDES AND GUIDEBOOKS

Much of what we know of travel during this early

Figure 2.1 The first Olympic Games, held in Greece. (*Courtesy National Tourist Organisation of Greece*)

Pausanias, a Greek travel writer, produced a noted 'Description of Greece' between AD 160 and 180 which, in its critical evaluation of facilities and destinations, acted as a model for later writers. Advertisements, in the form of signs directing visitors to wayside inns, are also known from this period. However, it was under the Roman Empire that international travel first became important. With no foreign borders between England and Syria, and with the seas safe from piracy due to the Roman patrols, conditions favouring travel had at last arrived. Roman coinage was acceptable everywhere, and Latin was the common language of the day. Romans travelled to Sicily, Greece, Rhodes, Troy, Egypt – and, from the third century AD, to the Holy Land. The Romans, too, introduced their guidebooks (*itineraria*), listing hostels with symbols to identify quality in a manner reminiscent of the present-day Michelin Guides. The Roman poet Horace published an anti-travel ode following his travel experiences from Rome to Brindisi in 38–37 BC.

It is interesting to note, too, the growth of travel bureaucracy at this stage. An exit permit was required to leave by many seaports, and a charge was made for this service. Souvenirs acquired abroad were subject to an import duty, and a customs declaration had to be completed.

Rome, too, suffered its share of 'cowboy operators'. Among the souvenirs offered to Roman travellers were forgeries of Greek statues, especially works bearing the signature of Greece's most famous sculptor, Praxiteles. Roman writers of the day complained of Athens as a 'city of shysters', bent on swindling the foreign tourist.

Domestic tourism also flourished within the Roman Empire's heartland. Second homes were built by the wealthy within easy travelling distance of Rome, occupied particularly during the springtime social season. The most fashionable resorts were to be found around the Bay of Naples, and there is evidence of early market segmentation between these destinations. Naples itself attracted the retired and intellectuals, Cumae became the resort of high fashion, Puteoli attracted the more staid tourist, while Baiae, which was both a spa town and a seaside resort, attracted the down-market tourist, becoming noted for its rowdiness, drunkenness and all-night singing.

period is due to the writings of Herodotus, who lived between c. 484 and 424 BC, a noted historian and early traveller who can be accurately described as the world's first significant travel writer. He has recorded extensively, and with some cynicism, the tall stories recounted to him by the travel guides of the day. It appears that these guides varied greatly in the quality and accuracy of the information they provided. The role of guides was divided between those whose task was to shepherd the tourists around the sites (the *periegetai*) and those whose function it was to provide information for their charges (the *exegetai*). Liberties with the truth included the story that the great pyramids at Giza extended downwards into the earth to the same extent as their height, and that the perfection of the white marble used in the greatest statues was such that viewers stood the risk of damaging their eyesight unless they averted their gaze. The philosopher Plutarch wrote to complain, a century before the birth of Christ, that guides insisted on talking too much about the inscriptions and epitaphs found at the sites, choosing to ignore the entreaties of the visitors to cut this short.

Guidebooks, too, made their appearance as early as the fourth century BC, covering destinations such as Athens, Sparta and Troy.

The distribution of administrators and the military during the days of the Roman Empire led to Romans making trips abroad to visit friends and relatives, setting a precedent for the VFR movements of the present day. The rapid improvement in communications which coincided with the Roman conquests aided the growth of travel; first-class roads, coupled with staging inns (precursors of the modern motels) led to comparatively safe, fast and convenient travel unsurpassed until modern times.

Travel in the Middle Ages

Following the collapse of the Roman Empire, and the onset of the so-called 'dark ages', travel became considerably less attractive: more dangerous, difficult and more synonymous with *travail* (literally, a painful and laborious effort, and the origin of the word). The result was that most pleasure travel was undertaken close to home, though this is not to say that international travel was unknown. Adventurers sought fame and fortune through travel, merchants travelled extensively to seek new trade opportunities, strolling players and minstrels made their living by performing as they travelled (the most famous of these must be Blondel, a native of Picardy and friend of King Richard I, the 'Lion-Heart', whom he is reputed to have accompanied on the latter's Crusade). However, all these forms of travel would be identified either as business travel, or travel from a sense of obligation or duty. In order for people to travel for pleasure, the conditions favouring travel must be in place.

Nonetheless, closer to home, holidays played an important role in the life of the public. The term 'holiday' has its origin in 'holy days', and from earliest times religion provided the framework within which leisure time was spent. For most people, this implied a break from work, rather than a movement from one place to another. The village 'wakes' of the Middle Ages, held on the eve of patronal festivals, provide an example of such 'religious relaxation'. Such public holidays were, in fact, quite numerous, and far more so than today – up until as recently as 1830 there were as many as thirty-three Saints' days in the holiday calendar, dispelling the myth of peasants engaged almost constantly in hard manual labour. For the pious intent on fulfilling a religious duty, pilgrimages would be undertaken to places of worship, and Chaucer's tale of one pilgrimage to Canterbury provides evidence that there was a pleasurable side to this travel, too.

Developments in road transport in the seventeenth to early nineteenth centuries

Before the sixteenth century, those who sought to travel had three modes in which to do so: they could walk (many who were too poor to afford any form of transport had to do so, regardless of the distance involved); they could ride a horse; or they could be carried, either on a litter (carried by servants, and restricted largely to the aristocracy) or on a carrier's wagon. This horse-drawn vehicle was slow and appallingly uncomfortable, being without springs. The roads of the time were poorly surfaced, potholed and in winter deeply rutted by the wagon wheels, which churned the road into a sea of mud, making the journey an endurance test for passengers. The journey was also unsafe: footpads and highwaymen abounded on the major routes, posing an ever-present threat to wayfarers. Apart from royalty and the court circle, who were always well guarded, only a handful of wealthy citizens, such as those with 'country seats' (second homes in the country) travelled for pleasure until well into the eighteenth century.

The development of the sprung coach was a huge advance for those who were obliged to travel. The invention in its most primitive form is traced to the Hungarian town of Kocs in the fifteenth century, and by the mid-1600s coaches were operating regularly in Britain, with a daily service recorded between London and Oxford. The concept of the stagecoach, for which teams of horses would be used and changed at regular points along the route, greatly aided mobility. These appeared in England as early as the seventeenth century, and were in use widely throughout the Continent by the middle of the eighteenth century (Austria, for example, introduced its first services in 1749). The construction of these coaches, in which the body of the coach was 'sprung' by being suspended from primitive leather straps, encouraged travel by offering a greater measure of comfort. In the eighteenth century the introduction of turnpike roads, which provided improved surfaces for which tolls would be charged, enabled stagecoaches carrying between eight and fourteen passengers to cover upwards of forty miles a day during the summer. However, this still meant that a journey to Bath from London would take some three days, while the 400 miles to Edinburgh took fully ten days. The later introduction of metal, leaf-spring suspension also added to comfort. Stagecoaches also greatly aided the development of the North American colonies, with a service between Boston and New York introduced in 1772, with other routes serving Providence (Rhode Island), Philadelphia and Baltimore. However, mail coaches, which were to provide additional passenger accommodation, were not to make an appearance until the 1780s in Europe and the USA.

Travel of some distance requires accommodation. At this time, such accommodation was basic. Inns sprang up to serve the needs of overnight guests and to provide fresh horses, while lodgings or 'chambers' were available for rent to visitors when they arrived at their destinations.

Around 1815, the discovery of tarmacadam revolutionised the road systems of Europe. For the first time, a hard surface less subject to pitting and ruts enabled rapid increases to be made in the average speed of coach services. *Char-a-bancs,* public coaches with rows of transverse seats facing forward, have been identified as far back as 1832; the term was later applied to the first motor-coaches used for leisure travel in the early twentieth century. By the 1820s, the horse-drawn omnibus was a common sight in London and Paris, greatly improving local city transport. Mail coaches were now covering the distance between London and Bath in twelve and a half hours, and the London–Brighton run was reduced to a little over five hours.

The Grand Tour

From the early seventeenth century, a new form of tourism developed, as a direct outcome of the freedom and quest for learning heralded by the Renaissance. Under the reign of Elizabeth I, young men seeking positions at court were encouraged to travel to the Continent to finish their education. This practice was soon adopted by others in the upper echelons of society, and it eventually became customary for the education of a gentleman to be completed by a 'Grand Tour' (a term in use as early as 1670) of the major cultural centres of Europe, accompanied by a tutor and often lasting three years or more. Travel for reasons of education was encouraged by the fact that under Elizabeth I a special licence had to be obtained from the Crown in order to travel abroad, though universities had the privilege of granting licences for the purpose of scholarship. The publication in 1749 of a guidebook by Dr Thomas Nugent entitled *The Grand Tour* gave a further boost to the educational tour, and some intrepid travellers ventured as far afield as Egypt. While ostensibly educational, as with the spas the appeal soon became social, and pleasure-seeking young men of leisure travelled, predominantly to France and Italy, to enjoy the rival cultures and social life of cities such as Paris, Venice or Florence. By the end of the eighteenth century, the custom had become institutionalised for the gentry.

As a result, European centres were opened up to the British traveller. Aix-en-Provence, Montpellier and Avignon became notable bases, especially for those using the Provence region as a staging post for travel to Italy. When pleasure travel followed in the nineteenth century, eventually to displace educational tours as the motive for Continental visits, this was to lead to the development of the Riviera as a principal destination for British tourists, aided by the introduction of regular steamboat services across the Channel from 1821 onwards. However, the advent of the Napoleonic Wars early in the nineteenth century inhibited travel within Europe for some thirty years. By the time of Napleon's defeat, the British had taken a greater interest in touring their own country.

Political hindrance to travel

Travel outside the boundaries of one's country had always been subject to restrictions, as we have seen from some of the constraints imposed by the state under the Roman Empire. Few people travelled any great distance, and those that did so were generally involved with affairs of state. Monarchs were suspicious of intrigues and alliances with foreign states, and vetted such travel carefully, issuing letters of authority to members of court, ostensibly to facilitate travel but equally to ensure that they were aware of the movements of their subjects.

Passports have their origin in the medieval *testimoniale*, a letter from an ecclesiastical superior given to a pilgrim to avoid the latter's possible arrest on charges of vagrancy. Later, papers of authority to travel were more widely issued by the state, particularly during periods of warfare with neighbouring European countries. However, when Belgium sought to require visitors to present passports for inspection in 1882, there was widespread indignation in the British press. The introduction of compulsory passports as a permanent requirement in Britain is of relatively recent origin, dating only from 1916, as a result of controls during the World War I. The institution of a formal immigration service in the UK is also a twentieth-century phenomenon, being established under the Aliens Act 1905.

We should not underestimate the importance of a common currency, and the difficulties and expense incurred when changing currencies while travelling abroad. As we have seen, under the Roman Empire the universal acceptance of Roman coinage proved to be a great facilitator for travel, in contrast to the wealth of currencies even within individual countries in the Middle Ages. Fynes Moryson, an academic who travelled extensively on the Continent, was to write in 1589 of finding over twenty different coinages in Germany, five in the Low Countries and as many as eight in Switzerland. Moneychangers cheated the visitor and were sometimes difficult to find. At a time when the European Union is planning the introduction of the Euro as a common currency throughout the Union's membership, it is worth our while considering the benefits that could accrue to tourists and the boost which this could give to tourism in the twenty-first century.

The development of the spas

Spas were already well established during the time of the Roman Empire, but their popularity, based on the supposed medical benefits of the waters, lapsed in subsequent centuries. They were never entirely out of favour, however; the sick continued to visit Bath throughout the Middle Ages. Renewed interest in the therapeutic qualities of mineral waters has been ascribed to the influence of the Renaissance in Britain, and elsewhere in Europe.

In 1562, Dr William Turner published a book drawing attention to the curative powers of the waters at Bath and on the Continent. Bath itself along with the spa at Buxton, had been showing a return to popularity among those 'seeking the cure', and the effect of Dr Turner's book was to establish the credibility of the resorts' claims. In 1626, Elizabeth Farrow drew attention to the qualities of the mineral springs at Chalybeate in Scarborough, which became the first of a number of new spa resorts. In the same year, Dr Edmund Deane wrote his *Spadacrene Anglica* which drew attention to what he claimed were 'the strongest sulphur springs in Great Britain' at Harrogate. This rapidly led to the popularity of the town as a spa resort, a role it continues to enjoy today. Soon, an astonishing number of spa resorts sprang up, sometimes in unlikely places; Streatham in South London, for instance, became briefly fashionable following the discovery of mineral springs there in 1659.

Taking the cure rapidly developed social status, and the resorts changed in character as pleasure rather than health became the motivation for visits. Bath in particular became a major centre of social life for high society during the eighteenth and early nineteenth centuries, aided by visits from the monarchs of the day. Under the guidance of Beau Nash at the beginning of the eighteenth century, it soon became a centre of high fashion, deliberately setting out to create a select and

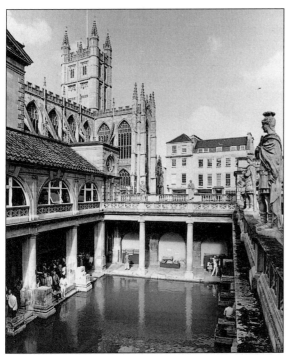

Figure 2.2 The Roman Baths at Bath. *(Bath and North East Somerset Council)*

exclusive image. The commercial possibilities opened up by the concentration of these wealthy visitors were not overlooked; facilities to entertain or otherwise cater for these visitors proliferated, changing the spas into what we would today term holiday resorts rather than watering places. The building of a Pump Room as a focal point within Bath was a key development leading to the town's success as a resort, while Harrogate similarly benefited by the construction of its own Pump Room in 1841–42.

Eventually, in the early nineteenth century, the common characteristic of resorts to go 'down-market' through their life cycle led to a changing clientele, with the landed gentry replaced by wealthy merchants and the professional class. By the end of the eighteenth century, the heyday of the English spas was already over, although they were to have a far longer life cycle on the Continent.

There are interesting parallels between the decline of the English spas and that of the English seaside resorts one hundred and fifty years or so later. The spa towns were seen as attractive places in which to live, and residents gradually sup-

planted visitors. These residents tended to be older, and their demand for more passive and traditional entertainment, with a preference for entertaining at home rather than seeking commercial entertainment, hastened the spas' economic decline. However, it was the rise of the seaside resorts which did much to undermine the success of the inland spas, just as later it would be the rise of the Mediterranean resorts which would lead to the decline of the British seaside resort.

The rise and fall of the seaside resort

Until the Renaissance, bathing in the sea found little favour in Britain. Although not entirely unknown before then, such bathing as occurred was undertaken unclothed, and this behaviour conflicted with the mores of the day. Only when the sea became associated with certain health benefits did bathing gain popularity. The association of sea water with health did not find acceptance until the early years of the eighteenth century, and initially the objective was to drink it rather than bathe in it. It is perhaps to be expected that health theorists would eventually recognise that the minerals to be found in spa waters were also present in abundance in sea water. By the early eighteenth century, small fishing resorts around the English coast were beginning to attract visitors seeking 'the cure', both by drinking sea water and by immersing themselves in it. Not surprisingly, Scarborough, as the only spa bordering the sea, was one of the first to exploit this facility for the medical benefits it was believed to offer, and both this town and Brighton were attracting regular visitors by the 1730s. But it was Dr Richard Russell's noted medical treatise *A Dissertation on the Use of Sea Water in the Diseases of the Glands, particularly the Scurvy, Jaundice, King's Evil, Leprosy, and the Glandular Consumption*, published in 1752 (and two years earlier in Latin), which is credited with popularising the custom of sea bathing more widely. Soon, Blackpool, Southend, and other English seaside resorts were wooing bathers to their shores. Blackpool, in fact, had attracted some categories of sea bather well before its growth as a resort; workers in the area are known to have travelled there by cart in order to wash off the accumulation of dirt resulting from their jobs. The heyday of these 'Padjamers', as they were known, was in the century between 1750 and 1850.

The growing popularity of 'taking the cure', which resulted from the wealth generated by the expansion of trade and industry in Britain at the time, meant that the inland spas could no longer cater satisfactorily for the influx of visitors they were attracting. By contrast, the new seaside resorts offered almost boundless opportunities for expansion. Moral doubts about exposing one's body in the sea were overcome by the invention of the bathing machine, and the resorts prospered.

Undoubtedly, the demand for seaside cures could have been even greater in the early years if fast, cheap transport had been developed to cater for this need. But in the mid-eighteenth century, it still took two days to travel from London to Brighton, and the cost was well beyond the reach of the average worker, at the equivalent of six weeks' wages. Accommodation provision, too, grew only slowly, outpaced by demand. But all this was to change in the early nineteenth century.

First, the introduction of steamboat services reduced the cost and time of travel from London to the resorts near the Thames Estuary. In 1815, a service began operating between London and Gravesend, and five years later, to Margate. The popularity of these services was such that other pleasure boat services were quickly introduced to more distant resorts. This development required the construction of piers to provide landing stages for the vessels; the functional purpose of the seaside pier was soon overtaken by its attraction as a social meeting-point and a place to take the sea air.

However, it was also the introduction of steamboat services linking Britain and the Continent which posed the first threat to the British seaside resorts. Brighton established a ferry link with Dieppe as early as 1761, and this was followed by links from Shoreham and Newhaven to France. By the 1820s it is estimated that some 150,000 visitors a year were travelling from Britain to the Continental mainland, many for the purposes of visiting coastal resorts. At first, from

about 1780 onwards, travel was concentrated along the Riviera, between the mouth of the Var and the Gulf of Spezia. The Italian resorts benefited from direct steamer services from London and Liverpool to Genoa. Soon, French resorts were attracting British visitors along the north coast between Boulogne and Cherbourg. The British visitors insisted on facilities which met their particular needs, including churches of favourite denominations and British shops, chemists, physicians and newspapers; the more successful French resorts quickly provided these. From 1880 onwards, the Train Bleu offered wealthy British visitors elegant sleeping accommodation from Paris to the Riviera, popularising not only summer, but also winter holidays to escape the cold of the British climate.

The conditions favouring the expansion of travel in the nineteeth century

From this brief history of travel from earliest times to the nineteenth century, we can see that a number of factors have been at work to encourage travel. We can divide these into two categories; factors that make travel possible (*enabling* factors), and factors that persuade people to travel (*motivating* factors).

In order for travel to be possible at all, people must have adequate time and money to undertake it. However, throughout most of history, and until very recently, both of these have been the prerogative of a very few members of society. Leisure time for the masses was very limited; workers laboured from morning to night, six days a week, and were encouraged to treat Sundays (and the not infrequent saints' days) as days of rest and worship. Wages were barely adequate to sustain a family and pay for the basic necessities of life. The idea of paid holidays was not even considered until the twentieth century.

Equally important, the development of pleasure travel depends upon the provision of suitable travel facilities. The growth of travel and of transport are interdependent; travellers require transport that is priced within their budget and that is fast, safe, comfortable and convenient. As we have seen, none of these criteria began to be met until the latter half of the eighteenth century; but from the early nineteenth century onwards rapid improvements in technology led to transport that was both fast and moderately priced.

The development of transport during the nineteenth century will be examined in greater detail shortly. But good transport must be complemented by adequate accommodation at the traveller's destination. The traditional hospices for travellers in the Middle Ages were the monasteries, but these were dissolved during the reign of Henry VIII and the resulting hiatus acted as a further deterrent to travel for everyone apart from those planning to stay with friends or relatives. The gradual improvement in lodgings that accompanied the introduction of the mail and stagecoaches went some way to correcting this shortcoming. However, the general inadequacy of facilities away from the major centres of population meant that towns such as London, Exeter and York, with their abundant social life and entertainment as a magnet, were to become the first centres to attract large numbers of visitors for leisure purposes.

Other constraints awaited those prepared to ignore these drawbacks to travel. In cities, public health standards were low and travellers risked disease – a risk compounded in the case of foreign travel. Exchange facilities for foreign travel were unreliable, rates of exchange were inconsistent and travellers were liable to be cheated, so they tended to carry large amounts of money with them, making them prey to highwaymen. Foreign currencies were, in any event, chaotic, as we have noted earlier – in the sixteenth century, for instance, Germany, with its multiplicity of small states, had no fewer than twenty coinages as well as the Reich's Dollar, while there were similar multiple coinages in other Continental countries; before unification, Italy alone, a popular venue for the cultural tourist, boasted sixteen different coinages. As we have also seen, travel documents of some kind were generally necessary, and at times not easy to come by; political suspicion frequently meant long delays in obtaining permission to travel.

Removing such constraints will encourage growth in travel. However, the real motivation for travel must be intrinsic, a wish to travel for its own sake, to get away from one's everyday surroundings and become acquainted with other places, cultures and people. It was the rapid urbanisation of the population in Great Britain which provided the impetus for travel in the nineteenth century. The Industrial Revolution had led to massive migration of the population away from the villages and countryside and into the industrial cities, where work was plentiful and better paid. This migration was to have two important side effects on the workers themselves. Firstly, workers became conscious of the beauty and attractions of their former rural surroundings for the first time. Cities were dark, polluted and treeless. Previously, workers had little appreciation of their environment – living in the midst of the natural beauty of the countryside, they accepted it without question. Now, they longed to escape from the cities in what little free time they had – a characteristic still evident among twentieth-century city dwellers. Secondly, the type of work available in the cities was both physically and psychologically stressful. The comparatively leisurely pace of life in the countryside was replaced by monotonous factory work from which any change of routine and pace was welcome.

The expansion of the British economy which took place as a result of the increased productivity created by the Industrial Revolution led to growth in real purchasing power for every worker, while worldwide demand for British goods created a huge business travel market. Increased wealth stimulated rapid growth in the population at this time, too.

In short, Britain at the beginning of the nineteenth century stood poised on the threshold of a considerable escalation in the demand for travel. The introduction of modern transport systems at this point in history was to translate this demand into reality.

The age of steam

THE RAILWAYS

Two technological developments in the early part of the nineteenth century were to have a profound effect on transport and the growth in travel generally. The first of these was the advent of the railway.

The first railway was built in England, between Stockton and Darlington in 1825. It was to herald a major programme of railway construction throughout the world, and a major shift in the facility to travel. We have noted the problems of travelling by road up to that point and, although travel by canal had been possible by 1760, it was too slow a mode to attract travellers, being used essentially for the carriage of freight. As a means of transport for all purposes, it was to suffer a rapid decline after 1825, when travel at 13 mph became possible for the first time – at least three miles an hour faster than the fastest mail coaches. In the decade following the introduction of a rail link between Liverpool and Manchester in 1830, trunk routes sprang up between the major centres of population and industry in Britain, on the Continent and throughout the world. In the USA, for example, passenger services on the east coast were being built from the 1820s, and by 1869 a transcontinental link was in place. One of the last great rail routes, the Trans-Siberian, opened in 1903, connecting Moscow with Vladivostok and Port Arthur.

In the UK, although the railways initially served the needs of commerce, new routes emerged linking commercial centres to the popular coastal resorts such as Brighton, bringing these within the reach of the mass of pleasure travellers for the first time. On the whole, though, the railway companies appeared to be slow to recognise the opportunities for pleasure travel offered by the development of rail services, concentrating instead on providing for the needs of business travellers. Certainly, in the 1840s, the growth of regular passenger traffic was enough to occupy them; between 1842 and 1847, the annual number of passengers travelling by train rose from 23 million to 51 million. Competition between the railway companies was initially based on service rather than price, although from the earliest days of the railways a new market developed for short day-trips. Before long, however, entrepreneurs began to stimulate rail travel by organising excursions for the public at special fares. In some cases, these took place on regular train services, but in others, special trains were chartered in order to take travellers to their destination, setting a precedent for the charter services by air which were to become so significant a feature of tour operating a century later. As an indication of the speed with which these opportunities were put into place, within twelve days of the rail line to Scarborough being opened in 1845, an excursion train from Wakefield was laid on to carry a thousand passengers to the seaside.

Thomas Cook, contrary to popular opinion, was not, in fact, the first entrepreneur to organise tours for the public. Sir Rowland Hill, who became chairman of the Brighton Railway Co, is sometimes credited with this innovation (others have suggested that the first package tour can be traced to a group of tourists taken from Wadebridge to Bodmin to witness a public hanging!), and there were certainly excursion trains in operation by 1840. However, Cook was to have by far the greatest impact on the early travel industry. In 1841, as secretary of the South Midland Temperance Association, he organised an excursion for his members from Leicester to Loughborough, at a fare of one shilling (the equivalent of five pence) return. The success of this venture – 570 took part – encouraged him to arrange similar excursions using chartered trains and by 1845 he was organising these trips on a fully commercial basis.

The result of these and similar ventures by other entrepreneurs led to a substantial movement of pleasure-bound travellers to the seaside. In 1844, it is recorded that almost 15,000 passengers travelled from London to Brighton on the three Easter holidays alone, while hundreds of thousands travelled to other resorts to escape the smoke and grime of the cities. The enormous growth in this type of traffic can be appreciated when it is revealed that by 1862 Brighton received 132,000 visitors on Easter Monday alone.

Supported by a more sympathetic attitude to pleasure travel on the part of public authorities such as the Board of Trade, the railway companies themselves were actively promoting these excursions by the 1850s, while at the same time introducing a range of discounted fares for day trips, weekend trips and longer journeys. By 1855, Cook had extended his field of operations to the Continent, organising the first 'inclusive tours' to the Paris Exhibition of that year. This followed the success of his excursions to the Great Exhibition in London in 1851, which in all had welcomed a total of three million visitors.

Cook was a man of vision in the world of travel. The success of his operations was due to the care he took in organising his programmes to minimise problems; he had close contacts with hotels, shipping companies and railways throughout the world, ensuring that he obtained the best possible service as well as cheap prices for the services he provided. By escorting his clients throughout their journeys abroad he took the worry out of travel for the first-time traveller. He also made the administration of travel easier by introducing the hotel voucher in 1867, which allowed tourists to prepay their hotel accommodation and to produce evidence to the hotels that this had been done. In 1873 he brought in the 'circular note', the precursor to today's traveller's cheque, which helped to overcome the problems caused by the many different coinages on the Continent. The latter was not a totally new concept: a certain Robert Herries set up the London Banking Exchange Company in 1772 in order to issue similar documents, but it was Cook (and later in North America, American Express) who popularised these ideas, which made travel far more tolerable for the Victorian traveller.

The coincidental invention of photography in the mid-nineteenth century further stimulated overseas travel for reasons of prestige. For the first time, visitors abroad could be photographed against a background of the great historical sites of Europe, to the envy of their friends.

The expansion of the railways was accompanied by a simultaneous decline in the stagecoaches. Some survived by providing feeder services to the nearest railway stations, but overall road traffic shrank and with it the demand for the staging inns. Those situated in the resorts were quick to adapt to meet the needs of the new railway travellers, but the supply of accommodation in centres served by the railways was totally inadequate to meet the burgeoning demand of this new market. A period of hotel construction began, in which the railway companies themselves were leaders, establishing the great railway terminus hotels which came to play such a significant role in the hotel industry over the next hundred years. The high capital investment called for by this development led to the formation of the first hotel chains and corporations.

Social changes in the Victorian era all encouraged travel. The new-found interest in sea bathing meant that the expanding rail network favoured the developing resorts, accelerating their growth. At the same time, Victorian society placed great emphasis on the role of the family as a social unit, leading to the type of family holidays for which the seaside was so well suited. The foundations of traditional seaside entertainment were soon laid – German bands, 'nigger minstrels' and pierrots, Punch and Judy shows, barrel organs, donkey rides, and the seaside pier all became essential components of the seaside holiday. Resorts began to develop different social images, partly as a result of their geographical location: those nearer London or other major centres of population developed a substantial market of day-trippers, while others deliberately aimed for a more exclusive clientele. These latter generally tended to be situated further afield, but in some cases their exclusivity arose from the desire of prominent residents to resist the encroachment of the railways for as long as possible. Bournemouth, for example, held out against the extension of the railway from Poole until 1870. Some areas of early promise as holiday resorts were quickly destroyed by the growth of industry – Swansea and Hartlepool, for example, and Southampton, where beaches gave way to the development of docks.

Health continued to play a role in the choice of holiday destinations, but the emphasis gradually switched from the benefits of sea bathing to those of sea air. Climate became a feature of the resorts' promotion. Sunshine hours were emphasised, or the bracing qualities of the Scarborough air, while the pines at Bournemouth were reputed to help those suffering from lung complaints. Seaside resorts on the Continent also gained in popularity and began to develop their own social images – Scheveningen near the Hague, Ostend, Biarritz and Deauville held the same magic for British holidaymakers as the Mediterranean resorts were to provide a century later. Some overseas resorts flourished in reaction to middle-class morality in Victorian England – Monte Carlo, with its notorious gambling casino, was a case in point. This desire to escape from one's everyday environment was as symptomatic of nineteenth-century life as it was to become in the middle of the twentieth century. Of course, these destinations on the Continent were to attract only the relatively well off, and the railways produced the service to cater for these high-spend tourists; trains such as the Blue Train, which entered service between Paris and the Côte d'Azur and Rome in 1883, and the Orient Express of the same year, operating from Paris to the Black Sea, provided unsurpassed levels of luxury for rail travellers on the Continent. Long-distance rail services became possible with the introduction of sleeping cars, invented in the USA by George Pullman in 1864 and introduced into Europe by the French Wagon-Lits company in 1869.

Other forms of holidaymaking, opened up by the advent of the railways on the Continent, arose from the impact of the 'Romantic Movement' of mid-Victorian England. The Rhine and the French Riviera benefited from their new-found romantic appeal, while the invigorating mountain air of Switzerland, combining the promise of better health with opportunities for strenuous outdoor activities, was already drawing tourists from Britain by the 1840s. Mountaineering became a popular pastime for the British in the 1860s, and was later spurred on by the introduction into Switzerland of skiing. The origins of skiing are lost in antiquity, but using skis as a sport is credited to a certain Bjorland Blom, Sheriff of Telemark, in the 1660s. By the beginning of the 1890s a number of individual British visitors to Norway had introduced the sport to Switzerland, while Mathias Zdardsky similarly brought skis to his native Austria in 1890. However, Sir Henry Lunn, the British travel entrepreneur, is credited with the commercialisation of winter ski holidays in Switzerland, having organised packages to Chamonix before the end of the nineteenth century. The railways made their own contributions to these developments, but above all they encouraged the desire to travel by removing the hazards of foreign travel that had formerly existed for travellers journeying by road.

STEAMSHIPS

Just as the technological developments of the early nineteenth century led to the development of railways on land, so steam was harnessed at sea to drive new generations of ships. Here, necessity was the mother of invention. Increasing trade worldwide, especially with North America, required Britain to develop faster, more reliable forms of communication by sea with the rest of the world. Although as we have seen, ferry services were operating as early as 1761 between Brighton and Dieppe, the first regular commercial cross-Channel steamship service was introduced in 1821, on the Dover–Calais route. The railway companies were quick to recognise the importance of their links with these cross-Channel ferry operators, and by 1862 they had gained the right to own and operate steamships themselves. Soon after, control over the ferry companies was in the hands of the railways, who rapidly expanded the cross-Channel services.

Deep-sea services were introduced on routes to North America and the Far East; the Peninsular and Oriental Steam Navigation Company (later P & O) is credited with the first regular long-distance steamship service, beginning operations to India and the Far East in 1838. This company was soon followed by the Cunard Steamship Company which, with a lucrative mail contract, began regular services to the American continent in 1840. Britain, by being the first to establish regular deep-sea services of this kind, came to dominate the world's shipping in the second half of the century, although it was soon to be challenged by other leading industrial nations on the popular North American route. This prestigious and highly profitable route prospered not only from mail contracts but also due to the huge demand from passengers and freight as trade with the American continent expanded. Later, the passenger trade would be boosted by the flow of emigrants from Europe (especially Ireland) and a smaller but significant number of American visitors to Europe. Thomas Cook played his part in stimulating the package tour market to North America, taking the first group of tourists in 1866. In 1872, he went on to organise the first round-the-world tour, taking twelve clients for 220 days at a cost of

Figure 2.3 Hindostan, built in 1842, opened P&O's service between Suez and Calcutta in 1843. *(Courtesy Peninsular and Oriental Steam Navigation Co.)*

some £200 – more than the average annual salary at the time.

The Suez Canal, opened in 1869, stimulated demand for P&O's services to India and beyond, as Britain's Empire looked eastwards. The global growth of shipping led, in the latter part of the century, to the formation of shipping conferences, which developed cartel-like agreements on fares and conditions applicable to the carriage of traffic. The aim of these agreements was to ensure year-round profitability in an unstable and seasonal market, but the result was to stifle competition by price, and eventually led to excess profits which were to be enjoyed by the shipping companies until the advent of airline competition in the mid-twentieth century.

Other late-nineteenth-century developments

As the Victorian era drew to a close, other social changes came into play. Continued enthusiasm for the healthy outdoor life coincided with the invention of the bicycle, and cycling holidays, aided by promotion from the Cyclists' Touring Club, which was founded in 1878, enjoyed immense popularity. This movement not only paved the way for later interest in outdoor activities on holiday, but may well have stimulated the appeal of the suntan

as a status symbol of health and wealth, in marked contrast to the earlier association in Victorian minds of a fair complexion with gentility and breeding. The bicycle offered for the first time the opportunity for mobile rather than centred holidays, and gave a foretaste of the popularity of motoring holidays in the early years of the following century.

As tourism grew in the later years of the century, so the organisers of travel became established institutionally. Thomas Cook and Sir Henry Lunn (whose name is retained in the company Lunn Poly) are two of the best known names of the period, but many other well-known companies became established at this time. Dean and Dawson appeared in 1871, the Polytechnic Touring Association (the other half of the Lunn Poly name) in the following year, and Frames Tours in 1881. In the United States, American Express (founded by, among others, Henry Wells and William Fargo of Wells Fargo fame) initiated money orders and travellers' cheques, although the company did not become involved in making holiday arrangements until early in the twentieth century.

Mention has already been made of the impact of photography on nineteenth-century travel. As the century drew to a close, the vogue for photography was accompanied by the cult of the guidebook. No British tourists venturing abroad would neglect to take their guidebook, and a huge variety of these soon became available on the market. Many were superficial and inaccurate, but the most popular and enduring of those published were those of John Murray, whose Hand-books appeared from 1837 onwards, and Karl Baedeker, who introduced his first guidebook (of the Rhine) in 1839. By the end of the century Baedeker had become firmly established as the leading publisher of guidebooks in Europe.

QUESTIONS AND DISCUSSION POINTS

1 What factors inhibited travel in the Middle Ages? Are there any similarities you can detect with factors that still inhibit travel in the latter half of the twentieth century?

2 Could spas be successfully rejuvenated in

Britain? What form of support should government, local authorities or other bodies offer which would help to regenerate the use of spas? Explain why spas in Britain have fallen into disuse, while those on the Continent remain popular.

3 What differences and similarities can you find between modern tourism and travels of the earlier Greeks and Romans? Are there lessons for twentieth-century tourists that can be learned from these early travellers?

4 History reveals many examples of adaptation by entrepreneurs to changing tourist needs and circumstances. Discuss what changes are currently required by present-day entrepreneurs to meet the needs of twenty-first century tourists.

ASSIGNMENT TOPICS

1 Prepare a set of notes, and deliver a talk, on either the Grand Tour or the spas in Britain. The research for these notes should have a complete and properly constructed bibliography (use the bibliography at the back of this book as a guide for the correct presentation of a bibliography). Draw on some verbatim comments from the research material to enliven your talk.

2 Write a short article (about 800 words) for your local newspaper which argues that travel in earlier times was more exciting and rewarding than travel today.

3

Tourism in the Twentieth Century

OBJECTIVES

After studying this chapter, you should be able to:

- describe the growth of the mass tourism movement;
- explain the origins and development of the package holiday;
- analyse the factors influencing travel in the twentieth century.

The first fifty years

THE ORIGINS OF MASS TOURISM

In the opening years of the twentieth century, travel continued to expand, encouraged by the increasing wealth, curiosity and outgoing attitudes of the post-Victorian population, and by the steady improvement in transport. Travellers had become safer from disease and physical attack, the Continent was relatively stable politically, and documentation for British travellers uncompli- cated – since 1860, passports had generally not been required for travel to any European country. The popularity of French Riviera resorts as places for wealthier British visitors to spend the winter is evidenced by the fact that by 1913–14 some 50,000 UK tourists are estimated to have been wintering on the coast.

World War I, disastrous though it was, proved to be only a brief hiatus in the expansion of travel, although it led to the widespread introduction of passports for nationals of many countries. The prosperity which soon returned to Europe in the 1920s, coupled with large-scale migration, meant unsurpassed demand for travel across the Atlantic, as well as within Europe. The first-hand experi- ence of foreign countries by combatants during the war aroused a sense of curiosity about foreign travel generally among less well-off sectors of the community for the first time. These sectors were also influenced by the new forms of mass com- munication which developed after the war: the cinema, radio and ultimately television, all of which educated the population and encouraged an interest in seeing more of the world.

Forms of travel also began to change rad- ically after the war. The railways went into a period of steady decline, following the introduc- tion of the motor car. Motorised public road transport and improved roads led to the era of the charabanc – adapted at first from army sur- plus lorries and equipped with benches to provide a rudimentary form of coach. These vehicles achieved immense popularity in the 1920s for outings to the seaside, but their poor safety record soon resulted in licensing regu- lations governing road transport. For those that could afford superior public transport, more lux- urious coaches also made an appearance: Motorways offered Pullman coaches, generally accommodating fifteen people in comfortable armchairs with tables, buffet bars and toilets. These coaches operated to many parts of Europe and North Africa, were used on safaris in East and Central Africa, and even provided a twice- weekly service between London and Nice, taking a relaxing five to six days for the trip.

However, it was the freedom of independent travel offered by the private motor car which contributed most to the decline of the railways' monopoly on holiday transport. The extensive use of the motor car for holidaying has its origins in the United States, where, in 1908, Henry Ford introduced his popular Model T at a price which brought the motor car within reach of the masses. By the 1920s, private motoring was a popular pastime for the middle classes in Britain, and the threat to domestic rail services was clear, although Continental rail services survived and prospered until challenged by the coming of the airlines. In an effort to stem the decline, domestic rail services in Britain were first rationalised in 1921 into four major companies – the London, Midland and Scottish Railway (LMS), London and North Eastern Railway (LNER), Great Western Railway (GWR) and Southern Railway (SR) – and later nationalised following World War II, remaining under public control until they were again privatised in the mid-1990s.

The arrival of the airline industry signalled the beginning of the end, not only for long-distance rail services but, more decisively, for the great steamship companies. British shipping lines had been under increasing threat from foreign competition throughout the 1920s with French, German and US liners challenging British supremacy on the North Atlantic routes particularly. The first commercial air routes were initiated as early as 1919 within Europe, but the infant air services were expensive (nearly £16 between London and Paris, or equivalent to several weeks' average earnings) and uncertain (passengers were warned that forced landings and delays could occur); it was therefore many years before air services achieved the reliability and low price which would make them competitive with world shipping routes. Pan American Airways introduced transatlantic air services in the 1930s (initially using flying boats), but in addition to their expense the aircraft proved unreliable, uncomfortable by modern standards and long-distance journeys necessitated frequent stopovers. In the early years, commercial aviation was more important for its mail-carrying potential than for the carriage of passengers. Only with the technological breakthroughs in aircraft design achieved during and after World War II did air

services prove a viable alternative to shipping for intercontinental travel.

THE ARRIVAL OF THE HOLIDAY CAMP

Among the major tourism developments of the 1930s, the creation of the holiday camp deserves a special mention. Aimed at the growing low-income market for holidays, the camps set new standards of comfort, offering 24-hour entertainment at an all-inclusive price, were efficient in operation and included child-minding services – a huge bonus for young couples on holiday with their children. This was in marked contrast to the lack of planned activities and the often surly service offered by the traditional seaside boarding houses of the day.

The origin of these camps goes back to early experiments by organisations such as the Co-operative Holidays Association, the Workers' Travel Association and the Holiday Fellowship (although summer camps for boys such as that run by Joseph Cunningham on the Isle of Man have been dated as early as 1887). However, their popularity and widespread acceptance by the public have been commonly ascribed to the efforts and promotional flair of Billy (later Sir Billy) Butlin. Supposedly Butlin, who built his first camp at Skegness in 1936, met a group of disconsolate holidaymakers huddled in a bus shelter to avoid the rain on a wet summer afternoon. It is thought he was also infuenced by a visit to Trusville Holiday Village in Mablethorpe, Lincolnshire, which had been opened and operated successfully by Albert Henshaw since 1924. Butlin determined to build a camp with all-weather facilities, for an all-in price. The instant success of the concept led to a spate of similar camps built by Butlin and other entrepreneurs such as Harry Warner and Fred Pontin in the pre-war and early post-war years. On the Continent, pre-war Germany had introduced the concept of the highly organised and often militaristic health and recreation camps which enabled many to enjoy holidays who would otherwise have been unable to afford them.

In France, the 'villages de vacance' arose from similar political and social influences. The success of this concept of all-in entertainment was later to be copied by hotels, and the hotel with its leisure

Figure 3.1 The early days of the holiday camp – Butlin's luxury holiday camp at Clacton-on-Sea, 1940s (*Courtesy Butlin's Holiday Worlds*)

complex became a popular development in the United States even before the war.

Interest in outdoor holidays and healthy recreation was also stimulated by the Youth Hostels Association in 1929 (the French equivalent opened in the same year), which provided budget accommodation for young people away from home.

THE POPULAR MOVEMENT TO THE SEASIDE

In spite of the rising appeal of holidays abroad, mass tourism between the wars and in the early post-World War II era remained largely domestic. This period saw the seaside holiday become firmly established as the traditional annual holiday destination for the mass of the British public. Suntans were for the first time seen as a status symbol, allied to health and time for leisure. Blackpool, Scarborough, Southend and Brighton consolidated their positions as leading resorts, while numerous newer resorts – Bournemouth, Broadstairs, Clacton, Skegness, Colwyn Bay – grew rapidly in terms of both visitors and residential population. Until the Great Depression of the 1930s, hotels and guest houses proliferated in these resorts. The tradition of the family holiday, taken annually over two weeks in the summer, became firmly established in Britain at this time.

The growing threat of competition from the European mainland was already apparent, for those who chose to take note of it. From the 1920s onwards, the Mediterranean Riviera had begun to attract a summer, as well as a winter, market from the UK, while the resorts of northern France were seen as cheaper and began to offer competition for the popular south coast resorts of Brighton, Hove, Folkestone and Eastbourne. These nearby French resorts, however, were seen primarily as places for short summer holidays, rather than the longer winter stays which had been popular with wealthy British clientele in the nineteenth century.

THE GROWTH OF GOVERNMENT INVOLVEMENT

It was in this period that Britain experienced the first stirrings of government interest in the tourism business. Britain was well behind other European countries in this respect: Switzerland, for example, had long recognised the importance of its inbound tourism and was actively involved in both tourism promotion overseas and gathering statistics on its visitors.

The British Travel and Holidays Association was established by the government in 1929, but with the theme 'travel for peace', its role was seen as essentially promotional, and its impact on the industry relatively light, until its change in status some forty years later. By the outbreak of World War II in 1939, the British government had at least recognised the potential contribution tourism could make to the country's balance of payments; equally, it had recognised the importance of holidays to the health and efficiency of the nation's workforce. The French government had already introduced holidays with pay in 1936; publication of the Amulree Report in 1938 led to the first Holidays with Pay Act for Britain in the same year. This encouraged voluntary agreements on paid holidays and generated the idea of a two-week paid holiday for all workers. Although this ambition was not fulfilled until several years after the end of World War II, by the outbreak of war some 11 million of the 19 million workforce were entitled to paid holidays – a key factor in generating mass travel.

Tourism since World War II

THE AVIATION INDUSTRY AND THE POSTWAR DESIRE FOR TRAVEL

As had occurred after World War I, World War II also led to an increased interest in overseas travel, arising from a desire to see the sites of such battles as those fought on the Normandy beaches and at St Nazaire. The extensive theatre of war had introduced combatants not only to new countries but to new continents, generating new friendships and an interest in diverse cultures. Another outcome of the war, which was radically to change the travel business, was the advance in aircraft technology, which was soon to lead to a viable commercial aviation industry for the first time. With the ending of the war in 1945, the first land-based commercial transatlantic flight took place between New York and Bournemouth, calling at Boston, Gander and Shannon. This flight, operated by American Overseas Airlines using a Douglas DC4, served to point the way ahead, although cost and the time involved, due to the frequent stops, ensured that long-haul flights would not become popular for some time.

The surplus of aircraft in the immediate post-war years, a benevolent political attitude towards the growth of private sector airlines, and the appearance on the scene of the early air travel entrepreneurs such as Harold Bamberg (of Eagle Airways) and Freddie Laker, aided the rapid expansion of air travel after the war. But more significantly for the potential market, aircraft had become more comfortable, safer, faster, and, in spite of relatively high prices in the early 1950s, steadily cheaper by comparison with other forms of transport. Commercial jet services began with the ill-fated Comet aircraft in the early 1950s, but already by that time advances in piston-engine technology had ensured that air travel prices would fall substantially. With the introduction of the commercially successful Boeing 707 jet in 1958, the age of air travel for the masses had arrived, hastening the demise of the great ocean liners. The number of passengers crossing the Atlantic by air exceeded those by sea for the first time in 1957, and although the liners continued to operate across the Atlantic for a further decade, their increasingly uncompetitive costs and the length of the journey time resulted in declining load factors from one year to the next. The new jets, with average speeds of 800–1,000 kph, compared with older propeller driven aircraft travelling at a mere 400 kph, meant that an air traveller could reach a far more distant destination within a given time. This was particularly valuable for business journeys where time was crucial.

THE DEVELOPMENT OF THE PACKAGE TOUR

The package tour depends upon the ability of tour operators to charter aircraft for their clientele, in order to drive down prices. The purchase of new jets by the large airlines left a large supply of good, second-hand propeller-driven aircraft, which were often purchased cheaply by smaller companies to undertake charter operations. These were able for the first time to transport holiday tourists to Mediterranean destinations both faster than, and almost as cheaply as, trains and coaches. These new charter services soon proved highly profitable. Initially, government policy ensured that charters were restricted to troop movements, but as official policy became more lenient, the private operators sought new forms of charter traffic. The package holiday business resulted from cooperation between these carriers and entrepreneurs in the travel business. Although there are instances of charter flights as early as the 1920s (Thomas Cook, for example, had organised an escorted charter, believed to be the first, to take fans from New York to Chicago in 1927 to see the Dempsey–Tunney heavyweight title fight), and the National Union of Students is known to have been organising charter flights for its members as early as 1949, Vladimir Raitz is generally credited with establishing the mass charter air movement as we know it today. In 1950, under the Horizon Holidays banner, he organised an experimental package holiday trip using a charter flight to Corsica. By chartering the aircraft and filling every seat instead of committing himself to a block of seats on scheduled air services, he was able to reduce significantly the unit cost of his air transport and hence the overall price to his customers. While carrying only 300 passengers in the first year, he repeated the experiment the following year and was soon operating profitably.

His idea was copied by other budding tour operators, and by the early 1960s the package holiday to the Mediterranean had become an established product for the mass holidaymakers. While the Spanish coastline and the Balearic Islands received the great proportion of these tourists, Italy, Greece and other Mediterranean coastal regions all benefited by the 'rush to the sun'. Other northern European countries were also soon setting up their own package holiday arrangements to the Mediterranean, and began to compete with Britain for accommodation along the Mediterranean coast. In Denmark, Pastor Eilif Krogager conducted a group of package tourists by coach to Spain in 1950, using the name of his village, Tjaereborg, as the company name. In 1962, Tjaereborg Travel moved into the air charter market with the formation of Sterling Airways, which was to become Western Europe's largest privately owned charter airline.

In Britain, difficulties in the economy forced the government to impose ever stricter control over the purchase of foreign currency. By the late 1960s the foreign travel allowance had been cut to only £50 per person. There was, however, a silver lining to this particular cloud; it encouraged people to take package holidays rather than travel independently, and the industry continued to flourish. The limits were relaxed from 1970 onwards, and with further liberalisation of air transport regulations, and longer paid holidays which encouraged a growing number of tourists to take a second holiday abroad each year, a new winter holiday market emerged in the 1970s. Through the more even spread of package holidays throughout the year, operators found that they were able to reduce their unit costs still further, and package holiday prices continued to fall, boosting off-season demand. It should be recognised, however, that Britain was not alone within Europe in imposing currency restrictions during these years; indeed, exchange controls were not totally abolished in France until as recently as 1990.

A further technological breakthrough in air transport occurred in 1970, when the first wide-bodied jets (Boeing 747s), capable of carrying over 400 passengers, appeared in service. The unit cost per seat fell sharply, and the result was an

Figure 3.2 A wide-bodied jumbo jet. (*Courtesy Adrian Meredith Aviation Library*)

increased supply of seats at potentially cheaper fares. This innovation meant that once again the aviation industry had to unload cheaply a number of obsolescent, although completely airworthy, smaller aircraft, and these were quickly pressed into service for charter operations.

THE MOVEMENT TO THE SUN

By the 1960s, it was clear that the future of mass market leisure travel was to be a north–south movement, from the cool and variable climates of North America and northern Europe, where the mass of relatively well-off people lived, to the sunshine and warmth of the temperate to tropical lands in the southern part of the northern hemisphere (see Figure 3.3). These southern countries were also for the most part less developed economically, and offered low-cost opportunities for the construction of a tourism industry. The new breed of tourism entrepreneurs involved with packaging tours recognised this trend very early on. Major hotel corporations, too, were quick to seize the opportunities for growth in these countries, and chains such as Sheraton and Hyatt in the USA quickly expanded into Mexico and the Caribbean, as well as into Florida and Hawaii, the states offering the most attractive climates for tourism development. In Europe, British and German tour operators such as Thomson and TUI developed bulk inclusive tours to the Mediterranean and North Africa, while, with steadily falling transport costs, operators were

Figure 3.3 Changes in destination trends for mass-market holidays, 1930s to 1980s

able to attract a fast-growing long-haul market. Florida, boosted particularly by the attractions of Disneyworld and Miami Beach, and by cheap charters across the Atlantic, has become a destination for Europeans almost as popular as major Mediterranean destinations.

The expert packaging of these tours has been extended to many other types of destination in the past twenty years. Tours to cultural and heritage sites, to capital cities such as London, Paris, Rome or Brussels, or river cruises on the Rhine or Danube have all been efficiently packaged and sold to the northern European market. The result was that by the end of the 1960s, some 2.5 million Britons were taking packaged holidays abroad each year. By the end of the 1980s, this had grown to over 11 million, with over 70 per cent of the British population having been abroad on holiday at least once in their lives.

Other trends in the flow of international tourism are also evident. There is, for example, a strong north–south movement in the flow of Japanese tourists to Australia. While the expansion of Japanese tourism generally is noteworthy and most European countries have benefited from it, travel time to Australia is shorter and, equally important, because the travel is largely within the same longitude there is no time change or jet lag to face. With typically only eight days of holiday, avoidance of jet lag becomes an attractive bonus for the market, and makes Australia doubly interesting to the Japanese. Absence of jet lag also promises to accelerate tourism to South Africa from the European nations, providing that the twin threats of growing crime and political disturbance can be overcome.

Destinations in the Pacific are beginning to attract Europeans in significant numbers, and have long attracted the Japanese and Australian markets. However, a large proportion of these visitors

Figure 3.4 An identikit destination: the Mediterranean beach. (*Courtesy Thomson Holidays*)

The larger the mass market, the less distinctive destinations are likely to be, especially if the destination is small and recently developed. One can find newly built 'marina' type resorts with yachting basins, hotel/apartment/villa accommodation, similar restaurants, cafés and shops, and golf, tennis, watersports, folk singers and barbecue nights in any one of a dozen countries around the Mediterranean, the Caribbean, North Africa and the South Pacific. These 'identikit' destinations are the result of comprehensive market research amongst various generating markets to find products with guaranteed mass demand. They may be compared with the piecemeal development of resorts two or three generations ago which may have had purely local or domestic attractions.

Not all destinations are similar, of course. While many may be 'down-market' in their attraction – that is they may offer cheap tourism to a large number of people, with the image of great popularity – others may offer an 'up-market' identikit image, allegedly offering higher quality and thus more expensive services to fewer people. So in the former category we may think of Benidorm, Magaluf, Benitses in the Mediterranean; Miami Beach in Florida; or Seefeld in Austria; while in the latter category we may think of Tahiti, Fiji, Malindi in Kenya, or Barbados. Many identikit destinations have been developed through the activities of multinational tour companies such as France's Club Méditerranée, Germany's Robinson Club or the United States' Sheraton Hotel chain. Within their establishments the tourist will find a comforting degree of uniformity.

Mass tourism has therefore demanded, and been supplied with, products designed specifically for its needs as revealed through the process of market research, i.e. products which are *user-orientated* as opposed to *resource-orientated* (that is, based on the resources available at a destination).

use the Pacific islands as stopover points for a night or two, rather than a holiday base. The impact of technology can be seen when for the first time aircraft became capable of flying direct between the USA and Sydney, with the introduction of the Boeing 747-400SP aircraft. Tahiti, slightly off the direct route between these continents and long established as an attractive stopover point but expensive for longer holidays, immediately suffered a sharp decline in visitors as the airlines concentrated their promotion on direct services between Los Angeles and Sydney or Auckland.

IDENTIKIT DESTINATIONS

The net result of these developments in tourism for the mass markets has been the establishment of destinations for particular market segments which, in all but their location, are very often remarkably similar. A convention centre, for example, may contain a conference building which may be usable for other purposes, with committee/lecture rooms, modern single or twin-bedded hotel rooms with private facilities, restaurants with banqueting rooms, bars, exhibition space, indoor and outdoor sports facilities and good scheduled transport links. The location may be Portsmouth, Basel or Rio – once inside their hotel or conference centre, delegates may not even notice where they are.

PRIVATE MOTORING AND HOLIDAYS

After a slow postwar recovery, standards of living rose steadily in the 1950s and after. Many people could consider buying a motor car for the first time, even if it were second-hand. For the first time, the holiday masses had the freedom to take to the roads as a family in their own private car, and the popular routes between London and the resorts on the south coast were soon clogged, in these pre-motorway days, with weekend traffic.

The flexibility which the car offered could not be matched by public transport services, and both bus and rail lost the holiday traveller. In 1950 some two out of every three holidaymakers took the train for their holidays in Britain. This fell to one in seven by 1970. In this period, private car ownership in Britain rose from 2 million to over 11 million vehicles, while by the end of the 1980s it had risen to some 20 million.

This trend led in turn to a growth in camping and caravanning holidays. Ownership of private caravans stood at nearly 800,000 by the end of the 1980s (excluding static caravans in parks), while 13 million holidaymakers in the UK took their holidays in a caravan. This development is a cause for some concern, however; the benefits to a region of private caravan tourism are considerably less than most other forms of tourism (owners can bring most of their own food with them, and do not require accommodation), while caravans tend to clog the holiday routes in summer. Both mobile caravans and static caravans at their sites are also something of an eyesore.

The switch to private transport led to new forms of accommodation to cater for this form of travel. Britain saw the development of its first motels, modelled on the American pattern, the contemporary version of the 'staging inn' catering for transit passengers. The construction of a new network of motorways and other road improvements brought the more distant resorts closer to centres of population, changing in some cases both the nature of the market served and the image of the resort itself. The ever resourceful tour operators met the private car threat to package holidays by devising more flexible packages such as 'fly-drive' programmes. Hotels, too, spurred on by their need to fill their rooms off-peak, devised their own programmes of short-stay holidays tailored to the private motorists' needs. Demand for hire cars abroad rose, as the overseas holidaymaker was emboldened to move away from the hotel ghettoes, and the car rental business benefited accordingly.

THE SHIPPING BUSINESS IN THE POSTWAR PERIOD

In the passenger shipping business, hit by rising prices and competition from the airlines, shipping companies were gradually forced to abandon their traditional liner routes in the 1960s. Some companies attempted to adapt their vessels for cruising, though not entirely successfully: vessels purpose-built for long-distance, fast, deep-sea voyages are not ideally suited for cruising, either economically or from the standpoint of customer demand. Many were incapable of anchoring alongside docks in the shallow waters of popular cruise destinations such as the Caribbean. Companies that failed to embark on a programme of new construction, either due to lack of resources or lack of foresight, soon ceased trading. Others, such as the Cunard Line, were taken over by conglomerates outside the travel or transport industries. However, many new purpose-built cruise liners, of Greek, Norwegian and later Russian registry soon appeared on the market to fill the gaps left by the declining maritime powers. These vessels, in spite of their registry, were to be based primarily in the Caribbean or Mediterranean waters. British shipping was not entirely without innovations at this time, however; Cunard initiated the fly-cruise concept in the 1960s, with vessels based at Gibraltar and Naples, where passengers flew out to join their cruise in chartered aircraft.

If the rapid escalation of fuel and other costs during the 1970s threatened the whole future of deep-sea shipping, the ferry services, by contrast, achieved quite exceptional levels of growth from the 1950s onward. This largely resulted from the increased demand from private motorists taking their cars abroad, influencing particularly routes between Scandinavian countries and Germany, and between Britain and the Continent. Growth in demand was also better spread across the seasons, enabling vessels to be in service throughout the year with respectable load factors (although freight demand substantially boosted weak passenger revenue in the winter period). Regular sailings, with fast turnarounds in port, encouraged bookings, and costs were kept down by offering much more restricted levels of service than would be expected on long-distance routes. Hovercraft and jetfoil services were introduced across the Channel, although their success was limited by technical problems and their withdrawal in rough weather.

GOVERNMENT POLICY IN THE MASS MARKET ERA

In Britain, the end of the 1960s was marked by a new direction in government policy towards tourism, with the introduction of the 1969 Development of Tourism Act. This Act, the first in the country specifically and uniquely devoted to tourism, established a new framework for public sector tourism, which took into account the industry's growing importance to the British economy. For the first time, also, conservation became an issue, as the number of foreign visitors to Britain leapt. The former laissez-faire attitude of successive governments gave way to recognition of the need for adequate planning and control in order to balance supply and demand, to maintain the quality of the tourist product, and to safeguard consumers' rights. Thus, tour operators became licensed by the government for the first time in the 1970s, and government incentives were introduced for the construction of hotels and other tourist facilities. The first serious efforts were made to categorise and register the accommodation sector, although resistance by hoteliers eventually led to a voluntary form of registration only. The failures of public sector planning and control in other countries (notably Spain) where exceptionally high growth rates in visitors were recorded, added fuel to the government's concern.

By the 1980s, however, the Conservative government's attitude to tourism had shifted to passive encouragement rather than active financial support. Grants provided under the terms of the 1969 Act were discontinued in England, and policy became one of encouraging partnerships between the private and public sectors. Responsibility for tourism was in turn transferred, first from the Department of Trade and Industry to the Department of Employment, and then in 1992 to the newly created Department of National Heritage. In 1997, following a Labour victory in the elections, this department's name changed to the Department for Culture, Media and Sport, within which a Minister for Film and Tourism reports to the Secretary of State.

Some efforts were made to coordinate the various government departments' interests in tourism through the establishment of committees such as the Inter-Departmental Tourism Coordinating Committee. On the whole, however, the government adopted a 'market forces' approach to tourism development, and increasingly by the end of the 1980s people were looking towards the European Union for legislation governing the industry. The Union responded through the introduction of a number of measures designed to liberalise air and road transport, to harmonise hotel classification, to ease frontier controls and to bring into line VAT and duty-free regulations throughout the Union. Most important, from the standpoint of the consumer, though, were measures aimed at providing greater protection for the traveller buying package holidays. These measures will be discussed at greater length in Chapter 15.

THE GROWING IMPORTANCE OF BUSINESS TRAVEL

The growth in world trade in these decades saw a steady expansion in business travel, individually and in the conference and incentive travel fields, although the recession of the late 1980s and early 1990s caused cutbacks in business travel as sharp as those in leisure travel. As economic power shifted between countries, so emerging nations provided new patterns of tourism generation: in the 1970s, Japan and the oil-rich nations of the Middle East led the growth, while in the 1980s, countries such as Korea and Malaysia expanded both inbound and outbound business tourism dramatically.

CHANGING PATTERNS IN TOURISM DEMAND

It is fitting to complete this chapter by examining some of the current trends and developments in the holiday market. Certainly, patterns of holiday-taking are changing quite rapidly, and the trade must take account of cultural, social and technological change, as well as numerical growth.

Special interest holidays in particular have been developed to cater for the widening range of interests of a leisure-orientated society. Activity holidays have become increasingly important, especially to workers whose jobs are desk-bound; and as service jobs fast replace manufacturing, such jobs become more common. Young people especially are seeking greater thrills from their adventure holidays, and hang-gliding, power-gliding, bungee jumping and sundry other thrill holidays are becoming commonplace.

In the 1970s, as prices soared, tour operators attempted to restrain prices through budget offers which often fell below the quality levels anticipated by consumers. Selling on price became the keynote for the industry, and inevitably the rising toll of complaints forced companies to consider value for money and quality assurance by the end of the 1980s.

Self-catering has become an increasingly popular form of package holiday, partly as a cost-saving measure but equally as a means of overcoming the constraints imposed by package holidays in general and the accommodation sector in particular. Set meals at set times gave way to 'eat what you please, where you please, when you please'. In reply, the package tour industry provided the product to meet this need: self-catering villas and apartments flourished across southern Europe, while in the UK, resort hotels gave way to self-catering flats. Hundreds of thousands of Britons invested in timeshare property in order to own their own 'place in the sun', or increasingly found their own accommodation abroad, while the operators provided 'seat-only' packages on charter aircraft to cater for their transport needs. There is some evidence that the decline in hotel accommodation may have been arrested, with hotels more popular than self-catering in 1997 package holiday bookings for the first time in five years.

The market for short-break holidays of between one and three nights has expanded rapidly during the 1990s. In Britain, about 3 million people now take short breaks, frequently in addition to their main holidays, although many are taken within the UK. This has been a boost to the British hotel industry, as foreign holidays usurped the traditional seaside holiday at home. Overseas destinations featured are expanding rapidly, with the traditional destinations of Paris, Amsterdam and Brussels giving way to Barcelona, Rome, Budapest, Prague, Cracow, Reykjavik, even New York.

Long-haul traffic in particular has shown a huge rise as growing disposable incomes are matched by ever-reducing air fares, especially across the Atlantic. Holidays to Florida and other parts of the USA, and to the Dominican Republic (one of the cheapest destinations in the Caribbean, and recently well developed by European tour operators) have boomed, while many holidaymakers are no longer content merely to lie on the beaches of the Mediterranean, and are travelling as far afield as Pattaya Beach and Phuket, Thailand, Goa in India and Mombasa, Kenya, to enjoy their traditional sun, sea and sand holiday.

The importance of the 'grey panther' market is finally being recognised by the industry, as the growing market of over-50s spend increasing sums on international travel. In Britain, 18 million

Figure 3.5 The linear tour: an example of the 'milk run' around Britain over-50s control 60 per cent of the nation's wealth, and their number will rise to nearly 20 million by 2001, a third of the population. These already account for nearly 40 per cent of overseas holidays purchased, and many over-50s are retiring earlier to indulge in travel, especially long-haul and cruising.

The traditional 'law of tourism harmony', in which every aspect of the tour would be broadly of similar standard and quality, is now giving way to a 'pick and mix' approach, in which savings may be effected in one area in order to indulge oneself in another. Tourists may decide, for example, to choose cheap B&B accommodation while eating out in expensive restaurants. The term 'Hilton Hippies' has been used to describe those who may want to engage in rough activities such as mountain biking by day, but look for luxury in their overnight accommodation. The travel industry will have to respond by providing more flexible packaging for their clients in the future. Many are already doing so, and tailor-made divisions, especially among the specialist tour operators, have been formed to meet this demand.

THE ALL-INCLUSIVE HOLIDAY

Another major factor appearing in the mid-1990s has been the trend towards the *all-inclusive* holiday. As the term indicates, this holiday includes everything – food, alcoholic drinks, watersports and other entertainment at the hotel. The attractions of this form of tourism are obvious – it is seen by tourists as offering better value; they can pay up front for the holiday, know what their budget will be well in advance, and be unconcerned about changes in the value of foreign currency, or the need to take large sums of money abroad. For the more timid foreign traveller, or those who are concerned about being badgered by local souvenir sellers and 'beach salesmen', there is the added reassurance that they do not even have to leave the hotel complex to enjoy their holidays. However, there are clearly serious implications for the local economy, as local bars, shopkeepers and others no longer stand to benefit from the influx of tourists, while greater profits flow back to the operators in generating countries who control the leisure site. This form of tourism may be judged far removed from the concept of sustainable tourism, although operators themselves would argue that by keeping tourists in 'ghettoes' they are in fact helping to reduce the negative impact of tourism on locals.

This form of tourism originated in the Caribbean, and up-market tour operators such as Sandals have promoted these programmes very successfully to the US and European markets. The concept has now moved down-market, though, and is growing rapidly in key European resorts such as those of the Balearic Islands, where it is threatening the livelihood of many in the traditional coastal resorts.

The pace of change in the tourism world is speeding up all the time, and just as the generating countries are having to learn to adjust to rapidly fluctuating economic swings, so must entrepreneurs who have to cater for these changes learn to identify them as they occur, and to react quickly by providing the products their clients seek, in the face of ever-increasing competition They must, however, at the same time ensure that any new initiatives are in line with the need for sustainable development.

QUESTIONS AND DISCUSSION POINTS

1. What changes have occurred in the holiday camp business in the past fifty years? What accounted for these changes? Do you foresee further changes in the next few years?

2. As an in-coming tour operator, suggest ways in which you would plan to cater for the particular needs of American tourists visiting Britain.

3. Compare the advantages and disadvantages of travelling through the Channel Tunnel as opposed to using ferries. What kinds of market are attracted to each, and why?

1 As a research officer in the Planning and Development Department of Sunny Tours, you have been asked by your Head of Department, Lucia Lamamoor, to provide her with a report on the relationship between sun-bathing and skin-cancers. She is interested in knowing whether this is a factor that might influence the development of the company's tours over the next few years.

Trace any references you can find to the subject, and see if the number of articles appearing in newspapers and magazines on the subject have increased over the past ten years. Identify the main issues discussed in the articles. Design and undertake a pilot survey which will help you to know whether the public are aware of the problem and if they are taking action of any kind. Write a short report to your Head of Department, giving the main findings and suggesting what further research should be undertaken.

2 As an assistant in the Marketing Department of New Wave Tours, a medium-sized tour operator, you have been asked to give your Marketing Manager, Jimmy Murphy, your views on the growth destinations for the next few years. The company has largely dealt with the traditional sun, sea and sand tours to the Mediterranean, but is thinking of going further afield. Examine trends, particularly in long-haul tours, and summarise these in a report to Murphy, supported by figures where possible.

Murphy is also concerned about a possible drop-off in the sale of package tours generally, in favour of independent travel. Within your report, give your views, and suggest what action the company should take.

4

The Economics of Tourism

OBJECTIVES

After studying this chapter, you should be able to:

- identify the economic benefits of tourism for a nation, both nationally and regionally;
- be aware of the principal trends in tourism, as they affect Britain specifically, and the world generally;
- understand how tourism is measured statistically;
- recognise the limitations of statistical measurement.

Introduction

Tourism is a human activity which arises in part from the economic circumstances of the consumer. It also has an economic impact upon nations and regions. For both these reasons, we need to study and understand the economic nature of tourism. This is a topic which is complex, and can only be touched on in this text; readers who wish to examine the subject in depth are referred to texts designed for this purpose, such as Bull (1995). The aim of this chapter will be primarily to explore the economic impact of tourism resulting from national and international tourist flows, and the ways in which this is measured and recorded. In later chapters, the economics of the firm, the industry and its various sectors will be examined.

First, however, we will look at the movement of tourists internationally, and some of the economic factors influencing these flows.

The international tourist market

Travel and tourism is probably the single most important industry in the world. It currently accounts for at least 6 per cent of the world's Gross Domestic Product (GDP), and employs 127 million people around the world, one job in every fifteen. According to the World Tourism Organisation, nearly 592 million international trips were taken in 1996, an increase of 4.3 per cent over the previous year. Worldwide tourism receipts (excluding the cost of international fares)

Table 4.1 A profile of international tourism 1950–96

Year	Arrivals (m)	Receipts ($bn)
1950	25.3	2.1
1960	69.3	6.9
1970	159.7	17.9
1980	284.8	102.4
1990	459.2	264.7
1991	466.0	271.8
1992	503.6	308.6
1993	518.3	314.0
1994	546.3	346.7
1995 (R)	566.4	393.3
1996 (E)	591.9	423.0

Note: excludes international fares.
(R) = Revised (E) = estimated
Source: TIQ Aug 97/World Tourism Organisation

rose 7.6 per cent, to $423 billion. These figures do not include the vast number of people taking trips within their own country; probably six times this number will take a trip lasting at least four nights. (see Table 4.1)

The rapid increase in international travellers during the early postwar years, exceeding 10 per cent per annum from 1950 to 1960, could not be permanently sustained, of course, and it reflected the pent-up demand which the war years, and the slow economic recovery after the war, had constrained. Nevertheless, it is worth noting that between 1990 and 1996, the average annual growth was around 4 per cent, still a quite remarkable increase year on year, especially taking into account the worldwide recession of the early 1990s. The good news for the tourism industry is that world tourism is expected to continue to rise for the foreseeable future. According to the World Travel and Tourism Council, tourism will represent 11.5 per cent of world GDP by the year 2006, at $7.1 trillion, and will then employ some 385 million people.

International tourism is generated for the most part within the nations of Europe, Canada and the United States, the result of low prices, frequent flights, and large, relatively wealthy populations (see Tables 4.2 and 4.3). However, in recent years

Table 4.2 Leading tourism generating countries, 1995 (based on tourism expenditure)

Country	Expenditure ($bn)
1 Germany	50.7
2 USA	45.9
3 Japan	36.8
4 UK	24.7
5 France	16.3
6 Italy	12.4
7 Austria	11.7
8 Russia	11.6
9 Netherlands	11.6
10 Canada	11.2

Source: World Tourism Organisation

Table 4.3 Leading tourism receiving countries, 1995 (based on receipts)

Country	Receipts ($bn)
1 USA	61.1
2 France	27.5
3 Italy	27.5
4 Spain	25.7
5 UK	19.1
6 Germany	16.2
7 Austria	14.6
8 Hong Kong	9.6
9 Switzerland	9.4
10 China	8.8

Source: BTA Digest of Tourism Statistics/World Tourism

Japan has been fast overtaking some European countries in generating tourism, the result not just of its wealth but also of the increased willingness of its population to take holidays. Traditionally, the Japanese have been unwilling to take all the holidays to which they are entitled, but encouraged by the Japanese government to do so in order to reduce the huge surpluses on their balance of payments, they are now travelling abroad in greater numbers and for longer periods of time. As a result, Japan is now among the top five generating countries which together are responsible for well over half the total expenditure on foreign travel.

It is interesting to note the changes occurring over time between the order of these countries. While the leading generating countries change little from one year to another, Taiwan in 1995 was surprisingly in twelfth place, with $8.4 billion, while Korea was in fourteenth place, with $5.9 billion. This reflects the growth of the 'tiger economies' of the Pacific, a region from which we can expect to see huge increases in international travel in the future. Poland is the second former Eastern Bloc country, after Russia, to engage in prolific overseas travel, lying in fifteenth place.

Simply looking at receipts will not give a sound picture of the value of tourism to an economy. The countries with the highest per capita receipts are Sweden, with over $4,000 spent for every tourist visiting, followed by Denmark and Japan – the UK would not even appear in the top forty of these countries. Similarly, the highest per capita spend by tourists coming to Britain is the Icelandic, at £92 a day, while Eastern Europeans spend only £27 on average. In economic terms, the financial value of tourism to a country is more important than the number of tourists it receives, so it is important to assess the average daily spend of tourists from different countries and the average length of time tourists from a particular country spend when visiting a country.

One must also always take account of factors likely to lead to the growth or decline of tourists from each country. The potential for growth, for example, is currently high for those living in former Soviet bloc countries, although their per capita expenditure will in many cases be small. On the other hand, a growing élite in these countries are high-spend tourists whom receiving countries are eager to cultivate. The potential from Japan remains high also, as only 9 per cent of the population have travelled abroad. What is more, Japanese are the highest spenders per capita when travelling abroad, spending in excess of $2,200 per person (their high spend on shopping and souvenirs for friends and relatives may account for this). Australians are the second-highest spenders, followed by tourists from Thailand, Taiwan and Singapore. In spite of the high revenues received from Americans travelling abroad, only 11 per cent of the population actually possesses a passport; most American tourists tend to travel to adjacent countries which do not require them to possess passports, and because of the size and diversity of landscape a large proportion of the US market is content to take their holidays within their own country, so the *propensity* to take holidays abroad is another important characteristic to take into account.

While (as we shall see in the next chapter) there are many factors which motivate people to travel abroad, the major factor will be the relative cost, compared with their income. As greater demand also leads to lower prices, with transport and accommodation costs falling for each additional person booked, there is a direct relationship between cost, price and demand (see Figure 4.1).

This helps to explain the vicious price wars in

Figure 4.1 The relationship between cost, price and demand

the travel industry, designed to capture market share and increase numbers, especially during the difficult years of the late 1980s and early 1990s, when Britain was experiencing a severe recession.

Britain's place in world tourism

Britain has enjoyed comparable growth with other western nations, both in its outbound and inbound markets. At the beginning of the 1950s, Britons were only taking some 5.5 per cent of their holidays abroad; but by 1995 this had risen to 44 per cent. In 1996, British residents took 43.2 million trips abroad, of which 27.4 million were holidays. Of these, some 14.2 million were package holidays. The proportion of holidays taken as package tours, 52 per cent, has fallen somewhat over the past decade, from a high of 63 per cent in 1988, reflecting a greater willingness to travel independently, as tourists gain confidence in foreign travel. UK visitors to France slightly exceed those to Spain, but the proportion of those on package tours is far greater in the case of the latter destination. France's appeal, because of its proximity to England and the nature of its tourist attractions, is for self-drive holidays in particular, and the country continues to receive the greatest number of British visitors abroad – nearly 10 million in 1995, compared to Spain's 8.3 million – but the growth in long-haul holidays has also been marked, particularly to the United States, which received 2.7 million visitors from Britain in 1995.

The propensity of the British to take a holiday – that is, the ratio of those taking holidays out of the total population – is high. Around 60 per cent

Table 4.4 Trends in British holidaytaking: foreign holidays and inclusive tours 1987–95

Year	Holiday (000s)	Inclusive tours (000s)
1987	19 703	11 980
1988	20 700	12 596
1989	21 847	12 590
1990	21 255	11 391
1991	20 630	10 646
1992	23 100	12 600
1993	25 133	13 600
1994	27 337	15 164
1995	28 110	15 305
1996 (P)	27 441	14 182

Source: Business Monitor MQ6/BTA Digest of Tourist Statistics

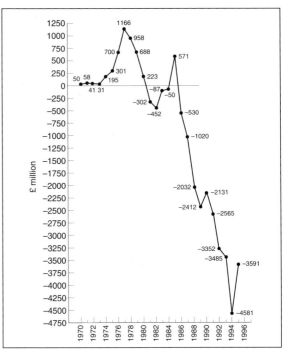

Figure 4.2 Britain's balance of payments on tourism account, 1970–95

of Britons take a holiday of four nights or more, and this figure has remained relatively unchanged for many years, having peaked in 1980 at 62 per cent. However, this is not as high as many of our European partners. Over 80 per cent of Switzerland's population, and a similar number from Sweden, take a holiday every year; this northern participation rate is almost certainly due to the inhospitable climate and long winter nights, leading to a desire on the part of many in the population to take a holiday in the sun.

Future trends for British travel appear healthy. The British have now firmly adopted the habit of taking an annual holiday, and nearly a quarter take two or more holidays of four nights or more each year (10 per cent take three or more). Not only are disposable incomes growing; inherited wealth is also having an impact on holiday spending, as those in middle age inherit properties from the first generation of parents to own their own homes on a wide scale. The Henley Centre forecast in 1997 that overseas holiday spending would rise to over £20 billion in 1998, £22.7 billion in 1999, £25.7 billion in the year 2000 and £28.8 billion in 2001.

Britain received around 26 million visitors in 1996, a peak year for incoming visits. Nevertheless, expenditure by British residents abroad continues to exceed receipts from foreign tourists in Britain, and the result is a steady balance of payments deficit on the tourism account over the past decade (see Figure 4.2). However, Britain does benefit substantially from incoming and domestic tourism; about two and a half million people, or one in ten of the working population, are estimated to work in tourism or a related activity, and tourism accounts for just over 5 per cent of all export earnings. This compares with over 20 per cent in Spain, which, in view of the volatile nature of the business, might appear to many observers to be an overdependence upon tourism in the economy.

The value of economic data

Gathering data on tourists is a vital task for the government of a country, both for use by its own national tourist office and for the benefit of the providers of tourism services. Governments need to know the contribution which tourism makes to the economy in terms of income, employment, investment and the balance of payments. Concern with regional development requires that these statistics be sufficiently refined to allow them to be broken down by region. Governments will also wish to compare their tourism performance with that of other countries, as well as to establish their performance in attracting tourists to the country over a period of time.

Tourism organisations, whether in the public or the private sector, need such data to enable them to forecast what will happen in the future. This means identifying trends in the market, patterns of growth and changing demand for destinations, facilities or types of holiday.

On the basis of this knowledge, future planning can be undertaken. The public sector will make recommendations and decisions regarding the *infrastructure* and *superstructure* needed to support growth. Infrastructure will include, for example, the building of new airports or the expansion of existing ones; the provision of new or improved roads to the growth destinations; or the improvement of other services such as public utilities, including water or electricity, which will be needed to cope with the expected expansion of tourism. The superstructure will comprise the tourist facilities needed – hotels, restaurants, shops and other services the tourist takes for granted. It cannot necessarily be assumed that these services will be provided by developers in the private sector. If a new destination is being developed, there will be a degree of risk involved while the destination becomes established, and developers may be reluctant to invest in such projects as hotels until there is proven demand for the destination. Governments or local authorities can themselves undertake the construction of hotels, as often occurs in Third World countries, or they can encourage hotel construction by underwriting costs or providing subsidies of some kind until the destination becomes established. Similarly, private companies can use the statistics which demonstrate growth or market change by extending or adapting their products to meet the changing needs of the marketplace.

To show how this information can be used, let us take the example of a destination such as London, which attracts a high volume of overseas visitors. The flow of these visitors will be affected by a great many different factors; if tourists can purchase more pounds sterling for their own currency, or if air fares have fallen to the destination, or if a major event such as an international exhibition is being organised, this will encourage tourism to the city. If London is being hit by a spate of terrorist bomb attacks, as occurred in late 1992, this may dissuade visitors from travelling, especially from generating countries such as North America, where there is particular sensitivity to the threat of terrorism. Negative first impressions, such as air pollution in the city, extensive littering, a decaying and overcrowded public transport system, even large numbers of homeless on the streets, can affect tourism adversely, and tourists may decide to go elsewhere, or recommend to their friends that they do so. Recessions may be hitting countries to different extents, so that in one year the forecast might be for a reduced number of tourists from the USA, but a growth in the number from Japan. Companies will have to take this into account in their promotional campaigns – and may need to consider employing staff with the appropriate languages to deal with the new incoming market.

These statistics are of particular importance in guiding the marketing plans of an organisation, whether a national tourist office or a private company. On the basis of the forecasts made, organisations must decide where they will advertise, to whom, and with what theme. To give just one example, it has been revealed that in recent years the Japanese market has been tempted to Paris rather than London, as Paris is seen by the many female Japanese visitors as being more a 'feminine' destination, and therefore less challenging. This might require the London Tourist Board, as part of its marketing campaign in that country, to set itself the task of generating a softer image for the city.

It will be seen from this last example that international tourism depends on more than merely economic behaviour of tourists; it will also be influenced by motivation arising from the tourists' efforts to meet their psychological or sociological needs. These latter motivations will be examined in the following chapter. It is the concern of this chapter to reveal the economic effects of tourism, and how these are measured.

The economic impact of tourism

Like other industries, tourism affects the economy of those areas – whether regions, countries or continents – where it takes place. These are known as tourist *destinations*, or *receiving areas*, and many become dependent upon an inflow of tourism to sustain their economy. This is especially true of Third World countries, some of which are largely or almost totally dependent upon tourism. The areas from which the tourists come to visit these destinations are known as *generating* areas, and of course, as the tourists are taking their money with them to spend in other places, this represents a net loss of revenue to the generating area, and a gain to the receiving area.

Students of tourism must understand the effect of the flow of tourists between generating and receiving areas, which can be measured in four distinct ways. We must examine the effect on *income*, on *employment*, on the area's *balance of payments* and on *investment and development*. We will look at each of these in turn.

INCOME

Income is generated from wages and salaries, interest, rent and profits. In a labour-intensive industry such as tourism, the greatest proportion is likely to be derived from wages and salaries paid to those working in jobs either directly serving the needs of tourists or benefiting indirectly from the tourists' expenditure. Income will be greater in those areas which receive large numbers of tourists, where visitors tend to stay for longer periods, where the destination attracts an up-market or more free-spending clientele, and where there are many opportunities to spend. A destination such as the Côte d'Azur, for example, satisfies most of these criteria, attracting not only many overseas visitors for a fairly long season (even through the winter some tourists will be attracted to the milder climate) but also bringing in many domestic tourists from other areas of France. A number of up-market resorts such as Nice, Cannes, Antibes, St Tropez or Juan les Pins provide a good range of relatively expensive

hotels; there are also expensive shops and restaurants, casinos, night-clubs and discos where the high-spend tourists can be relieved of their money. There are opportunities for water-based activities such as yachting or fishing, with marinas to attract the wealthy motor yacht owners; and there are numerous attractions nearby which bring in the day excursionists by coach or private car. Finally, the area is also well served with conference and exhibition halls, which will draw the high-spend business tourists.

It is important to recognise that, while income may be greatest where wage levels are high and there is relatively little unemployment in the area, tourism may in fact be of greater value in those areas where there are few other opportunities for employment. In Britain, for example, tourism is of prime importance in areas where there is little industry, such as the Scottish Highlands, western Wales and Cornwall. The tourism industry is often criticised for providing only low-wage, seasonal employment, but this is in fact a gross exaggeration, and many posts associated with the tourism business are neither seasonal nor temporary. As to low-wage jobs, one must take into account that were there no tourism in the area, many workers would be unemployed, as there may be few alternatives.

Income is also generated from interest, rent and profits on tourism businesses. This could include, for example, the interest paid on loans to an airline in order to buy aircraft, or rent paid to a landowner for a car park or campsite near the sea. We must also count taxation on tourism activities, such as VAT on hotel bills or the direct taxation which some countries levy on tourists to raise additional public income. In Austria, to give one example, there is a *Kurtaxe* imposed on accommodation to raise money for the local authority. Many countries, including the UK, levy a *departure tax* on all international travellers, and in the USA airline taxes are levied on both departing and arriving travellers.

The sum of all incomes in a country is called the national income, and the importance of tourism to a country's economy can be measured by looking at the proportion of national income created by tourism. In Britain this is estimated to be about 4 per cent, including income from accom-

Table 4.5 Percentage of national income represented by tourism in selected countries

Country	Percentage
Antigua and Barbuda	87
Maldives	82
Balearics	81
St Lucia	46
Barbados	33
Bermuda	29

Source: Spiegel Special, 'Urlaub Total' No 2 1997

modation, tourist transport and all kinds of extras for which tourists pay. This may seem a small percentage, but even engineering, the country's largest industry, contributes only about 8 per cent to the national income. By contrast, some regions of the world, particularly the Caribbean countries, are heavily dependent upon the income from tourism, as the Table 4.5 demonstrates. Some might see this as an unhealthy overdependence upon one rather volatile industry.

Attempts to measure the impact of tourism are always difficult, because it is difficult to distinguish the spend by tourists and the spend by others in restaurants or shops, for example. In resorts, even such businesses as laundromats – which we would not normally associate with the tourism industry – might be highly dependent upon the tourist spend where, for instance, a large number of visitors are camping, caravanning or in self-catering facilities. Furthermore, tourism's contribution to the income of an area is enhanced by a phenomenon known as the *tourism income multiplier* (TIM). This arises because money spent by tourists in the area will be re-spent by recipients, augmenting the total. The multiplier is the factor by which tourist spend is increased in this process. This is easiest to demonstrate by way of the following example.

Example

A number of tourists visit Highjinks on Sea, spending £1,000 in hotels and other facilities

there. This amount is received as income by the hoteliers and owners of the facilities, who, after paying their taxes and saving some of the income, spend the rest. Some of what they spend goes to buy items imported into the area, but the rest goes to shopkeepers, suppliers and other producers inside the area. These people in turn pay their taxes, save some money and spend the rest.

Let us assume that the average rate of taxation is 20p in the pound, that people are saving on average 10p in the pound of their gross income, and are therefore left with 70p in the pound to spend on goods and services. Let us further assume that of this 70p in the pound spend, 20p is spent on goods and services imported from other areas, while the remaining 50p is retained within the local community. The original £1,000 spent by the tourists will then circulate in the local community as shown in Figure 4.3, in the category 'first circulation'.

Of the 50p spent within the community, some will go to local suppliers of such items as food. The shopkeepers or restaurateurs then pay their employees who in turn shop in other shops locally, although some of what they purchase will have been brought into the region from outside. This second circulation will be further spent by the recipients, and so the cycle goes on, with a declining expenditure at each level of circulation. These cycles are illustrated in Figure 4.3 under the categories of second circulation, third circulation, and so on.

Each time the money is circulated in this way, some will be lost to the area. Taxes paid are transmitted outside the area, some of the savings may be similarly removed from the area, and some of the spend has gone to pay for goods imported into the area from other regions of the country or even from abroad. Expenditures in which the money is lost to other areas are known as *leakages* from the system.

So far, how much income has been created? From Figure 4.3 we can see that it is £1,000 + £500 + £250 + £125 + ... A progression is developing, and by adding up all the figures or by using the appropriate mathematical formula, we will find that the total sum is £2,000. The original injection of £,1,000 by tourists visiting the area has multiplied by a factor of 2 to produce income of £2,000.

Figure 4.3 The tourism income multiplier at work

It is possible to forecast the value of the multiplier if one knowns the proportion of leakages in the local economy. In the example above, tax was $^{20}/_{100}$ths of original income, savings were $^{10}/_{100}$ths of income and imports were $^{20}/_{100}$ths of income. Total leakages therefore amount to $^{50}/_{100}$ths, or half the original income. The multiplier can be found by applying the formula:

$$\text{Multiplier} = \frac{1}{\text{proportion of leakages}}$$

In the example given, the multiplier was $^1/_{0.5}$, or 2.

So in an economy with a high proportion of leakages, such as high tax rates (although we must remember that the government may choose to reinvest this tax money in the local economy, so much of it may not be lost for all time), or where many of the goods demanded by consumers are imported, TIM may be quite low, and the economy will not benefit greatly from tourism. Local hotels may also be foreign-owned, so that profits achieved are then transmitted to the hotel chain's head office and so lost to the area. This might be true of other tourist facilities in the area, or even

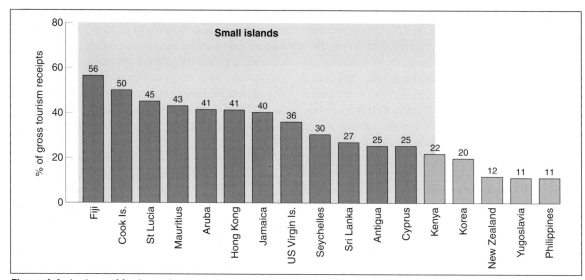

Figure 4.4 Leakage of foreign exchange earnings: seventeen countries. (*Source: WTO*)

local ground handling agents or coach operators may be owned by companies based elsewhere, leading to further losses in the multiplier effect. On the other hand, where many firms are in the hands of locals, and leakages are minimised in this way, the TIM may be quite high, and tourism will contribute far more than the amount originally spent by the tourists themselves. The principal reasons for leakages include:

- cost of imported goods, especially food and drink
- foreign exchange costs of imports for the development of tourist facilities
- remittance of profits abroad
- remittance of wages by expatriates
- management fees or royalties for franchises
- payments to overseas carriers and travel companies
- costs of overseas promotion
- additional expenditure on imports resulting from the earnings of those benefiting from tourism

Many studies have been undertaken of the tourism multiplier effect in different areas, ranging from individual resorts such as Eastbourne and Edinburgh to entire countries such as Barbados and Fiji. In most cases, the multiplier has varied between 1 and 2.5 (estimates have put it at about 1.7 for Britain as a whole, and around 1.2–1.5 for individual towns and regions in the UK), although in the case of some Third World destinations which depend heavily on outside investment and must import much of the food and other commodities demanded by tourists, the figure may be well below 1. The TIM for Barbados, for instance, has been estimated at 0.60. Leakages in Western developed nations are generally estimated at around 10 per cent of tourism income, while in developing economies with strong tourism dependency such as Fiji, the Cook Islands, Mauritius and the Virgin Islands, estimates suggest that imports consume 36–56 per cent of gross tourism receipts.

EMPLOYMENT

Tourism is also important to an economy because it generates employment. In some tourism-dependent economies, such as the Caribbean, as much as 25 per cent of all jobs are associated with the tourism industry. Jobs will be created in travel agencies, tour operators and other intermediaries which supply tourist services in both the generating and destination areas. Transport companies such as airlines will also employ staff to serve tourists in both areas. But the bulk of employment will be in the destination country, with jobs ranging from hotel managers to deckchair attendants, from excursion booking clerks to cleaners employed in the stately homes that are open to the public, or maintenance staff who will maintain the rides at leisure centres or theme parks in the resort.

Many of these jobs are seasonal or part-time, so that tourism's contribution to full-time employment is considerably less than its contribution to 'job-hours'. Whilst this is a criticism of the industry in economic terms, and one that has resulted in large sums of money being spent in an effort to lengthen the tourist season in many resorts, one must be reminded that these jobs are often being created in an area where there is little alternative employment. It is also worth making the point that many of the jobs attract those who wish to work seasonally, such as students seeking the job of resort representative during the summer, or householders who wish to open their houses for summer periods only as bed and breakfast establishments.

Earlier, it was pointed out that Britain has some 2.5 million workers involved in 'tourism or an associated activity'. The gist of the problem lies in estimating exactly what is to be included in the tourism statistics. A high proportion of jobs will be in hotels and catering, and estimates of those actually employed in the more narrowly defined 'travel and tourism industry' in Britain are thought to number around 125,000 only. In 1991, ABTA's National Training Board undertook a study of the travel services sector, embracing tour operating, retail travel and business travel, concluding that around 80,000 were directly employed in these fields, of whom perhaps 12 000 were in management posts (*An Occupational Mapping of the Travel Services Industry* 1991). This figure will have changed very little in the intervening period.

Clearly, for countries which are major receiving destinations or enjoy a strong domestic demand for tourism, employment figures will be far higher. Even if tourism is defined more narrowly, the UK employs at least 1.8 million in tourism. On balance, tourism as a form of employment is economically beneficial, although efforts must be made to create more full-time jobs in the industry. The extent to which tourism benefits employment can be seen when it is appreciated that roughly one job in fifteen in the world is directly ascribed to tourism, according to estimates by the World Travel and Tourism Council. Recent estimates (1996) by the WTTC indicate that tourism employs around 255 million people, with tourists spending $3.6 trillion annually, thus generating 10.7 per cent of worldwide gross domestic product (GDP) – a measure of the total value of goods and services produced by the world's economy. Tourism is already acknowledged as the largest industry in the world. If global tourism expands as forecasted, by the year 2006 worldwide employment will be as high as 385 million, with annual expenditure of $7.1 trillion. This would represent 11.5 per cent of GDP.

Just as tourism is globally important, so it is important for regions within an economy. The multiplier which affects income in a region affects employment in the same way. If tourists stay at a destination, jobs are directly created in the tourism industry there. These workers and their families resident in the neighbourhood must also buy goods and services locally; their families require education and may need medical care. This in turn gives rise to jobs in shops, schools, hospitals to serve these needs. The value of the employment multiplier is likely to be broadly similar to that of the TIM, assuming that jobs with average wage rates are created.

However, recent developments in technology are threatening labour opportunities in tourism. For example, computer reservations systems (CRS) are rapidly replacing manual reservations systems, and booking clerks in large companies such as airlines, tour operators or hotel chains are therefore becoming a thing of the past. Fortunately for the future of the industry, at the 'sharp end', where the tourist seeks a high level of personal service at the destination, the nature of the tourist experience will ensure that technology cannot replace many jobs.

The success of tourism in a country will be in part dependent upon an adequate supply of skilled labour, with the right motivation towards employment in the industry. Here, Britain has some way to go. Turnover of labour is high (attributable to relatively poor salaries and working conditions compared with many other fields of business) and training, while having improved considerably over recent years, still lags behind that of many other countries. Attitudes towards working in a 'service industry' make recruitment of good staff difficult as many people in Britain still equate service with servility.

BALANCE OF PAYMENTS

In a national context, tourism may have a major influence on a country's balance of payments. International tourists are buying tourist services in another country, and these payments are noted in a country's accounts as 'invisibles'. A British resident going on holiday to Spain will be making an invisible payment to that country which is a debit on Britain's balance of payments account and a credit to Spain's balance of payment. The money spent by an American visitor to Britain is credited to Britain's balance of payments, becoming an invisible receipt for Britain, while it is debited as a payment against the American balance of payments. It is important to understand that the outflow of British money being spent abroad by our residents counts as an *import*, while the inflow of foreign holidaymakers' money spent in Britain counts as an *export*.

The total value of receipts minus the total payments made during the year represents a country's *balance of payments on the tourism account*. This is part of the country's entire invisible balance, which will include other services such as banking, insurance and transport. This latter item is of course also important for tourism. If the American visitor to Britain decides to travel on a British airline, then he is contributing to Britain's invisible receipts; while if the Briton going on holiday to Spain does so on Iberia Airlines, that fare is credited to Spain, and represents a payment on the British balance of payments account.

Throughout the 1970s, Britain enjoyed a surplus on its tourism balance, reaching a peak during 1977, the year of the Queen's Silver Jubilee. Since then, however, spending by British tourists travelling abroad has increased faster than receipts the country has gained from overseas tourists, with the result that there has been a net deficit since 1986 (see Figure 4.2).

For a country like Britain, which has experienced a steady decline in the terms of trade (amount of our goods sold abroad, compared with the amount of goods we import) it is important to try to redress the balance by a better showing on our invisible exports. As can be seen, however, tourism is not producing a net gain for Britain either – a matter about which we should be concerned. The government will attempt to resolve this deficit by encouraging more visitors to visit Britain, through the marketing efforts of the national tourist boards, or by encouraging more Britons to stay at home and enjoy their holidays in their own country. But the lure of the sun is a strong magnet for British tourists, and the tourist boards may find it easier to attract the overseas tourist to Britain. Some countries, particularly Third World countries, could not afford this kind of drain on their financial resources, and would be forced to impose restrictions either on the movement of their own residents, or on the amount of money which they may take abroad with them. Other countries suffer severe deficiencies in their tourism balance of payments, but can offset this with manufacturing exports. The German travel budget deficit in 1995 was $35.8 billion, while Japan was not far behind with a deficit of $30.7 billion. Both countries, however, enjoy a strong pattern of exports in other fields. By contrast, Spain achieved a surplus of $20.4 billion, and Italy a surplus of $15.6 billion, in the same year. Both are popular receiving countries and neither generates a large overseas holiday market.

Important though tourism is to Britain, it still represents a far smaller proportion of the total GDP, at around 5 per cent, than in countries like Spain. Caribbean countries, as we have seen, have invested heavily in tourism at the expense of their traditional farming and fishing economy, and may depend for between a quarter and a third of their total foreign receipts on tourism.

INVESTMENT AND DEVELOPMENT

One factor helping to determine the success or otherwise of tourism in a region is the level of investment, whether private or public, in the industry. Unfortunately, tourism and leisure generally are seen by private investors as high-risk investments. Banks are reluctant to lend money for tourism projects and developers are less willing to take investment risks. This will often mean that tourism cannot take off until the public sector is prepared to 'kick-start' the economy, that is, to invest risk capital in order to encourage tourism development. This might take the form of grants or low-interest loans to private developers, or in some more centrally planned economies it may mean that government itself builds and operates facilities such as hotels for tourists.

A good example of this 'partnership' between the public and private sectors is the development of the Disneyland site near Paris, involving investment of many hundreds of millions of dollars. The French government, in order to ensure that the Disney Corporation built in France rather than in competitive European countries, provided subsidies to attract the company to the site near Paris which was eventually selected.

Investment is something of a 'chicken and egg' situation. There may be an unwillingness to invest until a flow of tourists to the area can be demonstrated, while the area will in turn attract few tourists until they can see evidence of sufficient facilities to attract them. However, once tourism is shown to be successful, private developers or government agencies are often willing to invest even further in the area – in short, success breeds success. Economists refer to this as the *accelerator* concept. Areas which have benefited from this phenomenon include Spain in the 1960s, Hawaii, Tunisia and the Languedoc-Roussillon area of France in the 1970s, and Turkey and Greece in the 1980s and 1990s. Naturally, the attraction of these regions to tourists also draws other industries, which recognise the benefits to be gained from a large inflow of consumers, and the appeal of a pleasant working environment for staff. Resorts such as Bournemouth and Brighton in Britain, or the fast-expanding resorts of Florida in the USA or the Gold Coast in Queensland, Australia, have all benefited from this process.

Unfortunately, the relationship between tourism growth and economic development is uneven, due to other complicating factors such as the rate of inflation, the ability of an area to diversify and attitudes to work among the local labour force. Consequently, risk in investment remains high, as it does in many other areas of the economy.

Statistical measurement of tourism

Gathering data on tourism is a vital task for the government of a country. Governments need to know the contribution which tourism makes to the economy in terms of income, employment, balance of payments and investment. Figures must be available in sufficient detail to know how tourism has affected regional, as well as national, economies. Governments will wish to examine trends over time, not only within the country, but in comparison with the performance of other, competing countries. National tourist offices will use this information to forecast growth, to plan for tourism in their areas, and as a guide to their promotional campaigns.

Information must be both quantitative and qualitative in nature; that is, data should be provided not only about the numbers and composition of tourists but also about their nature and purpose. For example, British statistics should include:

(a) the number of visitors to Britain
(b) how these are distributed over the months of the year
(c) the countries generating these tourists, and the number of tourists they generate as a proportion of the whole
(d) the growth, year on year, of these tourists
(e) their spend in Britain, in absolute terms and how they distribute the spend between accommodation, transport, shopping, catering, etc.
(f) their mode of travel; i.e. what form of transport they use, whether they are travelling independently or on an inclusive tour
(g) the type of accommodation they use
(h) the purpose of their visit; whether leisure, business, VFR, etc.

(i) demographic profiles: age, group composition, social class
(j) sociographic profiles: personality, lifestyle, interests and activities; and
(k) what these tourists seek, and the extent to which they are satisfied with what they find.

This is a great deal of information, and when one remembers that it must also be collected for British residents travelling abroad and for British residents taking their holidays within Britain, the task of collecting the data is daunting. Nevertheless, it is vital that governments undertake this collection of data, and that, as far as is possible, the data that are collected are based on commonly defined characteristics, so that meaningful comparisons can be made between countries. The collection of data allows the nation to know what trends are developing over time, what patterns of growth are taking place, and how tastes and preferences are changing over time. This information will enable governments to determine where to site roads and airports, where to plan for expansion in local government plans, and in what countries to increase or decrease the spend on advertising (as well as how to redirect the theme of advertisements, when it is found that new types of tourist are being reached). The private sector will benefit from this information in deciding whether and where to invest in hotels or tourist attractions, and the form these facilities should take. Similarly, those in the industry require an understanding of the propensity to take holidays. They need to know the proportion of the population choosing to take a holiday each year, in particular a holiday abroad, and the proportion taking more than one holiday a year. They need to know, too, how this propensity is affected by a growth in disposable income. Public sector planners must be aware of the multiplier effect, which will call for sophisticated research techniques if measurement is to be accurate.

We will examine the most commonly used measurements of tourism here, under two categories: international surveys and national surveys.

INTERNATIONAL SURVEYS

Statistics of intra-European and transatlantic tourist flows were collected even before World

War II. However, the systematic collection of tourism data on a global scale can be dated to the early postwar years, and methods of measurement have been gradually refined and improved in recent years, particularly in those developed countries which have seen tourism expand rapidly.

Global tourism statistics, covering traffic flows, expenditure and trends over time, are produced and collated annually by the World Tourism Organisation (WTO) and the Organisation for Economic Cooperation and Development (OECD). Figures are published in the WTO's *World Tourism Statistics Annual Report* and *Tourism Compendium*, and in the OECD's annual *Tourism Policy and International Tourism*. These statistics are not always strictly comparable, as data gathering methods vary and differences in definition of terms remain.

In Britain, information on travel into and out of the country is obtained in a variety of ways. Until the early 1960s, most basic data on incoming tourism were obtained from Home Office immigration statistics. However, as the purpose of gathering such data was to control immigration rather than to measure tourism, the data have major weaknesses, including failure to distinguish the purpose of travel – obviously a key statistic in surveying tourists. The government therefore decided to introduce a regular survey of visitors entering and leaving the country. The *International Passenger Survey* (IPS) has enabled data to be collected on tourists since 1964, and the survey, which interviewed 248,000 visitors in 1995, includes a record of the number of visitors, the purpose of their visit, the geographical region visited, their expenditure, mode of travel, transport used and duration of stay. Information is based on country of residence; so, for example, the large number of British visitors living in America and travelling to visit friends and relatives in Britain each year would be counted as American visitors. This information is published quarterly, and compounded annually, in the government's *Business Monitor* series (MQ6, *Overseas Travel and Tourism*).

Numerous other surveys, both public and private, are undertaken, and these provide additional data on tourism volume and expenditure. The English Tourism Council carries out in an annual Holiday *Intentions Survey* before Easter, which greatly aids the process of forecasting anticipated levels of tourism within the UK and overseas by British residents for the coming summer. The same board also carries out regular hotel occupancy surveys. Commercial research organisations such as STATS MR also carry out research on overseas tourism, the results of which are available on subscription.

NATIONAL SURVEYS

In Britain, as in other countries in Europe, surveys are regularly carried out on tourism flows within the country. The most important of these is the *UK Tourism Survey* (UKTS). The survey is carried out on a monthly basis under the auspices of the English Tourism Council and the Scottish, Wales and Nothern Ireland Tourist Boards. Some 82,000 UK residents over the age of 15 are interviewed in their homes, and information is collected on the volume and value of all trips involving at least one overnight stay. This survey, in its present form, has been carried out since 1989, but the origins of the survey go back to the *British Home Tourism Survey* (BHTS) which was carried out between 1960 and 1972, and the *British Tourism Survey Monthly* (BTS-M), which covered the period 1973–1988. The dating of these surveys is important because either the methods or the scope of the information collected changed, and the data are therefore not strictly comparable over time. The most recent surveys cover all regions of the UK, and due to a greatly increased sample size the level of statistical error is much smaller.

is the *British Tourism Survey Yearly* (BTS-Y), formerly the *British National Travel Survey*, which produces data on holidays only, with a duration of at least four nights. The origins of this survey, which is funded by the travel trade and carried out under the auspices of the BTA, go back to 1951, with data collected annually since 1960, but once again changes have taken place in the way the research is carried out, and care must be exercised when making conclusions about long-term trends.

Information on day visitors is less complete. The tourist boards do not carry out regular surveys on this market, although an ad hoc survey was undertaken by the BTA and the Department of Employment at the end of the 1980s. However, surveys are undertaken biannually by the Countryside Recreation Network (CRN), involving structured home interviews, to gain information on both the leisure and business travel markets.

TECHNIQUES AND PROBLEMS OF TOURISM MEASUREMENT

From the descriptions of the methods of gathering UK tourist statistics outlined above, it can be seen that most research employs quantitative methods, in order to provide descriptive information about issues such as when and where tourists travel, where they come from, how long they stay and how much they spend. In some cases, this information is available in considerable detail; for instance, expenditure can be broken down into sector (shopping, food, accommodation, etc) and data on visits can be identified by tourism region within the country. Although the data collected are not above criticism, by and large there is a sufficient body of information on which to make decisions.

However, research dealing with why people travel is far more limited. This is beginning to change, as organisations become more concerned with understanding the behaviour of tourists: how they choose their destinations; what they do when they arrive and why; what satisfies them; their purchasing patterns (preference for booking direct rather than through an agent, or for booking early rather than close to departure time). None of these questions is easily answered by use of the structured questionnaire and a more qualitative approach to research is needed. This can involve lengthy interviews in the home or in 'panels' or groups of up to eight consumers who will talk about their behaviour under the guidance of a skilled interviewer. Some information is best obtained by observation rather than questioning, for example, by watching how customers visiting a travel agency choose their brochures from the racks. All these types of research are expensive, and time-consuming to administer. What is more, unlike quantitative methods, they cannot be subjected to tests of statistical probability in order to 'prove' the accuracy of the findings, no matter how carefully and scientifically the information is collected. Many organisations are therefore reluctant to commission research involving qualitative methods, although a growing number of research experts are now recognising that they may produce richer and more complete data than the more common survey. After all, the information provided by the use of questionnaires will only be as accurate as the honesty of the answers, and it is particularly difficult to know if respondents are answering questionnaires honestly or with sufficient thought about the questions. This problem is compounded where mailed questionnaires are used.

Asking questions of arriving passengers at a destination is in reality an 'intention survey' rather than an accurate picture of what those passengers will actually engage in while in the country, while surveys carried out on departing travellers will require recall – at best, guesswork, especially where the aim is to assess the expenditure which the tourist has incurred.

Even if common definitions are used, direct comparisons may be misleading. An international journey may require an American resident to make a trip of several hundred kilometres, or to cross a stretch of water, which will usually mean forward planning, while a resident of Continental Europe may live within a couple of kilometres of an international border and think nothing of crossing it regularly for shopping or a meal out. In some cases, it is difficult to think of border crossings as international; no border control has existed for some years, for instance, between the Netherlands, Belgium and Luxembourg. The freedom to cross borders unrestricted within the European Community will make the measurement of tourist flows within EU countries increasingly difficult. Some countries still use hotel records to estimate the number of visitors – a system known to be notoriously inadequate – visitors travelling from one hotel to another are double counted, while those visiting friends and relatives will be omitted entirely from the count.

Accurate measures of tourist expenditure are equally difficult to make. Shopping surveys have problems distinguishing between residents and tourists, and tourists themselves frequently under- or overestimate their expenditure.

While international standards for methods of

data collection and definition of terms have become widely accepted, particularly among the developed countries, small variations continue to make genuine comparison difficult, not only between countries but within a country over a period of time. Above all, if specific types of tourist activity are being examined as part of a larger sample of general tourists, limits of confidence may fall sharply. Certain BTA survey material will produce results that are accurate only to within 20 per cent either way, due to the small number of respondents in the particular category being examined.

As a final observation, it can be argued that we are far too concerned with measuring the economic impact of tourism on a region at the expense of the social or environmental impact. The industry's sole concern with growth in annual trends may conceal the very real danger that the number of tourists visiting a region will eventually exceed the number which the region can comfortably contain. Statistics on the ratio of tourists to residents, for example, or the number of tourists per square kilometre would provide some guidance on the degree of congestion experienced by the region. However, the social impact of tourism is also the outcome of many other variables, and statistical measurement is still a comparatively recent art which will require continual refinement in the future for the purposes of both economic and social planning.

QUESTIONS AND DISCUSSION POINTS

1 What are the main purposes behind the collection of tourism statistics?

2 How serious is the deficit on the balance of payments on the tourism account for the British economy? What steps could be taken to improve the position?

3 Is the decline in the proportion of holidaymakers taking inclusive tours inevitable? What could tour operators do to reverse this trend?

ASSIGNMENT TOPICS

1 You have recently taken up the position of Assistant Tourist Officer in a county of your choice. The county has only recently created a tourism department, and your immmediate supervisor is preparing a plan of action to increase the number of visitors over the next five years. He has asked you to provide him with a brief report which:

   a) looks at trends in domestic and incoming tourism over the past decade
   b) identifies significant trends and forecasts for the future flow of tourism within Britain
   c) suggests the relative advantages and disadvantages the county has to offer in attracting more visitors.

   Your report should specifically indicate the shortcomings you find in the amount and quality of the statistical data you seek, and what further research you think will be needed to guide the department in its activities.

2 You are shortly to attend an interview for a post in the National Tourist Office of a lesser developed country which is a popular tourism destination. At the interview, you will be asked to make a five-minute presentation about the economic advantages of tourism for the country, identifying some of the key statistics which will support your evidence.

   Prepare for your talk, and write it up in the form of a set of notes, with supporting data. You may choose the country concerned.

5

Tourist Motivation and Behaviour

Introduction

An understanding of why people buy the holiday or business trips they take, how they go about selecting their holidays, why they choose one particular company over another, and why they choose to travel when they do, is vital to those who work in the tourism industry. Yet, curiously, we know relatively little about tourist motivation and although we gather numerous statistics which reveal a great deal about who goes where, the reasons for these choices are little understood. This is not entirely the result of a lack of research, because many large companies do commission research into the behaviour of their clients, but as this is 'in-house' research, the information it reveals is confidential to the company concerned and seldom becomes public knowledge.

Motivation and purpose are closely related, and earlier in this book the principal purposes for which tourists travel were identified. These are grouped into three broad categories: business travel, leisure travel and miscellaneous travel, which would include, inter alia, travel to visit friends and relatives, travel for one's health and religious travel. However, simply labelling tourists in this way only helps us to understand their general motivation for travelling; it tells us little about their specific motivation, nor about their needs and wants which are a reflection of that travel, and how these needs and wants are met and satisfied. It will be the purpose of this chapter to examine these terms, and the complex interrelationship of factors which go to make up the choice of trips taken by tourists of all kinds.

The tourist's needs and wants

If we ask the prospective tourist why they want to travel to a particular destination, they will offer a variety of reasons, such as 'It's somewhere I've always wanted to visit', or 'Some friends recommended it very highly', or 'It's always good weather at that time of the year, and the beaches are wonderful; we've been going there regularly for the past few years'. Interesting as these views may be, they actually throw very little light on the real motivation of the tourists, because they have not helped to identify the tourists' *needs* and *wants*.

People often talk about their 'needing' a holiday, just as they might say they need a new three-piece suite for the lounge, a new dress, or a better lawnmower. Are they in fact expressing a

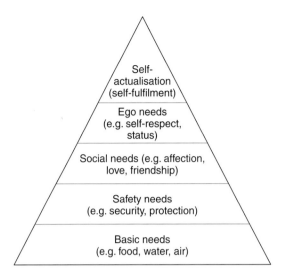

Figure 5.1 Maslow's hierarchy of needs. (*Source: A Maslow, Motivation and Personality, Harper & Row, 1984*)

need, or a want? Needs suggest that the products we are asking for are necessities for our daily life, but this is clearly not the case with these products. We are merely expressing a desire for more goods and services, a symptom of the consumer-oriented society in which we live. So let us start by examining what it is we mean by a need.

People have certain physiological needs, which are essential for their survival: they need to eat, to drink, to sleep, to keep warm and to reproduce, all needs which are essential to the survival of the human race. Beyond these needs, we also have psychological needs which are important for our well-being, such as the need to love and be loved, the need for friendship, the need to value ourselves as human beings and to have others value and respect us. Many people believe we also have inherently within us the need to master our environment, and to understand the nature of the society in which we live. Abraham Maslow conveniently grouped these needs into a hierarchy (see Figure 5.1), suggesting that the more fundamental needs have to be satisfied before we seek to satisfy the higher-level needs.

The difficulty in exploring these needs is that many people may actually be quite unaware of their needs, or how to go about satisfying them. Others will be reluctant to reveal their real needs; for example, few people would be willing openly

to admit that they travel to a particular destination to impress their neighbours, although their desire for status within the neighbourhood may well be a factor in their choice of holiday and destination.

Some of our needs are *innate*, that is, they are based on factors inherited by us at birth. These include biological and instinctive needs such as eating and drinking. However, we also inherit generic traits from our parents which are reflected in certain needs and wants. Other needs and wants arise out of the environment in which we are raised, and are therefore *learned*, or socially engineered. The early death of parents, or their lack of overt affection towards us, may cause us to have stronger needs for bonding and friendship with others, for example.

Travel may be one of several means of satisfying a need, but although needs are felt by us, we do not necessarily express them, and we may not recognise how travel actually satisfies our particular needs. Consequently, if we re-examine the answers given earlier to questions asking why we travel, it may be that in the case where respondents are confirming the desire to return to the same destination year after year, they are actually expressing the desire to satisfy a need for safety and security by returning to the tried and tested. The means by which this is achieved, namely a holiday in a resort well known to them, reflects the respondents' 'want', rather than their need.

The process of translating a need into the motivation to visit a specific destination or to undertake a specific activity is quite complex, and can best be demonstrated by a diagram (see Figure 5.2)

Figure 5.2 The motivation process

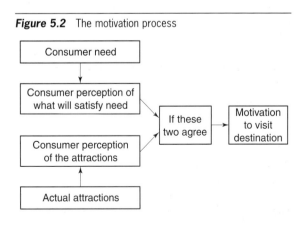

A potential consumer must not only recognise that they have a need, but also understand how a particular product will satisfy it. Every consumer is different and what one consumer sees as the ideal solution to the need will be rejected by another. A holiday in Benidorm, which Mr A thinks will be something akin to Paradise would be for Mr B an endurance test; he might prefer a walk in the Pennines for a week, which Mr A would find the nearest thing to purgatory. It is important that we all recognise that each person's perception of a holiday, like any other product, is affected by their experiences and attitudes. Only if the perception of the need and of the attraction match will a consumer be motivated to buy the product. The job of the skilled salesperson behind a travel agent's desk is to subtly question their clients in order to learn about their interests and desires, and find the products to match.

General and specific motivation

We have established that motivation arises out of the felt wants or needs of the individual. We can now go on to explain that motivation is expressed in two distinct forms, known as *specific motivation* and *general motivation*.

General motivation is aimed at achieving a broad objective, for example that of getting away from the routine and stress of the workplace in order to enjoy different surroundings and a healthy environment. Here, health and relief of stress are the broad motives reflecting the needs discussed above. If the tourist decides to take their holiday in the Swiss Alps, where they will be able to take walks in fresh mountain air and enjoy a varied scenery, good food and total relaxation, these are all specific objectives, reflecting the means by which their needs will be met. Marketing managers sometimes refer to these two forms of motivation as 'push' factors and 'pull' factors; the tourist is being pushed into a holiday by the need to get away from their everyday environment, but other factors may be at work to pull, or encourage, them to travel to a specific destination. For this reason, marketing staff realise that they will have to undertake their promotion

at two distinct levels to persuade the consumer of the need to take a holiday, and also to show the consumer that the particular holiday or destination the organisation is promoting will best satisfy that need.

If we look at the varied forms of leisure tourism which have become a part of our lives in the past few years, we will quickly see that certain types of holiday have become popular because they best meet common, and basic, needs. The 'sun, sea and sand' holiday, which caters to the mass market, is essentially a passive form of leisure which entails nothing more stressful than a relaxing time on the beach, enjoyment of the perceived healthy benefits of sunshine and saltwater bathing, good food and reasonably priced alcohol (another relaxant). The tendency among certain groups of tourists abroad to drink too much and to misbehave generally is again a reflection of need, even if the result is one which we have come to deplore because of its impact on others. Such tourists seek to escape from the constraints of their usual environment and to enjoy an opportunity to 'let their hair down', perhaps in a more tolerant environment than they would find in their own home country. Those travelling on their own might also seek opportunities to meet other people, or even find romance (thus meeting the need to belong and other social needs). In the case of families, parents can simultaneously satisfy their own needs while also providing a healthy and enjoyable time for their children on the beach; parents may also be given the chance to get away and be on their own while their children are being cared for by skilled child minders. What is provided is therefore a 'bundle of benefits' and the more a particular package holiday or a particular destination can be shown to provide the range of benefits sought, the more attractive will that holiday appear to the tourist compared with other holidays on offer. In this case, the 'bundle' will be made up of benefits which are designed to cater to both general and specific needs and wants.

Today, there is a growing demand for holidays which offer more strenuous activities than are to be found in the traditional 'three S' holidays, such as trekking, mountaineering or yachting. These appeal because they attract those whose basic needs for relaxation have already been satisfied (and whose desk-bound jobs may involve mental, rather than physical, strain); they are now seeking something more challenging. Strenuous activities provide opportunities for people to test their physical abilities and, while this may involve no more than a search for health by other means, there may also be a search for competence – another need identified by Maslow. Because these holidays are also purchased by like-minded people and are often provided for small groups, they can also help to meet other ego and social needs.

It must also be recognised that many tourists are constantly seeking novelty and different experiences. However satisfied they might be with a previous holiday, they will be unlikely to return to the same destination, but are forever seeking something more challenging, more exciting, more remote. This is in part an explanation for the growing demand for long-haul holidays. For other people, these increasingly exotic tourist trips satisfy the search for status.

The need for self-actualisation can be met in a number of ways. At its simplest, the desire to 'commune with nature' is a common trait among tourists, and can be achieved through scenic trips by coach, by 'fly-drive' packages in which routes are identified and stopping-off points recommended for their scenic beauty, by cycling tours, or by hiking holidays. Alternatively, the quest for knowledge can be met by tours such as those offered to cultural centres in Europe, accompanied by experts in particular fields such as archaeology. Self-actualisation can be aided through packages offering painting or other artistic 'do-it-yourself' holidays. Some tourists seek more meaningful experiences through contact with foreign residents, where they can come to understand the local cultures. This process can be facilitated through careful packaging of programmes arranged by organisers, who build up suitable contacts among local residents at the destination. Local guides, too, can act as 'culture-brokers', in overcoming language barriers or helping to explain local culture to inquisitive tourists.

As people come to travel more, and as they become more sophisticated, or better educated, so will their higher-level needs predominate in their motivation for a particular holiday. Companies in the business of tourism must always recognise this and take it into account when planning new programmes or new attractions for the tourist.

Motivators and facilitators

We have dealt up to now with the factors that motivate tourists to take holidays. However, in order to take a holiday, the tourist requires both time and money. These factors do not motivate in themselves, but they make it possible for prospective tourists to indulge in their desires. They are therefore known as facilitators.

Facilitators play a major role in relation to the specific objectives of the tourist. The availability of more money, for instance, means that the choice of destination is wider for the tourist. Better access to a destination, more favourable exchange rates against the pound sterling, easier entry without political barriers, friendly locals speaking the language of the tourist, will all facilitate the choice of destination.

If all consumers responded in the same way to given stimuli, the life of marketing managers would become a great deal easier. Unfortunately, consumer behaviour is by no means an exact science, and individual influences on motivation which help to explain the behaviour of tourists as they become aware of, search out and choose their holiday destinations are extremely complex. Nevertheless, we can identify the major factors behind these influences and they are either psychological or sociological in nature.

Psychological and sociological factors influencing motivation

BUYING BEHAVIOUR AND DECISION-MAKING

Before anyone can choose to undertake a holiday, they must become aware of the destinations from which they can choose and obtain information about these destinations. They then have to develop a favourable stance towards particular destinations, and finally become sufficiently committed to one over other choices to buy a

```
• Awareness
• Interest
• Desire
• Action
```

Figure 5.3 AIDA model

particular holiday. Marketing theorists have developed a number of models to explain this process of buying behaviour, some of them extremely complex, as they try to integrate more and more factors into the model. Perhaps the best known, as well as simplest model, is known as AIDA (see Figure 5.3).

Marketing aims to move the consumer from a stage of unawareness, either of the product (such as a specific destination or resort), or the particular brand (such as an individual package tour company, or a hotel), through each of these stages to a point where the consumer is persuaded to buy a particular product and brand.

The first step in this process is to move the consumer from unawareness to awareness. This entails an understanding about the way in which the consumer learns about new products.

If you, the reader, think for a moment about how you came to learn about a particular destination you have visited, you will quickly recognise how difficult it is to pinpoint all the influences – many of which you may not be consciously aware of. Every day, consumers are faced with hundreds of new pieces of knowledge, including information about new products. If we are to retain any of this information, the first task of marketing is to ensure that we perceive it, i.e. become conscious of it.

Perception is an important part of the process by which we learn. It involves the selection and interpretation of the information which is presented to us. As we cannot possibly absorb all the messages with which we are faced each day, many are consciously or unconsciously 'screened out' from our memories. If we are favourably predisposed towards a particular product or message, there is clearly a greater likelihood that we will absorb it. Thus if, for example, our best friend has just returned from a holiday in the Cayman Islands, and has enthusiastically talked to us about

the trip, if we then spot a feature on the Cayman Islands on television this may arouse our interest, even though, up to the point when our friend mentioned the place, we had never even heard of it. If what we see on the television programme reinforces the image of the destination which we gained from our friend, we might be encouraged to seek further information on the destination, perhaps by contacting the tourist office representing the destination. At any point in this process, we might be put off by what we find – for instance, if we perceive the destination as being too far away, too expensive, too inaccessible for the duration of the trip we are contemplating, we may search no further. If, on the other hand, the search process leads us to form a positive image of the destination, we may start mentally comparing the destination with others towards which we were favourably disposed. The process of choice involves constant comparison, weighing up one destination against others, estimating the benefits and the drawbacks of each as a potential holiday destination. As this process goes on, three things are happening.

THE TOURISM 'IMAGE'

First, we are developing an image of the destination in question. This image may be a totally inaccurate one, if the information sources we use are uninformed, or deliberately seek to distort the information they provide. We may then find that we become confused about the image itself – for example, in 1993, the media carried many reports of tourists being mugged in the Miami area, while the destination itself continued to try to disseminate a positive image of the resort and brochures of the tour operators likewise concentrated on selling the positive benefits with little reference to the potential dangers faced by the tourist.

Images are built around the unique attributes which the destination can claim. The more these help to distinguish it from other similar destinations, the greater its attraction will be for the tourist. Destinations which offer truly unique products, such as the Grand Canyon in the USA, the Great Wall of China in Beijing, or the Pyramids at Giza, Egypt, have an in-built advantage, although in time the attraction of such destinations may be such that it becomes necessary to 'demarket' the site to avoid over-popularity. In 1993 the Egyptian Tourist Office faced the problem of negative publicity associated with attacks against tourists by fundamentalists in other parts of the country, closely following on the over-popularity of the area with international tourists during the early 1990s. Much of the promotion undertaken by tourist offices has the long-term objective of generating a positive image of a destination, so that when it is being considered by the tourist, the favourable image generated will give the destination an edge over its competitors.

By contrast with the above examples, many typical seaside resorts suffer from having very little to distinguish them from their competitors. Simply offering good beaches, pleasant hotels, well-cooked food is not enough in itself; in some way, an image must be *induced* by the tourist office to distance the resort from other similar resorts, so that, for example, if changes in exchange rates or inflation rates work against the destination, it may still be seen as having 'added value', and will retain a loyal market.

ATTITUDES TO THE PRODUCT

So much for image. Next, we find we are developing an attitude towards the destination. This attitude, which is a mix of our emotional feelings about the destination and our rational evaluation of its merits, will help to determine whether we would consider it a possible location for a holiday. It should be stressed at this point, however, that we may have a negative image of the destination, but still retain a positive attitude towards travel there, because we have an interest in seeing the destination. This was often the case with travel to the Communist Bloc countries before the collapse of their political systems at the end of the 1980s. The troubles in Northern Ireland throughout the 1990s also led to new expressions of interest, partly again on account of the negative, but frequent, press publicity the area received.

RISK AS A FACTOR IN TOURISM CHOICE

Finally, in this process of consumer choice, we will also be weighing up the perceived risk we run in travelling to the destination. All holidays involve risk in some way – risk of illness, of bad weather, of being unable to get what we want if we delay booking, of being uncertain about the product until we see it at first hand, about its representing value for money. We will be asking ourselves what risks we are running, whether there is a high likelihood of their occurrence, whether they are avoidable, and how significant would be the consequences. Some tourists, of course, will relish a degree of risk, as this gives an edge of excitement to the holiday, so the presence of risk is not in itself a barrier to tourism. Others, however, are 'risk averters' and will studiously avoid risk wherever possible. Clearly, the significance of the risk will be a key factor; there will be much less concern about the risk of poor weather than about the risk of crime. Risk averters will book early; they may choose to return to the same resort they have visited in the past, knowing its reliability; they will book a package tour, rather than travel independently. The American Hilton and Holiday Inn chain hotels have been eminently successful throughout the world by offering some certainty about standards, in countries where Americans might feel at risk from 'foreign' food, poor plumbing or other inadequacies of a tour which can become preventable by good forward planning. Travel businesses such as cruise lines, which offer a product with a reassuring lack of risk, can make this an important theme in their promotional campaign.

SOME THEORIES OF DECISION-MAKING

The process of sorting through the various holidays on offer and determining which is the best to choose is inevitably complex, and individual personality traits will determine how the eventual decision is arrived at. Some people undertake a process of *extensive problem-solving*, in which information is sought about a wide range of products, each of which is evaluated and compared with similar products. Other consumers will not have the patience to explore a wide variety of choices, and will deliberately restrict choice, with the aim of satisfying rather than being certain of getting the best possible product. This is known as *limited problem-solving*, and will provide the benefit of saving time. Many consumers engage in *routinised response behaviour*, in which choice changes relatively little over time. This is a common pattern among brand-loyal consumers, for example, and some holidaymakers who have been content with a particular company, or destination, in the past may opt for the same again. Finally, some consumers will buy on *impulse*. While this is more typical of products costing little, it is not unknown among holiday purchases, and is a pattern of behaviour that can be stimulated and serviced by late availability offers particularly.

PRESSURES FROM SOCIETY

We are all members of society, we are influenced by others in society and we react to the norms and values reflected in society. We all like to feel that we are making our own decisions about the products we choose, without always realising how other people's taste influences our own, and what pressures there are on us to conform.

When we claim that we buying to 'please ourselves', what exactly is this 'self' that we are pleasing? We are, in fact, composed of many 'selves'. There is the self that we see ourselves as, often highly subjectively; the ideal self, representing how we would like to be; there is our self as we believe others see us, and the self as we are actually seen by others; and there is – perhaps? – a real self, the unknown self that we are objectively. Whether that real self actually exists is questionable. Readers will be aware that they put on different 'fronts' and act out different roles according to the company in which they find themselves, whether family, best friend, lover, employer. Do any of these relationships truly reflect our real self?

The importance attached to this theory of self, from the point of view of this text, is the way in which it affects those things we buy and with which we surround ourselves. This means that in the case of holidays we will not always buy the kind of holiday we think we would most enjoy, or even the one we feel we could best afford, but instead we might buy the holiday which we feel will give us status with our friends and neigh-

bours, or will reflect the kind of holiday we feel that 'persons in our position' should take. Advertisers will frequently use this knowledge to promote a destination as being suited to a particular kind of tourist, and will perhaps go further, using as a model in their advertisements some well-known star of TV or films, who will reflect the 'typical tourist at the destination' with whom we can then mentally associate ourselves.

In the same way, status becomes an important feature of business travel, as business travellers are aware that they are representing their company to business associates and must therefore create an impression. Since the company also accepts this view and is paying their bills, it can be seen why business travel generates more income per capita than does leisure travel!

FASHION AND TASTE

Many tourism businesses, including destinations, suffer from the effect of changing consumer taste, as fashion changes and as 'opinion leaders' find new resorts to champion. It is difficult to define exactly what it is exactly which causes a particular resort to lose popularity with its public, although clearly, if the resources it offers are allowed to deteriorate, the market will soon drift away to seek better value for money elsewhere.

Sometimes, however, it is no more than a change in fashion which causes tourism to fall off; this is likely to be the case where the site was a 'fashionable' attraction in the first place. This hap-

Figure 5.4 The life cycle of a resort

Number of visitors/expenditure (vertical axis)

| Few visitors as resort becomes known | Number of visitors accelerates rapidly | Number of visitors continues to increase, but at a slower rate | Number of visitors peaks and falters | Number of visitors starts to decline |

LAUNCH   GROWTH   MATURITY   SATURATION   DECLINE

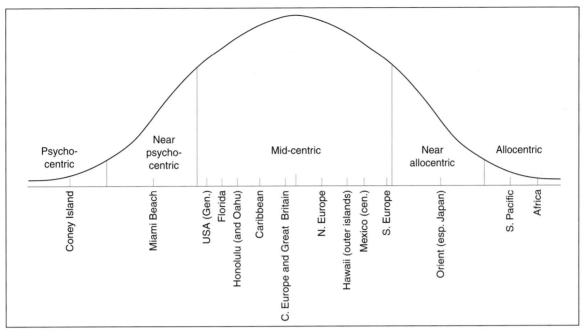

Figure 5.5 Personality and travel destination choice: the allocentric-psychocentric scale. (*Source: S Plog. 'Why destination areas rise and fall in popularity', paper presented to the Southern California Chapter of the Travel Research Association, 1972*)

pened to Bath after its outstanding success as a resort in the eighteenth century, and can be seen again in the case of several seaside resorts in the twentieth century, such as St Tropez (fashionable when Brigitte Bardot, who chose to reside there, was a star). It is the case, however, that all products, including tourism, will experience a life cycle of growth, maturity, saturation, and eventual decline if no action is taken to arrest it (see Figure 5.4). Generally, this will entail some form of innovation or other investment helping to revitalise the product.

LIFESTYLE AND MARKETING

Marketers are paying much more attention now to people's lifestyle, which may better reflect the kind of products they will purchase than many other factors more traditionally associated with purchasing patterns, such as socio-economic class (based on occupation and education) or age. Lifestyle is a more complex concept, and is therefore more difficult to measure, but several theorists suggest that this can best be done by looking at the activities (or attitudes), interests and opinions of the individual – hence this measure of lifestyle has come to be known as the 'A–I–O Model'. An awareness of the benefits sought from a particular product will also reveal something of the lifestyle of an individual, and will then allow the marketer to segment markets by the benefits sought – a more accurate targeting of the market than a judgement based on socio-demographic variables alone.

PERSONALITY TRAITS

Several researchers have attempted to measure the impact of personality on choice. Perhaps the best known, in the field of tourism research, is Stanley Plog (see Figure 5.5).

Plog developed a theory which classified the United States population by the extent to which they are either *allocentrics*, meaning those seeking variety, self-confident, outgoing and experimental; or *psychocentrics*, meaning those who tend to be more concerned with themselves and the small problems of life, are often anxious, and inclined to seek security. Psychocentrics would therefore be more likely to return to resorts which are familiar to them, to stay closer to home and to use a package holiday for their travel arrangements,

- A   Higher managerial, administrative or professional
- B   Middle managerial, administrative or professional
- C1   Supervisory or clerical, junior managerial
- C2   Skilled manual workers
- D   Semi- and unskilled manual workers
- E   Those at lowest levels of subsistence

Figure 5.6   Socio-demographic segmentation by occupation

while allocentrics would be disposed to seek new experiences, in a more exotic destination, travelling independently. Of course, these are extreme examples, and in practice most holidaymakers are likely to fall somewhere between the extremes, as *mid-centrics*. Those tending towards the psychocentric were found by Plog to be more commonly from lower-income groups, but it is equally these groups who are more constrained financially as to the kind of holiday they can afford to take. Whether Plog's findings are similarly applicable to European markets is by no means certain.

Plog recognised that personalities change over time and that, given time, the psychocentric may become an allocentric in their choice of holiday destination and activity, as they gain experience of travel. It has long been accepted that many tourists actually seek novelty from a base of security and familiarity. This would enable the psychocentric to enjoy more exotic forms of tourism and can be achieved, for instance, by coaching tourists through novel destinations in their own 'environmental bubble'. The provision of a familiar background to come home to after touring, such as is offered Americans at Hilton Hotels or Holiday Inns (referred to earlier in this chapter) is a further means of reassuring the nervous while in unfamiliar territory.

SOCIO-DEMOGRAPHIC FACTORS

By far the most common means of segmenting markets and assessing the likely appeal of different products to different types of tourist is by examining the socio-demographic distinctions between travellers. These include differences of age, gender and occupation, and are the easiest form of information to obtain about tourists. They are therefore a popular set of data to be collected in all tourist market research.

Market differentiation by occupation is one of the most common ways of categorising consumers (see Figure 5.6). These particular categories are employed by the National Readership Survey and the Institute of Practitioners in Advertising.

To an extent, this approach is helpful, and indeed vital, if the aim is, say, to develop holidays with particular appeal to young people, or it is known that the particular attraction one is marketing appeals significantly more to the AB socio-economic tourist than to the CDE. As we have seen, however, it is often not enough in itself to explain the variation in choice between different tourist products, and we must look to consumer psychographics for a fuller explanation of motivation and behaviour.

Future trends

Those charged with the task of marketing to tourists must be fully aware not only of existing patterns of tourist behaviour, but also of trends which might indicate possible changes of behaviour in the future. Some of these changes will be generated by tourists themselves, others will come about as a result of changes taking place in the business environment. Many can be readily forecasted simply by projecting existing trends. For example, statistics provided by the government will identify changes in the make-up of the population and we know that as the 1990s give way to the twenty-first century, older people will form a greater proportion of the population. What we must also take into account is other complementary changes. Older people are much fitter and more adventurous than they were a few years ago and will be looking for more activity holidays. They will also enjoy a higher income than in the past; far from retiring on a modest pension, many will have inherited homes which they will translate into disposable cash to invest or to spend on long-haul holidays. An increasing number are also likely to opt for early retirement, thus gaining the opportunity to travel extensively. The older market is therefore a particularly attractive one for tourist businesses.

In most developed countries, those in work are likely to enjoy increased disposable incomes and a higher propensity to travel abroad. On the other hand, there will continue to be a relatively high number of unemployed in the population, most of whom will be unable to take holidays of any kind. Single-parent families will form an ever larger segment of the population and efforts will be made in the holiday trade to cater for the needs of this group, too. In the past, those with spouses who have not wished to travel abroad have tended not to do so themselves, but lifestyle changes could mean that an increasing number of happily-married couples will choose to holiday separately, 'doing their own thing'.

The dangers of skin cancer arising from extensive exposure to the sun are already well documented and, as the depletion of the ozone layer heightens risk, so tourists will be forced to reconsider the attraction of the beach holiday – at least, in the format in which it has been offered up to the present. The fashion for suntans may well disappear; this was, after all, a twentieth-century phenomenon, for until the early part of this century tans were disparaged by the middle class as indicative of those working outside, i.e. 'the labouring classes'. However, in spite of widespread media coverage on this subject, it is proving difficult to change long-standing attitudes, and it is recognised that few younger readers are likely to absorb this lesson!

Other behaviour changes which may well impact on tourism include the growing interest in health and personal well-being. Physical fitness is already playing a larger role in our lives and holidays will need to cater for this increased demand. Activity and outdoor holidays, in particular, stand to benefit from these developments. Greater concern about what we eat must lead to better food, better preparation, better hygiene, and a cuisine which caters for increasingly segmented tastes, from veganism and vegetarianism to gluten-free and fat-free diets. An interest in personal development and creativity, and a growing desire to lead a full, rich life promise well for those planning special interest and activity holidays of all kinds, especially the arts.

Finally, one must recognise the impact of new technology and how this will affect the industry and the consumer over the next few years. The development of the Internet and World Wide Web as sources of computerised information will have immense repercussions on the distribution systems in use. Until the latter part of the 1990s, these systems were relatively undeveloped and most holidaymakers, who had not been brought up in the computer age, were content to visit a travel agent for advice and to arrange their bookings. However, in Britain today it is possible, as a member of the public, to book a holiday through interactive terminals in the home. Increasing familiarity with computer systems, coupled with the growth of databanks and reservations systems accessible directly by the public, will significantly change patterns of booking behaviour over the next few years.

Just a few examples of some of the possible repercussions of societal change for the travel industry have been explored in this section. We live in a period of rapid and vast change as we approach the end of the twentieth century. If those in the tourism industry are to make a success of their business, their first task must be to recognise change when it takes place and to be capable of responding quickly to meet new threats and opportunities as they arise.

QUESTIONS AND DISCUSSION POINTS

1 What 'image' does the town in which you live or work have? Pool the opinions of about twenty people (if possible, find a few who are not originally from the town, and obtain their views on how they felt about it before coming there). How would you use the information if you were planning to encourage tourism to the town?

2 What makes a resort 'fashionable'? Compare and contrast one currently unfashionable and one fashionable resort. What is it that distinguishes the successful one? Can 'fashion' in a tourist resort be manipulated?

3 In a group, discuss your own personal preferences for a holiday destination and activity. How far do these reflect your own personality?

Would you sometimes choose a holiday that appears an allocentric choice and sometimes one that appears more like a psychocentric choice? What might account for this?

ASSIGNMENT TOPICS

1 You are working in the Sales and Development section of a large tour operator, which plans to launch a new programme of long-haul tours next year to some of the smaller Caribbean islands.

   (a) Compile information about the long-haul market in general, and find out as much as you can about the market profile for the Caribbean or similar holidays.

   (b) You will be expected to arrange for an educational study-trip for some key 'opinion leaders' (not including travel agents) to the destination. Draw up a list of fifteen people (by job, if not by name) whom you would plan to invite for the trip, and plan a four-day itinerary for them.

   Produce a short report with your findings on both of the above tasks for your Head of Department.

2 You are interested in the relationship between the sun and skin cancer, and want to know what young people know about the issue and their feelings. Is it affecting their behaviour on holiday? If so, how?

   Draw up a questionnaire to find out as much information as you can about the issue and carry out a survey on thirty young people. Analyse the responses and present the results in a brief presentation.

6

The Structure and Organisation of the Travel and Tourism Industry

OBJECTIVES

After studying this chapter, you should be able to:

- identify the integral and associated sectors of the tourism industry;
- understand the chain of distribution and how this is applied within the tourism industry;
- distinguish between the different forms of integration within the industry, and identify the reasons for this integration.

The tourism chain of distribution

The demand for tourism is met by the concentrated marketing efforts of a wide variety of tourist services. Together, these services form the world's largest and fastest-growing industry. Because some of these services are crucial to the generation and satisfaction of tourists' needs, while others play only a peripheral or supportive role, defining what is meant by a 'tourism industry' is fraught with difficulties. Several services,

Figure 6.1   The network of sectors in the tourism industry

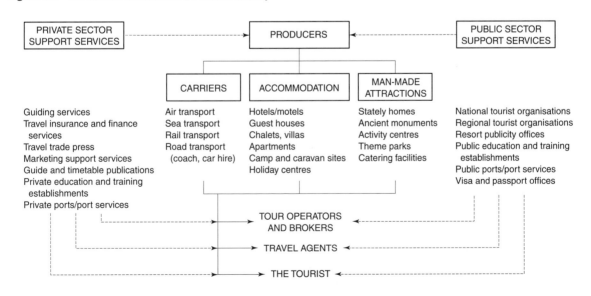

such as catering and transport, obviously serve the needs of other consumers apart from tourists. Other services, such as banks, retail shops and taxis – or laundrettes in a resort where a significant number of tourists are in self-catering facilities – may only serve tourist needs incidentally to local residents' needs, although at certain times of the year their revenue may be heavily dependent upon the visitors. Inevitably, what one decides to include under a definition of the tourism industry must be to some extent arbitrary, but Figure 6.1 provides a framework for analysis based on those sectors commonly seen as forming the core of the industry. An examination of these sectors will form the basis for the bulk of this book.

Figure 6.1 is also an illustration of the *chain of distribution* in the travel and tourism business. This term is used to describe the system by which a product or service is distributed from its manufacturing source to the eventual consumers; the alternative term *marketing channel* is also used to describe this system. Traditionally, products are distributed through a number of intermediaries who link producers, or manufacturers, with consumers. These intermediaries are either wholesalers, who buy in large quantities from suppliers and sell in smaller quantities to others further down the chain, or they are retailers, who form the final link in the chain and sell products individually to the consumer. The structure of the chain of distribution is shown in Figure. 6.2.

Producers, of course, are not obliged to sell their products through the chain. They may choose to sell direct to consumers, or direct to retailers, thus avoiding some or all of the intermediaries. Wholesalers, in turn, sometimes sell products direct to the consumer (a common example being the 'cash and carry' companies), avoiding the retailer. All these alternatives can be found in Figure. 6.1, and all are commmon forms of distribution within the tourism industry.

As we have seen earlier, the tourism product consists essentially of transport, accommodation and attractions, both man-made and natural. The producers, or 'manufacturers', of these services include air, sea, road and rail carriers; hotels or other forms of tourist accommodation; and the various forms of man-made facilities designed to

Figure 6.2 Marketing channels, or the chain of distribution

attract the tourist, such as stately homes or heritage sites, amusement parks and purpose-built activity centres such as skiing resorts. These services can be sold to the tourist in a number of ways, either direct, through travel agents (the retailers of the tourism industry), or through tour operators or brokers, who can be described as wholesalers of tourism.

Tour operators can be accurately viewed as wholesalers because they buy a range of different tourist products, such as airline seats, hotel rooms or coach transfer facilities, in bulk, 'packaging' these for subsequent sale to travel agents or direct to the tourist. By buying a number of individual services in this way and packaging them into a single product – the 'package holiday' – they are seen by some theorists as *producers* of a new product rather than wholesalers of an existing product. This is a debatable point, but in the author's view they are best viewed as intermediaries, in the sense that their fundamental role is to bulk-purchase, and then sell individually. This view is reinforced by the trend for tour operators increasingly to sell seat-only aircraft flights rather than a total package. In this sense, they are coming closer to the role of the *broker*.

Brokers are most actively involved in the distribution system in the air transport sector, although they may also be involved with bulk purchase of hotel rooms or certain other services. As with tour operators, by purchasing aircraft seats in bulk they are able to negotiate much lower prices. The seats can be sold on to tour operators or travel agents either individually or in quantity, at net prices, allowing the other intermediaries to determine their own profit level and selling price for them. One of the commonest forms of broker-

Figure 6.3 Card and travel services provided by American Express. *(Courtesy American Express)*

and timetables, and a number of specialist marketing services such as travel consultants or brochure design agencies.

The success of the tourism industry is dependent upon a close working partnership between the private and public sectors. Many tourist attractions, such as heritage sites, are publicly owned, either by the state or by local authorities, while public authorities are also frequently responsible for the promotion and distribution of information about tourism (through, for instance, their tourist information centres). This interrelationship between the private and public sectors, which is an important aspect of the dynamics of the tourism industry, will be explored in later chapters.

ing in the travel industry is found in the role of the *consolidator*. These are specialists working in airline brokerage who bulk-purchase unsold charter aircraft seats for sale through intermediaries, thereby helping airlines to clear unsold 'stock'.

Travel agents form the retail sector of the distribution chain, buying travel services on request by their clients. They carry no stock, simply acting as an intermediary between the consumer and the supplier, or *principal*, and their main role is to provide a convenient network of sales outlets for the travelling public. Agents do not normally charge for their services, receiving their remuneration in the form of a commission on each sale they negotiate.

A wide variety of support services interact with this central distribution system of producers, wholesalers and retailers. For convenience, these can be divided between public sector organisations (those directly controlled or organised by central or local governments) and those privately owned. The former include national tourism organisations such as tourist offices, government-operated airports or seaports, passport and visa services, and other ancillary services such as public education and training institutions offering courses in tourism. The private sector includes services offered by freelance guides, travel insurance and financial services (including foreign exchange and credit card facilities), privately operated airports or seaports, travel trade newspapers and journals, publishers of travel brochures, guides

Common interest organisations

A feature of the tourism industry is the extent of association, voluntary or otherwise, that has taken place between businesses and/or public sector bodies that share similar interests or complement one another's interests in some way. Such associations can take a number of forms, but typically three can be identified:

1 *Sectoral organisations* based on the interests of a particular sector of industry (or link in the chain of distribution)
2 *Destination organisations* concerned with a specific tourist destination, whether resort or region
3 *Tourism organisations* based on a concern with tourism activity as a whole.

These can, in turn, be sub-divided into trade organisations and professional organisations. The latter are normally composed of individuals whose common interest is likely to be based on objectives such as establishing educational or training qualifications for the industry or the sector, devising codes of conduct to guide members' behaviour, and limiting or controlling entry to the industry or sector. Membership of such bodies is often associated with a personal drive to enhance status and prestige. Trade bodies, by contrast, are groupings of independent firms whose common purpose will include such aims as the opportunity to exchange views, cooperation (especially in the functions of marketing), representation and negotiation with other organisations, and the provision of identifiable services to their members. At times, such organisations will become involved in activities more generally associated with professional bodies, such as entry to the industry or sector, or the provision of appropriate education and training.

It should be noted that the structure of these bodies may vary considerably. In some cases, particularly the larger organisations, there may be a paid administrative staff to carry out the functions of the organisation. In the case of smaller bodies (such as local marketing consortia) there may be no full-time staff, and the administration of the organisation is often carried out by volunteer staff seconded from member companies. An important characteristic of trade bodies, is that their membership is made up of autonomous companies or other organisations subscribing to the common purpose of the body concerned.

SECTORAL ORGANISATIONS

Probably the most numerous organisations are those which reflect sectoral interests. As we have seen, there is a wide range of sectors making up the tourism industry, and each of these can be expected to have at least one common-interest association. Professional bodies catering for sectoral interests include the Chartered Institute of Transport (CIT), and the Hotel, Catering and Institutional Management Association (HCIMA). The Chartered Institute of Marketing (CIM) has a section devoted to hotel industry members, known as the Hotel Marketing Association (HMA), while tourism educationalists and consultants each have their own professional bodies – The Association of Tourism Teachers and Trainers and the Tourism Society Consultants' Group (both autonomous divisions of the Tourism Society, see page 72).

Sectoral trade bodies may be national or international in scope. One of the most influential among international bodies will be the International Air Transport Association (IATA), which is global in scale, while the International Federation of Tour Operators (IFTO) draws its members from European national tour operating bodies. Examples of British national bodies include the Association of British Travel Agents (ABTA, see Figure 6.4), which presently represents both tour operators and travel agents, the Federation of Tour Operators (FTO), an influential consultative body made up of around twenty leading British tour operating companies, or the British Hospitality Assocation (BHA). Similar bodies are to be found in all countries with a developed tourism industry. The American Society of Travel Agents (ASTA), for example, fulfils a similar role in the USA as does ABTA in Britain, but also draws on members from other sectors of industry, as well as overseas members, due to the importance and influence of the USA as a tourist generating country.

THE ROLE OF ABTA

The Association of British Travel Agents has in the past played a key role as a sectoral trade body in the British travel industry. For this reason it will be useful to examine the organisation's role here, and to consider its relationship with other sectors of industry. Its role with respect to its own members, whether tour operators or travel agents, will be dealt with in forthcoming chapters. As a result of legislation within the European Union which has had the effect of reducing the monopoly position enjoyed by ABTA in the past, its influence has waned to some extent in the latter half of the

Figure 6.4 ABTA logo

1990s, and other organisations are springing up to meet the needs of tour operator and travel agency groupings.

ABTA was founded in 1950, initially to represent the interests of travel agents, and later, as operating developed discretely from the retail sector, those of tour operators. It acts as a mouthpiece for these two sectors of industry and is consulted by government and by other bodies on issues of national concern and on legislation affecting the industry. It is governed by a Board of Directors composed of ten members drawn equally from its two subsidiary councils, the Tour Operators' Council (TOC) and the Travel Agents' Council (TAC). It operates through committees which liaise with other sectors of the industry, such as railways, airways, shipping and UK tourism, together with certain other committees dealing with issues of current importance such as technology. It is also responsible for training in the travel sector, a responsibility it discharges through the Travel Training Company. This body works closely with validating bodies in education such as the City and Guilds of London Institute (CGLI) and the Business and Technology Education Council (BTEC), helping to develop programmes of further education seen as relevant to industry's needs, in particular National Vocational Qualifications (NVQs) for the various functions of the travel business. The Agency is also responsible for administering government grant-aided training schemes for young people entering the industry.

TOC and TAC approve applications for membership in their respective sectors, and check the financial standing and competence of members. They have powers to discipline members who are in breach of the ABTA Codes of Conduct, by imposing a reprimand, a fine or, in extreme circumstances, suspension or termination of membership.

From 1965 until 1992, ABTA was legally permitted to operate a 'closed shop', whereby tour operating members were required to sell their products exclusively through travel agents belonging to ABTA, who, in turn, could only sell packages organised by tour-operating members. This process, known as Stabiliser, was overturned by an EU Directive which, in common with broader EU policy, required tourism products to be available to consumers without restraint on channels of distribution. As a result, ABTA has had fundamentally to rethink its role as a trade body, as membership is no longer an essential to trade for tour operators and retailers. Many felt that such a re-evaluation of its role was long overdue, given that the interests of ABTA's members have often been in conflict. The interests of tour operators, for example, will inevitably conflict with those of travel agents, and it becomes difficult for the trade body to represent both these sectors' interests equally. Conflicts also emerged between the larger tour operators and the smaller independents, as well as between the retail agency chains, which are responsible for about half of all the bookings in the UK, and the smaller independent travel agencies. In the case of tour operating, this led to the establishment of a separate body to represent the interests of independent operators, the Association of Independent Tour Operators (AITO). Where retailing was concerned, the widening gap in interests between the so-called 'multiples' (travel agency chains such as Lunn Poly, Going Places, Carlson/A T Mays, Thomas Cook and Co-op Travel, which operate hundreds of branches) and the independent agents made a reassessment of the ABTA role inevitable. Since the demise of Stabiliser, a number of alternative associations of independent retailers have been established, including ARTAC WorldChoice, which held a 6–7 per cent share of the package tour retailing market in 1996 (and which upset some independents by uniting in 1997 with retail chain A T Mays to form the new 1,000-strong chain WorldChoice), Advantage Travel Centres and the Global Travel Group, while others are seeking to attract membership from agents largely in order to offer alternative arrangements for the financial protection of consumers and tour operators dealing with smaller agencies.

ABTA also claims to serve the interests of travel consumers, although this must inevitably clash at times with its principal role in serving the needs of its members. However, in one respect, ABTA has served the travelling public exceptionally well. Apart from ABTA's 'Stabiliser' role, it has undertaken the responsibility of protecting the consumer through a system of bonding, so that consumers booked through ABTA members have had their holidays protected in the event of the collapse either of the agent or operator concerned before or during the holiday. This insurance, which has worked so effectively in the British package tour market, was extended by the government, as part of the requirements contained in the European Union's Package Holiday Directive, to other forms of travel, and now embraces non-ABTA bookings, too. Nevertheless, ABTA continues to offer its bonding scheme to members, and remains the major force within the British travel scene. Details of the ABTA Codes of Conduct and bonding arrangements, and the implications of the EU Directive, are discussed in Chapters 12 and 13.

DESTINATION ORGANISATIONS

A destination organisation is one drawing its membership from public or private sector tourism bodies sharing a common interest in the development or marketing of a specific tourism destination. That destination may be a resort, a state or region, a country or even an area of the globe. Membership of such bodies is open to firms or public sector organisations rather than individuals. These bodies generally share two common objectives:

1 to foster cooperation and coordination between the various bodies that provide, or are responsible for, the facilities or amenities making up the tourism product
2 to act in concert to promote the destination to the travel trade and to tourists.

Consequently, these organisations are trade, rather than professional bodies. Examples range from such globally important regional marketing bodies as the Pacific Area Travel Association (PATA) and the European Travel Commission (ETC), to local marketing consortia made up of groups of hotels or tourist attractions within a particular region or resort. The Bournemouth Hotels and Restaurants Association, the Devon Association of Tourist Attractions, or the Association of Bath and District Leisure Enterprises are all typical examples of such limited-area groupings in Britain.

TOURISM ORGANISATIONS

The activities of some bodies transcend the sectoral boundaries within the industry. These organisations may have as their aim the compilation of national or international statistics on tourism, or the furtherance of research into the tourism phenomenon.

The World Tourism Organisation is undoubtedly the most significant global body concerned with the collection and collation of statistical information on international tourism. This organisation represents public sector tourism bodies from most countries in the world and the publication of its data makes possible comparisons of the flow and growth of tourism on a global scale.

Similarly, the Organisation for Economic Cooperation and Development (OECD) also has a tourism committee composed of tourism officials drawn from its member countries, and this committee provides regular reports comprising comparative data on tourism developments to and within these countries. Other, privately sponsored bodies have been set up to produce supporting statistics, such as the World Travel and Tourism Council (WTTC), whose members are drawn from some thirty-one leading airlines and tourist organisations. This body also regularly commissions and publishes research data. An equivalent body exists within the UK, known as the Council for Travel and Tourism (CTT).

Many countries with a strongly developed tourism industry will establish professional bodies composed of individual members drawn from several or all sectors of the industry. The purpose of these bodies is to promote the cause of the tourism industry, while simultaneously encouraging the spread of knowledge and understanding of the industry among members. In Britain, there are two professional bodies devoted to the tourism industry as a whole, although they tend to draw their membership from different sectors of the industry. The Institute of Travel and Tourism (ITT) has its origin as an institute designed to serve the needs of travel agents and tour operators, and still draws its membership largely from these sectors, while the Tourism Society, a more recently formed professional body, attracts its membership particularly from the public sector, tourist attractions and the in-coming tourism industry. As has been pointed out earlier, this body also draws significantly for its membership on tourism consultants and educationalists.

Occasionally, organisations are established outside the tourism industry, if tourism comes within their provenance. Such a body is the Confederation of British Industry's Tourism Advisory Group, set up in 1993 to help advance the interests of tourism as one area of business. This body has concerned itself principally with improving tourism career appeal and the quality of training on offer to new recruits to the industry; improving the marketing of tourism overseas to the UK; ensuring tourist attractions come up to expectations in their quality; and improving accessibility for tourism through an integrated transport system within the UK. In this work, the CBI complements many of the concerns of sectoral organisations within tourism.

Integration in the tourism industry

A notable feature of the industry over recent years has been the steady process of integration that has taken place between sectors of the tourism industry. If we refer to our earlier model of the chain of distribution, Figure 6.2, we can identify this integration as being either *horizontal* or *vertical* in character. Horizontal integration is that taking place at any one level in the chain, while vertical integration describes the process of linking together organisations at different levels of the chain.

All business is highly competitive and the tourism industry is no exception to this rule. Such competition, often encouraged by government policy, has been evident within the British tourism industry ever since the development of the mass market in travel, which began in the 1960s. The process accelerated in the 1980s, following policies of deregulation in the transport sector, which affected both airlines and coach companies. Competition forces companies to seek ways of becoming more efficient in order to cut costs. Integration makes this possible by enabling

companies to benefit from economies of scale: by producing and selling more of a product, the supplier reduces the unit cost of each product, since the fixed costs incurred are spread over a larger number of units, whether these are hotel bedrooms, aircraft seats or package tours. At the same time, buyers of these products, such as tour operators, can obtain lower net prices if they buy in larger quantities, just as airlines can negotiate lower prices if they order more aircraft from the manufacturers. The savings achieved through both these economies of scale can be passed on to clients in the form of lower prices, making the product more attractive to the consumer.

THE BENEFITS OF SIZE

Large companies offer other benefits to both the supplier and the tourist. Suppliers, knowing the reputation of the major companies in the field, are anxious to do business with them, secure in the belief that such corporations are least likely to collapse in the face of competition (a belief that is not always well founded, as shown by the collapse of the International Leisure Group at the beginning of the 1990s). The tour operator's operational risks are minimised, because suppliers, faced with an overbooking situation, will be less likely to turn away the clients of their best supporting companies. Similarly, hotels uniting into larger groups will be able to negotiate better deals through their own suppliers for the bulk purchase of such items as food and drink, while airlines will bring greater bargaining strength to the negotiating table in their dealings with foreign governments for landing rights or new routes.

Most companies, asked to identify their organisational goals, would cite market expansion as a major objective. Growth in a competitive environment is a means of survival, and history testifies to the fact that few companies survive by standing still. Integration is a means of growth, enabling a company to increase its market share and simultaneously reduce the level of competition it faces, by forcing less efficient companies out of business.

Greater sales mean more revenue, and therefore potentially more funds to reinvest in the company to assist expansion. This, in turn enables the company to employ or expand its specialist personnel. Nowhere is this more true than in those companies whose branches are individually quite small. A small chain of travel agents or hotels, for instance, may for the first time become able to employ specialist sales or marketing staff, or recruit their own legal or financial advisers. Higher revenue also releases more money for the marketing effort – a programme of national advertising in the mass media may become a real possibility for the first time. Few readers will have missed the frequent – and highly effective – post-Christmas TV advertising campaigns of the multiple travel agents which have enabled the market leaders to extend still further their share of the travel market at the expense of the independents.

In addition to these broad benefits offered by integration generally, there are other advantages specific to horizontal or vertical integration, and these will be examined in turn.

HORIZONTAL INTEGRATION

Horizontal integration can take several forms. One form is the integration between two companies offering competing products. Two hotels may merge, for example, or two airlines competing on similar routes may unite. Such mergers may result from the takeover of one company by another, or they may simply result from a voluntary agreement between the two to merge and obtain the benefits, identified above, of a much larger organisation. Voluntary unions, however, can be established which allow the companies concerned to maintain their autonomy while still obtaining the benefits of an integrated organisation. This is the case of a consortium – an affiliation of independent companies working together to achieve a common aim or benefit. One example of this affiliation is the marketing consortium, which allows independent companies to gain economies of scale in, for example, mass advertising or the publication of a joint brochure. Alternatively, the consortium may have its prime benefit in the purchase of supplies at bulk prices for its members – a feature of certain hotel consortia, and of groupings of independent travel agents like Advantage Travel, which in this way can negotiate higher commission levels from tour operators and other principals.

A second form of integration occurs between companies offering complementary rather than competing products. Tourism, as we have seen, is defined as the travel and stay of people. Close links therefore form between the accommodation and transport sectors, which are interdependent for their customers. Without hotel bedrooms available at their destinations, airline passengers may be unwilling to book airline seats, and vice versa. Recognition of this dual need has led many airlines to buy into, or form, their own hotel divisions, especially in regions of high tourist demand, where bed shortages are common. This trend was given impetus when the 'jumbo jet' era arrived at the beginning of the 1970s, and airlines woke up to the consequences of operating aircraft with 350 or more passengers aboard, each requiring accommodation over which the airline had little or no control. This led to the integration of several major airlines and hotel chains. However, with the intense competition between airlines during the 1970s and 1980s, which led to huge losses, coupled with the need to invest massively in new aircraft, many of these airlines were obliged to sell their hotel investments to raise capital, in order to survive. Since those days, the more common relationship has been through closely linked computer reservations systems (CRSs) which allow the airlines a measure of control over hotel bedrooms without major capital investment in the accommodation sector.

Airlines which are not directly competing may also seek the benefits of merging in order to feed one another's routes. British Airways' attempts during the latter part of the 1990s to buy into domestic airline businesses in the United States, which resulted first in the purchase of a minority interest in US Air, and later, an abortive attempt to integrate services with American Airlines (thwarted by European Union monopoly restrictions), provide a good example of one airline's recognition of the importance of complementary routes to its survival. BA's transatlantic routes provide 'feeder' opportunities into the US network of domestic routes, yet cabotage rules do not allow foreign companies to operate domestic routes within the USA. This placed British Airways at a disadvantage against its American competitors crossing the Atlantic.

The changing nature of tourism demand may also cause companies to diversify their interests horizontally. A few years ago, shipping companies woke up to the realisation that the future of long-haul travel lay with the airlines, and started to invest in the airline business as a means of survival. In most cases, though, the recognition came too late to save the companies, while the huge investments necessary to establish an airline were difficult to achieve at a time when the shipping companies' profits were dwindling or nonexistent.

At the retailing level, integration is also common, but because the traditional development of travel agencies has led in many cases to regional strengths, integration has tended to be regionally based, leading to the development of so-called 'miniples' – agencies with a significant number of branches within one region of the country only, which may well, within that region, outperform the multiple agents. Although the last few years have seen a huge growth in the number of branches of the big multiples, the miniples have been able to expand and strengthen their performance within their regions at the same time. In some cases, this has led to travel companies taking over a miniple as a means of building or strengthening their profile in a particular region, as was the case with the takeover of A T Mays, the prominent Scottish agency, by the US-owned Carlson Travel company.

Tour operating has also experienced growth through integration in the past decade, firstly between large companies in Britain, and later internationally. The most prominent takeover was the acquisition of Horizon Holidays by Thomson Holidays, while Airtours successfully took over Aspro Holidays in 1993. In 1992, the German airline LTU, which owns one of Germany's leading tour operators, LTU Touristik, took control of Thomas Cook, which itself took over Sunworld in 1996, while First Choice and Airtours have both purchased leading tour operators in Canada during the first half of the 1990s. Such integration in the principal travel sectors is likely to continue, with the emphasis on international mergers, both within Europe, as competition within the European Union is facilitated in the process of post-1992 harmonisation, and on a global scale, particularly where airlines and hotels are con-cerned. Aspects of this internationalisation process are discussed at the end of this chapter.

VERTICAL INTEGRATION

Vertical integration is said to take place when an organisation at one level in the chain of distribution unites with that at another level. This integration can be forward (or downward in the direction of the chain), as when a tour operator buys its own chain of travel agents, or it can be backward (or upward against the direction of the chain), as when the tour operator buys its own airline. Forward integration is obviously found more commonly, since organisations are more likely to have the necessary capital to buy businesses further down the chain of distribution, which require less capital investment. For example, a travel agent, even the largest chain, would be unlikely to have the capital needed to form its own airline. Generally speaking, the higher in the chain of distribution, the greater the investment required.

As with horizontal integration, organisations can achieve significant economies of scale by expanding vertically. Where total profits in individual sectors may be slight, an overall level of profit may still be made by a parent organisation controlling all levels in the chain. The package tour industry may be suffering in a year of intense competition, but those companies which control both airlines and retail sales outlets may nevertheless end up with an overall profit within the corporation as a whole.

As with the linking of complementary services in horizontal integration, many companies are concerned to ensure the continuation of their supplies. A tour operator, which depends upon a continuous supply of aircraft seats and hotel beds, and which may be facing international competition for such supplies, can best ensure adequate and regular supplies by directly controlling them, i.e. by 'buying backwards' into the airline and hotel businesses, as has Thomson Holidays. Until 1998 Thomson Holidays was itself a part of a much larger international organisation, the Thomson Corporation, which controlled newspapers and newsprint, as well as travel. However, the Corporation has now sold its travel interests to concentrate on its core businesses.

Such companies are well equipped financially to diversify their interests into new products when they see opportunities arise. Many large tour operators have followed just this process of vertical integration, either by integrating backwards or starting their own airline. Thus we find, for example, Cosmos Holidays (itself part of a large Swiss parent company) linked to charter carrier Monarch Airlines, while Thomson's chief rivals, Airtours and First Choice, each established its own charter airline, Airtours Aviation and Air 2000. These vertical links between airlines and tour operators are examined more fully in Chapter 12.

INTEGRATION LEADS TO CONTROL

In the same way, many large tour operators have in recent years sought to own and operate their own hotels in key resorts abroad, to ensure the availability of rooms at a reasonable price. This can be achieved either by direct purchase, or by setting up joint venture companies with partners in the hotel industry, or other sectors of the industry. Such integration offers the added advantage of greater control over the quality of the product. This is frequently difficult to achieve in the case of foreign hotels, and indeed, ensuring that standards are uniform, consistent and of the required quality is no easy matter in the case of a business composed of such diverse and disparate services. Clearly, the task becomes much easier when all these services come under the overall management of a single parent company.

Equally, the production sector will attempt to exercise control over the merchandising of its products. Airlines, shipping services and hotels are all multi-million pound investments, yet, curiously, they must each rely to a considerable extent on a fragmented, independent and frequently inexpert retailing sector for the sale of their products. Travel agents carry no stock, and therefore have little brand loyalty to a particular travel company. It is logical for the manufacturers to seek to influence the retail level by buying into retail agencies (British Airways has its own retail shops, for instance, as do many domestic US airlines, whose retail services compete with agents for the consumers' flight tickets). Thomson

Holidays, in addition to its own charter airline, also owns one of Britain's largest chain of travel agents, Lunn Poly, hence controlling all three key links in the chain of distribution; it also has interests in ground handling companies on the European mainland, having formed Viajes Cresta in Spain for this purpose.

Air carriers similarly try to help ensure demand for their seats by controlling tour operations. In Britain, British Airways operates its own programme of package tours, British Airways Holidays, while on the Continent, Air France linked up with Sotair and Jet Tour, as well as Meridien Hotels, and the major charter carrier in Germany, LTU, has its own tour operating division, LTU Touristik (LTT).

In Britain, and within the European Union, integration of this type has in the past had the added attraction of failing to draw criticism from bodies such as the Monopolies and Mergers Commission, compared with their closer inspection of horizontal integration. (For example the MMC investigated the horizontal takeover by Thomson Holidays of Horizon Holidays at the end of the 1980s, although ultimately viewing it as not against the public interest.) However, the MMC, in 1997, investigated the control of travel agent chains by UK tour operators, ruling that ownership by the latter must be made clear to customers. An organisation committed to growth and seeking to expand its operations in the tourism field is likely to be attracted to development of its interests across several sectors of the industry, providing it can be assured that this will not draw the attention of monopolies bodies.

In the long run, some danger is posed to travel agents themselves by this process of vertical integration downwards into the retailing sector. Airlines or tour operators opening their own retail outlets may, by competitive pricing or other marketing tactics, be able to attract the market away from the traditional agencies; it is concern with this aspect of trading in particular that encouraged the MMC investigation. Some travel agents, as we have seen, are competing through the establishment of consortia, within which they could sell their own 'brand label' tours. It is too early as yet to judge the likelihood of success of these ventures in competing with the larger chains.

Conglomerates and international integration

No discussion about the changing structure of ownership within the tourism industry would be complete without examining the growing role of the conglomerates. These are companies with investments in a diverse range of products which may include interests in travel and tourism businesses. This avoids the risks associated with investing in a single type of business. Although tourism has the reputation of being a highly volatile industry, the long-term growth prospects for leisure gener-ally have attracted many businesses from outside the tourism industry itself. Breweries, for example, have expanded into hotels and holiday centres (Center Parcs is owned by Scottish and Newcastle). Abroad, the trend is already firmly established, with most of Germany's travel and tourism businesses owned, through department stores, by the big banks.

Paralleling this diversification, the travel industry is also experiencing rapid internationalisation of ownership. This is a process which has been hastened within Europe by the process of harmonisation among members of the European Union. Travel businesses seeking to expand are eyeing opportunities within each others' countries. This process is already well advanced on the Continent, and is likely to become more common in Britain. The purchase of Thomas Cook by the German airline and tour operator LTU in 1992 clearly reflects the German parent's view of opportunities for expansion both horizontally, in the tour operating field, and vertically, in gaining a retailing toe-hold in Britain for the German organisation. Many examples of this ownership of, or more commonly, substantial investment in, cross-border companies can be cited; a few examples of these, based on the situation in the mid-1990s, will suffice. In Germany the largest tour operator, TUI, owned over three-quarters of the holding in Ultramar Express, a prominent tour operator and travel agency in Spain (a further small shareholding being held by Holland International Travel).

NUR Touristik, the second-largest operator, had a minority holding in Viajes Iberia of Spain. The French company Wagon Lits, one-time owners of Thomas Cook before its integration with US-owned Carlson, held nearly three-quarters of the equity of Viajes Ecuador, Spain's largest tour operator/travel agency combine, while Spain's second major company, Melia, was owned by Italian interests. The German Metro group, through their substantial shareholding in the Kaufhof department store, were not only outright owners of tour operator ITS, but had a 50 per cent shareholding in Swiss long-haul operator Kuoni Holidays. Many further examples of this growth in internationalisation could be cited, but these are issues which are in regular process of change, and in consequence are better examined in current articles in the travel press than here. Suffice it to say that, increasingly, British travel companies must look beyond their own borders to understand the nature of the competition they face.

QUESTIONS AND DISCUSSION POINTS

1   Operation Stabiliser was strongly defended by ABTA as the best means of protecting the travel client. With its removal, and in the light of current events, is the industry better run and the client better protected?

2   Identify the main patterns of integration which have occurred in the industry over the past year, both in the UK and in mainland Europe, and explain the reasons for these developments.

3   Large companies claim the benefits of economies of scale in the size of their organisations. Are there also diseconomies of scale which may inhibit their performance and productivity? Give examples where possible of tourism firms whose massive growth has led to problems for the organisation.

4   Who do you see as the next possible victim of a takeover bid in the British tourist industry? Give reasons for your choice.

1 As a student attending a full-time travel and tourism course, You are undertaking a short period of industrial work experience in the office of a local travel agent, a branch of a major multiple.

It is clear from the manager's attitude that she feels you are gaining no advantage in spending a long period studying tourism, declaring, 'I've usually found it preferable to take staff on direct from school and train them up in the way we operate here. My staff learn more in a week here than you will learn in a year at your college.'

Write a set of notes setting out how you would answer this, identifying the benefits of formal education in tourism. Make clear in your answer how you would distinguish between training and education.

2 As a retail agent and member of WorldChoice, you have been approached by that organisation for help in drafting a letter designed to encourage more companies to join.

Prepare a draft of your letter whihc will be sent to the proprietors of small agencies, citing the advantages they might achieve by joining. You should take account of topical circumstances which might influence the arguments you set out in the letter.

(Note: it may be helpful to discuss the benefits of WorldChoice membership with a present member of that organisation before tackling this assignment.)

7

Passenger Transport: the Aviation Industry

OBJECTIVES

After studying this chapter, you should be able to:

- understand the role that airlines and airports play in the development of tourism;
- explain how air transport is organised and distinguish between different categories of airline operation;
- understand the reasons for air regulation and the systems of regulation in force, both in the UK and internationally;
- explain how an air broker operates and the importance of this role to the industry.

Introduction

Tourism is the outcome of the travel and stay of people, and, as we have seen, the development of transport, both private and public, has had a major impact on the growth and direction of tourism development. The provision of adequate, safe, comfortable, fast, convenient and cheap public transport is a prerequisite for mass market tourism. A tourist resort's accessibility is the outcome of, above all else, two factors: price (in absolute terms, as well as in comparison with competitive resorts), and time (the actual or perceived time taken to travel from one's originating point to one's destination). Air travel, in particular, over the past thirty years has made medium- and long-range destinations accessible on both these counts, to an extent not previously imaginable. In doing so, it has substantially contributed

to the phenomenon of mass market international tourism, with its consequent benefits and, increasingly, as numbers multiply, drawbacks for the receiving nations.

Public transport, while an integral sector of the tourism industry, must also provide services which are not dependent upon tourist demand. Road, rail and air services all owe their origins to government mail contracts, and the carriage of freight, whether separate from or together with passengers, makes a significant (and sometimes crucial) contribution to a carrier's revenue. It should also be recognised that many carriers provide a commercial or social service which owes little to demand by tourists. Road and rail carriers, for example, provide essential commuter services for workers travelling between their places of residence and work. These carriers (and sometimes airlines, as in remoter districts of Scotland) provide an essential social and economic service by linking outlying rural areas with centres of industry and commerce, thus ensuring a communications lifeline for residents. The extent to which carriers can or should be commercially orientated while simultaneously being required to provide a network of unprofitable social routes is a constantly recurring issue in government transport policy.

Most forms of transport are highly capital-intensive. The cost of building and maintaining track in the case of railways, and of regularly re-equipping airlines with new aircraft embodying the latest technical advances requires massive investments of capital, which are likely to be available only to the largest corporations, and financial subsidies from the public sector may be essential. At the same time, transport offers great opportunities for economies of scale, whereby unit prices can be dramatically reduced. There is a high element of fixed costs, for example, for an airline operating out of a particular airport, whether that airline operates flights four times a day or once a week. If these overheads can be distributed over a greater number of flights, the costs of an individual seat on a flight will fall.

The question of economies of scale is one for caution, however. There comes a point where the growth of organisations can result in diseconomies of scale, which can well offset any benefits of size. The inability of some major airlines to compete with leaner, more efficient airlines is a case in point. Major airlines, for reasons of prestige, tend to opt for expensively furnished high-rent city centre offices, imposing added burdens on overheads.

The airline business

In Chapter 3 we explored the way in which the development of air transport in the second half of the twentieth century contributed to the growth of tourism, whether for business or pleasure. Travel by air has become safe, comfortable, rapid and, above all, cheap, for two reasons.

The first reason is the enormous growth of aviation technology, especially since the development of the jet airliner after World War II. Since the first commercial jet (the DeHavilland Comet) came into service in the early 1950s, seat cost per passenger kilometre (a common measure of revenue yield) has fallen both in absolute terms, and relative to costs of other forms of transport, particularly shipping, which up until that point had dominated the long-haul travel business. Both engines and aircraft design have beeen continuously refined and improved: wings, fuselage and engines have been designed to reduce drag, engines have become more efficient and less fuel-hungry. At the same time, increases in carrying capacity for passengers and freight have further reduced average seat costs. The current third-generation wide-bodied jumbo jets, spearheaded by

the Boeing 747 in 1970, have reduced seat costs substantially, as costs are now spread across as many as 400 passengers, rather than the previous 130–200. However, prices to passengers can only fall if a high proportion of these seats are filled; in some cases, the sudden jump in capacity posed problems for airlines until seat demand on routes finally caught up with supply.

Following the huge increases in fuel costs resulting from the oil crisis of 1973–74, research was stepped up to find ways of improving fuel economy. This was achieved by a combination of improved engine efficiency and reduced weight (some airlines went as far as reducing the number of pages in their in-flight magazines to trim weight!) Recent aircraft, such as the Boeing 757, introduced in the early 1980s, offer huge savings in fuel cost over earlier generations of aircraft. (Boeing claim their 757 is the most fuel-efficient of all aircraft flying.) Airlines facing low profits from competition seek any means possible to save cost, and are tempted to re-equip their fleet with the latest cost-saving aircraft, but the investment required is substantial; this problem will be discussed later in the chapter.

It is thought that the jet engine has now reached a stage of evolutionary sophistication which will make it increasingly difficult to produce further economies, and cost-cutting exercises have replaced technological innovation as a means of reducing prices to the public. However, the search for more economy goes on; there are promising developments in recent research which suggest that the problems of carrying liquefied hydrogen rather than kerosene as fuel have been largely overcome. This would provide three times the energy per unit, and allow aircraft to increase their range substantially. Given that world oil stocks will begin to run out between 2020 and 2040, the need to develop new sources of energy is paramount.

Other research is being directed towards size, with the leading aircraft manufacturers working on developments which will lead to a new generation of 'super-jumbos', capable of carrying 600–800 passengers on key long-haul routes such as Los Angeles–Tokyo or London–Sydney. These could be in operation before the turn of the century, but the motive for their construction lies as much in airport and air corridor congestion as in efforts to cut costs. Hub airports in Europe, particularly, are already so congested that expansion of competition to reduce airfares, politically encouraged through the liberalisation of air transport in 1997, is proving difficult due to shortages of slots.

During the 1980s, the technological focus changed to the development of quieter aircraft and aircraft capable of taking off from, and landing on, shorter runways. The emphasis on quieter engines originated in the United States, where controls on noise pollution forced airlines to re-equip their fleets, or to fit expensive modifications to existing aircraft. In turn, the airlines have pressed governments to relax controls over night flying, which would enable them to operate around the clock, easing congestion and increasing their productivity. The British government, however, has shown itself reluctant to permit more than a token increase in night flying, especially from the congested London airports.

Short take-off and landing (STOL) aircraft such as the De Havilland Dash-7, Dornier 228 and BAe 146 (later the RJ series of regional jet aircraft) have all helped to revolutionise business travel, allowing the siting of airports much closer to city centres. London City Airport, situated in the Docklands area (see Figure 7.1), is an example of such a development which is dependent upon STOL technology for success. (Although the airport has been hampered in its development by problems of poor overland access from the City, at the time of writing it is starting to move into profitability after a decade of losses partly owing to a shortage of slots at other London airports.)

The second factor in the development of mass travel by air has been the enterprise and creativity demonstrated both by air transport management and other entrepreneurs in the tourism industry. The introduction of net inclusive tour basing fares for tour operators, variable pricing techniques such as Advance Purchase Excursion (APEX) tickets and stand-by fares, and more recently 'frequent flyer' programmes, in which passengers collect additional free miles based on the mileage they accumulate with a carrier, have all helped to stimulate demand and fill aircraft seats. The key factor, however, has been the chartering of air-

Figure 7.1 RJ-85. (Courtesy London City Airport)

craft to tour operators, first on an ad hoc basis for weekly departures, and later in a time series basis (in which the aircraft is placed at the disposal of the operator throughout the season, or even for the entire year). Chartering aircraft in this way to operators who could achieve very high load factors on each aircraft helped to reduce unit costs to a point where low-cost package tours, especially to such destinations as the Spanish east coast and Majorca, brought foreign holidays within reach of millions in the UK and Western Europe.

The organisation of air transport

It is convenient to think of the civil aviation business as composed of a number of elements:

(a) equipment manufacturers
(b) airports
(c) air navigation and traffic control services
(d) airlines

As was mentioned earlier, however, each of these is not dependent on tourists alone for its livelihood. Apart from other forms of civilian passenger, they also serve the needs of the military, as well as those of freight and mail clientele. Nevertheless, tourists represent for each a significant element of the markets served, and therefore they must be counted as components of the tourism industry.

EQUIPMENT MANUFACTURERS

Equipment manufacturers are made up of companies manufacturing commercial aircraft and engines. The demand for airframes (fuselages and wings) can be conveniently divided between those used for large jet aircraft, carrying between 150 and 500 passengers, which provide the bulk of passenger services throughout the world, and those used for smaller aircraft seating as few as eighteen passengers, which are employed chiefly on business routes or provide feeder services from rural airports.

Within the former category, the world market is dominated by just two manufacturers: Boeing, which is responsible for the major proportion of aircraft manufacture and which recently swallowed the second-largest airframe manufacturer, MacDonnell Douglas; and the Airbus Industrie consortium of Aérospatiale (France), Daimler-Benz Aerospace (Germany), CASA (Spain) and British Aerospace (BAe) (UK), which is now the second-largest manufacturer. BAe also cooperates with other companies to compete more effectively in the global market; for example in 1997, as part of Aero International, a joint venture with Aérospatiale and Alenia of Italy, it gained a major order for RJ-85 jets from North West Airlines.

Aircraft engines are manufactured quite separately, and three companies also dominate this market: General Electric (USA), Pratt and Whitney (USA) and Rolls-Royce (UK). The last two have formed a consortium known as International Aero Engines (IAE), which also includes MTU (Daimler-Benz) and Aero Engines Corporation of Japan, a move once again designed to compete more effectively for world orders. As with airframes, we can see that this market, too, is effectively controlled by an oligopoly, and that the cost of aircraft development and production is now so high that international cooperation between leading companies is essential.

The world fleet in 1996 comprised some 11,700 Western-built aircraft, and this is expected to rise over the next twenty years to around 17,100, while the average seat capacity is also expected to increase over this time from 179 to 235, as economies of scale encourage the purchase of larger and larger aircraft. When it is revealed that a single Boeing 777 currently costs around $160 million, and even a 'discounted' Boeing 737 will cost at least $20 million, while an Airbus report in 1996 estimated the forthcoming demand for new aircraft by the largest 214 airlines as 14,966 aircraft at a cost of over $1,000 billion (80 per cent of which would be to replace existing aircraft), it can clearly be seen that the manufacture of aircraft is one of the world's largest businesses, which can play a vital role in the economy of aircraft manufacturing nations. Small wonder that other fast-developing Third World countries are also seeking to enter this lucrative market.

The manufacture of small aircraft is, however, far more fragmented, and with the world's airlines increasingly equipping their fleets with larger aircraft at the expense of the smaller, supply is now outstripping demand in this field. Several of these smaller manufacturers are facing financial difficulty, led by the Dutch Fokker company which ceased production and went into administration in 1996. Leading competitors in the market include the Swedish Saab, which niche-markets the thirty-seven-seat 340 and fifty-eight-seat 2000, both turboprops; Daimler-Benz's Dornier division which produces a high-cost, high-quality aircraft now deemed too expensive for the marketplace; the Candian Bombadier which swallowed up Short Brothers of Belfast and produces the 50-seat Canadair Jet and the 36-seat Dash-8 turboprop; and the recently formed consortium of Aero International Regional, comprising British Aerospace, Aérospatiale of France and Alenia of Italy, which currently offers the Avro RJ 80 100-seat jet, the turboprop ATR 42 and 72 (fifty and seventy-four seats) and the Jetstream 41, a turboprop with twenty-nine seats. These manufacturers face challenges from Third World manufacturers with lower cost bases, such as Brazil's Embraer which offers the new EMB-145 fifty-seat regional jet, and Indonesia's IPTN, which has formed an alliance with CASA of Spain to produce a fifty-seat turboprop.

The smaller of these aircraft are mainly twin turboprops, while the larger aircraft, seating up to fifty or more, tend to be pure jets. After the advent of deregulation in the USA, the demand for smaller aircraft rapidly increased to fill the need for feeder services from rural airports into 'hub' airports, where connections would be made for long-haul or intercontinental flights. However, the trend to regional city-to-city services calling for somewhat larger aircraft, and the stabilisation of the US airline business after initial expansion, has led to overcapacity among the regional aircraft makers.

AIRPORTS

Ownership of airports may be under the control of the state or of local authorities, or in private hands. In some cases, as in many German airports, local and state governments may share the responsibility for running the airport, while in other examples, such as Milan, control is exercised by a combination of local government and private enterprise. In Britain, many regional airports are in local authority hands, while seven of the major international airports are owned and operated by BAA, a private corporation formed by the denationalisation of the former state-run British Airports Authority, under the terms of the Airports Bill (1985). Bristol International is one example of a privately owned airport, in common with many of the smaller regional airports. The City of Bristol, which owned the airport until 1997, released a substantial shareholding to the First Group Bus Company in order to finance expansion. The significance of ownership is that where airports are under the control of the public sector, it may be possible for some of the overheads and direct costs to be concealed, so that the airport's performance figures are improved. The leading six airports in Britain, based on passenger throughput in 1996, were:

London Heathrow	55,723,000
London Gatwick	24,106,000
Manchester	14,473,000
Birmingham	5,471,000
Glasgow	5,471,000
Stansted London	4,811,000

Heathrow is the busiest airport in the world, in terms of international passengers; however, Chicago O'Hare takes the lead when domestic air passengers are also included.

Airports require a good balance of passengers and freight to be profitable, although they may also earn a substantial proportion of their revenue and profits through other commercial activities, such as the sale of duty-free goods (where international flights are involved), catering services or franchises for local car rental companies. Their earnings from the airlines are based on a complex set of landing charges, which are designed to cover parking charges, landing fees, and a per capita fee for passengers carried – thus a jumbo aircraft will be charged a considerably higher landing fee than a small aircraft. In cases where civil aviation authorities pass on the cost of air traffic control to the airports, or where the airport itself is responsible for this (as at Jersey Airport), a share of these costs will also be charged to landing aircraft.

The threat to duty-free sales within the European Union, which are set to be abandoned after mid-1999, is obviously of concern to both airlines and airports. Estimates based on research in 1997 by the Duty-Free Confederation, a lobby supporting its continuation, suggest that the loss of this revenue could force up airport charges by 20–40 per cent, while package holidays would rise by between £10–£14 per person and scheduled air fares would rise by up to 20 per cent. However, the EU has shown no inclination to step back from this legislation, and BAA has instead built up its duty-paid retailing, in 1997 taking over the largest company in the USA dealing with duty-free goods, in an effort to protect its profit levels. Evidence suggests that many travellers are willing to spend time and money on the purchase of goods at airports. A study by Select Service Partners in 1997 found that airport profits rise by 20 per cent for every ten minutes passengers are kept waiting by delayed aircraft – so it is not in an airport's interest to reduce congestion! In the mid-1990s, average 'dwell' time at European airports was 94 minutes.

The congestion problem at major international airports is becoming so intense that efforts are being taken to improve technology which will help to improve ground handling. Increased automation is helping to speed up the throughput of passengers and two forms of ticketing are being introduced, albeit gradually. One is the Automated Ticketing and Boarding Pass (ATB), a ticket printed on card which allows check-ins as short as 20 minutes; while 'E-Tickets' are virtual tickets which can be issued at airports by swiping credit cards of E-Ticket Access cards, avoiding the need to check in by the normal method. However, these systems only allow passengers to by-pass check-in counters when they have no hold baggage and are on a domestic trip (passports still have to be checked for international movements). British Airways were forced to reverse their decision to work only with electronic tickets when these proved unpopular with a large proportion of agents and passengers. In spite of these developments, there are finite limits to the number of passengers for which an airport can cater, and those such as Heathrow are already close to their capacity. The addition of a further runway (Heathrow plans a fifth runway within the next few years, if local objections can be overcome) may postpone the inevitable point where capacity is reached, but air corridors are already overcrowded in Europe, and increasingly aircraft are forced to 'stack' at busy periods, wasting fuel. This creates a knock-on effect, delaying later take-offs, which combined with poor weather, lightning air traffic control strikes and the need for increased security in checking baggage at times of terrorist activity, has led to serious problems of congestion at busy airports all over the world.

In Britain, the pressures on London airports have encouraged the Government to seek to disperse traffic to regional airports, while Schiphol Airport in Amsterdam has sought to benefit from London's congestion by picking up British regional passengers, particularly those bound for intercontinental connections. The regional airports have shown their enthusiasm for expansion, but have not always had the support promised by the British government, which has shown itself reluctant, for example, to give approval to American carriers wishing to expand into regional airports. Some as well face difficulty due to local authorities' unwillingness to expand facilities in the face of opposition from local residents.

Airlines have great difficulties at the congested airports in gaining take-off and landing slots for new services they plan to operate. Slots are awarded to airlines through processes of negotiation, which usually take place in November each year, to cover flights in the following year. Scheduled services receive priority over charter, and the so-called 'grandfather' rights of existing carriers tend to take precedence over new carriers – so much so that at airports such as Heathrow, a new airline which seeks to gain slots may find it necessary to take over an existing airline in order to do so. This accounted for the high paper value of companies like Pan Am, with its access to Heathrow, even when they were upon the point of collapse.

NAVIGATION AND AIR TRAFFIC CONTROL

The technical services which are provided on the ground to assist and control aircraft while in the air, and in landing or taking off, are not normally seen as part of the tourism industry. However, their role is a key one in the operation of aviation services. Air traffic control has the function of guiding aircraft into and out of airports, giving pilots (usually in the form of continually updated automatic recordings) detailed information on ground conditions, windspeed, cloud conditions, runways in use, and the state of navigation aids. ATC will instruct pilots on what height and direction to take, and will be responsible for all flights within a geographically defined area.

ATC sytems are being updated throughout Continental Europe to allow many more aircraft movements to take place within a given period, as a means of overcoming congestion. Key air corridors such as those between London, Paris and Frankfurt have been the first to gain the benefits of this investment. Another innovation has been made possible by the improvement in altimeters on board aircraft; those flying transatlantic and fitted with the latest equipment are permitted to halve the vertical distance between aircraft, from 2,000-foot intervals to 1,000. The present horizontal distance apart which aircraft must maintain, nose to tail, is ten minutes' flying time (at a height of 29,000 to 41,000 feet), with aircraft held at least 60 miles apart laterally. If these lateral gaps could also be halved, this would permit an eightfold increase in the number of flights operating, although the problems of congestion at the airports themselves would remain to be solved.

AIRLINE SERVICES

The services provided by airlines can be divided into three distinct categories: scheduled services, non-scheduled, or charter services; and air taxi services.

Scheduled services

Scheduled services are provided by some 650 airlines worldwide, of which just over 250 are members of IATA. They operate on defined routes, domestic or international, for which licences have been granted by the government or governments concerned. The airlines are required to operate on the basis of their published timetables, regardless of passenger load factors (although flights and routes which are not commercially viable throughout the year may be operated during periods of high demand only). These services may be publicly or privately owned, although there is now a global movement among the developed nations towards private ownership of airlines. Where state-owned airlines continue to operate, as in the case of Air France, or many Third World countries' airlines, the public airline is recognised as the national *flag-carrier*. Some European airlines, such as SAS in Scandinavia, are partly state-owned, but in the UK, all airlines are now in the private sector, since British Airways was privatised in 1987.

Airlines operating on major routes between 'hub' airports within a country are known as *trunk route* airlines, while those operating from smaller, often rural airports into these hubs are referred to as *regional* or *feeder* airlines. In the case of the USA and certain other regions, these may also be termed *commuter* airlines, as their prime purpose is to serve the needs of commuting businesspeople, many of whom regularly use these routes. The growing development of 'hub and spoke' routes will be discussed later in the chapter.

Charter services

Charter services, by contrast with scheduled services, do not operate according to published timetables, nor are they advertised or promoted by the airlines themselves. Instead, the aircraft are chartered to middlemen (often tour operators) for a fixed charge, and these middlemen then become responsible for selling the aircraft's seats, leaving the airlines only with the responsibility for operating the aircraft. The middlemen can change flight departures, or even cancel flights, transferring passengers to other flights.

With the liberalisation of air service regulations within Europe – a key element in European Union policy for air transport – the distinction between scheduled and charter services is becoming less clear-cut. Efforts have been made by some charter companies to operate scheduled services – although with mixed success, as they have neither the marketing experience nor the organisational structure to support selling directly to the public. However, the growth of 'seat-only' sales on charter aircraft (estimated at up to 20 per cent of the total inclusive tour market from the UK into European destinations) is a clear indication of the direction in which the market is moving. Many scheduled carriers have their own charter subsidiaries; for example, Lufthansa operates a charter subsidiary known as Condor.

Air taxi services

Air taxis are privately chartered aircraft accommodating between four and eighteen people, and used particularly by business travellers. They offer the advantages of convenience and flexibility; routings can be tailormade for passengers (for example, a feasible itinerary for a business day using an air taxi might be London–Paris–Brussels–Amsterdam–London, a near-impossible programme for a scheduled service), and small airfields close to a company's office or factory can be used. There are some 350 airfields suitable for air taxis in Britain alone, and a further 1,300 in Western Europe (see Figure 7.2), compared with only about 200 airports receiving scheduled services. Flights can be arranged or routings amended, at short notice, and, with a full flight, the cost for chartering can be commensurate with the combined business class fares for the number of staff travelling.

Aircraft in use range from helicopters like the Bell Jet Ranger, or the piston-engined Piper twin Comanche (each seating three to four people, with

Figure 7.2 Airports and airfields of Europe

Figure 7.3 Air taxi: Gates Learjet 35A, seating eight passengers. *(Courtesy Northern Executive Aviation Ltd, Manchester)*

a range of between 350 and 900 miles, up to aircraft such as Embraer's Bandeirantes which are capable of carrying eighteen passengers up to 300 miles. Larger aircraft can also be chartered as needed. Most air taxi journeys are in the range of 500–600 miles, and therefore these aircraft are ideal for many business trips within Europe. In the UK alone, some 150 air taxi companies are available to meet the needs of the market.

Some corporations which formerly ran their own fleet of executive aircraft have switched to using air taxis, as purchase is difficult to justify unless the aircraft concerned have a very high usage.

Air transport regulation

THE NEED FOR REGULATION

With the growth of the airline industry, regulation on both national and international routes has become necessary for a number of reasons. First and foremost there is the question of passenger safety, which requires that airlines be licensed and supervised. For reasons of public concern, other regulations will also be needed in such areas as noise or pollution control.

Since air transport has a profound impact on the economy of a region or country, governments will take steps to encourage the development of routes which appear to offer prospects of economic benefits, and to discourage those which appear to be suffering overcapacity. While the policy of one government may be to encourage competition, or to intervene where a route monopoly is forcing prices up, another government's policy may be directed to rationalising excessive competition in order to avoid energy waste, or even to protect the profitability of the national flag-carrier. Some governments are tempted to provide subsidies in order to support their inefficient flag-carriers; private airlines in Europe have long complained of this unfair protection against competition which, although forbidden by the Treaty of Rome within the EU, has been widely ignored by those member countries which retain public ownership of the flag-carrier. The state airlines of France, Spain and Italy have all received subsidies in the mid-1990s, in spite of protests by British Airways and other private carriers operating within the Union.

Another characteristic of such protection is the *pooling* arrangements made between airlines operating on certain international routes, whereby all revenue accruing on that route is apportioned equally between the carriers serving the route. This may appear to circumvent competition on a route, but is also one means of safeguarding the viability of the national carrier operating in a strong competitive environment. In Third World countries, where governments are anxious to earn hard currency, the support of the national carrier as an earner of hard currency, through arrangements such as this, may be justifiable. Pooling arrangements are often entered into, where the airlines are not of comparable size, in order to safeguard the smaller carrier's capacity and revenue. By rationalising schedules, pressure is reduced on peak-time take-off slots, and costs are reduced. Financial arrangements between the pooled carriers usually limit to a fixed maximum the amount of revenue transferred from one carrier to the other, to reduce what may be seen as unfair government support for an inefficient carrier. The USA has made such pooling agreements illegal.

In some areas, air transport is an essential public utility which, even where commercially nonviable, is socially desirable in order to provide communications with a region where geographical terrain may make other forms of transport difficult or impossible (as is the case with areas such as New Guinea, Alaska, or the Hebrides in Scotland). In some cases, governments may provide airlines with subsidies in order to ensure a service is maintained.

SYSTEMS OF REGULATION

Broadly speaking, air transport operations are regulated in three ways:

1 Internationally, scheduled routes are assigned on the basis of agreements between governments of the countries concerned.
2 Internationally, scheduled air fares are now subject to less and less control, as in both North America and Europe airlines are free to set their own fares. However, governments can still intercede where they suspect predatory pricing is involved, and in practice within Europe, fares

are permitted to fluctuate between acceptable maxima and minima. In Third World areas, however, the extent of regulation is often far greater, with airlines agreeing fares which may be then mediated through the traffic conferences of the International Air Transport Association (IATA). Agreed tariffs arrived at in this way are then subject to ratification by the governments of the countries concerned. Generally, less direct control is exercised over domestic fares.
3 National governments approve and license the carriers which are to operate on scheduled routes, whether domestically or internationally. In the UK, the CAA has this responsibility and is also responsible for the licensing of charter airlines and of tour operators organising package holidays abroad.

The worldwide trend is to allow market forces to determine the shape and direction of the airline business. Regulation is today less concerned with routes, frequency, capacity or fares, and more concerned with aspects of safety.

Air transport regulations are the result of a number of international agreements between countries dating back over many years. The Warsaw Convention of 1929 first established common agreement on the extent of liability of the airlines in the event of death or injury of passengers, or loss of passenger baggage, with a limit of $10,000. The limitations on liability soon led to inflation reducing the value of claims, and liability was reassessed by a number of participating airlines, first at the Hague Protocol in 1955, where the figure was increased to $20,000, and again at the Montreal Agreement in 1966, when the United States imposed a $75,000 ceiling on flights to and from the USA and it was agreed that the maximum liability would be periodically reviewed. In 1992, Japan waived all limits for Japanese carriers, and in the following year, the UK government unilaterally required British carriers to increase liability to a limit of 100,000 SDRs (Special Drawing Rights, a reserve currency operated by the International Monetary Fund, and equivalent to about $140,000). Finally, in 1995 IATA negotiated an *Intercarrier Agreement on Passenger Liability* which was designed to enforce a blanket coverage for all member airlines, whereby any damages would be determined according to the laws of the country of the airline affected. However, only some fifty-five carriers have so far agreed to this and implemented it.

THE FIVE FREEDOMS OF THE AIR

Further legislation concerning passenger aviation resulted from the Chicago Convention on Civil Aviation held in 1944, at which eighty governments were represented in discussions designed to promote world air services and to reach agreement on standard operating procedures for air services between countries. There were two outcomes of this meeting: the founding of the International Civil Aviation Organisation (ICAO), now a specialised agency of the United Nations; and the establishment of the so-called *five freedoms of the air*. These comprise the privileges of:

1 Flying across a country without landing
2 Landing in a country for purposes other than the carriage of passengers or freight, e.g. in order to refuel
3 Off-loading passengers, mail or freight from an airline of the country from which those passengers, mail or freight originated
4 Loading passengers, mail or freight on an airline of the country for which those passengers, mail or freight are destined
5 Loading passengers, mail or freight on an airline not belonging to the country for which those passengers, mail or freight are destined, and off-loading passengers, mail or freight from an airline not of the country from which these originated.

These privileges were designed to provide the framework for bilateral agreements between countries and to ensure that carriage of passengers, mail and freight between any two countries would normally be restricted to the carriers of those countries.

THE MOVE TO GREATER FREEDOM OF THE SKIES

Other freedoms not discussed by the convention, but equally pertinent to the question of rights of operation, have been termed 'sixth and seventh freedoms'. These would cover:

6 Carrying passengers, mail or freight between any two countries on an airline which is of neither country, but is operating via the airline's own country
7 Carrying passengers, mail or freight directly between two countries on an airline associated with neither of the two countries.

These various freedoms can best be illustrated using examples (see Figure 7.4).

While a handful of countries expressed a preference for an 'open skies' policy on regulation, most demanded controls. An International Air Services Agreement, to which more than ninety countries became signatories, provided for the mutual exchange of the first two freedoms of the air, while it was left to individual bilateral negotiations between countries to resolve other issues. The convention agreed not to regulate charter services, allowing countries to impose whatever individual regulations they wished. Few countries, in fact, were willing to allow a total 'open skies' policy for charters.

The Anglo-American agreement which took place in Bermuda in 1946, following the convention, set the pattern for many of the bilateral agreements which followed. This so-called *Bermuda Agreement*, while restricting air carriage betweeen the two countries to national carriers, did not impose restrictions on capacity for airlines concerned. This was modified at a second Bermuda Agreement reached in 1977 (and ratified in 1980), in line with the tendency of many countries in the intervening years to opt for an agreement which would ensure that a percentage of total traffic on a route was guaranteed for the national carriers of the countries concerned. It was Britain's intention, in this renegotiated agreement, to avoid overcapacity on the route by restricting it to two British and two American carriers. A further agreement in 1986 extended the agreed capacities across the Atlantic, following a three-year moratorium on new services by the UK and American governments. However, in line with the policy of deregulation which both the North American and European nations have introduced, the tight control over capacity has been relaxed and new routes have been agreed. The concept of *reciprocity* nevertheless remains important, with

Figure 7.4 Some examples of the freedoms of the air

the British government only willing to concede new routes for American carriers if reciprocal routes are granted to British carriers.

Carriage on routes within the national territory of a country (known as *cabotage* routes) is not subject to international agreement, and is normally restricted to the national carriers of the country concerned. However, this provides opportunities for a country's national carriers to operate exclusively on international routes, in cases where these countries have overseas possessions. This is the case, for example, on routes out of the UK to destinations such as Gibraltar, or on services between France and Réunion Island. Under the EU's programme of liberalisation of the air within member countries, the cabotage regulation, the final barrier to total freedom of operation, was dropped on 1 April 1997. Any airline of any member country can now file to operate services between cities within another member's borders. Thus, for instance, British Airways can now choose to operate between Paris and Milan, or between Milan and Rome, while Alitalia or Air France can provide a service between Manchester and Aberdeen. In theory, this liberalisation should open up competition and encourage a wealth of new services throughout the EU. In practice, the difficulty of getting slots at congested airports, as well as delaying tactics by some governments attempting to support their own national carriers, has meant that few new services were introduced in the immediate aftermath of the Act, and virtually none at hub airports.

European carriers operating across the Atlantic are, of course, restricted by US cabotage laws from carrying passengers domestically within the US. Their rival US carriers can, however, operate between European cities as an extension to transatlantic flights, giving US airlines an advantage over Europeans. The British government, inter alia, has been attempting for a number of years to overturn this restriction and obtain rights for their country's airlines to operate within the US as an extension to their own transatlantic flights, so far without success.

THE ROLE OF IATA

For many years, effective control over air fares on international routes was exercised by the International Air Transport Association, a trade body comprising some 80 per cent of the world's airlines which operate on international routes. The aims of this organisation, which was restructured in its present form in 1945, have been to promote safe, regular and economic air transport; to provide the means for collaboration between the air carriers themselves; and to cooperate with the ICAO and other international bodies for the promotion of safety and effective communications. However, it was IATA's fare-fixing role which aroused most controversy, since the association has in the past acted as a legalised cartel. Fares were established at the annual fare-fixing Traffic Conferences by a process of common agreement between the participating airlines, subject to ratification by the airlines' governments. In practice, this ratification became largely automatic.

Critics of IATA argued that, as a result, fares became unnecessarily high on many routes and competition was stifled. Often, the agreed fares were the outcome of political considerations in which the less efficient national flag-carriers pushed for prices unrelated to competitive costs. IATA also controlled many other aspects of airline operation, such as the pitch of passengers' seats, which dictated the amount of leg-room they could enjoy, and even the kind of meals that could be served on board. As a result, the airlines were forced to concentrate their marketing effort on such ephemeral aspects of the product as service, punctuality or even the design of cabin crew uniforms, rather than providing a genuine measure of competition.

It was widely felt that this had led to inertia among the participating carriers, with agreements resulting from a desire to avoid controversy among fellow members. Nor had the cartel ensured profitability for its members, since they faced open competition from non-IATA carriers who successsfully competed on both price and added value.

Led by the United States, and soon followed by other countries, airlines chose to withdraw from this price-fixing mechanism, and as a result IATA was restructured in 1979 to create a two-tier organisation. The tariff section dealt with fare-fixing, for those nations which wished to continue doing so, and the trade section provided the benefits which an international airline body could offer. IATA's role in price-fixing has become steadily less important, and airlines have also been left also to determine their own service and catering arrangements. The principal benefit offered by IATA today is its central clearing house system, which makes possible financial settlements between members, in the same manner as the

British clearing banks. Tickets and other documents are standardised and interchangeable between IATA members, compatibility is established between members in air fare constructions and currency exchange rates, and other procedures, such as the appointment, through licensing agreements, of IATA-recognised travel agents, are standardised throughout the world. The computerised Bank Settlement Plan, introduced in the UK in 1984, permits the monthly settlement of accounts with appointed agents through a single centre rather than with each individual airline, and has enabled financial transactions to keep pace with the enormous growth in airline travel.

BRITISH REGULATION OF AIR TRANSPORT

In the UK, the Civil Aviation Act of 1971 led to the establishment of the Civil Aviation Authority (CAA), which has five regulatory functions:

1 It is responsible for regulating air navigation services (jointly with the Ministry of Defence), through Britain's air traffic control services.
2 It has responsibility for the regulation of all British civil aviation, including air transport licensing, the award of licences (ATOLs) to air travel organisers, and approval of air fares.
3 It is responsible for the airworthiness and operational safety of British carriers, including certification of airlines, airports, flight crew and engineers.
4 It acts as advisor to the government in matters concerning domestic and international civil aviation.
5 It has a number of subsidiary functions, including the research and publication of statistics, and the ownership and management of eight airports in the Highlands and Islands of Scotland.

Prior to the Civil Aviation Act, no clear long-term government policy had been discernible in respect to aviation in the UK. As governments changed, so attitudes to the public or private ownership of carriers changed. With the aim of providing some longer-term direction and stability, a committee of enquiry into civil air transport was established, under the chairmanship of Sir Ronald Edwards. The report, *British Air Transport in the Seventies*, appeared in 1969. This became known as the Edwards Report, and recommended that the government should periodically promulgate civil aviation policy and objectives; that the long-term aim should be to satisfy air travellers at the lowest economically desirable price; and that a suitable mix should be agreed between public- and private-sector airlines. The state corporations (BOAC and BEA) were confirmed in their role as flag-carriers but were recommended to merge and to start charter and inclusive tour operations. The idea of a major second-force airline in the private sector, to complement and compete with the new public airline, was proposed, as was the suggestion that a more liberal policy be adopted towards the licensing of other private airlines. Finally, the report proposed that the economic, safety and regulatory functions carried out by the previous Air Transport Licensing Board, the Board of Trade and the Air Registration Board should thereafter come under the control of a single Civil Aviation Authority.

The Civil Aviation Act, which followed publication of this report in 1971, accepted most of these proposals. BOAC and BEA were merged into a single corporation, British Airways, while British Caledonian was confirmed as the new second-force airline, following the merger of Caldonian Airways and British United Airways; and the new Civil Aviation Authority (CAA) was formed.

The CAA is financed by the users of its services, which are mainly the airlines themselves. Any excess profits are expected to be returned to the users through lower charges for its services. A subsidiary of the CAA is the Air Transport Users' Council (ATUC), which acts as a watchdog for air transport customers. There is also an international body serving this purpose, known as the International Foundation of Airline Passenger Associations (IFAPA), which has its headquarters in Geneva.

UK GOVERNMENT POLICY AFTER 1971

In its proposal to introduce a second-force airline in Britain, the Edwards Report clearly saw this as a mechanism to compete with the publicly owned flag-carrier across the North Atlantic. After the formation of British Caledonian, the government granted the carrier North Atlantic routes in 1973. Within two years, however, government policy had changed to 'spheres of influence', with the second-force airline licensed for complementary rather than directly competitive routes. Ignoring British Caledonian's claim that two British carriers on the North Atlantic routes would increase the British share of the total market by taking away business from American carriers, the CAA redistributed routes, giving British Caledonian South American routes and restricting the North Atlantic largely to British Airways. A White Paper in 1976, *Future Civil Aviation Policy*, indicated the prevailing policy to end dual designation – a policy later overturned by the Conservative government during the 1980s as support for a totally deregulated air transport system gathered momentum. An 'open skies' policy, favoured by both the US and British governments in the 1980s, led to effective deregulation on fares and capacity across the Atlantic, as well as on domestic routes in both countries. British Airways was privatised in 1987, and the subsequent redistribution and licensing of routes for smaller British carriers set the scene for liberalisation throughout Europe.

Deregulation of air transport

Deregulation, or 'liberalisation' as it has come to be known in Europe, is the deliberate policy of reducing state control over airline operations and allowing market forces to shape the airline industry. The US led the way with the Airline Deregulation Act of 1978, which abolished collusion in air pricing. The US regulatory body, the Civil Aeronautics Board (CAB), progressively relinquished control over route allocation and fares, and was itself disbanded at the end of 1984. Market forces were then to take over, the government expecting that inefficient large carriers would be undercut by smaller airlines with lower overheads and higher productivity.

In fact, the actual outcome was very different, and has caused advocates of deregulation in Europe to reconsider the case for total freedom of the air. The opening years of deregulation saw a rapid expansion of airline operations, with a threefold increase in new airlines. Among the established airlines, those that expanded prudently, such as Delta, prospered, while others, such as Braniff, became overambitious and committed themselves to a programme of expansion which, as fares became more competitive, they could not support financially. While a few routes saw substantial early rises in fares, especially on long-haul domestic flights, on the whole fares fell sharply, attracting a big increase in passengers. This growth was achieved at the expense of profitability, forcing airlines to cut costs in order to survive. New conditions of work and lower wage agreements were negotiated, some airlines abandoning union recognition altogether. Some airlines reverted to propeller aircraft on short-haul routes to cut costs, and worries began to emerge about safety and airlines cutting corners to save on maintenance. Indeed, air safety violations doubled between 1984 and 1987.

Within a decade of deregulation, more than a hundred airlines (including two out of three of the newly launched airlines) had been forced out of business or absorbed, as profits changed to losses. Poor morale among airline crew, due to uncertainty about their future job security, led to indifferent service.

Supplementals, as the charter operators are known in the USA, were particularly badly hit, as scheduled services dropped their fares. They had neither the public recognition nor the marketing skills to embark on an expansion in their operations, and many simply ceased to operate. In the longer term, what has occurred has been the growth of a handful of huge 'mega-carriers'. By the end of 1991, a total of some 200 carriers had disappeared, leaving the field to fewer than ten major airlines, of which the 'big three' – Delta, American and United – had the lion's share of the air travel market. Far from expanding opportunity, deregulation had led to small airlines being squeezed out, or restricted to less important routes, by the marketing power of the big carriers.

The second major characteristic of deregulation has been the development of a 'hub and spoke' system of operation, in which feeder air services from smaller 'spoke' airports provide links to connect with long-haul flights of the 'mega-carriers' out of the hubs. This pattern has enabled the airlines to keep prices down. Airports such as New York, Chicago, Atlanta, Fort Worth/Dallas and St Louis became major hubs for domestic and international flights, some dominated by a single carrier.

DEVELOPMENTS IN THE 1990S

In the early 1990s, the struggle to survive became more acute. Famous names such as Pan American disappeared, and one in four of the US domestic carriers were operating under America's Chapter 11 bankruptcy regulations, which permit an airline to continue to operate although officially bankrupt, while restructuring its finances. The huge losses sustained by even the biggest airlines led to cancellations of new aircraft orders, the sale of assets, and the formation of alliances with major international carriers, such as that between US Air and British Airways (see the section on the economics of airline operation later in this chapter for a fuller examination of this phenomenon). Airline retrenchment led to great difficulties for manufacturers of aircraft, who experienced widespread cancellation of orders in favour of leasing, and to the purchase of second-hand equipment, while the traditional leasing market dried up.

In the early 1990s, after fifteen years of deregulation in North America, US airlines had suffered greater losses (over $4 billion in the period 1990–92 alone) than the entire profits made by all carriers since the inception of passenger travel by air. Price-cutting had reduced profitability to a point where break-even was pushed from around the 50 per cent mark common in 1960, to around 65 per cent.

Evidence is also emerging that the expected hub and spoke development will be increasingly challenged by new, low-cost regional carriers operating city-to-city on less significant routes. One of the most successful of these carriers has been South West Airlines, which had grown to become the seventh-largest US carrier by 1995. South West is a low-cost airline offering 'no frills' flying at budget fares, operating medium-size aircraft spoke to spoke, and on the routes on which it operates it has cut into the market share of the dominant carriers operating hub and spoke connections.

By the mid-1990s, stability was returning to the US airline industry; TWA, once a leading US carrier, but one which had difficulty in surviving the deregulation period, was able to emerge from Chapter 11 restrictions in 1993. The pattern that has since emerged is still very much one of dominance of the US industry by a very small number of carriers, notably United Airlines, Delta Airlines, American Airlines and North West Airlines, on key domestic and international routes. These carriers are now becoming more profitable, but will need to keep fares up in order to expand and invest in new equipment needed for the beginning of the new millennium.

EUROPEAN LIBERALISATION

Elsewhere in the developed countries, governments have also supported the steady erosion of state regulatory powers. In Australia, liberalised air policy has led to the establishment of new airlines, and for the first time a competitively priced domestic air service. Europe's airlines have also moved slowly towards a 'market forces' policy, although those countries with the strongest involvement of the state in national flag-carriers, such as Italy, Spain and, to a lesser extent, Germany, were slower to accept the liberalisation policy of the European Commission; Iberia received significant public subsidies in 1992, as did Air France in 1993, in spite of this being technically contrary to EU regulations. Air fare collusion is also technically forbidden under the free trade clause of the Treaty of Rome, but forcing the airlines of these countries to adopt more liberal policies proved difficult, even after the introduction of the 'harmonisation' regulations imposed on EU members in three stages, over the ten-year period from 1987 to 1997. The third stage, introduced in 1997, allows EU carriers to fly anywhere within the EU, including cabotage routes, at any fare.

However, the UK government had long supported the cause of airline deregulation, and from 1984 onwards adopted a number of individual agreements with member states, starting with the Netherlands. Domestically, the CAA freed most routes from regulation in 1985, exempting only certain trunk routes out of London due to airport congestion. This policy led to a substantial growth in the number of domestic carriers (some fifty now operate), as well as the numbers of passengers travelling.

Britain enjoyed its share of new low-fare airlines created in the more liberal climate of the 1990s, but the significant new carriers such as Debonair and easyJet were based in less popular airports, like Luton, due to shortages of slots at the major airports. From the beginning of airline liberalisation in 1987, eighty new airlines appeared within the EU, but of these, only twenty were still operating by 1997, suggesting competition at a level of intensity similar to that in the USA after deregulation. Most survivors are airlines that chose not to compete directly with established carriers.

Reasons for the slow take-up by new challengers are not hard to find. Apart from the difficulty of gaining slots at main airports, there are high start-up costs for operators joining dense routes, high marketing costs to establish a new name in the public eye; the success of 'frequent flyer' programmes among the large carriers is a further constraint on support for small carriers. The latter also find it difficult to get travel agency support, particularly against overriding commissions paid to the leading agencies by larger carriers. New airlines were therefore forced to concentrate on niche marketing or less competitive routes.

One side effect of liberalisation was the virtual demise of the 'bucket shops' – non-appointed travel agents who sold off illegally discounted airline tickets dumped on the market at short notice by airlines with spare capacity. Their place has been taken by brokers (see page 103) who may legally contract with the airlines for spare capacity and sell this cheaply through travel agents (who were formerly forbidden to deal with the bucket shop operators).

The growth of passenger traffic resulting from liberalisation poses problems, however, by increasing congestion. Europe is rapidly approaching saturation, in terms of the number of aircraft movements that can be handled within a given time: runways and terminals are stretched to the maximum at peak times. One report produced early in 1991 suggested that by the middle of the decade, twenty-two out of forty-six major international airports in Europe would have reached saturation of runway capacity, hindering the exploitation of civil aviation by new carriers. Air corridors are also overcrowded in Europe, and the 'stacking' of aircraft above airports prior to landing is costing airlines huge sums of money in wasted fuel. Air traffic control systems in Europe are becoming coordinated and improved to handle greater numbers of flights. As we have seen, progress has been made in increasing the efficiency of air corridors by reducing height intervals between aircraft on some routes, and it may be possible to reduce nose-to-tail intervals as technology improves. The easing of restrictions on night flights would be a further aid to growth (as would approval for a fifth terminal at London's Heathrow Airport) but local resistance, organised into powerful lobbies, has to be overcome first.

Building larger aircraft is another short-term solution to the problem. Both Boeing and Airbus are working on a new generation of super-jumbo aircraft; the planned Airbus A3XX, with 550 seats, should be flying by 2003, and there are also plans to stretch this to 800 seats. Such aircraft are ideal for use on key long-haul routes such as Los Angeles–Tokyo and London–Sydney (there are also tentative steps to introduce an up-graded Concorde II by 2006, capable of carrying 300 people 6,500 miles, bringing both Tokyo and Los Angeles in reach of London non-stop). However, the problems of having to emplane and deplane up to 800 passengers, as well as cleaning and refuelling, in a short space of time will have to be overcome. The opening of the Channel Tunnel, coupled with new, fast rail services between the European capitals, may help by reducing short-haul air congestion on routes of up to about 500 miles. However, the worldwide growth of air transport – 1.4 billion passengers travelled by air in 1996 – is outstripping the airports' capacity to cope in many regions.

One further worry about the results of liberalisation should receive a mention; that of air safety. Cost competition is driving some airlines to use older aircraft, or aircraft registered outside the UK. While the CAA has imposed restrictions on

British scheduled airlines using foreign aircraft, there are no restrictions on UK tour operators chartering such aircraft to operate into and out of the UK, nor is any firm control exercised over the use of foreign aircraft registered in other EU countries. In the mid-1990s there were worrying trends among some UK operators to contract for old, even obsolete, aircraft from Third World, and especially former Communist bloc countries.

The economics of airline operation

The development of an airline route is something of a 'catch-22' situation. Airlines require some reassurance about traffic demand before they are willing to commit their aircraft to a new route, while air travellers in turn look for regular and frequent flights to a destination in order to patronise a route. There is usually an element of risk involved in initiating a new route, especially since seat prices are likely to be high to compensate for low load factors (the number of seats sold as a percentage of total seats available) and high overheads (for both operating and marketing costs) before traffic builds up. When a route has proved its popularity, however, the pioneer airline is faced with increasing competition, as other airlines are attracted to the build-up of traffic – unless governments decide to control the market entry. In an open market economy, the original airline faces lower load factors, as the market is split between a number of carriers, requiring it either to increase fares, or reduce profit margins; yet it may well have kept prices artificially low initially, in order to build the market before recouping launch costs. Key routes such as those across the North Atlantic attract levels of competition which can make it difficult to operate any services profitably, and the airlines have suffered massive losses and low load factors on these routes for many years.

THE DEVELOPMENT OF 'HUB AND SPOKE' SYSTEMS

Major airlines in the United States recognised that attempting to serve all airports with maximum frequency city-to-city flights was uneconomic, and developed the concept of the *hub and spoke* system. The hub airports provide transcontinental and intercontinental services, while the spokes are designed to offer connections from regional airports to meet these long-haul services. The latter services can be provided in smaller, cheaper-to-operate aircraft (often turboprops) by low-cost carriers, often working in strategic alliances with the major carriers. Flights are then banked into complexes, and in theory greater efficiency is achieved; a hub with fifty-five spokes can create 1,500 'city pairs' in this way; larger aircraft can be used between hubs themselves and higher load factors and better utilisation of aircraft are achieved. Some forty hubs have since been established in the US alone, serving twenty-five of America's largest cities. The popularity of this new development is revealed in the fact that by 1995, three-quarters of all passengers at Atlanta airport were transferring to other flights, while half those at Chicago, Denver and Dallas/Fort Worth were on hub and spoke flights.

These systems are clearly better suited to long-haul flights, as the additional stopover time called for by joining via a spoke is only a small proportion of the total journey. However, it became apparent that there are also diseconomies in operating these systems. The organisation of hub and spoke flights requires the establishment of frequent waves of closely spaced banks of arrivals and departures, resulting in peaks and troughs at the hub airports. This puts further pressure on congested air and terminal space, and leads to delays. It also requires larger numbers of ground handling staff during peaks, and involves further peaking expenses. Obviously, on-time performance becomes even more significant under these circumstances, and if airlines are forced to delay departures while waiting for delayed inbound flights, costs also rise. Some airports are clearly better suited than others to this problem; for example, Schiphol Airport in Amsterdam has benefited by hub and spoke flights being based in the same terminal, so that delays in connection are less catastrophic than at Brussels airport, where connections have to be made between terminals by airport bus.

There is now growing evidence that in some circumstances, airlines remaining outside the hub and spoke system can be more profitable, by charging a higher fare for non-stop services, so that smaller demand may still be equally profitable. This particularly applies to business flights, where non-stop services are seen as critical. We have noted elsewhere the success of South West Airlines, particularly, in gaining market share by flying city-to-city within the USA. However, there are clear limits to the extent to which city-to-city services can be viable, based on the distances to be travelled.

THE GROWTH OF STRATEGIC ALLIANCES

As the problems arising from open competition are obviously going to be long-term, a huge global restructuring exercise is now taking place, as airlines jockey to be among the survivors in a war of attrition. As we have seen, observers expect perhaps as few as a dozen mega-carriers, of which only three or four will be European, to survive beyond the year 2000.

European airlines had seen, and taken account of, developments in the North American market; they recognised that size, providing economies of scale and economies of scope, would be crucial to survival in the future. They also noted that US domestic carriers were expanding into transatlantic routes, some benefiting from fifth freedom rights in Europe, and posing further threats to market share. The way forward for the European carriers was seen as either mergers and takeovers, or the development of strategic alliances with US carriers.

Alliances were easier to establish, but experience showed that they could prove less durable. Political differences and differences of management style frequently hindered effectiveness. The short-lived relationships between British Airways and United Airlines, and between Lufthansa and Air France were cases in point, while the much-vaunted attempt in 1993 to form an alliance between Swissair, Austrian Airlines, SAS and KLM, known as Alcazar, also foundered before being implemented, due to failure to agree on a US partner.

Evidence now points to the success of strategic alliances as being dependent upon expansion in three stages. First, there is a need to secure a dominant share in the home market. British Airways undertook expansion especially through franchising, absorbing 100 per cent of Brymon Airways and soon holding six franchises in the UK, as well as a further four overseas. Air France absorbed Air Inter, TAT and UTA (although it was forced to unload TAT to secure UTA, France's second-largest carrier). KLM absorbed Netherlines, and a share in Transavia. The second step is to gain a strong foothold in the main European countries, especially the UK, France and Germany; this was achieved, for example, by SAS, which controlled 40 per cent of British Midland by 1993, while KLM Royal Dutch Airlines has purchased Air UK. BA meanwhile established a German carrier, Deutsche BA, with a 49 per cent interest by 1992, bought almost 50 per cent of French carrier TAT in 1992; acquired a 49 per cent interest in GB Airways and, most recently, took a controlling interest in French carrier Air Liberté in 1996/7. The final stage is the globalisation of the carrier, especially by investments in North America and the Asia/Pacific region. Again, BA has been a leader in this strategy, taking a minority investment in Australian carrier Qantas in 1992, and a 24.6 per cent share of US Air in 1993. The shaky position of the latter carrier, however, soon caused BA to switch to a merger with American Airlines, planned in 1996 but still held up at the time of writing by resistance from both US and EU authorities. BA also announced an agreement with US carrier Air West, the ninth-largest American carrier, in 1996. Meanwhile, Virgin Atlantic has formed a link with Delta, while Iberia has chosen to form links with South American airlines. The so-called 'Star Alliance' recently formed between Lufthansa, United Airlines, Air Canada, SAS, Thai Airways and Varig of Bazil is a clear indication of the way in which global airlines are cooperating to provide a global operation.

A strategic alliance offers opportunities for growth and for marketing benefits that cannot be achieved as an individual airline. For example, it allows domestic 'spokes' to be tacked onto international routes, as the alliance between the US carrier North West and Dutch carrier KLM has demonstrated; it increases the viability of marginal routes, and it allows carriers to compete on routes where separately they do not hold rights. An example of the latter is the Air Canada/Cathay Pacific alliance permitting AC to carry passengers from Toronto to Vancouver, with onward connections via CP to Hong Kong, thus competing with the Toronto–Hong Kong route held uniquely by Canadian Airlines International. Alliances enable companies to reduce costs by using larger aircraft to meet overall demand, and by sharing operational costs such as counter space at airports and baggage handling. Marketing costs such as advertising may also be shared.

Such alliances may range from the marginal, such as having an interline agreement to accept one another's documentation and transfer of passengers, to marketing agreements such as joint 'frequent flyer' programmes and operational agreements such as blocking space on one another's aircraft to sell their seats. However, the most common advantage to be gained is that of code-sharing.

CODE-SHARING

Domestic code-sharing was in practice within the United States as long ago as 1967, but was first introduced internationally in 1985, when American Airlines and Qantas agreed to share codes on routes across the Pacific. Under a code-sharing agreement, two airlines agree to share codes on through routes, for example between New York and San Francisco and from San Francisco to Sydney. This has the marketing advantage of appearing to be a single through flight, but there are also very concrete advantages for passengers, in that flight timings are coordinated; transfer times between stopovers may be reduced (and carriers will often hold connecting flights for up to 20 minutes for passengers connecting from flights which are code-shared); and baggage can be checked through to the final destination, reducing baggage loss. Carriers can sell each other's flights as if they were their own, and will frequently block off space to do so. A further advantage is that code-shared flights are featured on computer reservations systems before other connections, as these offer the passenger 'best choice'. They may also benefit from multiple listing on the CRS, since they will be listed under both carriers' services. By the mid-1990s, over 400

code-sharing alliances were in operation worldwide, and it is clear that these offer airlines a major marketing and operating advantage.

The establishment of code-sharing across the Atlantic has been crucial to the successful marketing of long-haul travel, and has been extensively used by European carriers to gain access to US domestic destinations. European airlines recognise that US airlines will continue to dominate the global marketplace, partly due, of course, to the huge demand for both domestic and international travel by American travellers. Success for the European carriers will depend upon establishing closer links with at least one of the major US carriers.

AIRLINE COSTS

The selection of suitable aircraft for a route is the outcome of the assessment of the relative costs involved (of which there are two kinds), and the characteristics of the aircraft themselves.

Capital costs

When supply outstrips demand, as is the case where there are many second-hand aircraft on the market, and intense competition for sales between the remaining aircraft manufacturers, airlines can drive very hard bargains in purchasing new equipment. It must be remembered that costs for new aircraft are usually a package embracing not only the sale of the aircraft itself, but also the subsequent provision of spares.

According to the ICAO, the global growth in demand for passenger services between 1997 and 2016 will exceed 5 per cent annually, while in the Asia/Pacific region this will reach 7 per cent. As we have also seen, the expected investment in aircraft over the next two decades is in excess of $1,000 billion. Attractive loan terms are likely to be a key factor in closing sales, and some manufacturers are willing to offer very favourable trade-ins on old aircraft in order to sell their new models. Nevertheless, airlines are increasingly cutting back on orders for new aircraft, and leasing instead of purchasing their aircraft (or even selling their existing aircraft and leasing them back, in order to release capital).

Operating costs

Mile for mile, short-haul routes (up to 1,500 miles) are more expensive to operate than are long-haul, due to two factors. First, short-haul travel requires a greater frequency of take-offs and landings, and in taking off, an aircraft consumes substantially more fuel than it does once it attains its operational ceiling during the flight. Aircraft are charged by airports for landing and parking, so naturally they will have to absorb more landing charges, also. Second, short-haul aircraft spend a proportionately greater time on the ground. Aircraft are only earning money while they are in the air, and depreciation of their capital cost can only be written off against their actual flying time. For this reason it is important that they are scheduled for the maximum number of flying hours each day. According to the efficiency of the airline, and of the airports into which the airline operates, productivity can be increased without impairing the (legally determined) minimum service and maintenance time required (Boeing 747 servicing entails 35–60 man-hours, with a complete overhaul involving 10,000 man-hours, after 6,000 hours of flying). Here, the American carriers appear to be more successful than the European, with the Big Three US carriers flying at least 10 hours per day on short- and medium-haul flights, against a European average of only 7 hours (although there are marked differences between the productivity of the various airlines within Europe). In the USA, aircraft turnarounds (time spent on the ground between landing and take-off) can be as low as 30 minutes, while in Europe a minimum of 45 minutes is the norm.

Long-haul aircraft normally operate at a ceiling of 30,000–40,000 feet (supersonics at 50,000–60,000 feet), while short- and medium-haul aircraft will operate at lower ceilings. While the cost of getting the long-haul aircraft to its ceiling will be higher, once it is at these heights there is little wind resistance and the rate of fuel burn falls considerably.

Costs can be subdivided betwen the direct costs of operating and indirect costs. The former will include flight expenses (salaries of flight crew, fuel, in-flight catering), plus maintenance, depreciation, aircraft insurance, and airport and navigation charges. Airport charges will include landing fees, parking charges, navigation charges (where these are passed on to the airline by the airport) and a per capita cost according to the number of passengers carried. Navigation charges vary according to the weight of the aircraft and the distance flown over a particular territory.

From 1998, the notional weight of passengers is to be increased, adding to costs. The current 75 kg for males and 65 kg for females will be replaced by a notional weight of 84 kgs per capita (already adopted by US and some other carriers), in recognition of the trend to increased body weight internationally. Japanese airlines operate on a notional body weight of 73 kgs (regardless of the nationality of those carried) – which will enable Japanese carriers to gain advantage over others by providing more seats.

Depreciation is the cost of writing off the original purchase price of the aircraft against the number of hours it flies each year (which may be as high as 4,000 hours per year). Total depreciation periods vary; in the case of smaller, relatively inexpensive aircraft it may be as short as eight to ten years, while wide-bodied jets may be depreciated over periods as long as fourteen to sixteen years. A residual value of typically 10 per cent of the original purchase price is normally allowed for. In some cases, it might be considered prudent to write off aircraft more quickly, because obsolescence can overtake the operating life, and airlines must keep up with their competitors by re-equipping at regular intervals. However, with falling profits, few airlines find it easy to re-equip, and the tendency is to extend depreciation time. On top of this, insurance costs will range around 3 per cent per annum of the aircraft's purchase price.

Indirect costs include all non-flight expenses, such as marketing, reservations, ground handling, administration and other insurances such as passenger liability. These costs will vary very little however many flights are flown, and large airlines will clearly benefit from economies of scale here.

Fuel costs globally are quoted in US dollars, and will therefore vary not only according to changing oil prices but also according to changing currency exchange rates. Airlines can contract to buy fuel in advance if they fear rising costs; again, larger airlines with bigger financial reserves are better placed to do so.

All airlines are seeking new means of trimming their costs to stay competitive. Typical techniques noted in the 1990s include reducing the labour force, while renegotiating wage levels and conditions of service (BA has been notably successful in achieving this, but met particularly strong union opposition in 1997, leading to air crew strikes). International carriers have moved some activities to low-wage countries – for example, Swissair, based in a high-wage economy, moved its accounts to India and some of its maintenance to Ireland, while contracting out its cleaning services. KLM contracted out its catering services, while American Airlines has moved its accounts department to Barbados. Smaller airlines are contracting out their maintenance to foreign countries. Savings can also be achieved by forming low-cost subsidiaries, a move which BA has successfully exploited, alongside other high-cost European carriers.

AIRCRAFT CHARACTERISTICS

These will include the aircraft's cruising speed and 'block speed' (its average overall speed on a trip), its range and field length requirements, its carrying capacity and its customer appeal. In terms of passenger capacities, airline development tends to occur in leaps; thus, with the introduction of jumbo jets, the number of seats on an aircraft tripled, and the proposed super-jumbos will see a further doubling of capacity. While average seat costs fall sharply as seat numbers are increased, this can only be reflected in lower prices to passengers if sufficient seats are filled.

Carrying capacity is also influenced by the *payload* which the aircraft is to carry, i.e. the balance between fuel, passengers and freight. An aircraft is authorised to 'take off at MTOW (maximum take-off weight)', which is its empty operating weight plus fuel and payload. At maximum payload, the aircraft will be limited to a certain range, but can increase this range by sacrificing part of the payload – i.e. by carrying fewer passengers. Sacrificing both fuel and some passenger capacity may allow some aircraft to operate from smaller regional airports with short runways.

Cost savings can be made in a number of ways when using larger aircraft. It is a curious fact that the relative cost of pushing a large aircraft through the air is less, per unit of weight, than a small one (incidentally, this principle also holds true in shipping operations, in that large ships are relatively cheaper per unit of weight to push through the water). Larger aircraft experience proportionately lower drag per unit of weight: they are more aerodynamic. They can also use larger, more powerful engines. Equally, maintenance and cleaning costs per seat are lower.

The marketing of air services

Aside from economic considerations, the customer appeal of an aircraft depends upon such factors as seat comfort and pitch, engine quietness and the interior design of cabins. In a product where, generally speaking, there is a great deal of homogeneity, minor differences such as these can greatly affect the marketing of the aircraft to the airlines, and in turn the appeal the airline can make to its prospective passengers.

It is for the marketing division of an airline to determine the destinations to be served, although these decisions are often influenced by government policy and regulation. Marketing personnel must also determine levels of demand for a particular service, the markets to be served and the nature of the competition the airline will face. Routes are, of course, dependent upon freight, as well as customer considerations, and a decision will have to be reached on the appropriate mix between freight and passengers, as well as the mix of passengers to be served – business, holiday, VFR, etc.

Flight frequencies and timings will be subject to government controls. For example, it is common to find that governments will limit the number of flights they will allow to operate at night. Where long-haul flights, and hence changing time zones, are involved, this can seriously curtail the number of flights an airline can operate. Traffic congestion will have an additional 'rationing' effect.

It is particularly important for business travellers to be able to make satisfactory connections

Figure 7.5 Small planes, such as this Islander, are used for short flights from the British mainland to surrounding islands. (Courtesy Adrian Meredith Aviation Library)

with other flights. To gain a strategic marketing advantage over competitors, an airline will want to coordinate its flights with complementary carriers, with which it must have interline agreements (allowing the free interchange of documents and reservations). In planning long-haul flights, the airline must also weigh up whether to operate non-stop flights, or to provide stopovers to cater for passengers wanting to travel between different legs of the journey (known as 'stage' traffic). Stopovers will permit the airline to cater for, or organise, stopover holiday traffic – which might be particularly attractive for passengers across the Pacific, for instance, allowing additional duty-free shopping. However, it may dissuade business passengers from booking, if their prime interest is to reach their destination as quickly as possible, and an alternative non-stop flight exists. Tahiti experienced a sharp drop in visitors when the stretched 747-400 was introduced on the transpacific route, and it first became possible to fly non-stop between Australia and North America.

YIELD MANAGEMENT

Following the planning stage, the airline must determine its pricing policy. Fixing the price of a seat is a complex process, involving consideration of:

(a) the size and type of aircraft operating
(b) the route traffic density and level of competition
(c) the regularity of demand flow, and the extent to which this demand is balanced in both directions on the route
(d) the type of demand for air service on the route, taking into account demand for first or business class, economy class, inclusive tour basing fares and other discounted ticket sales
(e) the estimated break-even load factor (the number of seats which must be sold to recover all costs). Typically, this will fall at between 50 and 60 per cent of the aircraft's capacity on scheduled routes. The airline must aim to achieve this level of seat occupancy on average throughout the year.

The last two points are critical to the success of the airline's marketing. The marketing department is above all concerned with *yield management*, the overall revenue which is to be attained on each route. Yield can be defined as the *air transport revenue achieved per unit of traffic carried*, or the total passenger revenue per revenue-passenger mile. It is measured by comparing both the cost and revenue achieved per available seat mile (ASM). Balancing the proportion of discounted seats and those where full fares can be charged, whether in economy or business class, is a highly skilled undertaking, since there is a need to ensure that any reduction in full fare will lead to an overall increase in revenue. This is achieved through a combination of pricing and the imposition of conditions governing the fares.

Business class, for example, will achieve much higher levels of profit than economy or discounted tickets; an airline with 10 per cent of its seats given over to business class may achieve 40 per cent of its income from the sale of these seats. However, expected demand for seats on a particular route will call for fine judgement. Discounted tickets must attract a new market, not draw higher-paying passengers to save money, so they must be hedged with conditions making them unattractive to prospective business class passengers.

BOOSTING YIELD THROUGH 'FREQUENT FLYER' PROGRAMMES

In order to boost overall yield, many airlines introduced the concept of 'frequent flyer' programmes, by which passengers purchasing airline tickets were entitled to extra free travel, according to the mileage covered. The success of this marketing campaign has been tremendous; it was estimated that by the mid-1990s, there were over eighty 'frequent flyer' programmes in operation around the world, with some 120 million members benefiting – American Airlines' AAdvantage scheme alone boasted 28 million members). British Airways' Air Miles programme allows miles to be accumulated on the value of products purchased at other outlets, including shops, hotels and petrol stations. This, coupled with the high number of points served by the airline and links with 'frequent flyer' programmes of other allied carriers, has given rise to concern among EU authorities, as the economies of scope achieved can provide an unfair advantage over smaller carriers. However, the popularity of these schemes has led to so many free seats being offered that airlines are now imposing limitations on their use, and some believe the schemes will shortly be phased out in favour of other, less expensive forms of promotion.

DEEP DISCOUNTING

All scheduled services operate on the basis of an advance reservations system, with lowest (APEX) fares being available on routes where the booking can be confirmed some time in advance of departure. This allows the airline to judge its expected load factors with greater accuracy. To fill up the odd seats that are not pre-booked, the airline offers stand-by fares, available to those passengers without reservations who are prepared to take their chance and turn up in the expectation of a seat being free. On many routes, particularly business routes, the chances of seats being available are good, because business passengers frequently book more than one flight, to ensure they can get back as quickly as possible after the completion of their meeting. Airlines will overbook to allow for the high number of no-shows (up to 30 per cent on some routes), but must exercise caution in case they end up with more passengers than they can accommodate. If this occurs, they can upgrade to a better class, or compensate the overbooked passengers financially, while providing seats on

another flight, but this may not be sufficient to satisfy the irate business passenger.

An alternative system, employed on high-density routes, is the 'shuttle', for which no advance reservations are needed, and on which all passengers are guaranteed a seat. If need be, an extra flight is added to cope with surplus demand. Such a service can only be commercially viable on those routes experiencing a high level of regular (typically business) demand in both directions, such as between Los Angeles and San Francisco in the USA, or between London and Glasgow in Britain.

THE COMPUTERISED RESERVATIONS SYSTEM

Of crucial importance to the airline's reservations system has been the introduction of the computerised reservations system, or CRS. Agents and clients clearly depend upon the provision of a fast and accurate indication of flight availability and booking service, together with rapid fare quotations so that the best prices for a given route combination can be secured. The new generation of airline CRSs provide exactly this. However, the cost of developing such a system is enormous, and in consequence the stakes are very high for those airlines whose system is adopted by most agents. Just as the airlines themselves are battling for survival in the skies, so their reservations systems are battling for supremacy as the major system of distribution through agents. Currently, the market leaders in the US are Sabre, the system developed by American Airlines, and Apollo, the United Airlines system, which are now rapidly expanding into Europe and developing into global distribution systems (GDS), to include worldwide hotel, car rental and other reservations facilities. In Europe, two leading contenders for a global reservations system are Galileo and Amadeus. The former, established by British Airways in conjunction with Alitalia, Swissair and KLM, is now linked with Apollo to provide a truly global network, while the strength of Amadeus, established by Lufthansa, Air France, Iberia and SAS (which later withdrew), lies largely in the Continent, but is also making strong inroads into the UK market.

The importance of dominance in this field lies in the way in which agents use the information displayed. Access can be made through the system to a large number of major world airlines, and 75–80 per cent of all bookings are made from the first page of information; although bias in the way information is displayed is illegal under US and EU law, it is still technically possible to present some information in a manner that favours particular carriers. Airlines are now seeking to expand the information providers in order to give agents access to tour operators and other travel services' booking systems. Ultimately, it is likely that a single global distribution network will dominate the travel scene, a clear distribution and marketing triumph for the successful airline.

One significant aspect of the new CRSs is their relative user-friendliness. These systems are at the time of writing just beginning to become available direct in consumers' homes, using the Internet and World Wide Web connections, and although only 1 per cent of air travellers from the UK are booking in this manner, there is little doubt that this will increase significantly over the next few years. The introduction of 'smart cards' (credit cards with built-in microchip memories) and debit cards (under test in the UK at the time of writing) will not only allow passengers to book direct, but will also allow the airlines to direct-debit cardholders for the purchase of airline tickets, further threatening the travel agent as the traditional distributor of air tickets. Given that distribution costs average 18 per cent of an airline's total costs, the global distribution system is likely to see rapid development as a means of cutting carriers' costs.

A notable feature of recent years, with the growth in intensity of competition, has been the evidence of 'dirty tricks', or unethical means of competing against rival carriers. British Airways lost an important battle with Virgin Atlantic in 1993, when it was forced to concede responsibility for illegally poaching Virgin's passengers. The negative publicity from this case, with its echoes of the British Airways–Laker Airways battle of an earlier generation, did for a period have a marked effect on British Airways' image in the marketplace.

THE ROLE OF THE AIR BROKER

One comparatively little-known role in the airline business is that of the air brokers. These are the people who act as intermediaries between aircraft owners and their customers. They provide a level of expertise to business clients, travel agents or tour operators who may not have the time or the knowledge to involve themselves in long negotiations for the best deals in chartering aircraft seats. They maintain close contact with both airlines and the charter market, and can frequently offer better prices for charters than tour operators could themselves obtain. They play an important role in securing aircraft seats in times of shortage, and in disposing of spare capacity at times of oversupply. The broker takes charge of the entire operation, booking the aircraft and taking care of any technical requirements, including organising the contract and arranging any special facilities. In their role as *consolidators*, brokers assist in consolidating tour operators' flights to ensure maximum load factors are achieved (see Chapter 12). The body representing their interests in the UK is the Air Brokers' Association.

QUESTIONS AND DISCUSSION POINTS

1 Is the growth of the mega-carrier an inevitable development in global air transport? And how effective are government or other controls over 'dirty tricks' campaigns similar to that which British Airways was accused of running against Virgin Atlantic in 1993? Might we see more of these tactics globally as airlines grow in size and power? What alternative scenarios could you envisage?

2 European countries have looked at the possibility of redistributing 'slots' at airports in order to allow new carriers to gain access. What are the arguments for and against this practice? Would doing so improve airline operations for the passengers?

3 An increase in flight delays at peak times in Europe seems inevitable, given the congestion on key routes. Will this force more people to use land transport, e.g. the Channel Tunnel?

1 As a member of staff with responsibility for route planning at Gemini Airways, a new scheduled airline planning to start up in Britain shortly, you have been asked to assess the impact of deregulation in the United States, and to consider how far patterns established there are being repeated following liberalisation in Europe. Produce a report for your Director, Route Planning and Development, which:

(a) examines the short- and long-term effects of deregulation in North America
(b) analyses the airline business environment in Europe, and the policies of the EU and Britain in particular.

Your Director is particularly keen to know whether you believe that the hub and spoke development is the way forward in Europe as it was in North America.

2 As a member of Gemini's team, you have been asked by the Director of Operations to stand in for him at a visiting lecture to be given to a mixed group of students of tourism and transport studying at a nearby educational institution. The theme of the talk is 'Problems of managing yield in scheduled airline operations'. Prepare a set of notes for your talk, which is intended to last about 20 minutes.

8

Waterborne Passenger Transport

OBJECTIVES

After studying this chapter, you should be able to:

- identify the categories of waterborne transport and the role they play in the tourism industry;
- understand the economics of cruise and ferry operations;
- be aware of principal world cruise routes;
- be familiar with other forms of leisure transport by boat, and their appeal to tourists.

Introduction

Although air services today play the leading role in providing transport for tourism, transport by waterborne vessels of all kinds continues to play an important role in the industry. While air transport offers the advantage of speed, which is often a critical factor in the choice of long-haul travel, travel by water still offers many unique advantages. Cruising, in particular, is enjoying a popularity boom that has not been seen since the heyday of the inter-war period – it offers the advantage of total relaxation and an all-inclusive price which allows the passenger to be carried from one destination to another in comfort and safety, without the need constantly to pack and unpack. Short-sea (ferry) vessels have achieved new standards of comfort on many routes, to a point where they will now attract tourists not just in order to travel from one point to another, but to enjoy a 'mini-cruise' which provides food and entertainment that a few years ago could only be found on a luxury cruise liner.

Technological developments have helped to reduce high operating costs, while new forms of waterborne transport have been developed, such as the hovercraft, jetfoil and the twin-hulled catamaran ferry. These have provided rapid communication over short sea routes and sometimes, as in the case of the hovercraft, across difficult terrain.

The pleasure that people find in simply being afloat has spawned many recent tourist developments, from yacht marinas and self-drive motor craft to dinghy sailing in the Mediterranean and canal barge holidays in Britain and on the European mainland. The continuing fascination with steam engines has led to the renovation and operation of lake steamers in England and paddle steamers in the USA. Increasingly, we find that the division between transport and entertainment is becoming blurred, as the journey, or even the vessel, becomes an end in itself, rather than merely a means of arriving at one's destination.

In this chapter, we will investigate the appeal and operation of a variety of waterborne forms of transport, ranging from seagoing vessels to river, canal and lake craft. We can divide these into five distinct categories: 'line voyage' liners; cruise liners; short sea, or ferry, vessels; inland waterways and other excursion vessels; and privately chartered or owned pleasure craft. These will be examined in turn.

The ocean liners

Line voyage services are those offering passenger transport on a port-to-port basis. This form of transport has declined to a point where very few such services exist any longer, and those that do tend to be seasonally operated. The reasons for this decline are not hard to identify.

From the 1950s onward, advances in air transport enabled fares to be reduced, especially on popular routes across the Atlantic, to a point where it became cheaper to travel by air than by ship. The shipping lines, which until the advent of aircraft had no competition from alternative forms of transport, could not compete: they faced rapidly rising costs for fuel and labour in a labour-intensive industry. The gradual decline in passengers, as these switched to the airlines, led to losses in revenue for the shipping companies which made it impossible to consider renovating ageing fleets or replacing them with new vessels. By 1957, more passengers were crossing the Atlantic by air than by sea, and the demise of the worldwide passenger shipping industry was imminent. Leading routes, such as Cunard Line's transatlantic services, P&O's services to the Far East and Australia, Union-Castle and British India Lines' services to South and East Africa, were either withdrawn or reduced to a skeleton service. The resulting shake-up in management led to attempts to regenerate traffic, mainly by extending cruising, but vessels built for fast line-voyage services are not ideally suited to alternative uses, and the appeal of cruising was also entering a period of decline. A small but loyal demand for sea transport remained among those, usually older, passengers who suffered from fear of flying, or who enjoyed sea voyages and had time to spend in reaching their destinations, and a few lines were able to continue to operate to serve these markets. The *Queen Elizabeth 2* of Cunard Line (see Figure 8.1) provides a regular summer service between Southampton and New York, cruising for the balance of the year, while the *St Helena* (built with a British government subsidy to provide a connection between the UK and the island dependencies of St Helena and Ascension) operates a regular passenger–cargo service between South Wales and South Africa, via the island colonies. The latter ship is as important for its freight capacity as its passenger. A handful of other passenger-cum-freighter services exist around the world, such as the the Mauritius Shipping Corporation's services

between Mauritius, Réunion Island and South Africa; services from Tahiti carrying up to sixty passengers to the Marquesas Islands and Tuamoto Archipelago in the South Pacific; and vessels, some carrying nearly 1,200 passengers, operated and subsidised by the Indian government, which connect the mainland to the Andaman and Nicobar Islands.

Most of the remaining passenger-carrying vessels operating around the world are built essentially to carry cargo. A maximum of twelve passengers is carried on such vessels (the limitation is due to the requirement of the International Maritime Organisation that the crew include a doctor if more than twelve passengers are carried), while some vessels are fitted only with an owner's suite, carrying two passengers; but they are all clearly designed for the lovers of sea travel for its own sake. Freight demand means that neither departure dates nor ports of call can be guaranteed, nor can it be certain that passengers will be allowed to disembark to visit the destinations en route. Entertainment is limited on board, and passengers dine with the ships' officers. However, these ships do attract an enthusiastic market, and often bookings have to be made a year or more in advance.

With hindsight, it is easy to pinpoint the inevitability of shipping's decline. However, it must be said that shipping management must bear the blame for failing to adapt its product to changing needs. Ships built for operating in the 1950s failed to meet the needs of the postwar market; insufficient cabins with private bathrooms were available to meet the needs of the American market in particular, and the vessels' specifications and size made them inflexible and unsuitable for routes other than those for which they were built. Because shipping companies did not recognise early enough the threat that the airlines posed for the future of their companies, they were slow to move into that sector themselves, and those that eventually attempted to do so found the capital investment required was beyond them. Shipping companies were also hampered by the existence of a number of old-fashioned and bureaucratic 'traffic conferences' which limited competition and restricted any attempt at creative marketing. In the 1970s, these conferences were swept away, and

Figure 8.1a The *Queen Elizabeth 2*, flag ship of the Cunard Line. *(Courtesy Cunard Line Ltd)*

Figure 8.1b The chart room in the *Queen Elizabeth 2*. *(Courtesy Cunard Line Ltd)*

shipping associations became more concerned with promotion than with regulation. In Britain, the Passenger Shipping Association, which represents all shipping interests, concerns itself principally with marketing and training on behalf of its members.

Cruising

After the 1950s, the passenger shipping industry shifted its emphasis from line voyages to cruising. Initially, this transformation proved difficult; vessels in service at the time were for the most part too large, too old and too expensive to operate for cruising purposes. Their size was a limiting factor in the number of ports they could visit, and they were built for speed rather than leisurely cruising. Fuel bills can be cut by operating vessels at slower speeds, but ideally cruise ships should be purpose-built to achieve their maximum operational efficiency. During the 1960s and 1970s, this meant ships of 18,000–22,000 tons, carrying some 650–850 passengers. However, changes in demand and advances in marine technology have enabled recent cruise ships to be purpose-built in a variety of sizes. Providing there is sufficient demand, optimum profits can be achieved by employing larger vessels, and the trend in the 1980s and 1990s has been to build ships of steadily increasing tonnage, first in the range of 50,000–70,000 tons, and later in excess of 100,000 tons, and capable of carrying up to 2,600 passengers.

By the mid-1990s, there were over 260 cruise ships operating worldwide, with a total tonnage of 4,435,000 gross registered tons. Of these, over 150 were based at US ports, Americans representing by far the largest proportion of the 6.5 million world cruise market. The UK held about 5 per cent of the share of world cruise ships – a marked decline over past years. Britain's share of the world cruise market is around 6.5 per cent, closely followed by Germany. All the developed countries are experiencing a noticeable increase in demand for cruising, after a long period of decline, and estimates suggest a world cruise market of about 8.9 million by the year 2000. Growth in this market has averaged around 9 per cent per annum since the early 1990s. Even more encouraging, extrapolations by the Cruise Lines Industry of America (CLIA) forecast a potential long-term market for cruising of around 35 million passengers, stimulating the ship-building boom of the 1990s. At the start of 1997, there were thirty-one new ships in the process of being built, and due for delivery within the next three years. Twenty-three of these were designed to be larger than the *Queen Elizabeth 2*, while the largest on order, two vessels for Royal Caribbean International, will be of 130,000 tons, carrying some 4,000 passengers. Allowing for the anticipated withdrawal of older ships, a net increase of 23,000 berths is expected by the turn of the century, which will further challenge profitability as the supply of berths outstrips demand.

One company, with support from a major hotel chain, has announced plans to build one ship, the *America World City*, with a tonnage of 250,000, carrying 5,600 plus 2,400 crew – a veritable floating city and a very different image of cruising from that of the past. But the whole concept of a cruise holiday is changing; cruise ships are coming to be seen as floating holiday resorts which conveniently move from one destination to another, offering new scenery every day and non-stop entertainment on board.

At the other end of the scale, vessels between 5,000 and 10,000 tons and carrying around 100 passengers have been introduced to offer a 'yacht-like' form of cruising for those who are prepared to pay the higher costs such vessels are obliged to charge. Such ships are able to enter harbours far smaller than would be possible for the traditional cruise ships, opening up new ports of call for cruising, such as Cadiz; the 11,000 ton *Ocean Princess*, for example, can navigate as far as 1,000 miles up the Amazon River. Small ships can also negotiate constricted canals, such as the Corinth Canal in Greece, or even the Panama Canal.

There is an important issue related to size of cruise vessels, and that is the question of *sustainability*. It is debatable whether building ever-larger cruise ships is an appropriate strategy for the tourism business, whether or not these could be profitable. The effect on small island economies of vessels disgorging up to 4,500 passengers simultaneously at a port, and within a strictly limited time period, must be judged against the possible benefits of visitor spend. However, the logistics and viability of putting such large numbers of people ashore and organising shore excursions for them is another factor that will have to be examined carefully.

CRUISE ROUTES

Broadly, the major cruise routes of the world can be located in seven regions of the globe (see Figure 8.3). These are:

- the Caribbean, Bermuda and the Bahamas, including the coast of Central and South America
- the west coast of North America, including Mexico, the USA (including Alaska) and Canada
- the Mediterranean, divided between the western and eastern sectors
- the Pacific islands and Far East
- the Baltic Sea, northern European capitals and the North Cape
- West Africa and the Atlantic islands of the Canaries and Madeira
- round the world.

Most cruising takes place either in the Mediterranean or Caribbean, which are responsible for 40 per cent and 21 per cent respectively of all UK cruising. Scandinavia and the Baltic are visited by 8.5 per cent of cruises, while other destinations (particularly the growing Far East destinations) take the balance of 30 per cent.

Most of these routes are seasonal and this will mean that shipping companies may be obliged to move their vessels from one region of the globe to another to take advantage of peak periods of cruising demand. The Baltic and North Cape cruises, for example, are operated during the northern hemisphere's high summer, with the North Cape cruise in particular operating in July to offer passengers the advantage of seeing the midnight sun. This is also true of Alaskan cruises, which have grown in popularity with passengers from the North American market, partly as a reaction to the perceived danger of terrorist activity against cruises in the Mediterranean. The Caribbean, by contrast, enjoys year-round market demand, although the winter period, when the cli-

Figure 8.2 Royal Viking line cruise liner off Waterford Harbour, Ireland. *(Photographed by the author)*

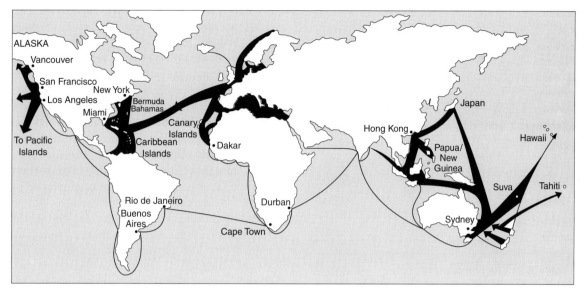

Figure 8.3 Major cruise routes of the world

mate is more temperate than in summer, attracts the most passengers. The fact that the Caribbean islands are situated so close to the principal cruise market of the USA accounts for ports in Florida, such as Fort Lauderdale, Miami/Port Everglades and Port Canaveral, having become by far the most important bases for the world cruise industry.

Competition is encouraging operators to seek new routes. Recent growth is found in Canada and New England; the east coast of Africa, to include Madagascar, the Seychelles and Mauritius; and the Indonesian Spice Islands. New bases where costs are low are also sought; Carnival's Windstar division, for example, switched their *Wind Song* from Tahiti to Costa Rica in 1997.

Another factor contributing to the rapid expansion of cruising was the introduction of fly-cruises, in which passengers are carried by the cruise company on chartered aircraft to a warm-water base port from which they can cruise directly. Fly-cruises were introduced by Cunard Line in the late 1960s, flying passengers into Gibraltar or Naples for a Mediterranean cruise. This overcame the problem of poor weather and rough seas (the Bay of Biscay, off northern Spain, can be a notoriously unpleasant stretch of water

to cross at any time of the year) and ensured that passengers could be enjoying the sunshine and calm seas of the Mediterranean from the first day of their cruise. Although the traditional, often older, cruise passengers at first resisted this move, it soon proved popular among an increasingly younger cruise market.

The search for new destinations led to new routes opening up in the 1980s, including Pacific inter-island cruises and even the Arctic and Antarctic – smaller, purpose-built vessels are often used for the latter destinations, with specially strengthened hulls to overcome ice problems. These long-haul routes were popularised by the fly-cruise concept, and Singapore in particular has sought to expand as a cruise base for the world cruise market which is now turning to the attractions of the Far East; however, these are largely aimed at the top end of the market, with prices starting as high as £500 or more a day. The past decade has seen a rapid increase in the total of British passengers taking a cruise (around 522,000 in 1997), as well as a steady rise in demand among British passengers for traditional ex-UK port sailings. A number of innovative cruises within the British Isles have been introduced, including cruises round Britain and to the Hebrides.

Table 8.1 The largest markets for cruising, 1996

Country	Cruises taken
North America	4 476 926
UK	429 201
Germany	357 004
Italy	157 000
France	153 813
Spain	27 000
Other Europe	112 000

Source: Travel Weekly 16 July 97

Table 8.2 The British cruise market, 1990–2000

Year	Cruises taken
1990	186 490
1991	193 010
1992	228 728
1993	264 940
1994	283 394
1995	352 179
1996	429 201
1997	522 000
2000	700 000+ (e)

Note: the 1997 figure has been boosted by more accurate calculation of river cruises, estimated at some 140 000.
Source: PSA

THE NATURE OF THE CRUISE MARKET

The key factors determining cruise demand are price, length of cruise, and destination; however, a number of other factors are also important. Cruising, although expanding, also continues to attract a significant number of repeat purchasers, who have demonstrated in the past a high degree of brand loyalty towards shipping companies and even towards individual vessels. Cruising appeals on a number of levels. The all-inclusive nature of a cruise, in which unlimited – and often excellent – food is on offer; the general ambience on board; the high levels of security that isolation on a ship can provide; the attraction of travelling with 'like-minded people' with whom it is easy to make friends, being thrown together within a confined space; the absence of constraint on the amount of baggage carried, all offer significant benefits. Indeed, for those with a fear of flying, cruising provides the only means of travelling abroad.

While the concept of a floating hotel has become of importance in selling cruises, passengers still expect ships to look like ships. A great deal of care goes into the design of a modern cruise liner to provide the illusion of greater space as well as maximum revenue-earning opportunities for the shipping company, in the form of shops, hairdressing facilities, casinos and bars. Design also takes account of the nationality of those travelling: cruise ships aimed predominantly at the US market tend to make greater use of plastics, gilt stairways, mirrors, neon lights and bright colours, while the more traditional European, and particularly British, market will expect greater use of wood (although safety standards at sea encourage the use of more fire-retardant materials today) and quieter, more refined decoration.

Cruising is still seen as an older person's holiday, but this image is beginning to fade, as new cruise companies such as Carnival encroach on the traditional cruise market and reach a younger group of holidaymakers. Carnival claims an average age on board in the mid-20s for its 'disco' ships operating short cruises in the Caribbean. Such cruises are sold in the US as package holidays, comparable to the all-inclusive resort on land; the result is that cruising represents about 6 per cent of all US package holiday business, compared to only 2 per cent in the UK.

In Britain, on average 50 per cent of the market for cruising is still between forty-five and sixty-five, while a further 29 per cent are over sixty-five. This pattern can be expected to change as greater numbers of young people are attracted to budget Caribbean cruising, and particularly to the new budget cruises offered by UK mass market tour operators like Airtours and Thomson Holidays.

Shipping companies have recognised the difficulty of appealing to varied markets, and varied nationalities, on the same vessel, however appealing this might be economically. Multinational passenger mixes call for multilingual announcements, as well as entertainment, on board, which will not be an attractive selling point; while passengers from different countries have widely varying habits and preferences in on-board entertainment. Passengers from Latin countries, for instance, prefer to take dinner later than those from the UK or US. One result of these differences is that cruise companies are tending to *niche market,* whether by price, by brand, or by type of cruise offered. Carnival Cruise Lines, for example, the world's largest cruise company, offers four distinct brands, while Britain's P&O Line distinguishes between its Princess cruise liners and other vessels in the fleet. The Disney Corporation provides an excellent example of niche marketing, in introducing two liners in 1998 to serve the family market which Disney caters for so successfully. Cruises on these liners, which are to operate out of Florida, will be sold in conjunction with stays at Disneyworld Florida. At the other end of the scale, Saga Holidays, the UK company catering to the over-50s, purchased a vessel from Cunard in 1997 for cruises marketed exclusively to the older holidaymaker.

Shipping companies are laying emphasis on product differentiation, while continuing to introduce new on-board facilities to meet the expectations of an increasingly sophisticated cruise market. One noted trend is to wider variety in catering on board. P&O's new *Oriana*, to take one example, introduced a pizzeria on board, while Crystal Cruises offered a choice of Italian, Japanese and Chinese restaurants on its vessels.

THE ECONOMICS OF CRUISING

In spite of the rise in popularity of cruising, it remains a highly volatile market, and is quickly affected by adverse events, as was witnessed during the Libyan crisis and the hijacking of the *Achille Lauro* by terrorists in the Mediterranean in 1986, which resulted in the collapse of the Mediterranean cruise market. The area was only just recovering when the 1991 Gulf War, and consequent threat of Iraqi terrorist strikes, again frightened away the Mediterranean cruise bookings, particularly those from the US market. Americans are cautious travellers and seek security abroad; the perception of danger in the Mediterranean caused many to switch bookings to safer waters in the Caribbean and Alaska, both of which experienced something of a boom in those years. Cruise companies were forced to reposition their vessels to the Caribbean, which already suffered from overcapacity, so that in spite of rising demand, the acute competition led to deep discounting in the region, and profits suffered.

Cruising is both capital-intensive and labour-intensive. A modern cruise liner can easily exceed $250 million to build, with some costing as much as $400 million (costs for the projected 250,000-ton vessel are likely to exceed one billion dollars); although the life expectancy of a cruise ship is far greater than an aircraft, and allowing for rebuilding and complete renovation, a fifty-year productive life would not be unusual. Vessels also need a substantial number of crew – a four- or five-star cruise liner would carry as many as one member of crew for every two passengers carried. With such labour costs, it is not difficult to see why luxury cruises are selling at several hundred dollars a day. However, once again economies of scale can pare costs, and companies operating large fleets, such as Carnival Cruise Lines in the USA, can reduce the cost per unit of marketing and administration. It is also more economic to operate large ships than small ones, and the trend, as we have seen, is to build bigger and bigger vessels to take advantage of this. Nevertheless, some in the industry feel that there are diseconomies of scale in operating ships over 110,000 tons, and it is likely that the current spate of new ships in the region of 100,000–110,000 tons will be the largest in general use for cruising.

Large companies also benefit by receiving greater support from travel agents, who prefer to deal with companies having a greater number of ships, and therefore a larger choice of both sailings and destinations.

Large ships are able to pare costs by reducing the ratio of crew to passengers, and by providing smaller cabins, with larger areas given over to public use. This provides space for shopping and other sales opportunities. Diningrooms accommodate large numbers within relatively confined spaces either by having two sittings for meals, or by providing only large tables; tables for two are rare on board ships. However, some companies have capitalised by designing their ships to permit all passengers to be accommodated in the restaurant at a single sitting – an attractive marketing advantage.

A useful rule of thumb in judging the relative luxuriousness and spaciousness on board ship is to ascertain the size to passenger ratio (SPR), based on the vessel's gross registered tonnage. If 20 or less, the ship is likely to appear crowded.

Further economies are obtained by calling at a greater number of ports on any itinerary, and spending more time in port, both of which help to reduce fuel burn while at the same time increasing the passengers' satisfaction. A reduction in speed also saves on fuel, but if vessels are to travel slowly and also call at numerous ports, it is essential that these ports are grouped closely together. For this reason, the Caribbean, with its many islands of differing nationality, makes an ideal cruise destination.

One example of effective cost reduction in the shipping business is demonstrated by Cunard which, in 1996, took the decision to extend the journey time for its *Queen Elizabeth 2* between the UK and New York from five to six days. While this achieved significant savings on fuel burn, reducing average speed from 28.5 knots to 23 knots, it also offered other marketing advantages: higher on-board spend was encouraged, while the passengers themselves saw an additional day's cruising as an added benefit; it also allowed the ship to arrive at a more convenient time of day for those with onward travel arrangements.

Economies can also be achieved by putting passengers ashore by tender (ship's launches), rather than tying up alongside. This may be a practical alternative when islands are forcing up mooring costs, although it does delay disembarkation and will be a less attractive selling point.

Cruising will be severely damaged by any rapid rise in fuel prices, as occurred during the oil crisis of 1973/4. It will also be affected by escalating labour costs, and the decline in the fleets of the established maritime nations such as Britain can be partly accounted for by their uncompetitive operating costs compared with their cheaper competitors. Lower-cost nations such as Greece and Russia have in turn built up their own fleets, while the more expensive nations have been forced to cut costs by registering their fleets in Third World countries such as Panama or Liberia, and by recruiting crews from these countries, often to the chagrin of the trades unions representing maritime crews in the developed nations.

Finally, cruise lines have to ensure that their ships are used for the maximum amount of time during the year (just as airlines do) – although this will not necessarily mean their use for cruising only. Some companies have done well by chartering out their cruise ships to tour operators, while other companies have successfully chartered some of their ships for use as a floating hotel when accommodation pressures force tourist destinations to find alternative accommodation for special events. Cunard was even successful in chartering its largest vessel, the *QE2*, for a period for Japan to use as a hotel; this represented a substantial saving to the company on operating costs, as it required no use of fuel for transport.

THE CRUISING BUSINESS

The level of competition between cruise lines during the 1990s has been such that few companies can claim to be making profits, in spite of the rapid rise in demand they have experienced; even top-brand, high-priced cruises have been heavily discounted in the late 1990s. The result is almost certainly that the future will lie, as with so many other sectors of the tourism industry, in greater market concentration. By the mid-1990s, three companies were coming to dominate the world cruise market, together holding nearly half the market share: Carnival Cruise Line, with a market share estimated at about 21 per cent in 1996; Royal Caribbean International, with around 14 per cent; and P&O Line, with 13 per cent. Trends are for these companies to get still larger: Royal Caribbean announced the forthcoming takeover of Celebrity Cruises in 1997, which will have the effect of increasing its share of the cruise market to around 20 per cent by the year 2000, while Carnival Cruises absorbed Costa Cruises in the same year, giving it forty-two ships with a further seven on order by the end of that year, and ensuring its continuing market leadership.

Carnival Cruise Line deserves special mention

in this text because of the way in which it has changed the face of cruising since the mid-1970s. The company was formed in 1972, and at the time of writing operated twenty-two ships, spread over four distinct brands: Carnival, a budget-priced mass market operation; Holland America Line, a middle-priced company; Seabourn Cruises, the up-market end of the company's cruise business; and Windstar, a specialist company offering luxury sail-assisted ships. The parent company also owns a minority holding in the UK's second-biggest tour operator, Airtours, and is expanding the cruise market with them in Europe.

Carnival has in particular been able to attract a much younger than average market for its major division, which offers relatively cheap cruises of short duration, using large vessels of typically 70,000–100,000 tons or more; its most recent vessels will accommodate around 3,400 passengers. The fanciful names of the ships (*Carnival, Festivale, Mardi Gras, Holiday, Jubilee, Celebration, Fantasy, Ecstasy, Sensation, Fascination, Imagination, Carnival Destiny* and *Carnival Triumph*) are pointers to the expectation of their passengers as to the kind of experiences these cruise ships promise. They are sold as 'fun cruises' offering a wide range of on-board facilities, including shops and casinos (Carnival has claimed that some 14 per cent of its total revenue is on-board spend). It attracts young, relatively high-spend passengers (the company claims that 30 per cent of their cheaper market is under thirty-five). This may be compared with Cunard's market, whose average age is over sixty.

Carnival has also taken care to market to recognised niches. Its Fiesta Marina division of Hispanic-oriented tours was developed to tap into Spanish- and Portuguese-speaking markets in the US and Latin America, based on a home port of San Juan, Puerto Rico, a US dependency. Food, wine and entertainment on board have been designed for Hispanic tastes, and dining hours are later than usual, in accordance with Hispanic preferences.

Over-tonnage in American waters has forced cruise companies to turn increasingly to Europe to fill ships. Widespread 'deep discounting' has been common on cruise ships since the early 1990s, due firstly to the recession and the aftermath of the

Gulf War, and more recently to the imbalance between supply and demand. Many carriers now offer free flights to the Caribbean to join cruise ships based there, as an incentive to attract the European market.

HEALTH AND SAFETY

The dominance of the Americans in the world cruise market, and American concern with both safety and hygiene, has resulted in strict standards being imposed on all foreign flag carriers operating out of, or calling at, US ports. All such ships are subject to unannounced inspections from the US Vessel Sanitation Program; vessels are rated for the quality of their water, food preparation, cleanliness, storage and repairs. An acceptable rating is 86 points out of 100, but it is not uncommon for even leading cruise ships of the world to be given grades considerably lower than this. Owners are then required to raise their standards; adverse publicity in the press is a further incentive not to fail these tests. Owners are also required to be bonded against financial collapse. More recently constructed vessels incorporating higher standards of safety can attract lower insurance premiums. These vessels are also more technically advanced and have lower operating costs, with the result that older ships find it difficult to compete. In this respect, the shipping and airline businesses are experiencing similar problems. As in the airline industry, forecasts in the USA suggest that by the turn of the century there may be no more than three mega-cruise lines. This suggests that those three brand leaders will gradually absorb their smaller competitors or force all those out of business who cannot afford the high cost of re-equipping their fleets, leaving only the niche market cruise operators to survive in the field.

TOUR OPERATOR CRUISING

While cruises are sold as package holidays in the United States, and tour operators there have also played a part as intermediaries in bringing the product to the notice of the travelling public, British tour operators were slower to move into the cruise market. During the 1970s, some operators, including Thomson Holidays, did charter or part-charter cruise ships which they incorporated into their programme of inclusive tours, but these attempts ran into a number of problems. Efforts to bring down the overall prices of cruising led to dissatisfaction with standards of service and operation. More recently, Airtours, Britain's second-largest operator, decided to take advantage of the trend towards cruising in the UK, and in 1995 introduced its own ship, *Carousel*. Selling Mediterranean cruises at lead-in prices of £399, and marketing them as merely alternatives to the traditional package holiday but with all meals and entertainment thrown in, for little more than the price of a package holiday, Airtours brought Carnival-style low-budget cruising holidays to the British holiday public, and proved to be enormously popular, carrying over 100,000 passengers in its first year of operation. This encouraged the company to enlarge its fleet to three ships (with a fourth planned for 1998), while Thomson Holidays soon emulated Airtours' success with its own chartered vessels; three were in operation by 1997, with a fourth to be chartered in 1998. Britain's third-largest operator, First Choice, is also investigating the potential of chartering ships for cruising in 1998, at the time of writing.

The entrance of tour operators into the mass market cruise business has changed the face of British cruising. Airtours claimed an average age for its customers of 45 years, and 80 per cent of these were first-time cruisers.

It is still likely, however, that most cruising will retain an up-market image in the UK. Although Airtours (and its partner Carnival Cruise Lines) can be expected to exploit fully the low-budget cruise holiday market to the Mediterranean, the bulk of sales is likely to remain centred on middle-price cruising, sold direct or through a limited number of specialising travel agents – indeed, it is in the middle-priced accommodation that cruise demand is expanding fastest. The market for this form of cruising is very loyal – both P&O and Cunard, Britain's second-biggest operator, claim 60–70 per cent of their market to be repeat bookings. One difficulty in expanding sales through agents is the specialised knowledge required of the cruise product; less than one in ten of British travel agents is productive in cruise bookings, and counter staff lack the expertise and experience in selling cruises. In recent years, the Passenger Shipping Association, the marketing arm of the passenger shipping business in the UK, has attempted to overcome this problem by mounting a special campaign to train agents, and has successfully trained staff in some 1,000 branches to provide a professional cruise sales service to their clients.

The future of the cruise industry looks healthy, in terms of the growth in numbers booking, if less so in terms of profitability. Greater efforts are now being made to differentiate products, rather than depending upon discounting to sell unsold cabins. Certainly, Carnival, with its niche marketing among the younger holidaymakers in the US, has led the way in this direction, but other companies have focused on theme cruising to survive. (Cruise lines now offer a huge variety of special interest cruises, ranging from botanical cruises to 'classical civilisations' cruising in the Mediterranean accompanied by specialist, often well-known, guest lecturers; and from classical music cruises to jazz cruises, with on-board orchestras). Some cruise companies, including the Disney Corporation with its two 85,000 ton liners *Disney Magic* and *Disney Wonder* are targeting the family market, while other shipping operators have experimented with new types of vessel; Radisson has introduced twin-hull catamaran vessels, and both Windstar Cruises and Club Méditerranée offer a new generation of luxury sail-assisted ships to attract a new market. Companies such as Society Expedition Cruises offer luxury cruising for around a hundred passengers to exotic destinations such as the Amazon and Antarctic, while Cunard's Sea Goddess ships offer a retractable platform at the stern from which passengers may swim, snorkel or sail while the ship lies at anchor.

The longer-term future of the shipping industry may be boosted by new marine technology now under development, such as the SES-200 Surface Effect Ship, which rides above the surface of the sea, or superconducting electromagnetic propulsion vessels under test in Japan in 1992 and potentially capable of speeds above 100 knots. Such developments could eventually lead to the reintroduction of line voyages between major ports in the world, although not in the near future.

While the expansion of the cruise business is to be welcomed for the benefits it can bring to holidaymakers and companies alike, there are down sides which have to be taken into account, too. The emphasis on on-board spend and the creation of ships which are virtually leisure complexes in their own right, with all the amenities provided at an 'all-inclusive resort' means that destination countries suffer from the same drawbacks as those experienced from the growth of such resorts. On-board spend simply means less spend ashore, less money going into local shops, bars, transport companies. Some companies have purchased their own, usually deserted, islands on which they can land their passengers for barbecues and lazy 'beach days', ensuring once again that no expenditure goes into the local economy. At the same time the growth in size, as we have seen, threatens massive congestion at small island ports. Leisure transport generally is also beginning to draw criticism for its pollution effects. Large cruise vessels are fuel-hungry (if not to the same extent as thirty years ago), and one estimate has suggested that marine engines in total account for about 8 per cent of all the world's nitrous oxide emissions. Admittedly, a large proportion of this would be accounted for by the enormous growth in private ownership of luxury motor yachts, but cruise vessels must bear their share of responsibility for increasing atmospheric pollution, as must passenger aircraft.

Ferry services

The term 'ferry' is one which embraces a variety of forms of short-distance waterborne transport. They provide a means of urban transport which may incidentally attract tourists, either as a feature of the urban environment or because they offer an original way of viewing the city. Some, such as the Staten Island Ferry in New York, which links Manhattan with the borough of Staten Island, or Hong Kong's Star Ferry, have become world-famous and a 'must' for tourists visiting these cities. Other notable ferries include the Bosphorus ferries linking Europe and Asia in Istanbul, the Manly ferry between Sydney and Manly in Australia, the Niteroi ferry in Rio de Janeiro, the Mersey ferry in Liverpool (immortalised in pop music), the Bainbridge Island ferry in Seattle, the Oakland ferry in San Francisco, the Devonport and Waiheke Island ferries in Auckland, New Zealand and the Cacilhas ferry in Lisbon. Most of these, of course, are designed to provide an essential service for local commuters, but inevitably they also provide important attractions for tourists either wishing to get a different view of the city or planning to visit more remote areas of a country, and where convenient links by air may not be possible. Examples of the latter include the Greek islands, or the Hebrides off the west coast of Scotland, the Isle of Wight off the south coast of England, or the Strait of Messina, between Italy and Sicily.

The key ferry routes for tourists are those major links between countries separated by water, such as across the English Channel, or between the Scandinavian countries, or across the Adriatic between Italy and Greece. These routes may be vital for those wishing to take their car on holiday, and also provide an attractive alternative to flying for those with time to spare. Additionally, there are many places in the world where transport is dependent upon good national ferry services, due either to the number of islands belonging to the territory or to the difficulty of reaching coastal destinations by air or sea. Examples include the east coast of Sweden, the west coast of Norway, the west coast of Canada and Alaska and, in Britain, the Hebrides.

The significance of the short-sea ferry market can be appreciated when it is learned that by the mid-1990s some 2,150 ro-ro (roll on-roll off) ferries were estimated to be in operation worldwide; from the UK alone around 50 million passengers were using ferries to travel to other countries, while services out of British Columbia in Canada will be carrying 24 million passengers a year by the year 2000. Of course, not all these will be counted as tourists, and this is an important point to remember; typically, ferry services provide a communication network for local populations, while taking advantage of visitors to boost numbers and become profitable.

The growth of short-sea voyages within Europe during the past decade can be hailed as a

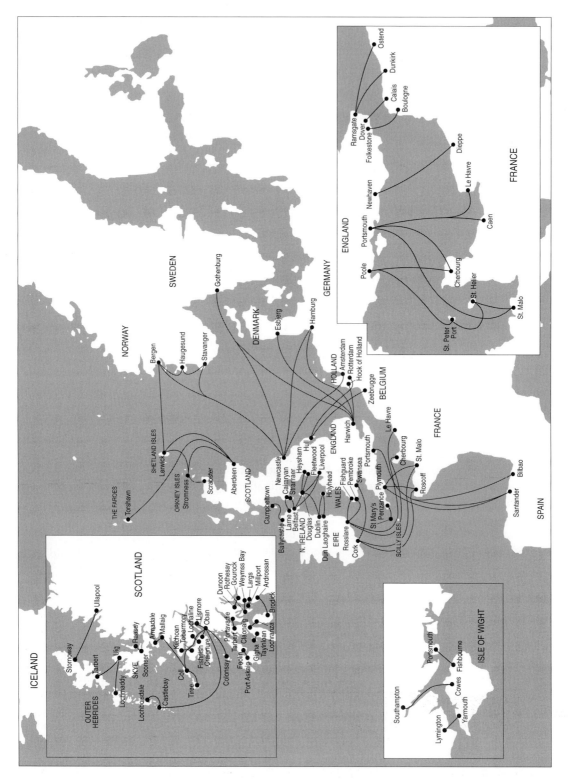

Figure 8.4 Major passenger/car ferry services from Britain
Source: Travel Weekly

major success story. The rise in demand for ferries during the 1980s and 1990s can be partly attributed to the general growth of tourism and trade in this region, especially of trade between European Union countries; but growth of private car ownership has also played a significant part in rising demand. France, in particular, has always been a destination with a strong attraction for independent British holidaymakers travelling with their cars, and the strengthening of the pound against the franc in 1997 played a major role in attracting UK holidaymakers back to France in large numbers. There has also been a large rise in coach transport between Britain and the Continent, as coach companies introduced long-distance coach routes linking London with the capitals of Europe.

In spite of the challenge offered by the Channel Tunnel linking Britain and France since 1994, Dover remains by far the most important of the ports serving the Continent, and was the only port offering carrier choice. However, in 1998 P & O and Stena Line formed a new joint company for the Dover–Calais route. Nearly 18 million passengers and nearly 3 million cars crossed the Channel between Dover and the Continent in 1995 (*Travel and Tourism Analyst* 1/1997) and some estimates suggest that the total number of cross-Channel passengers could reach as many as 94 million by 2003. However, given the growth of le Shuttle services through the Tunnel, how many of these passengers would continue to use ferries is more difficult to estimate.

Ferry companies have played their part in stimulating this growth in traffic. New routes have been developed to tap regional markets and to provide greater choice, so that passengers have been able in recent years to choose to travel to the Continent from Portsmouth to Caen, from Plymouth to Roscoff and from Sheerness to Vlissingen, as well as on the longer established routes out of Harwich, Dover, Folkestone and Newhaven (see Figure 8.4). Not all these routes have proved viable, as price-slashing attracts tourists to the most popular, even if not the most convenient, routes.

From Britain, routes can be conveniently grouped into four geographical regions:

- English Channel (short-sea crossing) routes, including services from ports such as Ramsgate, Dover, Folkestone, Newhaven and Brighton
- Western Channel routes, including services from Portsmouth, Southampton, Poole, Weymouth and Plymouth
- North Sea routes, including services from North Shields, Hull, Felixstowe and Harwich
- Irish Sea routes, including services from Swansea, Pembroke, Fishguard, Holyhead, Liverpool, Stranraer, Cairnryan and the Isle of Man.

It should be stressed that while these have been identified as key ports, services operating out of these ports do vary from time to time, as competition forces out some companies and others attempt to operate new routes in their place. The expectation that a route, once announced, will continue to operate for many years is no longer true; within the period 1995–97 one has seen the demise of the Brighton–Fécamp route, Eurolink's Sheerness–Vlissingen service, Sally Ferries' Ramsgate–Dunkirk service and Brittany's Poole–St Malo route. The Belgian operator RMT ceased trading in 1997, while Stena dropped its close twenty-six year working partnership with French carrier SNAT in 1995, forcing that company to relaunch independently as SeaFrance. Stena withdrew its Southampton–Cherbourg service in 1996, replacing it with a service between Portsmouth and Cherbourg in the following year.

In addition to these major routes, there are a number of important smaller ferry services operating in the UK, such as those linking the islands of Scotland, the Orkneys and Shetlands; and shorter services to the Isle of Wight, Isle of Man, the Scilly Isles and Lundy Island in the Severn Channel.

About 60 per cent of the market chooses to travel to the Continent on the short-sea routes, encouraged by the regular improvements made by Dover in particular to retain that port's market share. Another 22 per cent use the North Sea routes to Europe, while 18 per cent travel on the western Channel routes.

THE ECONOMICS OF FERRY OPERATING

As with cruising, operating short-sea ferry routes is expensive in both capital investment and in direct operating cost. Profitability is achieved through a combination of maximum usage of equipment, plus on-board sales (duty- and tax-free sales were estimated in 1997 to contribute as much as 45 per cent of ferry operators' revenues on the Dover Straits sailings). This means, in the first case, rapid turnarounds in port at the end of each journey, and round-the-clock sailings, with, ideally, an even volume of business all year round and a balanced flow of demand in both directions. In practice this is, of course, difficult to achieve, and in winter, when much of the pure holiday traffic dries up, the ferry services become very dependent upon freight carrying to achieve profitability.

The shorter sailings to France, Belgium and Holland attract much better market demand than do the longer routes to Scandinavia, Germany and Northern Spain, although the ferry companies on the latter routes have achieved considerable success in marketing the longer (24 hours or more) sailings as mini-cruises. Their success is modelled on the enormously popular service between Stockholm, Sweden and either Turku or Helsinki, Finland, which, in addition to providing one of the most scenic routes anywhere in Europe for a ferry service, also attracts customers through the sale of relatively cheap on-board drinks, in a region where alcohol is prohibitively expensive. As a result, the ferry market between these two countries is now approaching 10 million passengers a year, with the two major carriers, Silja and Viking Lines, together attracting over 6 million with twelve luxury jumbo vessels, the largest of which, at 60,000 tons, is capable of carrying in excess of 3,000 passengers on twelve decks.

Off-peak sailings on the shorter routes can be boosted by low fares, with a wide range of discounted prices aimed at differing market segments. Quick round-trips on the same vessel, or short stopovers of one to three nights have expanded, particularly those offering shopping expeditions to the French hypermarkets before Christmas. The removal of customs barriers on most duty-paid goods within the European Union, and the relatively low cost of duty-paid alcoholic drinks in France compared with Britain, have also had the effect of boosting cross-Channel traffic,

and about one in four passengers from Britain to France is now on a shopping expedition.

At extreme off-peak periods, and for night sailings which attract fewer bookings, it may be the ferry companies' intention only to price the product to make a contribution to fixed costs, rather than to ensure profitability on every crossing. Low fares may nonetheless stimulate on-board spend which will make a useful contribution to total revenue. Although the European Union has extended the date for ending the right to duty-free purchases until July 1999, the ferry companies have anticipated the move by increasing the general shopping facilities in their newer ships, in the hope that this will continue to stimulate the desire to shop on board, even at prices which are no longer duty-free.

Both the leading British carriers have made strenuous efforts to cut their operating costs in recent years, particularly their labour costs. First P&O, and later Stena, introduced new labour practices into their companies, which have increased the efficiency of crewing, but only after serious confrontations with the seaman's union. Against this, however, the SOLAS (Safety of Life at Sea) regulations, which came into effect following the Stockholm Agreement, signed in 1997 between Great Britain and six northern European countries, have substantially added to building costs. The objective of these regulations was to increase the safety and stability of ro-ro ferries, following the disastrous *Herald of Free Enterprise* sinking at Zeebrugge in 1987, but the shipping companies won a compromise from the government on the timing of their introduction, which meant that regulations would be introduced in stages, with the final implementation delayed until December 2004. In the meantime, concern over ferry safety remains an important factor. The subsequent sinking of the ferry *Estonia* in the Baltic in 1994 with a loss of around 1,000 lives revealed that there is still good reason for concern. The Stockholm Agreement requires vessels operating into and out of ports in the seven countries to be capable of remaining upright in waves up to four metres high and with 50 centimetres of floodwater on the car deck. It will require the fitting of all vessels with transverse bulkheads which will improve stability in rough seas, but the ferry companies are having to face major bills (around £1 million per vessel) and the further worry that the obligatory modifications will both reduce car capacity and slow down the loading and unloading of vessels, delaying turnrounds.

THE CHANNEL TUNNEL AND THE FERRY SERVICES

The Channel Tunnel, perhaps the greatest threat to the ferries since their inception, was opened to passenger traffic at the end of 1994, although the build-up to its full operation has been slow. The background to this is described more fully in Chapter 9, but here we should examine the impact upon ferry services of this new form of cross-Channel service.

Eurotunnel, operators of the Channel Tunnel, have suffered a number of setbacks in building and operating the Tunnel, including repeated delays in opening, delays in obtaining equipment to run through the Tunnel, and a disastrous and costly fire in a freight wagon at the end of 1996 which caused a great deal of damage to the interior of the Tunnel and led to reduced services over a number of months. Nevertheless, the success of this new alternative has been proved in its first years of operation, and on the Eurostar rail services in particular it has attracted a substantial amount of traffic between London and Paris which would formerly have travelled by air. Independent forecasts have estimated that the Tunnel could attract up to 40 per cent of all cross-Channel traffic, and by 1997 Eurotunnel, the car-carrying rail transporter service operating between Cheriton, near Folkestone, and les Coquelles, near Calais, had already won this share of the surface market. While early forecasts by Eurotunnel proved inaccurate and were rapidly condemned by the ferry companies as wildly optimistic, these companies privately agreed that the loss of a significant proportion of their traffic to the Tunnel would be unavoidable. In order to combat this threat, the two major ferry companies took steps to ensure their survival as competitors to the Tunnel.

Firstly, both P&O and Stena invested heavily in their short-sea operations; P&O spent some £400 million between 1987 and 1992, including the introduction of a new, 28,000-ton ship which, coupled with its existing fleet, enabled it to offer round the clock sailings every 45 minutes between Dover and Calais. Improvements in passenger handling facilities at Dover were effected, which would allow passengers to check in just 20 minutes before sailing. Stena likewise invested £250 million during 1991–92 to improve its own cross-Channel services, and introduced a 29,000 ton luxury mega-ferry to the route. But this was seen to be insufficient in itself to put the companies on a viable footing for their long-term future, so the two companies planned to amalgamate their services between Dover and Calais to form a single company operating regular round-the-clock hourly services which would not necessitate advance booking. To their dismay, the scheme was initially rejected by the Monopolies and Mergers Commission, and again on a number of subsequent applications. However, approval was finally granted in November 1997, with stringent conditions applied to control prices, as the merged company now controls over 40 per cent of the market. The new company will operate independently of its two parents.

Emphasis is being placed, in marketing these services, on encouraging passengers to treat the crossing as part of their holiday, a time to relax and unwind on board. The opposition is disparaged with references to the amenities they offer being no more than 'a toilet and a light-bulb'. Larger, more luxurious ships scheduled for this service would reinforce the idea of a short-sea crossing as a mini-cruise. To this end, P&O withdrew its Folkestone–Boulogne service in 1992 in order to concentrate its resources on the Dover service.

In the meantime, while the two leading companies believe they can continue to provide an effective alternative to the Tunnel that will appeal to the British traveller, they are taking advantage of the cost overruns experienced by Eurotunnel to slash prices and undercut le Shuttle's services. Eurotunnel has been obliged to retaliate with similar price cuts, with the result that profits for the ferries have slumped, while Eurotunnel has had great difficulty in reaching agreement with its creditors to continue in operation, to delay repayment of interest on its £9 billion loan, and to postpone any dividends to shareholders till well into the next century. Savage discounting on the short-sea ferry services has also raised a question mark over the future of other short-sea routes, which have been forced to lower their own fares to prevent diversion of traffic. Further amalgamations are likely, especially for services operating in the western Channel. The worry for the market leaders out of Dover must be whether they can attract sufficient trade during the winter months, when the Tunnel is coming to be seen by many passengers as a preferable choice to a rough sea crossing, even if only 75 minutes long. The joint service envisaged by P&O and Stena will have a daily capacity of some 190,000 passengers and 50,000 cars – more than twice the peak day sailings carried in the summer of 1992. The massive investment made by the two companies in past years will have to be recovered, and the worry for the ferries must be for a continuation of the price war between the two modes of travel – something that will be in the interest of none of the companies.

In 1996, P&O is estimated to have carried 9 million passengers and 1.6 million cars on the Dover–Calais route, while Stena accounted for 5.6 million passengers and 978,000 cars on the same route.

NEW MODES OF CROSSING

Other alternatives to ferries crossing the Channel also exist, in the form of the hovercraft, hydrofoil and catamaran. These offer the benefits of a faster crossing, and a certain degree of novelty, although hovercraft have now been operating across the Channel since 1968. The hovercraft rides on a cushion of air just above the surface of the water, and its ability to travel over land as well as water avoids the usual capital costs associated with dock facilities, as the craft can simply be beached on any convenient and obstacle-free foreshore. Unfortunately, it offers its passengers a somewhat bouncy and noisy ride by comparison with the more traditional ferry, and it cannot operate in rough weather. It has also suffered many technical problems in its development and throughout the years of its operation, and shortage of further research and development expenditure must mean that it is unlikely to provide a viable means of cheap transport in the long run, except over difficult terrain such as marshland.

The hydrofoil offers better prospects for future development, even though it, too, suffered from technological teething problems, and it was withdrawn from the Brighton–Fécamp route because of the high number of enforced cancellations on technical grounds. This vessel operates with a conventional hull design, but when it is travelling at speed the hull is raised above the surface of the water on blades, or 'foils' (see Figure 8.5). This enables the vessel to travel at speeds of up to 60 knots. Recent models have been powered by jet engines ('jetfoils').

Finally, wave-piercing catamarans (WPC) have been operating on cross-Channel services since 1991, and now threaten to take the place of the hovercraft. These are twin-hulled vessels large enough to accommodate cars, travelling at speeds up to 40 knots (comparable with the hovercraft). Although these, too, suffered from technical difficulties when first introduced, they are now operating successfully from Britain to Ireland and the Continent, and have been introduced on such key routes as Stena's Newhaven–Dieppe and Harwich–Hook of Holland routes. These vessels offer a valuable service for those who want the fastest possible crossing to the Continent but who might find the Channel Tunnel claustrophobic. As with other high-speed craft, however, this vessel can experience difficulties sailing in bad weather conditions, and it remains to be seen whether it

---

Table 8.3 The short-sea cross-Channel route; market shares Jan–July 1996

	Passengers %	Cars %
le Shuttle (Eurotunnel)	35	36
P&O	28	31
Stena	16	16
Hoverspeed	10	6
Sally Line	7	7
Sea France	4	4

Source: The Times 15 Aug 96, © Times Newspapers Ltd., 1996

Figure 8.5 Jetfoil. *(Courtesy P&O European Ferries Ltd)*

Figure 8.6 Hoverspeed 'Sea Cat' catamaran. *(Courtesy Hoverspeed Ltd)*

can provide a viable alternative to the Tunnel during the winter period. What is becoming clear, however, is that for a great many holidaymakers the trend is to choose faster surface vessels which can compete with the Tunnel on time.

Work on more advanced vessels is under way; in France, a 40-knot quadrimaran, operating on four hulls which offer a much smoother ride, has been under development since the early 1990s. Although this vessel is seen primarily as a freight carrier, it offers potential ultimately for development as a passenger carrier. Foil-catamarans, a hybrid of the jetfoil and hovercraft, are also under test at the time of writing, and a prototype was operated successfully on the Elbe in 1994. Capable of speeds of 30–40 knots, their low resistance in the water leads to 30 per cent greater fuel efficiency, and they would therefore make a very useful contribution in the competitive UK ferry market. Finally, a Hoverplane prototype was tested in 1997, which combines elements of catamaran, hovercraft and wing-in-surface-effect (WISE) in its design. WISE operates on the principle that a stable cushion of air is generated by a wing flying close to ground or water; by travelling on this dense layer of air, the craft benefits from reduced drag and increased lift, thus achieving high fuel economy. Speeds of up to 100 mph are anticipated, at one-fifth of the normal fuel cost of a ferry, which should enable prices to be much lower than at present. Craft should be capable of carrying between 80 and 150 passengers distances

of up to 250 miles. An added advantage of such a vessel is that it requires neither runway nor port in the accepted sense of the words.

OTHER EUROPEAN FERRY OPERATIONS

While this text has focused primarily on connections between the UK and its Continental neighbours, the continuing importance of other routes, especially within Europe, must be recognised. In the Mediterranean, ferries provide not only vital connections for travellers on a port-to-port basis, but also the opportunity to package these routes as mini-cruises calling at a variety of different countries. By way of example, services are available in the eastern Mediterranean between Venice, Dubrovnik, Piraeus, Iraklion and Alexandria, or between Istanbul, Piraeus, Larnaca, Lattakia (Syria) and Alexandria. Similarly, those tourists who traditionally think only of travel by air to Majorca may be unaware of the alternatives of travel from Barcelona by catamaran with Transmediterranea.

The Greek economy is heavily dependent upon its shipping interests, and the significance of this area of the economy to Greece, both in the cruise and ferry markets, is such that the country has received temporary dispensation from the lifting of cabotage restrictions which have opened up competition elsewhere within the European Union. Cruises operating out of and back to Greek ports are protected for Greek companies until 1999 and coastal shipping such as ferry services will be further protected until 2004. In spite of EU opposition, some member countries continue to subsidise their shipping interests; Britanny Ferries received a £40 million subsidy from the French government in 1996 despite protests from UK companies.

The other major area in Europe for ferry operations is in the Baltic, where services connect the Scandinavian countries, and in turn provide vital connections for travellers between these countries and Germany. Independence for the three Baltic states of Latvia, Estonia and Lithuania has renewed interest in these destinations for tourists, and both cruise ships and ferry crossings have achieved considerable growth in this area. The benefit of having St Petersburg in Russia as a major port in the Baltic has further stimulated interest in the region. The Helsinki (Finland)–Tallinn (Estonia) ferry route, being a comparatively short crossing, offers the tourist the opportunity for an attractive mini-cruise, but as reported earlier, the major draw in this area is the Stockholm–Helsinki route, which now operates with 60,000 ton mega-ferries carrying up to 2,800 passengers at a time. The obvious success in this region, in selling what were originally merely transport connections as luxury mini-cruises has established a trend which the British ferry operators are anxious to emulate.

Coastal and inland waterways tourism

The attraction of water offers many other opportunities for tourist activity, both independently and in forms which have been commoditised and packaged for the tourist. Inland waterways in particular – lakes, rivers and canals – provide exceptional opportunities for recreation and tourism, and in Britain the renovation of former canals, derelict locks and similar watersites has added in recent years to the many opportunities for river and lake recreational travel.

The major waterways of the world have long attracted the tourist. The Nile River, in Egypt, has provided inland waterway cruising for many decades, and in recent years the popularity of this stretch of waterway led to an enormous expansion in the number and size of cruise ships operating as package holiday products up to the early years of the 1990s. However, the volatility of the tourism business is well illustrated by the collapse of the Egyptian inland cruise market in the mid-1990s when the country was hit first by terrorism in which tourists were explicitly targeted, and then by drought, causing navigational difficulties in the upper Nile region. Other popular river cruises are those provided along the Danube (between Passau in Germany and Constanta in Rumania), the Rhine in Holland and Germany, the Mississippi in the USA (where traditional paddle wheelers offer a nostalgic cruise experience) and the Yangtze and Li Rivers in China. In South America, the Amazon River is sufficiently large to allow ocean-going ships to navigate as far inland as Iquitos in Peru. All of these services are packaged as tours and sold to tourists throughout the world.

Public craft also play an important role in tourism on inland waterways as well as along coasts. Excursion boats, such as the paddle steamer *Waverley* and the traditional steamer *Balmoral,* carry tourists on coastal trips in Britain during the summer from ports in Scotland, South Wales and the West Country. The lakes steamer remains a familiar sight in many parts of the world, providing an important tourist attraction in the US and Canadian Great Lakes, the Swiss and south German lakes, and the Scottish lochs and English Lake District in Britain.

Figure 8.7 The *Waverley* sails on a coastal excursion from Bristol. *(Photographed by the author)*

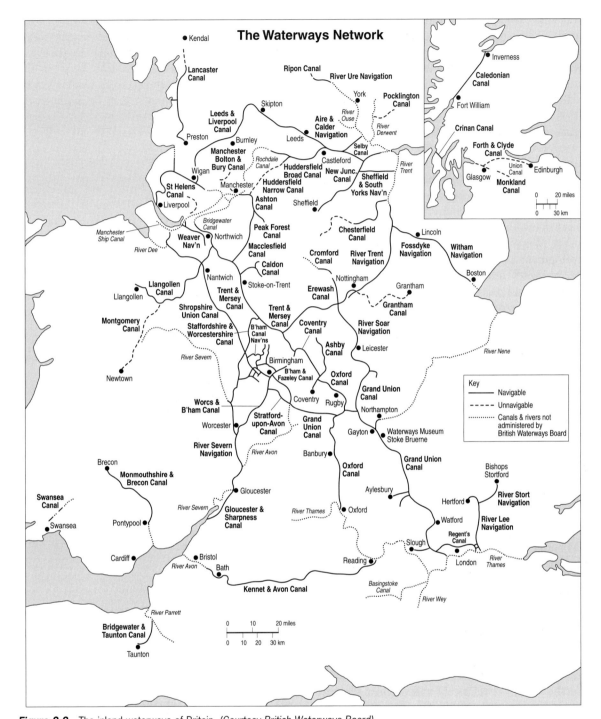

Figure 8.8 The inland waterways of Britain. *(Courtesy British Waterways Board)*

However, it is the growing attraction of rivers and canals for the independent boating enthusiast which perhaps holds the greatest potential for development over the next few years. The networks of rivers and canals in countries such as Britain, Holland and France have been redeveloped and exploited for tourism in recent years. Canals such as the Burgundy canals and the Canal du Midi in the South of France, and the Gota Canal in Sweden are also being discovered by British tourists in growing numbers.

Britain itself is particularly well-endowed with canals and rivers suitable for navigation (see Figure 8.8). In the mid-1800s, the nation could boast of some 4,250 miles of navigable inland waterways, many of which had been developed for the movement of freight. As these became redundant with the advent of the railways, they fell into disrepair and many stretches became no longer navigable. However, in recent years the British Waterways Board has encouraged the development and use of these waterways for pleasure purposes and, in partnership with private enterprise, and aided by voluntary bodies, it has helped to restore and reopen many formerly derelict canals. This has generated enormous interest in domestic waterways tourism in Britain.

Of course, the British have a long-standing tradition of enjoying holidays afloat, and the popularity of areas such as the Norfolk Broads for water-based tourism dates back to the early twentieth century; but the reopening of many formerly derelict waterways has made it possible for boat hire companies to organise packages which allow enthusiasts to follow a circular route during a one- or two-week holiday, without the need to travel the same stretch of water twice.

The British Waterways Board maintains some 2,000 miles of inland waterways, and a further 1,250 miles of navigable waterway are preserved by other bodies. Over 200 miles of formerly derelict canals have been returned to use, and another 100 miles are under development. Now foreign, as well as British, tourists are becoming attracted to the tourism potential these waterways offer.

This form of tourism does suffer from the fact that the market has become highly competitive and the season is relatively short. Most pleasure boat companies are small, family-run concerns, achieving low returns on capital invested and generally low profits. Effective marketing, especially to the overseas tourist, is a problem where companies' budgets for promotion are small, and the destination being sold is linear (the Kennet and Avon Canal, for instance, runs through different regional tourist board areas, making unified marketing difficult). In such circumstances, cooperative promotion between the small boat companies themselves, working with other private sector interests, may be the best solution.

WATERSITE DEVELOPMENT

In a similar fashion, the closure and subsequent dereliction of many of Britain's major docklands offered another opportunity for redevelopment of these sites for recreation and tourism. Although primarily a consequence of urban redevelopment policy, the restoration of waterfront property in sites such as Bristol's Historic Floating Harbour, Salford Quays, Liverpool's Albert Docks, Southampton's Ocean Village and, of course, the London Docklands, has in turn generated tourism to these sites, following the construction of marinas and the subsequent introduction of waterbuses and ferries, scenic cruises, floating restaurants and other leisure attractions. Notable developments in this direction have also taken place abroad, especially within the USA and Canada. The astonishing success of Baltimore's Inner Harbor development sparked off similar schemes in New York, San Francisco, Boston and Toronto, all of which now attract tourists in large numbers. In Europe, Stockholm and Oslo have both restored their decaying harbour sites, and in Australia, Sydney's Darling Harbour has likewise been the subject of extensive renovation, making these cities more attractive for visiting tourists. While most of these sites are, of course, planned for multiple use, including shops, offices and residential communities, the leisure use of the sites will inevitably attract the tourist and generate new forms of income for the cities concerned.

Seagoing pleasure craft

This section would not be complete without some mention of the growing demand for holidays aboard seagoing pleasure craft, a demand which is now being met by the travel industry. It has been estimated that there are more than 400,000 boat owners in Britain, and some two million people sail for pleasure. This is naturally leading to demand for institutionalised boating holidays. On the one hand, a growing band of small private companies offer package holidays aboard small sailing ships or steamboats, with facilities ranging from the luxurious, where the passengers are guests, to the more basic, where passengers play an active part in crewing the boat. On the other hand, tour operating companies are catering to the mass demand for boating holidays by offering flotilla cruising holidays, especially in areas where there are many small islands, which provide a sheltered anchorage and good weather conditions. The Greek islands, and certain Caribbean islands such as the Windward and Leeward groups, offer ideal conditions for these types of package holiday, in which individually hired yachts sail together in flotilla formation from island to island. In this manner, the tourist has the benefits of independent use of the yacht while enjoying the social life of the group when together at anchor (see Figure 8.9).

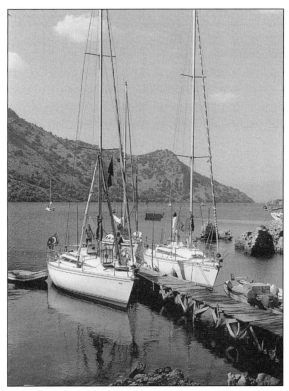

Figure 8.9 Flotilla sailing in Turkey. *(Courtesy Sunsail Worldwide Sailing Holidays)*

QUESTIONS AND DISCUSSION POINTS

1 Explain why cruising enjoys a higher level of demand in North America than in Britain, and suggest what more needs to be done by British shipping companies to increase the cruise market.
2 Will the new P & O Stena service between Dover and Calais compete successfully with Eurotunnel services? Should the MMC have permitted them to operate a joint service?

3 Compare and contrast the two ferry routes,

   (a) Britain to France, and
   (b) Sweden to Finland

Both routes are extremely popular, but for different reasons. Explain why this is, and suggest what conclusions can be drawn about the nature of ferry services in general.

ASSIGNMENT TOPICS

1 You are employed in the Cruise Planning Department of a major British shipping company. Your manager has asked you to prepare a study to investigate the possibility of operating a new cost-cutting 'cheap and cheerful' line voyage service across the North Atlantic between Britain, France and New York. He believes that there will be a substantial market among young people for a low-priced transatlantic crossing with buffet-style 'pay as you go' meals and minimum service on board.

   Investigate the possibility of this and prepare a short report to him, giving your views; some indication of what might be charged should be included.

2 As a result of the closer ties which have developed between Britain and the rest of the EU, a German leisure corporation, Gesellschaft für Internationalen Reiseverkehr, is examining opportunities to expand into the British market. They already have interests in inland waterways cruising on the Continent, and have asked you, as a research officer with a firm of consultants retained by the company, to carry out a study of the opportunities in Britain. They are contemplating setting up, or purchasing, a company operating a hire fleet of narrow boats based on a section of Britain's inland waterways network, which would enable holidaymakers to hire vessels for circular trips, avoiding the necessity of retracing their journey over the same route.

   In the first instance, you are asked to provide a brief report to the company identifying one or more suitable locations. You should also present evidence of factors favouring growth of this particular form of leisure activity. Your report should be suitably illustrated with maps and graphs.

9

Road and Rail Passenger Transport

OBJECTIVES

After studying this chapter, you should be able to:

- understand the role and scope of public and private railways in the UK, in terms of their importance to tourism;
- be aware of the role and significance of the coach industry in tourism;
- recognise the importance of the private car for tourism;
- understand the role of car hire in tourism, both in the UK and abroad.

The role of the railways in tourism

Considering their long lead over other carriers in providing public service transport, it may be thought surprising that the railways in Britain have taken so long to adapt to the needs of mass-market tourism in the late twentieth century. Certainly, the railways played a major role in the provision of tourist transport throughout the first half of this century, but as ownership of private cars grew, so tourist traffic on the railways fell. The process had already become noticeable before World War II and accelerated after 1947, when the railways were nationalised in Britain. The switch to private passenger transport, coupled with the rapid expansion of freight transport by road, led to severe difficulties for British Rail during the 1950s and 1960s, which it attempted to solve by substantial reductions in its routes. This resulted in its focusing on the main intercity routes, and cutting back their unprofitable branch lines. Many smaller resorts and other destinations that could have attracted the tourist became no longer accessible by rail. The alternative of coach links connecting with the rail termini makes tourist travel inconvenient and time-consuming, and this, coupled with continuing fare increases on the railways, soon made the railways an unattractive choice for many destinations. However, railways have continued to play an important role in bringing tourists to key English resorts such as Brighton, Bournemouth and Torquay.

In the 1970s and 1980s, British Rail became more marketing-orientated, and helped by the escalation in fuel prices following the oil crisis of 1973, succeeded in winning back some of the domestic tourists from private car travel. Packages using rail transport were introduced on a larger scale than for many years. The packages proved to be particularly popular for the short-break market, particularly to London, but by the mid-1980s, tourists were reverting to car trips, and the sale of rail packages declined. British Rail eventually sold off its loss-making Golden Rail Holidays division to the private sector. However, its efforts to entice the rail travel enthusiast proved more successful, even though these were limited in scale. Nostalgic day trips and excursions using famous old steam trains proved popular, as did short breaks using Intercity trains, and packages aimed at the over-55s. Recognising that unsold off-peak seats represent substantial lost revenue, the cor-

poration used variable pricing policies and promotions, sometimes in cooperation with retail
stores such as Boots, to attract the tourist and
excursionist back to the railways.

Unlimited travel tickets were also made available for inbound tourists buying tickets before
departure from their own countries. These
allowed overseas tourists to travel freely over the
rail networks of Britain, while Eurailpass offered
similar benefits for travel within Continental
Europe. Such schemes proved highly popular with
independent tourists visiting Europe, especially
the young back-packer market.

THE PRIVATISATION OF RAIL TRANSPORT

In the early 1990s, the decision was taken by the
Conservative government then in power to dena-
tionalise the railways. Private companies were to
be allowed to bid for individual routes within the
British Rail system, while Railtrack, the state-run
body responsible for the maintenance and operation of all track and signalling, was also to be
sold off as a separate company. The government's
belief was that a privatised railway system would
be more efficient, would end the drain on government funds through subsidies and would compete
effectively against other forms of transport by
attracting travellers back onto the railways.
Therefore, by early 1997 some twenty-five train-
operating units in the UK had replaced the former
monolithic rail system.

While there is some evidence that passenger
traffic has increased on most services through
more attractive marketing, passengers themselves
are confused about the range of choice facing
them, and journeys involving the services of more
than one rail company have become more complex to organise in some respects, due to the lack
of integrated marketing. The impact of these
changes on tourist traffic has yet to be analysed,
but concern has been expressed over the lack of
promised investment by the rail companies and
the impact of cost-cutting by some companies in
order to boost profits. Distribution systems for rail
tickets have also suffered; travel agents were
already abandoning the sale of rail tickets as
unprofitable before the advent of privatisation;
this has been hastened by the additional complex-

Figure 9.1 Two high-speed train services: a) Japan's
Shinkansen (Bullet Train) *(Courtesy Japan Information Centre,
London).* b) France's Train à Grande Vitesse (TGV). *(Courtesy
SNCF. CAV photo Bruno Vignal)*

ities of dealing with a score of different rail
companies.

However, the ambition to serve the needs of
the tourist market remains; the Special Trains division of British Rail is now in private hands too,
and continues to provide special steam and electric

excursions which have proved popular with domestic and foreign tourists alike in the past. A handful of domestic tour operators also continue to specialise in offering domestic and Continental rail travel, but although the potential exists for a greatly expanded market for rail travel within the European Union, this is not really being tapped in Britain as yet. The success of the Eurostar service through the Channel Tunnel, and developments on the Continent, may well change this in the future.

THE CHANNEL TUNNEL AND THE RAILWAYS

In Chapter 8 we examined the impact of the Channel Tunnel on ferry operations from the UK. Here, we must examine its impact on rail and road services in Britain and the Continent.

The Channel Tunnel is one of the great engineering feats of the twentieth century – although, contrary to popular belief, not the longest underwater rail tunnel in the world; Japan's Selkan Tunnel, 32.5 miles long, has been carrying rail traffic for a number of years. The first direct rail link between Britain and France was completed and opened to traffic in 1994, after frequent delays. It offers passengers the choice of two forms of transport: regular rail connections on Eurostar from London to either Paris or Brussels, calling at Ashford in Kent and Lille in northern France and beyond; and Eurotunnel, a vehicle-carrying rail service operating between Cheriton (near Folkestone) and les Coquelles (near Calais), a distance of some 50 kilometres, of which 37 kilometres is under the Channel itself. Cars are carried in double-deck carriages (higher cars, those with trailers, and coaches are accommodated in single-deck carriages). They can be transported across the Channel and drive directly onto the connecting French motorway in a little over thirty minutes.

At the insistence of the Conservative government the Tunnel was privately financed without any contribution from the state. Its construction involved leading-edge technology, and the project ran into delays and huge cost overruns, leaving the parent company, Eurotunnel, with massive debts of some £9 billion.

Overambitious estimates of traffic and revenue were not realised, but this is not to say that the Tunnel has not been a success. Within two years of operation, it had made sufficient inroads into the share of the short-sea market to badly worry the ferry companies, which were obliged to slash prices to compete. A severe fire in the Tunnel during November 1996 disrupted traffic for six months, but Eurostar still carried some 5 million passengers during 1996, and was attracting 50 per cent of the former London–Paris air traffic. In 1996, Eurotunnel was used by 13 million passengers in all (up from 8 million in 1995), and the company held 50 per cent of the entire short-sea market. This market share, however, was badly hit by the Tunnel fire, falling to only 36 per cent in the first six months of 1997. Eurotunnel is confident that market share will have fully recovered by 1998. The rail route from London has been particularly attractive for the business traveller, for whom a first-class service is available, and who can travel city centre to city centre in around three hours, compared with closer to four hours by air, allowing for check-in time and the inevitable delayed departure. A journey time of two hours from London Waterloo to Lille enables the tourst to connect with the French TGV (*Train à Grande Vitesse*) high-speed trains for onward travel to Southern France (Lille–Bordeaux is a five-hour trip), or contiguous European countries. Through trains from London beyond Paris have been delayed due to technical problems with equipment, but at the time of writing some are expected to be in service in 1998. Eurostar plans services to operate eventually from London to Amsterdam, and from Glasgow, Manchester, Swansea and Plymouth to Paris, although earlier plans for sleeper services on some of these routes have been shelved.

High-speed trains are available between Calais and Paris, and since 1997 between Calais and Brussels (bringing the latter to within 2 hours 40 minutes of London). Government indecision about the route and financing of a high-speed connection for the 68-mile journey from London to the Tunnel entrance has meant a long delay in the construction of new track, which is expected to start in 1998 and will not be completed until at least 2004. This will cut a further half-hour from existing journeys, making these routes still more

Figure 9.2 Unloading cars from Eurotunnel. *(Courtesy @ Eurotunnel)*

attractive to present air passengers. Estimates in France have shown, for example, that for journeys of up to two hours, rail will capture some 90 per cent of all traffic, while for journeys of up to three hours, rail will still capture 75 per cent. The research also revealed that 25 per cent of the passenger traffic carried by the first TGV service was newly generated traffic.

The advent of the Tunnel has led to a substantial increase in the numbers of people travelling between Britain (particularly London and the South East) and the Continent. Popular tourist destinations such as Canterbury, which are now brought into reach for the day and short break visitor, are under pressure from the huge increase in tourism, leading to considerable difficulties for the local authorities in managing congestion and catering for increasing numbers of cars on these roads.

Eurotunnel's debt creates obvious difficulties in attempting to compete on price with the ferries.

A price war would be disastrous for the Tunnel company, given that interest payments of some £700 million have to be met before considering operating costs. Eurotunnel has successfully negotiated with the banks to delay repayment of interest, but has to convince its bankers that it can be viable in the long term. While the ferries' high investment in new equipment must also be recovered, they appear to be prepared to wage a price war to retain their market shares – although the evidence of the early months of 1997 is that a degree of rationality in pricing is returning to the market. Certainly, if independent estimates for the increase of passengers over the next twenty years prove to be correct, the Tunnel's future looks promising. The novelty factor has undoubtedly boosted carryings in the first years of operation, and although some believed that this would be offset by many travellers' fear of taking long underwater rail journeys, this does not appear to

Figure 9.3 Eurotunnel terminal at Folkestone. (*Courtesy @ Eurotunnel*)

have been a major barrier in practice, and many of those who have used it have become committed to this form of travel. Ultimately, when the massive capital costs of the Tunnel have been recuperated, and the benefits of its low operating costs against those of the ferries are taken into account, its success seems assured. In particular, the ferries will have to demonstrate that they can still attract the market during the winter months, when weather conditions will put them at a disadvantage to the Tunnel. Indeed, some forecasts are already suggesting that traffic growth will require a second tunnel to be built within twenty years.

THE EUROPEAN RAIL NETWORK

By contrast with the lack of rail investment in Britain, our Continental partners have for the most part recognised the importance of an effective rail network as an element of an integrated public transport policy for their countries, and have been prepared to invest heavily to achieve this. The present 4,000 km of high-speed track in Europe will double by 2002. France has invested some £22 billion to build its 300-kph TGV service, while Germany found £54 billion to build its own network of 280-kph ICE (Intercity Express) trains. Italy has introduced its *Pendolino* 250-kph tilt-body train on the Milan to Rome route, while Spain's AVE (Alta Velocidad Espagnola) offers a high-speed service between Madrid and Seville. Thalys, a consortium of Belgian, French and Dutch rail interests, is developing similar high-speed links between its member countries. Sweden's hugely successful X2000 high-speed train which reduced the journey between Stockholm and Gothenburg to less than three hours increased rail's share of this market from 30 per cent to 52 per cent, and is being extended to Oslo, Norway, as well as to other Swedish cities.

The French TGV network in particular has proved very attractive to the tourist market, with British tourists able to connect at Lille for Belgium, Holland, Germany and southern routes; the 1,216-km route between London and Nice can now be covered in a little over ten hours, and between London and Valence offers the longest high-speed train journey in the world. One contender to build the high-speed rail link between London and the Channel Tunnel is considering the possibility of operating overnight ski-trains from London to the Alps.

Improved equipment and service, rapid connections between major cities, and the avoidance of delays in congested airports are making European rail services appear increasingly attractive to the tourist market, and there is little doubt that rail services will figure prominently in the future of European tourism.

THE GLOBAL RAIL NETWORK

Although routes and standards of service have declined in many countries, railways still have a useful role to play in the carriage of both passengers and freight, and for the many tourists who are enthusiasts, railways continue to exercise a fascination. Countries in which steam trains still operate, such as India and China (although sadly they are now being phased out in India), attract both independent travellers and the package tour operator. Luxury rail travel on restored or recreated early-twentieth-century rolling stock, drawn by steam locomotives – much romanticised on television – continues to attract tourists to destinations such as India, which offers 'The Palace on Wheels', and to Spain, whose Al Andalus Express provides rail cruises in 1920s carriages which are berthed on sidings at night to allow passengers a restful and uninterrupted sleep. Hungary has introduced the Imperial Explorer, employing carriages built originally for the use of high-level party members under the Communist regime, as a feature to attract tourists to destinations outside Budapest. Long intercontinental rail journeys reminiscent of an earlier age of travel, such as the trans-Siberian route, have been exploited by specialist tour operators to provide unusual packages for rail aficionados.

In North America, rail travel in the 1960s and 1970s declined in the face of lower air fares and poor marketing by the railway companies themselves, which chose to concentrate on freight revenue at the expense of the passenger services. The continuing losses suffered by most US rail companies, and the importance of the rail network in social communications, led the government to integrate rail services in the country into a centrally funded public corporation known as AMTRAK. This organisation has achieved some success in reversing the decline of passenger traffic, although many of the great names of the past, such as the Santa Fe Superchief and the 20th Century Ltd, have gone for ever, and with them, some of the mystique of North American rail travel. Nonetheless, North American railways still travel through some of the most splendid scenery in the world, such as the Canadian Rockies and the western states, providing a base for future regeneration of interest in rail trips for the European tourist and tour operator alike. Rail journeys to the Rockies already form an important element in excursions for those booking cruises out of west coast North American ports.

In Japan, the *Shinkansen* (popularly known as the Bullet train: see Figure 9.1(a)) has changed the face of high-speed transport, and its reliability and high levels of service have proved immensely popular with tourists. The journey between Tokyo and Osaka, for example, takes three hours from city centre to city centre by train, compared with an hour's flying time between airports, and 80 per cent of all passengers now use the train for this journey.

The future of high-speed trains is promising for tourism. Both Germany and Japan are developing Magnetic Levitation (MAGLEV) trains, and in 1997 Japan's MLX-01 broke the world speed record for a train, travelling at 280.3 mph. In the US, rail authorities are currently testing the Cybertran, a cross between a high-speed train and a light railway system, which will provide fast, non-stop service at speeds up to 150 mph between US cities. Russia and America have held talks to discuss the construction of a 50-mile tunnel under the Bering Strait and a 4,600-mile rail track to provide a surface transport link between the two countries. While designed primarily as a means of competing with shipping across the Pacific for the carriage of freight, it would enable the rail enthusiast to travel by rail between London and New York in 14 days. However, the costs of all these developments are substantial (the US–Russian project is estimated at £27 billion alone), and they are unlikely to materialise until well into the twenty-first century. Some of these initiatives will provide strong competition for short-haul air services, particularly on major business routes. In view of the existing congestion in air routes, which can only get worse as the integration of Europe progresses, the development of alternative high-speed land routes is vital if trade – and tourism – are to prosper.

THE PRIVATE RAILWAYS

With the electrification of the railways in Britain, nostalgia for the steam trains of the pre-war period has led to the re-emergence of many private railways. Using obsolete track and former British Rail rolling stock, enthusiasts have painstakingly restored a number of branch lines to provide an alternative system of transport for travellers as well as a new attraction for domestic and overseas tourists. In Britain alone, there are over 250 railway preservation societies, and some forty private lines are in operation (see Figure 9.4), with a further 400 other projects either in hand or under consideration. Some of these depend largely upon tourist patronage, while others also offer a service to commuters; their profitability, however, is often dependent upon a great deal of voluntary labour, especially in the restoration of track, stations and rolling stock to serviceable condition. Since these services are generally routed through some of the most scenic areas of Britain, they attract both railway buffs and tourists of all kinds, and undoubtedly enhance the attractiveness of a region for tourism generally.

Meanwhile, the nostalgia boom has supported the resurrection of the former Venice–Simplon–Orient Express, extensively renovated and providing a level of luxury and service seldom seen since

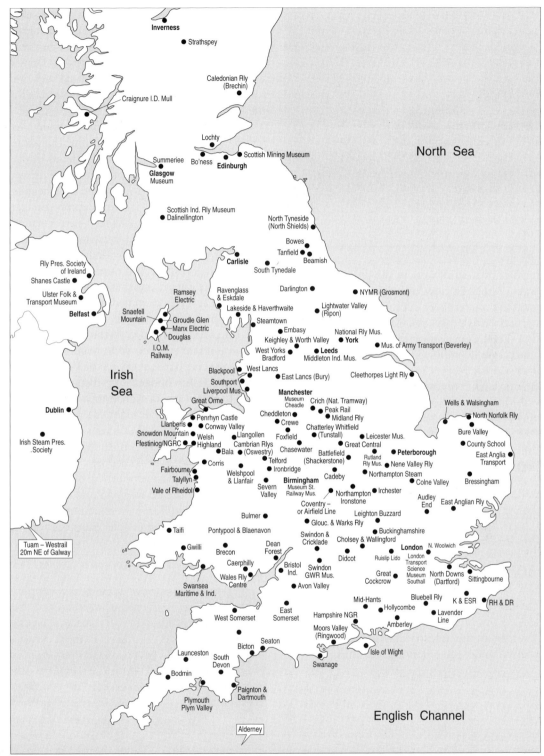

Figure 9.4 The private railways and railway transport museums of Britain and Ireland. Over fifty private railways offer tourists pleasure trips of between one and twenty miles. *(Courtesy The Heritage Railways Association)*

Figure 9.5 The *Royal Scotsman. (Courtesy Abercrombie and Kent Ltd)*

the heyday of the railways in the period between the wars. Although now operating only as far as Venice, the train has been successfully marketed to the US and British markets. Carriages used on the London–Folkestone leg of the journey have also been successfully employed for nostalgic day trips to other British resorts like Bath. In Scotland, a second successful venture has been the introduction of the 'Royal Scotsman' (see Figure 9.5). Although without benefit of a genuine pedigree, the 1920s-style train has been packaged with success in the American market, offering a very up-market tour of the Scottish Highlands. These two enterprises have proved that market niches exist for unusual rail programmes, which can undoubtedly be emulated in other tourist regions.

Coach travel

Coach operators today offer a wide range of tourist services to the public, both directly and through other sectors of the industry. These services can be categorised under the following headings:

(a) express coach routes, both domestic and international
(b) private hire services
(c) tour and excursion operations
(d) transfer services

Statistics relating to the coaching industry in the UK are not easy to obtain, because the Department of Transport does not distinguish between regular bus services and coach services in gathering data. However, estimates suggest that 8 per cent of overseas holidays from the UK in 1996 were taken on coaches, and some 8.3 million tourists take a coach holiday each year, either in the UK or abroad.

Long-distance coach services provide a cheap alternative to rail or air travel, and the extension of these both within the UK and from the UK to points in Europe and beyond has drawn an increasing number of tourists at the cheaper end of the market, particularly among the younger age groups. Younger passengers have also been attracted to adventurous transcontinental coach packages which have provided, for a low all-in price, both transport and minimal food and lodging en route (often under canvas). These services have been severely curtailed in recent years due to political problems in transit countries such as Iran and Iraq. An alternative is the sleeper-coach, an innovation scarcely known in Britain, although on the Continent, particularly in the German market, it is popular for budget long-distance coach holidays. In this form of transport, the coach pulls a sleeper trailer which at night can accommodate all the passengers in sleeping bunks (see p151).

However, for the most part coach travel remains the mode of transport of the older traveller, and the highest proportion of coach holidays are taken by those between 55 and 64. Two-thirds of all coaching holidays are taken by the over-45s, despite efforts by the coach operators themselves

Figure 9.6 Continental touring by coach. (*Courtesy Thomas Cook*)

to attract a younger market. This is perhaps unsurprising, given the advantages which coach services offer to the older market – not just low prices (reflecting low operating costs vis-à-vis other forms of transport) but the convenience of door-to-door travel when touring, overcoming baggage and transfer problems; courier assistance, especially in overseas travel, where the elderly avoid problems of language and handling documentation; and now, arrangements are often made to pick up passengers at points convenient for their homes. One result of this is that coach companies traditionally benefit from high levels of repeat business. Coach companies are now taking the view that their marketing efforts are best spent on raising the frequency of sales to the older market, rather than on trying to attract a new younger market; the former market is expanding rapidly, as people retire earlier in increasing numbers. The most popular holiday destinations for British clients are Germany's Rhineland and Bavarian regions, the Austrian Tyrol and Swiss Alps. While the long-distance coaching market on the Continent is holding up reasonably well, the trend is towards short-break holidays by coach, in keeping with the growth of short-break holidays in general.

The operation of coach tours is a highly seasonal one, however, and companies are often forced to lay off drivers and staff out of season, unless they can obtain sufficient ad hoc charters or contract work (such as school busing). Most coach companies specialise in certain spheres of activity. While some operate and market their tours nationally, others may concentrate on serving the needs of incoming tourists and tour operators, by providing excursion programmes, transfers between airports and hotels, or complete coach tours for overseas visitors. These coach companies must build up close relations and work closely with tour operators and other intermediaries abroad or in the home country.

LEGISLATION IN THE COACH BUSINESS

Under the terms of the Transport Act 1980, in order to set up or operate a coach service, it is necessary to apply for a coach operator's licence. This is granted by the Traffic Commissioners, with conditions which limit the operation to a specified number of vehicles. Licences normally run for five years, although under some conditions the term can be shorter. Before granting a licence, the Traffic Commissioners must be satisfied that the applicant has a good financial record and adequate resources to operate the number of coaches for which the licence has been requested. At least one responsible member of the company must hold an individual transport operator's licence, which is essentially a certificate of professional competence based on management experience and appropriate educational qualifications (for example, membership of the Chartered Institute of Transport). The Commissioners must also satisfy themselves that the operator will provide satisfactory maintenance facilities (or in lieu, a contract with a supplier of such facilities), and the operating centre where the vehicles are to be garaged must be specified.

Coach operating conditions now fall into line with EU directives, which are designed to ensure adequate safety provisions for passengers. The concern with safety has been highlighted by recent incidents in the coaching industry, most notably a series of serious accidents on the Continent involving holiday coaches. The EU regulation governing drivers' hours (No. 543/69) dictates the maximum number of hours' driving permitted for each driver per day. These regulations apply automatically to all express journeys by coach with stages over 50 kilometres. The controversial tachograph, introduced in the EU in 1970 and adopted by Britain in 1981, following the Passenger and Goods Vehicles Recording Equipment Regulations 1979, provides recorded evidence of hours of operation and vehicle speeds by individual drivers. While there can be little doubt that implementation of these regulations has led to higher safety standards in the industry, the effect has also been to increase the cost of long-haul coaching operations, making it more difficult to compete with rail or air services. To permit through journeys without expensive stopovers, two drivers must be carried; or, more commonly, since rest periods must be taken off the coach, drivers are exchanged at various stages of the journey. With the constraint of a limited number of seats on each coach, this pushes up costs per seat by a significant amount.

The financial security of coaching operations has been increased through the Confederation of Passenger Transport UK (formerly the Bus and Coach Council), requiring that members be bonded for 10 per cent of their touring turnover, as insurance against the financial collapse of a member.

DEREGULATION AND ITS AFTERMATH

Substantial changes occurred in the UK coach industry following the 1980 Transport Act, which ended the licensing regulations affecting express coach services on routes of more than 30 miles.

Prior to this, the licensing system favoured the development of national and regional oligopolies; the trunk routes were effectively controlled by three major carriers, the National Bus Company, Wallace Arnold and Ellerman Bee Line. National, however, dominated the market. Apart from these three, some 220 licensed coach companies shared the regional routes, the result of historical developments within the coaching industry. Companies wishing to compete with the established carriers had to apply for a licence to the Traffic Commissioners, who were generally prepared to consider granting one only where a new service was envisaged, or a new market tapped. Applications could be refused on the strength of existing operators' complaints that their business would suffer. This obviously inhibited competition, and there was little incentive for creative marketing. Similar restrictions applied to all coach tour operations (with the sole exception of tours operated by coach companies on behalf of overseas tour operators on which all passengers had been pre-booked abroad).

With the ending of regulation, a spate of new coach services of all types was introduced in 1981. A number of important regional coach companies came together to form British Coachways, a consortium designed to compete with the National Bus Company on the express routes. National responded to the challenge by expanding into the formerly restricted regional territories to compete with the monopolies there. British Rail became the immediate target of the coach operators, which introduced new, low-priced express services between major city centres, initially attracting a considerable amount of traffic away from British Rail, until that organisation responded with its own highly competitive discounted fares.

The chief beneficiary of deregulation appears to have been the National Bus Company, which was able to make substantial gains at the expense of its rivals through its ability to offer greater frequency of service and flexibility. With its huge fleet of coaches and a national network of routes, it was able at short notice to replace a defective vehicle with little inconvenience to its passengers, an advantage denied to its smaller rivals. However, smaller companies operating newer or 'unusual' vehicles (such as luxurious foreign-built coaches costing up to £250,000 apiece) provided the larger companies with some competition, although in time most companies found that, given the prices they were forced to charge to recover their investments, they simply could not generate adequate demand for the luxury coaches, and many suffered large losses due to these investments.

The British Coachways consortium was also unable to maintain its challenge to National Bus Company's operation, and went into liquidation in 1982. Fears were expressed that the cut-throat competition the coaches were being forced into would lead to falling standards of maintenance and safety. Few small companies had the resources to engage in a major price war.

Before deregulation, the market for coach services had been virtually static. The deregulation of the industry stimulated demand, but also led to an even greater supply of new coach seats on the market, with the result that load factors for most operators actually fell. While the National Bus Company was able to strengthen its market share of coaching operations, the Monopolies and Mergers Commission felt disinclined to investigate coach operations, taking the view that the coach operators' principal competitor was British Rail, and that competition between rail and coach was driving down fares.

A general concern about coach standards and quality control led in 1985 to the formation of the Guild of British Coach Operators, a commercial body whose aim was to promote high standards of service, safety and maintenance, and to reassure the travelling public of the continuing benefits of travel by coach.

Subsequently, the 1985 Transport Act set the scene for almost total deregulation of Britain's bus industry by the end of 1986, opening to competition all local bus routes outside London (provision for later deregulation in London was made in the Act). Passenger Transport Executives and district councils were required to transfer their bus companies to private companies covered by the Companies Act. The Transport Act had two important implications for the tourist industry. First, it required the break-up and privatisation of the sixty subsidiaries of the National Bus Company, providing small bus operators with greater scope to compete with the former NBC empire. This process, which was completed in 1988, led to the establishment of seventy-two separate companies, more than half of which were sold to their own management. Second, the resulting competition on the short bus routes led to an overall growth in the number of vehicles, for which operators tried to find alternative uses outside of peak travel periods. Equally, of course, the long-distance coach operators became free to operate their equipment on bus routes.

While the Act led to random fluctuations in fares, as bus companies competed in the lucrative city commuter routes, no systematic change in pricing policy has become evident. The major result of the Act has been the reinforcement of an oligopolistic market among the national carriers which bears comparison with the deregulation of the US airlines a decade earlier. The beneficiaries of deregulation were, firstly, National Express, the company formed out of the erstwhile National Bus Company which not only retained its identity in the long-distance route market, but went on to establish Eurolines as a division of its continental services, at the same time buying out rival Euroways from Wallace Arnold in 1988. Secondly, deregulation saw the phenomenal rise of Stagecoach, a small private company which, through acquisitions, was to become one of Britain's leading bus and coach companies by the 1990s. Finally, a third company appeared on the scene, First Bus (later renamed FirstGroup), which, through acquisitions of prominent local companies such as Badger Line in the South West, was to form the third major force in this triumvirate. This company also invested in railways, operating the Great Eastern Railway and a stake in Great Western Trains. In 1997 they also bought a major shareholding in Bristol Airport.

Concentration also occurred in the package coaching business, with Wallace Arnold taking over the Bee Line operation and forming a powerful competitor to Shearings, the other market leader. Shearings itself attempted to take over Wallace Arnold in 1997, but was unsuccessful.

Thus the pattern in the coaching industry has been that deregulation, just as with the US airline industry deregulation a decade earlier, has had the opposite effect to that intended, by favouring the establishment of a handful of major carriers on trunk routes. However, British coach deregulation also led to a significant involvement by these leading companies in the UK railway network, following the privatisation of rail services. National Express took a financial interest in the Eurostar services providing rail connections with the Continent, while Stagecoach also took over some domestic rail services in the face of considerable public concern about the danger of a monopoly developing in the transport operations of some areas of the country.

On the international scene, an interesting development has been the growth of 'shuttle' services between Britain and the Continent. These international stage journeys enjoyed a huge boom in the early 1980s, although profitability went into sharp decline in 1984, with a narrowing of the differential between coach and air fares. Subsequently, profitability recovered, due to a decline in capacity and price increases.

The success of coach tours to the Continent from Britain tends to depend upon the relative strength of sterling against Continental currencies, and on the differential between air and coach fares. With the recovery of the pound in 1997, coach holidays experienced an upturn, following the setbacks of the early 1990s when sterling was weak.

Also on the international scene, mention should be made of the importance of coach operations in North America. Two powerful coach companies, Greyhound Lines and Continental Trailways, dominated the domestic coach market in the USA, and their low fares enabled them to compete successfully against both the huge network of domestic air services and the private car. However, in 1982, road passenger transport was also deregulated in the USA, leading to a flood of small low-priced coach companies, against which neither of the two giants could compete. Trailways cut services in an effort to remain profitable, but ultimately merged, under new management, with the Greyhound Corporation in 1987. The restructuring of the company and the introduction of new vehicles, including minibuses, appear to have halted the decline of the latter company.

Finally, it is worth mentioning the Gray Line organisation, an American franchise offering coach excursions and tours not only within the USA and Canada, but also in numerous other countries. Franchising globally on this scale is a comparative rarity in the tourism business, but offers a pointer to the possible direction which the industry will take in the future, as large companies go multinational.

The private car

Undoubtedly, the increase in private car ownership has done more to change travel habits than any other factor in tourism. It provided families in particular with a new freedom of movement, with increased opportunities to take day excursions as well as longer trips. From the 1950s onwards, the costs of motoring fell in relative terms, and car owners also tended to take into account only the direct costs of a motoring trip, rather than the full cost which would include depreciation and wear and tear. Thus, car transport was favoured over public transport.

The effect of this preference on the travel industry has been considerable. The hotel and catering industry responded by creating motels, roadside cafés and restaurants, while formerly remote hotels and restaurants suddenly benefited from their new accessibility to the tourist. Car ferry services all over Europe flourished, and countries linked by such services experienced a visitor boom (France remains, for the British, the leading holiday destination, being seen primarily as a destination for the independent and mobile tourist). Camping and caravan holidays also boomed, and tour operators reacted by creating flexible self-drive car packages, including packaged camping and 'gîte'-style holidays in France. Fly-drive and rail-drive packages were introduced. In the USA, a market developed for motor homes or motorised caravans, which have become widely known in that country as RVs (recreational vehicles). These originated with the invention of the Curtiss Aerocar in the 1930s, but have grown in popularity to a point where today some 25 million Americans make use of them each year. The industry responded by providing new and more luxurious camping facilities, with the franchise company Kampgrounds of America ensuring water and electricity were available on all sites. The railways, too, adapted to meet the needs of the motoring tourist, introducing motorail services which allowed tourists to take their cars by rail with them on longer journeys, such as to the South of France.

In the 1990s, the desire for greater flexibility, coupled with the introduction of the Channel Tunnel, suggests that the demand for motoring holidays is unlikely to fall, providing energy costs do not increase dramatically. However, this growth is by no means entirely beneficial for tourism. The need for new roads to cater for the explosion in car ownership has meant that many by-passes have been built around towns and villages. Apart from the environmental damage

Figure 9.7 A line-up of coaches from seven countries at Oslo's famous Vigeland Sculpture park. *(Photographed by the author)*

sustained by the countryside, this also has the effect of discouraging the impulse visitor from stopping and spending money in the towns. At the same time, the expansion of motoring and private car ownership in a small country such as Britain is leading to enormous problems of pollution and congestion. In 1996, car ownership in Britain stood at 21.5 million, with sixty-seven vehicles for every kilometre of road in the country (compared with an EU average of forty-four). Forecasts indicate a rise to 25 million by the end of the century, and 31 million by the year 2025. Small resorts and scenic attractions cannot expand sufficiently to meet the demand for access and parking facilities without damaging the environment which the motorist has come to see. The growing interest in our society in ecologically friendly tourism will inevitably discourage motorists from taking their cars to such destinations. Greater control can be expected in the future through developments such as 'park and ride' schemes, already provided at congested resorts like Bath, Oxford and St Ives in Cornwall, which require visitors to park their cars outside the resort and use public transport to travel into the centre. Much greater interest is also being shown in the 1990s in bicycle tourism, which is seen as ecologically friendly, and several specialist holiday firms have been established in recent years to cater for those seeking organised cycling holidays in Britain and on the Continent. There are fears that the rise in car numbers on rural roads, resulting from drivers seeking relief from the growing congestion on trunk roads in Britain, will make cycling far more dangerous on such roads, and will discourage the individual cycling holiday. Efforts are being made to compensate for this by creating new traffic-free cycle routes, and Millennium funding has been provided by the British government towards the construction of a 6,500-mile network of cycle routes throughout the UK. The first stages of these routes are to be seen in Fig 9.8.

THE CAR RENTAL BUSINESS

It has been estimated that there are over 1,000 car hire companies operating in Britain, with more than 130,000 cars available for hire (many being fleet cars on hire to private companies). The car rental business owes a substantial proportion of

Figure 9.8 Traffic-free routes due to be in place for cyclists by the year 2000 in the UK

its revenue (and in resorts, virtually all its revenue) to the tourist. While in total only 30–40 per cent of car hire is associated with leisure, small companies and local car hire operators get a disproportionate share of this, while the large corporations have the lion's share of the business travel market.

Car rental companies can be divided into two categories:

1. the large international companies, or franchise operators
2. small, generally locally based independent hire companies.

Most of the larger companies charge broadly similar prices, but offer a choice of cars, hiring locations, and flexibility (for example, the ability to pick up a car at one location and drop it at another). This flexibility and convenience makes them more attractive to business travellers, who are less sensitive to price, but who insist on speed of service, reliability and a more luxurious standard of car.

On the other hand, there are literally hundreds of small local hirers, who generally offer limited choice but low price and the convenience of a local pick-up – although perhaps from only one or two locations. Because of their reliance on the leisure market, these operators work in a highly seasonal business, where they may be unable to maximise their opportunities for business in summer because they have insufficient vehicles. In addition, there are a handful of specialist car hire operators who provide very luxurious vehicles, high-powered sports cars, or even classic vehicles, for a small up-market leisure or business clientele.

The competitive nature of the industry has once again resulted in good marketing playing a key role in the success of individual car rental companies. The expansion of outlets has been greatly aided by the introduction of franchising – Budget was the first car hire company to franchise in Britain, as long ago as the 1960s, but all the large corporations now do so. Three other factors have been critical:

1 Contracts with airports and railways. This allows the car rental company to maintain a desk at the airport or terminal. Opportunities for business which are provided by desk space in these locations make contracts very lucrative, and they are fought for between the major corporations, occasionally changing as competitors offer higher bids at the termination of a contract agreement.
2 *Links with airlines and hotels.* This establishes good relations with, and hence referrals from, hotel chains and larger airlines, generates huge volumes of business, and is critical for maximising sales opportunities for business travel bookings. Large hotel chains may also offer desk space for the car rental company in their reception area.
3 *Computer Reservations Systems (CRS).* The development of a good CRS (and increasingly

Global Distribution Systems – GDSs), together with accessibility to these systems via major airline GDSs such as SABRE or GALILEO, plays an increasingly important role in the success of the larger car rental companies, which cannot afford not to be linked to major systems. Some car rental systems are now starting to take live bookings on the Internet; this form of reservation, which will be extended to the general public also, will play an increasing role in car rental sales in the future, and will have an impact on travel agency sales.

Car rental companies also court the travel agents, who can provide a good proportion of advance sales for business and leisure travel. Attractive rates of commission of 15 per cent or more are offered to gain agency support. However, a comparatively small proportion of bookings for car rental are made through the trade in the UK, when compared with the USA. The growing 'seat only' airline reservations market has helped to expand the demand for car hire overseas, as has the increasing confidence shown by British package tourists abroad in hiring cars at their destination.

The car hire business in the UK was severely damaged by the recession in the early 1990s. Estimates of the number of closures suggest that these could have been as high as 500 locations, and competition continues to keep prices low, in spite of increased costs. In 1992, most car manufacturers, themselves suffering in the recession, withdrew the special subsidies they provided to car rental firms, increasing the difficulties for the industry.

QUESTIONS AND DISCUSSION POINTS

1 How successful have the newly privatised railways been in tapping into the potential tourist market in the UK? What major changes affecting tourists have there been as a result of the changeover to privatisation? Could the railways do more to tap this market?
2 In the early years of the Channel Tunnel, a great deal of criticism was expressed about the marketing of the Eurostar and le Shuttle services.

What problems did customers of the Tunnel experience and have they now been overcome?

3   Given the forecasted increases in private cars on the British roads by early in the twenty-first century, how will the country cope with this increase? What action has been taken to implement an integrated transport system since the election of the Labour government in 1997? Evaluate the likely success in particular of (a) road pricing, and (b) motorway tolls as means of improving the transport system. How would the introduction of such systems affect tourists visiting Britain?

ASSIGNMENT TOPICS

1   As a member of the planning team of Universe Tours, a company specialising in coaching holidays on the Continent, you have been asked by your boss to investigate the possibility of running a new series of tours to the former Eastern Bloc countries of Poland, Hungary and the Czech and Slovak Republics. Undertake research to identify the main attractions for the British market in these countries, and plan at least three different tours, with a maximum length of 14 days, to one or more of the countries. You should also discover any possible pitfalls of arranging tours to these areas, and bring these to the attention of your manager in the report.

2   Universe Tours is considering whether to move their clients between Britain and the Continent by Eurotunnel or by ferry. Investigate the relative advantages and disadvantages of each, together with prices, and prepare a short report for your manager outlining your recommendations, and giving your reasons.

3   You are employed with a small in-coming tour company based in London, dealing mainly with the American market. Your boss has asked you to draft a sales letter which will be sent to leading American tour companies with which your organisation works, explaining that you are starting to provide, from next year, a new programme of tours by rail in Britain, using chartered trains and carriages. Write the letter, concentrating on the appeal of a rail journey, the benefits it could offer and why the American tourist could be expected to enjoy it. The letter should close with a sales pitch which will ensure that the operator comes back to you for more information – the principal aim of your message.

10

The Hospitality Sector: Accommodation and Catering Services

OBJECTIVES

After studying this chapter, you should be able to:

- explain the structure and nature of the hospitality sector, distinguishing between the various categories of tourist accommodation and catering services;
- describe how accommodation is classified and the problems involved in classification;
- understand the nature of demand for accommodation, and how the sector has responded to changing patterns of demand over time;
- be aware of the relationship between the hospitality sector and other sectors of the tourism industry.

Introduction

In this chapter, we are principally concerned with examining the commercial accommodation and catering sector. It must not be forgotten, however, that this sector must compete with a large non-commercial hospitality supply which is equally important to tourism. The VFR (visiting friends and relations) market is substantial, and in addition there is a wide variety of other forms of accommodation used by tourists, including the tourists' own camping and caravanning equipment, privately owned boats and even second homes, of which there are more than 70,000 in the UK alone. There is also a growing market for home exchanges, and the swapping of timeshare accommodation, which the industry has encouraged through the establishment of timeshare exchange companies.

It is, in fact, difficult to distinguish between the strictly commercial and non-commercial aspects of the hospitality business. Youth hostels and YMCAs, for example, are not necessarily attempting to make a profit, but merely to recover their operating costs, while it is increasingly common to find educational institutions such as universities and schools hiring out their student accommodation to tourists outside the academic terms, in order to make some contribution to the running costs of the institutions.

Other forms of tourism which by their nature embrace accommodation would include privately hired yachts, or bookings on a cruise; and, as we saw in the previous chapter, there are certain forms of long-distance coach operation which include sleeping berths, while in many countries it is possible to take a holiday on a specially chartered train which also serves as the tourists' hotel throughout the trip. To what extent should all these services be counted as elements of the commercial accommodation available to tourists? Certainly, any study of tourism must take account of these forms of overnighting. Tourists staying in private accommodation away from their homes are nonetheless engaging in tourism, and may also be making a contribution to the tourism spend of the region, through their spend on local travel and entertainment. They must therefore be counted in the tourism statistics for the region. Apart from this, they may also be commercially exploited. Tour operators, for instance, provide flight-only sales to meet the needs of those who own villas and apartments abroad, while airlines, recognising that home exchanges can represent a healthy source of flight revenue, have developed and commercialised the home exchange business by establishing directories to assist people in arranging exchanges. Some national or regional tourist offices keep directories of home owners who are prepared to make exchanges, and others maintain lists of local householders willing to invite guests from overseas into their homes for a meal (a particular feature of US hospitality).

The structure of the accommodation sector

The accommodation sector comprises widely differing forms of sleeping and hospitality facilities which can be conveniently categorised as either serviced (in which catering is provided) or self-catering. These are not watertight categories, as some forms of accommodation, such as holiday camps or educational institutions, may offer serviced, self-service or self-catering facilities, but they will help in drawing distinctions between the characteristics of the two categories. Figure 10.1 provides an at-a-glance guide to the range of accommodation which a tourist might occupy.

Hotels are the most significant and widely recognised form of overnight accommodation. They also form one of the key elements of most package holidays. However, what constitutes a hotel and distinguishes it from other forms of accommodation is not always clear. The English Hotel Occupancy Survey defines it as an establishment having five or more bedrooms, not identified as a guesthouse or boarding house and not listed as providing bed and breakfast accommodation only. *Travel and Tourism Intelligence* estimates the total stock of beds in the world at around 12.6 million, with an average occupancy level of 44 per cent, while the UK, with around 440,000 rooms, holds just under 3.5 per cent of this stock.

A feature of the industry is that, as mass tourism has developed, so have the large chains and corporations in the accommodation sector. The hotel and motel business has reached a stage

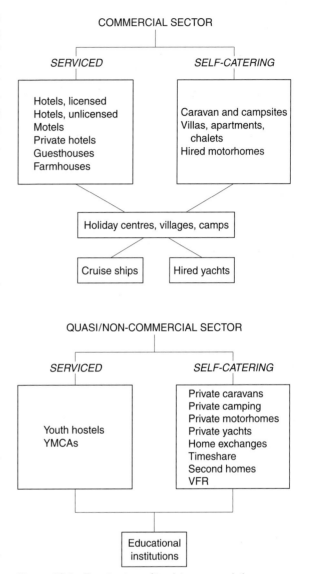

Figure 10.1 The structure of tourist accommodation

of maturity in which a few major companies have come to dominate the international market. In Britain, about a third of hotels with eleven or more rooms are now part of big chains, mainly British-owned, and similar patterns can be detected in other developed countries. This expansion has been achieved not only through direct ownership, but also through the process of franchising, whereby hotels and motels are operated by individual franchisees paying royalties to the parent company for the privilege of operating under a brand name. This form of expansion has been used with great success around the world by the largest international hotel company, Holiday Inns. Since these chains market their products more aggressively, advertising extensively, working closely with large tour operating organisations globally and providing an effective distribution network using computer reservations systems linked to the airline CRSs, they tend to play an even more significant role in the industry than their market share might suggest. (In total bed terms, their accommodation is still minimal by comparison with the many small independently owned facilities, which have less ready access to the other sectors of the tourism industry.)

STYLES OF HOTEL ACCOMMODATION

Leading world chains include the American companies Marriott, Hyatt, Ramada, Holiday Inns of North America and Sheraton. Such hotels aim to create an international and uniform marketing image to assist their sales around the world. Chains are also strong in Britain, with leading brands such as Granada (which absorbed Forte in 1996 and owns Meridien, Heritage and Exclusive Hotels, as well as the London Savoy), Mount Charlotte Hotels, Queens Moat Hotels, Hilton Hotels and Jarvis, but the French, who have expanded rapidly in the hotel business in the past decade, have become major players in the field and are creating a strong presence in the British market too. The largest French hotel company is the Accor group, which owns the Sofitel, Novotel, Mercure, Ibis, Formule 1 and Etap chains, and has brought a number of these brands to the UK, while the Envergure group, owners of the two-star Campanile Hotels along with the Première Classe, Bleu Marine and Clarine chains, has been expanding the Campanile chain rapidly in the UK. In the Pacific Rim area hotel mega-chains such as the Mandarin group are also becoming well established in the international tourism market. As with other sectors of the tourism industry, there is a growing belief that a handful of mega-chains such as these will come to dominate the world tourist market within a few years, while independents will seek to exploit niche marketing opportunities.

A recent trend within the large chains has been

Figure 10.2 The new budget hotels: a B&B chain hotel at Joue le Tours, France. *(Photographed by the author)*

concentration on the development of budget-price properties, long left to the independent sector. In Britain, well-established leisure corporations such as Granada or catering subsidiaries of the big brewers like the Beefeater chain were leaders in this development. On the Continent, Accor Hotels developed the super-budget chains Formule 1 and Etap, and other low-budget names such as B&B Hotels, Mister Bed, Villages Hotels, Unhotel and Fimotel are also expanding in France. The very low-priced hotels in France have managed to reduce costs by developing a unitary design and automating many of the services provided; reception desks are only manned for short periods of the day, and at other times entry is by the insertion of credit cards into a machine on the external wall. Similarly, breakfasts are self-service and highly automated. The introduction of this style of hotel into the UK has not been simple; land costs push up prices in Britain, while furnishings and service appeared too basic for the British market: for example, carpet soon replaced the linoleum which French hotel guests seemed more willing to accept.

The large hotels, as they develop different market niches, are increasingly employing branding to distinguish their products and to position them in the minds of the public. Holiday Inns, for example, now offers the Crowne Plaza brand for its global 'upper-middle' market, its Express brand for the 'upper-economy' US middle market and its Garden Court brand for the 'upper-economy' European middle market. At the other end of the market, the competition between luxury hotels is leading to market segmentation, introducing country house hotels with the emphasis on personal atmosphere, or all-suite hotels such as those provided by Marriott in the USA and Hilton's Conrad Hotel in London. The days of the monolithic concrete block, favoured in the development of new resorts in the Mediterranean and elsewhere in order to permit rapid construction and cheap operation, are ending, as the sophisticated travel market seeks better service and more character in their lodgings.

Hotels that can offer attributes that are unique to the country visited are enjoying much greater popularity. The *paradores* in Spain, or the *pousadas* of Portugal, national chains of state-operated inns located in historic properties, are proving highly successful in spite of their premium prices, while traditional haciendas in Mexico and the ryokans of Japan, which offer an authentic flavour of the country's culture, greatly appeal to the independent travel market. In Britain, individual character properties owned by the National Trust, the Landmark Trust and similar organisations are greatly in demand: one of the National Trust's most popular properties is Peel Bothy, a tiny former shepherd's home at Steel Rigg, Northumberland offering only very basic facilities – but seen as full of character.

In an effort to counteract the influence of the large chains, a number of independent hotels have banded together to form marketing consortia which will allow them to obtain some of the economies of scale achieved by the large chains, such as benefits of mass purchasing or mass marketing. Some of these consortia, such as Best Western Hotels and Inter Hotels, now operate on a global scale, while other national brands, such as Flag Hotels of Australia, have established a strong image in their overseas marketing. Similarly, some of the leading privately owned hotels in Britain have banded together to create consortia in order to market themselves more effectively at home and abroad. This is a highly appropriate strategy when developing a niche approach; for example, 'Small Luxury Hotels of the World' has focused on building an image of high-standard but personal hotels around the UK, while Grand Heritage Hotels, an American-owned

Figure 10.3 The stately home as commercial accommodation: The Lords of the Manor Hotel, Upper Slaughter, Gloucestershire. *(Photographed by the author).*

consortium which is now drawing membership from high-graded UK hotels, emphasises luxury and status.

For the business traveller, the concept of town house hotels has proved popular in large cities; they now constitute around 10 per cent of all the hotel beds in London. These provide a more personal and homely atmosphere for the businessperson away from home, with the emphasis on private space rather than public facilities. Other developments for the business traveller include designer hotels, which attempt to get away from the bland, often mediocre furnishings of the international hotel chains by incorporating interior decor themes styled by top designers. As brand image has become more important in marketing hotels, so are hotels attempting to distance themselves from their competitors through the use of innovative design, both internally and externally.

For the leisure traveller, the switch away from faceless concrete hotels of the 1950s and 1960s coincides with a rising interest in the country cottage style of accommodation, which is now being exploited by major tour operators. This may be a direct outcome of the interest in French gîte accommodation in the 1980s. Another grouping, 'Mansions and Manors' consists of around 200 manor house owners who will offer bed and breakfast accommodation on a selective basis to the 'right kind of clients' but do not wish to commercialise their product or advertise it directly to the public. This product is therefore marketed directly through tour operators in the USA.

CLASSIFYING AND GRADING ACCOMMODATION

It is no simple matter to differentiate between accommodation units of differing types and standards. The process of classification in the hotel and catering industry, either for purposes of legislation or for the systematic examination of business activity, has been attempted on several occasions in Britain in the past (for example, under the Standard Industrial Classification System). The purpose of these attempts was mainly to distinguish hotels and other residential establishments from sundry catering activities. Statistics seldom distinguish, for example, between guests staying at hotels and motels. Within the small independent sector, the problem is even greater. There is a broad spectrum of private accommodation which ranges from the 'private hotel', through boarding house and guesthouse accommodation to bed and breakfast establishments, and in Britain, under law there is no clear distinction between the private hotel and the boarding house. The only distinction between these two and the guesthouse is that the latter will have not more than four bedrooms, or accommodation for a maximum of eight guests. This distinction is important for legislative purposes, but need not concern us further here. However, tourists are interested not only in what different grades of hotel offer in the way of facilities, but also in the *quality* of the accommodation and catering they are being offered. To clarify these features, we need to distinguish between three terms: categorisation, classification and grading. Although these terms are often used interchangeably, the following are their widely accepted definitions:

(a) *Categorisation* refers to the separation of accommodation by type, that is, distinguishing between hotels, motels, boarding houses, guesthouses, etc.

(b) *Classification* distinguishes accommodation on the basis of certain physical features, such as the number of rooms with private bath or shower, etc.

(c) *Grading* identifies accommodation according to certain *verifiable objective features of the service offered*, such as the number of courses served at meals, whether 24-hour service is provided, etc.

Readers will note that none of these refers to the assessment of quality, which calls for subjective evaluation, and is therefore far more difficult – and more costly – to validate, especially when standards, particularly in catering, can change so rapidly over time.

Provision was made under the Development of Tourism Act 1969 for the compulsory classification and grading of hotel accommodation in Britain, but this was widely resisted by the industry itself, and the British Tourist Authority made no attempt to impose it, instead relying upon a system of voluntary registration first introduced in 1975. The separate National Tourist Boards of England, Scotland and Wales were left to devise their own individual schemes; however, urged on by the Scottish Tourist Board in particular, the three boards in 1987 agreed a common scheme which graded hotels into six categories: either 'listed', for the most basic property, or with from one to five 'crowns', depending upon the facilities offered. The system remained a voluntary one, but hotels taking part received regular checks from inspectors, and could only display their blue and white signboard or advertise in Regional Tourist Board publications after they had been approved. The hotels are charged an annual fee. While the system was clearly an improvement on the previous form of classification, in which the hotels themselves were responsible for advising the tourist boards of the facilities they provided, because it remained voluntary, only a very small proportion of the total accommodation sector in Britain became registered.

Two years later, the boards agreed a unified system of grading quality, additionally awarding the symbols 'Approved', 'Commended', 'Highly Commended' or 'Deluxe' in ascending order of quality. This was planned to take into account such subjective issues as hospitality, service, food and decor. These awards take no account of the facilities or status of the unit, which allows even a humble 'listed' unit to be rated as 'Deluxe', if meeting the quality criterion. Other types of accommodation subsequently received symbols, too; moons were awarded to lodges, keys to self-catering accommodation, and 'Q's to holiday centres. Wales, however, chose to develop its own scheme separately from England and Scotland.

Figure 10.4 Contrasts in accommodation: a) hotel in London. (*Courtesy Holiday Hospitality*); b) bed and breakfast in the country. (*Courtesy Scottish Tourist Board*)

The self-catering scheme was applied to a range of different units, including cottages, flats, bungalows, houseboats and chalets, and quality was assessed using the same form of assessment as was used for the hotels. Grading became based on such features as the appearance of the building, the decor and lighting, heating and furnishing, floor coverings, and the crockery and utensils provided.

This system also proved far from satisfactory, given that the private sector had devised its own schemes for grading hotels, some national, some international in scope, and these were often more widely recognised by members of the public than were the public sector designations. Of the private sector schemes, the best known in Britain were those offered by the two motoring assocations, the AA and RAC, both of which provided a star rating. In addition to these schemes, there were a number of guides on the market which provided subjective assessment of catering in hotels and other establishments, of which the best known are the *Michelin Guide*, *Egon Ronay's Guide* and the *Good Food Guide*.

Over the years, further attempts were made to introduce legislation for a common grading scheme for hotels. The harmonisation process within the EU gave an additional boost to these initiatives. Although some member countries do impose compulsory registration within their own borders, different grading schemes have been in use throughout the EU, each involving different criteria, so the problems of standardising within Europe remain. Clearly, however, no attempt to standardise throughout the EU could be considered unless the UK could itself put forward an agreed standard within its own boundaries. Consequently, talks were held in 1996 between the tourist board representatives and the two motoring organisations in order to try to achieve a commonly recognised system throughout the UK. The outcome of these talks was only a partial success. The English Tourist Board and the two motoring organisations agreed to adopt a common scheme from the year 2000, based on hotel ratings of one to five stars; the Scottish Tourist Board rejected the scheme on the principle that they wished to lay greater emphasis on quality rather than facilities, and therefore adopted their own scheme in parallel, to operate from 1999. Wales is expected, at the time of writing, to follow the Scottish Tourist Board's lead. In consequence, Britain remains without a commonly agreed scheme, nor will any attempt be made to register hotels compulsorily for the foreseeable future. However, agreement was reached between the three boards and the motoring organisations to adopt a common classification scheme for bed and breakfast establishments from the year 2000.

As far as common systems across Europe are concerned, the British Hospitality Association feels that comparisons between hotels of similar status in different countries are virtually impossible to make. There are further complications, for example, in the fact that some countries impose higher rates of VAT on their five-star properties, making it unattractive for hotels in those nations to upgrade their property, even if standards were comparable with a five-star property in Britain. In the meantime, tour operators have devised their own systems of assessing those properties used on package tours abroad, to meet the needs of their own clients, leading to additional confusion among the travelling public. Thomson Holidays, for example, uses its 'T-rating', based in part on its own customers' assessment of the accommodation.

The nature of demand for accommodation facilities

The hotel product is made up of five characteristics: its location, its mix of facilities (which will include bedrooms, restaurants, other public rooms, function rooms and leisure facilities); its image; the services it provides (including such indefinable features as the level of formality, personal attention, speed and efficiency of its staff); and the price which it is prepared to charge.

The location of a hotel will invariably be the first consideration, when the tourist is selecting a hotel. Location implies both the destination (resort for the holidaymaker, convenient stopover point for the traveller, city for the business traveller) and the location within that destination. Thus businesspeople will want to be accommodated in a city-centre site close to the company they are visiting, while the seaside holidaymaker will seek an affordable hotel as close as possible to the beach, and transit travellers will want to be accommodated at a hotel convenient to the airport from which they are leaving. In economic terms, a trade-off will occur between location and price, as the leisure traveller looks for the hotel closest to the beach which still fits the budget, or the transit traveller will opt for a more distant hotel which is prepared to offer a free transfer to the airport. Location is, of course, fixed for all time; if the resort itself loses its attraction for its visitors, the hotel will suffer an equivalent decline in its fortunes.

The fact that high fixed costs are incurred in both building and operating hotels compounds the risk of hotel operating. City-centre sites are extremely expensive to purchase and operate, requiring high room prices. The market may resist such prices, but is nevertheless reluctant to be based at any distance from the centres of activity, even when good transport is available. This has been evidenced in the problems faced by incoming tour operators in accommodating American visitors in central London at prices competitive with other city centres. The reluctance of many overseas tour operators to base their clients in accommodation on the outskirts of the city has led to loss of business in favour of other European capital cities.

Again, the demand for central London hotels, leading to high capacity and profits, has caused those in the hotel business to maximise profits by upgrading their accommodation and appealing to the business client, rather than catering for the leisure tourist's demand for budget accommodation. The French Accor Group was among the first to identify this market gap and as we have seen, set about catering for the lower-price bracket with its Formule 1 and Etap brands.

Hotels will seek to maximise their revenue by offering a wide range of different tariffs to different market segments they serve. By way of example, one city hotel provides, apart from the normal rack rate, at least nine other rates, including special concessions to corporate bookings, conference rates, air crew, weekender traffic and tour bookings. In the climate of recession experienced by hotels in the early 1990s, it has also been possible for clients to negotiate substantial discounts if they book late in the day: the hotel management, recognising that any sale is better than none, allows the desk clerks to come to an agreement on any realistic offer, which may be as much as 50 per cent lower than rack rate.

Hotel companies may be further constrained by the need to meet building codes present in the location where they are building. Increasingly, concern about the environment, and widespread recognition of the damage done to the architectural styles of resorts swamped by high-rise hotel building have led local authorities to impose stringent regulations on new buildings. This may mean

Figure 10.5 International hotel chains designed to complement the vernacular architecture of their cities: a) Ibis Hotel, Belgium; b) Novotel Hotel, Belgium. *(Photographed by the author)*

using local (often more expensive) materials in place of concrete, limiting the height of hotels to four or five floors (some tropical destinations restrict hotel building to the height of the local palm trees), or restricting the total size of the building to ensure it is in keeping with surrounding buildings (see Figure 10.5).

SOME CHARACTERISTICS OF THE HOTEL PRODUCT

The demand for hotel bedrooms will come from a widely distributed market, nationally or internationally, whereas the market for other facilities which the hotel offers will often be highly localised. In addition to providing food and drink for its own residents, the hotel will be marketing these services to other tourists or members of the local population at a short distance from the site. Clearly, a very different market segment will be involved, calling for different marketing techniques of advertising, promotion and distribution.

Another characteristic of the hotel product is that it is seldom uniformly in demand throughout the year. Tourist hotels suffer from seasonality, involving high demand during summer peaks and little or no demand during the winter troughs, while hotels catering chiefly to businesspeople may find business dropping off during the summer. Business hotels also suffer from periodic-

ity, in which demand is focused on the Monday to Thursday nights, while there is little demand from Friday to Sunday night. The lack of flexibility in room supply, coupled with the perishable nature of the product (if rooms are unsold there is no opportunity to 'store' them and sell them later) mean that greater efforts must be made to unload unsold accommodation by attracting the off-peak customer, or the leisure market to business hotels at weekends.

Even with creative marketing and high discounting, many tourist hotels in highly seasonal resorts will find their occupancy levels falling alarmingly in the winter, and must then face the decision whether it is better to stay open in the winter, in the hope of attracting enough customers to make some contribution to overheads, or to close completely for several months of the year. The problem with the latter course of action is that a number of hotel costs, such as rates, depreciation and salaries for management staff, will continue whether or not the hotel remains open. Temporary closure may also result in difficulties in recruiting good staff, if jobs are known to be only seasonal. In recent years, more hotels, especially the larger chain hotels, have opted to remain open, and to offer special packages for those willing to come off-season. The increase in second holidays and off-season short breaks in Britain has helped to make more hotels viable year-round, although room occupancy remains low out of season in many of the more traditional resorts. Here, the hotel sector is also heavily dependent on the extent to which the public sector is willing to invest in order to make the resort attractive out of season. Towns such as Bournemouth, through a process of continuous investment and a deliberate attempt to attract the conference and non-seasonal market, have been able to draw in a high number of winter tourists, making it possible for many more hotels to remain open year-round. This in turn stimulates further business, as local attractions and events are also encouraged to stay open throughout the year.

While we have talked chiefly in terms of the physical characteristics of the hotel, the psychological factors which attract the visitor are no less important. Service, 'atmosphere', even the other guests with whom the customer will come into contact, all play a role when the choice of hotel is made. Only about 22 per cent of British holiday-makers choose to stay at hotels or guesthouses when holidaying in the UK, compared with some 47 per cent who do so when abroad. This is obviously the result of the large VFR market in the UK, as well as the growing demand for camping, caravanning and self-catering holidays. According to the Overseas Visitors' Survey, 59 per cent of overseas visitors stay at hotels at some point when visiting the UK, although the pattern varies, and many will choose a variety of different forms of accommodation during their tour. Some 20 per cent choose to stay in bed and breakfast accommodation, with 14 per cent staying in unlicensed hotels or guesthouses. Factors such as class, age and lifestyle will also have a bearing on the choice of sleeping accommodation. In particular, the nature of, and consequent demand for, large hotels will be quite different from that of the small guesthouse or bed and breakfast unit. A large hotel may well provide attractions of its own, distinct from the location in which it is situated; indeed, in some cases the hotel may be a more significant influence on choice than the destination. This is often true of the large hotel/leisure complex providing a range of in-house entertainment as in the case of a number of North American and, increasingly, European hotels. Similarly, some hotels are so closely linked with the destination

Figure 10.6 The hotel–resort complex: Chateau Lake Louise, Banff National Park, Canada. *(Photographed by the author)*

they serve that the combination of stay at hotel/destination becomes the established pattern. This is seen in Canada, where resorts such as Lake Louise and the Chateau Lake Louise Hotel are inextricably linked (see Figure 10.6). This type of hotel and resort combination is still a rarity in Britain, although Gleneagles Hotel in Perthshire, Scotland, with its golfing links, provides one example. It is, however, increasingly a characteristic of the package holiday hotels in the 1990s, and has been taken a stage further with the growth of the 'all-inclusive' packaged hotel at which all food, drink and entertainment are included in the price. The Sandals Hotel chain based in the Bahamas and Caribbean was a major initiator in this development.

By way of contrast, a noticeable trend in recent years has been the fall-off among guests staying at non-licensed accommodation in the UK, although licensed hotels have been able to retain their overall share of the accommodation market.

The provision of a good range of attractions, as well as a drinks licence, can help to offset the disadvantages which result from the unavoidable impersonality of the large hotels. As the chains increase their hold on the total pool of hotel beds, an increase in the average number of rooms in each hotel follows, since larger hotels benefit from economies of scale. However, in Britain, hotels of more than 100 rooms remain the exception, and British hoteliers still emphasise the personal nature of their service as a feature of their marketing. As we have already noted, the trend to smaller hotels, as the travel market becomes more sophisticated, is hurting those resorts which have concentrated on building the modern concrete block style of mass market hotel; this is particularly noticeable in the former Soviet Union countries, where small hotels of Western standards are virtually unknown. However, the large hotel operators have been sensitive to changes in fashion, and in the USA, where change and novelty is a feature of market demand, hotel companies deliberately 'theme' their properties to distinguish them from others, either through the style of their architecture or their interior decoration. This, as was pointed out earlier in the chapter, is now becoming a common approach in expensive hotels around the world. The chains also provide in their budget for regular changes of decor to keep up-to-date. More traditional hotels have responded by emphasising their traditional values and style. With the current boom in nostalgia, older hotels which can retain the style of yesteryear while nevertheless incorporating modern features such as good plumbing which Western tourists demand, can find a ready market for their product. A good example here is the recently restored Raffles Hotel in Singapore, which reopened after an extensive facelift which successfully blended modern comforts with the traditional architecture of the colonial era.

Increasingly, the search for 'character' properties is leading consumers to seek something different in their sleeping arrangements, and this is being catered to, especially in the package holiday market. For example, long-haul travellers can book into an authentic and traditional native long house in Malaysia (that at Skrang, Sarawak, has been adapted for tourist use since 1981), while tourists to Canada have the choice of staying in a North American Indian tepee in Manitoba or an Inuit igloo in the Hudson Bay area. At Oak Alley, Georgia, the former slave quarters have been refurbished to accommodate tourists, while Bandera, Texas, offers a wide range of dude ranches. In Prague, the former secret police detention centre has become one of the most popular youth hostels in Europe, while Jukkasjärvi in Swedish Lappland provides visitors with an opportunity to sleep in a hotel carved entirely out

Figure 10.7 Contrasts in accommodation in India: (a) The Umaid Bhawan Palace, luxury hotel in Jodhpur and home of the Maharajah; (b) Basic overnight accommodation at Sam Dunes, near Jaisalmer; (c) Rotel Tours of Germany offer 'sleeping buses' on Indian tours. *(Photographed by the author)*

of ice – it is rebuilt each year after the summer thaw!

The point which must be emphasised here is that accommodation is seen by the customer as much more than simply a 'room to sleep in'. Rather, it is a total leisure experience, comprising a range of different services and emotional experiences which together go to make up the holiday or business stay.

THE DOMESTIC HOLIDAY HOTEL

The traditional British domestic holiday in a small seaside guesthouse or hotel has been under threat now for a number of years, and many of these types of accommodation unit have been forced out of business. First, there has been the steady trend to taking holidays abroad, where packages can often be no more expensive than in the UK, but provide much better value for money and, of course, guaranteed sunshine. As a result of their experience, British holidaymakers are now demanding the same facilities in their UK hotels as they found abroad, including better food, a better choice of entertainment, and a private bathroom. This has meant that hotel proprietors have faced a huge increase in capital investment in order to raise their standards; not all have been able to find the means to do so. The Section 4 grants available for hotel construction and improvement under the 1969 Development of Tourism Act were withdrawn in England in 1989 (although they continue in Scotland and Wales), and high interest rates made loans more difficult for hoteliers to consider. The introduction of the Uniform Business Rate (UBR) in 1990 had the effect of raising many hotels' rates at a time of recession when they could least afford such increases. The hoteliers' difficulties have been compounded by the trend for domestic holidays to be of shorter duration, even though short breaks have helped to extend the season. Shorter stays raise room costs, which cannot easily be recovered by higher prices, particularly in a recession where the market is extremely price-sensitive.

Liberalisation of the licensing laws in 1988, permitting alcoholic drinks to be served on weekday afternoons, has been one of the few rays of sunshine in an otherwise difficult period for the industry. This has also helped to boost sales in pubs and inns catering to the tourist, which can now compete more equally with their European neighbours. Traditional accommodation units also face the challenge of a shift to self-catering, both in Britain and abroad. This has come about partly in an effort to hold down holiday prices, but

of at least equal importance is the demand from tourists for more flexible types of accommodation and catering than have been available in the small hotels and boarding houses. The once-popular fully inclusive holiday comprising three meals a day, taken at fixed times of the day in the hotel, no longer meets the requirements of the modern tourist, who may wish to tour the surrounding area by car during the day, and will therefore want to eat irregularly, or even forgo a midday meal. Self-catering accommodation meets these needs effectively, and its popularity abroad with British tourists has led to rapid expansion of similar facilities in the UK, at the expense of the boarding houses. Many smaller hotels have adapted their premises to provide self-catering units in order to survive. Motels have also expanded in number to meet the need for flexibility in touring holidays – the UK has some 150 motels – but these units are really better suited to larger countries, where they serve the needs of the long-distance motorist travelling on a motorway network.

THE B&B UNIT

The increasing desire of many tourists, particularly overseas visitors to Britain, to 'meet the people' and enjoy a more intimate relationship with the culture of the country they are visiting has benefited the smallest forms of accommodation unit, such as the guesthouse or bed and breakfast establishment. These are generally family-run, catering to business tourists in the

Figure 10.8 A farm holiday. *(Courtesy Irish Tourist Board)*

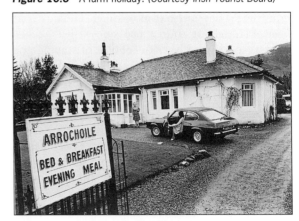

towns and to leisure tourists in the country towns, rural areas and the seaside. B&Bs in particular provide a very valuable service to the industry, in that they can offer the informality and friendliness sought by many tourists (many have no more than three bedrooms), cater for the impulse demand that results from holidaymakers touring by car or bicycle, and conveniently expand the supply of beds during peak periods of the year in areas which are highly seasonal, and where hotels would not be viable. There are estimated to be about 11,500 B&Bs in the UK, of which more than one-third have been certified under the tourist boards' grading systems. Most have six or fewer guests, since this obviates payment of business rates, and neither a fire certificate nor public liability insurance is required to operate.

This form of accommodation was virtually unknown in North America until relatively recently, but has boomed since the 1980s, as the Americans and Canadians brought back with them the experiences they had gained in Europe.

FARMHOUSE HOLIDAY ACCOMMODATION

Farmhouse holidays have also enjoyed considerable success in recent years, both in the UK and on the Continent. Farmers have catered for tourists for many years in Britain, but as they have found greater difficulties in paying their way through farming, with the reduction in agricultural subsidies, so they have turned increasingly to tourism as a means of boosting revenue, particularly in the off-season. A study of farm tourism carried out in 1991 reveals that 15 per cent of all farms in England (and 24 per cent in the West Country) have some form of tourism project on their land. The simultaneous trend to healthier lifestyles, and the appeal of natural food and the outdoor life, have also helped to make farm tourism popular. Within the Assisted Areas, and particularly in Wales, tourist boards have provided financial assistance and training for farmers interested in expanding their accommodation for tourism. Ireland and Denmark have both been notably successful in packaging modestly priced farm holidays for the international market, in association with tour operators and the ferry companies. In the case of Denmark, this has been a logical

development to attract tourists to what is generally recognised as an expensive country for holidays based on hotel accommodation.

The market for camping and caravanning holidays in the UK is substantial, with some 12 per cent of holidays in Britain taken in caravans in 1992, and a further 4 per cent in campsites. While many holidays are, of course, taken in private caravans (of which there are over 500,000 in Britain – down from a peak of 650,000 twenty years ago), caravan parks remain popular, and have become an accepted part of the holiday scene. Holiday parks entered the tourist boards' grading schemes in 1987, with the introduction of agreed codes of practice for operators, and quality designated by ticks (a maximum of five ticks can be awarded) accompanied by the letter 'Q' for quality. Over 1,000 caravan parks are so graded in the scheme. A trade body, the British Holiday and Home Parks Association (BH&HPA) has been formed to represent the interests of operators.

HOLIDAY CENTRES

Holiday camps were very much a British innovation, introduced on a major scale in the 1930s by three noted entrepreneurs, Billy Butlin, Fred Pontin and Harry Warner. The aim was to provide all-in entertainment at a low price in chalet-style accommodation which would be largely unaffected by inclement weather. The Butlin–Pontin–Warner style of holiday camp became enormously successful in the years prior to World War II and the early postwar era, but all three organisations have now been absorbed into large corporations. Market leader Butlins, with about two million guests a year and a 22 per cent share of this market (five sites), together with the joint Haven (fifty-one sites) and Warner (eleven sites) centres, were absorbed into the Rank Organisation in 1972 and 1991 respectively. Pontins (twenty-two sites) has been owned by Scottish and Newcastle Breweries since 1991.

For the most part, the balance of the market is split between a large number of independent companies operating a small number of sites. The market for holiday centres remains highly seasonal, falling almost entirely between May and September. It had been customary for centres to

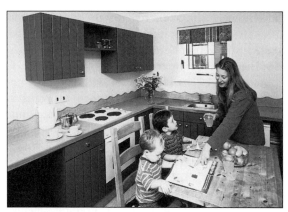

Figure 10.9 Butlin's three-star country suite accommodation. *(Courtesy Butlin's Holiday Worlds)*

close during the winter months, but improved marketing, including mini-breaks and themed events, has helped to extend sales into the 'shoulder' months of spring and autumn. As a percentage of the total accommodation used in domestic tourism, though, holiday centres are relatively insignificant.

Holiday centres have been affected as much as any other accommodation facilities by changes in public taste for holidays. Before the war, they attracted a largely lower-middle-class clientele, but in the postwar period their market became significantly more working-class, and the canteen-style catering service and entertainment provided reflected the needs of this market segment. Bookings were made invariably from Saturday to Saturday, and most clients booked direct with the companies. Each company had a quite distinct image for its clientele, who were strongly brand-loyal and booked regularly with their favourite company.

More recently, these camps have attempted to move up-market, a process heralded by a change in their names from camps to holiday centres, villages or parks. The former working-class orientation has been modified to cater for wider social tastes. Large chalet blocks have given way to smaller units with self-catering facilities. A choice of catering styles has been introduced, ranging from fully serviced through self-service to self-catering, the latter enjoying the greatest rates of growth. Butlins in particular have invested huge sums of money to redevelop their remaining five centres and give them a more up-market image, which was initially successful in

regenerating sales after a decline in trade for holiday centres during the early 1980s. However, sales are suffering in the mid-1990s, in the face of competition from the new wave of holiday centres, spearheaded by Center Parcs, which now have fourteen sites in Europe and offer a very different kind of holiday experience. Rank has itself entered this market with its Oasis Forest Holiday Village. At the time of writing, the company was seeking to combat the erosion of sales in its Butlins division by a massive new investment in three sites, at Minehead, Skegness and Bognor Regis, which will enable them to be relaunched with a new image in 1999; the other two sites, at Ayr and Pwllheli, are expected to revert to the Haven brand. The new Butlins image is not designed, however, to compete with the Oasis product, which is aimed at a different market.

THE NEW HOLIDAY VILLAGES

The Center Parcs phenomenon represents one of the most interesting developments in domestic holiday centres in the past two decades. The first of these up-market holiday villages was introduced into Britain in 1987, since when two further villages have been built in the UK. The Dutch company responsible for bringing this innovation to Britain operated a number of sites on the Continent, but later sold out to Scottish and Newcastle Breweries. Offering a wide choice of all-weather facilities (most notably a vast indoor pool designed to resemble a tropical beach), the villages had an extraordinary measure of success in their early years, with an average 96 per cent occupancy year-round. Later, competition from other large leisure companies, most notably the Rank Organisation with its Oasis Forest Holiday Village, has lowered occupancy and there is now some danger of overbuilding in this field. Oasis has plans to build a further village in Britain, if a suitable site is found.

Billy Butlin's early attempts to introduce his holiday camp concept to the Continent were unsuccessful, but the more up-market holiday village has been highly successful. Market leader is Club Méditerranée, French-owned and with a worldwide spread of holiday villages, from France to Tahiti. The success of this organisation, which started its package programmes in 1950, has been attributed to its unique approach to its clients, who are referred to as 'gentils membres'. It has been the practice for beads to be used instead of hard currency to purchase drinks on site; this has heightened the feeling for the holidaymakers of being 'divorced from the commercial world' while on holiday. However, this organisation has also experienced a decline in the latter half of the 1990s, having failed to keep pace with holiday centre development, and is currently undergoing a restructuring in an effort to restore its position in the holiday centre field.

SECOND HOME AND TIMESHARE OWNERSHIP

Some word is also appropriate here about the growth of second home ownership, which is influencing the tourism industry. In Britain, increasing disposable income, especially among those living in London and the South East, has led to massive growth in second home ownership, both within Britain and in overseas countries such as Spain, France and Greece. Where an outright purchase is beyond people's means, the concept of timeshare offers an alternative means of taking a holiday in one's second home in the UK or abroad. Estimates place timeshare ownership at around one million, with 37 per cent of properties located in the Canary Islands, 20 per cent elsewhere in Spain and 18 per cent in the UK. Together, this major new market has initiated substantial demand for seat-only sales on charter aircraft, and poses a new threat to the traditional accommodation sector – indeed, some hotels in Britain have responded to the challenge by converting some or all of their accommodation for timeshare ownership.

Timeshare is a scheme whereby an apartment or villa is sold to several co-owners, each of whom purchases the right to use the accommodation for a given period of the year, which may range from a week to several weeks. The initial cost of the accommodation will vary not only according to the length of time for which it is purchased, but also depending on the period of the year, so that a week in July or August, for example, may be three or four times the cost of the same accommodation in winter.

The scheme is reported to have been initiated at a ski resort in the French Alps in 1965, although the Ring Hotel chain in Switzerland was developing along similar lines some years before

this. By the early 1970s, timeshare had been introduced in the USA, and the concept had also arrived in Britain by the mid-1970s. Since then it has enjoyed enormous success, boosted by schemes allowing owners to exchange their properties for others around the world during their period of ownership. A number of timeshare exchange organisations have been established, of which the largest and best-known are RCI (Resort Condominiums International) and II (Interval International). These companies keep a register of owners, and for a fee will facilitate home exchanges around the world.

There are well over 2,000 timeshare resorts, with at least a hundred in the UK alone. Unfortunately, the sheer popularity of timeshare has led to high-pressure salesmanship by less reputable organisations using 'street touts' to approach tourists visiting resorts abroad, and this has led to some poor publicity for the scheme in the press. The Timeshare Developers' Association was formed to give the industry credibility, and to draw up a code of conduct for members, and since 1991 a Timeshare Council has overseen the regulation of timeshare within the UK. The Office of Fair Trading keeps a watching brief on development within the UK.

Timeshare is not without its problems. It has been found to be difficult to resell property, due to the amount of new timeshare property on the market, and in some cases management and maintenance fees have been high. There can be a problem in getting widely dispersed owners together to take decisions on the management of the property. Notwithstanding these difficulties, timeshare remains popular, and is likely to grow as a threat to the traditional package holiday.

EDUCATIONAL ACCOMMODATION

The significance of the educational accommodation sector must also be recognised. Universities and other institutions of higher education, seeking to increase the contributions to their revenue through the rental of student accommodation during the academic holidays, have marketed this accommodation for budget holidays to tour operators and others. Often situated in green field sites near major tourist destinations, such as Stirling or

York, the universities have experienced considerable success in this new venture, and have further expanded their involvement with the leisure market by providing other facilities such as activity centres and public rooms for themed holidays. More than 1.5 million holidays are now sold each year in the UK using the accommodation of educational institutions.

The distribution of accommodation

Large hotel chains enjoy substantial advantages in gaining access to their markets. Many international chains have close links, through ownership or financial interest, with the airlines, a situation dating back to the early 1970s when airlines, introducing their new jumbo jets, hastily set about establishing connections with hotels to accommodate their increasing passenger numbers. This relationship today gives the hotel chains access to the airlines' Global Distribution Systems (GDSs), computerised reservations networks which constitute a vital factor in selling rooms to the international market.

Large hotels depend upon group as well as individual business, so they must maintain contact with tour operators, conference organisers and others who bulk-buy hotel bedrooms. The tourist boards can play a part in helping such negotiations by organising workshops abroad to which the buyers of accommodation and other facilities will be invited.

Virtually all of the larger hotel chains, and many smaller hotel companies, have today installed their own computer reservations systems to cope with worldwide demand for immediate confirmation on availability and reservations. Some chains maintain their own offices in key generating countries (and of course each hotel will recommend business and take reservations for others in the chain), while independent hotels reach the overseas markets through membership of marketing consortia or through representation by a hotel representative agency. These hotel representatives are not merely booking agents; they are on contract to the hotels they represent and will offer a complete marketing service. Some agencies, such as William R Galley Associates, R M Brooker and Utell International, generalise in the hotels they represent, while others specialise, either choosing to represent hotels within a specific geographic area such as the Caribbean (as does Windotel), or dealing with niche market hotels, such as smaller, 'character' hotels.

Sales made through hotel representatives are normally commissionable at 10 per cent to the representative. This does not prejudice the commission normally allowable to travel agents, so a hotel being represented abroad may well find that a high proportion of its sales are costing as much as 20 per cent of the room price to obtain. The smaller hotel with low margins must consider carefully whether it can afford to pay out such a large share of the room price to obtain the business – yet alternative ways of reaching a foreign market are not easy to find. However, the promise offered by the Internet is beginning to change this. Even small companies today can be information providers on the World Wide Web, and as computer software becomes increasingly interactive, allowing the public to book rooms directly through the computer, global marketing becomes a reality for the independent hotel as well as the large chains.

Travel agents will be thought of as the first means of reaching the market, though few agents, apart from those dealing regularly with business travellers, are prepared to handle hotel bookings as a normal part of their activities. Domestic bookings are traditionally dealt with directly by the client, and agents are also unwilling to get involved as there is no common agreement on whether commission will automatically become payable on sales through an agent. Some hotels will pay a standard 10 per cent, but others will allow only a lower commission, or will restrict commissions to sales achieved outside their peak periods. Many agents are also unwilling to deal with overseas hotels without making a charge for the service (which will normally involve a fax or telephone call, resulting in a total handling cost which could well exceed the commission accruing on the sale). However, there is a growing tendency for hotels to package their product in the form of short breaks or longer holidays, which may be sold like any other package through the agent. Here, the agent is clear about the commission accruing, but may still be reluctant to stock the brochure due to the limited amount of rack space available to display such offers.

Clients for UK holiday centres have traditionally also been booked direct, but this pattern is changing, as the centres themselves make greater efforts to produce packages which can be sold through agents. Companies like Butlins can now expect to sell at least 60 per cent of their product through travel agents.

Finally, mention should be made of the sale of accommodation through public sector tourism outlets. This is commonly found on the Continent – the Dutch Tourist Offices (VVVs) provide a reservation service for tourists, and have done so for many years – and today tourist information centres (TICs) in the UK also offer a booking service, as one reflection of their increasingly commercial role. The 'Book a Bed Ahead' (BABA) system now allows visitors to book either hotel or farmhouse accommodation through local TICs, for which a fee is charged and for which the TIC receives a commission from the principal. Increasingly, such bookings can be undertaken using a local computer reservations system, which improves the service which the TICs can provide.

Environmental issues

All sectors of the tourism industry are becoming sensitised to the issue of eco-tourism, or ecologically sound tourism which can be sustained as tourist numbers continue to grow. Hotels are in a position to take a lead on this issue. They are also frequently the recipients of complaints by the eco-tourism lobby as a result of their practices; for example, hotels in Goa, in India, have been strongly criticised because of their profligate use of water for showers, swimming-pools, etc. in an area where the local inhabitants suffer from water shortages due to drought.

Where there are shortages of water, as for example in the Channel Islands in Britain, many hotels will encourage their guests to use water sparingly – to shower rather than bath, to ensure taps are turned off and to take other measures which reduce waste. Hotel proprietors have recognised, for instance, that many guests would prefer not to have their towels and sheets replaced daily, and savings can be effected by offering guests the choice of fresh linen (which they may indicate by leaving towels on the floor in the morning) or reuse of their linen (indicated by hanging towels up). One recent example of an eco-friendly approach in the industry is the introduction of the International Hotels Environment Initiative, in which a dozen major hotel corporations are collaborating. The initiative sets out to monitor environmental performance of the participating hotels, and to offer practical advice, especially to small independent hoteliers, on how they can manage their hotels in a more environmentally sensitive manner. This includes encouragement to reuse linen, the efficient use of energy in the hotel, consideration of methods of rubbish disposal and even the replacement of throw-away shampoo containers with shampoo dispensers in the bathroom. Such measures can provide substantial savings on costs for the hotels themselves, as well as helping to improve the environment as a whole and ensuring that as far as possible tourism in hotels is environmentally sustainable.

QUESTIONS AND DISCUSSION POINTS

1 Discuss the relative attractiveness of French 'gîtes' to the British market and British B&Bs to foreign visitors. What are the particular features of each which appeal to the respective markets? To what extent has each country tried to copy the other's unique accommodation concept, and have such attempts been successful?

2 Argue the case for and against compulsory registration and grading of accommodation in Britain. Should this include some attempt to assess quality? How should the cost of any such scheme be covered?

3 Does the concept of timeshare offer opportunities for the travel industry which it has not yet tapped? And what threats does its growth pose for the industry?

4   What can be done to correct an acute shortage of budget accommodation in major cities such as London? And how can cost, quality and value for money be reconciled?

ASSIGNMENT TOPICS

1   The Raymonde Hotel is a small county-town property which has recently benefited from the growing demand for rural tourism, especially short out-of-season breaks. As a result of three successful seasons, the hotel has received planning permission for an extension which will bring the total number of rooms up to eighty-two.

The result of this growth in capacity is that the General Manager, Jonathan Bromley, is keen to take advantage of sales opportunities wherever they can be found. Until now, little active marketing has taken place, beyond publication of the hotel's details in local tourist literature and ad hoc advertisements in the *London Evening Standard* (but no check has been kept on how much business these draw).

Mr Bromley has asked you, as a member of his back office staff, to investigate new ways of increasing sales. He is also interested in computerising the hotel's reservations systems for the first time. However, his administrative staff have expressed doubts that the introduction of computers will provide all the benefits that the computer companies promise, and some fear that it will mean cutbacks in staffing. He wants your advice on the benefits of installing a computer. Provide him with a report which examines both of these issues.

2   Following the submission of your report, Mr Bromley has complimented you on the care and detail that went into it. One outcome is that you have been appointed to the position of the hotel's first sales representative, with a commensurate increase in salary.

Mr Bromley has read in the trade press of the success enjoyed by some hotel proprietors, particularly abroad, who have 'themed' their properties or introduced special events to make them more attractive. He is particularly taken by the idea of the 'murder weekends' which a number of hotels in Britain have introduced. He asks you to look into the possibility of theming or developing special events, but wants to make the hotel distinctive rather than emulating what other hotels have done. His main aim is to increase the out-of-season trade, as the hotel is already getting very high occupancy rates between early June and late September.

Provide him with a report which suggests a theme, how it should be introduced and the market it is expected to attract.

11

Visitor Attractions and Visitor Management

OBJECTIVES

After studying this chapter, you should be able to:

- understand the range of opportunities provided by differing types of tourist attraction;
- differentiate between linear and nodal tourism, and man-made and natural attractions, and categorise them;
- appreciate the problem for attractions of changing taste and fashion, and propose solutions to overcome this;
- recognise the potential for new attractions.

Introduction

Any examination of the visitor attractions sector must start with a definition of what exactly is meant by this term. It is, after all, the attraction which prompts the tourist to travel in the first place; but the concept of an 'attraction' is a very broad one, encompassing a great many different sights – and sites. Often we use the term synonymously with 'destination': the attraction of a holiday by the sea is primarily that of warm water, a good beach and a pleasant climate. The attraction of a trip by car through the countryside is the scenery, but this will be heightened for some by the occasional stop at a village for a walk around and visit to a pub, while for others the pleasure of the trip may involve a picnic stop, where perhaps facilities have been provided for this purpose by the local council. At the other extreme, an attraction may be a very specific site: a stand-alone museum in the countryside such as the Blaenavon Big Pit in Wales, or the home of the composer Sir Edward Elgar near Worcester.

Some authorities suggest that the definition of an attraction should be that it has the primary purpose of admitting the public for entertainment, interest or education. This can hardly be the case of a seaside resort, however, which also serves the need of local residents; nor can it be the case of Buckingham Palace, an important tourist attraction for overseas visitors! Perhaps it is easiest just to accept that any site that appeals to people sufficiently to encourage them to travel there in order to visit it can be judged a 'visitor attraction'.

It will be helpful, however, to make some effort to categorise attractions. We can identify at least three categories which will help in examining the nature of attractions:

1. Attractions may be *man-made* or *natural*. The former will include buildings of all types, or attractions such as Hadrian's Wall or the Great Wall of China; the latter will include National Parks, waterfalls, lakes or other geographical phenomena. Natural attractions may also be subdivided according to whether they are in any sense 'managed', or are left entirely to nature to develop.

2. Attractions may be *nodal* or *linear* in character. Thus, the seaside resort or capital city will invite the tourist to focus their visit within a clearly designated and narrowly defined area, while linear tourism will involve the movement of tourists from one place to another – for example, by touring the countryside, or following a scenic coastal road.

3   Finally, attractions may be distinguished between those which involve a *site* and those involving an *event*. Some events are temporary, indeed some are of very short duration. These too can be either man-made or natural; the Changing of the Guard in London is a ceremony that attracts many overseas tourists, while the Spring high tides which create the famous Severn Bore along the River Severn, the annual migration of wildebeest across the Serengeti Park in East Africa, and the regular eruptions of Old Faithful, the geyser in Yellowstone National Park in the USA, are all examples of natural events that attract the tourist. Many sites, of course, owe their attraction to an event happening in the past: Liverpool became a place of pilgrimage for many overseas youngsters not because of any inherent attraction but due to its links with the Beatles in the 1960s. Lourdes, as a place of religious pilgrimage, owes its appeal entirely to an event occurring in 1858, when 14-year-old Bernadette Soubirous was said to have experienced a vision of the Virgin Mary.

The English Tourism Council, which regularly monitors visits to specific visitor attractions, rather than destinations, divides these broadly into the following categories:

- historic properties
- museums and art galleries
- wildlife parks
- gardens
- country parks
- workplaces
- steam railways
- leisure attractions
- other attractions

In all, there are nearly 5,600 such attractions in the UK for which entrance figures are maintained. Even during the recession of the 1990s, many new attractions continued to open each year; some of these have proved almost instant successes; the American Adventure theme park at Ilkeston, to take one example, soon drew more than a million visitors a year; however, at the other end of the scale, a significant minority attract fewer than 10,000 visitors each year.

It is important to recognise that many destinations owe their appeal to the fact that they offer a cluster of attractions within the immediate locality. The attraction of the seaside is heightened – particularly in Britain, with its uncertain climate – by its being able to offer, either within the town or within a short drive, a number of sites which are not weather-dependent, such as museums, amusement arcades, retail shopping malls, theatres or industrial heritage sites.

Seaside resorts

Britain suffers from an uncertain summer climate which ensured the decline of the seaside holiday as soon as the British tourist could afford to travel abroad in large numbers. In spite of this development, which we have examined in earlier chapters, by the beginning of the 1990s 32 per cent of Britons' holidays were still being spent at the seaside (compared with 45 per cent in 1975). Major resorts such as Blackpool, Bournemouth and Torquay have continued to invest in tourism, with the result that they remain attractive to the market; top resorts can still draw more than a million visitors a year, but the smallest may be attracting no more than 2,000 a week, and have been forced to find other means of raising revenue. All too often, in view of of the continuing flight of retired people to the seaside, this has meant converting former hotels and guesthouses into homes for the elderly, and the decline of many famous resorts is all too apparent to the present-day visitor. Some resorts have been able to attract a new type of tourist, the overseas visitor who has come to learn English. By the early 1990s, over 600,000 foreign visitors were arriving in Britain each year with this intention, and many of the 1,000 schools of English are situated in resorts such as Eastbourne, Worthing and Bournemouth to offer additional appeal to the market. The benefit of these visitors is also the length of stay, which averages thirty days, although average spend by most of these tourists (excluding, of course, business executives who come to improve their language skills) will inevitably be less per day than regular tourists on holiday.

The most successful British resorts are not only dependent upon their beaches and other seaside attractions. Bournemouth has grown into a town of some size, with shopping facilities which are now attractive enough to bring in the international tourist, while Blackpool has invested massively in recent years to ensure it continues to draw the largest numbers of tourists of any site in Britain. Blackpool's illuminations are internationally famous; first introduced as long ago as 1912, they represent an investment of nearly £2 million a year, and attract many tourists who would not dream in the normal way of holidaying in the town. Brighton, similarly, can attract both British and Continental tourists, partly due to its proximity to London, and partly owing to the appeal of its premier (and recently restored) attraction, the Royal Pavilion.

By contrast, many resorts which have lost tourists in recent years have chosen, or been forced through lack of funds, to go down-market. Unfortunately, this market was also badly hit by the recession of the late 1980s and early 1990s, and these seaside resorts suffered accordingly, as those who could afford a holiday were attracted to bigger and better-maintained resorts offering discounted prices.

Three-quarters of all tourists visit the seaside in Britain by car, and improved accessibility via motorways and road upgrading to resorts in the South West and North Wales has enabled many more tourists to consider day trips and short breaks to such destinations. These have helped to balance the decline in longer holidays.

The image of Britain's seaside resorts has also suffered a blow owing to publicity surrounding their increased pollution levels. Britain has some 450 recognised beaches, as listed in the *Good Beach Guide*, but of these, only a relatively small number are awarded Blue Flags each year. This award scheme, which is operated by the Foundation for Environmental Education in Europe, is based on criteria such as litter, graffiti and car parking facilities as well as water quality standards. Viewed against the standards achieved by other countries in Europe, even those bordering the Mediterranean with its notorious pollution levels, Britain's performance is poor, although councils are being forced to invest in cleaning up

in order to retain their markets. Blackpool, which has come in for particular criticism in the past, was forced to install new sewage treatment facilities in an attempt to improve the quality of the water, but has tended to take the view that, for this particular resort, its appeal rests not on swimming but in the entertainment provided on-shore.

THE BRITISH PIER

The idea of a pier is a particularly British phenomenon; very few are to be found abroad, while at one time Britain boasted more than a hundred. These soon proved to be an attraction in their own right at many of Britain's most popular seaside resorts. The first pier was constructed at Weymouth in 1812, soon followed by that at Ryde, Isle of Wight, in 1813. Their heyday, however, occurred between 1850 and the early 1900s. They were first constructed to serve as walkways to reach the numerous paddle steamers providing excursions by sea for the seaside holidaymakers, but were soon used for 'promenading', a popular Victorian pastime. There is a continuing nostalgia for them among the British public, and those that remain (some forty-three in the UK in varying states of preservation) are currently enjoying something of a revival. 1996 was declared the Year of the Pier in Britain, to encourage awareness of the pier and its historic and cultural role in British tourism; the formation of a National Piers Society to further the interest and regeneration of the piers has led to five piers being restored, two new ones being built, and others planned for restoration, including the outstanding West Pier in Brighton, closed since 1975 and the only Grade 1 listed pier in the country.

THE SEASIDE RESORT ABROAD

Seaside resorts elsewhere in the world, and particularly on the Continent, have faced problems in the last few years that are familiar to the British. With the development of mass tourism, it is inevitable that resorts will wax and wane in popularity, and continual upgrading of facilities to attract the mass tourist market is essential. The Spanish resorts, many of which were first developed for mass tourism in the 1960s, suffered from a lack of investment due to the complacency of local authorities in these resorts, which saw numbers increasing each year. Inevitably, deterioration of the fabric of the often poorly constructed concrete hotel blocks of the 1960s, coupled with inflation which made the country less attractive by comparison with other Mediterranean destinations such as Greece, and later Turkey, led to a downturn in visitor numbers from the traditional generating countries. The country was fortunate in some respects to be able to offset this development to some extent through the growth in tourism from Russia and other former Eastern Bloc countries, as tourists from these countries sought their first package holidays abroad. Nevertheless, the lower spend per capita of these markets made them less attractive to local tourist enterprises. Formerly popular resorts such as Benidorm on the east coast of Spain and Magalluf in Majorca became increasingly concerned that their traditional markets were drifting away in favour of more recent and better-kept developments in other countries of the Mediterranean. These resorts took steps, however, to recover their markets. Benidorm invested substantial amounts of money (over £300 million) to effect improvements. Magalluf and Palma Nova, major resorts in Calvia, where tourism was responsible for over 80 per cent of all income, started a process of eliminating their older hotels and replacing them with better-built ones. Regulations were tightened up; four and five-star hotels were required to provide at least 60 square metres of land for each bedroom, compared to only 15 square metres in 1990. There is evidence that the slide downmarket has now been halted.

THE FUTURE OF THE SEASIDE

The long-term future of seaside resorts must be questioned, in view of the growing alarm over the dangers of skin cancer, dangers which are increasing rapidly as the world's ozone layer is threatened. The fear has been recognised for some years in Australia, where one in three of the population is affected, and 140,000 new cases of skin cancer appear each year, while in the United States, over a half million new cases of skin cancer are reported each year. The problem has been well publicised in Britain, which now experiences over 40,000 cases each year, of which 1 500 end in death. However, many tourists either remain ignorant of the danger or choose to disregard it; the vogue for a 'healthy-looking' suntan remains a powerful motivator for sunbathing. Behaviour patterns, nonetheless, are expected to change gradually over the next few years, even if tourists do choose to continue to visit seaside resorts. There is evidence of increasing use of sun-block creams, with outdoor activities being reduced between eleven o'clock and three o'clock when the sun is at its greatest intensity. Resorts must certainly consider building more indoor facilities, and offering their visitors protection from the sun while on the beach, if they are to enjoy long-term popularity.

Spa tourism

Although Britain could boast of over a hundred active spas in the seventeenth century, by the 1990s only a dozen remained, and only one spa, that at Droitwich, continues to offer medical treatment today, with a private hospital offering an indoor brine bath. On the Continent, though, spa tourism remains popular. Countries such as Germany and the Czech and Slovak Republics continue to accept that thermal treatment, in mud or mineral water baths, can play an important part in health care (although the high cost of providing such care resulted in Germany, in 1996, cutting back on the amount of time its citizens were permitted to stay at spas when funding was provided by the state). Nevertheless, some 15 million Europeans daily immerse themselves in thermal waters in the belief that they will benefit, and the spas of Europe continue to benefit from this belief.

In Britain, which formerly attracted many domestic tourists to its spa towns, as we saw in Chapter 2, medical experts became more sceptical about the health benefits of spas in the twentieth century. Recent evidence concerning sufferers from osteoarthritis and osteoporosis, and a growing interest in alternative medicine generally, are causing some medical experts to re-evaluate their former views, and there is hope that some former spas will eventually be reopened to provide treatment for health tourists, even if this is limited to private health treatment. At the same time, the attractions of the former spa towns remain an important element in heritage tourism; towns such as Bath, Cheltenham, Harrogate and Buxton are still popular destinations for tourists due to the attraction of their infrastructure, which was originally built to serve the needs of health tourists. At Bath, plans are also at an advanced level to restore health care amenities.

In spite of the lack of medical facilities at British spas, a number of tour operators in the UK are featuring spa treatment abroad in their promotions, and two leading specialists in this field were carrying over 18,000 tourists abroad in 1996.

Urban tourism

Visitors are increasingly attracted to towns and cities, as the tourist attractions of these destinations become more widely recognised, especially for the short-break market, both in the UK and elsewhere. Britain is fortunate in that most in-coming visitors have as their motivation the desire to see the country's heritage, much of which is found in the urban areas. Apart from London and its myriad attractions, architecturally, historically and culturally, all the leading destinations in Britain are dependent upon their heritage to attract the overseas tourist. The university towns of Oxford and Cambridge, the Shakespeare connection with Stratford upon Avon, Windsor with its royal castle (attracting even more tourists since its well-publicised conflagration in 1992), the cities of Bath, York, Edinburgh and Chester, all feature on the standard 'milk-run' tours sold to the package tour market abroad. Apart from their beauty, all these cities benefit from having a clear-cut image in the public eye, and strong associations which are easy to market as products composed of a complex of benefits.

On the Continent, cities such as Amsterdam and Paris, which enjoy their status as capitals, also

Figure 11.1 The glass pyramid, the Louvre, Paris. (*Photographed by the author*)

benefit from their situation at the heart of Europe and their unique cultural attractions. Amsterdam offers the particular benefit of its canals and waterways, while Paris has enhanced its traditional attractions with a range of controversial but powerful modern buildings in recent years. These number at least a dozen, including the Pompidou Centre, the glass pyramid and new extension at the Louvre, the complex of new twenty-first century architecture at La Défense, the Musée d'Orsay, the science and technology complex at La Villette and the new Opera House at the Bastille.

While Paris and London have the capacity to absorb large numbers of tourists, smaller cities such as Oxford suffer from overpopularity, as thousands of foreign tourists visit by coach and car during the peak summer months, creating mammoth parking and congestion problems for the local authority. Marketing of these destinations will need to focus on tight planning and control, coupled with efforts to extend the holiday season, so that tourists can be more easily managed.

Aided by government urban redevelopment funds, the inner-city regions of several British towns have enjoyed a renewal; former warehouses, woollen mills in the north of England, and other sites of industrial strength in the eighteenth and nineteenth centuries have been converted into museums or other buildings to attract tourism and leisure. Notable among the successes have been the cities of Bradford and Glasgow, both suffering

Figure 11.2a Contrasting dockland redevelopment: Baltimore's Inner Harbor, USA. *(Photographed by the author)*

the worst features of urban decay at the beginning of the 1980s, but offering splendid examples of Victorian architecture, which has now become fashionable again after a long period out of favour. Bradford benefits from its location close to the Yorkshire Moors and Haworth, home of the Brontës, and now forms an ideal base for touring, with good shopping and entertainment.

Derelict waterfront sites have similarly been rejuvenated, with the aid of grants, following the success of the redevelopment of the Inner Harbour at Baltimore, USA and other American restoration schemes. Apart from the London Docklands, redevelopment work has taken place at Liverpool's Albert Dock, Bristol's Historic Harbour, Southampton Docks, and at Salford, Manchester, Swansea, Cardiff, Portsmouth, Plymouth, Newcastle, Gloucester, Glasgow and Dundee, all of which have expanded their tourist markets by adding dockland attractions. Many of these sites have a unique historical image to project, and using a combination of public and private fund-

ing, developers have introduced a range of amenities including shops, restaurants and entertainment to generate a new leisure market.

The illustrations here are drawn predominantly from British examples, but these are only symbolic of developments taking place in many countries where tourism is recognised as making, or capable of making, an important contribution to the local economy.

Rural tourism

The British climate, the bugbear of our seaside resorts, is also responsible for providing a major stimulus to tourism: the beauty of the countryside. A temperate climate, with frequent precipitation, provides us with the richness of green fields and abundant woodland which, coupled with rolling hills and stretches of water, make up the idyll of typical British rural scenery. In fact, Britain offers

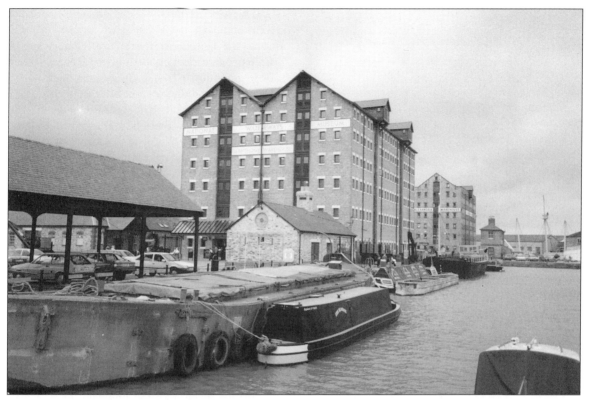

Figure 11.2b Contrasting dockland redevelopment: Gloucester Docks, UK. *(Photographed by the author)*

considerable diversity in its countryside, from the meadows and tightly hedged fields in the south and west of England to the dry-stone walls and bleak moors of the north, and from the flatlands and waterways of East Anglia and Lincoln to the lakes and mountains of Cumbria and the wild beauty of the Welsh mountains and the Highlands and Islands of Scotland.

As modern living forces more and more of us to live in built-up areas, so the attraction of the countryside grows, whether merely to take a day out at the weekend or to spend a longer holiday touring, or perhaps holidaying on a farm. Rural tourism attracts international tourists, too, with a growing number of Continental visitors coming to tour Britain by car while, in turn, Britons take their cars to France or Germany to tour. The attraction of contrasts is important here: the Dutch, Danes and Swedes, whose countryside is limited to flatland and waterways, find great appeal in the undulating hills and mountains of their European neighbours.

Hiking has become a popular pastime for tourists in recent years, and Britain is fortunate to possess many country footpaths with public rights

Figure 11.3 A popular rural attraction in Ireland: Glendalough Chapel, Co. Wicklow, Ireland. *(Photographed by the author)*

Figure 11.4 Major National Trails in Great Britain

NATIONAL TRAILS

1 Speyside Way
2 West Highland Way
3 Southern Upland Way
4 Pennine Way
5 Cleveland Way
6 Wolds Way
7 Pembrokeshire Coast Path
8 Offa's Dyke Path
9 Peddars Way and Norfolk
   Coast Path
10 Thames Path
11 Ridgeway
12 North Downs Way
13 South West Coast Path
14 South Downs Way

of way which the Ramblers' Association is anxious to protect, as pressures on the countryside grow. The National Parks and Access to the Countryside Act 1949 also created a network of long-distance footpaths which is enjoying growing popularity with hikers. These national trails are illustrated in Figure 11.4.

Walking holidays are packaged for the inclusive tourist not just in Europe, but as far afield as the Himalayas and the wilderness areas of North America. Cycling, too, has experienced a regeneration of interest, and now attracts both the independent traveller and the package tourist, with tour operators offering inclusive tours by bike to a growing number of countries. Both these forms of tourism are encouraged by the interest in 'green tourism', or environmentally friendly tourism, an issue which will be more fully explored in the final chapter of this book.

As we saw in Chapter 8, demand for leisure and recreation using boats has always been popular among the British, and the rural waterways of Britain provide ideal opportunities for water-based tourist activities, particularly at sites such as the Lake District and the Norfolk Broads, both of these now having National Park status. The canals and waterways of the Netherlands, France and Ireland, to name but three countries, all attract growing numbers of tourists seeking the pleasure of 'messing about in boats'. Waterfalls, too, exercise their own attraction, and major falls form unique settings for tourism. Those that are readily accessible, such as Niagara Falls on the Canadian/US border, or Victoria Falls on the Zambia/Zimbabwe border enjoy considerable popularity, but more inaccessible falls, including the world's highest, Angel Falls in Venezuela, do not yet attract the number of tourists that could be anticipated at such a unique scenic attraction, were adequate transport and other infrastructure available.

Mountains attract both passive and active tourists. The Alps in central Europe have long been a focus of tourism, both as objects of awe and beauty to be admired passively or as scenic attractions on gentle walks, or more actively by climbers and mountaineers. The setting of Glencoe in Scotland, noted for its famous massacre of the Macdonald clan by the Campbells in 1692, provides historic appeal in addition to its savage beauty. Activity holidays are one of the fastest-growing fields in tourism, so that both mountaineering and winter sports provide great opportunities for growth. However, the enormous expansion in winter sports holidays has also put huge pressures on the Alps, which have a fragile environment, easily damaged by overuse. The challenge of climbing major peaks in mountain ranges such as the Alps, Rockies or Himalayas has led to a number of specialist tour companies arranging special expeditions to destinations as far afield as Everest, where high levels of demand have now forced the Nepalese government to impose swingeing charges for climbing rights. Even packages costing in excess of £20,000 do not seem to stem the flow of demand.

Areas of woodland and other areas of dense foliage provide a different appeal for tourism. In

Britain, there are over fifty historic forests, and many further areas of woodland that attract the day tripper or walking tourist. Burnham Beeches, near London, is noted for the superb foliage of its beech trees, while forests such as the New Forest (a royal forest, with its memorial commemorating the spot where King William Rufus met his death in a hunting accident) and Sherwood Forest, associated with Robin Hood, have close links with history, myth and literature. In the USA, New England states such as Vermont, New Hampshire and Maine attract huge numbers of domestic and international tourists to witness the famous 'fall foliage' colours in the autumn. In South America and Africa, jungle and rain forests provide another form of attraction, and have been added to the list of exotic long-haul tourist destinations now offered by the inclusive tour industry.

Finally, mention should be made in this section of battlefields as tourist attractions, since most of these in Britain are located in rural areas. Many battlefield sites offer little for the tourist to see, the authorities feeling that the events taking place at the sites are best left to the visitors' imagination. As a result, they are relatively undisturbed, but this also means that they are often under threat from development, or to provide access roads. English Heritage has listed forty-three sites in England as of historical importance (Figure 11.5).

In North America, the National Park Service, established by Congress in 1916, has created fifty national parks throughout the fifty States, as well as the US Virgin Islands and American Samoa (see Figure 11.6). The service is also responsible for over 300 monuments and other cultural or historical sites.

All rural sites need careful management to ensure that tourism does not ruin them. As increasing numbers of tourists visit such sites, whether in the developed world or the more primitive countryside of the less-developed regions, greater control will need to be exercised to ensure that tourism is 'sustainable'. This is also an issue to which we will turn our attention in the final chapter.

Figure 11.5 English battle sites listed by English Heritage

LISTED SITES

English Heritage has listed 43 battle sites:

1 Maldon, Essex, 991; **2** Stamford Bridge, North Yorks, 1066; **3** Hastings, E. Sussex, 1066; **4** Northallerton, North Yorks, 1138; **5** Lewes, E. Sussex, 1264; **6** Evesham, Hereford & Worcester, 1265; **7** Myton, North Yorks, 1319; **8** Boroughbridge, North Yorks, 1322; **9** Halidon Hill, Northumberland, 1333; **10** Neville's Cross, Co. Durham, 1346; **11** Otterburn, Northumberland, 1388; **12** Homildon Hill, Northumberland, 1402; **13** Shrewsbury, Shropshire, 1403; **14** Blore Heath, Staffs, 1459; **15** Northampton, 1460; **16** Towton, North Yorks, 1461; **17** Barnet, N. London, 1471; **18** Tewkesbury, Glos, 1471; **19** Bosworth, Leics, 1485; **20** Stoke Field, Notts, 1487; **21** Flodden, Northumberland, 1513; **22** Solway Moss, Cumbria, 1542; **23** Newburn Ford, Tyne and Wear, 1640; **24** Edgehill, Warwicks, 1642; **25** Braddock Down, Cornwall, 1642; **26** Stratton, Cornwall, 1643; **27** Hopton Heath, Staffs, 1643; **28** Adwalton Moor, West Yorks, 1643; **29** Lansdown Hill, Avon, 1643; **30** Newbury, Berks, 1643; **31** Roundway Down, Wilts, 1643; **32** Winceby, Lincs, 1643; **33** Chalgrove, Oxon, 1643; **34** Cheriton, Hants, 1644; **35** Cropredy Bridge, Oxon, 1644; **36** Marston Moor, North Yorks, 1644; **37** Nantwich, Cheshire, 1644; **38** Naseby, Northants, 1645; **39** Langport, Somerset, 1645; **40** Rowton Heath, Cheshire, 1645; **41** Stow-on-the-Wold, Glos, 1646; **42** Worcester, 1651; **43** Sedgemoor, Somerset, 1685.

Man-made attractions

We now move away from the broader definition of a destination, to examine the role and functions of the purpose-built attraction. Attractions are not, of course, necessarily purpose-built for tourism; many, such as ancient monuments or historic buildings, served, or continue to serve, other purposes in their lives. Some – such as the great cathedrals – are open to tourists only as secondary users of their facilities; others, including some royal palaces, are not open to the public at all, but act as a magnet for tourists who merely seek to gaze at their exterior. Many, however, were con-

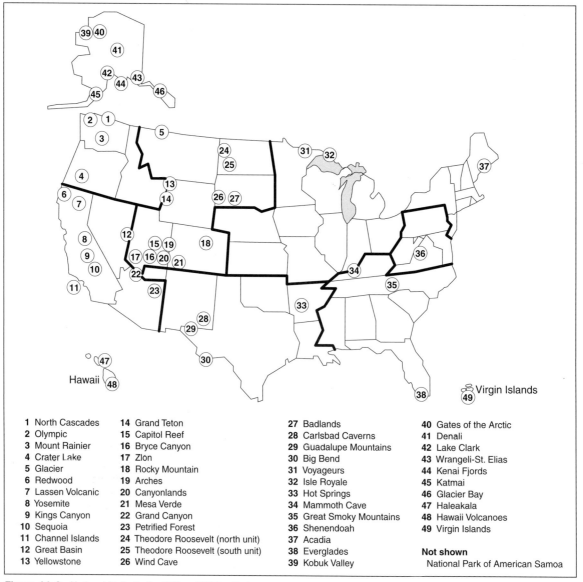

Figure 11.6 National Parks in the USA and US territories

1 North Cascades	14 Grand Teton	27 Badlands	40 Gates of the Arctic
2 Olympic	15 Capitol Reef	28 Carlsbad Caverns	41 Denali
3 Mount Rainier	16 Bryce Canyon	29 Guadalupe Mountains	42 Lake Clark
4 Crater Lake	17 Zion	30 Big Bend	43 Wrangeli-St. Elias
5 Glacier	18 Rocky Mountain	31 Voyageurs	44 Kenai Fjords
6 Redwood	19 Arches	32 Isle Royale	45 Katmai
7 Lassen Volcanic	20 Canyonlands	33 Hot Springs	46 Glacier Bay
8 Yosemite	21 Mesa Verde	34 Mammoth Cave	47 Haleakala
9 Kings Canyon	22 Grand Canyon	35 Great Smoky Mountains	48 Hawaii Volcanoes
10 Sequoia	23 Petrified Forest	36 Shenendoah	49 Virgin Islands
11 Channel Islands	24 Theodore Roosevelt (north unit)	37 Acadia	
12 Great Basin	25 Theodore Roosevelt (south unit)	38 Everglades	**Not shown**
13 Yellowstone	26 Wind Cave	39 Kobuk Valley	National Park of American Samoa

structed specifically to serve the needs of tourists, or at least to meet the recreational needs of locals, and these sites will include museums and art galleries, theme and leisure parks. Here, we will briefly examine each in turn, and discuss their importance to the tourism business.

ANCIENT MONUMENTS AND HISTORIC BUILDINGS

Many historic buildings of course continue to serve their daily task regardless of the interest or needs of the passing tourist. Towns and villages throughout the world frequently contain buildings that are old, or of architectural interest, and provide an attractive setting in which to sightsee, even though such buildings may now serve as homes, shops, offices or hotels (it is worth noting that over 2,500 hotels in Britain enjoy listed status as being of historic or architectural interest). Towns with an unusual number of such buildings – such as York, Bath or Oxford – will, naturally, attract the tourist, and inevitably some outstanding examples of these buildings will eventually lose their original purpose and will be adapted purely to serve the needs of the tourist. These are assessed as part of the 'national heritage'. Some may be identified by UNESCO as World Heritage Sites; there are over 500 such sites in the world now, in 105 countries. Most recently (1997) Salzburg's Old City and the Schonbrunn Castle in Vienna were listed, while in Britain, among other sites, both Stonehenge and Bath have been listed. Within Britain, buildings and sites are similarly listed on the grounds of their architectural or historical interest. In all, some 440,000 buildings have now been singled out by the Department of the Environment, the main result of which is to ensure that they are not razed or changed without recourse to the Department. The definition of 'building' can include everything from a stately home to a telephone box, and all are graded into three categories in descending order according to their architectural or historical merit: grade I, II* or II. Only about 2 per cent achieve the highest listing, with a further 5 per cent listed as grade II*.

Heritage sites will include fortifications and castles, palaces, churches, stately homes and gardens. It is also important to appreciate that our heritage is not only composed of ancient buildings; many recent buildings of historical or architectural importance are now protected, and have become attractions in their own right. Recent

history is exemplified by World War II sites, such as the Cabinet War Rooms in London, where Winston Churchill conducted affairs of state during aerial bombardments. Modern architectural heritage includes the striking black glass Willis Corroon Building in Ipswich, designed by Sir Norman Foster in 1975 and now a grade II listed building.

Most English castles and other ancient monuments are now in the care of English Heritage, while those in Wales are cared for by the Welsh equivalent Cadw, and in Scotland the Historic Buildings and Monuments division of the Scottish Development Department has responsibility. The Tower of London is by far the most visited heritage building, with well over two million visitors each year, due to its location in the heart of London and the added attraction of the Crown Jewels which are on display there.

Britain is also fortunate in having a large number of historic houses, many referred to as 'stately homes'. There are believed to be over 6,000 such houses in Britain, of which over 800 are open to the public. A surprising number are still in private hands, and others are under the care of the National Trust. These are prime tourist attractions for the excursion market, and are often sited in the heart of the countryside, attracting tourists to rural Britain. Some date from the period of the Norman Conquest, while others, such as Winston Churchill's former home, Chartwell in Kent, are much more recent.

The first such property to open commercially in Britain was Longleat, the home of the Marquess of Bath, in 1949. In order to pay the massive costs of upkeep and death duties, Lord Bath realised that he would have to generate a substantial income for the estate, and later added other attractions, including a drive-through wildlife park. Other aristocrats soon followed suit, such as Lord Montagu of Beaulieu, who added to the attraction of Beaulieu Palace a classic cars museum, a monorail and other forms of entertainment bordering on the funfair. Alton Towers, under the guidance of the entrepreneur John Broome, developed an entire theme park, and was receiving over three million visitors a year by 1994.

A growing interest in history has meant that the visiting public has gone beyond merely gazing

Figure 11.7 Modern architecture as tourist attraction: the Willis Faber and Dumas Building (1975) designed by Sir Norman Foster. *(Photographed by the author).*

in awe at the former wealth of Britain's aristocrats. Many quite humble homes which, through force of circumstance, have been little changed over the decades have now opened to the public. One of the smallest such attractions is Toad Hall Cottage, an eel catcher's home in the Norfolk Broads, which opened its doors in the early 1990s and immediately attracted over 35,000 visitors a year. But perhaps the smallest 'enterable' man-made attraction in Britain is the gypsy caravan owned by the former radio entertainer and story-teller 'Romany' (George Bramwell Evens), which has been restored in its location at Wilmslow, Macclesfield.

A list of the most popular historic buildings open to the public appears as Table 11.1.

It is also important to stress the significance of Britain's great churches for tourism. The numbers visiting sites such as Westminster Abbey are now so great that there are serious problems of congestion, and the constant flow of tourists threatens the prime purpose of these buildings as places of worship. Some cathedrals, such as Salisbury, have attempted to introduce charges to help pay for the upkeep and added wear and tear arising from visitors, although those visiting to worship are exempted. In 1993, King's College Chapel in Cambridge, one of the most celebrated of the University buildings, announced that charges would be introduced in order to regulate numbers and 'make visits a more pleasurable experience for tourists'.

Britain is fortunate in having such a wealth of historic attractions, particularly as, for the most part, they are not weather-dependent. Over half of all visitors to Britain participate in visits to heritage sites, while a quarter also attend performing arts events.

Abroad, historic homes play no less a part in tourism. In Germany, Bavaria attracts by far the most foreign tourists, and this is certainly accounted for in part by the Disneyesque castles, with their wedding-cake architecture, erected in the nineteenth century by mad King Ludwig II. In Spain and Portugal many former stately homes, known as *paradores* in Spanish and *pousadas* in Portuguese, have been converted into luxury hotels to attract the up-market touring visitors. Although history is much shorter in the New World, Americans take great pride in their heritage, and have carefully preserved many great buildings of the seventeenth and eighteenth centuries, including Monticello, in Virginia, home of Thomas Jefferson, third president of the United States, a building now dedicated as a National Shrine. Early colonial buildings at Williamsburg in Virginia have been restored with funds provided by the Rockefeller family, and the entire village has been preserved intact and is now a site of educational, as well as entertainment, value for tourists.

GARDENS

Any stately homes are noted as much for their magnificent gardens as for their buildings. Great landscape architects of the eighteenth century like Capability Brown or Humphrey Repton built splendid parks to complement the buildings, and even in the twentieth century famous gardens have been constructed, among others by the great landscape gardener Gertrude Jekyll, whose work was often used to complement the popular architect of great houses of the early part of this century, Sir Edwin Lutyens. Some houses, such as Stourhead in Wiltshire, are more famous for their gardens than for the house itself. Other gardens attracting

Table 11.1 Top ten historic buildings for paying visitors in England, 1996

Historic building	Visitors
Tower of London	2 539 272
Canterbury Cathedral	1 700 000
Windsor Castle	1 215 631
St Paul's Cathedral, London	1 002 000
Roman Baths and Pump Room, Bath	902 186
Warwick Castle	820 000
Stonehenge, Wilts	747 644
Hampton Court Palace	612 155
Leeds Castle	598 714
Blenheim Palace	419 902

Source: Travel Industry Digest 306 15 August 1997

Figure 11.8 Archaeological tourism: the 5,000-year-old neolithic houses at Skara Brae, Orkneys, have become a major tourist attraction in the islands. *(Photographed by the author)*

large numbers of tourists are Kew Gardens, with well over a million visitors each year, the grounds of Hampton Court, and Wisley Gardens – the proximity of all these to London helps to ensure their success, but the British are noted for their love of gardens and gardening, and will travel far afield to see unusual plants or particularly beautiful settings. Arboreta, which are essentially museums for living trees and shrubs, are particularly popular. Kew Gardens is the forerunner in this respect, but in Gloucester, Westonbirt Arboretum still manages to attract some 200,000 visitors every year.

ARCHAEOLOGICAL SITES

Archaeology is the study of human antiquities, usually through excavation, and is generally thought to be concerned with pre- or early history – although recently the term has come to be used in reference to industrial archaeology, relating to

study of the industrial relics of the eighteenth century. Areas where civilised man originated, such as the countries of the Middle East, are rich in archaeological sites, and Egypt in particular attracts visitors from around the world to sites such as the Pyramids at Giza, the burial sites at the Valley of the Kings, or the temples of Luxor. Great Britain is also rich in early history, with sites such as Chysauster prehistoric village in Cornwall, the Roman ruins such as the rich mosaic flooring at Fishbourne in Sussex or Skara Brae Neolithic site in the Orkney Islands (see Figure 11.8). Myth and history are closely interwoven in our heritage, and the legend of King Arthur, which locates his castle of Camelot at Tintagel, or the possible association of this mythical king with the archaeological digs at Cadbury Camp in Wiltshire, exercise a fascination for young tourists in particular.

In the early 1990s, the world's largest collection of palaeolithic art, embracing hundreds of ice-age drawings of animals, was discovered in a remote area of northern Portugal. A fierce battle then developed between those seeking to dam the area as a reservoir and others seeking to conserve the site for tourism; the latter won the day, and the Côa Valley Archaeological Park was opened to the public in 1996.

INDUSTRIAL HERITAGE

Britain was the seat of the Industrial Revolution in the eighteenth century, and over the past forty years interest has been awakened in the many redundant buildings and obsolete machinery dating back to this period. The fact that many of the early factories and warehouses were examples of splendid industrial architecture added zest to the drive to see these buildings preserved and enhanced for the purpose of tourism. Other European countries and the USA and Australia also quickly came to recognise the potential of redundant buildings. Lowell, in Massachusetts, where a number of early mills had survived intact, received massive federal government funding to be restored as an Urban Heritage Park, and since the conversion of its buildings into museums, offices and shops, it has enjoyed huge commercial success as an unusual tourist destination. A similar success has been recorded in Britain for Ironbridge, the site of the founding of the Industrial Revolution, where very large investments have been made on six sites spread over some six square miles. The importance of the site can be gauged by its accolade of World Heritage Site in 1986, and soon after that date the five museum sites were attracting over 400,000 visitors every year.

The variety of industrial sites is astonishing. Early mining sites such as the coal and slate mines of South Wales or the copper mines of Cornwall have been converted into tourist attractions, as have former steam railways, docks and manufacturing sites. The textile mills of the north of England, driven out of existence by the import of cheap textiles from Third World countries following World War II, have taken on a new life as museums – or in some cases have been converted to attractive new homes. The open-air museums which are based on a combination of industrial archaeology and industrial heritage provide settings which, to be properly appreciated, will require many hours, if not days, of

viewing, and have helped to turn former areas of urban decay into major tourist attractions. Apart from Ironbridge, other significant developments in Britain include Beamish Open-Air Museum in the north of England, and the Black Country Museum near Dudley, in the Midlands. The Big Pit Mining Museum at Blaenavon in South Wales, and the Llechwedd Slate Caverns near Blaenau Ffestiniog in North Wales have both made important contributions to the local economy of their region, with tourism helping to replace the former dependency upon mining.

Early transport has provided another focus for tourist interest. Sometimes the equipment can be restored and used for entertainment; this is particularly notable in the case of the many steam railways in private hands in Britain, especially in Wales, many of which travel through very scenic countryside. We have seen in Chapter 8 how older ships have been restored or maintained to offer trips, such as the *Delta Queen* on the Mississippi River in America, or the paddle steamer *Waverley* in Britain. In Bristol, the oldest surviving vessel built in Bristol's former shipping yards, the tug *Mayflower*, regularly provides trips through the floating harbour for visitors. Bristol is also the setting for I K Brunel's *SS Great Britain*, the first iron-hulled screw-driven vessel, launched in 1843, brought back from the Falklands as a rusting wreck in 1970 and now being extensively restored. Together with the city's famous suspension bridge, this early ship has now helped to create an image for the city to attract the tourist.

Earlier ships also provide unique attractions for their locations. Viking ships have been found in Scandinavia, and splendid museums created to display them – for example, at Roskilde in Denmark. The only seventeenth-century warship to survive is the Swedish *Vasa* which capsized and sank in Stockholm harbour soon after its launch in 1628. Raised in almost perfect condition, it is now a major museum attraction in Stockholm. Still in Scandinavia, Oslo in Norway provides the setting for the *Fram,* the vessel in which Roald Amundsen sailed in 1910, on his way to become the first person to reach the South Pole. Similarly, Captain Scott's vessel, the research ship *Discovery,* has now returned to Dundee where it was built in 1901, and serves as a museum.

Figure 11.9 The Vasa museum, Stockholm. *(Photographed by the author)*

The cost of preserving more recent vessels, due to their size, militates against their preservation. Perhaps the best-known of all twentieth-century ships, the *RMS Queen Mary*, has been converted into a dry dock hotel near Long Beach, California, but has persistently lost money for her developers since the ship was sold in the late 1960s. Britain, as a leading maritime nation, has sadly no examples of her great passenger vessels of this century on display, although there are numerous examples of fighting vessels from this and earlier centuries preserved and open to the public. *HMS Belfast*, a World War II cruiser, is moored near Tower Bridge in London, and receives over 200,000 visitors each year. Portsmouth is particularly lucky to have three great examples of our maritime history, including Nelson's flagship *HMS Victory*, the nineteenth-century *HMS Warrior* and the Tudor warship *Mary Rose*, raised from the sea in 1982 and still undergoing restoration. The combination of three vessels of historic value located close together in the same city acts as a powerful magnet for the day excursionist and helps to account for the high number of visits – approaching 400,000 in the case of the *Mary Rose*.

Other forms of transport have also become museum attractions. There are numerous vintage car museums throughout Britain, although that at Beaulieu is probably the best known. Vintage aircraft are preserved at Yeovilton, among other sites, while elsewhere, museums have been devoted to early carriages, bicycles and canal-boats. As with other artefacts which are too large to house indoors, the costs of preservation are very high, adding to the difficulties faced by museums which wish to focus on such attractions. This was a factor in the collapse of the Exeter Maritime Museum in 1996.

INDUSTRIAL TOURISM

Interest in our industrial heritage has now spread further to include an interest in modern industry. A number of companies have recognised the possibilities of achieving good public relations by opening their doors to the public, either to see work in progress in the factory, or to maintain a workshop or museum of some kind on site. Americans were the first to realise the value of this from the point of public relations, and car companies in particular soon organised visits to manufacturing plants where prospective purchasers could watch cars being built. Today, this practice is widespread in the USA, and is particularly beneficial for tourism in the sense that most automobile plants are not sited in areas which would normally attract tourists. Among those currently open to the public: General Motors' Chevrolet Corvette factory in Bowling Green, Kentucky, one of that state's major tourist attractions, while at Georgetown, Kentucky, the Toyota Assembly Plant attracts 37,000 visitors a year; GM's Saturn plant at Spring Hill, Tennessee, and the Nissan plant in the same state at Smyrna; BMW's plant at Spartanburg, South Carolina; and Ford's Lincoln plant at Wixom, Michigan, now the nearest such plant to Detroit, the traditional home of automobile manufacturing, which still remains open to the public. Some of these plants are booked months in advance, such is their popularity for visits.

There are other commercial benefits apart from public relations. Watching the production processes of, for example, modern china and glass will stimulate an interest in purchasing, and people can be encouraged to purchase direct at the factory shop. At Cadbury's, the chocolate confectioners located at Bourneville, England, hand-made chocolates are sold to members of the public individually by members of staff in traditional costumes.

In 1980, the Sellafield nuclear fuel plant was opened to visitors to help counteract much negative publicity about nuclear energy appearing in the media. This quickly became a major, and quite unexpected, draw for tourists in the area, since when other nuclear processing plants have also opened their doors for guided tours of the site. The variety of factories and workplaces open to the public is now considerable, from leading companies such as the car manufacturers to small individual workshops like Langham Glass in Norfolk, which makes lead crystal glassware by hand and received an industrial award in 1993, after attracting 100,000 visitors in the previous year. Another popular innovation has been access to the Scotch whisky distilleries in Scotland; of more than a hundred distilleries, over forty admit members of the public, and a distillery trail has been established for aficionados of single malt.

Many craftspeople depend upon tourists visiting their studios in order to sell their products, and as these studios are frequently set in the countryside, they will stimulate tourism to the area. For this reason, the Rural Development Commission will sometimes provide financial aid to companies willing to open to the public, as they did in the case of Langham Glass.

THEME AND AMUSEMENT PARKS

Purpose-built theme and amusement parks are, not surprisingly, the major attractions for tourism, receiving the greatest number of visitors. The appetite for entertainment parks seems never-ending, and in Europe has a very long history: London's Vauxhall and Ranelagh Gardens date back to the seventeenth and eighteenth centuries respectively, while Denmark's famous Tivoli Gardens, first opened in 1843, have become one of the best-known centres of entertainment in the world, attracting over four million visitors annually. Bakken, near Copenhagen, lays claim to being the oldest amusement park in the world, having opened in 1583, while in North America Coney Island's Luna Park in Brooklyn, New York, was established at the end of the nineteenth century and, by 1905 was drawing 250,000 visitors a day in the summer.

The United States is the home of the theme

park, and together US parks received over 150 million visitors in 1995, the top ten alone accounting for 76.4 million arrivals. It is the Walt Disney empire, and particularly its four US sites, with which one immediately associates the modern leisure park; entries to the Disney parks in California and Florida are by far the highest in the world, with over 14 million visiting Anaheim, California, alone. Disney has gone on to open theme parks in Japan and France, and has plans for further developments within these parks and on other sites, including a new Animal Kingdom at Orlando five times the size of the present Magic Kingdom, due to open in 1998. Disneyworld's group of sites at Orlando, Florida (the Magic Kingdom, Epcot and Disney-MGM Studios) attracts over 30 million visitors a year, over one million of whom are from the UK, and between the time of the site's first opening in 1971 and 1996 it has attracted a total of over 500 million visitors. Because of the clustering of these attractions, and the scale of each, visitors tend to spend several days in Orlando, so that entire packages can be built around a visit, and the area now boasts over 85,000 bedrooms to accommodate the visitors. After a shaky start at its site in France, launched in 1993, Disneyland Paris went on to achieve equivalent success, becoming Europe's

Table 11.2 Top ten attractions in Britain charging admission, 1996	
Attraction	Visitors
Alton Towers	2 749 000
Madame Tussauds	2 715 000
Tower of London	2 539 272
Canterbury Cathedral	1 700 000
Chessington World of Adventures	1 700 000
Natural History Museum	1 607 255
Science Museum	1 548 286
Legoland, Windsor	1 420 511
Windsor Castle	1 215 631
Blackpool Tower	1 200 000
Source: BTA/ETB Insights	

Figure 11.10 Event tourism: the annual Food and Drink Festival at Ludlow, Shropshire. *(Photographed by the author)*

major tourist attraction with over 11.7 million visitors in 1996, twice that of the nearest rival in France, the Eiffel Tower.

The initial problems at Disneyland Paris (originally called EuroDisney) were due partly to the weather – unlike the American sites, the French site is too far north to attract visitors to outdoor events in winter – and partly to a misjudgement of the market. Although EuroDisney pulled in plenty of visitors from Britain and Germany, the domestic French market proved more resistant, as the site failed to cater specifically for French tastes and was criticised as an inappropriate invasion of American culture.

The size of the US population, and demand for theme parks in the US market, has ensured a strong domestic market not just for the Disney enterprises but also for many other US parks. The Americans were among the first to develop the modern concept of the leisure park, and today there are over 2,000 such parks of all kinds in the USA, including the two Disney mega-parks (the first of which was built in 1955 at Anaheim) and some thirty-eight large regional parks.

Construction of theme parks in Europe has kept pace with American developments, with a dozen key sites on the Continent and at least half this number in the UK alone which could be termed of international stature. Figure 11.11 iden-tifies the major Continental sites and the larger UK sites. A number of the leading British theme parks attract over a million visitors every year, with Alton Towers in Staffordshire by far the biggest crowd-puller, but other notable attractions include the Chessington World of Adventures, Flamingoland in North Yorkshire, American Adventure World near Ilkeston in Derbyshire, Lightwater Valley near Ripon, North Yorkshire, Frontierland in Morecambe, Lancashire, Thorpe Park in Surrey and Pleasurewood Hills, near Lowestoft in Suffolk. Entry numbers for several of these exceed a million people each year, but it is questionable how many more such major attractions can be built and become viable; several big planned projects in recent years, including the massive Wonderland theme park planned as part of the redevelopment of the Corby steel mills site, have been abandoned or have not yet proceeded because of difficulty in raising capital. Britain also suffers from a poor winter for outside events, and many attractions do not attempt to remain open in winter.

The distinction between a theme park and a leisure park is not always a clear one, although the former is rather loosely based on some theme, whether geographical, historical or other – the future is a popular theme, as it can allow the development to focus on advanced technology to attract the public. One of the most recent examples in Europe is that of Futuroscope, near Poitiers in France, where imaginative architecture of the future is combined with advanced technology – for instance, theatre seats are fitted with hydraulic jacks which move in sympathy with what is showing on the screen, so that sporting events such as white water rafting can be experienced as well as observed. The park attracted over a million visitors in its first year, 95 per cent of whom were French.

Many theme parks incorporate elements of the funfair, with parks vying with one another to construct the largest white-knuckle rides to attract the younger visitors. Blackpool boasts the 'Pepsi Max Big One', the highest and fastest roller coaster in Britain at the time of writing, while a millennium coaster is planned to be Europe's longest at the Magical World of Fantasy Island, Skegness, by the turn of the century. Japan boasts the highest roller

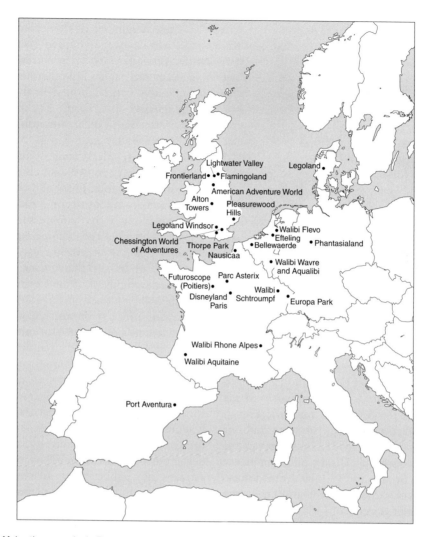

Figure 11.11 Major theme parks in Europe

coaster, the 'Fujiyama', at 259 feet, but the search for ever more gravity-defying rides has reached a point where the human body is now being subject to dangerous levels of acceleration, and engineers believe nothing higher than 300 feet is feasible.

However, these forms of entertainment can soon pall, and management must constantly update with new rides and other investment – perhaps at a level of some 5–10 per cent of the initial investment – to keep the attraction appearing 'new' to the public, and ensure repeat visits. Perhaps the ride to end all rides is that recently constructed in Las Vegas; known as the Stratosphere and built at a cost of $550 million, it offers brave (or foolhardy) tourists an inverse bungee jump, catapulting riders sixteen storeys to the roof in just 2.3 seconds, with four times the pull of gravity. The search for the ultimate funfair experience without actually doing permanent damage to the participant goes on!

WILDLIFE ATTRACTIONS

Wildlife is a growing attraction for tourists, and the industry has responded in different ways to meet this interest. At one time, the most prominent way

Figure 11.12 Major wildlife parks in South and East Africa

in which the tourist would see wild animals was in the numerous zoos which exist in most countries around the world. The keeping of collections of animals goes back at least two thousand years, but the present-day concept of a zoo dates back only to the eighteenth century. In Britain, although zoos are known to predate the turn of the nineteenth century, the founding of the Zoological Society in London by Sir Stamford Raffles at the beginning of that century led to the interest which Victorian England took in caged animals.

Today there are some 900 established zoos around the world, but attitudes to zoos have changed, as people in Western countries have come to consider it cruel to keep animals in captivity. Nevertheless, zoos still enjoy high attendance figures, although not at the peaks to be found thirty years ago; and they are adapting to the new perspective by stressing their curatorial role in preserving rare species of wildlife, rather than the former emphasis on displaying animals for the purpose of entertainment. There was a fear at the end of the 1980s, as attendances fell, that London's famous zoo in Regent's Park might be forced to close; although that fear receded with a massive private investment of capital, this sharpened awareness of zoos as a whole in Britain, renewing interest in visiting them, and encouraging the construction of better facilities to keep the animals in settings of less constraint.

With the growth of long-haul travel, more tourists are taking advantage of the opportunity to see animals in the wild, usually in safari parks, of which the best known are situated in Southern and East Africa (see Figure 11.12).

Some of these big game parks have become world-famous, such as Kenya's Maasai Mara, Tsavo, Amboseli and Samburu Parks, Tanzania's Serengeti National Park and South Africa's Kruger National Park. The attraction of these parks is the opportunity to see big game such as lion, elephant, leopard, buffalo and rhino (although poaching is rapidly diminishing the last of these). All of these parks feature in tour operators' long-haul programmes, although the political situation in South Africa and lack of tourism investment in Tanzania have favoured Kenya as a destination. This country, too, faces an uncertain political future at the time of writing, which may threaten tourism.

With the decline in zoo attendance, there have been some efforts to introduce the atmosphere of the safari park in Britain, notably at the Marquess of Bath's property at Longleat. Running costs for such projects are high, taking into account the need for maximum security to protect visitors; another safari park at Windsor was attracting close to a million visitors a year, but still proved a financial failure, closing in 1992.

Finally, mention must be made of wildfowl reserves and other miscellaneous centres where fauna are on display to the public. Ornithology is a popular pastime in Britain, and the Wildfowl Trust at Slimbridge in Gloucester has been a model for other sites around the country where birds can be viewed in their natural setting. Other attractions, for which tourism is a secondary consideration in some cases, include falconry centres and the New Forest owl sanctuary, while sanctuaries for other specific animals have been built in many places in Britain, such as the seal sanctuary at Gweek in Cornwall. Sanctuaries, of course, exist to protect animals and to tend to wounded animals, but most are open to visitors, who make a useful contribution in admission fees to the running costs of the project.

Bird-watching in particular is attracting the specialist long-haul market, with tour operators such as Noble Caledonia offering cruises to the Arctic and Antarctic to study unusual bird life, frequently accompanied by well-known ornithological experts who will lecture to cruise passengers en route.

Other site attractions

The scope for providing new attractions to feed the insatiable appetite of the tourist is almost never-ending, and would be quite impossible to cover in a single chapter. In many cases, attractions are unique within their destination, but share commonalities with others in other areas or countries, which offers scope for joint marketing schemes or twinning. For example, a number of towns around the world are noted for their towers – always an attraction for tourists, especially if they are open to the public and offer distant views of the countryside or city (see Figure 11.13). The CN Tower in Toronto, at 553 m, is currently the world's tallest (see Figure 11.14), and for that reason alone will draw tourists, but others are known for their historical interest, especially those that have become symbols of their city such as Paris's Eiffel Tower (381 m) and the Rotterdam Euromast (185 m). Such towns can band together to share contacts, or market their towers jointly. Another recent example is the Walled Towns Friendship Circle, established as a marketing association in 1992 by a group of European towns which benefit from an encircling fortification wall.

Cultural tourism

Cultural tourism – however that is defined – is one of the fastest-growing areas of tourism. In its widest definition, it encompasses both 'high' and 'low' culture: visits to museums and art galleries and to football matches; performances of music both popular and classical; pilgrimages to literary sites ranging from the Brontës' Haworth to the bridge in Sussex identified as that from which 'Pooh-sticks'

WORLD FEDERATION OF GREAT TOWERS
MEMBERS

① The CN Tower / La Tour CN Toronto Canada 1,815 ft / 553 m	② The Ostankino Tower / La Tour Ostankino Moscow / Russia Moscou / Russie 1,771 ft / 540 m	③ The Oriental Pearl Tower / La Tour Perle Orientale Shanghai P.R. China/R.P. Chine 1,535 ft / 468 m

(Towers 1–11, top row, left to right:)

① The CN Tower — La Tour CN — Toronto, Canada — 1,815 ft / 553 m
② The Ostankino Tower — La Tour Ostankino — Moscow / Russia — Moscou / Russie — 1,771 ft / 540 m
③ The Oriental Pearl Tower — La Tour Perle Orientale — Shanghai — P.R. China/R.P. Chine — 1,535 ft / 468 m
④ The John Hancock Centre — Le Centre John Hancock — Chicago — U.S.A. / États-Unis — 1,455 ft / 444 m
⑤ The Empire State Building — L'Empire State Building — New York — U.S.A. / États-Unis — 1,454 ft / 443 m
⑥ KL Menara — La Tour KL — Kuala Lumpur — Malaysia / Malaisie — 1,403 ft / 421 m
⑦ The Tianjin Tower — La Tour de Tianjin — P.R. China / R.P. Chine — 1,362 ft / 415.2 m
⑧ The Central Radio & TV Tower — La Tour Centrale de Radio et TV — Beijing — P.R. China / R.P. Chine — 1,329 ft / 405 m
⑨ The Tashkent Tower — La Tour de Tachkent — Uzbekistan/ Ouzbékistan — 1,230 ft / 375 m
⑩ The Fernsehturm — La Fernsehturm — Berlin — Germany / Allemagne — 1,207 ft / 368 m
⑪ The Tokyo Tower — La Tour de Tokyo — Japan / Japon — 1,092 ft / 333 m

(Towers 12–22, bottom row, left to right:)

⑫ The Sky Tower — La Tour CéLeste — Auckland — New Zealand/Nouvelle Zélande — 1,076 ft / 328 m
⑬ The AMP Tower — La Tour AMP — Australia / Australie — 1,000 ft / 304 m
⑭ The Barcelona Tower — La Tour de Barcelone — Spain / Espagne — 945 ft / 288 m
⑮ The Rialto Towers — Les Tours Rialto — Melbourne — Australia / Australie — 832 ft / 253 m
⑯ The Donauturm — La Donauturm — Vienna / Vienne — Austria / Autriche — 827 ft / 252 m
⑰ The Seoul Tower — La Tour de Séoul — South Korea / Corée du Sud — 777 ft / 237 m
⑱ The Telstra Tower — La Tour Telstra — Canberra — Australia / Australie — 640 ft / 195 m
⑲ The Euromast — L'Euromast — Rotterdam — Holland / Hollande — 607 ft / 185 m
⑳ The Latinoamericana Tower — La Tour Latinoamericana — Mexico / Mexique — 595 ft / 181 m
㉑ The Harbour Centre Tower — La Tour Harbour — Vancouver / Canada — 581 ft / 177 m
㉒ The Montréal Tower — La Tour de Montréal — Canada — 575 ft / 175 m

Figure 11.13 The World Federation of Great Towers. *(Courtesy WFGT)*

were played in A A Milne's Winnie-the-Pooh stories. The tourism industry has become adept at packaging and popularising culture in all its forms. France, noted for its predominance in the fine art field, has packaged art 'trails' covering Cézanne's sites at Aix-en-Provence, Monet's garden at Giverny, and areas associated with Gauguin, Manet, Renoir, Degas, Pissaro and Sisley. Embracing wider tours, the 'circuit Pissaro–Cézanne' and 'circuit Toulouse-Lautrec' have proved popular for cultural tourists. Major exhibitions draw an international audience of mass tourists; 1.1 million visitors attended the Barnes Foundation's exhibition 'A Century of Impressionism' held at the Musée d'Orsay in Paris in 1993, while a later showing of the Barnes Foundation's collection in Germany drew such crowds that the museum exhibiting the collection stayed open all night.

Where a place is popularly identified with an author or artist, tourist interest follows automatically; where the link is less well established, it can still be built upon. Dylan Thomas's disparaging comments about the town and people of Laugharne have not stopped a steady flow of 25,000 visitors annually to the Boathouse where he lived between 1949 and 1953, in spite of the locals' preference to play down this link. By contrast the town of Rochester in Kent, associated with Charles Dickens, has created a Dickens Festival and a Dickensian Christmas to attract tourism. Recently Crowborough in Sussex has endeavoured to promote itself as the home town of Sir Arthur Conan Doyle, establishing a Sherlock Holmes Festival in 1996.

Cultural tourism has been given a boost in Europe by the EU's naming of a European City of Culture each year; the title is to be given to no fewer than nine cities in the millennium year. A list of those named to date appear in Table 11.3.

Figure 11.14 The world's tallest tower: the CN Tower, Toronto, Canada. *(Photographed by the author)*

Table 11.3	European City of Culture
Year	City
1985	Athens
1986	Florence
1987	Amsterdam
1988	Berlin
1989	Paris
1990	Glasgow
1991	Dublin
1992	Madrid
1993	Antwerp
1994	Lisbon
1995	Luxembourg
1996	Copenhagen
1997	Thessaloniki
1998	Stockholm
1999	Weimar
2000	Avignon, Bergen, Bologna, Brussels, Cracow, Helsinki, Prague, Reykjavik, Santiago de Compostela

CULTURE, THE MEDIA AND TOURISM

Britain has not been slow to develop the association between culture and tourism, supported by the popularising of culture through the media, and most notably television and the cinema. Brontë country in Yorkshire offers its 'Great British Literary Tours', while the popularity of Jane Austen's books, following their filming in the mid-1990s, has been particularly noteworthy. Also, the attraction of top stars helps to boost appeal considerably; thus, Emma Thompson's and Anthony Hopkins' appearance in *Remains of the Day* was sufficient to boost attendance at Dyrham Park, Bath. In 1995, the BBC filmed *Pride and Prejudice* at Belton House, Lincolnshire, Sudbury Hall, Derbyshire and Lyme Park in Cheshire, the last of which enjoyed a tenfold increase in visitors in the first week after the screening. A 'Darcy Walk' was quickly initiated to take advantage of this interest. In the following year, a Hollywood production of *Sense and Sensibility*, starring Emma Thompson and Hugh Grant, achieved similar success in promoting tourism for Saltram House in Devon. The TV series of George Elliot's *Middlemarch* drew tourists en masse to Stamford, in Lincolnshire, where the series was filmed (in preference to the original site in the book, Coventry, which wartime bombs and post-war redevelopment had rendered no longer suitable); 'Dr Lydgate's house' at Barn Hill is particularly sought out. The town was not slow to take advantage: 'Middlemarch fudge' soon appeared for sale in the local sweet shops. The Alton Hotel in Birmingham, setting for part of the film *Four Weddings and a Funeral*, starring Hugh Grant, has enjoyed virtually 100 per cent occupancy since the film was released.

The popularity of certain cult films will guarantee a steady audience of aficionados to the locations where the films were shot. Hundreds now visit the telephone box near Pennan, Morayshire, featured in the film *Local Hero*, while the enduring 1945 film *Brief Encounter*, shot at Carnforth station in Lancashire, has enticed so many tourists, and from as far afield as Japan, that Railtrack are investigating the possibility of creating a theme park at the now deteriorating site. In France, Provence tourist authorities have established a 'Marcel Pagnol Route' to popularise the locations at which the French film *Manon des Sources* was filmed.

The power of Hollywood is of course most noted in its own territory, and tourists both domestic and foreign flock to locations of films made in the United States. To cite recent examples of areas that formerly drew few tourists and now, as a result of popular films, attract many: *Field of Dreams*, starring Kevin Costner, was filmed at Dyersville, Iowa (population 3,800) in 1988; 50,000 tourists a year are now attracted to view an empty cornfield with minimal tourist facilities. The popularity of Winterset (population 4,300) in the same state, and particularly the Northside Café, which featured prominently, was created by the film *The Bridges of Madison County* (1994), starring Clint Eastwood and Meryl Streep. These two remote sites are now the most visited destinations in Iowa.

Entire regions and countries can be similarly boosted by media exposure. Australia experienced a 20 per cent increase in visits from Americans as a result of the popularity of *Crocodile Dundee* in 1986. Scotland benefited from two feature films in 1995, *Rob Roy*, starring Liam Neeson, and *Braveheart*, starring Mel Gibson, and has promoted the district in which the first film was based as 'Rob Roy Country'. Tunisia, where both *Star Wars* and *Raiders of the Lost Ark* were filmed, enjoyed enormous popularity following the filming of *The English Patient* at Sfax, Mahdia and an oasis at Tozeur; the Tunisian Tourist Office spent £20,000 in sponsoring the UK première of the film, and is developing an 'English Patient Route'.

These are just a handful of examples to demonstrate the power of the media in influencing tourism, a factor that is, for the most part, fully taken into account and built upon by tourism authorities today, in their efforts to promote 'cultural tourism'.

MUSEUMS AND ART GALLERIES

Both museums and art galleries are visited by huge numbers of tourists each year. Many are established primarily to serve the needs of the local inhabitants, at least initially, while others have rapidly gone on to create an international reputation. Examples of the latter include the British Museum, the Ashmolean Museum in Oxford, the Louvre in Paris, the Smithsonian Museum in Washington DC and the Museum of Modern Art (MOMA) in New York.

Museums have a very long history, and in Britain date back to at least the seventeenth century, when some private collectors opened their exhibitions for a fee. Ashmole's gift of his collection to Oxford University provided the foundation for the Ashmolean Museum. In Britain alone now there are well over 3,000 museums, and of the 1,300 listed in the *Cambridge Guide to Museums*, 180 are in London alone. Some 77 million visits were paid to museums in the UK in 1991, of which 23 million were to those in London.

There are six categories of museum in Britain:

1 *National museums*, which are funded directly by the Office of Arts and Libraries, and include such famous museums as the Science Museum and the Victoria and Albert.
2 *Independent (charitable trust) museums*, financed by turnover; The National Motor Museum at Beaulieu is an example.
3 *Independent non-charity museums*, such as Flambards Museum in Helston, Cornwall.
4 *Regional museums*, which are funded by a mix of public and private funding. An example is the Open-Air Museum at Beamish in Northumbria.
5 *Local authority museums*, such as the Cotswold Countryside Museum in Gloucester, or the Georgian House and Red Lodge Museums, owned by Bristol City Council.
6. *Small, private museums*, which depend entirely upon private funding.

The period between 1970 and the mid-1980s was a boom time for museums in Britain, many of which were able to take advantage of government grant aid, coupled with charitable status which avoided taxation. A large number of redundant buildings, ideal for conversion into museums, became available during these years, and the nostalgia boom and a generally positive view towards urban renewal and heritage all encouraged new museums to open. Seventy per cent of the museums in the UK opened after 1970. A second, if lesser, boom arrived in the 1990s with the possibility of museums applying for National Lottery, or even Millennium, funding, although these funds tended to favour larger projects.

The problem for those who manage museums is that the initial capital investment is not the only financial consideration. Indeed, many collections are donated, or gifts of money are made to establish a museum, but steadily rising operating costs are seldom met by increases in revenue, and after the first two or three years, during which time the museum has novelty value, attendance figures slump. As new museums are opened, so the available market to visit them is more thinly spread. Museums have also been badly hit in recent years by the consequences of the Education Reform Act, which has made the financing of educational visits – the core business for many museums – more difficult.

Many museum curators argue in favour of subsidies, on the grounds that their museums help to bring tourists into an area, where they can be encouraged to spend. Certainly, clusters of museums and other complementary attractions such as shops do give rise to greater tourism demand. The Castlefield site at Manchester is a good example of a 'critical mass' of attractions sited close together which make the destination an attractive day out. Conference and exhibition halls have long been underwritten by local authorities on just these grounds, but local authorities are today much more constrained financially, and in some cases have been forced to reduce the support they formerly provided to the museums in their territory. Museums are having to become increasingly self-sufficient, and their curatorial role is now less significant than their marketing one. Even the major national museums such as those in South Kensington, London, have been obliged to introduce charges, or at very least 'suggested contributions'. The Science Museum started charging in 1989 and saw its attendance figures drop by 50 per cent between 1988 and 1990.

Those London museums which did not initiate a charge have benefited by a sharp rise in visitors, but those charging have been able to spend money on refurbishing which, with government subsidies alone, would not have been possible.

To attract new audiences, and bring back former visitors, many museums are moving away from the concept of 'objects in glass cases' in favour of better interpretation and more active participation by the visitors. New techniques include guides dressed in period costume, audio-visual displays, self-guided trails using cassette tapes, reconstructions of the past, and interactive programmes which provide opportunities for hands-on experience. In the kitchen of the oldest house in Toronto, for example, the guide demonstrates the making of soap, provides souvenirs of the finished product to the visitors, and reveals that the soap can be eaten, too! Some museums are fully interactive, such as the Bristol Exploratory, which is designed to explain science to the lay visitors by giving them the opportunity to become involved in practical experiments. At the Big Pit Mining Museum in Blaenavon, a former colliery transformed into a mining museum in 1980, former miners act as guides, providing vividly illustrated tours which draw on their own former experiences in the mines. An example of a 'living history' museum can be found at Llancaiach Fawr Manor, a sixteenth century fortified house in the South Wales valleys. Here, actor/interpreters (more correctly referred to on the Continent as 'animateurs'), dressed in costumes of the period, guide visitors around the site, using the language and speech patterns of the time and authentically recreating the year 1645.

It is debatable what distinguishes a 'museum' from an 'attraction'. Many museums, for example, are the former homes of famous people, and the trustees have a curatorial and research role in safeguarding and investigating documents of the previous owner, as well as promoting tourist trade to the house for commercial reasons. A good example of this is Gracelands, the former home of Elvis Presley in Memphis, Tennessee which, long after the former star's death, continues to attract huge crowds of fans to see his house, his former possessions and his grave (see

Figure 11.15 Visitors attend the graveside of Elvis Presley at Graceland, Memphis, Tennessee. *(Photographed by the author)*

Figure 11.15). On the twentieth anniversary of the pop idol's death in 1997, thousands queued for hours to see the house and gravesite, with European tour operators organising special air packages to the site. Gracelands has become one of the major tourist attractions in the United States, and is listed in the National Register of Historic Places; with over 700,000 visitors annually, it is now second only to the White House itself in terms of annual visits to these sites.

Retail shopping

While shops are not considered in the normal way part of the tourism industry, there can be no doubt that they exercise a considerable attraction for tourists, and in many cases may be the sole attraction. The flood of visitors to London to take advantage of the January sales (particularly that held by Harrods, the best-known department store in the world, which will attract shoppers from all over the globe) is just one example of the power of shops to influence tourists. Internationally, one can cite examples such as the weekend shopping flights to capitals such as Paris or Rome, or British shopping expeditions by ferry to the French supermarkets just before Christmas

(the liberalisation on duty-paid goods within the EU after the beginning of 1993 saw ferry bookings rise by as much as 18 per cent in some cases, as British shoppers flocked to the Continent to benefit.) The great department stores such as Saks Fifth Avenue or Bloomingdales in New York, or even the humble Marks and Spencers in Oxford Street (which has laid claim to the highest turnover per square foot in the world) exercise considerable influence on visitor spend, and of course expenditure on shopping features in the tourism balance of payments.

Increasingly, shopping is being combined with other forms of leisure in the design of attractive shopping malls, which can attract huge numbers of visitors prepared to spend several hours enjoying themselves in an environment that encourages people to spend. Perhaps the outstanding example of this development is the Mall of America, built in 1992 at Bloomington, Minneapolis and claiming to be the second most visited site in the USA, with some 40 million visitors a year. At 4.2 million square feet, and offering 400 stores, 45 restaurants, 14 cinemas, a 7-acre amusement park and a miniature golf course, the site provides everything that the leisure shopper could hope for. It attracts a global market, and most notably brings in shoppers on direct flights from London, Amsterdam, Korea and Japan. North West Airlines arranges flight packages between London and Minneapolis as 'shopping breaks', with on-site hotel accommodation provided. Many of the North American malls were developed underground as all-weather facilities where people could enjoy a leisurely shopping expedition even in winter; but they have since proved to be capable of attracting crowds from considerable distances away. In Britain, some towns have copied the American concept, and in recent instances have even gone as far as emulating the architecture of that continent, with 'New England'-style themes such as that found at Bicester, near Oxford. Bicester, and similar malls in Swindon, Wilts, and Ellesmere Port, South Wirral, have focused on the concept of 'designer outlets' selling up-market products which bring up-market shoppers from some distances away. Others focus on size and choice, including such well-established new sites as the

Figure 11.16 Event attraction: the annual Bristol to Bournemouth veteran car rally. *(Photographed by the author)*

Lakeside Shopping Centre at Thurrock, Essex and Merry Hill Centre in Birmingham. 'Factory outlet' malls such as those at Street in Somerset and Festival Park, Ebbw Vale in Wales offer direct sales to the public from manufacturers at discounts attractive enough to bring in tourists up to two hours' or more driving distance. The Gateshead Metro is the largest in the UK, but Covent Garden in London, which was developed out of the former fruit, flower and vegetable market, has been able to offer the equal attractions of a first-class set of nineteenth-century buildings tastefully restored as a shopping mall in the heart of London. With the added appeal of round-the-clock events such as buskers, this shopping facility has become an important addition to the visitor attractions of London's capital.

Events

Up to this point, we have mainly been talking about fixed-site attractions. It is important to remember that tourists will also visit a place in order to participate in, or observe, an event. In some cases, these events occur regularly and with some frequency (for example, the Changing of the Guard in London); in others, the events are intermittent, perhaps annually or even less frequently (arts festivals such as the

Venice Bienniale, held every two years, the four-yearly Olympic Games, or the Floriade flower festival which takes place in a different Dutch city every decade). In some cases, they may be one-off ad hoc arrangements to take advantage of a particular occasion (such as the all-day pageant event organised to celebrate the reopening, after refurbishment, of Castle Park in Bristol in 1993).

Many tourism sites use events as a means either of increasing the number of visitors to their destination, or helping to spread the demand to the shoulder seasons. One interesting example of this is the costume events mounted by the Sealed Knot Society in England, a voluntary body with an interest in English history of the Civil War period, which, *inter alia*, recreates battle scenes on the original sites, drawing very large audiences. Other sites such as towns which in themselves may not be seen as having any particular merit for tourism, may nevertheless mount a special event designed to bring the tourist there. Certain forms of event will be more likely to attract a market consisting of older or more wealthy people; these groups are more likely to have the freedom to choose the time of their travel and, indeed, may even wish to avoid the crowds that are common in the peak seasons. Some off-peak events have been so successful that the destination has managed to turn a low winter season into a peak attraction; the Quebec Winter Carnival is a case in point.

There is, of course, a direct relationship between the degree of attractiveness of the event and the distance visitors are willing to travel to visit it. The drawing power of the Olympic Games is so immense that huge crowds can be attracted from all over the world, and Atlanta was more than happy to spend some $250 million in its efforts to gain the right to host the Games in 1996. The success of Sydney in securing the Games in the Millennium year of 2000 was a major coup for Australia's tourism industry. International Expo exhibitions such as that held at Seville in 1992, which are often used as a showcase to promote the country, will also attract a global audience willing to pay the high gate fees that are charged for entry.

Smaller, but still significant events capable of boosting the local economy are prominent fea-

Figure 11.17 Site and event attraction: Snow White and the Seven Dwarfs parade at Disneyland, Paris. *(Photographed by the author)*

tures of many towns and villages around the world. Some have very long traditions. In Britain, ancient fairs continue to play a role in attracting visitors. Many trace their origins to the Middle Ages, often linked to the horse fairs organised by gypsies, and a strong element of Romany culture survives at these events. Notable examples include the Ballymena Fair in Northern Ireland, the Appleby Fair in Cumbria, the Stow Fair in Gloucestershire and the Nottingham Goose Fair.

ARTS FESTIVALS

Arts festivals, an important aspect of cultural tourism, have a long history in many countries, arising out of cultural and traditional festivals which often have local associations. In Britain alone, some 557 arts festivals have been identified, lasting from two days to several weeks in duration. More than a half of these have been founded since 1980, and over 60 per cent are professionally managed. Most depend upon sponsorship and financial support from their local authority. The leading events in terms of sales include the Edinburgh Festival and Fringe Festival, and the BBC Promenade Concerts.

The extent to which regions and cities, some little known on the tourist circuit, have embraced the arts festival concept will be apparent from Table 11.4, which provides a selection of those on offer in Europe during 1996.

It will be noted that many of these events are held outside the peak summer periods, for those destinations where congestion is a problem in high summer. Lengths of these festivals vary greatly, from two or three days up to, in the case of special events such as Copenhagen's Cultural Capital Year, the entire year.

Ad hoc events can always be built around a commemorative date; in 1993, for example, Norway celebrated the 150th anniversary of the birth of the composer Edvard Grieg, and special concerts were devised not only in his homeland and town (Bergen) but also in Britain and other parts of the world. The 100th anniversary of the death of the German composer Johannes Brahms in 1997 provided a similar opportunity for music festivals in his home country and abroad.

Table 11.4 Arts Festivals in Continental Europe 1996

Event	Location	Time
Brescia–Bergamo Pianistico	Brescia Italy	Apr–Jun
Budapest Spring (1100th year of Magyar settlement)	Budapest, Hungary	Apr/Jun–Aug
Cultural Capital Year	Copenhagen, Denmark	all year
Festival van Vlaanderen	Flanders, Belgium	all year
Printemps des Arts	Monte Carlo	Apr–May
Schwetzinger Festspiele	Schwetzingen, Germany	Apr–Jun
International Festival	Bergen, Norway	May–Jun
Dresdner Musikfestspiele	Dresden, Germany	May–Jun
Drottningholms Slottsteater	Drottningsholm, Sweden	Jun–Sep
Maggio Musicale	Florence, Italy	May–Jun
Holland Festival	Amsterdam, Netherlands	May–Jun
Ludwigsburge Schlossfestspiele	Ludwigsburg, Germany	May–Sep
Spring Festival	Prague, Czech Republic	May–Jun
Wiener Festworchen	Vienna, Austria	May–Jun
Arjeplog Lappland Festival	Arjeplog, Sweden	Jun–Jul
Kissinger Sommerfestival	Bad Kissingen, Germany	Jun–Jul
Feldkirch Schubertiade	Feldkirch, Austria	Jun
Festival Internacional de Musica y Danza	Granada, Spain	Jun–Jul
Ravenna Festival	Ravenna, Italy	Jun–Jul
Reykjavik Arts Festival	Reykjavik, Iceland	Jun
St Petersburg White Nights	St Petersburg, Russia	Jun
Schleswig-Holstein Musik Festival	Schleswig-Holstein, Germany	Jun–Aug
Festival dei Due Mondi	Spoleto, Italy	Jun–Jul
Umea/Korsholm Festival	Umea and Korsholm, Finland	Jun
Film Bienniale	Venice, Italy	Aug–Sep
Architecture Bienniale	Venice, Italy	Sep
Festival International d'Art Lyrique et de Musique	Aix-en-Provence, France	Jul
Arts Fiesta	Avignon, France	Jul–Aug
Bayreuther Festspiele	Bayreuth, Germany	Jul–Aug
Bregenzer Festspiele	Bregenz, Austria	Jul–Aug
Dubrovnik Festival	Dubrovnik, Croatia	Jul–Aug
Galway Festival	Galway, Ireland	Jul
Musiksommer Gstaad-Saanenland	Gstaad, Switzerland	Jul–Sep
North Sea Jazz Festival	The Hague, Netherlands	Jul
Kuhmo Festival	Kuhmo, Finland	Jul
Munich Bayerische	Munich, Germany	Jun–Jul
Orange Opera	Orange, France	Jul–Aug

Table 11.4 cont.		
Event	Location	Time
Pori Jazz	Pori, Finland	Jul
Salzburger Festspiele	Salsburg, Austria	Jul–Aug
Savonlinna Opera Festival	Savonlinna, Finland	Jul–Aug
Vadstena Academy	Stockholm, Sweden	Jul–Aug
Verona Opera Festival	Verona, Italy	Jul–Sep
Helsinki Festival	Helsinki, Finland	Aug–Sep
Festival Inter-Celtique	Lorient, France	Aug
Internationale Musikfestworchen	Lucerne, Switzerland	Aug–Sep
Rossini Opera Festival	Pesaro, Italy	Aug
Festival of Early Music	Utrecht, Netherlands	Aug–Sep
Aarhus Festival	Aarhus, Denmark	Sep
Berliner Festspiele	Berlin, Germany	Sep
International Music Festival	Brno, Czech Republic	Sep–Oct
Eisenstadt Haydn Festival	Eisenstadt, Austria	Sep
Linz Brucknerfest	Linz, Austria	Sep
Musiktage Mondsee	Mondsee, Austria	Sep

Of course, if the festivals are capable of drawing people from greater distances, and keeping them on site for longer periods of time, the average spend increases; visitors will need overnight accommodation and food, and will be tempted to spend money on other activities during their stay. Other festivals will embrace the fine arts, crafts, drama, dance, literature or poetry. Some will commemorate historical occasions, and may be highlighted with parades, pageants, or *son et lumière* events. Most provide an opportunity for hosts and guests to meet and get to know one another. As well as meeting a wide variety of tourist needs, they also fulfil an essential requirement of contemporary tourism, that of sustainable development.

Exhibitions of all kinds, cultural or otherwise, feature prominently in global tourism. The French, never slow to exploit their cultural tourism opportunities, mounted an unusual outdoor exhibition of controversial works by the Spanish sculptor Botero in 1992. What was unusual about this event was that the massive sculptures were arrayed along each side of the Champs Elysées, Paris's major arterial highway. So successful did this experiment prove, that four years later another sculptural display of fifty works by modern sculptors was similarly displayed along the same street, reinforcing Paris's reputation as *the* city of culture for the European visitor.

THE SCOPE FOR NEW IDEAS

The beauty of tourism is that the number of products that can be devised to interest the tourist is virtually unlimited. One reads regularly in the press of new ideas that have been promoted, of new – and frequently bizarre – reasons tourists advance for visiting a site. Perhaps our ideas of what is appropriate to view have changed a little since the nineteenth century, when the Coney Island amusement park displayed 300 dwarfs in 'Midget City' and publicly electrocuted Topsy, a performing elephant, as a tourist event. There remains, nonetheless, a fascination at times bordering on the macabre with observing scenes such as those exploiting sudden and violent death, sites which Chris Rojek (1) has termed 'black spots'. Rojek describes the flood of tourists to Scotland to see the scene of the Pan Am crash at Lockerbie in 1988. Similarly, following the earthquake which rocked the city of San Francisco at the end of 1989, visitors to the city were asking to be accommodated in hotels that 'overlooked the collapsed freeway'. The BBC reported in 1995 (2) that visitors to Blackpool were clamouring to 'ride the Alan Bradley Death Tram' after a character of this name was killed in front of the tram in the popular soap opera Coronation Street. More recently, the Sunday Times (3) described as 'Terror Tourism' the growing trend for tourists to plan visits to countries beset by political disturbances or even civil wars. Some of the more curious tourist attractions in recent years, as well as efforts to develop tourist interest in the banal or bizarre, are listed below:

- Corpses displayed as tourist attractions. Perfectly preserved bodies retrieved from bogs in Denmark are on display in museums at Silkeborg and Moesgaard; undoubtedly, when the scientists have finished with their research, the 4,000-year-old Bronze-Age corpse found on the Austro-Italian border in 1991 will in turn become an object of voyeuristic interest in a tourist museum. The exhibition of corpses in this manner, however, raises serious ethical questions.
- Enterprising Hungarians offering American tourists tours around an abandoned Soviet army base. One of the highlights on the three-hour tour is the latrine. Similarly, an Ossi Park has been proposed at a site north of the former East Berlin, where the trials and tribulations of life under the former German Democratic Republic could be experienced again, including barbed wire, searchlights, police with tracker dogs and the threat of arrest by the Stasi secret police. Perhaps unsurprising when day trips to the concentration camp at Auschwitz-Birkenau have become one of the mainstays of tourism in Cracow, Poland.

- The Northern Ireland Tourist Board considered developing tours to the trouble spots that were making news, until persuaded that this would be politically insensitive. The flow of tourists asking to see the Shankhill and Falls Roads area, Bogside and Crossmaglen in South Armagh reveals what the NITB describe as the 'curiosity factor' among visitors to Northern Ireland. Meanwhile, specialist operators are arranging tours to trouble spots around the world, and an Italian operator organises trips to sites of former conflicts in Yugoslavia, Somalia and Nicaragua.
- SATOUR, the South African Tourist Office, has introduced visits to Soweto Township, an impoverished suburb in which Nelson Mandela's former home is based. Visitors also glimpse Winnie Mandela's palatial house. Plans are under way to turn Robben Island, the scene of Mandela's imprisonment, into a Museum of the Freedom Struggle; Mandela's cell will feature prominently.
- China has opened the site of a hitherto secret armaments factory, to allow tourists to practise on the firing range with rocket launchers and anti-aircraft guns. The tour is particularly popular with Americans and Japanese. Meanwhile, a Leicester-based operator in Britain has established a programme to fly tourists to Poland where they can fly in aerial dogfights in MIG fighters.
- The world's first dung museum has opened at Machaba safari camp in Botswana. Necklaces of dried polished dung can be bought in the shop. In Sweden, moose droppings are sold as souvenirs to tourists visiting Lapland, and have been given as gifts to conference delegates. The reaction of the delegates was not recorded.
- Lignite pits near Hamburg attract tourists because of their resemblance to the lunar landscape.
- After the dramatic rescue of a group of British servicemen from Low's Gully in 1994, a remote region near Mount Kinabalu in North Borneo, which was widely covered by international TV, guided tours to the peak have been popular.

- Two-hour guided tours are available around the municipal rubbish dump at Fresh Kills, Staten Island, New York.
- A former V-2 bunker near St Omer in France is to reopen to tourists as the European History Centre of the Second World War. Over 200,000 visitors a year are expected. Similarly, in Britain former nuclear bunkers sold off to the public have in some cases been restored and opened as tourist attractions.
- Plans have been drawn up in the Cayman Islands to sink a Russian destroyer off-shore. This will not only attract scuba divers, but will also offer protection to the coral reefs.
- Special tours and cruises are arranged for visitors to approach active or recently active volcanoes. These include sites in Ecuador, Sicily, Crete, Nicaragua, Iceland and the Azores. Montsarrat in the Caribbean is exploring ways in which its own volcanic eruption in 1997 can be exploited for tourism. Iceland experienced considerable interest from tourists after the eruption under the Vatnajokull Glacier in 1995.
- Walking tours across the arches of Sydney Harbour Bridge are to be arranged. A wetsuit and safety cable are obligatory accompaniments. The organisers expect over 200,000 a year to take up the opportunity.
- Miniature submarine rides are available in Loch Ness to see 'Nessie', the mythical monster. Over 500 bookings were taken before the trial runs.
- Two-hour guided tours are on offer in Berlin's red light district, with off-duty prostitutes acting as tour guides. They will answer clients' questions on all aspects of the city, including their own activities.
- At Bovington in Dorset, the army medical team put on realistic displays of amputations for visitors.
- A light bulb that has been burning continuously since 1901 in Livermore Fire Station, California, and is featured in the Guinness Book of Records, has become a minor tourist attraction. The station maintains a visitors book for comments.

Hoteliers are noted entrepreneurs, and many have introduced special events to attract out-of-season tourists, or fill rooms during the recent recession. 'Murder weekends' have been popular, while one hotel offered heavy discounts for people whose surname was Smith. Perhaps the prize for originality should be awarded to the group of hotels situated near the M25, London's notoriously crowded orbital motorway. These developed a series of 'M25 theme nights', with a 'motorway madness' banquet. All of which only goes to show that in the tourism business, some far-out ideas can be made to work. No one believed that Bradford could be turned into a popular tourist destination in the 1980s; yet it went on to become one of the success stories of British tourism.

References

(1) Rojek C, *Ways of Escape: Modern Transformation in Leisure and Travel*, Macmillan 1993
(2) Technology Season, BBC2, 7 Nov 1995
(3) *Sunday Times*, 16 March 1997

QUESTIONS AND DISCUSSION POINTS

1   Blackpool now lays stress on its beachfront entertainment, rather than its attractions for swimmers and bathers. Is this the future marketing strength for the British seaside resort, and could other British resorts follow suit? Which seaside resorts are not largely dependent upon the attractiveness of their beaches?

2   Certain types of tourist attraction pose complex ethical problems for the industry. We have seen in this chapter how mummified corpses put on display have generated tourism, but not without criticism. Another example is the use of ecclesiastical buildings as tourist attractions, when their prime purpose remains that of a place to worship. Can the demands of tourists and worshippers be satisfactorily reconciled, and how? Can you think of other issues which raise ethical questions of this kind?

Figure 11.18 Recognition for a tourist attraction of the future. The Berlin Wall, photographed immediately prior to its destruction, bears a prophetic message. *(Photographed by the author)*

3 Identify any modern buildings in your area which could become the focus of tourist interest. How would you market these? Could visits to the interior be arranged, and what problems would be posed by efforts to organise this?

1   As an assistant in the local tourist office of your town, you have been asked to identify potential attractions in the town which have not yet received much promotional effort. Draw up a list for the Tourist Officer, which:

  (a) indicates priority in terms of the site's relative importance for tourism

  (b) makes clear what the particular features of the attractions are

  (c) identifies any problems and constraints in promoting them.

2   Pleased with your report, the Tourist Officer now asks you to become involved in two further projects. He wants to produce a brochure for the town which will offer two walking tours. The first is to be a 'tourist trail', which will suggest an itinerary around the town, taking in the key attractions, for those with only a limited time to spend. The second is to be a 'shopping trail', identifying unique shops that will be likely to appeal to tourists, for which an illustrated guide and map will be prepared. Detailed artwork is not required at this stage, but present the two guides in the form of plans or diagrams, with a suitable covering report justifying your choices.

NB. For the purpose of this assignment, you may choose any town in the area, and the two trails do not have to be in the same town.

12

Tour Operating

OBJECTIVES

After studying this chapter, you should be able to:

- define the role of a tour operator, and distinguish between different types of operator;
- explain the functions of different types of operator;
- understand how operators interact with other sectors of the industry;
- understand how the activities of operators are constrained;
- construct and market a package tour;
- understand the appeal of the package tour to its various markets;
- evaluate alternative methods of tour distribution, and the importance of computer reservations systems for an operator.

Figure 12.1   The place of the tour operator in the tourism system

The role of the tour operator

Tour operators perform a distinct function in the tourism industry; they purchase separate elements of transport, accommodation and other services, and combine them into a package which they then sell directly or indirectly to consumers. Their position in the market can be demonstrated by the diagram in Figure 12.1.

Tour operators are sometimes classed as wholesalers, in the sense that they purchase services, and *break bulk* (i.e. buy in large quantities in order to sell in smaller quantities). However, wholesalers do not normally change the product they buy before distributing it, and it is for this reason that some argue for an operator to be classed as a *principal*, or supplier, rather than a traditional 'middleman'. Their argument is based on the premise that by packaging a series of individual tourism products into a single whole new product, the *inclusive tour*, the operator is actually changing the nature of those products. In a sense, the operator becomes a 'light assembly' business, recognising that the customers could well put together the same package themselves, but not at the same price. The service which the tour operator provides is to buy in bulk, and thus secure considerable discounts from the suppliers, which could not normally be matched by the customer buying direct. The operator is then able to assemble and present to the customer a package – the 'inclusive tour' – which is both convenient to purchase and competitively priced.

This service is also valuable to the principals in the travel and tourism industry. The travel industry operates in a business environment in which supply and demand are seldom in balance; nor can supply expand or contract quickly to take advantage of changes in demand. Both the airline and hotel businesses operate in circumstances which make it difficult to adjust their capacity in the short term. A scheduled flight, for example, *must* operate regardless of whether one passenger or a hundred are booked on it. A charter airline with a single type of aircraft – say, a Boeing 757 with a maximum capacity of 239 passengers – cannot expand the number of seats to take advantage of peak opportunities, nor reduce capacity if demand falls slightly. We say that supply is 'lumpy'; that is, it cannot be expanded by a single seat, but must be expanded in blocks of seats, perhaps as many as 150 at a time in the case of aircraft. This is most clearly evidenced in the example of shuttle airline services, in which airlines have agreed to carry every passenger who turns up for a flight to a specific destination. If one too many passengers turns up for a flight, the airline must lay on another complete aircraft.

In these circumstances, carriers seek ways to adjust demand to fill available seats. This is important to keep down costs per passenger, and reduce waste of resources; the aircraft costs a certain amount of money to run, regardless of the number of passengers it carries, and this fixed cost is likely to be the major element in any transport costs. Tour operators have played a very useful role for the scheduled airlines, which can offer substantial discounts on seats which they know they themselves cannot fill. Let's look at one example to demonstrate this.

Example

Suppose that the fixed cost of flying a 140-seat plane from London to Athens and back is £20,000 (that includes capital costs, fuel, crew's wages, etc). Suppose also that the additional, or variable, cost per passenger is £20 (to cover administrative expenses such as writing the ticket, and providing in-flight refreshments, extra fuel, and so on). If the airline wants to budget for a small profit and estimates that at a price of £203 it can expect to sell 110 seats, then the cost and pricing looks like this:

Fixed cost	£20,000
110 passengers × £20	£2,200
Cost of return flight	£22,200
Sell 110 tickets @ £203 each	£22,300
Profit	£130

Of course, if only 109 passengers show up, then sales drop by £203, costs by only £20, and the airline ends up losing £53. This is a very risky business!

This is where tour operators prove themselves so useful. By agreeing to purchase in bulk say, twenty-five seats, they can virtually ensure that the airline will fly at a profit. The question arises, what should the ticket price be? As far as the airline is concerned, anything above £20 a head will be profitable, as the fixed costs are already paid for. Tour operators will want the lowest price possible to ensure they can resell all twenty-five seats. Obviously, customers are unwilling to pay anything like the original £203 that was being asked, or they would have already booked with the airline itself. Let's say that after negotiating, the airline agrees to sell the seats to the tour operator at a net price of £100 each. The airline's budget now looks like this:

Fixed cost	£20,000
135 passengers × £20*	£2,700
Cost of return flight	£22,700
Sell 110 tickets @ £203 each	£22,330
Sell 25 tickets @ £100 each	£2,500
Revenue	£24,830
Profit	£2,130

* assumes all 25 seats sold by tour operator.

The airline will now be very happy: it can afford to lose some of its standard fare-paying passengers and will still be in profit. What is more, it takes no responsibility for marketing the twenty-five seats which the operator must sell. The operator takes on this burden, which may involve it in heavy selling costs, but as long as it sets a sensible price which will still deliver a profit for the company after paying overhead costs, the customer will still be able to buy seats which represent good value. A figure of £140 might be considered reasonable under these circumstances.

To ensure that tour operators do not poach existing passengers, airlines usually impose various conditions on the resale of the tickets. The main condition is that the tour operator must build the trip into a package, or inclusive tour, and publish a number of brochures to prove it. However, the airlines themselves may also try to sell other seats to seat brokers, whose role is merely to buy seats in bulk and sell these off to any market they can find.

As the tour operators build their markets, so they can eventually decide that they will have enough customers to fill an aircraft, and can consider either part-chartering a plane with other operators, or even chartering a whole plane themselves. Eventually, they may be in a position to buy and operate their own airline to carry their customers, as leading British and other tour operators now do.

In exactly the same way, hoteliers attempt to use tour operators to fill their unsold bedrooms. They, too, have a high element of fixed costs in operating their properties, and are willing to provide substantial discounts to operators and others willing to commit themselves to buying rooms in bulk. As with airlines, once the fixed costs of the property have been covered by revenue, any price which more than pays for the variable cost will represent pure profit for the hotel. To this must be added the possibility that the operator, if the price is sufficiently attractive, may even be able to provide the hotel with guests during the winter period. This will mean that the hotel can retain staff year-round, possibly avoiding closing (closure means that no revenue is coming in at all, while the hotel will still attract costs for permanent staff, maintenance, etc). Hotels in the Mediterranean also find it difficult to reach the North European market direct, and so are delighted if their marketing is done for them by the tour operators in those countries. As a result, they have come to depend largely, and in some cases entirely, on tour operators to sell their rooms. In time, many larger operators started to run their own accommodation, but in practice this proved more difficult, and most operators eventually divested themselves of their overseas properties, preferring to sign contracts with overseas proprietors, often for the entire capacity of the hotel, and sometimes for several years in advance. The hoteliers' dependence upon these contracts and their inability to reach the market-place in any other way has made them overly dependent upon tour operators, who in turn have used their dominant positions in the market to force down prices. The low profit levels achieved by the hoteliers meant cost-cutting in the level of service they provided, with self-service menus offering clients limited choice. The number of complaints rose as a result. Unfortunately, at least as far as British clients are concerned, there is little apparent willingness to pay higher prices for better standards of service.

The specialised roles of tour operators

THE DOMESTIC OPERATOR

Tour operators fulfil a number of roles, and are not only concerned with carrying traffic out of the country, although this is the role with which we most frequently associate them. Operators also exist to organise package holidays domestically, that is, to a destination within the country in which the tourists reside, although these businesses form a much smaller element of the travel and tourism industry, because it is relatively simple for tourists to make their own arrangements within their country. It is comparatively rare today to find a tour operator who simultaneously organises both domestic and foreign package holidays, although of course the originator of the package tour, Thomas Cook, started as a domestic holiday organiser and later expanded into foreign holidays. However, the larger operators are now beginning to expand into the domestic market, and Thomson Holidays, the leading UK brand, has become a major player in the English country cottage market. The longest-established domestic programmes are coach tours, operated by such well-known companies as Shearings or Wallace Arnold. More recently, the larger hotel chains in Britain have also started their own package holiday programmes in order to help fill their rooms at weekends or in the off-peak seasons. The tourist boards have strongly supported this development, and all three boards have coordinated programmes of commissionable domestic inclusive tours in brochures available through retail travel outlets.

Fragmentation is evident in the sector organising domestic programmes. Most companies are relatively small in this sector, and few are members of ABTA, or indeed of any travel organisation. Most deal direct with the public, and are therefore not involved in retailing through the trade.

THE IN-COMING OPERATOR

Those countries such as Spain and Greece which are predominantly destination countries, rather than generating countries, will have an in-coming travel sector that is as important as the out-going. Organisations specialising in handling in-coming foreign holidaymakers have a rather different role to that of outbound operators. Some are merely ground handling agents, and their role may be limited to organising hotel accommodation on behalf of an overseas tour operator, or greeting in-coming visitors and transferring them to their hotels. Other companies, however, will offer a comprehensive range of services, which may include negotiating with coach companies and hotels to secure the best quotations for contracts, organising special interest holidays or study tours, or providing dining or theatre arrangements. In some cases, companies specialise by the markets they serve, catering for the inbound Japanese or Israeli markets, for example.

In all, there are well over 300 tour companies in Britain which derive a major part of their revenue from handling in-coming business. As with domestic operators, most of these are small companies, and more than a third are members of the British In-coming Tour Operators' Association (BITOA), which aims to provide a forum for the exchange of information and ideas among members, to maintain standards of service and to act as a pressure group in dealing with other bodies in the UK which have a role to play in the country's tourism industry.

In-coming tour operators' services are marketed exclusively through the trade, and organisations work closely with the tourist boards in marketing their services.

OTHER SPECIALISATION

Many operators recognise that their strengths can lie in specialising in some particular aspect of operating. Some outbound operators choose to specialise according to the *mode of transport* by which their clients will travel. Although our earlier example was based on air travel, other companies focus on coach transport, some (especially those involved in providing camping holidays abroad) organise package holidays for their clients which enable them to use their own private cars, and some have chosen to specialise in holidays using the railways. Ferry companies developed their own package tour programmes to promote sea travel using their services (although in recent years the British ferry operators have preferred to divest themselves of these activities in order to allow specialist operators to organise the programmes on their behalf). Naturally, the coach operators and railway companies have also sought to boost their carryings by building inclusive tours around their own forms of transport.

Finally, specialism among tour operators can be based on the markets they serve or the products they develop. The most common distinction is between on the one hand the *mass market* operators, whose product – typically the 'sun, sea, sand' holiday – is designed to appeal to a very broad segment of the market; and on the other hand the *specialist* operator, which aims at a particular niche market. By trying to distinguish their product from those of their competitors, the niche market operators are not in such intense competition as are those in the mass market, and the product is less price-sensitive as a result.

Specialists have a number of advantages over mass market companies in the marketplace. Most carry small numbers of tourists, and can therefore use smaller accommodation units, such as the small, family-run hotels in Greece which are popular with many tourists, but are too small to interest the larger operators. As the specialist companies generally use scheduled carriers and do not have the level of commitment to a particular destination that their larger colleagues have, they can be more flexible, switching to other destinations if the market sours for any reason. Staff can generally be expected to have a better knowledge of the products, and as the market is less price-sensitive, the intense price competition found in the mass marketplace is absent, allowing companies to make reasonable profits. However, if they are successful, there is always the danger that one of the larger operators will be attracted to their market and undercut them, as happened when Thomson Holidays decided to get into the Paris market and rapidly undercut the market leaders in that field.

Many companies do seek to specialise according to the geographic destination. However, the danger of this particular specialism can be demonstrated in the collapse of the holiday market to Yugoslavia, following civil war in the 1990s. Yugotours, the leading specialist to the area, was forced not only to change its destination, but even its brand name, in order to build a new market, but still failed to re-establish itself.

Specialism by market is common. Some companies chose to appeal to a particular age group, as do Saga Holidays, targeting the over-fifties market, or Club 18–30, targeting the younger client. The singles market – fast growing, as social changes increase the proportion of divorced people in our society – is also served by specialists such as Solo Holidays. Obviously, there will be ample opportunity to specialise according to the specific interests, activities or hobbies of clients, and tour companies have been established to cater for such diverse needs as those of vegetarians, those with an interest in various cultural activities, golfing or angling enthusiasts, even such highly specialised activities as textile weaving. One company which has proved itself highly successful in specific targeting is Cycling for Softies, which caters for tourists interested in using bicycles as a mode of transport but still seeking comfortable and well-equipped accommodation overnight. This company's main focus is on travel in France, and they are therefore specialising in both destination and market served.

THE ROLE OF AIR BROKERS

One other role should be examined here; that of those who specialise in providing seats in bulk to other tour operators. These specialists are variously known as *air brokers*, or where their

Figure 12.2 Specialist holidays 'on safari'. *(Courtesy Abercrombie and Kent Ltd)*

business is principally concerned with consolidating flights on behalf of operators which have not achieved good load factors for their charters, they are termed *consolidators*. These must also now obtain ATOLs from the CAA in order to operate.

Brokers negotiate directly with airlines, buying seats in bulk and arranging to sell these, either in smaller bulk blocks or even individually, to operators or travel agents. They provide the airlines, especially those companies which may find it difficult to obtain good load factors on some legs of their operations, with a good distribution service, and in return the airlines are willing to offer very low net rates to fill their remaining seats. The brokers put their own mark-up on the seats and take on the responsibility of marketing them for whatever price they can get. In doing so, they have largely replaced the former 'bucket shop' operators who performed a similar function but often infringed IATA regulations in 'dumping' tickets at discounted prices on the market. Deregulation on an international scale has now considerably reduced these illegal operations and made them 'respectable'. Many mark-ups are very low, the broker making money on the huge turnover of seats they achieve, and in short-term investments in the money market.

The British tour operating scene

THE STRUCTURE OF THE OUTBOUND TOUR OPERATING BUSINESS

The number of tour operators in Britain rose steadily in the years between 1992 and 1997, although the exact Figures are not strictly comparable due to changes in the conditions under which companies are required to obtain ATOLs (Air Travel Operators' Licences). In mid-1992 there were 603 ATOL holders with licences to operate using chartered carriers. Companies using scheduled carriers were brought under ATOL control in 1993, at which point 726 operators were licensed. This number grew to 1,227 by mid-1995, when the next change in regulations was imposed. However, with no further amendments to the conditions under which licences are necessary, the intervening two years saw a further rise to 1,719 by mid-1997, of which 1,332 were fully bonded and carrying charter passengers, suggesting that there is no shortage of eager applicants willing to invest in the tour operating business in spite of its well-recognised cutthroat competition and low profits. About 630 of these remain members of ABTA.

There are two important characteristics of the tour operating business. One has been an increasing tendency to concentration, with a handful of leading companies dominating the marketplace; this is a trend that is also evident in other European countries. The other characteristic is a trend to vertical integration, with a growing number of the largest companies owning and/or controlling their own airlines and retail travel agencies. This trend has been less apparent on the Continent, at least as far as airline and tour operator links are concerned.

These are outcomes of the rapid expansion which took place in the tour operating business after the 1960s in Britain, but occurred slightly later in Western Europe and North America. Leisure, and holidays in particular, were seen as substantial growth areas for the future by many industries in the 1960s, and encouraged many new companies to come into the business, while those already established expanded quickly to maintain their dominance in the field. This led to a cycle in which many companies collapsed, due to three main problems:

1. Growing too fast, overborrowing to finance the expansion and in some cases lacking the management expertise to operate larger companies
2. Making insufficient profit to survive, in the face of intense competition which drove down prices
3. Being hit by external problems such as rises in the price of fuel, political unrest in some of the destination countries, and economic recession at home.

This has been a pattern for the industry throughout the last thirty years. In 1964, the collapse of Fiesta Tours led to tighter controls imposed on members of ABTA. The failure of Court Line and its subsidiary Clarksons Holidays – Britain's leading holiday company – in 1974, stranded 50,000 passengers abroad at the height of the summer holiday season, and was a direct outcome of all three of the above factors. In 1991, the International Leisure Group, owners of Britain's then second-largest tour operator Intasun, was brought down by a combination of recession at home, the weakness of the pound, cutthroat pricing against the leading operator Thomson, and overambitious expansion, especially in the efforts of the company to develop scheduled services for the charter airline Air Europe. The collapse of Best Travel, another company within the top seven, in 1995 reveals the continuing inherent instability of the tour operating business.

Most of the 1,700+ operators in the UK are very small companies, with only the largest forty being of major importance in the market (these held about 86 per cent of the entire inclusive tour market in 1996). Furthermore, market share tends to be concentrated in the hands of the top five or six companies (see Table 12.1).

Table 12.1 Estimated market shares of Air Inclusive Tours held by leading tour operators, 1996 (%)

Tour operator	Total market	Sales via travel agents
Thomson Holidays	21.5	27.5
Airtours	14.5	17.5
First Choice	12.0	12.5
Cosmos/Avro	5.5	5.5
Sunworld	3.5	3.5
Top five:	57.0 (1995 61.5)	66.5 (69.5)

Source: Thomson Travel Group Annual Report 1996
*Sales via travel agents represent an estimated 70 per cent of all AITs sold

Elsewhere, estimates have placed Flying Colours' market share as high as 5.2 per cent for the year ending January 1997, with Unijet and Virgin Holidays responsible for 3.6 and 2.5 respectively.

An oligopolistic concentration of some two-thirds of the market revenue sold through agents lying in the hands of just five companies is of obvious concern, although in fact this represents a considerable reduction in market share over former years. While the Monopolies and Mergers Commission has investigated this concentration in the past (notably at the time of the takeover of Horizon Holidays by Thomson in 1988), they have judged that this *horizontal* integration was not against the public's interest, given that competition has still ensured that prices are kept down. In fact, the leading three operators have seen their market share fractionally reducing in recent years, with the share held by independent operators gaining ground, so it could well be that the situation is stabilising. The leading operator, Thomson, has actually seen its market share cut substantially, from a high of around 36 per cent, and is keen to ensure that its share of the market does not fall further; while Airtours, which has been primarily responsible for the fall in Thomson's market share, appears set on achieving the number one position, so the intense price-cutting of recent years is likely

to continue. Some companies have also been over-ambitious as regards the size of the potential market when forecasting their aircraft and accommodation needs for the coming year, and have contracted for too many seats and rooms, with the result that they are obliged to offload these at whatever price they can get during the season. This constant imbalance in supply and demand places severe pressures on profits in the industry. This is best demonstrated by examining the profits achieved by the leading thirty tour operators over a period of ten years (see Table 12.2).

Table 12.2 Profits of the leading 30 UK tour operators, 1986–95

Year	Turnover (£ million)	Profit (£ million)	Profit as % of turnover
1986	2 132	35.6	1.7
1987	2 791	−24.8	−0.9
1988	3 005	15.5	0.5
1989	3 048	−0.1	−0.003
1990	2 731	40.3	1.5
1991	2 743	104.8	3.8
1992	3 621	100.6	2.8
1993	3 826	99.1	2.6
1994	4 434	85.6	1.9
1995	5 073	−9.9	−0.2

Source: CAA Reports

It will be observed that, on the evidence presented, only once in the past ten years have profits exceeded 3 per cent, and during three of these ten years a net loss was recorded. There is a caveat to these figures, though, in that they have become increasingly distorted by different accounting practices among the companies listed, and the CAA has decided not to continue publishing these statistics in the future.

The leading operators believe that low-price strategies will eventually force the smaller and less efficient companies out of the market, leaving rich pickings to be shared among the remaining contenders. However, there is little evidence to support this view. As companies such as Horizon or Intasun have been absorbed or collapsed, so others have risen to take their place. The demise of ILG resulted in the formation of four new tour operating companies, each intent on picking up market share from their predecessor. While only two of these – Sunworld and Club 18–30 – were to survive the recession of the early 1990s, the growth of the former company in particular, and subsequent rise in market share by others within the top ten, tends to suggest there is more scope for competition at the top than might have appeared to be the case. This does not refute the evidence that key market share is typically shared between the leading three players, however.

Profit squeezes have resulted in constant restructuring throughout this sector of the industry in recent years, leading to the collapse of some well-established names while others grew through mergers and takeovers. A short resumé of the most significant of these events during the decade 1988–97 will be helpful here:

- Thomson Holidays took over Horizon Holidays, Britain's third-largest operator (1988).
- British Airways Holidays took over SunMed Holidays, a leading Greek specialist, integrating it with its own holiday brands (including leading brand names Enterprise and Sovereign) into a new division, Redwing Holidays (1988).
- Owners Abroad undertook a staged purchase of the Redwing Holidays group from BA (1990–91).
- ILG bought Sol Holidays, and from Granada the Quest group of brand-name holidays (1990).
- ILG collapsed (1991).
- Novotours, formed after the ILG collapse, itself collapsed (1992).
- Riva Holidays, the second company founded following the collapse of ILG, also went out of business (1993).
- Vic Fatah, former owner of the SunMed Holidays company, formed Inspirations.
- Airtours, which in 1992 bought the leisure division of multiple travel agency chain Pickfords, attempted to take over Owners

Abroad, but was foiled. Instead, Owners Abroad established a working relationship with Thomas Cook, which had recently been taken over by the giant German tour operating company LTU and in turn bought a 21 per cent share of Owners Abroad (1993).
- Owners Abroad was renamed and relaunched as First Choice Holidays; old brands Tjaereborg, Martin Rooks, Sunfare were eliminated, and new direct sell brand Eclipse launched (1993).
- Airtours bought the leisure travel branches of retailer Hogg Robinson Travel (1993). Hogg Robinson and Pickfords were renamed Going Places.
- Thomson Holidays acquired its first domestic operation, Country Holidays.
- Airtours absorbed Aspro Holidays, a leading Wales-based operator and seventh-largest in the UK; it also acquired Scandinavian Leisure Group (SLG) (1994).
- First Choice established International Travel Holdings in Canada, operating under the brand Signature (1994).
- Thomson extended its domestic holiday interests by the purchase of Blakes Country Holidays and English Country Cottages (1995).
- Best Travel, Britain's seventh-largest operator, collapsed, the biggest failure since ILG (1995). Other collapses in the same year included Vilmar Travel, draining the Air Travel Trust Fund (ATTF).
- Inspirations bought the charter carrier Caledonian from British Airways (1995).
- Formation of Flying Colours Group, which purchased Club 18–30 and linked this with their Sunset brand (1995).
- Airtours bought Canadian operator Sunquest Vacations (1995).
- Inspirations bought twenty-eight branches of John Hilary Travel, giving them control over eighty-eight A T Mays retail travel branches (1995).
- Collapse of The Flight Company and Go-Air plunged the ATTF further into the red (1996). Other collapses this year included All Jamaica, Sunstyle, Globespan and and its airline Excalibur Airways.
- Thomas Cook bought Sunworld (which also

controlled a Canadian operator) and Time Off (1996).

- Carnival Cruises, US leading cruise company, bought 29.6 per cent of Airtours. Airtours bought Scandinavian company Spies (1996).
- Flying Colours launched its own airline (1997).
- Rainbow Holidays collapsed (1997).
- Airtours bought Suntrips, a Californian tour operator (1997).
- Airtours bought Sun International, Belgium's largest operator and owner of British operators Cresta and Bridge Travel Group (1997).
- Suntours, specialist tour operator to Turkey, collapsed (1997).

The expansion abroad by British operators is a notable feature of the 1990s. The leading operators' purchases of North American companies is explained by their desire to spread the seasonal flow of traffic, thus obtaining better year-round usage of their aircraft. Airtours seeks as far as possible to ensure an even spread of revenue between their markets in North America, the UK and the Continent.

INTEGRATION IN THE INDUSTRY

The second characteristic of the industry is the integration between tour operators, their suppliers and their retailers. In Britain (although to a lesser extent in other European countries) the operators have sought to maintain control over their transport supply in particular, usually through direct owner-ship of an airline. This helps them to control over-all standards of the package, to increase overall profitability within the group, and at the same time ensures the operator a supply of air seats when demand is heavy, although operators are careful to ensure that some of their seats are obtained through other airlines. This will enable them, when demand is lighter, to retain their own aircraft seats while 'dumping' on other carriers unwanted seats for which they have contracted. There are further operational and marketing advantages in owning and controlling take-off and landing slots.

Operators need to be carrying around 400,000 passengers a year to secure the critical mass that will make it economically viable to consider establishing their own airline. The integration of Sunset Holidays and Club 18–30 under the Flying Colours Group in 1995 was largely to ensure the necessary critical mass to set up an in-house airline. However, pressure on profits in recent years has caused a number of operators to view leasing as a more attractive proposition to purchasing aircraft.

The extent of integration among leading UK tour operators is illustrated in Figure 12.3, which reveals that not only are the leading operators owners of the leading charter carriers in Britain, but that there are also close links between them and the top two British travel agency chains. Since the purchase of Sunworld by Thomas Cook, this agency has reduced its alliance with First Choice, which is now at a marketing disadvantage against its two

Figure 12.3 Integration between UK operators, airlines and travel agents (mid-1997)

Airline	Tour operator	Travel agent
Britannia Airways	Thomson Travel	Lunn Poly
Airtours Aviation	Airtours	Going Places
Air 2000	First Choice Holidays	Thomas Cook[a]
Airworld	Sunworld	Thomas Cook
Monarch Airlines	Cosmos Holidays, Avro	
Flying Colours Air	Flying Colours Leisure Group	
Caledonian	Inspirations	A T Mays[b]
British Airways	BA Holidays	BA shops
Leisure International Airways	Unijet	
Palmair Flightline	Palmair	Bath Travel

Notes:

a Thomas Cook is wholly owned by LTU of Germany, which has a minority holding in First Choice through Thomas Cook. A marketing agreement is in force between the UK operator and agent.

b Inspirations owns the franchise of some A T Mays shops, and has a marketing alliance with others. The A T Mays chain has been purchased by US chain Carlson, which bought Inspirations in 1997.

major rivals, and is believed at the time of writing to be negotiating with the A T Mays/ARTAC WorldChoice grouping of agents for 'preferred operator' status to redress the balance. Market shares of the carriers owned by the major tour operators are given in Table 12.3, while market shares of the agents appear in Chapter 13.

Table 12.3 Size and market shares of the UK's leading charter airlines, 1996

Airline	Aircraft	Seats	%
Britannia Airways	28	7 200	26
Monarch Airlines	20	4 800	17
Airtours Aviation	20	4 300	15
Air 2000	17	3 700	13
Caledonian Airways	8	2 500	9
Others	31	5 500	20

Source: Travel and Tourism Analyst 3/1997, Travel and Tourism Intelligence, London

In 1997, Britannia announced its intention of setting up a division in Germany to cooperate with a fast-growing German tour operating company in carrying charter passengers on long-haul flights.

While the Monopolies and Mergers Commission has not felt disposed to investigate the horizontal integration of tour operators in recent years, it has shown greater concern with the process of vertical integration, and the power now wielded by operators owning their own retail outlets. At the end of 1996, the Office of Fair Trading referred the principle of integration (essentially that of Thomson's and Airtours' operations) to the MMC, to investigate:

(a) whether agents under the control of tour operators sell those operators' programmes in preference to others, and whether they therefore offer the public biased advice on the purchase of inclusive tours
(b) whether vertically integrated companies control and fix prices of their programmes
(c) the failure of these agents to advise their customers of their links with tour operators
(d) the practice of agents of insisting that customers buy their own company's insurance

policies, often at inflated prices, in order to benefit from the discounts offered on the holidays they sell
(e) whether agents are removing, or threatening to remove, from display brochures of independent agents if commissions payable are deemed insufficient.

The MMC produced the results of its investigation at the end of 1997. Recommendations were that vertically integrated companies should make clear their operator–agency links, both externally (on agency fascias) and internally. At the same time, the linking of insurance sales to discounted package tours was to be banned. Details as to how these new conditions were to be imposed were under discussion at the time of going to press.

FACTORS LEADING TO THE CURRENT ECONOMIC SITUATION

The expansion of leisure time and greater discretionary income have seen a rapid rise in demand for overseas holidays, both winter and summer, throughout the 1980s and a small but steady increase year by year during the 1990s, apart from minor falls, in 1985, 1991–92 and 1996. The industry anticipated the last of these falls, and for the first time cut back capacity in order to bring supply and demand into balance; in doing so, it was able to ensure greater profitability. Estimated

Table 12.4 Package tours by air, 1990–96 (000s)

Year	Summer AITs	Winter AITs	Total AITs
1990	8.0	3.4	11.4
1991	7.3	3.3	10.6
1992	8.8	3.8	12.6
1993	8.8	4.5	13.3
1994	10.2	5.0	15.2
1995	10.3	5.0	15.3
1996	9.3	4.6	13.9
1997(e)	8.8		

Source: Travel and Tourism Analyst 3/1997, industry estimates for Summer 1997, Travel and Tourism Intelligence, London figures for the seven years 1990–96 appear in Table 12.4.

Tour operators, recognising the strong growth potential in the overseas holiday market, sought to gain significant increases in market share while at the same time attempting to increase the total size of the market by encouraging those who traditionally took domestic holidays to travel abroad. To achieve this, they slashed prices. Large companies used their purchasing muscle to drive down suppliers' prices (at some cost to quality in a number of cases); they introduced cheap, 'no frills' holidays through subsidiary companies such as Thomson's Skytours, which attracted the budget-conscious C2D market; and finally, profit margins were trimmed. Thomson and its leading competitors, each determined not to be undersold, engaged in the periodic repricing of their holiday programme during the selling season. Thomson, from 1983 onwards, introduced the strategy of brochure reissues with cheaper prices, and this became a regular feature of the tour operating price war. Holiday prices during the period remained relatively stationary as a result, while real buying power greatly increased.

While these moves certainly expanded the market, overoptimistic forecasts of traffic growth also led to huge growth in supply; capacity generally exceeded demand each year, and operators were then forced into offloading seats at bargain basement prices. This factor has been a key one in the growth of late bookings. Traditionally, bookings for package holidays have occurred in the weeks immediately following Christmas, allowing operators more time to balance supply and demand, and aiding their cash flow – deposits paid by clients in January would be invested and earn interest for the company until its bills had to be paid, which in some cases could be as late as September or October. Holidaymakers soon came to realise, however, that if they refrained from booking holidays until much nearer their time of travel, they could snap up late booking bargains. The development of computerised reservations systems allowed operators to update their late availability opportunities quickly, putting cheap offers on the market at very short notice, which made late bookings convenient as well as attractively priced. So encouraged were customers to make late bookings that estimates by industry research specialists STATS MR were that 57 per cent of all Summer 1996 holiday reservations were being made later than 1 March. The loss to the operators themselves was considerable, with the opportunity to invest revenue and earn interest now falling from a period of months to only weeks. Uncertainty about the forward booking position also made tour operations management more difficult. Operators therefore set about reversing this trend, by a policy of 'fluid pricing'. Introduced by Thomson Holidays in 1996 and soon copied by the other leading operators, this entailed offering holidays in the brochures at different prices, with high discounts for early booking and reduced discounts as the time of the holiday approached. Some operators even quoted prices above the highest brochure price, where demand was sufficiently strong, although the legality of this has been questioned.

THE LONG-HAUL MARKET

The tendency for all mass market operators to focus on low price rather than quality or value for money led these type of tours to move down market. As they did so, tourists at the top end of the market, particularly those who had travelled frequently, began to travel independently more frequently, and to more distant destinations. The demand for long-haul packages throughout the period expanded much faster than the growth of short-haul tours, and has continued to expand throughout the recent period of recession. About 20 per cent of all holidays are now taken to long-haul destinations annually, and this figure is expected to increase in the final years of the twentieth century. In 1995, more than thirty countries attracted over 25,000 tourists from the UK, with the USA, Canada, India, Australia, Tunisia, Kenya, South Africa, Pakistan, Israel, Thailand and Egypt all recording over 100,000. Fastest-growing has been the United States, with its particular appeal of Disneyworld, and Thailand, which has successfully sold the idea of long-haul sun, sea, sand holidays to destinations such as Pattaya Beach and Phuket, attracting over 125,000 visitors from the UK in 1995.

Market leader for long-haul packages is Swiss-owned Kuoni Travel, with about a quarter of the market, with the three leading tour operators Thomson, Airtours and First Choice taking another 25 per cent between them.

SEAT-ONLY SALES

The figures for inclusive tours by air given in Figure 12.4 also contain seat-only sales, in which passengers, although ostensibly buying a package, are in fact only using the air travel portion of the tour. This type of 'package' was originally introduced by operators to fill surplus charter seats; technically, to abide by international regulations, some form of basic accommodation had to be included in the package, although this was seldom used. After January 1993, EU legislation swept away the requirement to book accommodation within EU destinations. Seat-only sales have now become an important feature of the travel industry, as growing numbers of holidaymakers are either prepared to find their own accommodation abroad, or are seeking flights to carry them to their second homes, timeshare apartments or friends' accommodation on the Continent. Even business travellers seeking to save money during the recession are known to have made use of this facility. Subsequently, 'seat onlys' also became available on block-booked seats on scheduled aircraft, offering the additional benefits for clients of no consolidations and daytime flights. Sales peaked at around 20 per cent of the total air IT market, and have now stabilised. In 1996, Globus (Cosmos and Avro) held about 19 per cent of the seat-only market, with Airtours and Sunworld each holding a further 17 per cent, First Choice 16 per cent and Thomson 15 per cent. Thus, together the top five tour operators control 84 per cent of the seat-only market.

RECENT DEVELOPMENTS

The volatility of the tour operating business can be well illustrated by comparisons between the 1996 market and 1997 market. Holiday bookings were weak in 1996, for a number of reasons. First, sterling was weak, due to the strengths of other currencies such as the US dollar, the German mark and French franc. There was widespread job insecurity and financial worries in Britain, and potential consumers were tempted to hold off booking until the last possible moment, leading to 3 million unsold holidays by the beginning of May. Brochures had been launched later than usual in 1995, reducing the 'sales window', and a heatwave that year had also led customers to expect a good year for domestic holidays. As a result, operators were forced to cut back on holidays, substantially reducing the prices of unsold holidays and finding their average margins sharply reduced, too.

By contrast, the 1997 picture had greatly improved. Operators had restrained their buying, producing a better balance between supply and demand. The use of fluid pricing ensured a better forward booking position and higher profits. A May election returning a change of government led to a period of euphoria and increased optimism about the future of the economy. This was accompanied by windfall payments of some £35.9 billion to members of building societies converting to banks; about £6 billion of this went into consumer spending over the summer, and holidays, particularly long-haul, were in strong demand.

Operators sought new locations to develop, where hotel capacity was cheap and readily available; first, the more remote areas of Greece, then Turkey became boom destinations for the British seeking sun at rock-bottom prices. European travellers were also attracted to the low prices offered by British tour companies, and tourists from Holland, West Germany and Norway, among others, were drawn to booking summer holidays out of the UK. A package tour in Holland could be booked in Britain, using identical facilities, at a saving of over 30 per cent, a bargain even with the added cost of the flight between Holland and England. Still greater savings could be achieved on long-haul flights to the Far East or Florida.

The evidence suggests that the inclusive tour market for traditional 'sun, sea, sand' destinations peaked at the beginning of the 1990s, with 54 per cent of the population choosing a package when buying an overseas holiday, a proportion that is varying little from year to year. Seventy per cent of the UK population has now had a foreign holiday at some point in their lives, a figure which has remained constant for a number of years; thus, it is reasonable to assume that the first-time market has been captured, and the future growth of the IT market is likely to be concentrated on selling greater *frequency* of holidays, and with a focus on the variety of holidays offered: short breaks and city breaks, exotic long-haul, activity and adventure, all-inclusives, etc. In 1995, over 19 per cent of UK adults claimed to have taken two holidays in the previous year, while nearly 11 per cent had taken three or more. The market for more long holidays each year has by no means peaked yet.

CONSUMER COMPLAINTS

One inevitable consequence of the process of 'trading down' was the increase in customer complaints. Studies revealed that some 40 per cent of complaints arose from the 'bargain basement' holidays, often based on late availability without guarantee of which accommodation was to be provided. The large operators were responding to consumer pressure for low-cost packages by establishing budget brands, such as Thomson's Skytours and Airtours' Aspro; however, consumers were unwilling to accept the very rational argument that they got what they paid for: minimum standards provided simply failed too often to meet consumer expectations. Even more worrying to operators was the fact that only 40 per cent of those dissatisfied were prepared to make an official complaint; others simply refrained from booking with the company again. The use by British operators of non-British-registered aircraft has also led to concern over air safety, and in one notable occurrence in 1997, passengers refused to fly on one foreign-registered aircraft which had been subject to lengthy delays before take-off due to 'technical problems'. Older aircraft registered in central European countries such as Latvia are attractively priced for charter, but there may be less careful monitoring of maintenance and other safety factors such as crew hours, especially where these are chartered through other EU countries.

One source of customer irritation was the practice of operators applying surcharges to their final invoices. Inclusive tour costs are affected by changes in the inflation rate, exchange rates or costs of supplies, particularly aviation fuel, which is priced in US$ on the world market, and is there-fore affected by either increased costs or changes in the relative values of the pound and dollar. Tour operators have to estimate their costs for all services up to a year ahead of time. They can anticipate higher costs by raising prices, which may make them uncompetitive, or they can take an optimistic approach and price low, in the expectation of stable or declining costs. Until 1988, the latter was more attractive, as moderate cost increases could be passed on to customers (within established limits) in the form of surcharges. Such surcharges, however, are resented by travellers, and are in any case not applied to scheduled fares (which can respond to market prices more quickly). It also became apparent that a handful of operators were misusing this facility and adding fuel surcharges in excess of cost increases, or even when actual fuel costs had not increased at all, as a means of raising profits sliced by open competition. Fanned by the media, the issue received government attention in 1988, and pressure was applied to the industry to resolve the problem. ABTA responded by initiating a scheme whereby operators would absorb the first 2 per cent of any increase, and give passengers the freedom to cancel without penalty if surcharges exceeded 10 per cent. In the event, ABTA's scheme was presaged by the leading tour operators themselves, who determined to phase out surcharges by guaranteeing prices for the following year. Stability in price can be obtained by 'buying forward' the fuel required for the following year, but this is only practical for the largest operators with sufficient financial reserves. While there is no formal 'futures' market in aviation fuel, negotiation is possible on future purchases of fuel on an ad hoc basis, but clearly at a premium, and purchasing forward will further affect the operators' cash flow. However, the rapid increase in the value of sterling in mid-1997 made it well worthwhile to buy in advance fuel or accommodation required for the 1998 programme.

The introduction in 1996 by the government of an 'exit tax' for all flights out of the UK, amounting initially to £5 within the EU and £10 outside the EU (this rate doubled in November 1997) resurrected the issue of hidden charges, with many tour operators not absorbing these taxes in their total price structures. Some claimed that to do so would make their prices unattractive against scheduled air rivals, which never included the supplements. Eventually, both operators and scheduled airlines were persuaded by the Government to incorporate these taxes into their prices.

The nature of tour operating

At this point let us recap on the nature of the inclusive tour, and go into more detail about how these are operated. An inclusive tour programme, as we have seen, is composed of a series of integrated travel services, each of which is purchased by the tour operator in bulk and resold as part of a package at an all-inclusive price. These integrated services usually consist of an aircraft seat, accommodation at the destination and transfers between the accommodation and the airport on arriving and departing. They may also include other services such as excursions or car hire. The inclusive tour is commonly referred to as a 'package tour', and most are single-destination, resort-based holidays. However, tours comprising two or more destinations are by no means uncommon, and long-haul operators frequently build in an optional extension to another destination in their programmes. Linear tours, such as those offered by coach companies which carry people to different destinations or even through several countries, were at one time the most popular form of trip, and still retain a loyal following, mainly among older clients.

The success of an operator depends on its ability to buy its products, put them together and sell them at an inclusive price lower than the customers could obtain themselves. Operators are in some cases booking several million beds for a season, and can thus obtain very low prices from the supplier. It is important that this still represents value for money to the customers, as the package holiday has become increasingly a standardised product, differing little between destinations. The destination or country does not play a crucial part in customer choice, and they will readily substitute an alternative destination for their first choice if they feel that the latter is becoming overpriced.

Tour operators keep prices low either by restraining profits, or by cutting costs. Cost savings are achieved by chartering whole aircraft instead of merely purchasing a block of seats on a scheduled flight. Further savings can be made by time series chartering of the aircraft over a lengthy period of time, such as a whole season, rather than on an ad hoc basis. Ultimately, larger tour operators can further trim costs by running their own airlines, and this also allows them to exercise better control over their operations and the standards of their product. Owning your own aircraft ensures that when demand is there, you have the aircraft to meet it at a price you can afford. Emphasis then shifts to ensuring that the highest possible load factors – the percentage of seats sold to seats available – are achieved, and that the aircraft are kept flying for the maximum number of hours each day; aircraft are not earning revenue while stationary on the ground. This means careful planning to ensure turnarounds (time spent between arriving with one load of passengers and taking off with another) are as rapid as possible, commensurate with good standards of safety. Consequently, common flight plans involve establishing a 'W' flight pattern for the aircraft (see Figure 12.4), which produces the maximum usage of the equipment during a 24-hour period.

One problem arising from the tight scheduling of W-pattern flights occurs when different operators contract for morning, afternoon and evening flights. If one operator decides to cancel, the airline concerned has to find alternative users for the aircraft, which may mean a longer flight commitment, causing delays, or a change of flights, to passengers already booked. The knock-on effect of delays can become very apparent if air traffic

Figure 12.4 A typical 'W' flight pattern

Gatwick
0740

Palma
0955–1055

Bristol
1310–1410

Palma
1625–1725

Gatwick
1940–

controllers go on strike or mount go-slows. Tight flight scheduling means that a delay in one flight could have repercussions on flights using the same aircraft for the next two or three days.

High load factors are achieved by setting the break-even (the number of seats to be sold on each flight to cover all operating, administrative and marketing costs associated with the flight) at a point as close as possible to capacity. This brings down the average seat cost to a level which will encourage people to travel. On many well-marketed charter flights, break-even is set as high as 90 per cent or higher, while actual average load factors may be as high as 96–98 per cent. The company makes its profits on the difference between these two figures, and since clearly every extra person carried is almost pure profit (virtually all costs having been covered), then substantial reductions can be made for last-minute bookings to fill these final seats. Of course, if break-even load factors have not been reached, the operator will not cover all costs, but it will still be better to attract as many people as possible for the flight, because they will at least make a contribution to the fixed costs of operating the flight, even if all costs are not recovered. Passengers may also buy duty-free goods on board, which will make a further contribution to profit for the airline – or, taking a broader view, for the parent company of the jointly-owned airline/tour operator.

Productivity in airline operations can be aided, as we have seen, by the procedure of *consolidating* flights. Charter flights with unacceptably low load factors can be cancelled, and their passengers transferred to other flights, or even departures from other airports. This helps to reduce the element of risk for the operator, otherwise break-evens would have to be set at a lower level of capacity, and fares would be consequently higher. Such consolidations are not available for groups carried on scheduled airline services, and are in any case subject to considerable restrictions, such as adequate advance notice being given to the client. Inevitably, they are unpopular with clients, and many companies are now trying to avoid their use.

THE PROBLEM OF SEASONALITY

A problem facing all sectors of tourism is the highly seasonal nature of most tourist traffic. Nowhere is this more apparent than in the demand for package holidays in Europe. This market, however, is also highly price-sensitive, and longer periods of holiday entitlement over the past twenty years have helped to encourage many people to take their second holiday abroad, too – often outside of the peak periods of holiday demand. This meant that operators could spread their fixed costs more evenly over the entire year, rather than concentrating them into the summer periods, helping to reduce prices further. Most importantly, it allows the operator to contract for aircraft and hotels on a year-round basis. If a summer season only is programmed, the operator is left with a 'dead leg' twice in the year; an aircraft returning empty after the first flight of the season because it has no passengers to pick up, and an empty outbound flight at the end of the season to pick up the last clients returning home. The costs of these empty flights have to be built into the overall pricing structure of the programme, and if they can be avoided, by offering year-round programmes, clearly prices can be reduced.

Operators also use marginal costing techniques to attract their clients out of season. This means pricing the holidays to cover their variable costs and making some contribution to fixed costs. This recognises that many costs, in operating hotels, for example, continue whether the hotel is open or closed, and any guests that the hotel can attract will help to pay the bills. They will also enable the hotel to keep its staff year-round, thus making it easier to retain good staff. Some market segments – pensioners, for example – can be attracted to the idea of spending the entire winter abroad if prices are low enough, and hoteliers welcome these budget clients who can still be expected to spend some additional money in the hotel bars.

OPERATING SCHEDULED PROGRAMMES

Not all destinations allow charter flights to operate into their territory (often in order to protect bookings on the scheduled flights of the country's airline). Nor will there be sufficient demand for many destinations, such as those served by most long-haul programmes, to merit chartering an aircraft. For these forms of packaging, the net inclusive tour-basing (ITX) or group inclusive tour (GIT) fares can be used by the operator, which may in this way either contract for individual seats based on client demand (around which a tailor-made holiday can be constructed), or will contract for a block of seats on flights to satisfy the needs of a brochure programme.

Airlines will allow ITX fares to be applied subject to certain conditions attached to the programmes. A minimum number of brochures must be printed, and the programme must consist of a package of flight, accommodation and transfer or other feature. The tour programme can be organised using one or more carriers, but approval is usually sought through a particular carrier, who will validate the programme and provide a tour code number, which is contained on each ticket issued. Tour operators making a forward commitment on seats must also obtain an Air Travel Organisers' Licence (ATOL) through the CAA.

Control over tour operating

Regulations restricting tour operators were very limiting when the mass tour market developed in the 1960s. In particular, the regulation known as Provision 1 made it impossible to price package tours lower than the cheapest regular return air fares to a destination. The sole exceptions to this rule were in the case of affinity groups, which involved charters arranged for associations whose existence was for a purpose other than that of obtaining cheap travel. Members were obliged to have been members of the organisation for at least six months before they became eligible for low-cost flights. The rule was designed to protect scheduled carriers, and to ensure adequate profit for tour operators, but it severely hindered the expansion of the package tour business. It was also widely abused by club secretaries who back-dated membership, and many spurious clubs were formed in order to provide the benefits of cheap travel.

When the CAA was established in 1971, restrictions were lifted, initially only during the winter months (leading to a huge increase in off-season travel), but by 1973 this was extended to all seasons. However, at the same time the CAA tightened up control on tour operators themselves, in 1972 bringing in the requirement to hold ATOLs for charters and block-booked scheduled seats, and at the same time introducing a system for vetting operators on their financial viability. Licences are not required for domestic air tours, nor for travel abroad using sea or land transport.

Following the collapse of an important tour operator, Fiesta Tours, in 1964, which left some 5,000 tourists stranded abroad, the industry and its customers came to recognise the importance of introducing protection against financial failure. On the whole, in the UK successive governments in the past two decades have preferred to allow the industry to police itself rather than to impose additional controls, and this has been undertaken relatively effectively by ABTA on behalf of tour operators and travel agents in the UK. In 1965, ABTA set up a *Common Fund* for this purpose, anticipating legislation for the compulsory registration of tour operators. When this did not materialise, ABTA introduced its *Stabiliser* regulation, under which Common Fund provisions were to apply only to ABTA members' clients, and a reciprocal agreement was entered into whereby ABTA tour operators were restricted to selling their package holidays exclusively through ABTA travel agents. In turn, ABTA agents were restricted to selling tours operated by ABTA tour operators. Many agents, however, resented having to contribute to a fund to insure operators, and it also became clear that the provisions against collapse were inadequate. In 1967, the Tour Operators' Study Group (TOSG – later to become the FTO, Federation of Tour Operators), an informal group comprising approximately twenty of the leading tour operators, decided to establish their own bonding scheme. A bond is a guarantee given by a third party (usually a bank or insurance company) to pay a sum of money, up to a specified maximum, in the event that the company becomes insolvent. This money is then used to meet the immediate financial obligations arising from the collapse, such as repatriating tourists stranded at overseas resorts, and reimbursing clients booked to travel later with the company. TOSG's bonding scheme became a reality in 1970.

Later, ABTA itself introduced its own bonding scheme for all tour operating (and retail agency) members. The collapse in the peak of summer, 1974 of the Court Line group brought down Clarksons Holidays, Britain's leading tour operator, and revealed once again that protection was inadequate. At this point the government stepped in to introduce an obligatory levy of 2 per cent of operators' turnover between 1975 and 1977. This levy, imposed by the Air Travel Reserve Fund Act of 1975, established the Air Travel Reserve Fund (later, this became the Air Travel Trust Fund). However, these reserves were severely depleted by collapses in the early years of the 1990s, particularly that of the International Leisure Group. Collapses in the mid-1990s were still leading to difficulties for the ATTF, which had to call on the government for additional borrowing facilities when reserves were depleted in 1996. At the time of writing (end of 1997), the fund is some £5 million in debt, and levies may have to be reintroduced to place the fund back on its feet.

THE EUROPEAN UNION AND PACKAGE HOLIDAYS

Operation Stabiliser has been seen to work reasonably effectively since its introduction in the 1960s, although its effectiveness has been limited to members of ABTA, of course. The lack of control over other members of the industry, and one or two spectacular collapses of non-ABTA members in the early 1990s, revealed the weakness of the system for policing the industry in general.

This concern was shared by the European Commissioners, who were also looking at the problems of protecting consumers in other member countries. In 1991, the EC Directive on Package Travel was published, designed to extend responsibility to all sectors of the industry. The new regulations, which were to come into effect in 1993, covered non-air-based holidays also. The British Department of Trade and Industry (DTI) responded to the Directive with a Consultative Document to implement the Directive in the UK. The measures to be introduced included the following obligations:

(a) all tours to be licensed
(b) a public protection fund to be set up, similar to that offered by the Air Travel Trust, covering other forms of package holiday
(c) tour operators to be required to observe certain minimum standards in brochure descriptions
(d) travel agents to become responsible, not only for the information contained in brochures they stocked, but for providing necessary advice to clients on booking (e.g. health requirements, passport and visa requirements, insurance needs, etc)
(e) restrictions on surcharges and changes to bookings (although these were in effect weaker than those already imposed under ABTA regulations).

The imposition of these regulations brought considerable problems for operators and agents, not least because the interpretation of the regulations was unclear. In particular, it remained unclear what exactly constituted a 'packaged holiday' – was this to include business trips, and tailor-made holidays? Would all organisers of packages, such as clubs, or schoolteachers organising educational trips, be included? 'Occasional' organisers were to be excluded, but the interpretation of what constituted 'occasional' posed further problems. What was immediately apparent was that the long-standing 'Stabiliser' regulation could no longer be enforced, as all operators and agents were now required to be bonded.

The move to set up a Travel Protection Association to license surface operators was slowed by disagreements betweeen the partners concerned (FTO, ABTA, AITO, the Bus and Coach Council and the Passenger Shipping Association) about whether membership in the new body should be mandatory or voluntary. The FTO withdrew from discussions in order to implement its own scheme, and since then a number of alternative schemes have been introduced, either in the form of bonds or trustee accounts.

Initially, some believed that ABTA could no longer survive, but its significance and the need to have a body to represent the interests of tour operators and retailers as a whole has ensured that ABTA has survived, albeit in a much-weakened form of its former self. Many operators have chosen not to remain members.

What does appear clear is that the additional burden of responsibility placed on tour operators has led to some increases in cost for consumers, as operators attempt to cover themselves against any threat of legislation. Operators now become responsible for any negligence on the part of their suppliers overseas, or failure of their suppliers to provide any services for which the client has booked.

Planning, marketing and operating package tours

Planning for the introduction of a new tour programme or destination is likely to take place over a lengthy span of time, sometimes as much as two years. A typical time scale for a programme of summer tours is shown in Figure 12.5.

In planning deadlines for the programme, it is necessary to work backwards from the planned launch dates. One critical problem is when to determine prices. These have to be established at the last minute before material goes to printing, but inevitably this will be several months before the tour programme starts, and entails a good understanding (and some luck!) with regard to the movement of currency and the foreign exchange markets in the intervening period.

MARKET RESEARCH

In practice, the decision to exploit a destination or region for package tours is as much an act of faith as the outcome of carefully considered research. Forecasting future developments in tourism, which as a product is affected by changing circumstances to a greater extent than most other consumer products, has proved to be notably inaccurate. As we have seen, tourist patterns change over time, with a shift from one country to another and from one form of accommodation to another. With the emphasis on price, the mass tour operator's principal concern is to provide the basic sun, sea and sand package in countries that provide the best value for money. Transport costs

will depend upon charter rights into the country, distance flown and ground handling costs. They will also be affected by the relative demand for, and supply of, aircraft in any given year. Accommodation and other costs to be met overseas will be the outcome of exchange rates against sterling, and operators must consider these vis-à-vis other competitive countries' currency values when considering how many clients they can anticipate travelling to any one destination. Operators also have to take into account such qualitative issues as the political stability of the destination, the support given to developing tourism to the destination by the carriers, or tourist office, of the country, and the relationship between the host and destination countries. Increasingly, the effect upon the environment of such new development must be considered, and how this can be effectively managed by the operators, the hotels they work with and the local authorities.

Once the tour operators have narrowed the choice to two or three potential destinations, they must produce a realistic appraisal of the likely demand for these destinations, based on factors such as the number of tourists the destinations presently attract, growth rates over recent years, and present shares held by competing companies. The mass market operators are unlikely to be looking at a single year's programme – any commitment to a destination is likely to be for a substantial period of time, unlike the specialist operator, which may be more flexible in switching destinations according to changing demand. Mass market operators will be considering long-term contracts with their hoteliers abroad, or even establishing their own hotels.

Availability of suitable aircraft for the routes must be ascertained. This will in part dictate capacities for the programme, since aircraft have different configurations and on some routes where aircraft are operating at the limits of their range, some passenger seats may need to be sacrificed in order to take on board sufficient fuel to cover the distance. In some instances, provincial airport runways may be insufficient for larger, fully laden aircraft, and again, fewer passengers may be carried to compensate.

All planning is, of course, also dependent upon

RESEARCH/ PLANNING	YEAR 1	Summer	First stages of research. Look at economic factors influencing the future development of package tours. Identify likely selection of destinations.
		September/December	Second stages of research. In-depth comparison of alternative destinations.
	YEAR 2	January	Determine destinations, hotels and capacity, duration of tours, departure dates. Make policy decisions on size and design of brochure, number of brochures to print, date for completion of print.
NEGOTIATION		February/March	Tenders put out for design, production and printing of brochures. Negotiate with the airlines for charter flights. Negotiate with hotels, transfer services, optional excursion operators.
		April/May	Typesetting and printing space booked with printer, copy for text commissioned. Illustrations commissioned or borrowed. Early artwork and text under development at design studio, with layout suggestions. Contracts completed with hotels and airlines, transfer services, etc.
		June	Production of brochure starts.
ADMINISTRATION		July	Determine exchange rates. Estimate selling prices based on inflation, etc. Galley proofs from printer, corrections made. Any necessary reservations staff recruited and trained.
		August	Final tour prices to printer. Brochures printed and reservations system established.
MARKETING		September/October	Brochure on market, distribution to agents. Initial agency sales promotion, including launch. First public media advertising, and trade publicity through press, etc.
	YEAR 3	January/March	Peak advertising and promotion to trade and public.
		February/April	Recruitment and training of resort representatives, etc.
		May	First tour departures.

Figure 12.5 Typical time scale for planning a summer tour programme

the company having the necessary finance available to operate and market the programme.

The process of negotiating

Once the decisions have been made as to destinations to be served and numbers of passengers to be carried during the season, and dates of departure have been established, the serious negotiations can get under way with airlines, hotels and other principals, leading to formal contracts. These contracts will spell out the conditions for the release of unsold accommodation or (in the case of block bookings on scheduled services) aircraft seats, or the cancellation of chartered aircraft flights, with any penalties that the tour operator will incur. Normal terms for aircraft chartering are for a deposit to be paid upon signing the contract (generally 10 per cent of the total cost), with the balance becoming due on each flight after it takes place. In negotiating with charter services, the reputation of the tour operator is of paramount importance. If they have worked with that airline, or with similar charters, in previous years, this will be taken into account in determining the terms and price for the contract.

A well-established operator does not wish to be at the mercy of market forces in dealing with charter airlines. In any given year, the demand for suitable aircraft may exceed the supply, leading the larger tour operators to form or buy their own airline, just to ensure that capacity is available to them.

Part and parcel of the negotiations is the setting up of the tour operating flight plan, with decisions made on the dates and frequency of operations, the airports to be used and times of arrival and departure. All of this information will have to be consolidated into a form suitable for publication and easy comprehension in the tour brochure.

HOTEL NEGOTIATIONS

Hotel negotations, other than in the case of large tour operators which negotiate time contracts for an entire hotel, are generally far more informal than is the case in airline negotiating. Small and specialist tour operators selling independent inclusive tours (IITs) may have no more than a free-sale (or sell and report) agreement with hoteliers, by which the hotel agrees to guarantee accommodation for a specified maximum number of tourists (usually four) merely on receipt of the notification of booking from the tour operator, whether by phone, mail, telex or more commonly now, fax or e-mail. This arrangement may be quite suitable for small tour programmes, but it suffers from the disadvantage that at times hoteliers will retain the right to close out certain dates. As these are likely to be the most popular dates in the calendar, the operator stands to lose both potential business and goodwill. The alternative is for the operator to contract for an allocation of rooms in the hotel, with dates agreed for the release of those unsold, well in advance of the anticipated arrival dates.

Long-term contracts, either for a block of rooms or for the entire hotel, have the attraction of providing the operator with the lowest possible prices, but they carry a higher element of risk. Some contracts have been drawn up by operators for as long as five years, and while at first glance such long fixed-term price contracts may seem attractive, they are seldom realistic, and in an inflationary period may well have to be renegotiated to avoid bankrupting the hotelier. Such an event would obviously not be in the operator's interest.

In addition to the operator spelling out exact requirements in terms of rooms – required numbers of singles, doubles, twins; with or without private facilities; whether with balconies or seaviews; and with what catering provision, e.g. room only, with breakfast, half or full board – they must also clarify a number of other facts, including:

- reservations and registration procedures (including whether hotel vouchers are to be issued)
- accommodation requirements for any representatives or couriers (usually provided free)
- handling procedures and fees charged for porterage
- special facilities available or needed, such as

catering for handicapped customers, or special catering requirements such as kosher or vegetarian food
- languages spoken by hotel staff
- systems of payment by guests for drinks or other extras
- reassurance on suitable fire and safety precautions
- if appropriate, suitable space for a representative's desk and noticeboard.

It is also as well to check the availability of alternative hotel accommodation of a comparable standard in the event of overbooking. Of course, a hotel with a reputation for overbooking is to be avoided, but over the course of time some errors are bound to occur, and will require guests to transfer to other hotels. Tour operators must satisfy themselves that the arrangements made by the hotelier for taking care of clients in these circumstances are adequate. Any operator negotiating with a hotelier will be aware that they are likely to be sharing contracted space with other operators, not only within their own country but also from other countries. It is as well to be aware of one's own standing with the hotelier vis-à-vis other companies; for example, in Spain it is not uncommon to find that the German operators, who tend to pay higher prices for their rooms than do the British, will have their rooms protected in preference to British operators, when overbookings occur.

ANCILLARY SERVICES

Similar negotiations will take place with locally based in-coming operators and coach companies to provide coach transfers between airport and hotels, and any optional excursions. Car hire companies may also be approached to negotiate commission rates on sales to the tour operator's clients.

The reliability and honesty of the local operator is an important issue here. Smaller tour operators in the UK will not be in a position to employ their own resort representatives initially, hence their image will depend upon the level of service provided by the local operator's staff.

If the local company is also operating optional sightseeing excursions, procedures for booking these and handling the finances involved must be established, and it should be clarified whether qualified guides with a sound knowledge of the English language are to be employed on the excursions. If not, tour operators must reassure themselves that all driver-couriers will be sufficiently fluent in the English language to do their job effectively for the company.

The role of the overseas representative

Tour operators carrying large numbers of package tourists to a destination are in a position to employ their own resort representatives. This has obvious advantages in that the company can count on the loyalty and total commitment of their own staff. A decision must be made as to whether to employ a national of the host country or of the generating country. The advantage of a man or woman from the local community is that they will be better acquainted with the local customs and geography, fluent in the language of the country and will have good local contacts, which may make it easier to take care of problems (such as dealing with the police, local shopkeepers or hoteliers) more effectively. On the other hand, they are likely to be less familiar with the culture, customs or language of their clients, and this can act as a restraining influence on package tourists, especially for those on first visits abroad. Exceptional local representatives have been able to overcome this problem, and if they themselves have some common background with their clients, such as having lived for some years in the incoming tourists' country, they can often function as effectively as their counterparts from the generating country. However, some countries impose restrictions on the employment of foreign nationals at resorts, and this is a point which must be clarified before employing representatives.

The representative's role is far more demanding than is commonly thought. During the season, he or she can be expected to work a seven-day week and will need to be available on call for twenty-four hours each day to cope with any emergencies. Resort representatives are usually given a desk in the hotel lobby from which to work, but in cases where tour operators have their clients in two or more hotels in the resort, the representative may have to visit each hotel during some part of the day. Their principal functions include:

- handling general inquiries
- advising on currency exchange, shopping, etc.
- organising and supervising social activities at the hotels
- publicising and booking optional excursions
- handling special requirements and complaints, and acting as an intermediary for clients, interceding with the hotel proprietor, the police or other local authorities as necessary.

These routine functions will be supplemented by problems arising from lost baggage, ill-health (needing to refer clients to local dentists or doctors), even occasionally deaths, although serious problems such as these are often referred to area managers. The representatives must also relocate clients whose accommodation is for any reason inadequate, or when overbookings have occurred, and they may also have to rebook flights for their clients whose plans change as a result of emergencies.

The representatives' busiest days occur when groups are arriving or leaving the resort. They will accompany groups returning home, on the coach to the airport, ensuring that departure formalities at the hotel have been complied with, arrange to pay any airport or departure taxes due, and then wait to greet incoming clients and accompany them in turn to their hotels on the transfer coaches. They must ensure that check-in procedures operate smoothly, going over rooming lists with the hotel managers before the latter bill the company. Most operators also provide a welcome party for their clients on the first night of their holiday, and it is the representatives' task to organise and host this.

Representatives can also expect to spend some time at their resort bases before the start of the season, not only to get to know the site but to report back to their companies on the standards of tourist facilities and to pinpoint any discrepancies between brochure descriptions and reality. This

Figure 12.6 Overseas representative dealing with clients. *(Courtesy Thomson Holidays)*

has become increasingly important under the new regulations imposed through the EU Directive on Package Holidays, and representatives are also expected to inform their companies if any changes occur during the season of which the clients must be notified at the time of booking.

The importance of the representatives' job is recognised by companies, and today there are more opportunities for full-time posts, alternating between summer resorts and winter resorts, sometimes starting with positions as children's reps, but with promotional opportunities to representative, senior representative, area supervisor and area manager. Ultimately, progression must lie back in head office, where managers having overall responsibility for resort representatives must recruit and train staff, organise holiday rosters, provide uniforms and handle the administration of the representatives' department. Nevertheless, many posts are still dependent upon seasonal staff (the largest companies will employ thousands such staff each summer), and the drive to cut costs has affected these staff, too. Leading tour operators are reducing staff by developing a 'service centre' accessible to clients by phone, avoiding the need for large numbers of peripatetic staff. However, this is a practice which must be questioned, if one accepts that the only clear distinction between one operator and another at a resort is in the quality of its representation.

Pricing the package tour

A key requirement for success in a tour operator's programme is to get the price right. Price must be right for the market, right compared with the price of competitors' package tours, and right by comparison with the price of other tours offered by the company.

Specialist operators which offer a unique product may have more flexibility and the freedom to determine their prices based on cost plus a mark-up that is sufficient to cover overheads and provide a satisfactory level of profit. The mass operators, however, must take greater account of their competitors' prices, since demand for package tours is, as we have seen, extremely price-elastic, especially for programmes offered in the shoulder season or off-season. In the past in the UK there has been a tendency to follow the prices determined by the market leader, and economies of scale have been important in terms of reducing cost and undercutting rival prices. Below are two typical examples of cost-determined tour pricing.

MASS MARKET TOUR PRICING

This first example is based on time-series charter travel and a two-week holiday to a destination such as Spain.

	£
Flight costs, based on 25 departures (back to back) on Boeing 737 148-seat aircraft at £14 750 per flight:	368,750
Plus one empty leg each way at beginning and end of the season:	14,750
Total flight costs:	383,500
Cost per flight:	15,340
Cost per seat at 90% occupancy (133 seats), i.e. £15 340 ÷ 133	115.34
Net hotel cost per person, 14 nights half board:	225.80
Resort agent's handling fees and transfers, per person:	7.00
Gratuities, porterage:	1.00
Total cost per person:	349.14
Add mark-up of approx 30% on cost price to cover agency commission, marketing costs (including brochure, ticket wallet, etc), head office administrative costs and profit:	104.74
Selling price:	454.00

A small element of cost arises from VAT imposed on the relevant portion of the ground arrangements, and for operators whose company is not directly integrated with an airline, VAT must be added to the tour operator's margin under TOMS (the tour operators' margin scheme). Airport taxes (to include any security or other levies) would be added on a per passenger basis for both the UK departure point and the overseas destination. Many companies would add a further small fee, say £15, in order to build in a no-surcharge guarantee.

In estimating the seat cost for aircraft, operators must not only calculate the load factor on which this cost is to be based but must also aim to achieve this load factor on average throughout the series of tours they will be operating. This must depend on their estimates of the market demand for each destination and the current supply of aircraft seats available to their competitors. Since high-season demand will frequently exceed the supply of seats to these destinations, there is scope to increase the above price, and hence profits, for the high season months of the year, even if this results in the company being uncompetitive with other leading operators. However, as operators have in the past tended to overestimate forecasted demand, this is becoming a more risky procedure. In the off-season, meanwhile, supply is likely to exceed the demand for available packages, and the company may set its prices so low that only the variable costs are covered and a small contribution is made to the fixed costs (marketing, adminstration, etc), in order to fill seats.

Each tour operator must carefully consider what proportion of its overheads is to be allocated to each tour and destination. As long as these expenses are recovered in full during the term of operation, the allocation of these costs can be made on the basis of market forces, and need not necessarily be apportioned equally to each programme and destination. In practice, most operators now recover overhead costs by determining a per capita contribution, based on anticipated head office costs for the year and the total number of passengers the company expects to carry. Under this system, of course, each tour carries the same burden of office costs regardless of destination or price. However, there is a case for a more marketing-orientated approach to pricing, based on consideration of market prices and the company's long-term objectives. In entering a new market, for instance, it may be that the principal objective is to penetrate and obtain a targeted share of that market in the first year of operating, and this may be achieved by reducing or even forgoing profits during the first year, and/or by reducing the per capita contribution to corporate costs. Indeed, for some destinations the operator may introduce loss leader pricing policies, subsidising the cost of this policy from other more profitable routes in order to get a footing in the market to the new destination.

Detailed consideration of value-added taxation has not been included here for the sake of simplicity. However, VAT is applicable on profit margins of the operators operating within the EU countries, and the operator will also be paying VAT incorporated into hoteliers' and other services' contractual prices. Most tour operators (but not all) have agreed to pay commission to agents on revenue which includes the VAT cost (which the operator can later recover).

SPECIALIST TOUR PRICING

This second example is of a specialist long-haul operator which uses the services of scheduled carriers to Hong Kong, with a group inclusive tour basing fare.

	£
Flight cost, based on net group air fares, per person:	405
Net hotel cost per person, 7 nights, twin room (HK$750 per room, HK$12.50 = £1):	210
Transfers (£5 each way):	10
Sub-total:	625
Add agent's commission:	69
Total cost per person	694
Selling prices:	
'Lead price' (offered on only 1–2 off-season flights):	699
Shoulder season price:	750
High season price (summer, Christmas and Easter holiday periods):	950

It will be noted that in the case of this specialist operator, prices reflect market demand at different periods of the year, and there is no equal distribution of office overheads; profits and most overheads are recoverable in the peak season prices charged to the market. The lead price gives virtually no profit for bookings made through the trade, but is strictly limited to one or two weeks of the year. On the other hand, very high profits can be obtained over Christmas, Chinese New Year, during conferences and for other business committed to specific dates. This is quite a common policy among the smaller specialist operators who may use less sophisticated pricing techniques to arrive at target profits. Many specialists who operate in a climate where there is no exact competition for their product could be expected to charge a price which would give them an overall gross profit of 25 per cent or more, while many mass market operators, and some specialists, will be forced by market conditions to settle for much lower margins.

In developing a pricing strategy for package tours, operators must take into account a number of other variables in addition to those shown above. Earlier, the point was made that price had to be right compared with all competing products on the market; for example, when setting a price for departure from a regional airport, the operator will look at how much more the client will be willing to pay to avoid a long trip to a major airport. Similarly, if a flight is to leave at two o'clock in the morning, the price must be sufficiently attractive compared with others leaving during the day to make people willing to suffer this inconvenience. What special reductions are to be offered to children, or for group bookings? As seat and other costs will be unaffected, whatever reductions the company makes for these bookings will have to be recovered in profits achieved through sales to other customers.

As a general policy, members of the Federation of Tour Operators standardise the date each year on which rates of exchange are fixed against the pound sterling. This usually occurs at the end of June or beginning of July in the preceding year. This ensures that the public can make meaningful comparisons between the prices of tour programmes to similar destinations, and that the mass operators are competing 'on a level playing field'. However, operators can also *buy forward* the foreign currency they will require, to protect themselves against currency fluctuations. If they are involved in exchanging large sums of money, they can buy *futures* in the international money market. Needless to say, this involves speculation and an element of risk; if the operator guesses wrong, the company's prices may end up uncompetitive against those of other companies.

DISCOUNTING STRATEGIES

Discounts on published tour prices have become a widely accepted practice in the industry since retail price maintenance in the industry was curtailed in the 1980s. Originally applied to late bookings, in order to clear seats, the technique has more recently been used by the larger operators to persuade members of the public to book earlier, under a system of 'fluid pricing'. Other operators prefer to rely on guarantees to early bookers against any increases in price prior to their departure.

Since a legal challenge made in 1987 by one retailer, the Ilkeston Co-op's travel agency, against operators which forced agents to sell tours at prices determined by the operators themselves, retailers have been allowed to discount tours they sell by passing on to the clients a proportion of their commission. In practice, this has meant that the largest discounts can be allowed by the largest multiple travel agencies, who can negotiate target-overriding commissions well above the 10 per cent norm, and in effect can pass on to their clients almost all the 10 per cent basic commission. As this percentage represents the total commission which most independent agents receive from operators, the independents cannot match this and therefore find it very difficult to compete. However, many try to offer alternative benefits, such as free insurance, to attract business. The heavy discounting policy of Lunn Poly in particular has been a major factor in helping it to obtain its current share of the market, estimated at between 27 and 29 per cent of the summer 1997 inclusive tour market. The company's policy of refunding virtually all of its commission, but profiting in turn from high margins on the sale of insurance policies tied to the package, was one of the issues investigated by the Monopolies and Mergers Commission and condemned in its 1997 ruling.

THE ECONOMICS OF TOUR OPERATING

A tour operator must purchase three main inputs which will comprise an inclusive tour: transport, accommodation and services. The last of these will include transfers between terminals and the accommodation abroad, and the services provided by the company's resort representative at the site. The operator will also, of course, have to meet costs which arise within the company's headquarters; these will include administration, reservations, marketing and advertising, etc. Finally, the operator will have to meet the cost of commission allowed to retailers, and the cost of servicing those retailers. A typical inclusive tour from the UK might well have the kind of cost structure outlined in Table 12.5.

Table 12.5 Typical cost structure of an inclusive tour using charter air services

Costs	% of overall costs
charter air seat	45
hotel accommodation	37
other services at destination	3
head office overheads	5
travel agency commission	10
	100

As we have seen earlier, the profits achieved by most operators after allowing agency commissions are actually quite narrow – perhaps as little as 1–3 per cent of revenue, after covering all costs – and the operator will therefore seek to top up revenue in any other way possible. For the mass market operator, the bulk of revenue – in excess of 50 per cent, normally – is achieved through the sales of summer holidays. Perhaps another 15 to 20 per cent will be achieved through a winter tour programme, and the balance of revenue is achieved through a mix of sales of excursions at the destination, the interest received on deposits and final payments invested, foreign currency speculation, and sale of insurance policies.

The normal booking season for summer holidays starts in the autumn of the preceding year, reaching its peak in the three months following Christmas, so a large proportion of deposits will have been paid by the end of March. Although the operators themselves will have had to make deposits for aircraft charters at the beginning of the season, and may also have had to make some advance to hoteliers to ensure their rooms are held, the balance of payment will not fall due until after the clients have completed their holiday. Operators will have the use of deposit payments for anything up to a year in advance, and will have final payments at least eight weeks before they themselves have to settle their accounts. This money is invested to earn interest, and in many cases this interest will actually exceed the profits made by tour operating itself. Clearly, one effect of the growing tendency of British holidaymakers to book their holidays later, and to pay by credit card, will be a fall in earnings by the operators, which may be forced to compensate by raising the price of their holidays.

Further profits are achieved through the sale of ancillary services, such as excursions, car hire and (if the airline used is part of the parent organisation) the sale of duty-free goods on board flights. The intention of the EU to phase out duty-free sales within the Community by July 1999 will again lead to loss of revenue for operators, and could have an effect in forcing up prices. Equally significantly, it may affect the future pattern of tourist flows, since an undefined proportion of tourists may choose to switch to non-EU destinations in order to take advantage of the duty-free benefits. Countries such as Turkey or Malta could benefit from this development.

One further contribution to revenue is achieved by imposing cancellation charges. These charges will often substantially exceed any costs borne by the operator which result from the cancellation, and indeed the operator may well be able to sell the cancelled accommodation again, gaining double revenue. However, once again the EU Directive on Package Holidays now allows the substitution of names by the clients to replace cancelled bookings.

Finally, one must mention that a small proportion of package tours is sold direct to the public by the mass market operators. This avoids payment of commission to agents, so is highly profitable, particularly where unsolicited (so that no additional marketing costs have been borne by the operator). These direct sales may only account for 5–10 per cent of the total holidays booked, but obviously they result in very good profits for the operator. Companies must be careful, however, not to target clients directly, as they may antagonise their supporting agents.

YIELD MANAGEMENT

The high levels of competition for the summer tours will require the operator to take a great deal of care to get the price of the company's packages right, so that sufficient demand is generated to fill available seats, but prices are not so cheap as to threaten profitability. This skill of *yield management* is frequently defeated by the excess capacity available on the market generally, forcing companies to 'dump' packages at whatever price they can realise which will, at least, help to make a contribution to the company's overheads. Evidence that the companies are improving their skills at yield management is revealed through the generally increased profits achieved during the summer of 1996, when operators reduced their capacity to obtain a better balance between supply and demand. While this action was taken almost by implicit agreement between the major operators, there is always the risk that the smaller operators will see this as an opportunity to steal some market share from the brand leaders, and increase their own capacity.

If prices are set too low initially, and late demand in the season results in a 'sell-out', the company will not have maximised its profit opportunity. At the same time, if the company finds itself involved in added expenditure in the course of the summer – for example, in providing accommodation and meals for clients delayed through air traffic control strikes or go-slows, which cannot be foreseen – what might have been a slim but acceptable profit can soon be turned into an overall loss.

Another aspect of yield management is the

decision taken on when to launch the new holiday programme. Companies launching ahead of their rivals will always hope to steal a larger proportion of the early booking market, and of course have revenue which can be invested over a longer period. While the pattern in the past was for a launch in September, the larger operators have been progressively launching earlier, with some summer 1998 holidays available as early as May 1997. The objective in this instance was to take advantage of the post-electoral 'feel-good factor' and to soak up some of the windfall payments totalling £36 billion paid to investors as a result of the conversion of building societies to banks. In the event, the date proved too early; not only were bookings sluggish initially, both retailers and customers were confused about the range of holidays on offer, with retailer racks holding brochures simultaneously for three seasons – summer 1997, winter 1997/98 and summer 1998. While windfalls certainly accounted for the pick-up in holidays sales made during 1997, most of the bookings for the following year were made later in the summer.

The tour brochure

The tour operator's brochure is a vital marketing tool, being the main influence on the customer's decision to buy. Tourism is an intangible product which customers are obliged to purchase without having the opportunity to inspect it, and often from a base of very inadequate knowledge. In these circumstances, the brochure becomes the principal means of both informing customers about the product and persuading them to purchase it.

For this reason, very large sums are invested in the brochure itself, and in advertising, to persuade the customers to enter the travel agent's and pick up the brochure. In particular, the production of the brochure will represent a very significant proportion of the total marketing budget for the year, with print runs, in the case of the largest operators, running into tens of millions, at a unit cost of well over £1 a copy. Accordingly, it is essential for the operator to ensure that this large expenditure achieves its intended results. In spite of this, however, there is considerable wastage. Green Flag International, the environmental lobby, has estimated that of 120 million British travel brochures printed each year, 48 million are never used. This wastage rate, coupled with the high cost of each copy that is picked up and consulted free, puts approximately £20 on the price of the average package holiday.

BROCHURE DESIGN AND FORMAT

Larger companies will either have their brochures designed and prepared in their own advertising department, or they will coordinate the production with a design studio, often associated with the advertising agency they use. The agency will help to negotiate with printers to obtain the best quotation for producing the brochure, and will ensure that print deadlines are met. Other operators will tackle the design of the brochure themselves, and this process is being increasingly aided by computer graphics packages, which allow desk-top publishing, by which means the operator is able to produce the entire contents of the brochure, including all illustrations, on an in-house computer. The computer will organise the layout, selecting the best location of text and illustrations to minimise use of space, thus helping to reduce cost. Naturally, the financial investment in the technology necessary to undertake this work is considerable.

Smaller operators which do tackle the design of the brochure themselves are best advised to use the help of an independent design studio, which can provide the professional expertise in layout, artwork and copy that is so important in the design of a professional piece of publicity material. Most printers have their own design departments which can undertake this work for their clients, but unless the company has had experience of the standards of work of their printer, they are probably better advised to approach an independent studio for this work.

The purposes the brochure serves will dictate its design and format. A single ad hoc programme, for example for a foreign trade exhibition, may be printed on nothing more than a leaflet, or if a limited programme of tours is contemplated these may be laid out in the form of a folder.

Folders can take a number of different forms, ranging from a simple *centrefold* to more complicated folds (see Figure 12.9).

Larger brochures (or in printing parlance, *booklets*) consist of eight or more pages, printed in multiples of four sheets which require binding together in some manner. Smaller brochures are usually machine-bound by saddle-stitching (stapling through the spine), while larger brochures may be side-stitched with a glue-on cover, or bound as a book. It is not the purpose here to discuss printing methods in detail, and the reader is referred for further reading in the subject to the many excellent books on print publicity.

Package tour brochures can be described as falling into three categories: *shell folders*, *umbrella* brochures and *regular* tour brochures. The use of a shell folder is a convenient way to reduce printing costs, and is particularly suited for limited-capacity tour programmes or ad hoc specialist tours. Shells are blank folders interspersed with preprinted photographs, and are provided at low cost by airlines or national tourist offices to encourage smaller tour operators to run programmes using their services or destinations. The operators can overprint a suitable text describing their tour programme; since only the text needs to be added, a one-colour print run at low cost will meet the requirements of scheduled airlines for inclusive tour basing fares approval.

An umbrella brochure can be produced in order to allow a travel agent to become, effectively, a package holiday organiser. The brochure only covers the basic essentials to satisfy IATA airlines' requirements for independent inclusive tour operating, but this will allow the agent to build a tailor-made package around net tour basing fares. However, these brochures have largely fallen into disuse, as agents have the means of obtaining cheap airline tickets from a multitude of sources which may undercut regular inclusive tour basing fares.

The rest of the tour brochures are purpose-designed for regular package holiday series. They usually comprise all of an operator's summer or winter tours in a single brochure. However, many larger operators have diversified into a great many different types of holiday – long-haul and short-haul, coach tours as well as air holidays, lakes and mountain resorts as well as seaside resorts – and if all these were to be combined into a single brochure, it would run to hundreds of pages and be both clumsy to handle and very expensive to produce. There would also be high wastage, as clients who know the type of holiday they want will have to pick up the entire brochure to get their particular product. Operators have therefore produced individual brochures, even in some cases separate brochures by destination. As well as overcoming the problems identified above, this will have the added advantage of filling more of the agents' rack space, leaving less available space for competitors. If the leading half-dozen operators produce as many as seventy to eighty different brochures – all top sellers for agents – this will require the agents to devote as much as half their rack space to these brands.

The first task of a brochure is to attract attention. Operators have therefore developed a 'house style' for the covers of their brochures which is quickly recognised by customers, when displayed on the agents' racks. These are usually images of attractive models in beachwear combined with an eye-catching symbol and house name across the top of the brochure. While some might contend that there is a disappointing sameness among the leading operators' brochures today, taken individ-

Figure 12.7 Examples of tour folders

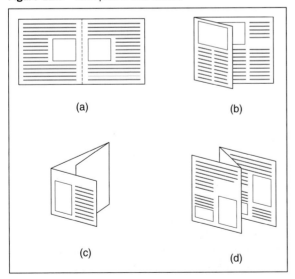

(a)

(b)

(c)

(d)

ually the quality and professionalism of their brochure design is outstanding. As brochures today must also reinforce an image of quality and reliability, the text and images contained in brochures must be not only attractive but also truthful, accurate and easily comprehended. Good layout, high-quality photography and paper are all essential if the brochure is to do its job effectively.

OBLIGATIONS AFFECTING TOUR BROCHURES

As was stated earlier, the brochure must both inform and persuade the potential tourist. Tour operators are selling dreams, and their brochures must allow consumers to fantasise a little about their holidays. But it is also vitally important that consumers are not misled about any aspect of their holiday. Care must be taken not to infringe the Trades Description Act 1968, section 14 of which deals with the offence of making false statements concerning the provision of services.

In the past, operators have invoked the law of agency in claiming that within their booking conditions they act as agents only in representing hotels, transport companies or other principals. However, the provisions of the Unfair Contract Terms Act 1977 went some way to placing the burden of responsibility on operators themselves for the services they represent, and this has now been enhanced by the EU Directive on Package Travel, which makes quite clear that operators must now take total responsibility for the care of their clients while abroad. This will simplify proceedings for the tourist, who can henceforth sue the operator for offences for which their suppliers abroad are responsible, requiring the operator in turn to sue the supplier in the destination country.

The Consumer Protection Act 1988 makes it illegal to give a misleading indication of the price of goods and services. Operators must therefore ensure that the price panels in their brochures provide full details of the tour costs. However, the larger tour operators had already introduced comprehensive price information in their brochures, and under ABTA pressure this became the norm for all member operators. ABTA's Tour Operators' Code of Conduct imposes specific obligations upon operators to provide honest and accurate information, and the new EU laws have strengthened this requirement.

INFORMATION REQUIRED IN THE BROCHURE

To satisfy not only the ITX conditions but also the clients' need for information on regular charter programmes, the operator should include the following information in the brochure:

- the name of the firm responsible for the IT
- the means of transport used, including, in the case of air transport, the name of the carrier(s), type and class of aircraft used and whether scheduled or charter aircraft are operated
- full details of destinations, itinerary and times of travel
- the duration of each tour (number of days/nights' stay)
- full description of the location and type of accommodation provided, including any meals
- whether services of a representative are available abroad
- a clear indication of the price for each tour, with any extras charged clearly shown on the same page (NB airport taxes should also be included in tour operators' pricing panels)
- exact details of special arrangements, e.g. if there is a games room in the hotel, whether this is available at all times and whether any charges are made for the use of this equipment
- full conditions of booking, including details of cancellation conditions
- details of any optional or compulsory insurance coverage (clients should have the right to select an alternative insurance from the operator's own scheme, of equivalent coverage)
- details of documentation required for travel to the destinations featured, and any health hazards or recommended inoculations.

A booking form is usually printed within the brochure for completing a reservation. The terms and conditions of the booking should appear in full in the brochure, but should not be printed on the back of the booking form, as they need to be retained by the customer.

NEGOTIATING WITH THE PRINTER

Printers will not expect their clients necessarily to be experts in printing methods, but those involved with the processing and production of a brochure should be reasonably familiar with current techniques in printing and common terms used. Printers will need to know:

(a) the number of brochures required
(b) the number of colours used in the printing. Full colour work normally involves four colours, but some cost savings should be possible if colour photography is not to be included
(c) the paper to be used: size, format, quality and weight. The choice of paper will be influenced by several factors, including the printing process used. Size may be dictated by the industry's requirements; for example, a tour operating brochure needs to fit a standard travel agency rack. Paper quality varies according to the material from which it is made. It may be glossy or matt, but will be selected for its whiteness and opacity. Inevitably, this requires some compromise, as very white paper tends to be less opaque, and one must avoid print showing through to the other side of the sheet. The weight of paper will of course depend upon its effect on the overall weight of the brochure, if this is to be mailed in quantity
(d) number and positions of illustrations (photos, artwork, maps, etc) used
(e) typesetting needs. There are over 6,000 typefaces from which to choose, and the style of type chosen should reflect the theme of the brochure, its subject and the image of the company
(f) completion and delivery dates.

When obtaining prices from the printer, operators should approach several companies, as quotes can vary substantially between printers. Many operators choose to have their brochures printed abroad, especially in Italy, where good-quality work can be produced at very competitive prices for long print runs, but obviously the operator will want to compare whether British printers can match price, since use of a domestic printer will reduce transport costs. Most importantly, operators must avoid cutting corners to save money, as an inferior print job can threaten the whole success of the tour programme. The progress of the printing must be supervised throughout, either by the operator itself or its advertising agency. Proofs should be submitted at each stage of production to check on accuracy and a final corrected proof should be seen before the actual print run to ensure there are no outstanding errors.

The printer should be asked to quote not only for the actual number of brochures that are expected to be required, but for the run-on price for additional copies. Once a brochure is set up for printing, the cost of running off a few extra thousand is very small compared to the overall price, and it may be better to do this rather than having to reorder at a later date.

BROCHURE DISTRIBUTION AND CONTROL

Tour operators must make the decision either to use all the retail agencies available to them, or to select those which they feel will be most productive for the company. Whatever decision is made, operators must also establish a policy for their brochure distribution to these agents. If equal supplies of brochures are distributed to every agent, many copies will be wasted.

Wastage can be reduced by establishing standards against which to monitor the performance of travel agents. A key ratio is that of brochures given out to bookings received. 'Average' figures appear to vary considerably among different operators; while one will expect to gain a booking for every three or four brochures given out (which may still mean that every booking carries a burden of marketing cost of some £6–7 in brochure production costs), specialist operators may have to give out as many as twenty-five to thirty brochures to obtain a single booking. The position is slightly improved when one remembers that each booking will involve typically between 2.5 and 3 persons. If figures consistently poorer than this are achieved by any of its agents, the operator should look for an explanation. The problem could be accounted for by the agent's lack of control over their own brochure distribution; do they merely stock their display racks and leave clients to pick up whatever numbers they wish, or do they make a serious attempt to sell to 'browsers'? Some agents go even further than this, and retain all stocks of brochures except a display copy, so that customers have to ask for copies of the brochures they require. This is instrumental in cutting down waste, as well as increasing sales opportunities.

It is now the practice of most operators to categorise their agents in some way, in terms of the productivity. This could typically take the following form:

		Bookings per year
Category A:	top producing agents, multiples	100+
Category B:	good agents	50–99
Category C:	fair agents	20–49
Category D:	below average agents	6–19
Category E:	poor agents, producing little	0–5

Of course, for a specialist operator, the sales categories might be considerably smaller; a good agent may be producing as few as ten bookings a year. However, the principle remains the same; the operator will determine, on the strengths of these categories, what level of support to give the agent. At the top of the scale, agents can expect to receive as many brochures as they ask for, while at the other end, perhaps the operator will be willing to provide only a file copy, or two to three brochures to work with. Many new or independent agents are finding it increasingly difficult to obtain any supplies of brochures from the major operators, which are increasingly narrowing the focus of their distribution policy.

The reservations system

In order to put a package tour programme into operation, a reservations system must be developed and implemented. The design of the system will depend upon whether reservations are to be handled manually (an increasingly rare system, with the development of low-cost computer programmes to handle bookings) or by computer, and on whether the operator plans to sell through agents or direct to the public.

Most tour operators continue to sell their tours through the high street travel agents who are responsible for handling 80–90 per cent of all bookings made. This being the case, the operator must provide the best and fastest reservations system possible for the agents' use.

Manual systems have several disadvantages. A travel agent needs to contact the operator quickly when serving a client at the counter. If telephone lines are engaged, or not answered for long periods of time, the agent may become frustrated and decide to deal with a competitor who is easier to contact. Installing an automatic call distribution (ACD) system, by which calls are automatically queued until a line becomes free, will not prove entirely satisfactory, as agents face mounting phone bills while holding on until the line clears. This has led most operators to opt for a computer-operated reservations system.

All the bigger tour operators (those carrying 50,000 or more clients) and virtually all smaller operators today have computerised reservations systems (CRSs); with advances in technology and declining costs for computer systems, reliance on a manual system even among operators carrying as few as 5,000 clients is becoming the exception rather than the rule.

Initially, the CRS operated only 'in-house', i.e. within the operator's own premises. Agents seeking to make a booking would telephone to the operator, who tapped into the company's computer to check availability. It was but a short step from this to link the agent directly into the CRS, using a Visual Display Unit (VDU) in the agent's office. Thomson, the market leader, was the first operator to decide that all bookings through agents should be handled in this fashion, forcing agents to invest in VDUs. Most other large companies rapidly followed suit.

These connections depended upon the use of telephone wires to link the agent's VDU to the operator's CRS. This posed problems of cost and time wasting for the agent, if lines were busy and there was difficulty in accessing a CRS. More recently, agents have been 'hard-wired' directly into the operators' CRSs, reducing time and allowing the agent to switch directly from one CRS to another without redialling.

The speed of development of technology in this field is too rapid to allow a thorough treatment of the subject in a textbook. Students of tour operating must keep abreast of such developments through the trade press or other media. Suffice to say that in addition to reservations systems, the computer is now used widely to provide accounts and management information quickly and accurately, and the larger operators have also introduced accounting systems which allow direct transfer of agency payments from the agents' bank account to that of the operator.

IMPLEMENTING A RESERVATION

The computer will allow the agent to see whether the particular tour required is available, or if it is not, will automatically display the dates or destinations nearest to the client's needs. Once the agent has established that a package is acceptable to the client, a booking is made (sometimes an option can be taken for 24 hours, but operators are now tending to accept only firm bookings). Any late changes to the programme which are not in the brochure can be drawn to the attention of the client and agent on the screen at this time. The agent is provided with a code number to identify the booking, and obtains a completed booking form from the client, together with a deposit.

The computer booking is sufficient to hold the reservation, and booking forms are now held in the agent's files rather than, as formerly, sent to the operator with the deposit. On receipt of the deposit, the operator will issue an interim invoice to confirm the booking, and a final invoice will normally be issued about ten weeks before the client is due to leave, requesting full payment eight weeks before departure. Changes to the programme cannot be made once the final invoice has been issued. After receipt of the final payment, the operator will issue all tickets, itineraries and, where necessary, vouchers, and despatch these to the agent, who forwards them to the client.

Prior to each departure, a flight manifest is prepared for the airline, with names of all those booked, and a rooming list is sent to the hotels concerned and to resort representatives where appropriate. The latter should go over the rooming list with the hotelier to ensure that all is in order prior to the clients' arrival.

Larger tour operators will have a customer relations department whose function is to monitor and handle passenger and agency complaints and ensure quality control in the operation of the tour programme.

LATE BOOKINGS

Tour operators are anxious to fill every seat in their tour programme. The ability to react quickly to deal with last-minute demand for bookings plays a key role in fulfilling this objective. Around 40 per cent of summer holiday bookings are now booked after 1 April, and a similar booking pattern has emerged for winter holidays. Coupled with the offer of last-minute discounts, many operators have introduced procedures designed to pick up these late bookings, including the rapid updating of availability on computer reservations systems, and a booking procedure which allows tickets to be collected at the airport on departure.

The distribution network

THE SELECTION OF RETAILERS

Basically, the tour operator has to choose between two alternative methods of selling its tour programmes – either through retail travel agents, or direct to the public. Larger operators whose product is of universal appeal and whose market is national in scope will expect to sell the bulk of their holidays through the retail trade, although many will be glad to receive the occasional booking direct from the customer, since this will enable them to retain the commission normally paid to the agent. While operators may be keen to increase the volume of bookings coming to them direct, they must also avoid generating any fear among the agents themselves that they are in any way attempting to 'poach' the business away from the retail trade, as agents may switch their loyalty to other operators if they suspect this is the case.

Few operators now deal indiscriminately with all retail agents. As with most products sold, some 80 per cent of package holidays are actually sold through 20 per cent of the retail agents, while a large number of agents will make very few sales (the so-called 'Pareto Principle'). The cost of servicing the less productive agents is often greater than the revenue they produce – they must not only be provided with expensive free brochures, but also receive regular mailings to update their information, and are supported by sales material and even, in some cases, visits from sales representatives of the operator. The operators must therefore decide whether to vary the support they offer to different agents, or even to dispense with the services of some agents altogether. We have already seen how brochure supplies will be varied according to the productivity of the agent. It is now increasingly common for operators to support their best agents by offering them an overriding commission of between 1 per cent and 5 per cent, in addition to the basic 10 per cent, for achieving target sales figures. The large multiples, due to the strength of their position in the retail trade, can negotiate the highest overrides, giving them the ability to discount substantially in order to attract yet more business.

Thomson's strategy in dealing with its agents is illustrative of the efforts now being made to cut costs and increase productivity. Seventy-five per cent of its business was achieved through just thirty-six major accounts, each selling over 5,500 holidays a year. Thomsons decided in 1995 to target the largest single-shop independent agents (each responsible for over 1,000 sales a year) through its Club 1000 scheme; and at the same time twenty key miniple agencies, each handling over 3,000 bookings a year (with a minimum of 500 per branch), were targeted. Additional sales support is now available to these agents, in the form of point of sale material, daily late availability updates, monthly merchandising calls, educational study trips, staff incentives and tactical promotional campaigns.

An even more worrying trend for the independent agent is the close links which now exist between the larger operators and multiple retailers. This was illustrated in Figure 12.4, and with the leading three operators now controlling or having close links with the top four multiple agents, selling will inevitably be directed to focus on the products of the parent companies. While leading tour operators earlier denied any intention of establishing this policy, in 1993 both Thomson and Airtours introduced incentives for their agents to sell their own products. Subsequently, Thomas Cook gave preference to First Choice, in which it

had a financial interest, and still later this was switched to Sunworld when Thomas Cook bought that company. This has had the effect of reducing choice for the customer, although there remains scope for some of the independent agents to increase their efforts to sell specialist or smaller tour companies' products. Some are focusing on the sale of holidays offered by the Association of Independent Tour Operators, whose products are niche marketed to avoid competing directly with the mass market holiday destinations. Leading operators who do not have the benefit of direct support from a multiple are also at a disadvantage; First Choice claimed that 'directional selling' reduced their bookings by over 40 per cent through the two leading travel agents (who were owned by Thomson and Airtours) in the months following the incentive offers to those companies by their parents. The Monopolies and Mergers Commission report, published in 1997, criticised this practice, although resolution of the problem is incomplete at the time of writing.

The smaller operators, those whose market strengths lie in certain geographic regions, or those catering for specific niche markets often involving quite a small number of customers in total, are obviously not in a position to support a national network of retailers. Most will choose to sell direct to their customers, although a handful may try to concentrate sales through a limited number of supportive agents.

RELATIONSHIPS WITH TRAVEL AGENTS

It is customary for tour operators to draw up formal agreements with the travel agents they appoint to sell their services. These agreements specify the terms and conditions of trading, including such issues as the normal rates of commission paid, and whether credit will be extended to the agent or settlement of accounts must be made in cash.

An ill-defined area in these agreements is that of the application of the law of agency. A contract is between the principal and the client, and this raises the question of whether a travel agent is acting as agent of the principal or agent of the client. Some agreements will suggest that the agent is the agent of the principal, but since the collapse of Clarkson's Holidays in 1974, when a large amount of money had been paid by customers to agents but had not yet reached the operator, it has generally been held that this 'pipeline' money is rightfully the clients'; some agreements go so far as to specify this.

Under the terms of these agreements, the agent agrees to support and promote the sale of the principal's services. In return, the operator agrees to provide the support and cooperation necessary for the successful merchandising of the company's products, i.e. provision of adequate supplies of brochures, sales promotion material and sometimes finance for cooperative regional advertising or promotion campaigns. Operators will also try to ensure that their retailers are knowledgeable about the products they sell. This will be achieved through the circulation of sales letters or mail shots, by invitations to workshops or other presentations, and by inviting selected agents on educational study trips.

THE EDUCATIONAL STUDY TRIP

The educational (or 'familiarisation trip', as it is known in North America) is a study trip arranged by principals (whether tour operators, carriers or tourist offices of the regions involved). Such trips are organised for a variety of purposes; for example, members of the media, or travel writers, will be taken to tourist destinations in order for the principals to gain free – and hopefully, positive – media coverage. Travel agents are also offered opportunities to undertake trips in order to improve their knowledge of the destinations, or to encourage them to sell the region or product. Visits to a destination are known to be one of the most effective means of encouraging agents to sell a particular package, and these organised trips also have a social function, enabling the operators to get to know their agents better and to obtain feedback from them. However, the cost of mounting educational trips is high, even if a proportion of the costs are met by the hotels in the destination, or the national tourist offices and carriers helping to organise the programme, and principals will try to do everything they can to ensure that the educational gives them value for money. This was not always the case in the past, where educational visits abroad were often treated as 'jollies', attractive as a social perk rather than an educational experience. The effectiveness of these educationals has been improved by more careful selection of candidates, by providing a more balanced mix of visits, working sessions and social activities, and by imposing a small charge for attendance, so that travel agency managers will take care to ensure that the expense is justified in terms of increased productivity and expertise among their staff.

Careful selection of candidates will ensure that all those attending share common objectives, and that, for example, senior agency managers and young counter clerks do not find themselves together on the same educational, to the discomfort of both. Monitoring performance, by soliciting reports from those attending, and by checking the sales performance of staff from those agencies invited to participate, will also help to ensure that the operators' money has been well spent.

THE SALES REPRESENTATIVE

Tour operators, like most larger travel principals, employ sales representatives to maintain and develop their business through travel agents, and to solicit new sources of business. The functions of the sales reps are to call on present and potential contacts, advise agents and others of the services they offer, and support their agents with suitable merchandising material.

The reps act as one point of contact between the agent and operator, when problems or complaints are raised, and the often close relationship that develops between reps and their contacts is valuable in helping to build brand loyalty for the company. The personal contact enables them to receive direct feedback from the marketplace about client and agency attitudes towards the company and its products. The reps are also likely to play a valuable role in categorising agents in terms of their potential, and selecting sales staff for educational trips. But, making sales calls in person is expensive, and most companies have now switched to telephone sales calls to keep in touch with all but their most productive agents. As with the resort representatives abroad, however, the sales rep is another means by which the company can be distinguished from its competitors, and the advisability of this trend to more impersonal contacts is debatable. It is true that many agents have mixed feelings about the merits of sales reps, who are sometimes seen as time-wasting socialisers. It goes without saying that if the reps are to do their job effectively, they must be well trained; reps who are not sufficiently knowledgeable about their companies' products or those of their competitors will relay a poor image of the company to the agent.

DIRECT-SELL OPERATORS

Apart from those operators who will inevitably sell direct to their clients, for the reasons outlined above, a handful of larger tour operators have chosen deliberately to market their product direct to the public. This movement was spearheaded by the Danish company Tjaereborg, which entered the British market in the late 1970s with a promotional strategy to the effect that directly booked holidays, by cutting out the agents' commission, would represent a saving to the customers. However, although isolated bargains were certainly on offer, many holidays were no cheaper, and sometimes more expensive than similar packages booked through an agent. The reasons for this are not hard to understand; while travel agency commissions are saved, huge budgets are required to inform and promote to the mass public. The company had to invest millions in heavy advertising in the media, and similar high costs were incurred by the need to have a large reservations staff and multiple telephone lines to answer enquiries from the public. These costs are, of course, fixed, while commissions are only paid to agents when the latter achieve a sale. Tjaereborg soon found, after initial success which was probably the outcome of curiosity, that they were unable to achieve greater market penetration, especially as Thomson Holidays had rapidly joined the competition with a direct-sell division, Portland Holidays. The total direct-sell market is thought to have stabilised, and has been estimated in total as between 20 and 30 per cent of all inclusive tour sales, and Tjaereborg, after turning in an indifferent performance for several

years, was sold to First Choice (then called Owners Abroad). That company later withdrew the brand, replacing it with another direct-sell operation, under the brand name Eclipse.

The evidence suggests that traditional buying patterns die hard among British holidaymakers, many customers still seeking the assurance of face-to-face contact with an agent, even if the product knowledge of that agent may be limited. There are, nonetheless, some interesting variations in the pattern of agency sales – for example, those in the London area demonstrate a higher propensity to buy their holidays direct than do other Britons, and certain types of package tour, such as ski holidays and coach tours, also experience a higher proportion of direct bookings. However, the advent of interactive booking of travel arrangements using the Internet may change this pattern dramatically over the next few years. A new generation of holidaymakers, brought up in total familiarity with the computer, can be expected to demonstrate more confidence to book their holidays direct, in preference to using the traditional avenue of the retail travel agent. What appears certain is that unless the distribution network can keep ahead of this threat by offering improved product knowledge together with rapid accessibility to a wider choice of holidays, the future of agents as distributors of the bulk of UK package tours could be jeopardised.

QUESTIONS AND DISCUSSION POINTS

1 The Monopolies and Mergers Commission's decision affecting vertically integrated companies will have been clarified by the time you read this. Discuss its decision and examine the consequences for tour operators, retailers and the travelling public.

2 Explain the difference between in-coming and outbound operators. Why is the former sector of the industry usually smaller and more fragmented? Why do the large outbound operators not get involved with in-coming tours too?

3 Find out who are the leading five tour operators currently, and their market shares. Account for any changes to the figures given in this text. Contrast developments with the tour

operating picture on the Continent, particularly in Germany and France. What attempts are being made to move into other EU members' countries by the major UK operators? Is this a useful strategy to expand revenue and profitability for the leading British operators?

4 What are the implications for the future of the industry in

(a) the use of fluid pricing?
(b) the expansion in demand for all-inclusive holidays abroad?

ASSIGNMENT TOPICS

1 Industrial Holdings plc is a conglomerate with a rising investment in leisure. The company has retained Marketsearch Ltd, a group of consultants with whom you are employed, to weigh up the merits of entering the outbound tour operating business, either by taking over an established small- to medium-sized company, or by setting up a new company. They have ample financial resources to invest, but have reservations about investing in a field where profit margins are generally thin and competition high.

You have been asked to provide an input into the preliminary report that Marketsearch is preparing for the company. Your employer has asked you to examine the profitability of the sector over the past five years, and to evaluate the current market and trends over the next five years. Prepare this section of the report in draft, with statistics that you plan to incorporate into the eventual final report.

2 As a former student of tourism, now employed by a seat broker, you have been invited back to your old college to talk to students on the subject of 'The seat-only market; where it's been, where it's going'. Prepare a set of notes for your talk, which will be expected to last about thirty minutes. As your talk will also make use of the overhead projector, you should prepare transparencies which you will use to illustrate your talk.

(Note: the trade press from time to time has special articles on seat-only sales, which will help you in gathering up-to-date material.)

13

Travel Retailing

OBJECTIVES

After studying this chapter, you should be able to:

- explain the role of travel agents as a component of the tourism industry and their relationship with other sectors;
- identify the functions performed by an agent;
- be aware of the qualities necessary for effective agency management and service;
- understand the considerations and the requirements for establishing and running a travel agency;
- be aware of the constraints and threats under which agents operate, and evaluate alternative solutions for their survival.

Introduction

Most travel principals sell their products to consumers through the medium of travel agents. Such agents have been in existence for more than a hundred years (indeed, the oldest, now the tour operator Cox and Kings, traces its origins back to the eighteenth century). Their main role in earlier times was to sell shipping and rail services, but with the coming of air transport and the development of the package tour business after World War II, travel retailers took on a new role.

Before the war, the shipping companies were able to provide a good reservations and ticketing service direct to the public, with sales outlets in their city offices and at leading ports. Railways and coach operators had similarly established city-

centre terminals, from which they could dispense tickets direct to the public. However, when the airlines arrived on the scene, their airport terminals were situated well away from centres of population, and as a convenient network of travel agents was by that time in place, they decided against setting up their own chain of direct sales offices in favour of appointing agents to handle their sales. In turn, the agents expanded their distribution outlets to handle the new demand for air tickets. Only in the case of North America, where the volume of domestic travel by air is so substantial, did individual airlines establish city-centre offices to deal direct with the public, and these continue to vie with agents for sales. In Britain, British Airways has established a number of outlets in the leading city centres, but is still dependent upon travel agents for the bulk of its sales.

Historically, of course, Thomas Cook, which is today best known as a retailer, originated as a tour operator, only expanding later to retail travel services. In more recent times, it was the travel agents themselves who developed the first air package tours, as we have seen in Chapter 12. A handful of retail entrepreneurs had the vision to see that if they could buy air seats in bulk and reduce the cost of air fares, a huge mass market for foreign tours would develop. The packages they developed were, in turn, sold through other agents, and eventually became the retailers' largest source of revenue. Today, the vast majority of airline tickets, and eight out of ten package holidays, are purchased by consumers through retail agencies.

At the beginning of 1997 there were close to

7,000 branches of travel agents affiliated to the Association of British Travel Agents (ABTA), the leading trade body which represents both tour operators and travel agents. This number, although around 500 less than that at the end of the 1980s, has remained fairly stable after an initial fall due to the recession at the beginning of the 1990s. The influence of the major travel agency chains played a role in this, a factor which will be examined later in this chapter. Apart from these ABTA agents, there are also a growing number of independent agencies operating outside the ABTA framework. Because of the constraints under which non-ABTA agents had to operate in the past, they were limited to selling fringe services such as coach trips, or operated as so-called 'bucket shops'. The latter term refers to outlets used by airlines to dump unsold tickets on the market at short notice and at heavily discounted prices. However, with increased deregulation in the airline industry and the growth of consolidators wholesaling air tickets, discounted tickets became more widely available through ABTA/IATA-appointed agencies, and the role of bucket shops has declined sharply in the past few years, although some continue to offer a technically illegal service in 'cross-border ticketing'. This is a scheme whereby the agent issues a ticket for a two-leg or multi-leg journey in which the through cost is lower than the price for a single leg, and discards the first coupon of the ticket. Thus, for example, if the fare between Athens and New York via London is less than the normal London–New York fare, a customer in London might be issued a through ticket with the section Athens–London discarded. This is contrary to IATA regulations, and is technically a legal offence.

With the removal of 'Stabiliser' regulations, agents are free to trade with all ABTA and non-ABTA tour operators, and are now subject only to legal requirements to carry satisfactory bonds against financial collapse. In the event, this has not led to the wholesale withdrawal of members from ABTA; the need for a powerful association to represent the interests of tour operators and retailers remains, and most retailers have chosen to retain their membership.

The role of travel agents

The travel agent's role is dissimilar to that of most other retailers, in that agents do not purchase a product for resale to their customers. Only when a customer has decided on a travel purchase do agents approach their principal on their customer's behalf to make a purchase. The travel agent does not, therefore, carry 'stock' of travel products. This has two important implications for the business of travel distribution. Firstly, the cost of setting up in business is comparatively small compared to that of other retail businesses, and secondly, agents are not seeking to dispose of products they have already purchased, so will therefore display less brand loyalty towards a particular product or company. However, in the past few years negotiations between principals and agents have led to higher commissions being paid to agents who achieve target sales, and this is causing agents to become more commercial in their approach to sales. Rather than the objective advice which customers could anticipate from an agency, it is now more common for them to be faced with a limited range of products which offer the agent the best return on sales. This is especially true in the case of the large agency chains, as we saw in Chapter 12.

Arguably, the main role of travel agents is to provide a convenient location for the purchase of travel. At these locations they act as booking agents for holidays and travel, as well as a source of information and advice on travel services. Their customers look to them for expert product knowledge and objectivity in the advice they offer; but as we have seen, they may be disappointed, as agents choose to deal with an increasingly limited range of products on which they can maximise their revenue. In one sense, this is inevitable; the competitive nature of retail travel is such that margins are extremely narrow, and agents must find whatever means they can of surviving. Nor is it realistic to imagine that sales staff can have a thorough knowledge of every product in the industry, with a product range of package tours alone drawn from well over 600 ATOL-holding tour operators.

The range of products that an agent will choose to offer will vary, not only on the basis of the commission each earns but also depending upon the demand within the catchment area, the degree of specialisation of the agency and the preferences and marketing policies of the proprietor. An agency that is attempting to provide a full range of services to the public will sell air tickets, cruise and ferry tickets, rail and coach transport, car hire, hotel accommodation and package tours (a growing number of which might be domestic). Ancillary services such as travel insurance, travellers' cheques and foreign exchange may also be offered, and some agents will also undertake to arrange travel documentation (such as procuring visas) for their clients. Some will even deal with theatre tickets.

However, these all-round agents are rapidly disappearing in the face of commercial pressure. Due to the small amount of revenue achieved on the sale of coach or rail tickets, many agents are now forgoing the sale of these types of transport, although there are agents who believe it to be better to offer a full range of services even if making a loss on some, on the grounds that the customer may return to buy other travel arrangements later. Nonetheless, research by Coopers and Lybrand in 1997 (Benchmarking Survey) which found that agents dealing with more than 200 operators generally had lower profit margins than those focusing on twenty preferred operators, tends to suggest that it makes sense to specialise.

Agents may specialise not only in the selection of products they offer, but in the markets they serve. The clearest distinction is between those who focus on business travel (serving the travel needs of the local business community) and those who focus on leisure travel. Serving the needs of the business community calls for additional skills and knowledge, and while some agents attempt to serve both markets, by establishing a separate business division within the company, they find it difficult to compete against the expertise and buying power that the specialist business agents can bring to bear. These large business travel specialists have come to dominate the market, led by American Express (which took over the business travel interests of Thomas Cook in 1994), Hogg Robinson and Carlson Wagonlit.

Setting up and running a travel agency

Travel agents are located in major city centres, in the suburbs of large towns, and less frequently in smaller towns. To be successful, they need to be sited close to the centre of the shopping district. They compete against other agents within a catchment area which, in the case of a large city, may extend only to the surrounding streets, while in the case of an important market town the catchment may draw on residents living within a radius of thirty or forty miles. Those agents whose location is close to city centres, or other centres of business and industry such as an industrial estate, will usually try to capture the business travellers within this field, and may go to the extent of providing an implant (or in-plant) office, based in the business client's premises but staffed by the agency, in order to handle the company's travel needs exclusively. To do so, the company must be certain of a substantial amount of business each year, as the cost of setting up another branch is not inconsiderable. Implants are usually only viable if the agency can be guaranteed sales in the millions of pounds each year. Commissions earned may well have to be shared with the client, through discounting to the company. Increasingly, commission payments are being replaced by management fees, with bonus payments for savings achieved for the companies represented. If this is coupled with a credit agreement whereby the company only pays for its tickets after thirty days (or even longer), the agency may well find that the cost of servicing the business is too high.

It is also worth noting that agents in city centres will draw their clients not only from residents in the area but also from workers employed in the area, who may find it more convenient to make their travel arrangements close to their place of work, rather than nearer to their homes. On the other hand, the agency is also faced with the likelihood that a number of workers in the area will choose to pick up their brochures from the city branch, but make their reservations at an agency near their homes. This may mean a high turnover of brochures with little return for the city agency, a problem particularly common in London.

Setting up a travel agency in Britain requires little capital, for reasons already noted, nor are formal qualifications a prerequisite (unlike other European Union members). Consequently, the business appears extemely attractive to outsiders, who see it as a glamorous occupation with wonderful opportunities for cheap travel.

Anyone contemplating opening a travel agency will have to consider the merits of buying an existing agency, or forming a new one. There are considerable advantages in taking over an existing agency. To begin with, trading figures for recent years can be examined, and the viability of the agency evaluated, in relation to the asking price. A going concern can be expected to retain its loyal clientele, if service remains comparable, but against this, if there is a strong loyal market already the asking price for the agency may be high to include the goodwill. 'Goodwill' embraces the reputation of the business and the expectation that existing customers will continue to buy there. In recent years, prices of independent agencies were pushed up by the eagerness of the chains to expand quickly by taking over independent local agencies. As this process has slowed, and there is now greater awareness of the difficulties of trading at a profit as an independent, so the value of agencies has dropped. Another advantage of buying an existing agency is that licences and appointments, once granted by principals, are generally retained under the new management. Staff, too, can be retained; even in the recession, good qualified and experienced staff were not easy to find, especially for those seeking to set up a new agency.

The attraction of starting from scratch is mainly a financial one; capital cost will be limited to office furnishings, fixtures, computers, phones, perhaps a new external fascia. However, persuading principals to provide you with brochures, to offer you an appointment and to pay a commission on sales may prove difficult, especially if the area concerned is already well served by existing agents.

A travel agent once declared, 'there are only three important things in setting up an agency: location, location and ... location'. He was driving home the fundamental point that, to the customer, the convenience of the location is the main criterion in their choice of a travel agent. Any agent choosing a little-used side street away from the main shopping area, merely because rents or rates are lower, can be at a major trading disadvantage. Equally, it can be a mistake to scrimp on floor space and decor. Clients are attracted to roomy shops with plenty of rack space and a bright, cheerful, inviting atmosphere to tempt them in. Increasingly, windows are designed not as setting to display brochures or destination publicity, but as living advertisements for the shop interior. Good lighting, warm colours, comfortable chairs, desks rather than impersonal counters, all affect the client's perception of the agency and their motivation to enter the shop. Once they are inside, a good agent takes advantage of the opportunity to make a sale; but enticing the client through the door is the first step in selling. Needless to say, a street-level shop is imperative; only an agency with a well-established clientele and not dependent upon the impulse purchaser (for example, agencies dealing largely with business or group travel) could risk moving to an upper floor.

Sites need to be researched carefully. Existing pedestrian flows should be noted (usually, one side of a major shopping street – often the sunny side – always appears to attract more people than the other) as should barriers, whether physical or psychological. For instance, shops on traffic 'islands' which involve pedestrians using subways

Figure 13.1 A branch of a multiple travel agency. *(Courtesy Lunn Poly Travel)*

to cross the road will find it more difficult to attract the passing trade. Parking is often difficult in town centres, but if there are too many restrictions, and no nearby car parks, this can be a further important disincentive to the shopper. The local planning office should be consulted to examine any plans for redevelopment in the area. Residential redevelopment in the immediate area could be an important plus for the site, while commercial redevelopment nearby may pose a threat; another travel agency could well open in competition with you when the site is opened, and if attractive and more accessible, could poach much of your business. It may be better, under such circumstances, to consider delaying your own decision to open until you can rent in the new shopping plaza.

In law, a travel agency is an office, rather than a shop. This is important beyond mere semantics, since in the case of *Ilkeston Co-operative Travel* v *Erewash Borough Council* (1988), it was determined that travel agents were exempt from the legal restrictions on Sunday trading applicable to retail shops, and could therefore open to trade. Some other agents, particularly the multiples, have followed suit, but this has been more common at key booking periods of the year, rather than a year-round policy.

Agents earn their revenue in the form of commission on sales. While levels of commission will vary over time and according to the travel product sold, typical commission rates at the time of writing are shown in Table 13.1.

These rates of commission are not inviolate. Airlines in particular, seeking ways of cutting costs to control prices, have been testing reducing commissions to their agents. In Germany, Lufthansa reduced the rate of commission to agents from 9 per cent to 7.5 per cent, and Ryanair made a similar reduction in 1997 for agents in the UK. KLM was considering, at the time of writing, cutting commission to agents in the Netherlands. Agents will fight back against this erosion of their revenue; the consortium Advantage Travel Centres in fact went so far as to investigate the possibility of setting up its own charter airline as a rival to Ryanair in 1997, when that company cut agency commission, but backed down when it realised the proposal was not viable economically. The introduction of 'ticketless travel' by some airlines, which not only saves airlines the cost of issuing tickets, but also encourages bookings direct, may further undermine agency profitability.

For most agents package tour sales represent by far the largest proportion of their sales, although an increasing proportion of these involve some tailor-made elements. Typically, overseas holidays account for 60 per cent of sales, air tickets another 25 per cent, and ferry tickets some 4 per cent. Domestic holidays, a growing area of potential sales, have been estimated to take up to 4 per cent, while the remainder is divided between cruises, rail and coach bookings and miscellaneous services.

Value added tax (VAT) is payable by travel agencies on the 'added value' of package tours, i.e. on the commission earned by the agent. Payment to Customs and Excise is usually undertaken on behalf of the agents by the tour operators, but agents devising their own packages will make their own returns to Customs and Excise. For example:

Tour price		£200.00
Agent deducts:		
commission	£20.00	
VAT due	£3.50	
		£23.50
Agent remits to tour operator		£176.50
Agent remits to C&E		£3.50

Table 13.1 Typical commission rates in 1997

Travel product	Commission (%)
International IATA airlines	9(a)
Domestic airlines	7
Railways	9
Tour operators	10–15(b)
Cruises	8.5–9(c)
Ferries	9–10
Insurance	35–50

Notes: (a) Overriding (incentive) commissions are payable on the sectors sold, and net fares are available, on which the agent determines own mark-up.
(b) Some operators pay higher commissions, especially to the multiples, on certain selected products, and for achieving targets. Trade bodies such as Advantage Travel Centres and Worldchoice have negotiated special deals for higher base commissions.
(c) Net premiums are also available, on which the agents can establish their own price.

Sales		1 378 708
Gross profit (commission at average 9.4%)		129 599

Expenditure

Personnel
Salaries, NHI, pensions	57 768	
Staff travel, training, subscriptions	2 700	
	60 468	(50.49%)

Establishment
Rent, rates, water	20 580	
Light and heat	2 640	
Insurance	1 875	
Cleaning	1 080	
	26 175	(21.86%)

Administration
Computers, telephone	9 510	
Postage	2 040	
Printing & stationery	1 320	
Hire of equipment	4 020	
Advertising and publicity	2 400	
Publications, timetables	1 992	
	21 282	(17.77%)

Financial and legal
Credit cards	3 288	
Bank charges	1 272	
Auditing and accounting	2 166	
Legal fees	324	
Bad debts	400	
	7 450	(6.22%)

Depreciation and amortisation
	4 386	(3.66%)

Total operational costs
	119 761	(100.00%)

Net profit before tax
	9 838	

Note: 0.71 as % of sales

Figure 13.2 Operational costs of an independent travel agency: a monthly profit and loss account to show typical expenditure

Most principals today will offer higher rates of commission to agents who are members of consortia banding together to achieve agreed sales targets, in order to compete with the multiples. This can add up to 2.5 per cent or more to the earnings of the agent, particularly for the sale of package tours. However, it is still rare to find an agent averaging more than 10–11 per cent on the total of the revenue they achieve during the year.

Since it became legal to discount the price of travel products at the point of sale, the independent agents have been under particular pressure from discounting by the multiples. These large chains, because of their substantial buying power, can negotiate higher overriding commissions with the major tour operators, which allows them to pass as much as 10 per cent – virtually the whole of the commission earned by the smaller agent – back to the client. This accounts for the phenomenal success of the Lunn Poly chain in particular (see illustration, Figure 13.2) in the early 1990s, when, as a result of heavy discounting and widespread television advertising, it was taking an estimated quarter of the total tour operating revenue of ABTA agents.

Out of an average gross profit of between 9 and 10 per cent, travel agents must pay all the running expenses of their agencies, including their own salaries (see Figure 13.2). Only after these expenses have been met can they judge whether they have made a net profit or a loss for the year. One measure of the profitability, and particularly the productivity, of agents is to examine their turnover per employee. The Coopers and Lybrand Benchmarking Survey, published in 1997, found that multiples were generally more profitable than independents, achieving a turnover of £253,000 per employee. However, if we take average commission to be just 10 per cent of turnover (a slightly conservative figure for the multiples), we are left with earnings of only some £25,000 per employee, before all costs, including salaries, are met.

Of increasing importance to the profitability of agents is their status as 'cash' or 'credit' agents. Agents who have credit arrangements with their principals have the advantage of simpler recording procedures and improved cash flow, since they will hold clients' payments for longer before transmitting funds to the principals.

Travel agency skills and competences

It follows that, owing to the extremely competitive nature of the retail travel business, two factors become paramount if the agency is to succeed: good management and good service. Good management will ensure that costs are kept under control, that staff are motivated, and that the agency goes out actively to seek business rather than wait for it to come through the door. Good service will ensure satisfied clients, help to build a regular clientele and encourage personal recommendation which will increase the local share of the market for the agent.

The vast majority of travel agencies are small, family-run businesses in which the owner acts as manager, and employs two or three members of staff. In such an agency there is little specialisation in terms of the usual division of labour, and staff will be expected to cope with all the activities normally associated with the booking of travel, which will include:

(a) advising potential travellers on resorts, carriers, travel companies and travel facilities worldwide
(b) making reservations for all travel requirements
(c) planning itineraries of all kinds, including complex multi-stopover independent tours,
(d) accurately computing airline and other fares
(e) issuing travel tickets and vouchers
(f) communicating by telephone and letter with travel principals and customers
(g) maintaining accurate files on reservations
(h) maintaining and displaying stocks of travel brochures
(i) interceding with principals in the event of customer complaints.

In addition to product knowledge, therefore, the main skills that counter staff require will include the ability to read timetables and other data sources, to construct airline fares, to write tickets and to have sufficient knowledge of their customers to be able to match customer needs with the products available. There is also today a growing need for staff who can competently operate computers, especially computer reservations systems (CRSs).

The correct construction of airline fares and issue of airline tickets is a far more complex subject than might be apparent to the uninitiated, and entails a lengthy period of training coupled with continuous exercise of these skills. A number of internationally recognised courses are available to develop these skills, including in Britain those offered by British Airways, which meet IATA requirements and can be taken up to the BA Fares and Ticketing Part II level, indicating full competence to meet any requirement for fare construction and ticketing.

However, airline CRSs increasingly include all the basic point-to-point air fares, and the ticketing function is also widely computerised so that fare quotations and ticketing skills are becoming less important for most staff than they once were. An understanding of the principles underlying the construction of fares can nevertheless be helpful – for example, in explaining complex fares to customers; and of course there will be a continuing need for fares experts in the industry. The large travel agency chains have in some cases centralised this role, so that a handful of experts can quickly determine the lowest fares for a particular journey by air on request from a member of their counter staff at any of the company's branches.

In addition to counter staff functions, agency managers (who frequently spend time at the counter themselves) are required to fulfil a number of administrative functions. On the financial side, these will include:

- maintenance and control of the company's accounts
- invoicing clients
- effecting bank reconciliations
- preparing and controlling budgets
- providing an estimate of the cash flow in the company on a month by month basis
- controlling expenditure.

The introduction of VAT has added to their workload, where returns have to be made to the tax authorities. Sales records must be kept, and sales returns completed regularly for travel principals. All these 'back office' jobs can today be computerised, even in the case of the smaller independent agency. Managers also have the task of safeguarding their stock of tickets and other negotiable documents, and in addition have the usual tasks of recruiting, training and supervising office staff, and promoting their business in-shop and externally.

CUSTOMER CONTACT SKILLS

The way in which staff communicate with clients is, together with the essential product knowledge they display, a key ingredient in the agency's success. These communication skills can be divided into three distinct categories:

1 language skills
2 personal and social skills
3 sales skills

Both employers and government are expressing concern over the lack of basic language skills demonstrated by many British workers; and this applies not merely to a lack of foreign languages, but to a lack of competence in the way we use our own mother tongue. Written communication to a client which demonstrates poor sentence construction, grammar or spelling reflects not just on the employee, but on the company itself. When such correspondence goes out under the signature of a senior member of staff, the image of the company suffers a still more serious blow.

Personal and social skills are still more important, but fortunately it lies within our own power, to a large extent, to exercise these skills. There is still a tendency in Britain to look down upon jobs which involve serving the public, which is all too often confused with servility. We are gradually learning as a nation that if we are to compete with our European colleagues, we must be prepared to offer the same level of 'service' in our service industries as they do. The acceptance of the credo 'the customer is always right' is the first move towards creating the right atmosphere for serving behind a counter, in a travel agency as in any other shop. Customers expect to be received warmly, and with a genuine smile of greeting; staff are expected to be unfailingly cheerful, whatever stress they may have experienced during their workday. These qualities need to become second nature to counter staff.

First impressions weigh heavily, and staff will also be judged by their dress and appearance. Tourism employees must be prepared to adjust to the constraints that the job imposes, if they wish to succeed in the industry. Employers will insist on neat hairstyles, suitably discreet make-up, overall good grooming and appearance – often to the extent that counter staff in agencies will be required to wear a uniform – and personal hygiene is essential.

Deportment, too, is important. The way employees sit, stand or walk says a great deal about them and their attitude towards their customers. Staff who are exposed to the clients' view will be expected to look alert and interested when addressing their clients, to avoid slouching when they walk, and to sit upright rather than slumped in their chairs. These non-verbal signals all say a lot about the attitude of the company to its customers. The scene of employees filing their nails and talking to their friends on the telephone, while customers try to attract their attention, is a common one in training videos, but one that encourages us to think about how we present ourselves in public. A warm, welcoming smile and friendly manner when greeting a customer approaching the counter will convey a positive view of the company, and make the customer feel at home and in a buying frame of mind. Attentiveness to the customer is not only polite, it ensures that vital client needs are recognised, enabling the employee to match needs with products. When talking to customers and greeting them, the employee should maintain eye contact and a manner which will breed confidence in the agency and its staff's product knowledge. Even handshakes are important cues to confidence; they should be firm and offered willingly. Use of the client's name enhances the relationship.

Even the way in which staff answer the telephone can help to generate the right image of the company. Telephones should be answered quickly and competently. As there are no dress and appearance 'cues' from which the client can make a judgement, the voice becomes the sole basis of judgement. Trainers emphasise the need to smile, even over the telephone, as an impression of friendliness can still be conveyed in the voice. If clients are asked to hold on, they should be given the reason, and regularly checked to ensure they are still holding. If the person they are trying to reach is busy, an offer should be made to call them back and there should be a follow-up to ensure that they have been called back. Similarly, if the employee cannot give an answer immediately to a problem, they should offer to call the client back with the answer in a short while, and do so. A failure to call back is one of the most common sources of frustration to clients, and can easily lead to a loss of business to a competitor.

THE SALES SEQUENCE

Travel agencies are no longer order-takers; to compete, they must go out and get the business. Good social skills build the atmosphere which encourages buying, but closing a sale requires an understanding of technique. Effective selling is the outcome of four stages in the selling process, which together make up the sales sequence:

1 establishing *rapport* with clients
2 *investigating* clients' needs
3 *presenting* the product to the clients
4 getting clients to take action, by *committing* themselves to the purchase.

Below, each of these stages is examined in more detail.

Rapport

To sell products successfully, one must first match them to the customer's needs. If the client buys a product they do not really want, or which does not provide the satisfaction they were looking for, they simply do not come back again. As no travel agency can survive without a high level of repeat business, achieving a one-time sale is clearly not enough; the customer must be satisfied in the longer term. To achieve this, the first step is to build a rapport, by engaging the client in conversation, gaining their trust and learning about their needs. This process allows the salesperson to judge how receptive the client is to new ideas, and how willing to have products sold to them. Some customers prefer to self-select, and should not be badgered into a sale, while others need and seek advice more openly.

To generate a two-way conversation, the opening phrase 'Can I help you?' has to be avoided – it simply invites the reply, 'No thanks, I'm just looking'. A more useful way of opening a conversation would be to use a phrase such as, 'Do you have a particular type of holiday in mind?', or, to a customer who has just picked up a brochure, 'That's a very good programme this year. Were you just looking for sun, sea, sand holidays, or had you something more adventurous in mind?' This forces a reply, and encourages the client to open a conversation.

Investigation

Once one has gained the client's trust, the next step is to investigate their needs more thoroughly. Once again, it is necessary to ask open questions, which elicit full answers. The sort of information needed to draw out the client will include:

- who is travelling, and the number in the group
- when they wish to travel, and for how long
- their preferred mode of travel
- their choice of destination
- what they expect to pay.

It must be recognised at the outset that the client will not necessarily have the answer to these questions. They may have only the vaguest idea about where they want to go, and what they want to do. Needs must never be assumed, even from a clear statement of intent: clients saying they do not want to take a package holiday may merely be revealing a deep-seated prejudice that such holidays are 'down-market', while on the other hand they may have had a bad experience of earlier such holidays. The salesperson's task is to tease out the real reason so that the appropriate product can be offered – for example, an IIT (independent inclusive tour) may suit, where the client would not be one of a crowd. In particular, one should never take for granted that the price the customer states they are willing to pay is the maximum; the industry has encouraged holidaymakers to believe that holidays are invariably cheap, but one is doing the clients a disservice not to point out that cheapness is not necessarily value for money, and that by paying a little more one might have a better guarantee of satisfaction.

Presentation

Once the salesperson is satisfied that they know exactly what the client needs, they may go on to the next stage, that of presenting the products that they feel will suit the client. The aim will be to present not only the features of the holiday being offered, but also the benefits:

> Travelling in the early spring, you have the advantage of lower prices, yet this can be the nicest time of the year in the Austrian valleys, with the blossom out and before the mass of tourists arrive in the height of the season.

Product knowledge is, of course, critical for success in gaining the client's confidence to a point where they are willing to accept one's recommen-dations. Even if the salesperson feels that what they are offering is exactly suitable to the client, it is always a good idea to offer an alternative, so that the client has the opportunity to choose. If the salesperson then demonstrates just how one holiday is a better buy than the other, this will make it easier for the client to decide on the choice they are recommending.

At this stage in the sales sequence, the salesperson will often have to handle objections. Sometimes objections are voiced only because the client needs reassurance, or because they have not yet fully understood the benefits being offered to them. At other times objections occur because not all the client's needs have yet been met, and here a process of patient questioning may be needed once again to draw out the possibly hidden motives for the objections.

Commitment

This final stage is the process leading to closing the sale. This means getting the client to take action – ideally to buy, but of course some clients will need more time to consider the offer. The aim of the counter clerk is to get the best possible outcome from the sales sequence – taking an option, getting the client to call back later, or getting them to agree that the salesperson may call them later to follow up the sale. The good salesperson is always looking for the buying signals that herald that the client is ready to buy: 'Would you like me to take an option on that holiday?' can prompt clients who are dithering to take action. Care must be taken, however, never to push the client into a sale before they are ready to buy, or they may be lost for ever.

Finally, having received the deposit for a firm booking, the salesperson must remember that the sales job has not been finished. They must continue to show interest and concern for the client, helping to reinforce the sale and their commitment to return for later travel arrangements. Many agents now send a 'Welcome home' card to their clients after their return from holiday, to invite them to come into the shop and talk about their experiences, and to ensure they will remember the agency in the future.

A good selling technique grows with experience, but it takes effort; effort to find out what the client really needs, effort to appear constantly friendly and interested, and effort to find the right product to match the needs.

THE PRODUCT PORTFOLIO

It is ironic that the travel product requires perhaps greater knowledge on the part of retail staff than does virtually any other product, while travel agents' salaries lag far behind those of other people in the distributive trade. This makes it particularly hard for agency managers to attract and retain qualified staff. Agents argue that competition and discounted prices make it impossible to pay higher salaries. Principals have come to accept that their retailers cannot be expected to have detailed product knowledge of every company's offerings, and concentrate instead on providing agents with easier access to information through CRSs and more informative brochures.

While the apparently unbiased service provided by the independent travel agent appears to be a marketing advantage, it is questionable whether clients themselves actually deal through an agent to gain this benefit, since the proportion of sales through travel agents is highest for the standard package holidays, which could arguably be booked direct with equal simplicity. One piece of evidence (the *Keynote Report on Travel Agents and Overseas Tour Operators,* 1990) revealed that while 86 per cent of sun, sea, sand holidays were booked through agents, the proportion of lakes and mountains holidays fell to 72 per cent, self-catering holidays to 69 per cent and winter sports (where expertise might be thought of particular value) to only 58 per cent.

The low proportion of bookings achieved by travel agents for domestic holidays owes much to the traditional pattern of booking holidays in the UK. Domestic holidaymakers have tended in the past to contact principals direct to make their holiday bookings, often by writing to resort tourist offices for brochures and details of hotels. Holidays in Britain were neither conveniently packaged, nor seen by travel agents as sufficiently remunerative to justify devoting precious rack space to brochures or training staff in domestic product knowledge. However, two factors have tended to increase sales through agencies. First,

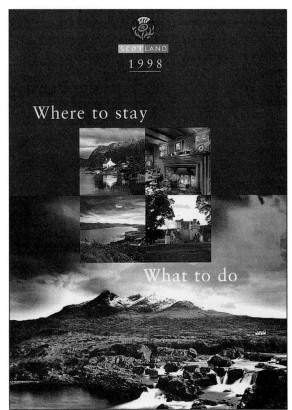

Figure 13.3 Scottish Tourist Board brochure offering commissionable domestic holidays. *(Courtesy Scottish Tourist Board)*

UK holidays have risen in price vis-à-vis foreign holidays, so that sales of a holiday at home can equal or exceed the 'bargain basement' prices now offered overseas. Secondly, UK holidays have been better packaged by middlemen in the past few years. For some years the three National Tourist Boards produced composite brochures of commissionable package tours for sale through travel agents. Although the English and Wales Boards found this uneconomic and have since decided to rely on operators to promote their packages through agents, the Scottish Board continues to produce a composite brochure (see Figure 13.3).

Business travel

Agents have made strong efforts in recent years to tap the lucrative business house travel market –

bookings for company employees travelling on business. The growth in the economy and in exporting has led to a parallel growth in corporate travel, often seen as highly profitable for the travel agent because capital spend is high and the market relatively price-insensitive. Nearly five million business visits are made abroad every year from Britain, and this clearly constitutes a very attractive market to tap. However, increasing competitiveness among agents soliciting business travel, coupled with the drive for greater cost-efficiency in industry, has made this sector of the market more price-sensitive. Business houses now seek, and usually can obtain, 'deals' with travel agents in exchange for agreements to place all their corporate business through the one agency. Agencies, in turn, attract business houses either by providing a standard rate of discount on all travel arrangements, or, more commonly today among the larger business agents, charging a management fee and negotiating a contract on which bonuses are paid for achieving a certain level of cost savings for the company. Extended credit terms, whereby companies may not have to settle their accounts until ten to twelve weeks after receiving their tickets, are also commonly on offer.

Businesses are extremely demanding customers. The level of service which an agent must offer to retain their patronage is considerable. Companies often require reservations at very short notice, and will need service outside the normal office hours of the travel agent. They will expect documents to be delivered to their offices, and may also require the agent to obtain visas or other help with documentation. Therefore the additional costs of handling these arrangements must be considered by the agent, particularly where credit is offered to the business house. It is not unusual for companies to delay payments until well beyond the dates due, while the agent must still make payments to the principals within the agreed times; thus the agent is helping to fund the company's cash flow at their own expense. However, the attraction of a large account which may in some cases exceed a million pounds a year will be sufficient to ensure that agents compete for the business by offering extra levels of service, implants, fares expertise to guarantee lowest prices, and financial incentives.

Since the highest discounts can be offered by agents negotiating the best deals with their principals, this has once again led to the multiple branch agencies dominating the business house market. The Guild of Business Travel Agents (GBTA), with just forty members, accounts for some 75 per cent of all airline tickets sold in the UK, while the bulk of these sales are in the hands of a few key players: American Express, Hogg Robinson, Carlson Wagonlit, The Travel Company, Portman and Britannic. Thomas Cook is also examining the viability of returning to the business travel market at the time of writing, having been prevented for doing so for three years after the sale of this division to American Express. Some business travel companies have joined international consortia of business travel agents, which offer them greater influence and purchasing power with principals. Hogg Robinson, for example, is linked in an international consortium of business travel agents known as Business Travel International, whose members include the largest French travel chain, Havas, the German chain Hapag Lloyd, and the US agency IVI, as well as Holland International of the Netherlands, Bennett Travel of Scandinavia and National Australia Travel. With the global buying power of this group, airline and other tickets can be purchased at the lowest possible price for business house clients. Hogg Robinson also strengthened its power in the global business travel market through the purchase in 1997 of Kuoni's business travel division on the Continent. The British Institute of Travel Management, whose membership is made up of those involved with making travel arrangements for their companies, seeks to use its influence to obtain better deals for its members, while the equivalent organisation in the USA, the National Passenger Traffic Association, has actually set up its own travel agency to make further cost savings for its members, and a Business Travel Contractors' Club has also been founded to improve on deals negotiated with travel principals. Large corporations in the UK have also recognised they have the buying power to control their own travel arrangements, and increasingly negotiate direct with airlines for their tickets and discount agreements. Galileo's 'Travelpoint' computer link allows corporate travellers to make their own bookings direct via the computer (although these are presently referred to the travel agent for completion).

Travel agency appointments

MEMBERSHIP OF TRADE BODIES

In the UK there are no legal requirements for setting up as a travel agent, but in some countries, including most of those within the European Union, governments do exercise licensing control over agencies. However, most principals license the sale of their services through a process of agency agreements, or appointments, which are in effect a licence to trade and to receive commission for sales achieved. Some principals dispense with this formality – hotels, for example, will normally allow commission on any sales made through a reputable travel agency, without any formal agreement.

Up to 1993, any travel agent wishing to sell the products of an ABTA tour operator had themselves to be a member of ABTA, while in turn ABTA tour operators could only sell their services through ABTA retailers. This reciprocal agreement, known as 'Stabiliser', and allowing ABTA to operate as a closed shop, was technically a constraint on trade, and as such was challenged by the Office of Fair Trading. However, the Restrictive Practices Court upheld the agreement in 1982 after appeal by ABTA, on the grounds that it was in the public interest; and certainly, ABTA's in-house scheme of protection for consumers against the collapse of a member company has been recognised as one of the best in the world. A common fund, provided out of membership subscriptions, was held by the association and drawn on to allow clients of a travel agency to continue with their holidays even if the travel agency they had booked with went into liquidation before the tour operator received payment for the tour. This complemented the protection offered by ABTA against the collapse of a tour operator, details of which have been outlined in Chapter 12.

New members of ABTA were required to take up a bond to cover a percentage of their revenue in the event of their collapse. The same conditions were not imposed on long-standing members, though, and this created difficulties in the case of one or two spectacular collapses such as that of Exchange Travel, in which ABTA had to meet the costs of lost revenue without adequate bonding. This imposed a drain on the reserve fund.

Thus membership of ABTA provided many advantages, but it also imposed obligations on its members. Premises were open to inspection, and agents were obliged to abide by a strict Code of Conduct complementing that of the tour operator. However, many earlier conditions imposed on members by ABTA, such as a prohibition on discounting, and on the sale of non-travel products ('mixed selling'), were overturned by the Restrictive Practices Court. There has, in fact, been a considerable increase in the sale of non-travel products since restrictions were relaxed, particularly in the sale of complementary products such as luggage and electrical goods.

ABTA will investigate the travel agent's financial standing and qualifications for entry prior to admitting the company to membership. This process can take between six and twelve weeks. ABTA also requires members to have at least one of their counter staff with at least two years' experience (a formal qualification such as COTAC or ABTAC counts in lieu of six months of this experience).

Since the EU Directive on Package Travel was introduced in 1993, ABTA has not retained the same measure of power it enjoyed formerly. The organisation no longer has the exclusive right to bond its members, although it remains paramount among the travel associations, and continues to represent the interests of both tour operators and travel agents, in spite of the conflicting interests of the two and the growing conflicts of interest between multiples and independents within the ranks of the retail agents. The Multiple Travel Agents' Association (MTAA) has taken on a more influential role outside of ABTA to represent the former, while many independents have linked themselves with the consortium which serves their interests best – Advantage (formerly NAITA), Worldchoice (formerly ARTAC) or one of the smaller regional consortia.

BONDING

New ABTA agents, during their first year of trading, and agents judged by ABTA, after inspection of their accounts, to be at risk financially, have been required to post a bond which indemnifies them to clients and customers against the risk of their failure. Certain principals may also require the posting of a bond, even if an ABTA bond is held – for example, if the agent plans to hold a principal's ticket stock. A significantly higher bond would normally be asked of agents who are without limited liability (i.e. trading as sole traders or partnerships). Additionally, if the retail agent operates tours, whether in the UK or overseas, they will also be required to put up a tour operating bond.

Bonding may be undertaken in one of three ways:

1 A sum of money equal to the value of the bond can be placed in a trust account. The agent can benefit from the interest accruing on the account, but cannot touch the capital itself. Since this could involve putting up a substantial amount of money, it is rarely chosen except by the largest corporations.
2 The agent can obtain an insurance policy for the amount required, paying an annual premium.
3 The agent's bank puts up the bond, against either company assets or, more commonly, the personal guarantees of the directors. A fee is charged which is substantially less than the premium paid for an insurance policy, but the directors become personally liable for the amount of the bond in the event of the company's failure.

As a safeguard, ABTA also runs a Travel Agents' Bond Replacement Scheme (TABRS). Agents pay into this scheme and money is paid out to help them in the event of collapse. If there is not enough money held by the scheme to cover the claims against the company, then all ABTA agents contribute to make up the shortfall. When there is enough money in the scheme then the agents are not required to pay anything. The scheme is further backed up by captive insurance companies set up be ABTA.

Following the introduction of the EU Directive which made bonding compulsory for any tour operator or agent, agents now have the alternative of trading outside of ABTA, and making their own bonding arrangements through banks or other organisations. Many have chosen to do so, following a very substantial hike in the cost of bonding through ABTA itself. One example of a successful alternative is that of the Travel Trust Association, which enables member agents to use a trust account to protect their clients' funds, rather than purchasing a bond through insurance companies or banks. The association monitors its members to ensure compliance with the trust fund regulations.

DEALING WITH PRINCIPALS

Most contracts with principals are non-exclusive; that is to say, they do not prevent the agent from dealing with the principal's competitors. Occasionally, however, a contract may offer the agency the exclusive right to sell the product, and may further restrict the agent's ability to deal with other directly competing companies.

Unless expressly stated in the contract, agents do not have the automatic right to deduct their commission from the monies due to the principal. If bonus commissions are paid for targets achieved, it is generally the case that these additional sums of money are paid to the agent at the end of the season, rather than immediately following the achievement of the target. These facts must be borne in mind by the agent in estimating cash flow.

A licence is required if commission is to be paid on the sale of services of members of the International Air Transport Association (apart from sales of purely domestic tickets). Since IATA travel makes up a substantial proportion of a typical travel agent's turnover, it is important for travel agents who wish to offer a full range of services (and doubly so for those dealing in business house travel) either to hold the necessary IATA appointment, or to have an arrangement with another agency that does so, whereby that agent will issue tickets on their behalf. At one time, agents could earn no income on IATA sales until they received IATA approval, and they were not permitted to obtain IATA tickets through recognised agents, splitting commission. This ruling, IATA Resolution 800, was overturned by the CAA in the UK, so that it is now possible for the new agent to trade and earn commission by agreement to split commissions with an established IATA agent.

Around 2,000 agency branches hold IATA appointments in the UK. IATA's Agency Distribution Office deals with applications for a licence, a process which can take up to forty-five days. A representative from IATA's Agency Investigation Panel visits the agent to judge whether the site is easily identified as a travel centre and suitable for the sale of tickets. (While proof of turnover is no longer required of agents, IATA wishes to satisfy itself that the agency has the scope to generate business.) The number and competence of staff will be judged; at least one member of staff will be expected to have two years' agency experience, and preferably hold COTAC, ABTAC and/or an equivalent qualification in fares and ticketing (ABTAC allows six months' remission in the experience required). The representative must also be satisfied that the agency premises are secure and ticket stock safeguarded.

If approved, a bond is taken out to cover the agency's anticipated monthly IATA turnover. An entrance fee is payable, and a small annual subscription. This approval enables the agent to sell the services of all IATA members. Separate plates are available for every IATA airline, and agents may hold stock of as many as sixty plates if they plan to draw tickets on each airline.

Approval is also required to make commissionable sales on the services of railways, National Coaches, domestic airline services and other principals such as shipping and car hire firms. Obtaining approval for most of these has been largely a formality for agents holding ABTA and IATA appointments. However, appointments to sell travel insurance will involve closer scrutiny, since the agent will be acting as a broker for the insurance service concerned. Insurance companies are tightening up in the face of evidence that some agents have taken insurance premiums from their clients but have withheld issuing certificates of insurance unless claims were filed.

Profitability of travel agents

There are surprisingly few studies of travel agency productivity and profitability in Britain, although ABTA undertakes occasional studies of profitability among its members. Unfortunately, the sample responding to research surveys has often been quite small, throwing into doubt the results. One study carried out in 1984 found that on average, ABTA members were managing to retain just 0.7 per cent of their total turnover after expenses. That report did not make clear that success in creating high turnover may be as much a factor of location as of efficiency, nor that fast turnover is not commensurate with a professional standard of advice and sales assistance. A better pointer to profitability can be found in the trading results of the leading chains such as Lunn Poly, whose negotiating power with the major principals has enabled them to discount package tours significantly, so that in spite of one of the highest spends on advertising in the industry, they have still been able to push profits well above the industry average, while simultaneously retaining or increasing their market share. The Coopers and Lybrand benchmarking survey published in 1997 produced some useful statistics revealing the generally larger profits achieved by the multiples and companies that chose to specialise in a limited number of suppliers' products.

It is becoming clear that the retail sector of the industry is now moving in two, or even three, distinct directions: towards specialist business travel; or towards the fast turnover 'leisure sales shop', a feature of the multiples' approach, which is essentially a booking service offering rock-bottom prices; or towards a more specialised advisory service for complex or expensive travel arrangements, without necessarily discounting. The latter move has its precedent in the USA, where for a number of years travel experts holding the Certified Travel Counsellor (CTC) qualification have dealt with the more lucrative end of the package tour business, often based in independent agencies.

Meanwhile, the traditional travel agent, attempting to provide a full range of services with little discounting, faces a future that is increasingly uncertain as other forms of distribution arrive on the scene, and opportunities are presented for the first time for members of the public to book direct with the suppliers using the Internet.

Evidence that many sectors of travel involve greater costs to the agency than the commissions it can achieve on sales has led a number of agents to move away from selling non-profitable products. At the same time, the proliferation of brochures, and the policy of leading tour operators to produce a range of different branded products each in its own brochure, has forced agents to re-evaluate their racking policies. With the typical travel agency only having rack space for around 145 brochures, of which up to 20 per cent may be filled with the products of the leading operators, there is little opportunity for the smaller and specialist operators to get their brochures racked. So far, only a handful of independent agents have attempted to redress the balance by niche marketing, and those that have done so have chosen to focus on the narrow long-haul and cruise markets. Some believe this may be the only way in which the independents will be able to compete with the multiples in the long run, although an alternative in the shape of large consortia will be discussed later in the chapter.

The move to fast turnover booking centres, typical of the large chains, is in part a recognition that salaries cannot be offered to provide the level of service demanded of a traditional travel agency. Efforts have been made to improve the quality of training in recent years, and skills-oriented NVQ qualifications have been introduced, although these are still not fully approved by ABTA itself, which has introduced its own qualification, ABTAC, to replace the former COTAC (Certificate of Travel Agency Competence) qualification to provide a yardstick against which quality can be measured. Nevertheless, the gap in salaries has, if anything, widened between travel and other forms of retailing. The fall in the number of young people coming onto the labour market in the early 1990s did not make it more difficult to attract staff, because the recession led to higher unemployment generally and some redundancies among existing travel staff. Counter clerks are now typically young and female, and staff turnover remains relatively high. Government-sponsored training schemes have helped to subsidise labour costs by providing a pool of young people to be trained in agencies, but promotion opportunities are limited. Within the chains, even the management responsibilities of branch managers have been down-graded, with policy, including marketing decisions, determined largely by head office.

THE MARCH OF THE MULTIPLES

The growth of the multiple travel agencies has been the key characteristic in this sector in recent years (see Table 13.2). Of the six leading multiples, Lunn Poly, owned by the Thomson Corporation, controlled 800 offices by the beginning of 1997, giving them some 12 per cent of all ABTA offices, while runner-up Going Places, owned by Airtours, controlled a further 10 per cent of the market with its 715 offices. A T Mays and Thomas Cook together accounted for a further 800 offices. In total, the leading four retail agencies were estimated by early 1997 to control nearly 34 per cent of ABTA outlets and more than 50 per cent of revenue.

It will be seen that First Choice, Britain's third-largest tour operator, is at a disadvantage in not controlling its own retail outlets. Following the purchase of Thomas Cook by the German tour operator LTU in 1994, and Cook's own small financial holding in First Choice, a strategic alliance was established between the UK agent and operator, but it was never a successful relationship, and First Choice later sought a closer relationship with A T Mays, owned by the giant Carlson Group, which has over 1,000 retail travel outlets in the USA. At the end of 1997 ARTAC

Table 13.2 The march of the multiples, 1996		
	Branches	*Market share (%)*
Lunn Poly	800	22.5
Going Places	715	14
A T Mays	416	5
Thomas Cook	385	10

Source: Thomson Travel Group Annual Report 1996

WorldChoice and A T Mays united to form a new 1,000-strong chain of agencies under the name WorldChoice, of which over 400 remain Carlson-owned. A link between the operator First Choice and retail chain WorldChoice would be a logical development for both parties.

The fear among the independents is that, as these multiples grow, their parent companies may choose to retain the exclusive sale of the leading tour operators' products through their own retail chains, cutting the independents' opportunities for sales. The likelihood of this development appears to be receding, with the recent announcement from the Monopolies and Mergers Commission ruling on vertical integration, which may require the two leading operators to modify their present situation.

COMPETING WITH THE MULTIPLES

Although the large number of branches owned by the leading chains appears to give them an insuperable advantage over the independents, this is not necessarily the case. In the first place, the market share held by the largest retailer, Lunn Poly, has actually declined during the mid-1990s, and Thomsons have declared their intention not to pursue the establishment of further outlets. Secondly, within the regions, the chains are not necessarily the most significant producers of booking. *Miniples*, independent companies controlling typically 40–100 shops, concentrate their branches in specific areas of the country; for example, the Bakers Dolphin chain, with some sixty branches, is a major force in the South West of England. Some believe these strong regional presences make the companies ripe for takeovers by the multiples, but so far the owners have shown reluctance to sell out. However, a scheduled seat wholesaler with a small tour operation, Gold Medal Travel, succeeded in taking over the 100-branch north of England miniple Travelworld in 1997.

The independents on their own face an almost impossible task in competing with the multiples. As we have seen, the multiples are in a position to discount and undercut the holiday products, and the market has become sensitised to price bargains through the marketing campaigns of the big companies, to the exclusion of other possible benefits available through a smaller agency. The chains can also invest substantially in high technology computer systems to improve their performance, and in national advertising campaigns to draw in customers.

Independent travel agents have done what they could to cut costs or to increase turnover in order to compete, and many have realised that only through close collaboration with others will they be able to compete. This has led to the establishment and growth of franchises and consortia. The latter have been more successful. The first chain in Britain to attempt to franchise on a wide scale, Exchange Travel, went into liquidation in 1990, and the Canadian-based Uniglobe chain has also found it difficult to attract members into a franchising arrangement in the UK, achieving only seventeen franchises by the middle of 1997, in spite of a chain of offices numbering more than 1,400 worldwide. The future of franchising remains uncertain. Arguably, a franchise, if it is to succeed, must offer a unique product of some kind which is not available through other distributive outlets; this, a travel franchise signally fails to deliver.

Agents forming consortia have had a greater degree of success. A consortium allows agents to compete with the multiples by negotiating with the mass tour operators for higher commissions on bulk sales, or even to set up their own tour operation or airline. The most successful of those established to date include Advantage Travel Centres, a chain formed under the name National Association of Independent Travel Agents (NAITA) in 1978, and now with over 700 members; and ARTAC WorldChoice, formed in 1995 out of the Association of Retail Travel Agency Consortia, which was founded in 1976. This body has over 650 outlets, and in 1997 it entered into an alliance with the A T Mays chain, to form WorldChoice, a new chain with approximately 1,000 branches, well in excess of the largest multiple in operation at present. The A T Mays branches relinquished their name, while remaining under Carlson ownership. A third association now challenging the multiples is the Global Travel Group, an organisation that selects members who have chosen to remain outside of ABTA.

The potential buying power of these groupings of independent agencies provides them with a very real chance to compete with the large UK chains in reducing their costs, as well as ensuring that the smaller tour operating companies are represented in the high street.

DISTRIBUTION POLICY

As we have seen, distribution policy among mass market tour operators in recent years has been towards selective distribution, the operator favouring distribution through a smaller number of productive agents rather than attempting to provide stock for all 6,800 ABTA members. This policy has also been favoured by the multiple agents themselves, in choosing to stock the products of a few key operators who are responsible for perhaps 80 per cent of the total revenue in the mass market. Naturally, Lunn Poly tended to discriminate against its parent company's rival Airtours, and similarly Going Places discriminated against the Thomson products, although both chains choose to trade in the rival operators' products. This 'directional selling', may account for the MMC ruling directing the two chains to make clearer to their clientele their links with the operators, principally by incorporating the name in the agency fascias. Efforts to force agencies to adopt their parents' names would not necessarily have worked to the advantage of the independents, as it may encourage the public to believe that Thomson Holidays or Airtours Holidays can only be purchased from the retail branches of those names.

Thomas Cook has introduced a policy of racking only 400 companies, of which thirty are identified as 'premium selection', while other companies have become even more selective, with the Holiday Hypermarket organisation emulating warehouse retailing practice by stocking just the leading twenty operators' products. Whether these developments become widespread in the next few years is a critical question for the future of travel retailing.

The decision on what products to stock is not based purely on what is expected to sell most quickly or easily. The introduction of tighter EU legislation over quality has forced many agents to reconsider the companies with which they deal; and while bonus commissions undoubtedly play a role in the decision, equally the service provided to the agent by the operator will be taken into consideration. Agents who encounter difficulty in getting through to operators on the telephone, or who find their complaints are not answered quickly, will feel less inclined to stock that operator's products. The personal relationship between travel agency staff and the principal is vital in this decision, and the role of a sales representative can be of immense importance in cultivating goodwill in the distributive trade. Here one must question the decision taken by so many principals to cut back their field representation as a cost-cutting measure during the industry's recession in the 1990s.

NEW MEANS OF DISTRIBUTION

At various points during the history of travel retailing, organisations from outside the travel world have looked at the scope for selling travel alongside, or ancillary to, their existing products. Few successes have been recorded among those who have braved the market. W H Smith, the newsagent and bookseller, and the most ambitious entrant to date, abandoned the sale of travel within a few years of entering the market. The complexity of selling travel has to be acknowledged, and this may well be a factor in the decision of so many other retail organisations to avoid the travel business; yet in the Netherlands, the sale of holidays through banks is well established, and they handle some 18 per cent of all package tour sales.

A new threat has appeared on the horizon in the UK, however, in the shape of the Post Office which, with relaxed regulatory mechanisms, had already branched into the sale of insurance and foreign exchange, and has sought to expand its sphere of activities. After testing the market for airline tickets in 1996 in its Trafalgar Square, London, branch, a decision was taken to expand these sales opportunities through some 600 of the 20,000 post office branches in Britain. Although sales will be limited to scheduled air tickets at present, there can be little doubt that the Post Office will continue to appraise the situation, and this new form of distribution could pose a further threat to agency profitability.

DIRECT SELL

Can travel principals sell their products direct to the public at lower cost without losing sales? This is a vital question for both carriers and tour operators. Travel firms which have traditionally sold their products direct, such as some of the railways, and others such as small tour operators whose total carryings are too small to consider using agents to distribute their product, do not have to take into consideration the possible retaliation of the retail trade against companies which choose to ignore them, or cut them out. However, even these direct-sell companies usually recognise that to antagonise the retail trade may jeopardise marginal bookings, and they will not deliberately ignore agent support.

There is an obvious attraction to the mass operator in selling their product direct to the public. Selling direct cuts out the high cost of servicing intermediaries and of paying commission on each sale. On the other hand, it involves considerable capital expense in setting up sales offices, and direct marketing costs can be high, especially if a national advertising campaign is to be mounted. There will be a need for a large reservations department to deal with enquiries direct from the public, and a huge telephone system to cope with enquiries and bookings.

If principals which presently deal through travel agents decide to sell direct for the first time, or to increase the proportion of direct sales they currently achieve, they risk antagonising their present distributors. Therefore any effort to increase sales in this way must be handled with extreme discretion, in order to avoid any loss of sales through ill-will. British Airways was forced to abandon its own efforts to expand implants in the headquarters of leading corporations in the face of strong reaction from ABTA members, who threatened to switch their sales to rival airlines. The airline, however, continued to expand its network of city-centre sales offices, in order to maintain control over sales, as much as to save on payment of commissions.

When the Channel Tunnel first opened, the management of Eurotunnel services largely ignored the strength of the trade, assuming that most clients would prefer to book their crossing direct, thus simultaneously antagonising the trade and reducing their own sales opportunities. Later, the company realised its mistake and placed greater emphasis on the role of the agent in providing tickets for the cross-Channel tourism market.

The larger tour operators depend upon travel agents for the sale of up to 86 per cent of their products. Smaller companies, generally offering less than 10,000 holidays each year, cannot afford to distribute their products through agents, nor would most agents be willing to stock brochures of these companies, in view of the small number of potential sales they would achieve. Consequently, these operators may adopt one of two distributive strategies: either to find a selection of key agents (likely to be independents rather than chains) who would be willing to stock the product, or to sell all their holidays direct to the public.

In addition to these, a number of mass market tour operators have created products which they distribute direct to the public. Foremost among these is Portland Holidays, a direct-sell division of the Thomson Travel Group. Other large direct-sell operators include Eclipse, the direct-sell division of First Choice, and Saga Holidays, the largest company specialising in holidays for the elderly.

It is significant that two major direct-sell operators are, in fact, divisions of two of the leading tour operators in Britain. Although agents might be thought to be concerned about the challenge of direct-sell operations, they have fought shy of any direct confrontation with these large operators, possibly out of fear that this could jeopardise their sales of the powerful mass market holidays marketed by the companies. They have also recognised that the proportion of direct sales made in the UK has largely stabilised. Early claims that direct sell would undercut the price of holidays sold through agents were shown to be inaccurate, as a close examination of the companies' pricing structure revealed that low prices were highly selective, rather than across-the-board. The market share of direct-sell operators reached about 20 per cent in the mid-1980s, but has since settled at no more than 15 per cent, with perhaps another 5 per cent achieved by direct selling of holidays normally sold through agents.

Agents today have much more to fear from advances in computerisation, which are now beginning to lead to direct access to operators' CRSs by the travelling public. This has already occurred to a limited extent in the USA and France, and as we have seen, it is already becoming a reality among business travellers. It is likely to be common for leisure travel bookings in the UK by the end of the century. This problem will be examined below.

Agents have every reason to be concerned about alternative methods of reaching the public with holiday sales, as we have seen in the section above dealing with distribution. New techniques are constantly emerging, such as direct-sell credit card Holiday Clubs, formed by a trading relationship between credit card companies and travel firms which handle the bookings. This scheme was initiated by a link between travel agents Page & Moy and Barclaycard, which has since taken over the travel company. Marketing is done by the credit card company through its direct mail contacts with cardholders, who place orders for travel by phone to Page & Moy's office. The travel company provides neither an advice service nor brochures; it acts purely as a booking office, and payment is made, of course, by credit card. The resultant cost savings can be passed back to the customer in the form of a discount on the regular price of the holiday (averaging about 6 per cent). The huge volume of business this has generated for the company has led to other similar links: Trustcard (TSB) with A T Mays, Access with Thomas Cook. The success of the various schemes has been limited, and it is thought once again that the market for this type of booking is unlikely to expand further. Nevertheless, a number of later developments have continued to worry agents, including direct sell to readers of local newspapers, and cooperative marketing promotions with other products.

THE IMPACT OF COMPUTER TECHNOLOGY

The industry has been profoundly affected by the development of computer technology over the past decade. Since such systems are constantly being launched or improved, information in this sphere of travel activity tends to date very quickly,

so there will be little benefit to be gained by examining the detailed merits of any existing system in this text. Suffice it to say that even the smallest travel agents can today benefit from computer technology to handle their back office and front office functions – in fact, many would argue that no agent can afford to be without back office computer aids, and in terms of making reservations, it is now mandatory to use computers rather than the telephone to make bookings with the leading companies.

The tourism industry is ideally suited for computer technology. It requires a system to determine availability of transport and accommmodation at short notice; to make immediate reservations, amendments or cancellations; to quote complex fares and conditions of travel; to process documents such as tickets, invoices, vouchers and itineraries rapidly. The back office also needs to process an ever-increasing amount of accounting and management information quickly. All of these functions are available today to any agent, and agents can be hard-wired to provide a direct link into the CRSs of tour operators and transport companies.

Computer systems in travel agencies are designed to offer three distinct facilities:

1 front office 'client relations' systems enabling a counter clerk to access principals' CRSs, check availability and make reservations
2 back office systems enabling documents such as invoices, vouchers, tickets and itineraries to be issued, and accounts to be processed with principals
3 management systems, producing updated figures on the company's performance to assist managers to guide and control operations.

Systems have now been developed which will provide all three facilities for even the smallest independent agent, at prices which continue to fall; or equipment can be leased to reduce capital investment and spread costs.

In considering systems which are designed to access travel principals' reservations systems, one can distinguish between those developed by carriers, and those developed by tour operators. In Britain, because of the importance of 'interlining' (common ticket issuing and ability to transfer bookings between carriers) any system used must be capable of booking seats on a large number of different airlines. Agents may now do so by using the recently developed systems of organisations such as Galileo or Sabre (details of these systems have been given in Chapter 7), while tour operators can be accessed live through either the Istel or MNS Fastrak networks. Thomson Holidays took the decision in 1993 to transfer their own live TOP system to Fastrak, and many agents are now hard-wired to these systems, which allow them to enter the CRS without using their telephone line to dial up each time.

Back office systems offer not only faster means of carrying out accounting and documentation procedures, but also the potential to cut costs. The new systems have brought computerised accounting procedures within reach of every agent. Thomson Holidays introduced an automatic banking system in 1988 which debits travel agency accounts for transactions effected through TOP. Although agents are still given some period of credit, this represents an example of the use of EFTPOS (Electronic Fund Transfer at Point of Sale) within the travel industry itself. The system can be expected to be adopted widely over the next few years, and will have a marked effect on travel agency cash flows.

Many agents have been slow to come to terms with the computer era, and there is some evidence that their customers also mistrust computer reservations procedures. Other agents, though, have recognised that the technological revolution will affect their business to a greater extent than almost any other industry. Most information, such as ABC air timetables and fares, is now accessible to the trade electronically, and agents are beginning to learn that the computer may be the key for survival.

However, just as computers offer great promise for agents, so they also pose a serious threat. Information sources do not have to be restricted to agents. The opportunity to place such systems in public areas where they can be used by members of the general public to make direct bookings cannot be ignored – indeed, Thomas Cook has already experimented with self-service booking kiosks in NatWest Bank branches and David Lloyd sports centres, which allow the public to book a range of travel facilities. Inevitably, over time this will progress to a situation where the public will be able to package their own tours simply by selecting from a choice of worldwide flights and hotels available on similar machines. Already in the USA the Sabre reservations system is available for public use, although bookings are at present still referred to a dedicated travel agent to protect commissions.

Agents have also looked for new ways to develop and protect their business. One example of this can be seen in the example of one high street travel agency which recruits home-based agents to visit customers in their homes, taking bookings through customised lap-top computers which are linked with the operators' reservations systems. A freelance sales force such as this, available at short notice 24 hours a day, may be the solution to ensuring the agent has a future role.

THE FUTURE OF TRAVEL RETAILING

With the ending of 'Stabiliser', agents no longer have the protection of ABTA that they enjoyed in the past. New methods of retailing travel products are certain to be introduced, perhaps through banks, department stores or petrol stations. In an effort to achieve better profit margins in an increasingly competitive business environment, principals will be constantly evaluating new ways

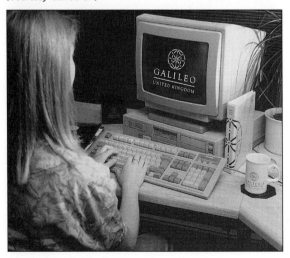

Figure 13.4 Galileo's computer reservation system in use. *(Courtesy Galileo UK)*

in which they can distribute their products to the public. The possibility of agents buying tours from operators in bulk and selling these under their own brand names will be explored (some agents, including Thomas Cook, are already doing so) while the squeeze on independents by the multiples can be expected to continue. Common promotional tactics of the past few years, such as 5 per cent deposits or even no deposit bookings, are likely to become typical rather than exceptional marketing ploys.

All of these developments suggest an end to the era of the traditional 'corner-shop' travel agent that we have known in the past. Agents in the future must be flexible, innovative, willing to move with the times and to make use of the new tools of marketing which technology has made available. They can no longer be expected to possess the range of product knowledge required by an increasingly sophisticated travelling public, but must find the means to access and make available this information to their clients more effectively, and at the lowest possible cost.

QUESTIONS AND DISCUSSION POINTS

1   Why has Britain not adopted the US strategy of the 'Certified Travel Counsellor'? Could it do so?

2   There is evidence that travel agents selling leisure services are separating into three categories: those that provide a traditional service, with limited discounts; those that specialise in serving certain 'niche' markets; and 'supermarket' agencies that provide little service or information, but will offer greater discounts. Can all three survive? Which is likely to be most profitable?

3   Travel agents have taken to stocking a variety of travel products in their shops in order to increase their profitability. Identify those products currently on offer, and discuss whether the variety of goods could be further extended. What other products could, or should, a travel agent sell? What are the implications of extending the range of goods and services?

1 Assume for the purposes of this assignment that you have been employed by a retail travel agency in your area (you may choose the company). You have been asked by your manager, in view of your studies, to undertake a study of the agency's brochure racking policy, to see whether it is adequate or could be improved. Undertake some field research in travel agencies in the area to estimate the typical number of spaces available for racking, and the various strategies adopted to categorise and display brochures. Taking into account present practice in your own agency, and the market which the agency draws, examine alternative solutions and produce a report for your manager which makes recommendations for changes. You should also consider the question of the 'marginal demand' brochures for which racking space cannot be found. Include a recommendation on tactics, such as whether a supply of brochures, or an individual brochure only, should be accommodated in each rack.

2 You are appointed as senior counter clerk in a small independent agency (three branches) in a large provincial town with a population of 350 000 people. The directors of the agency, aware of your educational background, have invited you to participate in discussions about the future of the agency. The Managing Director is keen to amend the company's policy by aiming at niche markets, but is uncertain which market to try to attract. Research the possible markets and write a brief report to her, making recommendations, and supported by the evidence of your research.

Your recommendations should be as detailed as possible, containing also an examination of the implications of the changes for brochure racking, layout and design of the agency, etc.

14

Ancillary Tourism Services

OBJECTIVES

After studying this chapter, you should be able to:

- understand the role of guides, couriers, insurance and financial services in meeting tourist demand;
- be aware of training and education available for those in the industry;
- understand the role and value of the trade press to the industry;
- identify the principal guides and timetables in use by travel agents, and their contents;
- be aware of marketing and consultancy services available to members of the industry.

Introduction

Attempts to analyse the tourism industry, as we have seen earlier, lead to the problem of defining the parameters of the industry. Some services depend entirely upon the movement of tourists, but are seldom considered to be part of the industry itself. Customs services or visa issuing offices are cases in point. Other services which derive much of their revenue from tourism and yet are clearly not part of the industry include companies specialising in the design and construction of hotels, theatres, restaurants or other centres of entertainment.

However, there is a further category of miscellaneous tourism services which deserve to be examined more closely here. We will call these *ancillary services*, and they are provided either to the tourist, or to the suppliers of tourist services. Each will be dealt with in turn.

Services to the tourist

GUIDE/COURIER SERVICES

Unfortunately, there is as yet no term which will conveniently embrace all the mediators whose function it is to shepherd, guide, inform and interpret for groups of tourists. Nor can one conveniently link their functions to one particular sector of the industry. Some are employed by carriers and tour operators, others work independently, or provide their services freelance to companies in the industry.

In an industry which is becoming increasingly impersonal, as companies grow in size, and tourism products themselves become more homogeneous, the role of those who interface with the tourist becomes more and more important. Indeed, it may be the only feature of the package which distinguishes one product from another; yet curiously, it is a role which is becoming progressively downgraded by the larger companies, often as a means of cutting costs. The role of the resort representative has already been discussed in this context. Here we will examine two similar roles, those of the courier and the guide.

Couriers are employed by coach companies or tour operators to supervise and shepherd groups of tourists participating in tours (either on extended tours or day excursions). As well as couriers, they may be known as tour escorts, tour leaders, tour managers or tour directors (the latter terms imply greater levels of responsibility and status). One of their functions will be to offer a sightseeing commentary on the country or region through which they are travelling, and to act as a source of information.

Some companies dispense with the separate services of a courier in favour of a driver-courier, who takes on the responsibility of both driving the coach and looking after the passengers. These, however, may be inhibited in their information-giving roles by less general knowledge and training, and by their need to focus simultaneously on driving the coach. There is also a safety issue here, and some countries frown on, or forbid, coach drivers who carry on commentaries while their coach is in motion.

Courier work offers little opportunity for careers, tending by its nature to be seasonal, and consequently it depends upon recruiting high numbers of temporary workers, although many of these do choose to return to the job year after year. In some cases, as in major cities where jobs are less seasonal, all-year-round work can be found, or couriers will be able to find alternative work during the winter season in winter sun or winter sports resorts.

Couriers are still employed largely on the strength of their prior experience. Qualifications applying to this sector of the industry are being introduced, although they are not widely accepted in the UK yet. The role is attractive to graduates with relevant qualifications such as languages, but companies tend to recruit couriers largely on the strength of their personality, their ability to handle clients with sensitivity and tact, and their stamina, both physical and mental. Increasingly, employers are emphasising sales ability, as couriers and resort representatives both play an important role in selling supplementary services such as optional excursions. Arguably, this is changing the nature of the role, as commercial acumen replaces sociability.

Couriers differ from guides in the sense that the latter stress their information-giving role, even though they may perform shepherding functions in their job. Guides, or guide lecturers, are retained by operators for their expertise in general or specialist subjects. Their employment is again generally freelance and intermittent, off-season

jobs being harder to come by outside the large cities. Guides take pride in their professionalism, and have well-established regional and national bodies to represent their interests. The largest of these is the London-based Guild of Guide Lecturers, which draws on a national membership. This body's efforts to establish agreed professional fees for members, however, ran counter to rulings by the Office of Fair Trading on price fixing in the industry, although the Guild continues to encourage the travel industry to employee professional guides with well-established training qualifications. These qualifications are achieved through formal courses of varying length, validated by the regional tourist boards for guiding within the region. In other European countries, such a qualification is often seen as vital

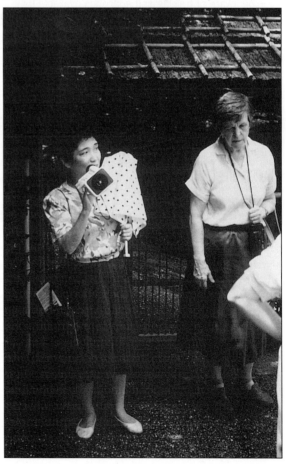

Figure 14.1 A guide addresses tourists with the aid of a hand-held microphone, Japan. *(Photographed by the author)*

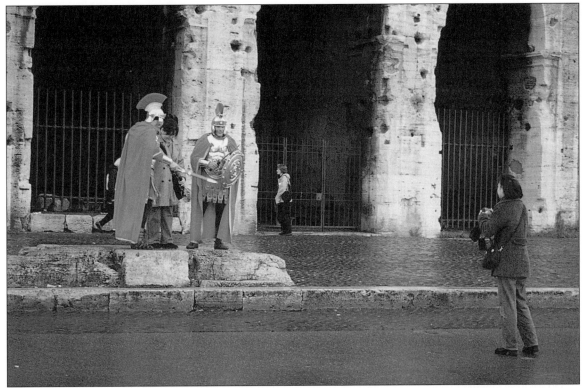

Figure 14.2 Animateurs, dressed as Roman soldiers, pose for tourists, Rome. *(Photographed by the author)*

if a guide is to be given the licence to operate; in France, for example, a local guide must be employed to guide in Paris, having demonstrated local knowledge in formally approved qualifications (although such qualifications can also be obtained by other EU member countries' guides, of course).

Obtaining registered guide status does not, of course, guarantee job security, and many coach operators continue to employ non-registered guides who will accept lower fees for their services. The 'added value' of a qualified guide is still seen by many employers as a luxury they cannot afford in a climate where cutting costs to achieve sales is imperative.

THE ROLE OF THE ANIMATEUR

The term 'animateur' is now becoming more widely known in the British tourism industry. It applies to those members of the industry who entertain tourists, either by acting out a role, or providing entertainment or instruction. The English term 'entertainer' is not strictly comparable, as this tends to be restricted to an acting role: the French term will also cover those whose task it is to interact with tourists to ensure that they enjoy themselves. They could be involved with instructing tourists in sports or hobbies, lecturing to cruise passengers or teaching them how to play bridge, or entertaining in the evening on stage at a European campsite. In Disney's theme parks there are a variety of animateur roles, the best known of which personify Mickey Mouse, but a host of other Disney characters is to be found on site, dressed as Alice in Wonderland, Snow White, even the Chipmunks. These workers normally have no speaking role, and are there to make friends with younger visitors, posing for photographs, etc. Others may take on a historical role, at a heritage site; for example, at Williamsburg in Virginia, a number of staff are dressed in eighteenth-century costumes, and will maintain this role if questioned by visitors. The job might be thought of as fairly basic, in terms of skills, but Continental Europeans take a different view, and animation appears on the syllabus of French tourism and leisure qualifications, to cite just one example. This reflects the seriousness with which Continental tourism employees view their roles as providing a professional service.

FINANCIAL SERVICES

This section will deal with three financial services for the tourist, those of insurance, foreign exchange and credit.

Insurance

Insurance is an important, and in some cases obligatory, aspect of a tourist's travel arrangements, embracing coverage for one or more of the following contingencies:

(a) medical care and hospitalisation (and, where necessary, repatriation, important where hospital services are of low standard)
(b) personal accident
(c) cancellation or curtailment of holiday
(d) delayed departure
(e) baggage loss or delay
(f) money loss
(g) personal liability.

Some policies are now also including coverage for the collapse of the travel agent or tour operator through which the tour was purchased – an increasingly important option in view of the growing instability in the industry.

Tourists may purchase insurance either in the form of a selective policy, covering one or more of the above items, or, more commonly, in the form of a standard 'package' which will include all or most of the above. The latter policy, although inflexible in its coverage, invariably offers the best value if comprehensive coverage is sought. Most tour operators encourage their clients to buy the operators' own comprehensive policies (often by requiring the client to indicate on the booking form if they do not require the policy). The operators' own policies, however, may be more expensive to purchase than a comprehensive policy offered by an independent insurance company, and since the travel agent can earn substantially more by selling independent insurance (up to 50 per cent commission, in the case of the largest travel agency chains, compared with the operators' own 10 per cent), agents have considerable incentive to sell insurance and to gain a sufficiently broad knowledge of the subject to be able to match the right policy to their clients' needs. Agents face a new challenge in selling insurance, though, as this now bears VAT at 17.5 per cent if bought in a travel agency, whereas it attracts only 4 per cent if bought direct from an insurance firm. This anomaly is being fought by the trade, but the government has not yet shown itself willing to lift the imposition.

Key issues in choosing a policy are to ensure that medical coverage is sufficient to meet the needs (in the USA, bills in excess of one million dollars are no longer unheard of for serious illnesses), and that loss of any treasured individual items will be covered in full. The normal comprehensive coverage will limit compensation to £200 for total valuables (with an excess of £25 against each claim), and as the value of most tourists' cameras alone exceeds this figure, holidaymakers need to consider covering such valuables within their house contents insurance, for which a premium is normally payable if the insurance is to cover their use outside the home.

Insurance remains a lucrative business for both operators and agents, although claims have been rising in recent years. Some reports estimate that 10 per cent of holidaymakers make claims, many fraudulent, against their policy, and this has led insurers to increase premiums to offset losses. Free insurance, or a deal involving insurance (such as reduced, or no, deposits for those buying the agent's insurance package) has become a regular form of incentive in recent agency marketing.

Agents are required to draw their clients' attention to insurance facilities and cover, but face the dilemma of deciding whether to sell those policies seen as in the customers' best interest or those producing higher revenues or similar benefits (such as extended credit facilities). The decision to sell the policies of one particular company is one to be taken by the branch manager, but in the larger chains it may rest with more senior management.

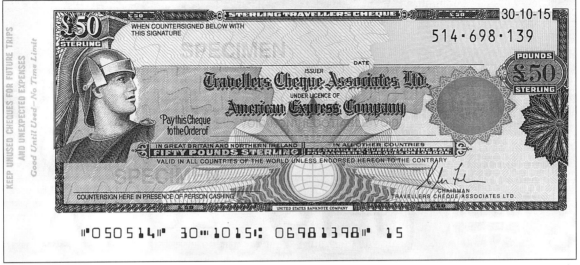

Figure 14.3 A traveller's cheque. (*Courtesy American Express*)

ABTA itself, in conjunction with leading travel insurance companies, recommends to its members a specific package, for which it receives an override commission from the company concerned. However, agents who aim to offer objective advice to their clients will have to weigh the benefits offered by the ABTA-recommended package against other insurance policies they represent.

Foreign transactions

Travellers today have an ever-widening choice of ways in which they can pay for services and goods while abroad. These include:

(a) taking sterling or foreign banknotes with them. This can lead to loss or theft, and certain foreign countries have restrictions on the import or export of their currencies
(b) taking travellers' cheques, in sterling or foreign currency
(c) arranging for the advance transfer of funds to a specified foreign bank, or for an open credit to be made available, through their own bank, at a foreign bank
(d) using National Girobank postcheques
(e) taking Eurocheques
(f) using travel vouchers
(g) using credit cards or charge cards.

Additionally, personal cheques can be cashed against a cashcard, but commission rates for this service can be quite high. As one example of developments in this area, Lloyds Bank has a 'payment card' which can be used worldwide to draw out local currency over the counter or from a cash machine in banks where Visa is displayed. The money is drawn direct from the drawer's home town branch.

Travellers' cheques are the most widely used, being readily acceptable throughout the world by banks or commercial institutions, and offering the holder guaranteed security with rapid compensation for theft or loss. For the tourist, this advantage outweighs the standard premium charged of 1 per cent of face value. The value of the system for suppliers is that there is generally a considerable lapse of time between the tourist purchasing their travellers' cheques and encashing them. The money invested in the interim at market interest rates provides the supplier with substantial profits. Market leaders in travellers' cheque sales in the UK are Thomas Cook (whose 'circular note', the predecessor of the traveller's cheque, originated in 1873), and American Express, which first introduced the concept in 1891. However, a growing proportion is being issued by the clearing house banks, and in 1997 Lunn Poly entered into an agreement with American Express to sell the latter's travellers' cheques through a number of its branches. Other major multiple agencies such as Going Places and WorldChoice also operate their own foreign exchange desks at many branches. In the USA, dollar travellers' cheques are widely used in place of banknotes, and may be the easiest way of carrying out transactions for many foreign visitors.

Holders of National Girobank accounts can draw postcheques for the equivalent in foreign currency of £100 a day at post offices in many countries around the world (Western Union providing this service in the USA).

The Eurocheque is still widely used throughout Europe, especially in Germany, and it has the advantage of allowing the holder to write a cheque in any local currency, again for the equivalent of approximately £100. As with credit cards and cheque cards, delays occur between the transaction and the debit to the holder's account, and in addition a charge of a few pounds is levied for the cheque card itself, plus a percentage for each cheque drawn abroad. Eurocheques also allow for cash to be drawn from banks abroad.

Travel vouchers such as Barclay's Visa and Citicorp provide for sterling prepayment for travel services like car hire and hotel accommodation. Although prepaid vouchers of this kind have been in existence in the travel industry for many years, the credit organisations have greatly boosted their use in recent years.

Credit cards such as those of Visa and Mastercard/Eurocard can be used to purchase goods and services overseas, or to obtain cash advances. Since transactions can take some time to filter through to one's bank account, users take a chance on the fluctuations of exchange rates. Charge cards such as American Express or Diners Club provide similar advantages and drawbacks (charge cards differ from credit cards in that accounts are due for settlement in full after receipt of an invoice from the company. Credit is not extended. However, the limit on charge card transactions is generally much higher than on credit cards – indeed, the company may impose no ceiling on the amount the holder may charge to their account).

In addition to Visa and Access, there are a large number of other credit cards issued for the purchase of specific goods and services, such as

Figure 14.4 A Eurocheque card

car hire or hotels. Among these, mention should be made of the UATP (Universal Air Travel Plan) card, used for the purchase of IATA tickets throughout the world (although more commonly in use in North America than Europe). However, with the growth in popularity of the two leading credit card organisations, the use of other cards for international credit transactions is likely to decline. Since agents are required to pay a fee to the card companies when accepting credit cards in payment for travel, there has been some reluctance to accept them, but credit card sales are increasing at such a rate that no agent can afford to turn this form of business away.

Some travel agents, notably Thomas Cook and American Express, provide facilities themselves for the exchange of currency, but travellers more commonly obtain their foreign exchange through their banks or specialist foreign exchange dealers. The large number of dealers in foreign exchange provides a very wide choice for the market, but charges fluctuate considerably, and both rate of conversion and fixed charges need to be compared to judge what represents best value for money.

Mention should also be made here of direct debit cards such as Switch cards, which have brought the reality of EFTPOS (Electronic Funds Transfer at Point of Sale) into travel transactions. Direct debit cards are now in widespread use, especially for the purchase of foreign currency, and their use can be expected to increase dramatically over the next few years. Work is under way to introduce 'smart cards' which have a microchip built into the card storing credit. These have been in use in France for some years, and supermarkets in the UK are undertaking regional testing to judge their viability. Again, it is likely that we shall see these in use for travel purchases within a short period of time.

INCENTIVE TRAVEL VOUCHERS

Incentive travel has shown considerable growth over the past few years, with companies providing their employees or dealers with attractive travel packages as rewards for achievement. One alternative taken up by some companies is the travel voucher, issued in various denominations, which allows the recipient to choose the travel arrangements. This is simply another form of monetary reward for achievement, but the appeal of travel has proved to be a stronger motivator than cash or consumer durables, and is also more flexible, and can be given in smaller denominations – to reward, for example, low absenteeism or the achievement of weekly targets. Some of these certificates can only be exchanged against specific travel products, or through certain travel agents, while others can be used to pay for any holiday arrangements purchased through agents.

DUTY-FREE SHOPPING

Under the category of services to tourists, mention should also be made of duty-free shopping facilities. The purchase of duty-free goods at airports, on board ships and aircraft, or at specially designated duty-free ports has always exerted a strong attraction for tourists. Duty-free purchases of spirits and tobacco in particular have been effectively marketed by airports and carriers alike, and the profits and sales of such items are substantial, accounting in some cases for half the total operating profits of airports.

This has led in some quarters to criticisms of profiteering, but the principals' reply to such criticism is that without these profits, airports would have to increase their landing charges, and airlines their fares. As a result, transport fares would rise appreciably; estimates range from 10 per cent to as high as 30 per cent. BAA reduced its estimate of increases in charges to airlines using its airports after expanding its retail shopping outlets and

forecasting rapid increases in duty-paid sales (rising congestion at airports, requiring earlier check-in times, and flight delays will all enhance sales in airport shops).

With the introduction of tax harmonisation in the European Union in 1992, it was intended that the practice of duty-free purchases for travel between member countries would cease. The European Commission has agreed, under intense lobbying from interested parties, especially in Britain, to delay the termination of duty-free privileges until July 1999; however, powerful lobbies are at work to extend this further, or even to retain duty-free shopping, and some doubt has arisen as to whether the EU will enforce the regulation by the deadline set. If, in fact, this privilege is terminated it will be interesting to observe how this affects the patterns of travel between countries in Europe, as profit declines are compensated for by rises in fares, and travellers readjust their holiday arrangements to take advantage of duty-free opportunities outside the Union. Countries such as Tunisia, Malta or Turkey could well benefit from this change.

Services to the supplier

EDUCATION AND TRAINING

The approach to training in the tourism industry has been historically a sectoral one. In the past, each sector of the industry was primarily concerned with training staff to become competent within its own sector, focusing on narrowly job-specific abilities. In an industry comprising mainly small units with entrepreneurial styles of management, formal education and training was little recognised. Most employees of travel agencies, tour operators and hotels were trained on the job, often by observing supervisors at work, although some companies, such as Thomas Cook, were notable for their early recognition of the need for more formal, although in-house, training.

With the growing institutionalisation of sectors, greater emphasis is placed on professionalism, the introduction of national standards and more formal modes of training. The professional bodies within industry introduced their own programmes of training and vocational education leading to membership and often carried out through full-time or part-time courses at local colleges of further or higher education. Examples of these early developments included courses offered by the Hotel Catering and Institutional Management Association (HCIMA), the Chartered Institute of Transport (CIT) and the Institute of Travel and Tourism (ITT). However, with the rapid expansion of nationally validated travel and tourism courses in colleges of further and higher education which occurred during the 1970s and 1980s, the ITT decided to drop its own courses and to offer approval to those nationally validated courses meeting the Institute's own criteria for membership.

In-service training for travel agents was formalised with the introduction of a Certificate of Travel Agency Competence (COTAC), nationally validated by the City and Guilds of London Institute (CGLI), and offered at two levels. These programmes were introduced with the support of ABTA's National Training Board, (which was later to become the Travel Training Company). In 1997, with the government's intention to reduce the role of the Industry Lead Bodies and replace these with National Training Organisations, the TTC joined forces with the English Tourist Board in a joint bid to become the National Training Organisation for the travel and tourism industry. Approval is awaited for this development at the time of writing.

The National Training Board, as it then was, widened the scope of its activities to include approval for a number of courses such as COTOP (Certificate of Tour Operating Practice) and COTICC (Certificate of Tourist Information Centre Competence), extending the scope of these courses into management with the introduction of COTAM (Certificate of Travel Agency Management). Coupled with suitable periods of industrial experience, these ABTA-approved courses led to the award of the Diploma in Travel Studies or Diploma in Advanced Travel Studies and the Licentiateship of the City and Guilds (LCG). However, the City and Guilds- (and BTEC-) validated courses have given way to National Vocational Qualifications (NVQs), offered at three levels, foundation, intermediate and advanced, which are designed to test skills and competence as much as knowledge. As these were designed to be tested in the workplace rather than an educational institution, they were favoured by some employers – although others expressed concern about the absence of formal examinations, and the added burden faced by employers in assessing students. Modifications were made to the programmes to allow a greater measure of examinable content, in the hope that this would satisfy employers. However, ABTA itself has been unwilling to fully recognise the new NVQ programmes, instead introducing its own qualification, ABTAC, as the approved replacement to COTAC.

The difficulty of organising day release for employees of smaller travel companies encouraged the development of distance-learning packages. British Airways fares and ticketing courses, for example, which are offered either full-time or through self-study packs, have found national acceptance as a standard for those seeking to work in travel agencies and airlines, while Lufthansa provides similar nationally accepted courses in Germany. The World Tourism Organisation (WTO) and International Air Transport Association (IATA) have organised internationally recognised distance-learning packs for students of tourism throughout the world.

As we have seen earlier, courses for registered guides have been created in the UK and elsewhere; but these are validated individually in Britain by the regional tourist boards and national standards have not yet been laid down for such courses. With vocational courses of this nature, the question of balance between job-specific skills and broader conceptual knowledge has long taxed employers and educationalists alike. Unlike most countries on the Continent, Britain does not hold formal qualifications in high respect, preferring to provide the job skills that are seen as essential to fulfil basic, sector-specific roles in the industry. However, public sector colleges have offered courses since the late 1960s which were designed to provide not just essential skills, but a broader knowledge of the industry and the world of business, and although these were slow to achieve credibility with employers, the eventual approval of ABTA for BTEC National Diplomas in tourism helped to establish credibility for formal education. In 1986 the first degrees in travel and tourism were introduced, to join the already well-established higher national diplomas (HNDs), postgraduate diplomas and masters' degrees in the subject, so that tourism can now be studied formally at all levels of post-school education. The popularity of degree-level tourism programmes led to a huge expansion of courses on offer in the new universities during the 1990s, with an output of qualified students far in excess of suitable posts available. Only some 20 per cent of graduates educated in tourism in the UK actually enter the industry. This pattern, however, is similar to that found in many countries on the Continent; for instance, only about 10 per cent of those educated in tourism in the Netherlands enter the tourism industry.

Within the school system itself, GCSEs in travel and tourism have also been introduced, with the support of key members of the industry, in order to interest school leavers in a career in travel. Attitudes among careers counsellors in schools are slow to change, though, and tourism continues to be seen by many as a career for the less academically able. Low salaries paid to those on the lower levels of employment tend to reinforce this attitude.

THE TRADE PRESS

In addition to specialised academic journals, there is a large selection of weekly and monthly journals devoted to the travel and tourism industry. The weekly trade papers *Travel Trade Gazette* and *Travel Weekly* provide an invaluable service to the industry, covering news of both social and commercial activities, as well as providing the heaviest concentration of advertisements for jobs in the industry.

In an industry as fast-moving as tourism, employees can only update their knowledge of travel products by regular reading of the trade press. The newspapers complement the work of the training bodies, while for untrained staff they may well act as the principal source of new information.

The trade press depends largely upon advertising for its revenue, as the two weeklies are

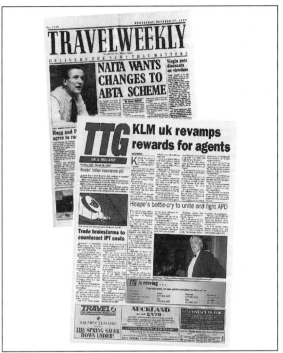

Figure 14.5 The weekly trade papers. *(Courtesy Travel Weekly and Travel Trade Gazette)*

distributed free to members of industry; in return, they support the industry by sponsoring trade fairs, seminars and other events. Within the general category of the press one must also include publications such as travel guides and timetables. The major publications in the field are shown in Table 14.1, and are those most commonly used in travel agencies. The task of updating the information is obviously immense, especially in view of the worldwide scope of many of these publications. Since their production becomes more complex each year, this is also a field which lends itself to computerisation. ABC Guides now provide access for agents to their air timetables and fares information electronically, and within a few years most of these travel data can be expected to be retrieved electronically by the trade at least; and no doubt even by members of the general public.

Table 14.1 Travel publications

Publication	Details
British publications:	
ABC World Airways Guide (monthly)	Flight and fares information, car hire
ABC Rail Guide (monthly)	Timetables between London and all stations
ABC Shipping Guide (monthly)	Worldwide passenger and cargo–passenger
services	
ABC Guide to International Travel (quarterly)	Passport, visa, health, currency regulations, customs, climate, etc.
ABC Hotel and Travel Index (quarterly)	Hotel and trade information.
Thomas Cook Continental Timetable (monthly)	Rail and passenger shipping services throughout Europe and the Mediterranean
Thomas Cook Overseas Timetable (bi-monthly)	Road, rail and local shipping in America, Africa, Asia, Australia
National Express Coach Guide (biannual)	Express coach services for British Guide Isles
Travel Trade Directory	Directory of travel industry in UK/Eire
IATA Travel Agents' Directory of Europe (annual)	Agents, airlines, hotel groups, car hire, tourist offices
Britain: Hotels and Restaurants (annual)	BTA official guide
AA Guide to Hotels and Restaurants (annual)	Listing of 5,000 recommended establishments in the British Isles
A–Z Worldwide Hotel Guide (biannual)	Comprehensive listing of international hotels and reservations offices
Agents' Hotel Gazetteer	
Resorts of Europe	CHG Publications. Details of resorts and
Apartments Gazetteer	accommodation in Europe and elsewhere
Alpine Resorts Gazetteer	
USA Resorts Gazetteer	
Holiday Guide (annual summer and winter edition)	Identifies tour operators providing package holidays to specific hotels and resorts worldwide
Car Ferry Guide (annual)	Index of car ferry routes and operators
International publications	
International Hotel Guide (French annual)	Worldwide guide published by International Hotel Association
Michelin Red Guides	French annual guides to GB and Ireland, France, Benelux, Spain, Portugal, Italy and Germany
Europa Camping and Caravanning (annual)	Guide to campsites
Jaeger's Intertravel (annual)	Directory of world's travel agencies

Marketing services

A number of services exist either wholly or in part to provide marketing support to members of the travel industry. These include marketing consultants, representative agencies, advertising agencies, brochure design, printing and distribution services, suppliers of travel point-of-sale material, and research and public relations organisations. To this list must now be added the organisations which provide the hardware and software for the travel industry's computer systems.

This book does not propose to discuss in depth the marketing of tourism. The subject is fully covered in a companion text (*Marketing for Tourism*, Holloway and Robinson, Longman, 1995). Other texts dealing with the topic can be found in the bibliography at the end of this book. The point to be made here is that both large and small companies in the industry can benefit by employing these specialist agencies, while the services of some are seen as indispensable.

GENERAL MARKETING CONSULTANTS

Management and marketing consultants offer advice to companies in the organisation and operation of their businesses. They bring to the task two valuable attributes, expertise and objectivity. Most tourism consultants have years of experience in the industry on which to draw, and have been successful in their own fields before turning to consultancy. As a result of the recession of the 1990s and the inevitable rise in the number of companies either failing or being taken over, the pool of those former managers in industry turning to consultancy work has increased significantly; the consultants' group affiliated to the Tourism Society alone now includes some 300 individuals.

Consultants, not being directly involved in the day-to-day running of the companies they are employed to help, can approach their task without any preconceived ideas. They can therefore advise the companies either on the general reorganisation of the business or on some ad hoc issue such as undertaking a feasibility study or the introduction of a new computer system.

REPRESENTATIVE AGENCIES

For a retainer or payment of royalties on sales, these organisations act as general sales agents for a company within a defined territory. This is a valuable service for smaller companies seeking representation abroad, for example. In the travel industry it is most commonly found in the hotel sector, but carriers, excursion operators and public sector tourist offices all make use of the facility in marketing their services abroad.

ADVERTISING AND PROMOTIONAL AGENCIES

Many large travel companies, and an increasing number of smaller ones, retain an advertising agent, a number of whom specialise in handling travel accounts. An advertising agent does much more than design advertisements and place them in the media. They should be closely involved in the entire marketing strategy of the company, and will be involved with the design and production of the travel brochures. Many are equipped to carry out marketing research, the production of publicity material and merchandising or public relations activities. Some larger agencies also produce their own hotel/resort guides, using their own staff's extensive knowledge.

Travel companies may have their brochures designed by the design studio of their advertising agent, they may arrange for them to be produced by an independent design studio, or in some cases their printer's studio may undertake the work. However, a growing number of brochures are now put together in-house, with the aid of sophisticated computer software available for the purpose. Advertising agents can also help and advise in the selection of a printer for the production of brochures or other publicity material.

One recent innovation in publicity material for the trade is the use of video cassettes to supplement, and perhaps in time even to replace, the travel brochure. They are designed to help customers reach a decision on holiday destinations and services, and are already being used by agents, who loan them out to their clients. The cost of the cassette production is borne by the principals whose services are being promoted in this way. A number of companies are now specialising in the production of these travel aids.

Finally, in the area of marketing services mention should be made of direct mail and distribution services, some of which specialise in handling travel accounts. The companies design and organise direct mail promotional literature aimed at specific target markets, or at travel retailers. They can also undertake distribution of a company's brochures to travel agents in the UK.

MICROPROCESSOR ORGANISATIONS

The rapid spread of computer use within all sectors of the travel industry has led to the establishment of specialist computer experts, who concentrate on designing and implementing purpose-made systems for their travel industry clients. Such systems include not only travel information and reservations functions, but also accounting and management information. Other computer organisations have been set up to provide networks which allow agents to access principals' computer reservations systems.

QUESTIONS AND DISCUSSION POINTS

1   Is there a potential conflict between the commercial role and the pastoral role of a resort representative? Does the increased emphasis which companies are now putting on selling excursions and other 'add-ons' compromise the traditional role of the rep, and can this be avoided in a trade where revenue has become the priority?

2   Evaluate the two weekly trade papers, *Travel Trade Gazette* and *Travel Weekly*. As manager of a small travel agency whose staff are always too busy to read both, which would you recommend they read regularly, and why?

3   Does the prospect of high commission levels on the sale of certain comprehensive travel insurance policies encourage agents to sell insurance to their clients which is not necessarily the best value for money? Should ABTA or another organisation step in to control this practice and make certain that insurance policies are sold objectively? Should tour operators exercise the right to insist that customers buying their package tours must buy the operator's own insurance with the package?

4   Evaluate the new NVQs for travel and tourism and weigh up their strengths and weaknesses compared with previous vocational education courses. Which is better (a) for employers, and (b) for prospective employees?

ASSIGNMENT TOPICS

1   Mrs H, a client of your travel agency who is not well travelled, has come into a small inheritance, and is proposing to spend it in a way she has always dreamed of – by taking an independent around-the-world holiday by air. She plans to stop over in Bangkok, Sydney (touring Australia), New Zealand, Rarotonga, Fiji and Tahiti before visiting relatives in Los Angeles and flying home. Her previous trips abroad have been limited to short visits to France and Belgium, booking a prepaid package tour where very little personal spending was necessary, and these costs she met by changing sterling notes into local foreign currency as the need arose.

Her planned tour will cost £5,000–£6,000. She is on her way to your shop to ask you about alternative ways of meeting her expenses while abroad. Some of her hotels will be prepaid, but most expenses will have to be settled en route. She is normally careful with money, and wants your advice on the cheapest way of handling these financial transactions, but does not want to forgo security and convenience.

Prepare a set of notes which will give her the guidelines she seeks on alternative methods of taking money abroad and changing it.

2   As a member of the travel industry of some standing, and a Fellow of both the travel and tourism professional bodies, you have been invited by your local college to talk to their new students of tourism about the two bodies, the Institute of Travel and Tourism and the Tourism Society.

Prepare a set of notes to guide your talk, which discusses the present and future advantages of membership in these organisations. Indicate which of these bodies you would recommend the students to join if they are only willing to join one.

15

The Structure and Role of Public Sector Tourism

OBJECTIVES

After studying this chapter, you should be able to:

- understand the part played by local and central governments in the planning and promotion of tourism in a country;
- recognise why governments are becoming increasingly involved with all aspects of tourism in some countries;
- understand the meaning of the term 'social tourism' and its importance;
- show how governments and local authorities in Britain and elsewhere control and supervise tourism;
- explain how public sector tourism is organised in Britain.

Introduction

In the opening chapter of this text, it was shown that tourism can play an important part in a nation's economy by providing opportunities for regional employment, by contributing to the balance of payments and by stimulating economic growth. On the other hand, countries that experience an influx of large numbers of tourists also suffer the environmental and social consequences of mass tourism, unless care is taken to plan for and control the flow of tourists. For both economic and social reasons, therefore, governments take a direct interest in the development of tourism within their countries, and the more a nation becomes involved in tourism, whether domestic, inbound or outbound, the more likely it is that the government will play a role in the industry.

The nature of government involvement

The system of government of a country will of course be reflected in the mode and extent of government intervention. At one end of the scale, centrally planned economies will exercise virtually complete control, from policy-making and planning to the building and operating of tourist facilities, the organisation of tourist movements and the promotion of tourism at home and abroad. Since the collapse of the Soviet empire, such central control is limited to very few countries, and even those nations still ostensibly operating centrally planned economies, such as China, Cuba or Vietnam, are showing signs of recognising and accepting the power of market forces, and the benefits of private investment, in their tourism planning. Thus China, for example, has cooperated with privately owned American hotel corporations to establish chains of tourist hotels in major centres of tourism within the country.

Most other nations have mixed economies in which public and private sectors coexist, and collaborate in the development of tourism within their borders; only the balance of public versus private involvement will vary. Thus the United States, with its belief in a free enterprise system and a federal constitution, delegates much of the responsibility for overseas promotion of the nation either to individual states or even to private organisations created for the purpose. Central government intervention is limited to measures designed to protect the health and safety of its citizens (such as aircraft safety and air traffic control).

The *system* of government is not the only factor dictating the extent of state intervention. If a country is highly dependent upon tourism for its economic survival, its government is likely to become far more involved in the industry. Spain, for example, has a Ministry of Tourism, Transport and Communications, while in Kenya, the Ministry of Tourism and Wildlife takes on this responsibility. In these countries, tourism as an economic activity will feature prominently in policy-making and planning directives. Britain, where tourism is important but to a lesser extent than in the Mediterranean countries, has an undersecretary with responsibility for tourism within the Department for Culture, Media and Sport.

Countries where tourism has only relatively recently become a significant factor in the economy, and where this sudden growth has become problematic, are likely to exercise stronger control over tourism development than are those where tourism is either in its early stages of development or has developed slowly over a long period of time. Mauritius, for example, recognised that the sudden surge of interest it experienced in the early 1980s could lead to the country being swamped, destroying the very attractions that brought visitors to the islands, unless the country took steps to control such key activities as hotel construction. Tunisia, too, learned the lesson and introduced control over hotel and other tourism construction early in the development of mass tourism to that destination. Unfortunately, however, the potential for quick riches can exercise a greater influence than the long-term interests of the country, and there are all too many examples of countries which have suffered from lack of sufficient control over building and development, leading eventually to a drop in visits as tourists turn to less exploited destinations. Overbuilding in Spain was held up as an example in the late 1960s, and could have

influenced subsequent development in other Mediterranean countries to which tourists turned en masse somewhat later. Nevertheless, in the 1980s and 1990s we have seen overdevelopment in key regions of first Greece, then the Portuguese Algarve, and later (in spite of initial efforts to control hotel building) in Turkey. Corruption and nepotism – the significance of having influential 'connections' to overcome planning controls should never be underestimated – are very real enemies of sustainable tourism policies.

All countries depend upon the provision of a sound infrastructure in order to encourage tourism in the first place, and this is a role which must be undertaken by government. Adequate public services, roads, railways, airports must all be in place before the private sector can become interested in investing in the equally necessary superstructure of hotels, restaurants, entertainment, attractions and other activities which will bring in the tourists.

Less developed nations may have a further incentive for government involvement; private developers will be reluctant to invest in speculative tourist ventures, preferring to concentrate their resources in countries where there is already proven demand. In this case, it may fall to the government either to aid private developers, in the form of grants or loans for hotel construction, or even to build and operate the hotels and other tourist amenities which will first attract the tourist. Where the private sector can be persuaded to invest, it is often companies from the generating countries which become involved, with the result that profits may be repatriated rather than benefiting the local economy. There is also the danger that private speculators will be overly concerned to achieve a quick return on their investment, rather than the slow but secure long-term development which will benefit the country most.

The state is called upon to play a coordinating role in planning the provision of tourist amenities and attractions. Supply should match demand as closely as possible, and the state can ensure that facilities are available when and where required, and that they are of the right standard.

As tourism grows in the economy, so its organisation, if uncontrolled, can result in the domination of the market by a handful of large companies. Even in a capitalist system, the state has a duty to restrict the power of monopolies, in order to protect the consumer against malpractice such as unfair constraints on trade or exorbitant prices.

Apart from these economic reasons for which governments become involved in tourism, there are also social and political reasons. In many countries, especially in less developed states, national airlines are state-owned and operated. While, of course, the income accruing from the operation of the airline is important to the state, there is also the political prestige of operating an airline, even if the national flag-carrier is economically non-viable. In other situations, certain airline routes may be unprofitable, but since they may provide an important economic lifeline to the communities they serve, they will therefore be subsidised by the government.

Governments also have a duty to safeguard a nation's heritage. Buildings of historical or architectural interest, particularly those of international importance such as Stonehenge, must be protected and maintained, as must sites of exceptional landscape merit. Sometimes governments are caught up in a conflict between the needs for economic development and for protection of a cherished site, as in the case of Twyford Down, a cherished English beauty spot in Hampshire, which, in the face of an outcry from conservationists, was destroyed in 1993 in order to build an extension to a motorway. The long search for a third London airport was extended by several years while the government weighed up the relative merits of the economic benefits of a particular site and the environmental damage which the development would cause. In the latter half of the 1990s, the conflict between conservation and economic development is noted in the UK in the cases of the construction of a fifth terminal at London's Heathrow Airport and the expansion of Manchester Airport. Needless to say, the power of political lobbying may be the deciding factor in the decision taken by the public authorities, as it was in the case of London's third airport.

We can sum up by saying that a national government's role in tourism can be manifested in the following ways:

(a) in the planning and facilitating of tourism, including the provision of financial and other aid
(b) in the supervision and control of the component sectors of the tourism industry
(c) in direct ownership and operation of components of the industry
(d) in the promotion of the nation and its tourist products to home and overseas markets.

These issues will be examined in the balance of this chapter.

Planning and facilitating tourism

Any country in which tourism plays a prominent role in national income and employment can expect its government to produce policies and plans for the development of tourism. This will include generating guidelines and objectives for the growth and management of tourism, both in the short and the long term, and devising stategies designed to achieve these objectives.

British government policy on tourism has fluctuated considerably in recent years. The Conservative government's approach was initially to support tourism through grant aid and other strategies, but after the early 1990s the government took the view that they had undertaken the necessary pump priming, and the private sector should itself take on the role of development. The British Tourist Authority (BTA), as a quasi-autonomous national government organisation with the responsibility of promoting Britain abroad, had as its aims not just an increase in the total number of tourists to Britain but also a more even spread of visitors throughout the region and across the months, to avoid the congestion of demand in the south and during the summer months. In Spain, since demand had already been created by the private sector for the popular east coast resorts and the Balearic Islands, national tourist office policy focused on promoting the less familiar north west coast and central regions of the country, while coastal development became subject to increasing control.

Tourism planning calls for research, first to assess the level of demand or potential demand for a particular region, secondly to estimate the resources required in order to cater for that demand, and finally to determine how these resources should best be distributed. As we have seen, demand is unlikely to be generated to any extent until an adequate infrastructure and super-structure are in place, but it is not sufficient simply to provide these amenities. Tourists also need staff to service the facilities – hotel workers, travel agents, guides – trained to an acceptable level of performance. Planning therefore implicitly includes ensuring the availability of a pool of labour, as well as the provision of training through hotel, catering and tourism schools, to provide the skills and knowledge the industry requires.

In some cases, providing the facilities which tourists want can actually have a negative impact on tourism to the region. To take one example, while the building of airports on some of the smaller islands in Greece opened up these islands to larger flows of tourists, it made the islands less attractive to up-market high-spending tourists who preferred the relative isolation achieved when accessibility was restricted to ferry operations.

Much earlier in the text, we examined the need for accessibility as a key factor in the development of tourism. This depends not only on adequate transport, but also the absence of any political barriers to travel. If visas are required for entry to a country, this will discourage in-coming tourism. At the beginning of the 1990s, the British imposed a visa requirement on citizens of Turkey seeking to enter Britain; the Turks retaliated by imposing a visa requirement on British visitors to their country. However, the flow of tourists is almost entirely one-way, and the Turks emerged as the clear losers, as the visa requirement dissuaded tourists from visiting their country. In 1988, the USA abandoned visas for many visitors from Western Europe (albeit with some limitations which continued to hinder the free flow of tourism), having recognised the barrier that this bureaucratic constraint exercised at a time when other factors, such as relative exchange rates, were favouring the rapid expansion of tourism to North America. Similarly, the ending of visa require-ments for the Baltic States following the collapse of Communism led to a substantial increase in

tourist visits, while Russia continued to insist on visas, and consequently failed to benefit by a simi-lar increase in tourism.

Taxation can also hinder tourism flows. In 1993, Greece increased its airport departure tax threefold, to 5,200 drachmas (roughly £15), suffi-cient to antagonise tour operators and to persuade the 'marginal' tourist to switch to other Mediterranean destinations. The British govern-ment's imposition in the 1993 budget of an airport departure tax of £5 in the European Union and £10 elsewhere was widely criticised in the press; the decision to double this rate from November 1997 provoked fury in the trade. When one sets such figures against the new low-cost fares offered within Europe by carriers such as easy-Jet, it is apparent that airport taxes can account for as much as 25 per cent of the air transport costs. Likewise, heavy airport tax bur-dens were introduced in 1997 both into and out of the state of Florida, which would result in a family of four flying to Disneyworld paying another £70 in taxation – a very considerable proportion of their flight costs.

Another important factor determining tourism flow is the attitude of nationals of the host country towards visitors in general, and towards visitors from specific countries in particular. Many coun-tries heavily dependent upon tourism have had to mount political campaigns aimed at their resi-dents, to encourage them to show more friendliness towards foreign visitors. Those resi-dents who most frequently come into contact with tourists, such as customs officers, immigration officials, shopkeepers and hotel staff, must be trained to be polite and friendly: first impressions are important for long-term image-building of a country. The USA has introduced campaigns to improve the politeness and friendliness of officials dealing with incoming visitors, while countries of the Caribbean have been forced to mount cam-paigns to deal with growing xenophobia among the local population. The British tourism industry has also taken steps to improve its own handling of foreign tourists through training programmes such as Welcome Host, and encouragement has been given to learning foreign languages, a major weakness among personnel in the industry.

One difficulty which faces governments in the

planning of tourism is the split between the responsibilities of central and local government with respect to issues affecting tourism. In Britain, local authorities have direct responsibility for planning new developments, for the provision of car and coach parking, and for a host of other issues relating to tourist projects. These responsibilities are to some extent split between city and county councils, and conflicting views may appear between local authorities, as well as between local and central government. Local authorities are, of course, greatly influenced by the views of their ratepayers, who are often unsympathetic to the expansion of tourism in their area.

Although tourism in Britain comes within the area of responsibility of the Department for Culture, Media and Sport, no single government department is responsible for all facets of the industry. The Departments of Transport, of the Environment, and of Agriculture, among others, will have some role to play in the development of tourism. In practice, coordination between these various departments is difficult to achieve, hindering the overall planning of tourism within the country.

FINANCIAL AID FOR TOURISM

Governments also contribute to tourism growth through financing development of new projects. On a massive scale, developments such as those of Cancun, Mexico or the regional development of the Languedoc-Roussillon area in the South of France demonstrate the effectiveness of massive private and public sector cooperation in developing entirely new tourism resorts, with the public sector providing the huge funds necessary for land acquisition and infrastructure. On a smaller scale, many governments aid the private sector by providing loans at preferential rates of interest, or outright grants, for schemes which are in keeping with government policy. One example of the way such schemes operate in less developed countries is for loans to be made on which interest only is paid during the first three or four years, with repayment of capital postponed until the later years of the project, by which time it should have become self-financing. Other forms of government aid include subsidies such as tax rebates or tax relief on operating expenses.

Financial aid for tourism projects can also be provided internationally from a number of sources. Less developed countries have received aid from the International Development Association (IDA) – a subsidiary of the World Bank – which provides interest-free or low-rate loans, while another World Bank subsidiary, the International Bank for Reconstruction and Development (IBRD) offers loans at commercial rates of interest to countries where alternate sources of funding may be difficult to find.

On a regional scale, within Europe the European Investment Bank (EIB) provides loans at commercial rates of interest to small companies (normally those employing less than 500 staff). These loans have been provided for up to 50 per cent of fixed asset costs, with repayment terms up to eight years. Interest rates may be slightly lower in areas designated 'Assisted Areas' within the EU.

The European Regional Development Fund offers financial assistance (usually up to 30 per cent of the capital costs) for tourism projects generated by public sector bodies within the Assisted Areas. This money can be used not only as pump priming for direct tourist attractions such as museums, but also for infrastructure development to support tourism, such as airports, or car parking facilities. Northern Ireland in particular has greatly gained from this fund.

Financing available within Great Britain will be dealt with a little later in this chapter.

SOCIAL TOURISM

Reference should also be made here to the government's role in encouraging *social tourism*. This has been defined as the 'furtherance of the economically weak or dependent classes of the population', and is designed to provide aid for low-income families, single-parent families, the elderly, handicapped and other deprived minorities within a population. Aid may be offered in the form of finance (grants, low-interest loans and the like) or in direct support through the provision of free coach trips or holiday accommodation.

Countries with planned economies naturally place greater emphasis on the provision of social tourism. Holidays are seen by these countries as necessary to maintain the health and well-being of the working population. In Europe, a number of countries have been active in providing subsidised tourism for their deprived citizens, led by Belgium, France and the southern countries of the EU. The Brussels-based International Bureau of Social Tourism (BITS) has been active since 1963 as a base for the study and debate of social tourism issues, and maintains a databank, issues publications and conducts seminars on the subject. There are well-established programmes of aid on the Continent for holidays for the mentally, physically and socially handicapped.

By contrast, comparatively little support of this kind is provided in Britain for the disadvantaged, although Britain has over six million registered disabled people. Responsibility for providing this service is delegated to local authorities (the Chronically Sick and Disabled Act 1970 imposed a statutory duty on local authorities to fund holidays for the disabled). Many authorities provided coach outings for the elderly and other disadvantaged groups, but with the recession of the 1980s and 1990s, cutbacks in local authority funding sharply reduced these services, and the number of those receiving financial help from local councils has slumped. The result has been that social tourism has largely become the responsibility of the private sector in recent years. Sponsored by the English Tourist Board, and with the full support of the travel industry in the UK, the Holiday Care Service was set up in 1981, essentially to provide information about holiday opportunities for the disadvantaged, but it has recently introduced training programmes for members of the tourism industry. A number of specialist operators have turned to catering to the needs of these groups, or providing discounted holidays for those with limited means. Holidays are also organised by the Trade Unions in Britain, which have established holiday homes and subsidise holidays for their members; other bodies arranging holidays for the disadvantaged include Mencap, the Red Cross, the Multiple Sclerosis Society and the Winged Fellowship Trust. Both the Spastics Society and the Spina Bifida Association own holiday homes where holidays can be provided for those suffering from these illnesses.

Control and supervision in tourism

The state plays an important part in controlling and supervising tourism, as well as helping to facilitate it. This is necessary to restrain undesirable growth, to maintain quality standards, to match supply and demand and to protect tourists against industrial malpractice or failure.

A government can act to restrain tourism in a number of ways, whether through central directives or local authority control. Refusal of planning permission is an obvious example of the exercise of control over tourism development. However, this is seldom totally effective, since if an area is a major attraction for tourists, the authorities will be unlikely to dissuade them from visiting the district simply by, say, refusing planning permission for new hotels; the result may be that overnight visitors are replaced by excursionists, or that private bed and breakfast accommodation moves in to fill the gap left by the lack of hotel beds. Cornwall has had measures to control caravan sites since 1954, but the local authority has still found it difficult to prevent the growth of unlicensed sites.

The option of failing to expand the infrastructure is taken by some authorities. This can be partially effective, but unfortunately its effects are felt equally by local residents, whose frustrations with, say, inadequate road systems may lead to a political backlash. The price mechanism can also be used to control tourist traffic. This has the added advantage of raising revenue for the government; for example, selective taxation on hotel accommodation or higher charges for parking can be imposed, but these moves are criticised on the grounds that they are regressive, affecting the less well-off but having little effect on the wealthy.

A more acceptable form of control is exercised by effective marketing, concentrating publicity on less popular attractions or geographical regions, and promoting the off-season. Thus the BTA will stress the appeal of the North East of England in its marketing abroad, making little reference to the South West, which already attracts a high proportion of domestic tourists. However, attempts to do this may be frustrated by private sector promotion. Airlines, for example, will prefer to concentrate on promoting those destinations to which they already fly and which attract strong markets. There is always the danger, too, that if the public sector strategy is successful, the amenities and attractions at the more popular sites may well suffer a serious downturn in business. London has been the great Mecca for the majority of overseas visitors to Britain, but on occasions it has experienced fall-offs in the number of visitors which have seriously affected the theatres, taxis and other amenities that depend upon tourist support. Due to the cost of living in London, hotel accommodation has tended to move up-market, since the high costs of building and running a hotel can only be viable when high room charges are levied. The result has been a serious dearth of good-quality, modern, budget-priced hotels for the price-conscious tourist – a problem which may lead to the overseas tourists switching their travel arrangements to Paris instead. Some tourism experts have called for a new government-sponsored initiative in the UK, similar to the 1969 Act discussed later in this chapter, to pump more public funds into the hotel industry, in effect subsidising the capital costs in order to retain this important sector of the tourist market. However, the Labour government elected in 1997 soon made it clear that, while they supported the tourism industry and recognised its contribution to the economy, they would be unlikely to pump more money into the industry in the immediate future.

To some extent, planning for the more extensive use of existing facilities can delay the need to de-market certain attractions or destinations, but it has to be recognised that some tourist destinations are the victims of their own success. An extreme form of control, limiting or denying access to tourists, may become necessary. This can be imposed by some form of visa system, by rationing, by restricting access by private car, or by a total ban on tourist access. Local authorities are already considering one or more of these options for key sites such as Dovedale and the Lake District. In areas of Britain where traffic has reached saturation point, it is now common to find *park and ride* schemes which require the visitors to leave their cars and proceed into the centre

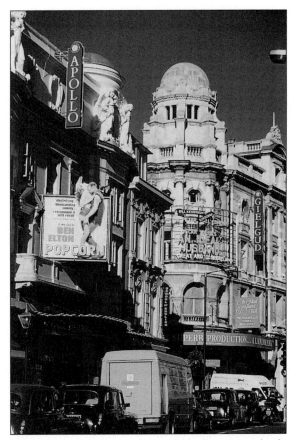

Figure 15.1 Downturns in the tourism business can seriously affect London's theatres. *(Photographed by the author)*

by public transport. In France, the prehistoric cave paintings at Lascaux have been so damaged by the effect of countless visitors' breath changing the climate in the caves that the French government has been obliged to introduce a total ban on entry to the site. However, an artificial replica of the site has been built, and continues to attract many visitors.

Britain has not yet followed the example of some of its Continental neighbours in attempting to stagger holiday-taking by legislation. In Germany, the *Länder* (states) are required to take their holidays on a rota basis over an eleven-year cycle, thus avoiding the holiday rush which is common in Britain at the end of the school summer term. Factories, schools and businesses all plan their closures in keeping with the rota. France, too, divides the country into three zones, each of which takes the summer holiday at a different time. While this policy helps to avoid national peaking, it is not without drawbacks (for example, the mass exodus of German holiday-makers clogging the motorways from their particular *Land* when their turn arrives!). In Britain, no proposals have been advanced for a similar scheme, but thoughts are being given to a four-term academic year in the schools, which would spread holidays and reduce the concentration of tourists in the high summer months.

Sometimes governments exercise control over tourism flows for economic reasons. As we saw earlier in this text, governments may attempt to protect their balance of payments by imposing currency restrictions or banning the export of foreign currency, in an attempt to reduce the numbers of their citizens travelling abroad. The last significant control of this kind in Britain occurred in 1966, when the government of the day imposed a £50 travel allowance, and France also imposed restrictions on the amount of currency that could be exported in the early 1980s. There is little evidence to suggest that these controls are particularly effective in preventing the outflow of foreign currency, and since the advent of the free movement of currency within the European Union, the right of its members to travel within the Union will no longer be restricted. The movement towards a single European currency, whether or not Britain decides to join this initially or later, will still benefit all tourists, including the British, who will no longer be involved in the high costs of changing their currency from one country to another.

Governments also exercise control over the various sectors of the tourism industry. As we have seen, the need to ensure passenger safety in transport leads to the licensing of transport companies, and tour operators are also subject to control through the imposition of Air Travel Operators' Licences (ATOLs). The government's introduction of the Air Travel Reserve Fund (later becoming known as the Air Travel Trust Fund) between 1975 and 1977 was designed to protect consumers against possible collapse of package holiday companies, funds provided by ABTA being seen as insufficient for the purpose. In many countries (although not yet in the UK), travel agencies are required to have a government licence

to operate, and as we saw in Chapter 14, tour guides are licensed by the government in some countries. In France, those using motorboats are also required to be licensed, even if visiting from abroad, owing to an increase in accidents caused by poor navigation. At the time of writing, there is also a move to introduce legislation to control the use of so-called 'wet bikes', which have been the cause of a number of off-shore accidents at EU sites.

The British government will also intervene where it is thought that the takeover or merger of large companies could result in the emergence of a monopoly. The Monopolies and Mergers Commission exists to investigate such situations, but it is interesting to note that in the attempt in 1993 by Airtours, then Britain's third-biggest tour operator, to take over Owners Abroad (later First Choice Holidays), then the second-largest operator, the Trade and Industry Secretary did not feel justified in referring the bid to the MMC.

Perhaps the most common form of government supervision of the tourism industry in all countries is to be found in the hotel sector. Apart from safety and hygiene requirements, many governments also require hotels to be compulsorily registered and graded, prices must be displayed, and the buildings are subject to regular inspection. Camping and caravan sites may also be subject to inspection to ensure consistent standards and acceptable operating conditions.

The organisation of public sector tourism

For the most part, government policies and objectives for tourism are defined and implemented through national tourist boards (although in many cases other bodies directly concerned with recreation or environmental planning will also have a hand in the development of tourism). The functional responsibilities of a national board are likely to include all or most of the following:

Planning and control functions

- Product research and planning for tourism plant and facilities

- Protection or restoration of tourism assets
- Manpower planning and training
- Licensing and supervision of sectors of the industry
- Implementation of pricing or other regulations affecting tourism.

Marketing functions

- Representing the nation as a tourist destination
- Undertaking market research, forecasting trends and collecting and publishing relevant statistics
- Producing and distributing tourism literature
- Providing and staffing tourist information centres
- Advertising, sales promotion and public relations activities directed at home and overseas markets.

Financial functions

- Advising industry on capital investment and development
- Directing, approving and controlling programmes of government aid for tourism projects.

Coordinating functions

- Linking with trade and professional bodies, government and regional or local tourist organisations
- Undertaking coordinated marketing activities with private tourist enterprises
- Organising 'workshops' or similar opportunities for buyers and sellers of travel and tourism to meet and do business.

In some countries, some of these activities may be delegated to regional tourist offices, with the national board coordinating or overseeing its implementation.

National tourist boards will generally establish offices overseas in those countries from which they can attract the most tourists, while their head office in the home country will be organised along functional lines. As one example, the Netherlands Tourist Board operates fifteen offices abroad, together with a home office responsible for promoting the country domestically. The various functions of the board are divided between six departments (see Figure 15.2)

Public sector tourism in Britain

Britain has long been at the forefront of international tourism, both as a destination and a generating country, though before 1969 tourism played little part in government policy-making. Forty years earlier, the government of the day had provided the first finance for tourism marketing, by funding (to the tune of £5,000) the Travel Association of Great Britain and Northern Ireland, in order to encourage travel to Britain from overseas. During the inter-war years this evolved into the British Travel Association, which was given the additional task of promoting domestic holidays for British residents. No clear policies were laid down for its activities, however, and its powers were limited.

Voluntary tourist boards were established in Scotland in 1930, and in Wales in 1948, the same year in which a board was first established in Northern Ireland. It was to be more than twenty years later, however, before a coordinated framework for public sector tourism was to be established in the United Kingdom as a whole.

THE DEVELOPMENT OF TOURISM ACT

By the late 1960s, following the rapid growth in popularity of Britain as a tourist destination, it was clear that a new framework for tourism was needed in the country. This was manifested in the Development of Tourism Act 1969, the first statutory legislation in the country specifically concerned with tourism.

The Act, in three parts, dealt with the organisation of public sector tourism, with the provision of financial assistance for much-needed hotel development, and also provided for a system of compulsory registration of tourist accommodation. The last part of the Act, which was designed to include rights of inspection by government officials, has never been fully implemented, although the compulsory display of prices was subsequently introduced. The accommodation sector preferred to follow a system of voluntary

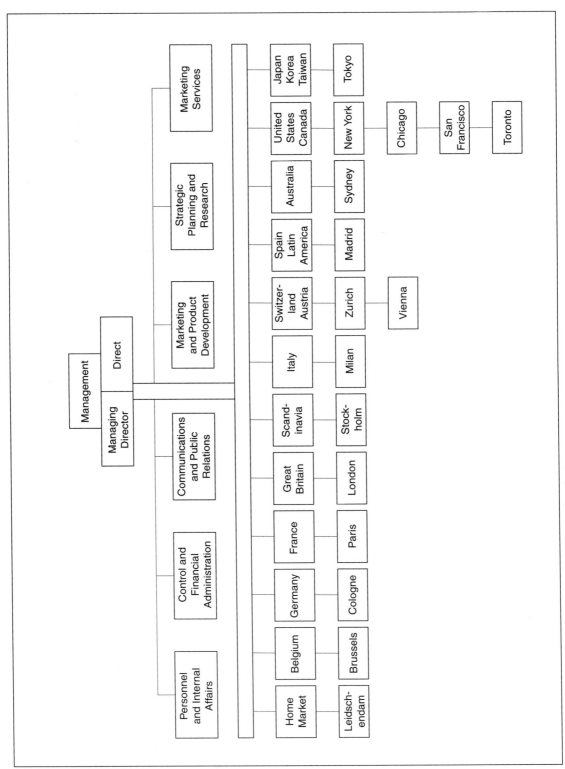

Figure 15.2 The Netherlands Tourist Board's organisation chart

classification and grading of tourist accommodation, persuading the government not to enforce a compulsory system. The result was a mixed success, as the voluntary system fails to embrace a substantial amount of the stock of available accommodation in the UK; however, the implementation of the first two parts of the Act were to have far-reaching consequences for tourism in Britain.

The part of the Act dealing with financial assistance for the hotel industry was designed in the short term to improve the stock and quality of hotel bedrooms, in order to meet changing demand and overcome scarcity. Grants and loans, administered by the three new national tourist boards, were to be made available for hotel construction and improvement until 1973 (during which time some 55,000 bedrooms were added to the stock). Unfortunately, because the Act failed to specify the location in which new hotels were to be built, much of the increased stock was located in London, leading to temporary overcapacity in the city, while areas where hotel construction involved greater financial risk, such as Scotland and the north of England, did not benefit to anything like the extent needed.

The first part of the Act called for the establishment of four national boards to become responsible for tourism, and defined the structure and responsibilities of each of these. At the apex, the British Tourist Authority, to replace the old British Travel Association, was to be the sole body responsible overseas for the marketing of tourism to Britain, and would also advise ministers on tourism matters in general. Tourism issues that concerned Britain as a whole were to be dealt with by the BTA, while three further boards – the English Tourist Board (renamed the English Tourism Council in 1999), Scottish Tourist Board and Wales Tourist Board – became responsible for tourism development within their own territories, and for the marketing of their territories within the UK. Scotland was later given the freedom to undertake overseas marketing itself, under the terms of the Tourism (Overseas Promotion) (Scotland) Act, 1984, and Wales followed suit in 1992.

Northern Ireland was not affected by this Act, having established its own tourist board under the Development of Tourist Traffic Act (N Ireland) in

1948. Subsequent legislation, the Tourist Traffic (Northern Ireland) Order 1972, amended the Act to allow local authorities to provide or assist in the provision of tourist amenities. Similarly, the Isle of Man Tourist Board and the States of Jersey and Guernsey Tourist Committees operate independently outside the jurisdiction of the Act.

Initially, both the BTA and the English Tourist Board were responsible to the Board of Trade, while the Scottish and Wales Boards were responsible to their respective Secretaries of State. Later, responsibility of the BTA and ETB passed to the Department of Employment and subsequently, in 1992, to the newly created Department of National Heritage, which absorbed a number of other related interests, including the royal parks and palaces, arts and libraries, sport, broadcasting and the press as well as heritage sites. This department became known as the Department for Culture, Media and Sport when the Labour government came to power in 1997.

All four bodies were established by the Act as independent statutory bodies, and were to be financed by grants-in-aid from the central government. They were empowered in turn to provide financial assistance for tourism projects (the so-called 'Section 4' scheme within the Act).

REGIONAL TOURIST BOARDS

The Act made no provision for a statutory regional public sector structure for tourism. Before the Act, some attempt had been made to establish regional tourist associations, these being more advanced in Scotland and Wales than in England. However, following the establishment of the three national boards, each set about creating its own regional tourism structure. The result was the establishment of twelve regional tourist boards in England, to be funded jointly by the ETB, local authorities and contributions from local private sector tourism interests. This number was reduced to ten during the 1990s, as the ETB determined they could no longer afford to fund twelve boards; firstly by the financial collapse in 1992 of the Thames and Chilterns Tourist Board, whose territory was allocated to the adjoining regions; and in 1996, by the formation of the East of England Tourist Board, constructed from the former East

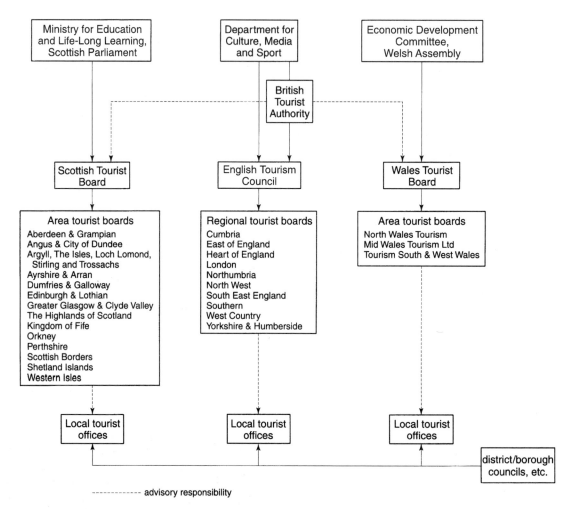

Figure 15.3 Structure of public sector tourism in Britain (incorporating changes introduced in 1999)

Midlands and East Anglian Tourist Board regions, coupled with Lincolnshire.

The Wales Tourist Board established three regional offices in North, Mid- and South Wales, which became responsible for the management of most of the tourist information centres in Wales, in conjunction with local authorities. Three tourism councils were also created, one in each region, supported by the regional offices, and designed to advise the board on a wide range of tourism-related issues. The councils draw their membership from local authorities and the tourist industry.

In Scotland, the picture was more complicated. Before the Act, regional tourism promotion was in the hands of the eight regional councils, with a separate voluntary association (Dumfries and Galloway) and a statutory development board responsible for the Highlands and Islands. This board subsequently established fifteen area tourist boards within its region. Under the terms of the Local Government and Planning (Scotland) Act 1982, the district councils in Scotland were empowered to set up area tourist boards which would become responsible for marketing tourism and running the tourist information centres in their region. The Highlands and Islands scheme was used as a model for the extension of the scheme throughout Scotland, and the new boards were established as a co-partnership between the

Cumbria Tourist Board
Cumbria

East of England Tourist Board
Cambridgeshire, Essex, Hertfordshire, Bedfordshire, Norfolk, Suffolk, Lincolnshire

Heart of England Tourist Board
Gloucestershire, Hereford & Worcestershire, Shropshire, Staffordshire, Warwickshire and West Midlands, District of Cherwell and West Oxfordshire, Derbyshire, Leicestershire, Northamptonshire, Nottinghamshire and Rutland

London Tourist Board
Greater London

Northumbria Tourist Board
The Tees Valley, Durham, Northumberland, Tyne & Wear

North West Tourist Board
Cheshire, Greater Manchester, Lancashire, Merseyside High Peak district of Derbyshire

South East England Tourist Board
East Sussex, West Sussex, Kent, Surrey

Southern Tourist Board
East and North Dorset, Hampshire, Isle of Wight, Berkshire, Buckinghamshire, Oxfordshire

West Country Tourist Board
Bath, Bristol, Cornwall and the Isles of Scilly, Devon, West Dorset, Somerset, Wiltshire

Yorkshire Tourist Board
Yorkshire, North East Lincolnshire

Figure 15.4a   Regional tourist boards in England. *(Courtesy ETB)*

Figure 15.4b   Regional tourism councils in Wales. *(Courtesy WTB)*

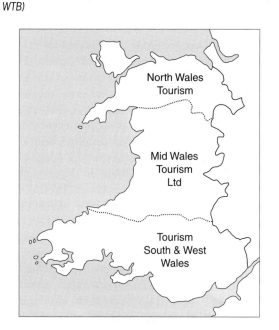

Scottish Tourist Board, one or more district councils and the tourist trade, with finance provided by grant aid and private contributions. Thirty-two area tourist boards were established, with four district councils deciding to retain their autonomy over tourism matters, while a further six districts failed to decide whether to participate in the scheme. The Highlands and Islands retained an interest in tourism within its territory, but changed its title to Highlands and Islands Enterprise. However, scarcely had this new structure been put into place before a further revision was introduced in legislation in 1993, replacing the thirty-two boards with fourteen new boards, all with greatly expanded territories. These were in place by 1996. Accompanying financial constraints led to the closure of a number of the tourist information centres in the country. Local enterprise companies were now given the role of operating the financial assistance programmes which were formerly the responsibility of the Scottish Tourist Board. At the same time local authority tourism marketing was required to be

AREA TOURIST BOARD AND
PARTICIPATING COUNCILS

1. **Aberdeen and Grampian Tourist Board**
   Moray
   Aberdeen City
   Aberdeenshire
2. **Angus and City of Dundee Tourist Board**
   Angus
   City of Dundee
3. **Argyll, the Isles, Loch Lomond, Stirling and Trossachs Tourist Board**
   Argyll and Bute
   Clackmannanshire
   Dumbarton and Clydebank
   Falkirk
   Stirling
4. **Ayrshire and Arran Tourist Board**
   South Ayrshire
   North Ayrshire
   East Ayrshire
5. **Dumfries and Galloway Tourist Board**
   Dumfries and Galloway
6. **Edinburgh and Lothians Tourist Board**
   City of Edinburgh

  East Lothian
  Midlothian
  West Lothian
7. **Greater Glasgow and Clyde Valley Tourist Board**
   City of Glasgow
   East Dunbartonshire
   East Renfrewshire
   Inverclyde
   North Lanarkshire
   Renfrewshire
   South Lanarkshire
8. **Highlands of Scotland Tourist Board**
   Highland
9. **Kingdom of Fife Tourist Board**
   Fife
10. **Orkney Tourist Board**
    Orkney Islands
11. **Perthshire Tourist Board**
    Perthshire and Kinross
12. **Scottish Borders Tourist Board**
    Scottish Boarders
13. **Shetland Tourist Board**
    Shetland Islands
14. **Western Isles Tourist Board**
    Western Isles

– – – Tourist board boundaries

Figure 15.4c Area tourist boards in Scotland. *(Courtesy STB)*

channelled through the new statutory, but private sector-dominated, boards.

The structure of public sector tourism appears in Figure 15.3, while the regional distribution of tourist boards is illustrated in Figure 15.4(a) (England), Figure 15.4(b) (Wales) and Figure 15.4(c) (Scotland).

GOVERNMENT POLICY AND TOURISM IN THE UK

The new structure of public sector tourism in Britain was to improve greatly the planning and coordination of tourism in the UK. Nevertheless, the diverse nature of tourism and its impact on so many different facets of British life make cohesive planning difficult. Quite apart from the fact that tourism issues cut across the interests of many dif-

ferent government departments, there are a number of public or quasi-public bodies whose roles also impinge in one way or another on tourism. The water authorities represent one obvious example, since water-based recreation plays such an important part in leisure and tourism planning. In this respect, it is interesting to note the extent to which tourism featured in the planning and development of the Kielder Reservoir in Northumbria, by comparison with earlier reservoir development. Local authorities, and the water authorities themselves, are now fully aware of the commercial leisure opportunities associated with large expanses of water.

Bodies such as the Countryside Commission, the Forestry Commission, the Nature Conservancy Council, the Arts and Sports Councils, the National Trust and the Council for the Preservation of Rural England, to take just a few examples, each have an interest in issues relating to tourism, yet there is no common coordinating body to bring these interests together.

Within the government, we have already seen how several departments may have responsibilities for some features of tourism, even though ostensibly this is the brief of the Department for Culture, Media and Sport. Again, coordination between the various interests at government level is not easy. An all-party Interdepartmental Tourism Coordinating Committee was established with the aim of facilitating this, but in practice this committee meets very seldom – it did not meet on a single occasion between 1992 and 1996. However, when one thinks of some of the issues under discussion within the government which impact on tourism, the full extent of the problem will be apparent: issues such as the recent reform of licensing, which extended drinking hours and had a huge impact on tourist spend, or legislation ending the long-standing ban on Sunday shopping, which also supported tourism. Efforts were made to bring Britain's clocks into line with the rest of Europe by changing to Central European Time; in the event, this motion was defeated, but the extra hour of daylight this would have given in the early evening would have greatly benefited the tourism industry – industry estimates suggested it would have enhanced spend by some £500 million per annum. The Department of Transport, quite apart from its public transport responsibilities, exercises control over certain types of signposting, and the signposting of attractions is of immense importance to the success of tourism. In January 1996, the relaxation of control over brown and white directive road signs for tourism sites led to information about these sites becoming far more readily available to passing tourists, enhancing tourist spend.

CHANGING GOVERNMENTS, CHANGING POLICIES

The Conservative government came to power in 1979, and during its term of office, which was to last eighteen years, there were marked changes of direction in terms of tourism policy, with a noted failure to produce a clear and consistent policy. The early years of the Thatcher government were notable for outspoken support for the tourism industry, and recognition of the contribution which tourism makes to the British economy, following reviews of the industry in 1983, and promises were made to expand Section 4 grants nationwide. In 1985, the Young Report (*Pleasure, Leisure and Jobs: the Business of Tourism*, issued by the Cabinet Office Enterprise Unit) promised to 'remove unnecessary obstacles' in the path of tourism development, and emphasised the role which small firms and self-employment would continue to play in the industry. Importance was attached to encouraging young people to enter the industry, and to ensure they were well trained. In the same year, the House of Commons Trade and Industry Committee proposed a radical restructuring of public sector tourism in Britain, which although not adopted in its entirety, influenced government thinking in its later policies.

Towards the end of the 1980s, the commitment to tourism was wavering; tourism, which had already moved from the Department of Trade and Industry to the Department of Employment, was transferred to the newly created Department of National Heritage. This Department was given a new name, and new priorities, under the Labour government when it came to power in 1997. However, the Department for Culture, Media and Sport, which fails to incorporate tourism in its title, suggests a further sidelining of the industry. Within the Department, direct responsibility for

tourism falls to a Minister for Film and Tourism, so that tourism still remains without a minister whose sole responsibility is for this major sector of the British economy. During the past few years, ministers with responsibility for tourism came and went with increasing rapidity, giving them little opportunity to familiarise themselves with the role and its responsibilities. The fact that many ministerial appointments were in the House of Lords, rather than the Commons, suggested a further downgrading in the importance government attached to tourism in the economy.

By the 1990s, the Conservative government was propounding the belief that sufficient effort had been made in regenerating the industry with public funds, and that the future lay in cooperation between the private and public sectors, with private enterprise playing the major role in funding any future development. Section 4 grants were discontinued in England, although political sensitivities in Wales and Scotland ensured that these privileges were not withdrawn from those areas also. Annual grants-in-aid for the already much-reduced ETB were cut, forcing a total restructuring of the BTA and ETB in 1995; departments were brought closer together to avoid duplication and to combine resources, and many services previously undertaken by the national boards were handed over to private enterprise. Increasing contributions from the private sector, which had been adopted as policy by the Wales Tourist Board by the end of the 1980s, were introduced for the English regional tourist boards, which faced cutbacks not only in NTB funding, but in support from cash-starved local authorities. Lack of public cash ensured that the regional tourist boards would have to contemplate privatisation or, like the Thames and Chilterns Board, they faced the prospect of bankruptcy.

The belief that private enterprise money can replace public support is questionable, based on the record of the industry to date. When the regional tourist boards (RTBs) were established, it was the intention that these would be a means for collaboration between the private and public sectors, with a third of the income to come from the private sector. In the event, as Ken Robinson, Chairman of the Tourism Society, has pointed out, of the 226,000 businesses involved in tourism in the UK, only 16,000 are actually members of their RTBs.

English boards have moved towards becoming more enterprising during the 1990s. In Northampton, to cite one example, the local tourist information centre (TIC) established an ETB-backed travel agency in 1996 as a pilot project to sell domestic tourism products, and a similar move was taken by Chester TIC in 1997. However, direct intervention by the public sector into commercial activities is not necessarily the best way forward. Efforts by the Wales Tourist Board to establish commercial tour operations to support tourism into Wales have failed to generate the support of the retail trade, in spite of ensuring that a commission-able domestic product would be available for agents to sell. However, it is proving difficult to change attitudes towards selling and stocking domestic products in the retail agencies; only 8 per cent of domestic holidays are sold in this way.

The illogicality of government policy towards tourism over the past twenty years has been a noted feature: the promise of support, while funds were simultaneously cut, the lack of development grants for tourism in depressed regions while manufacturing could benefit, the withdrawal of grants in poor English regions such as Cornwall while grants were awarded in Wales and Scotland regardless of the state of local economies, the decline in support for the English Tourist Board in particular vis-à-vis the other national boards, all suggest a failure on the part of successive governments to think through rational policies for tourism. Pressures on government spending in the 1990s will, nevertheless, make it unlikely that the policy of self-support will be reversed, in spite of a steady and substantial deficit in the balance of payments on the tourism account.

However, it is important to note that areas designated by the Government as 'Assisted Areas' do qualify for economic aid, which can, of course, include aid for tourism projects. There are some 125 Intermediate and Development Areas in Britain, the latter qualifying for higher grants. Funding can be provided through two schemes:

(a) Selective Assistance schemes, aimed at investment projects which create or safeguard jobs

(b) Regional Enterprise Grants, providing aid to small firms.

The expansion of the Assisted Areas in 1993 brought some of England's fading seaside resorts into the scheme, including Kent resorts such as Broadstairs, Margate and Ramsgate, which have benefited from funds.

Criticism has focused on the unfavourable rate of VAT in the UK compared to other countries, especially as it applies to hotel accommodation; on the imposition of passenger levies on air transport, which are now seen by governments as a comparatively painless means of raising extra revenue, and have already been doubled since their introduction; and on the failure to provide an integrated transport policy which would facilitate tourism.

DEVELOPMENTS UNDER A LABOUR GOVERNMENT

In the run-up to the 1997 election, the Labour Party focused particularly on tourism as an industry that had not received sufficient support under the previous government. In spite of the fact that employment in tourism had risen by 31 per cent between 1986 and 1995, the Conservative government appeared to do little more than pay lip service to the value of the industry to the UK economy. Grants-in-aid to the BTA/ETB, after allowing for the effects of inflation, fell in real terms in each of the years between 1993 and 1998 (see Table 15.1).

Table 15.1 UK grants-in-aid to BTA & ETB, 1993–98

Year	Sum awarded (£m)
1993/4	47.0
1994/5	44.0
1995/6	44.5
1996/7	45.5
1997/8	44.9

This joint allocation of funds to the BTA and the newly renamed English Tourism Council (ETC) conceals the fact that the distribution of funds between the organisations has changed dramatically. Generally, the BTA funding has been enhanced, or at least stabilised, while that of the ETB has been substantially reduced.

In 1996, the Labour Party raised a number of 'strategic issues' for tourism, including the need for

- increased understanding in the party of the tourism industry and its problems
- coherence of policy towards tourism across all government departments
- review of tourism policy in consultation with members of the industry
- the enforcement of statutory registration of accommodation
- improved performance of the industry in meeting the needs of foreign visitors
- review of VAT rates applicable to products in the industry
- review of transport policy affecting tourism
- examination of the issue of sustainable tourism in the UK
- consideration of the implications of the Social Chapter for tourism.

The Labour government has indicated its intention to introduce new legislation which would amend the structure of the regional and national tourist boards yet again. The expectation is that this will entail the establishment of some form of Regional Development Agency for each region, to promote economic growth in the regions, and that the RTBs would be reconstituted to parallel these agencies' activities.

However, at the time of writing, and since their election to power, Labour has disappointed the industry in its failure to give the support expected. It has maintained the airline departure tax, has not enhanced the grant-in-aid to the BTA/ETC (formerly ETB), and the failure to give tourism a higher profile in the reconstituted Department for Culture, Media and Sport, as noted earlier, suggests that the party may well follow Conservative policies in believing that the industry has reached a level of maturity where it is largely capable of fending for itself.

LOCAL AUTHORITIES AND TOURISM

At local authority level, the county councils and district councils have diverse statutory responsibilities and interests in the provision of tourist facilities. The Local Government Act 1948 empowered local authorities to set up information and publicity services for tourism, and this was reinforced by the Local Government Act of 1972, giving local authorities the power to encourage visitors to their area and to provide suitable facilities for them.

The organisation of tourism at local level is often curiously piecemeal. Counties and districts on the whole relegate responsibility for tourism to departments which are concerned with a range of other activities, with the result that it is seldom given the significance which its economic impact on the area merits. Evidence suggests that less than 50 per cent of local authorities include any strategy relating to tourism in their planning, although Circular 13/79 urged them particularly to consider providing for tourism in local structure plans, and the ETB drew up guidelines which local authorities should follow, emphasising the following key points:

- Assess the number and distribution of tourists in the area
- Estimate future changes in tourism flow, and implications of this for land use
- Identify growth opportunities
- Assess the impact of tourism on employment and income in the area
- Assess the tourists' effect on traffic flows
- Assess the tourists' demand for leisure and recreation
- Identify the need for conservation and protection
- Evaluate the contribution tourism could make to development, especially in the use of derelict land and obsolete buildings.

Local plans, too, should take into account the impact of tourism, in terms of the provision of car and coach parks, toilets, information centres, tourist attractions and the demand for local accommodation. The inadequacy of parking and toilet facilities in resorts has been a frequent topic of criticism, and cutbacks in local funding have magnified the problem recently.

By the beginning of the 1980s, tourism needs were beginning to find their way into several Local Authority Structure Plans, and local authorities were coming to appreciate the economic contribution which tourism could make even in traditionally non-tourist areas. Training courses such as COTICC (Certificate of Tourist Information Centre Competence) were developed to cover the need for basic skills among TIC staff, and some local authorities were even starting actively to recruit staff with formal tourism education or experience.

The principal responsibilities of county and district authorities which bear on tourism are as follows:

(a) provision of leisure facilities for tourists (e.g. conference centres) and for residents (e.g. theatres, parks, sports centres, museums)
(b) planning (under town and country planning policies). Note that district councils produce local plans to fit the broad strategy of the county council Structure Plans. These plans are certified by the county council
(c) development control powers over land use
(d) provision of visitor services (usually in conjunction with tourist bodies)
(e) parking for coaches and cars
(f) provision of caravan sites (with licensing and management the responsibility of the district councils)
(g) production of statistics on tourism, for use by the regional tourist boards
(h) marketing the area
(i) upkeep of historic buildings
(j) public health and safety issues.

Local authorities may also own and operate local airports.

Local authorities which have set out actively to encourage tourism have a number of objectives, some of which may conflict, and each of which will compete for scarce resources. Local tourist officers will need to identify the resources they require to achieve their stated objectives, and to determine their priorities. Typical objectives might include:

- increasing visitor numbers
- extending visitor stays
- increasing visitor spend
- increasing and up-grading local attractions
- creating or improving the image of the area as a tourist destination
- stimulating private sector involvement in tourism.

Local tourist officers act as catalysts between the public and private sectors and voluntary-aided bodies. As a focus for tourism in the area or resort, they become a point of reference, advising on development and grant-aided opportunities. Officers will help the local authority to determine and establish the necessary infrastructure which will allow tourism to develop, and they will carry out research and planning activities themselves. In some areas, they may become involved in the provision and training of tourist guides. In addition, they will undertake a range of promotional and publicity functions, including the preparation of publications such as guides to the district, accommodation guides, information on current events and entertainment, and specialist brochures listing, for example, local walks or pubs. The cost of most of these publications will be met in part by contributions from the private sector, either through advertising or, as in the case of the accommodation brochures, through a charge for listing. Many resorts also now produce a trade manual, aimed at the travel trade and giving information on trade prices, conference facilities and coach parking. Tourist officers organise familiarisation trips for the UK travel trade and press, and, if the resort shows sufficient potential, they may invite representatives of the overseas trade and press. They play a part in setting up and operating local tourist information centres, and may also offer a local bed-booking service. Finally, on occasion they even take a part in actively packaging holidays for clients, such as activity weekends or special interest short breaks. It should be noted that all of these functions are frequently the responsibility of a very small team, on occasion no greater than a single tourist officer and a secretary.

Unlike the regional tourist boards, whose aims are essentially promotional, the local authorities bear responsibilities for protecting the environment, and for tourism planning generally. They may consequently be as concerned to reduce or stabilise tourism as to develop it (particularly when, as is so often the case in the popular tourist resorts, local residents are opposed to increases in the numbers of tourists attracted). In providing for leisure, the authorities must be sensitive to local residents' needs as much as to those of incoming tourists. They must convince the residents of the merits of public sector funding for tourist projects. The development of conference centres in resorts such as Bournemouth and Harrogate was a controversial issue with local residents, since very few conference centres are viewed as viable investments for the private sector, and public sector funding of this kind will greatly increase the burden of debt on the council initially. It is hard to convince local residents of the wisdom of investments that do not appear to provide a direct profit; however, conferences do generate a healthy flow of indirect revenue through additional spend by delegates in local shops, hotels and restaurants, with the added bonus that much of this revenue will accrue outside the traditional holiday season.

The funding and staffing of local tourist information centres (TICs) is often the joint responsibility of local authorities and the regional tourist boards, with material drawn from the regional and national boards. Many of these local TICs also provide a booking service for tourists seeking accommodation in the area, and they also manage a scheme for booking accommodation from one TIC to another. This is known as the Book-a-Bed-Ahead scheme (BABA). Local authorities contribute directly to RTB funds, and clearly will expect to play a role in the board's policy-making. They will normally be represented on the board's committees or sub-committees dealing with tourism development in the area. However, since representatives of the private sector, such as local hoteliers, are also members of these committees, and their interests and objectives may well differ from those of the local authority's, this can lead to conflicts in policy-making within the regional boards.

NATIONAL HERITAGE BODIES

In Chapter 11 we examined the significance of man-made attractions for tourism. These play a particularly important role in Britain, with its rich heritage of monuments, historic homes, cathedrals and similar attractions. While many of these remain in private hands, or are the responsibility of bodies such as the Church Commissioners, a number of quasi-public or voluntary organisations exist to protect and enhance these heritage sites. These bodies therefore play their part in the tourism industry.

According to estimates made by the BTA/ETB, there are well over a million buildings in Britain of architectural merit, broken down into categories (see Table 15.2).

Table 15.2 Buildings in Britain of potential interest to tourists

* Listed buildings of architectural and historical merit	395 377
* Sites of archaeological interest	635 000
* Ancient monuments	12 875
* Ecclesiastical buildings	16 622
* Hotels of historical or architectural merit	5 202
* Conservation areas of architectural or natural interest	5 902
Total:	1 070 978

Source: Sightseeing, 1986, ETB

One might be surprised by the very high number of valued buildings, but a walk through any country town in Britain will soon reveal a wealth of buildings worth more than a passing glance. While many are not open to the public, they are nevertheless attractive to view from the outside. Key sites such as grade 1 listed buildings or internationally renowned sites such as Stonehenge will draw people from all over the world, and are carefully protected. Many of our great national monuments were under the control of the Department of the Environment until recently, but growing concern about their protection and maintenance led to the establishment of the Historic Buildings and Monuments Commission in 1983, following the National Heritage Act in that year. This body, more famil-

Figure 15.5 Stonehenge: one of the English Heritage's responsibilities. *(Photographed by the author)*

iarly known as 'English Heritage', which integrates the functions of the former Historic Buildings Council for England and the Ancient Monuments Board, has a dual conservation and promotion function. In 1993 it came under criticism for attempting to hive off some of its minor properties in order to concentrate an eroded budget on protecting its key sites. The organisation is seeking to make the budget stretch further by efforts to raise financial support from industry and the public, either through sponsorship of individual buildings or subscriptions to a national membership scheme similar to that of the National Trust. There is an equivalent body, Cadw, in Wales, with similar responsibilities, while Heritage Scotland is responsible for that territory.

Apart from these key quasi-governmental bodies, the National Trust (and an equivalent body in Scotland) plays a vital role in protecting buildings of significant architectural or historic interest. Founded in 1895, the Trust cares for over 190 properties and a quarter of a million hectares of land, acquiring properties for the most part through inheritance. Its properties include villages, nature reserves and woodland, and it also operates a campaign, under the title Enterprise Neptune, to buy up and protect stretches of British coastline; to date, it has acquired over 500 miles of coast. Operational costs are met by subscriptions from the very large number of members in Britain, but the Trust also anticipates that properties left to it will be accompanied by sufficient money for their upkeep.

Apart from these key organisations, a great many smaller bodies exist to protect the British heritage. One of the earliest to be founded was the Society for the Protection of Ancient Buildings, dating back to 1877; other bodies include the Ancient Monuments Society, the Georgian Group, the Victorian Society, the National Piers Society and SAVE Britain's Heritage. To these we must add a number of diverse trusts, all of which share an interest in the protection of sites of touristic appeal, including the Civic Trust, the Monument Trust, the Pilgrim Trust, the Landmark Trust and many others (over a thousand local amenity societies are known to exist in England alone). Some of these, such as the Landmark Trust and Pilgrim Trust, actually rent out their properties for holidays, so play an active part in the tourist industry.

THE NEW TOURISM

As we saw in Chapter 11, success in preserving our industrial heritage is evidenced in such sites as Ironbridge. Few would have believed, a few years ago, that vast numbers of tourists could be attracted to the former 'dark, Satanic mills' of eighteenth- and nineteenth-century Britain. The success of sites like Coalbrookdale and Blists Mill can be ascribed to a combination of nostalgia for a lost past with which many can still identify, and a growing awareness of our historical heritage in all its forms. It took the public sector to recognise the potential for tourism of this new kind which could be generated in Britain's decaying inner cities. The tourist boards, in partnership with local authorities and private enterprise, successfully established such unlikely places as Bradford ('A Surprising Place'), Glasgow ('Glasgow's Miles Better') and Liverpool's Merseyside ('Full of Magic Memories') as worthy of a visit and, even better, an overnight stay. Wigan took advantage of an old music-hall joke (and the popularity of George Orwell's book *The Road to Wigan Pier*) to recreate a former coaling wharf as 'Wigan Pier', while the resurrection of Liverpool's Albert Dock has included a new wing of London's Tate Gallery to make it a place of pilgrimage for the culture-seeker. Living history museums have been created at Beamish in Northumbria and Quarry Bank Mill, a former cotton mill at Styal, Cheshire. Not only the inner cities, but derelict waterfront sites,

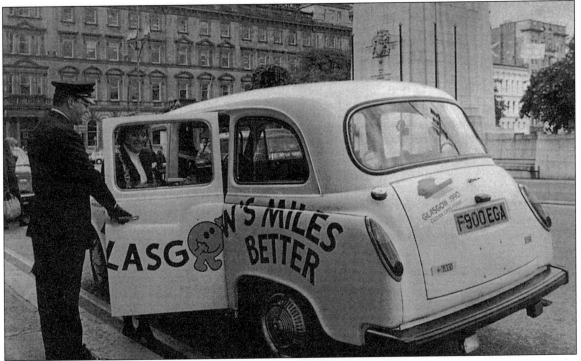

Figure 15.6 Glasgow's successful marketing strategy. *(Courtesy Glasgow City Council)*

have lent themselves to careful and tasteful restoration to create residential and leisure complexes which also attract tourism.

The way in which government policy has shifted from support for traditional tourism towards the encouragement of new forms of tourism in the economically depressed areas is among the most interesting fields of study for the tourism specialist, since it opens up the concept of what we understand tourism to be, and provides almost unlimited new opportunities to generate it.

The origins of this new policy can be traced to public sector policy to establish 'Tourism Growth Points' in the early 1970s, following a review of tourism policy. Areas like the Bude–Wadebridge area of Cornwall were identified as regions for planned tourism growth. While the growth points programme enjoyed mixed success, the development grants they attracted were later directed into Tourism Development Action Plans (TDAP), generally linked to inner cities; Bristol's floating harbour became the first of many such schemes to receive TDAP finance to help resurrect its decaying waterfront areas. The success of similar efforts at restoration in the United States, particularly in Baltimore, San Francisco and Boston, has spurred such programmes in Britain.

The TDAP is a phased programme of planned redevelopment, usually over a period of one to three years, undertaken as a cooperative venture between the English Tourist Board and local auth-

Figure 15.7 Fisherman's Wharf, San Francisco: an area revitalised through redevelopment. *(Photographed by the author)*

orities. The pump priming funds which are invested in the schemes by the public sector are designed to act as a spur to additional private investment in the area. Small tourist enterprises such as speciality retail shops, excursion boats and eating places are attracted to the site, which then generates its own momentum to become a focal point for the city as an area for leisure and recreation. Unfortunately, this scheme has been affected by the cutback in funding for tourism projects, in particular the ending of Section 4 grants in England.

Tourism can, however, still benefit from the terms of Urban Regeneration Grants, designed to restore life to the decaying inner cities. Where the value of a completed project may be less than the initial cost of its development, government grants can be made available to bridge the gap, making the project possible where a feasibility study might indicate that a purely private venture would be uneconomic.

New funding opportunities appeared on the scene in the late 1990s, with the introduction of the National Lottery, from which funds were allocated for the development or enhancement of tourism attractions around the country. From 1995 onwards, funds were allocated to celebrate the Millennium in the year 2000. Substantial sums of money were designated by the government to support schemes which would enhance the celebrations, including funding in excess of £500 million for a major site at Greenwich designed to attract millions of visitors. There has been some criticism of the disproportionate amount of these funds finding their way to London, compared with the more distant provinces.

Modern industry, too, offers scope for tourist enterprise, as we saw in Chapter 11. The initiative owes much to British Nuclear Fuels, which opened their Sellafield (formerly Windscale) processing plant to visitors in order to assuage public concern about nuclear energy safety. The success of this venture (which now attracts over 178,000 visitors annually) led to the government holding discussions with the CBI (Confederation of British Industry) with a view to opening factories to tourists, to allow them to observe the processes of manufacture of British products. The public relations value of this exercise has appealed to

Figure 15.8 Sellafield Visitors Centre – The Interatom. *(Courtesy British Nuclear Fuels plc)*

many firms; Ford Motors has opened its plant, and interest has been expressed by Jaguar Motors and other leading businesses.

The Thames Barrier at Woolwich was recognised as having tourist potential even while under construction, and plans for tourist visits were incorporated into the operating programme. In Cheshire, the local authorities planned visits to such 'attractions' as power stations and fire stations, under the 'Insight into Industry' banner. Such initiatives are expected to show considerable growth in the next few years.

Our recent history has also been successfully exploited for tourism, with the public opening in 1984 of Churchill's War Cabinet rooms below the streets of Whitehall, dating from World War II. Such schemes pay tribute to the astuteness of the public sector in recognising and developing the tourism potential of sites in its charge.

TOWN TWINNING AND TOURISM

No discussion of public sector tourism can be complete without exploring the role of town twinning, even though this aspect of travel is seldom considered as an aspect of the tourism business. The concept of town twinning emerged in the aftermath of World War II, as a means of forging greater understanding between communities in different countries. Usually, the selection of a twin town is based on some common characteristics such as population size, geographical features or commercial similarities. Local authorities and chambers of commerce arrange for the exchange of visits by residents of the twinned towns. Although conceived as a gesture of friendship and goodwill, the outcome has commercial implications for tourism, as visitor flows increase between the two twinned towns. While accommodation is normally provided in private homes, expenditure on transport, shopping and sightseeing can have a significant impact on the inflow of tourist revenue for the towns concerned – some of which have virtually no other form of tourist traffic. Friendships forming as a result of these links will also lead to subsequent travel demand. So far, no studies appear to have been made as to the financial contribution resulting from these links, but it is likely to be considerable.

Functions of the tourist boards

THE BRITISH TOURIST AUTHORITY

As we have seen, the Development of Tourism Act empowered the BTA to promote tourism to Britain in overseas countries. With the agreement of the respective territories, the Authority will also undertake foreign promotion on behalf of the tourist boards of Northern Ireland, the Isle of Man and the Channel Islands. With general responsibility for tourism throughout Great Britain, the Authority acts as adviser to the government on tourism issues, and is financed by an annual grant-in-aid from the Treasury, channelled through the Department for Culture, Media and Sport.

Stated objectives of BTA marketing policy have included extending the tourist season in Britain, promoting areas of high unemployment which can demonstrate tourist potential, and seeking to develop new markets and market segments for tourism to Britain. This has included, in recent years, a focus on business travel and 'adjustment' of established markets. Thus, any fall-off of the US market, for example – a country which provides the main source of Britain's overseas visitors – can be offset by promoting Britain harder to Germany, to Japan or other European markets which promise growth. It is interesting to note that in spite of paying lip service to quality

improvements, the Authority's policy has been repeatedly to emphasise an increase in the numbers of tourists it wishes to attract to Britain; at no time has any finite limit been suggested to the number of visitors which Britain, or specific parts of the country, can absorb.

Apart from maintaining offices in more than twenty countries abroad, the BTA carries out research and liaises with the other national tourism bodies in the UK. The overseas offices help UK companies to reach foreign markets, for example, by circulating details of inclusive packages to travel companies bringing tourists to Britain. The BTA also mounts workshops, either in Britain or in major centres of population in tourism-generating countries abroad, which are designed to bring together the buyers and sellers of travel services; for the smaller British company in the travel business, this may be the most effective way to reach the overseas market with a limited budget. Typical workshops include those for European coach and tour operators, special interest travel or English language schools. Limitations on funding, particularly in recent times, mean that the Authority must necessarily restrict what it can do for travel companies, and this means that little help is available for the smaller independent companies. However, the Authority will provide certain services at commercial rates, such as distribution abroad of a company's brochures, or advising on overseas marketing.

Other functions include the publication of numerous sales and information guides and directories, and the magazines *In Britain* and *Hello Britain*. The Authority's Product Marketing Department has also initiated 'theme years' as an incentive to visit Britain in a particular year – a common promotional initiative used by national tourist boards around the world. Recent examples include 'Britain for all seasons' and 'Britain's Treasured Landscapes'. The Authority also sponsors an annual 'Come to Britain' trophy for top new tourist attractions or facilities.

THE ENGLISH TOURISM COUNCIL AND SCOTTISH AND WALES TOURIST BOARDS

Under the terms of the Development of Tourism Act, the functions of these national boards were established as:

- encouraging residents of the UK to travel within their own country
- encouraging the provision and improvement of attractions and facilities for tourists in Britain
- administering the Section 4 grants,
- advising the government on matters concerning tourism within their territory.

As we learned earlier, Section 4 grants are no longer available in England, and the ETC's role has increasingly had to become one of advice and encouragement rather than of dispensing financial assistance.

Like the BTA, the ETC (formerly ETB) is financed by a grant-in-aid from central government, administered by the Department for Culture, Media and Sport (in the case of the Wales and Scottish Tourist Boards, the regional governments are responsible for the distribution of these funds). While this funding is still discrete, recent policy has been to integrate wherever possible the offices and administration of the BTA and ETB/ETC to avoid duplication and to improve efficiency. By comparison with the BTA, however, the ETC funding was severely curtailed in its funding in the early 1990s. Section 4 grants, which are available only through the Wales and Scottish Boards, have been primarily directed to improvements in hotel accommodation in the two countries, although they have also been used for such miscellaneous purposes as developing farmhouse tourist accommodation, and supporting tourist attractions which would be unlikely to become viable without some initial subsidies. Part of the ETC funding is automatically allocated to the Tourism Development Fund which is controlled by the regional tourist boards.

Like the BTA, the ETC, along with the other two boards, undertakes research and publishes a range of statistical data covering national as well as regional information. Much of these data are now collected by the four boards in collaboration. The ETC also develops themes for visits to England, and in recent years has emphasised sustainability and the needs of the disabled and disadvantaged in its theme years. It, too, has encouraged better standards by sponsoring an award, the England for Excellence scheme. All the boards publish a great variety of promotional literature, including guides on where to stay, short breaks and activity holidays. The ETC introduced its own annual workshop for buyers and sellers of travel products, known as MOOT, in 1985, but subsequently integrated this activity with the other national boards in a national Travel Trade Fair.

Shortage of funds has meant that the boards are increasingly having to become more commercial in their approach. The Wales Tourist Board, as we have seen, has farmed out some of its activities by establishing private limited companies to undertake some of its functions. One example of this is the establishment of Tourism Quality Services Ltd, which acts as the Wales Tourist Board's agent in carrying out inspection of holiday accommodation and attractions, and has widened the scope of its activities to carry out inspections outside of Wales, at commercial rates. The WTB has also attempted to promote holidays to Wales commercially, by the publication of a commissionable 'Holiday Wales' tour operating programme, for distribution through agents, though with only limited success.

THE TOURIST INFORMATION CENTRES

TICs play a particularly important role in disseminating information about tourism, in the UK as elsewhere. There are well over 800 official tourist information centres in Britain, with some 600 in England alone. Funding now comes largely from the local authorities, assisted to some extent by the national tourist boards through the provision of support material and publications via the regional boards. The national boards oversee the standards of each TIC, to provide it with formal recognition. This has entailed, among other criteria, a requirement to employ salaried staff rather than relying upon voluntary labour, as had been the practice in some TICs. Improved access, especially for the disabled, and agreed minimum hours of opening have also become important benchmarks for recognition.

The TICs, like the boards, have been forced to become more commercial in the light of government policy of the 1990s, and with the decline in funding by cash-strapped local authorities, which do not, in any case, have a statutory duty to provide these services. Apart from the now

Figure 15.9 Tourist information centres can themselves attract the tourist: (a) the award-winning Cardiff Bay information centre. (*Photographed by the author*)

(b) Gloucester TIC in a converted church. (*Photographed by the author*)

(c) A heritage building for a French TIC. (*Photographed by the author*)

(d) Tourist office in North Portugal with historic granary. (*Photographed by the author*)

well-established Book-a-Bed-Ahead scheme, TICs are increasingly introducing commercial products for sale within their shops, while seeking ways of cutting costs to remain viable. The Labour government has expressed an interest in exploring the possibility of privatising all TICs to ensure their closer collaboration with local authorities and travel agents.

One means of providing information cheaply is through the tourist information points (TIP), unmanned stands providing information about local facilities. In some parts of the world, these will include sophisticated booking systems for local hotels, either using telephone connections or computer links.

A final point to make is the valuable contribution which TICs can make through their design. In many cases, TICs will occupy buildings of outstanding architectural or historic interest in a city, and the careful preservation and adaptation of the buildings for this purpose has ensured that they are not only put to good use, but provide an additional point of focus for the visiting tourist, who is able to see the interior of a building which might otherwise be restricted. Increasingly, local authorities have come to recognise the important role which the TIC can play in drawing attention to modern design as well, whether in the traditional style and materials of local building or in a more modern concept where the new building can itself become a stimulus for tourist interest. The award-winning Cardiff Bay information centre is an example of the latter, and has acted as a tourist magnet in its own right. Examples of this centre and other TICs are illustrated in Figure 15.9.

INFORMATION TECHNOLOGY INITIATIVES IN THE PUBLIC SECTOR

The computer-linked accommodation reservation system is just one example of the important role which information technology is now coming to play in providing tourist services. Public sector tourism interests have not been slow to take advantage of the computerised information revolution.

ETNA is one outcome of this development. Developed jointly by the ETB and the RTBs, it provides a thorough database of information which will allow the counter clerk to match accommodation to the client's needs, indicate availability and print a confirmation for the client after the clerk has confirmed the reservation (presently, in the UK, this latter function has usually to be performed by telephone). The system will also build a database of names and addresses of those booking accommodation, allowing mailing lists to be developed which can be used in later campaigns. Information is also provided on local attractions and events.

At a macro level, the BTA and ETB have cooperated to develop a computerised tourism database, TRIPS, which allows the ETB's own national database to be integrated with that of the BTA. UK destination information is also available to travel agents worldwide via British Airways BABS computer reservations system.

Few can doubt that the CRS will become common for domestic hotel bookings within the space of the next few years, just as it is today for inclusive tour arrangements. Plans have been proposed for some local authorities, acting as coordinators, to allocate rooms within their districts to tour operators for package tour arrangements. Such a centrally controlled allocation of hotel rooms would enable hoteliers to reduce their individual commitments to tour operators, and therefore minimise wastage in the reservations process.

Perhaps one of the more noticeable features of the advance in information technology development within the public sector has been the emergence of electronic marketing units (EMUs) at TICs. These are databases accessible to passers-by outside the TICs, and therefore their use is not limited to the opening times of the TICs themselves. Although the range of information available through these units is still limited, it is expanding fast, and is already equipped to provide the basis for interactive communication between tourists and tourist facilities, which would allow visitors to make reservations for hotels, theatres, and a host of other amenities.

FUNCTIONS OF THE REGIONAL TOURIST BOARDS

While the example given here refers to the operation of the ten regional tourist boards established by the ETB in England, the area tourist boards in Scotland and the three tourism councils in Wales operate in a similar fashion.

Financing of regional boards was originally planned to be provided by a mix of national board, local authority and private sector funds, although private funding never achieved the levels anticipated by the national boards.

The objectives set for the regional tourist boards when they were established were:

- to produce a coordinated strategy for tourism within their regions in association with the local authority
- to represent the interests of the region at national level and the interest of the tourist industry within the region
- to encourage the development of tourist amenities and facilities which meet the changing needs of the market
- to market the region by providing reception and information services (in concert with the NTB), producing and supplying suitable literature and undertaking miscellaneous promotional activities.

Typically, an RTB will work with a very small staff of perhaps ten to fifteen members (although the London Tourist Board, due to its importance in the tourism economy, has a much larger number of employees). Coordination between the RTB, local authorities and the tourist trade is through policy-making panels, or committees, as exemplified below:

Development panel	*Publicity and promotions panel*
County council officers	Resort officers
District council officers	RTB members
RTB members	Local trade members
Local trade members	

Many RTBs also undertake the role of validating guiding courses for 'Blue Badge' guides within their regions.

RTBs have a particularly difficult role in their relations with local authorities. They must work with these authorities and cooperate with them in tourism planning, but the RTB's aims may be in conflict with those of the local authority, which is often apathetic or negative towards the growth of tourism in its area. Moreover, local authorities are charged with certain functions which have a direct bearing on tourism, as we have seen. They can hinder the expansion of tourism by refusing planning permission, for example. However, local authorities do also play an important role in safeguarding the countryside and coastal areas within their regions.

Geographically, RTB areas are often diverse and cannot be logically promoted as a single destination. The West Country Tourist Board, to take one example, represents counties ranging from Cornwall at its western extremity to Bristol on its northern boundary, and parts of West Dorset on its eastern boundary. It is responsible for the promotion of all these regions, although Bristol's council makes no financial contribution to the board's funds, while the promotion of Dorset would arguably be better handled as an integral destination. To produce a coordinated strategy for the promotion and development of tourism in the face of these diverse interests is no easy matter.

COOPERATIVE MARKETING ORGANISATIONS

We have seen how private and public sector interests can differ in tourism, the common lack of a coordinated tourism policy, the severe and growing constraints being imposed by government upon tourism financing, and the areas of potential conflict which can arise in the public sector. As one means of overcoming some of these problems, several areas have opted for the formation of a marketing board, made up of representatives from both public and private sector interests. This could be seen as the first step in privatising the public sector of tourism in the UK. Plymouth was the first city to launch a joint venture of this kind, in 1977. The city's marketing bureau draws its members from those nominated by the city council and others elected by the private sector. The bureau is financed by a grant from the city council, by membership subscriptions and by commercial activities. Other cities have followed suit, and although not all have proved successful, this 'joint venture' approach appears to be an appropriate way forward, and has also been successfully introduced at national levels. The BTA, for example, cooperates in a great many joint marketing schemes abroad each year, in association with British and foreign interests in the private sector. The public sector also cooperates to undertake joint overseas promotion, as in the case of that between the BTA and regional tourist organisations. The British Travel Centre in Regent Street, London, is an example of joint funding between the BTA and the railway networks.

THE ROLE OF THE EUROPEAN UNION

By contrast with some European Union nations where tourism makes an equally important contribution to the economy, Britain has chosen largely to allow the free market economy to operate in the tourism field, with little attempt to centralise policy-making. However, as Britain becomes more integrated with the Union, British travel and tourism interests are increasingly affected by EU legislation. Most importantly, since harmonisation came into force at the beginning of 1993, any constraints of trade have been largely abolished, allowing travel firms to compete within the Union on an equal footing and without legal hindrance. So far, the evidence suggests that fellow Europeans are faster in taking advantage of the opportunities that this presents than is the UK, although the British airlines have continued to expand into the Continent (see Chapter 7).

Within the European Commission, at least ten of the twenty-three Directorates General (the Commission's departments) have some responsibilities that impact upon the tourism industry, although the tourism unit itself is located within DGXXIII, Enterprise Policy, Tourism and Social Economy. This is a relatively small unit, formed in 1989, and prior to that date tourism was located within the Transport Directorate General. As with government departments in Britain, there is no system for coordinating tourism interests across the Directorates General. Unfortunately, the performance of the tourism unit has been marred by corruption, and the head of the unit faced charges in 1995 of extortion of bribes in funding tourism projects within the Union.

The principal stated objectives of the EU as regards tourism include:

- the facilitation of tourist movements, through abolition of frontier controls, deregulation of transport, ease in transfer of foreign currencies, reciprocal health coverage and

better information and protection for tourists themselves

- more effective promotion, through state aid and other means
- help in distributing the flow of tourists better, both geographically and seasonally, through emphasis on such features as rural tourism, and by staggering school holidays
- other measures, to include better tourism training, easing taxation, etc.

Many of these ambitions were already achieved to some extent before the introduction of harmonisation. The scheduled airline industry, as we saw in Chapter 7, has been fully deregulated, and there have been no controls over charter flights within the Union. Shipping is also largely deregulated, apart from rules of cabotage, which will be gradually eroded by the end of the century. The free movement of capital and labour promises the possibility of huge changes in the way some sectors of industry, such as tour operating and travel agencies, are run. The easing of the allowance of duty-free goods and the termination of a ceiling on duty-paid goods within the EU provide further opportunities for tourism growth, especially in the short-break shopping market – although attempts to rationalise excise duties on liquor throughout the EU could lead to substantial increases in the price of drinks in the traditional tourism resorts of the Mediterranean in Greece, Spain and Portugal. The effect on travel may also be partly offset by the imposition of VAT on transport within the Union, which is still under consideration.

As we have noted earlier in the text, however, the most immediate impact has resulted from the introduction of the Package Travel Directive, adopted after amendment in 1990, which was designed to provide tourists with better, more accurate information and greater protection. The additional burden placed on tour operators and travel agents has caused problems for the industry, and the measures have been costly to introduce. Nevertheless, the requirement for operators to bear the responsibility for virtually anything happening to their clients while they are abroad has undoubtedly marked a great advance in consumer protection for travellers within the Union.

Undoubtedly, regulations coming from Brussels will continue to impinge on the way the tourism industry is run, as well as affecting the decisions of the tourists themselves as to where they travel to, how they book and what they do while on holiday.

QUESTIONS AND DISCUSSION POINTS

1 Should tourist information centres be service-orientated or profit-orientated? Can the two objectives coexist? Pay a visit to your nearest TIC to see the extent to which it is commercially involved, then discuss the case for and against TICs becoming more commercial in their efforts to pay their way.

2 Examine the impact of the Package Tour Directive on (a) tour operators and (b) travel agents, and discuss the benefits or disbenefits of this regulation for the industry and for the consumer.

3 Are sources of financial aid for tourism in Britain adequate as they stand? What needs to be done to improve the situation, and how should more public sector funds be spent to benefit tourism? Why do you think it is that many developers appear reluctant to invest in leisure and tourism enterprises?

4 Discuss the ways in which Conservative and Labour policies have differed in respect to tourism since the Conservative government came to power in 1979. How have these policies affected the industry?

The Labour Government elected in 1997 introduced regulations imposing a minimum wage of £3.60 an hour (£3.00 for those under 21 years of age) in 1999. What impact has this had on the tourism industry? The industry argued at the time that this move would adversely affect employment and profitability. To what extent has this claim been justified?

ASSIGNMENT TOPICS

1 You have recently been appointed Assistant Tourism Officer in a South Coast resort with a strong traditional market among the C2DE population. In taking stock of the present patterns in tourism, you are interested to find out whether social tourism plays a role in bringing visitors to your resort. As a first step, you need to discover what support social tourism currently has in towns where there are a significant number of underprivileged or disadvantaged people.

Undertake some research within the local authority nearest you which has a significant number of deprived residents, and see what the authority's attitudes are towards social tourism. What funds are there available, and how are they spent? How has this funding changed over the past decade? What recommendations would you make on spending a limited amount of money, and how would you allocate this between the various deprived groups?

Prepare a short report for your Tourist Officer with suggestions of how the resort should cater for these groups.

2 As Tourism Development Officer of a town of your own choice with tourism potential, draw up a tourism strategy for the town which:

(a) reviews the existing provision by public and private sector
(b) identifies the potential for tourism in the town
(c) provides a basis for future action in collaboration with other bodies, by defining targets and priorities for action
(d) identifies how the plan will aid the town and its residents economically.

Present your findings in a report to the council.

16

Tourism Design and Management

Introduction

This chapter will introduce the reader to issues which are often ignored or overlooked in textbooks of tourism, although some will feature in complementary studies such as museum or attraction management. Others, such as architecture and landscaping issues, are more likely to be dealt with in studies in town and country planning. The purpose of introducing them here is to increase awareness among students of tourism of the cross-disciplinary nature and complexity of the tourism business, and to encourage both students and practitioners to think more broadly about what it is that actually appeals to tourists, encourages them to visit specific sites and allows them to derive satisfaction from the experience. The discussion will necessarily have to be limited in a textbook of this nature, particularly in examining the role of features such as architecture and landscaping in tourism, but it is hoped that touching on these issues will whet readers' appetites to learn more about them and will help to widen discussions on the nature of tourism generally.

The role of design in tourism

ARCHITECTURE AND DESIGN

Although all of us are affected by design, much of its effect on us is unconscious. Local architecture, the layout of our public parks, the design of signposts with which we have become familiar in our own home surroundings mean that we see these objects in a different light from the way visitors will see them. When we, in turn, visit other destinations, we will critically examine things we tend to take for granted in our own environment. Yet everything we see is designed, from the buildings to the shopfronts, from roads to lamp posts, from street signs to ticket booths, and all these objects affect us and mould our attitude to our surroundings.

Design therefore represents a crucial element in tourism planning, whether we are designing a tourist attraction from scratch, such as Disneyworld, or modifying a feature of the landscape to make it more attractive or suitable for tourist use, such as one of the principal approach roads to a town; or even arranging for a few cosmetic changes to the housing stock of the town, by encouraging residents to do a spot of painting. (President de Gaulle mounted a drive in the 1960s, for the stone fascia of Paris buildings to be cleaned. The result was that Paris became vastly more attractive for tourism, and Parisians took a new pride in their city.)

Design has two roles. One is *functional*, in the sense that if something is well designed, it should do its job better; the other is *aesthetic*, meaning that it should look right, in itself and in its setting, and that it should have visual appeal. However, when we refer to 'good' or 'bad' design, to some extent we are expressing subjective views. The controversy surrounding the rebuilding of Windsor Castle after the tragic fire of 1992 shows the depth of feeling about this heritage site. For some people it is sacrosanct, and should be reconstructed exactly as it was (even though most architects agree that much of what was lost was no masterpiece, and the castle had in any case grown over the years into a mishmash of architectural styles). Others argued that the fire had produced an opportunity to add modern extensions reflecting the best of twentieth-century architecture. The fact that overseas tourists come to see our heritage does not rule out the potential that modern buildings have to attract their own audience, and the best of these, too, will in time become part of the heritage.

RESTORATION, RENEWAL AND 'HERITAGE'

In the matter of architectural design, the private and public sectors often have quite different objectives. The private sector developer is interested in good design only to the extent that it operates functionally, and that it satisfies the consumer and encourages them to return. The developer will generally try to produce the design which does these things at the lowest possible cost. The public sector can, if it chooses, exercise greater control, not just by insisting on sympathetic restoration instead of rebuilding, or by requiring buildings to make use of local building materials, but by rewarding and encouraging good design. Too often, however, local authorities take a short-sighted view of their role in promoting good design; in the 1960s, for example, the developers

of the Seagram Building in New York were horrified to find they would be taxed far more heavily by the city because of the added value of their investment, which had created what was quickly hailed as a masterpiece of twentieth-century architecture. This rapidly discouraged other developers from spending more than they needed to on good design.

The extent to which a 'heritage building' should be restored also leads to considerable controversy. When reconstruction of the medieval Barley Hall in the centre of York was completed in 1992, architectural critics were enthusiastic about the care with which the work had been carried out, and the accuracy of the reconstruction; yet the Chairman of the Society for the Protection of Ancient Buildings quickly attacked the project for producing a replica of the original building and destroying many of the later additions which had made it organic. He dismissed the end result as 'another contribution to our Disneyland heritage'. Similar attacks have been launched on reconstructions of Roman fortifications along Hadrian's Wall, and of the Temple at Knossos in Crete (which in spite of overelaborate reconstruction has provided many thousands of tourists with a valuable insight into how some of the world's oldest buildings actually looked in their heyday).

In Britain we are criticised for adopting a provincial attitude to new building which suggests that most of us are happier with the designs of the past. The result is that pastiche neo-Georgian or mock Tudor is more popular than the contemporary buildings that are springing up all over Europe. But often criticism is directed not at the form of the building, but at its unsympathetic use of material, such as raw concrete, or the fact that it is out of scale against other buildings in the area. Modern materials do not age attractively, while natural materials will become more attractive with the passing years.

Some of the issues surrounding the design of modern buildings have been examined in Chapter 11, where the potential of modern design to attract tourism was discussed. Certainly, issues of size and scale must be taken into consideration, as must the use of local materials in construction, which can be a major feature in attracting tourists. On the other hand, given the right setting, and in

Figure 16.1 Finlandia Hall, Helsinki. *(Photographed by the author)*

Figure 16.2 Modern office building, Bremen, Germany. *(Photographed by the author)*

the hands of a master architect, an uncompromisingly modern building can become the pride of its residents, and an international draw. Figure 16.1 is one such example, Saarinen's Finlandia Hall in Helsinki, Finland, a country noted for the excellence of its design (which it promotes extensively to attract tourists to the country).

The building succeeds in part because, set in its own landscaping and away from city-centre buildings, it is not required to merge with the local traditional architecture. However, where this is required, modern adaptations of vernacular design can be undertaken and will merge sympathetically with their surroundings (see Figure 16.2).

From the point of view of the tourist, the significance of such design is not only that it reflects the traditions of the local architecture and therefore merges effectively with the surrounding buildings, but that it is also built on a human scale which does not dwarf the passer-by. Most visitors to a town will explore it on foot, and good street-level design is vital to maintain the visitor's satisfaction.

Local building materials are, unfortunately, often more expensive to use in construction, but the additional cost is well justified in the long run. In Britain, examples may be found in the use of Bath stone in Bath, Cotswold stone in the same area, thatch in the West Country, and slate in the West and Wales. Even for such mundane construction as public toilets, the use of local and natural building materials can greatly enhance the

Figure 16.3 Modern public toilet in natural stone with slate roof, Ireland. *(Photographed by the author)*

end result (see Figure 16.3). The use of natural materials specific to the locality will help to reinforce the uniqueness of the tourist image which the attraction is trying to create.

The importance of public toilets for tourists is an issue which is frequently overlooked, yet the subject of their inadequacies is regularly touched upon by those concerned with promoting tourism to the UK, such as BITOA. Many tourist sites suffer from an inadequate supply of toilets, while others have had their toilets locked or shut down due to shortages of money for maintenance and supervision. While Britain is not unique in facing this problem, it is interesting to note that in Japan, architectural competitions are promoted for public toilets, and the Chinese encourage architects to design toilets with the needs of American tourists in mind. The interest generated by the construction of the 'superloo' with an attached flower shop at Westbourne Grove in London, designed by architect Piers Gough in 1993, reveals just how important good toilet design can be for tourism. This particular example not only won design awards, but was featured in English Heritage's advertisements in 1997. It should come as no surprise, therefore, that over eighty public toilets around Britain are actually listed buildings.

Shopping is a prime motive for tourism, and the design of shopfronts can do much to increase the pleasure of the tourist experience, particularly for window-shoppers. Figures 16.4, 16.5 and 16.6 illustrate three very contrasting ways of attracting the shopper. The first shop is an innovative and unashamedly modern design in Paris – controversial, given its siting between more traditional shopfronts, but guaranteed to rouse interest. The second, a design for David Mellor's store at Shad Thames in London's Docklands, is also simple and modern, but is designed principally to give a good view to the passing visitor of both the shop contents and the distant renovated warehouses across the water. The third picture is of a much more traditional design; the carefully restored shopfront of a jeweller's in Lillehammer, Norway, which retains the vernacular architecture of the area (even down to the rust-red colour of its paintwork).

In many cases, modern architecture may be

Figure 16.4 Shopfront in Paris. *(Photographed by the author)*

actively disliked, but still provide a draw for tourism. The Pompidou Centre in Paris is certainly not everybody's idea of a good modern building, but it is a major magnet for tourists. On a smaller scale, the highly controversial Cube Houses of Rotterdam, designed by Piet Blom, and their adjoining Potloodflat (pencil flat) building have become important features to attract tourists to Rotterdam, and are now featured extensively in tourist literature produced by the city. The Netherlands is a country which has experimented extensively with modern buildings throughout the twentieth century, and this is now paying off by attracting a growing number of tourists, whether out of architectural interest or for novelty. One private house, the Rietveld-Schröder house in Utrecht, designed by Gerrit Rietveld and recently restored as a museum, now

Figure 16.5 Shopfront in London. *(Photographed by the author)*

brings students of architecture to visit from all over the world.

LANDSCAPE DESIGN

No building can be divorced from its setting, and just as thought must go into the design of the

Figure 16.6 Shopfront in Lillehammer, Norway. *(Photographed by the author)*

building itself, so the site must be landscaped attractively to maximise visitor appeal.

Part of the attraction of an English village is the way in which the houses lie in the landscape, blending in as if they were made for the setting. Where a site for development is sloping, it becomes even more important to ensure that the buildings blend with the background, and if the buildings are to be exposed to view – for example, a group of self-catering chalets high in the Alps – great care has to be taken to integrate them into the landscape. Buildings should not stand out on the skyline, but if it is essential that they do, then their lines should be broken up by the use of trees and shrubs. On sloping sites, buildings can be 'stepped' or terraced up the hillside to keep their scale in harmony with the environment. Similarly, on watersite developments, buildings should be sited well clear of the waterfront itself, to allow for walkways along the banks that will attract both residents and visitors, and to ensure that those using the waterway are not intimidated by high buildings alongside.

Figure 16.7 Effective landscaping for a picnic site at a reservoir: Lake Clywedoc, Mid-Wales. *(Photographed by the author)*

Figure 16.8 The art of catching the visitor's attention: a car park at Bordeaux, France. *(Photographed by the author)*

The appeal of water is evident in the conversion of so many redundant harbours and waterways in Britain for leisure use. Here, the local authorities must determine whether the site is best retained as a dockland environment, or themed as an urban parkland. Enlightened authorities have come to recognise that retention of the traditional bollards, cranes and other paraphernalia of a dockside will provide a unique setting and a better lure for the visitor, with the addition of a modest number of trees or shrubs.

In the countryside of England, boundaries are a prominent feature, giving the landscape much of its character. They range from the hedges of southern England (a significant proportion of which have sadly been lost since the end of World War II, as farmers tried to increase productivity on their land) to the dry-stone walls of the North which, using virtually no mortar, allow ferns and lichen to grow on their surfaces and soften their appearance. Fences also have characteristic local designs, complemented by the traditional five-barred gate; these designs can be incorporated into tourist settings, too. Public sector grants have been made available to retain and restore dry-stone walling and hedging where these are characteristic of the local landscape.

Car parks are a particular problem for the tourism designer, since they occupy large areas of land and are visually intrusive. In the countryside, efforts are now made to ensure that the park appears as natural as possible: logs can be used to separate the bays, and substantial shrubbery planting will help to conceal the cars themselves. Good, but not instrusive, lighting is important, while the surface itself can be retained as a gravel site rather than asphalted. In some small parks, it may be possible to use honeycombed concrete blocks which allow the grass to grow through them, rendering the concrete surface almost invisible.

Car parks must, of course, be situated well away from any high-grade heritage sites, and this may mean that special provision must be made for the disabled. In cities, the urban setting will mean the use of more man-made materials in car park construction, but this no longer means high-rise concrete. Designs have become more fanciful in recent years, including in one case a mock mediaeval fortification, while parks on open land have been attractively furnished with decorative modern lamps and plenty of trees to break up the land mass.

Telephone and public utility lines can disfigure even the most beautiful town or village. Fortunately, in Britain local authorities have generally taken an enlightened view about hiding these ugly necessities, but a visit to Spain or Greece will soon illustrate how much visual pollution is caused by overhead wires along streets and linking into houses. The cost of burying wires is much higher, but again in the long run it is worth the investment if it leaves the site much more attractive to visitors.

STREET FURNITURE

Street furniture is something we all take for granted, yet it plays an important part in reflecting the national landscape, too. One has only to think of the classic red telephone kiosks or letter boxes in Britain, or the nineteenth-century 'pissoirs' (now sadly disappearing) and the classic design green boulevard chairs and tables still to be found on the streets of Paris, to realise that such items play a part in formulating our ideas about national characteristics. In Britain, a great deal of attention has been paid in recent years to designs of public seating and litter bins, but any item of street furniture, from post boxes to telephone kiosks, from litter bins to bus shelters, from public toilets to refreshment stalls, from lamp posts to railings, needs to be carefully designed to be in harmony with the surroundings and reflect the image of the area in which it is sited.

Local authorities must first determine whether to adopt a classic or modern design for their setting. Heritage sites such as York or Chester are most likely to opt for a traditional and classic design to blend with the architecture of the area. Unfortunately, this has led to the development of

(b) a 'traditional' telephone kiosk in Stockholm. *(Photographed by the author)*

Figure 16.9 Different approaches to street furnishings: (a) a modern public toilet in Sweden. *(Photographed by the author)*

a ubiquitous design in cast iron with gold motifs, frequently bearing the crest of the city, which, while tasteful and elegant, does little to distinguish the city's streets from countless others in the country. However, these designs are to be welcomed over some of the the products they replace, such as the plastic litter bin (all too often cracked or misshapen), in a choice of battleship grey or garish yellow. Litter bins in particular need to be big enough to accommodate the huge amounts of litter created today by take-away shops, and the council must have a policy of emptying these frequently, or the benefits of good design will be lost, as rubbish piles up around the base of the bin.

Cities on the Continent, particularly those whose centres were substantially rebuilt after the war or which wish to promote a modern, dynamic image, will adopt more modern designs. These can work equally well in the appropriate setting.

(c) a 'classic' letter box in Bremen. *(Photographed by the author)*

(d) a modern bus shelter and litter bin in Brussels. *(Photographed by the author)*

Figure 16.9 illustrates four different approaches to design in the street.

The green granite and metal modern toilet in Stockholm represents an expensive investment, but will clearly last, and be relatively easy to maintain. By contrast, in the 'Gamla Stan' (old town) of the same city, the council has opted for a more traditional design for its telephone kiosks, a slightly whimsical reworking of the nineteenth-century design found in the area. A similar theme is evident in the design for a 'classic' letter box in Bremen, while Brussels chooses to project a more modern image with its contemporary bus shelters and litter bins. These well-designed features still manage to blend successfully with the more conservative buildings which surround them.

Providing seating in a town is a problem for councillors, as it tends to attract vagrants. However, the use of simple-to-maintain materials which will provide a brief respite for residents and tourists, but not a level of comfort encouraging longer stays, can be the answer to the problem, as demonstrated in Figure 16.10.

PEDESTRIANISATION

Many towns popular with tourists have pedestrianised some of their principal thoroughfares. The result can greatly enhance the atmosphere of a street and encourage visitors to come shopping. Some of Britain's most attractive town centres, such as such as those of York, Brighton, Bath and Chester, and many Continental towns, feature narrow pedestrian walkways which have never been wide enough to support motor vehicles. In these towns, the narrowness of the lanes is their very attraction. But, pedestrianising will not in itself be enough to make the street a focal point for shoppers; the shops themselves must be appropriate for the setting, and the street must be enhanced by well-designed street furniture, tree planting and the display of flowers or shrubs in tubs or other containers. When this is done tastefully, the end result can transform a street. However, the fact that it will also attract much larger numbers of pedestrians can lead to congestion and to a litter problem which the council must be prepared to tackle.

Figure 16.10 Polished marble 'rest areas' in downtown Toronto, Canada (note the stainless steel litter bins). *(Photographed by the author)*

Figure 16.11 A pedestrian shopping lane in Bremen, Germany ('the Schnoor'). *(Photographed by the author)*

HORTICULTURAL DISPLAYS

The use of hanging baskets, floral beds in the centre of main access roads, extensive tree planting along the pavements and similar horticultural displays can make a pretty village outstanding, and an ugly town bearable. Some of Britain's towns have made such a feature of their floral displays that they have become famous internationally: Bath's hanging basket displays are highly attractive features for the summer visitors, while the massed floral beds which highlight the seafronts of towns such as Eastbourne and Worthing are characteristics which draw many older visitors to the resorts year after year. Aberdeen is noted for its display of formal rose beds along the main roads, while on the Continent, the flower-bedecked chalets of Switzerland and Austria are features that are automatically associated with these countries' villages, and highlighted in their tourist brochures.

The cost of transforming a town in this way is considerable, but any town seeking to attract the tourist can at very least consider investing funds to make the main approach roads more attractive, both those carrying visitor traffic to the centre and those which provide the principal access for pedestrians to the centre from bus or train terminals.

Figure 16.12 Three examples of pedestrianisation – note the substantial use of street furniture in the first example and the use of patterned brickwork to add interest in all three: (a) Gloucester. *(Photographed by the author)*

(b) St Helier, Jersey. *(Photographed by the author)*

ART AND TOURISM

There is a growing recognition today that art has a role to play in the tourist industry, not just through the museums, galleries and arts events organised to attract tourists, but in the everyday surroundings in which the visitors find themselves. Ostensibly, 'street art' is designed to heighten the visual appeal of a town for its residents, but once again, such embellishment will add to the attrac-

(c) Lillehammer, Norway (with Christmas decorations). *(Photographed by the author)*

tion of the destination for visitors, too. If the work displayed is by artists of international reputation, this will widen the appeal of the destination to international visitors. Sculptures by Henry Moore in Yorkshire or at the Serpentine in London attract a dedicated audience of overseas and domestic visitors. Cities in the United States enforce local regulations requiring a small percentage of the total cost of any new development to be spent on 'public art' at the site, and the prestige offices of major corporations will also judge it appropriate to enhance their forecourts with sculptures by leading artists of the day. In London, prominent British artists such as Eduardo Paolozzi were recruited to design the wall tiling during the renovation of the Central London Underground railway stations.

Towns can reinforce their images by the imaginative use of sculpture or art. In Germany, for example, Hamelin will have its sculpture of the Pied Piper, while Bremen has greatly enhanced its pedestrian streets with scenes from Grimms' fairy tales, such as the Brementown Musicians (see Figure 16.13).

Britain is becoming more aware of the importance of art and the way in which it can serve the interests of the tourism industry. Notable features include two water fountain sculptures by William Pye, 'Slipstream' and 'Jetstream', commissioned by BAA at Gatwick Airport; a 130-foot long sculpture, 'Train' by David Mach, a monument to the record-breaking Mallard train and comprising 185,000 bricks, unveiled in Darlington in 1997 (to considerable local criticism but widespread national publicity); and the gigantic sculpture entitled 'Angel' by Anthony Gormley which is at the time of writing under construction and will shortly be mounted on a hillside near Gateshead. This will be clearly visible to hundreds of thousands of travellers and tourists using the nearby motorway each day. While controversial, such works draw the attention of the public to regions not normally seen as worthy of a touristic visit.

LIGHTING

External street lighting can play an important role in enhancing a town, both in respect of the design of the lights themselves and in the effect they can

Figure 16.13 Street sculpture drawing on Grimm's Fairy Tales, Bremen, Germany. *(Photographed by the author)*

create at night. Again, a choice must be made between traditional and modern lamps. Some towns have reinforced their quaintness by reverting to authentic gas lighting, which has great popular appeal for tourists. In Norwegian villages in the weeks leading up to Christmas, the shopping streets are illuminated with real flares, giving visitors an impression of warmth and cosiness at a time when the long periods of darkness could otherwise easily depress.

Floodlighting major attractions, long a recognised practice for the great monuments in leading cities, has become much more widespread, and its use can encourage tourists out onto the streets at night, thus extending the 'tourist day'. White lights are normally recommended; the use of coloured lights, apart from where a fairground atmosphere is appropriate, such as at the Blackpool illuminations, is best avoided. The use of coloured lights to floodlight Niagara Falls, many observers feel, turned a great spectacle into

an example of down-market kitsch. Limited use of coloured lighting can be helpful in highlighting horticultural displays at night, however. Care must be taken not to overlight; strong lights are particularly inappropriate in a village setting, for example.

SIGNPOSTING

All visitors look for signposts, so they become the most visible of all forms of street furniture. They serve three purposes.

Directional

Traffic signs direct vehicles or pedestrians in particular directions, and to specific sights. They must therefore be clearly legible, especially from a distance, in the case of vehicle signs. They should be identified by use of a standard, immediately recognisable colour, and their size and shape should

Figure 16.14 (a) Open-air sculpture on display at Cheltenham, Gloucestershire: 'Hare' by Sophie Ryder. *(Photographed by the author)*

(b) Artists demonstrating their skills to tourists enhance art exhibitions: Sophie Ryder meets the public, Cheltenham Art Gallery. *(Photographed by the author)*

also be uniform. Generally, standards for road signs will be set by local authorities or government departments of transport for road signs.

Within towns, signposts directing tourists to specific attractions have received a lot of attention in Britain in recent years. Once again, a 'traditional' classic signpost has been devised, with modest variations in design, constructed of cast iron with white lettering (some towns have produced a variation on this; Bristol, for example, has introduced Royal Blue as the standard colour).

Informative

These are of two types. They may be used to alert tourists passing in vehicles to a particular attraction in the vicinity, and they will also be provided at a particular site, such as a viewpoint or monument, to give information about the site itself.

In the former case, following a long period where signposting was arbitrary and often banned from main roads, in Britain the Department of Transport introduced white-on-brown signs in 1986, with thirty-five different pictographs representing every conceivable variety of tourist attraction. Regulations on the use of these and other signs is complex and quite restrictive. The use of white-on-brown signs, for example, is dependent upon the numbers visiting the site (for

example, historic houses must attract a minimum of 5,000 visitors a year for a road sign to be approved). This, of course, introduces a 'catch-22' situation, where already well-established attractions are favoured over newly developed ones.

Signs outside a particular attraction may also be subject to local government regulations. For example, attractions in North America, which are generally very well signposted, often adopt a standard format for imparting information about national monuments (see a typical Canadian cast-iron-with-crest 'interpretation' plaque in Figure 16.15a). Visitors to such sights will also need to receive information about the layout of larger sites, together with details of opening hours and price of admission. Examples of signs bearing this information are given in Figures

Figure 16.15 Examples of signposts bearing different types of information: (a) Old City Hall, Toronto, Canada (a national monument with historical information). *(Photographed by the author)*

(b) Historic Mackenzie House, Toronto (an attractively displayed sign bearing information on opening hours and admission prices). *(Photographed by the author)*

16.15b and 16.15c. Such signs must still be clearly legible, but may have more character in their design.

Mention should be made of the traditional blue plaques which are widely in use in Britain to advise the visitor of the fact that a property has been the home of some well-known person in the past. These are invariably of great interest to foreign visitors in particular, and the fact that they are often encountered by the tourist quite by chance in walking around the streets of a city gives them added appeal.

Utility

These signs are designed to direct visitors to public utilities such as toilets and telephone kiosks. They can be smaller in scale, and will often make use of symbols, as do the white-on-brown signs – a particular boon to foreign visitors. They may have their own design and colour, but are also often incorporated into information signs in popular tourist towns.

Within specific tourist attractions, imagination gives rein to a great variety of signs and symbols. In medieval times, as few people could read, this led to many shops hanging out symbols of their trade. These have been retained, and sometimes resurrected, by shops in tourist centres, adding visual appeal to the streets. The example shown (Figure 16.17) is one of a number of original street signs in the 'Old Village' of Aarhus in Denmark which has been restored in its entirety as a historic museum. The individual buildings within the site and open to the public make good use of characteristic directional signs in the folk idiom, as illustrated in Figure 16.18.

(c) Mont Orgueil Castle, Jersey (historical information coupled with a plan of the site). *(Photographed by the author)*

Figure 16.16 Good management means ensuring key facilities are working: public urinals 'out of service' and poorly signposted, France. *(Photographed by the author)*

The management of tourism sites

This textbook is not the place for a detailed examination of management techniques; but anyone studying tourism needs to be aware of some of the specific issues of management that are unique to tourism, and recognise the problems that arise. We will examine two issues here which are central to the study of tourism: those of interpretation and of visitor management.

INTERPRETATION

The days when visitors expected no more than to stare passively at exhibited artefacts or buildings are now over. Today, visitors to tourist sites expect to be both educated and entertained, and the managers of tourist sites, especially those involving 'heritage' (however we interpret this term), must find ways of getting the visitor involved, and bringing the site 'alive' for them. This implies finding ways to impart information successfully, and is seen as giving added value to any tourist visit.

Interpretation has come a long way in the past few years, and whole courses of study are now devoted to understanding it. Back in the 1970s, it would have meant no more than producing some attractive graphic design and handing out a few leaflets. Today, attempts are made to transport the visitor into another age, through the use of costumed animateurs and the careful staging of settings to make them as realistic as possible. By way of example, barmaids in period costumes will pull pints of real ale in the pubs at the Ironbridge Gorge Museum; and at Wigan Pier, an actor taking the role of a Victorian schoolmaster will invite the visitors to participate as pupils in a role-play demonstrating school life of the period. At the Blaenavon 'Big Pit' Mining Museum in Wales, visitors have to don mining helmets and lamps in order to accompany genuine ex-miners who guide them around the site; travel to the coal face is in an original mining cage, and the life and full horror of working underground are effectively communicated by the guides during the tour. At the Robin Hood Story exhibition in Nottingham, visitors have to find out the answers to a series of questions about Robin Hood, based on information contained in the interpretation plaques found throughout the exhibition, and those answering the questions correctly receive a 'good' certificate. A museum opened in Neasden, North London, in 1993, as a direct response to local demand, with an exhibition of 'Brent people'. Visitors are able to tap into audio history tapes by telephone, photos can be called up on screens by computer, and children are allowed to dress up in costumes of the 1920s, rather than observing them at a distance on dummies. Interactive communication of this kind is ideal as a means of involving children; however, such attractions all have to face one problem: is a single form of interpretation suited to every one of the variety of markets to which the attraction appeals? Plaques designed to be read by children will be dismissed by adults as patronising, while too much information, provided for those seeking the detailed background to a site, will put off those enjoying an entertaining day out. The answer is to provide a variety of different forms of communication, to cater successfully for each market segment served.

MANAGING VISITOR FLOWS

Most attractions share a common problem in managing their visitors: that of uneven flows. Demand at a particular site will fluctuate, and cannot easily be spread over time. The result is that managers face problems of scheduling and queuing to which their own preferred solutions may not be those which most appeal to the customers themselves.

Popular attractions such as major exhibitions which are mounted for a limited period of time (e.g. Tutankhamen and the Treasures of Egypt at

Figure 16.18 Directional sign at a house in Gamle By, Aarhus, Denmark. *(Photographed by the author)*

the British Museum, the Matisse Retrospective in Paris and London) or the key attractions at a Disney theme park, where demand will always outstrip supply, pose particular problems. One solution is to require advance reservations for entry, and to determine the maximum number to be admitted at any given time (admitting too many people to an exhibition of paintings will result in enormous disappointment if people are unable to see the paintings). Overpricing to reduce demand is seen by many as an injustice, and is a solution seldom enforced. At sites where advance bookings are less feasible as a solution, queues will have to be organised, and the tedium of waiting reduced as far as possible. Very long queues form for attractions like the Crown Jewels at the Tower of London, and the management of this site must find a means of getting the right balance between its own desire to move the crowds quickly past the display and the need to avoid antagonising its customers, who will have waited a long time and expect to take their time seeing the attraction.

Large events designed to cater for many thousands of people every day must ensure that they have the means to admit them quickly. This means sufficient numbers of ticket booths to avoid long lines queuing to buy tickets (see Figure 16.20). Where queues are inevitable, such as on public holidays, a variety of techniques can be employed to reduce the tedium of waiting. At the aquarium at the Inner Harbour at Baltimore, an elaborate 'maze' is devised to handle the queues. This has the result of making the queue appear shorter than

Figure 16.17 Street sign for a tobacconist in Gamle By (Old Village), Aarhus, Denmark. *(Photographed by the author)*

it is, and also allows it to be contained under a relatively small roof area as shelter from intense heat, or rain (see Figure 16.21).

At Alton Towers theme park in Staffordshire, where the management has had a great deal of experience in handling queues, a variety of different approaches are taken. Queues are segmented to make them appear shorter; buskers are used to entertain those waiting; estimates of how long they can expect to wait are given to those in line; barriers are in place to keep the crowd orderly, and the snaked queues (similar to those at Baltimore) not only appear shorter, but are designed to allow members of the public to engage in conversation while they wait.

Once inside, further problems of crowd control arise. Many visitors prefer to tour sites in their own time, independently. This raises problems of managing the crowds (who will tend to take longer watching some displays than others) and of security – where exhibitions contain highly valuable artefacts, such as at stately homes, guides are nor-mally assigned to accompany groups. However, at Aarhus's Gamle By, an original means of safe-guarding treasures against theft or vandalism by independent visitors has been devised; rooms are 'sealed off' with huge transparent plastic screens (see Figure 16.22).

At sites such as Jorvik in York, Tralee in Ireland and the Robin Hood Story in Nottingham, where visitors are taken around in 'time carts' on a journey through history, the carts control the flow of visitors, and determine the ceiling on the number of visitors who can be admitted. At stately homes, or sites like the Roman Baths at Bath, guides who accompany the visitors can delay or speed up the passage of visitors from one section of the building to another as the need arises. While this permits greater crowd control, it fails to over-come the resistance that many tourists feel towards being herded. Tourists like to feel in con-trol of their own movements, and if they are conscious of being unduly directed, their level of satisfaction will fall.

Figure 16.19 The use of wax figures in historical settings to portray the period is increasing: Chinon Castle, France. (Photographed by the author)

Figure 16.20 Multiple ticket booths permit the smooth flow of large numbers of visitors at the Ebbw Vale Garden Festival, Wales, 1993. *(Photographed by the author)*

We have now seen some of the problems which managers of tourist sites must contend with. Solving these problems, and the day-to-day operational difficulties associated with running any form of attraction, while delivering satisfaction and maintaining the level of quality which the tourist has come to expect, is what tourist management is about. Let us complete this chapter with a look at one site owned and managed by a highly professional organisation in the tourism business, Madame Tussauds, and highlight some

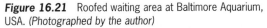

Figure 16.21 Roofed waiting area at Baltimore Aquarium, USA. *(Photographed by the author)*

Figure 16.22 Room secured from the public by clear plastic screens, Gamle By, Aarhus. *(Photographed by the author)*

of its practices designed to enhance the overall quality of the tourist experience.

THE CASE OF WARWICK CASTLE

Warwick Castle is one of the leading tourist attractions in Britain, and is managed professionally by one of the country's leading tourism organisations, Madame Tussauds. The following are key elements in its strategy to attract and satisfy its large number of visitors.

Accessibility

The attraction is open every day from 10 a.m., apart from Christmas Day. This overcomes any uncertainty on the part of impromptu visitors about whether they will find the site open – a common problem with many heritage sites which have widely varying opening times. There are ample and clear road signs around the site, and adequate parking for cars and coaches on all but high peak days of the year. Car parks are hard-surfaced and attractively landscaped.

Utilities

There are ample toilets for the numbers visiting, strategically placed at the entry to the site. Litter bins are positioned throughout the site. It is the policy of the organisation to ensure that the site is kept clean at all times, and litter is picked up constantly. Particular attention is given to catering for the elderly, and for families with young children. Staff are trained in first aid emergency treatment.

Signposting and interpretation on site

All attractions are well signposted, and warning signs are posted outside the site if any facilities have to be closed for the day. A leaflet with comprehensive information about the site is given out with tickets.

Crowd control

Visitors are directed, by additional signs, away from the most popular areas at times when queueing is likely to occur. Staff are on hand to supervise tourist flows, and queue warnings are given on peak days. Extra events, such as morris dancing, are mounted to entertain queues on these occasions.

Pricing

The policy is for an all-inclusive single payment for entry into every facility within the site. This has been found to achieve the highest level of satisfaction among visitors. The normal discounts are made available to those qualifying.

QUESTIONS AND DISCUSSION POINTS

1 Discuss the relative importance of design in each of the following tourism services: (a) a travel agency, (b) the public railway, (c) a local museum. Take into account both functional and aesthetic issues of design.

2 Taking as an example any popular event which you have recently attended (e.g. special exhibition, open-air pop festival, concert), describe how well crowds were handled, and look at ways in which their handling could have been improved.

3 How important is it to include foreign languages in messages directed at tourists in Britain? Identify the difficulties of doing so, and consider why more local authorities or private operators do not do so. Taking any three contexts (e.g. directional signs, tourist attraction leaflets, information signposts, etc.) discuss which languages would be most important, and how many languages should be used.

1 Using as your model any tourist attraction (or local museum) in your area, undertake an analysis of its relative strengths and weaknesses, in terms of:

    (a) functional design
    (b) aesthetic appeal
    (c) information and interpretation for visitors
    (d) management of visitor flows.

Write a short report to the organisation's executive in which you make recommendations for improving any of these, and determine the priority for action. Consider particularly any ways in which improved design could lead to increased revenue for the organisation.

2 As an Assistant Tourist Officer for your local town, you have been asked to assess the quality of the environment for the visitor. Present a report to the council which will include your evaluation of:

    (a) the street furniture
    (b) facilities for seating
    (c) lighting, including any floodlighting or other attempts to improve the cosmetic appeal of the town after dark
    (d) any pedestrian walkways or other attempts to improve street materials (e.g. use of coloured bricks or patterns in the roads, etc.) Take into account the quality of the construction, too.

Your report should consider particularly the possibility of improvements to those routes used by actual or potential visitors on foot in the town. Make recommendations for action where urgent improvements are needed.

17

The Social and Environmental Impact of Tourism

OBJECTIVES

After studying this chapter, you should be able to:

- understand the various ways in which tourism can impact on the environment;
- be aware of the socio-cultural effects of tourism on indigenous populations and on tourists;
- identify and evaluate different approaches to finding solutions to these problems;
- understand the concept, and the importance, of sustainable tourism;
- recognise the need for adequate planning, and for cooperation between the private and public sectors, as means of overcoming problems;
- be aware of future trends in tourism, and their likely impacts.

Introduction

In this closing chapter we will look at a different, and in many ways a darker, side of the tourism business: its impact on those who participate in tourism, on the residents of those countries subjected to tourist flows, and the effects of tourism on the the destination itself.

Tourism, as we have seen, can be a potent force for economic and social good, creating employment and wealth, and widening our understanding of other societies. In this book, many illustrations have been given of the way in which tourism has benefited a particular place, building or cultural activity. In Britain, many great buildings, particularly those serving the needs of eighteenth- and nineteenth-century industry, would have been lost had it not been possible to convert these factories, mills and warehouses into living museums for the tourist. Whole inner cities and dockland areas have been restored and developed to make them attractive as tourist sites. Even a city like London would be a poorer place without the tourist; 40 per cent of West End theatre tickets are bought by tourists, and undoubtedly the wealth of theatres available to Londoners owes much to their patronage by visitors. In rural areas and small seaside resorts, many of the smaller shops could not be economically viable without the summer tourists, who also make it feasible to provide public transport such as rural bus services. The battle to save the Settle–Carlisle branch line, one of Britain's most scenic railway routes, was won when British Rail recognised that the line could be profitable if based on the expectation of increasing tourist revenues. Country crafts, pubs, even the restoration of traditional pastimes such as morris dancing, all owe their survival to the presence of the tourist.

However, the rapid growth of tourism in the twentieth century has produced problems, as well as opportunities, on a vast scale for both developed and Third World countries. The governments of these countries have come to realise that unrestrained and unplanned tourist development can easily aggravate these problems to a point where tourists will no longer wish to visit the destination. In short, without adequate planning tourists may destroy what they have come to see. This problem is compounded, as long-haul travel to previously unaffected destinations increases. Now, such remote areas of the globe as the Antarctic continent are appearing on the tourist trail – a 100-bed hotel was recently opened in Antarctica by the Chilean armed forces to cater to tourists who are looking for diversions such as snow-mobile riding, and some 10,000 tourists are now visiting the continent each year, spurred on by the availability of cruises using Russian ice-breakers. One unexpected result of this influx has been that among the huge colonies of penguins inhabiting the area, a number are falling prey to chicken disease, thought to be the result of food carelessly discarded by tourists paying visits to the colonies. Ecologically sensitive regions such as the Galapagos Islands, Costa Rica and Belize are now controlling tourism development and introducing the concept of *sustainable tourism* to ensure that their environments are not destroyed by mass tourism. We will examine the environmental and social problems created by tourism in turn, and look at their possible solutions.

The environmental effects of tourism

POLLUTION

The technological complexity of twentieth-century living has led to various forms of pollution which are both initiated and compounded by tourism development, and by travel in particular. Large-scale tourist movement requires the use of mass transportation, and the fuel burn from air-craft adds to air pollution; civilian aircraft are said to account for the emission of 3 per cent of all carbon dioxide created by man, and a similar amount of nitrous oxide (see L. Archer, *The Environmental Impact of Aircraft on the Atmosphere*, Oxford Institute for Energy Studies, 1994). The introduction of quieter, more fuel-efficient and cleaner jet engines unfortunately has the side-effect of increasing the emission of nitrous oxide. Emissions from the exhausts of cars or boats used in tourism compound the problem. All three forms of travel can also contribute to unacceptable levels of noise, whether in rural

surroundings or in residential areas, and noise, too, must be considered a form of pollution. Noise, and possible danger to life, have been factors in attempts to reduce the use of water-bikes off-shore. Waterborne vessels, by dumping fuel or waste overboard, also contribute to water pollution, which, in turn, affects the wildlife on the rivers.

Beaches give particular cause for concern, in that polluted waters can lead to serious illness among bathers. Britain fares badly in the quality of its offshore water, which is seriously affected in many regions by raw sewage and other pollutants. The EU monitors closely the condition of European beaches, under its Bathing Water Directive of 1976; only a little over 80 per cent of Britain's beaches reach the minimum standards approved by the EU, a lower proportion than Ireland, Spain, Greece, Belgium, France or Italy. Major tourist beaches such as those at Blackpool and Weston super Mare have failed to meet these standards – perhaps it is as well that only some 7 per cent of those spending time on beaches in the UK actually indicate an intention to bathe.

Environmental 'pollution' is as much aesthetic as physical. An area of scenic beauty attracts greater numbers of tourists, so more and more of the natural landscape is lost to tourist development. The countryside retreats before the growth of hotels and other amenities which spring up to cater for the tourists' needs, with the eventual result that the site is no longer seen as 'scenic', and the tourists move on to find somewhere more tranquil as well as beautiful. Similarly, without careful control, the stately home which tries to meet the needs of its visitors will provide an ever-expanding range of facilities such as larger car parks, cafés, shops, directional signposts and toilet facilities, all of which detract from the appeal of the main attraction. Extreme examples of the scenery being marred by signposting are readily found in the United States where, with fewer controls than are exercised in Britain, both countryside and towns can be destroyed by directional signs and advertising hoardings. (However, some might argue that, at night, the forest of illuminated signs in towns such as Reno or Las Vegas is very much part of the attraction of the resorts.)

Noise pollution is a problem of twentieth-century living, especially in towns, but tourism has also made a significant contribution to the problem. In the resorts of the Mediterranean, the peace of the night is destroyed by late-night disco bars catering to tourists. At the Treetops Hotel in Kenya's Maasai Mara National Park, animals visiting the adjacent water hole at night are driven from the site by the careless loud talk or laughter of a minority of the visitors waiting in watch to see them. Noisy motorboats disturb the tranquillity of yachtspeople on the waterways, while aircraft taking off and landing at busy airports severely disturb local residents, especially if there are no restrictions on night flying.

Authorities have recognised the problem of air traffic noise, and some have taken action to reduce it. For example, aircraft are categorised under three classes, known as chapters, according to the noise levels they emit. Under government regulations, especially in the United States, the most recently introduced chapter 3 aircraft, such as the Airbus, are 85 per cent less noisy than were chapter 1 aircraft, and are consequently allowed greater freedom to operate. At a different level, Spanish police are now patrolling down-market resorts such as Magalluf and take action against pubs or nightclubs registering noise levels higher than 65 decibels.

Visual pollution can also be ascribed to insensitivity in the design of buildings for tourism. Lack of planning control is very often to blame, as developers prefer to build more cheaply, leading to high-rise concrete hotels lacking character and out of keeping with the surrounding architecture. Today, the skyscraper hotel is ubiquitous, from Wiakiki in Hawaii to Benidorm in Spain, with a conformity of architecture which owes nothing to the culture or traditions of the country in which it is built. More far-seeing authorities recognised the damage potential, and brought in controls to limit it. Some authorities have insisted that hotels must be built in local materials, or conform to 'vernacular' styles of architecture, that is, those indigenous to the region. Others require buildings not to exceed a certain height – for example, Tunisia requires that new hotel developments in tourism resorts should be no higher than the normal height of the palm-trees which will surround them. Mauritius has imposed constraints

on both the architectural style and the materials employed in hotel building. While some critics have questioned the rather 'staged' results, with thatched cottages vaguely resembling African kraals, no one questions the appeal which these accommodation units have for tourists.

Such legislation clearly must apply to all buildings, not just those for tourism. On Lanzarote, in the Canary Islands, all housing, apartments and hotels are required to conform to rigorous building regulations imposed by the Department of Tourism on the island. These control not only the style of the buildings but the colours in which doors and windows may be painted; only white, blue and green paintwork is permitted. Sometimes, planning controls will have the effect of restricting innovation in architecture, leaving developers to play it safe by falling back on 'pastiche' or bland designs attractive only to the most conservative visitor. The attempt to protect local building styles and materials can sometimes have unexpected results, as in Ireland, where traditional corrugated roofs have now become such a familiar feature of the landscape that they have been designated 'vernacular' building material! (See Figure 17.1.)

Sometimes, the problem of scale can relate to far smaller buildings than hotels, but the significance of the problem is no less. During the early 1990s, two historic properties were both under threat due to plans either to build or to expand

Figure 17.1 'Traditional' corrugated roofs on a restaurant in Ireland. (*Photographed by the author*)

visitors' centres adjacent to the site. The Haworth Parsonage, home of the Brontë sisters in the Yorkshire Moors, was threatened with a massive expansion of the visitors' centre which would have greatly exceeded the size of the original house; the project resulted in an outcry from the public, and a rethink of the plans. Similarly, trustees of the birthplace of Sir Edward Elgar, in the Malvern Hills, submitted plans for a new visitors' centre adjacent to, and much larger than, the composer's original cottage. This, too, led to a public outcry in the media. Nevertheless, one building was constructed (likened by one architectural critic to a Tesco supermarket), and this soon proved too small; to extend the site, plans for an even larger building were drawn up, creating further outrage among local residents, and the issue remains unresolved at the time of writing. However, the problem of providing sufficient room to accommodate all the visitors, who now exceed 10,000 each year, has no easy solution – or at least, no cheap solution. One plan proposed at Haworth was to conceal the new visitor centre underground, which although an ideal solution, proved to be too costly for the funds available.

Other common forms of visual pollution by tourists include littering, particularly in areas around picnic sites, and graffiti on buildings. It is a curious fact that even those tourists who come from large cities, where they are so used to seeing litter that they become unconscious of it, immediately become aware of the effects of litter in a tourist destination. Resorts which have made the effort to improve their image in recent years tend to start by undertaking a drive against both rubbish in the streets and graffiti on buildings. An important point here, discussed in Chapter 16, is that litter bins should be not only readily available, but themselves attractively designed. Unfortunately, at many sites not only in Britain but also elsewhere, the fear of terrorist bombs has caused rubbish bins to be sealed or removed, creating further difficulties in disposing of rubbish.

Graffiti has become a common problem in the Western world, with thoughtless tourists defacing ancient monuments with spray-painted, or even chiselled, messages. This of course is no new development: the Romans were chiselling their names on Greek monuments two thousand years ago. But the sheer scale of modern tourism has forced authorities to take action. In extreme cases, this had led to denial of access, as in the case of Stonehenge, where visitors are no longer permitted to walk among the stones themselves, but must be content to view them from a distance.

PROBLEMS OF CONGESTION AND EROSION

Mass tourism has led to a new problem in the second half of the twentieth century; that of congestion. This is a complex problem, because it exists at a *psychological* level as well as a *physical* one.

The latter is more easily measured, in terms of the capacity of an area to absorb tourists: car parks, streets, beaches, ski slopes, cathedrals and similar features all have a finite limit to the number of tourists which they can accommodate at any given time. However, it is also necessary to understand the psychological capacity of a site. This is the degree of congestion which tourists will tolerate before the site starts to lose its appeal. Quantifying this is far more difficult, since the perception of capacity will differ, not only according to the nature of the site itself but also according to the market which is attracted to it. A beach in, say, Fiji will be judged overcrowded much more quickly than, say, Bournemouth, while in a resort such as Blackpool a much higher level of crowding may be tolerated, or even welcomed as part of the 'fun experience'. One attempt to measure the psychological capacity of a beach was carried out at Brittas Bay in Ireland in the early 1970s. Aerial photographs were made of the number of tourists on the beach on a crowded Sunday afternoon, and a questionnaire was circulated to those on the beach to receive their views about the congestion. It was found that most visitors would accept around 1,000 people per hectare (ten square metres per person) without feeling the beach was overcrowded.

In so-called *wilderness* areas, of course, the psychological capacity of the region may be very low. From the viewpoint of the hiker, areas such as the Derbyshire Peak District may not support more than a handful of tourists per square kilometre, although the mass influx to its major centres such as Dovedale on an August Bank

Holiday fails to act as a deterrent for the majority of day trippers. Indeed, it has been demonstrated in the case of Cannock Chase, the beauty spot near Birmingham, that this area draws tourists from the Midlands as much for its role as a social meeting place as for its scenic beauty.

The behaviour of tourists at wilderness sites will be a factor in deciding their psychological capacity. Many trippers to an isolated area will tend to stay close to their cars, and hikers who are prepared to walk a mile or so away from the car park will readily find the solitude they seek. This is obviously a key for tourism planners, since by restricting car parking and access by vehicle in the more remote areas they can maintain the solitude the walker seeks.

Some authorities have tried to set standards for particular types of tourist activity as a guide to planners. Table 17.1 offers one attempt, by the World Tourism Organisation (WTO), to lay down guidelines, in terms of visitors per day per hectare.

The ecological capacity of an area to absorb tourists must also be taken into account. While too many tourists in a built-up area such as the narrow shopping lanes of York or Brighton can detract from tourism, the physical wear and tear on the environment is limited – at least, in the short term. However, too many tourists in a rural or otherwise fragile environment can destroy the balance of nature.

Some idea of the effect of erosion can be gained from a report in *The Guardian* (27 January 1990, 'Everyone a tourist now') which revealed that 400 tons of sand are removed from the beach of Benidorm each year on the soles of holiday-makers' feet!

Some sites are particularly fragile. Many sand dunes have been destroyed or seriously eroded in the United States by the use of beach buggies, and in the UK by motor cycle rallying, which can uproot the few clumps of dune grass on which the ecosystem depends. On the Great Barrier Reef off the coast of Queensland, Australia, fragile coral reefs can be easily damaged by divers or snorkelers – even touching or standing on live coral can be sufficient to kill it, and some visitors go so far as to break off pieces for souvenirs. Coral can also be damaged by boats anchoring. However, the bigger companies taking tourists out to the reef by boat are taking on the responsibility of educating the visitors, and during the boat trip the tourists are given instructions on the fragility of the site and how it can be preserved by careful use.

Buildings which face very high levels of demand from tourism pose even greater problems, unless authorities take very strong measures to control access, which can, of course, lead to disappointment for the tourists. In 1997, crowds visiting the Uffizi Gallery and Galleria dell'Accademia, the site of Michelangelo 'David' in Florence during Easter became so great that the local authorities took the unusual step of temporarily closing the buildings. Florence and Venice face especially heavy demand from international tourists; the latter welcomes over one and a half million tourists each year to the Doge's Palace and St Mark's Square, while on some days as many as 40,000 tourists have visited the Baptistry of San Giovanni and the adjoining Duomo in Florence. Such crowds produce high levels of condensation which affects the thirteenth- and fourteenth-century mosaics. The authorities have responded by reducing coaches to the city from 500 to 150 a day, coaches being charged high fees for the privilege and spot checks taking place on arterial roads out of the city to enforce compliance. Numbers admitted to the Baptistry

Table 17.1 Visitor capacity for selected sites

Site/Activity	Visitors per day/hectare
forest park	15
suburban nature park	15–70
high-density picnicking	300–600
low-density picnicking	60–200
golf	10–15
fishing/sailing	5–30
speedboating	5–10
waterskiing	5–15
skiing	100 (per hectare of trails)
nature trail hiking	40 (per kilometre)
nature trail horseriding	25–80 (per kilometre)

Source: E Inskeep (1991)

Figure 17.2   Coral reef, Whitsunday Islands, Great Barrier Reef, Australia. *(Courtesy Queensland Tourist and Travel Corporation)*

are reduced to 150 at a time, and charges are now being applied for entry.

CONGESTION IN BRITAIN'S NATIONAL PARKS

Many popular rural sites such as National Parks are at risk from the number of visitors they receive – and in the case of Britain, their proximity to centres of high population. Well over 100 million visitors enjoy the eleven UK National Parks each year, the Peak District being the most popular with over 22 million visitors – claimed to be the second-most-visited national park in the world, after Mt Fuji in Japan. Key points in the Park, such as Dovedale, reach saturation in midsummer, and so serious had the problem of over-use become by the end of the 1980s that, in a rare example of collaboration between tourism bodies,

the English Tourist Board, the Regional Tourist Board, the Park Authority, the Countryside Commission, the Rural Development Commission and eleven local authorities took the decision to appoint a Project Officer with the specific brief of seeking solutions to the problem.

In the parks themselves, overuse of footpaths can lead to soil becoming impacted, causing grass and plants to die; or soil being loosened and lost by wind erosion. One attempt was made in 1993 to counteract the effect on the footpath across the Moors near Haworth; some 25,000 visitors had turned parts of the Brontë Way into a quagmire, making it necessary for flagstones to be set into the track. Other running repairs have had to be made to long-distance footpaths such as those on the Pennine Way and Cleveland Way. Such artificial landscaping, of course, creates a very different visual landscape from the wild moorland it replaces, but it is a solution being used more widely, as such footpaths have to deal with greater numbers of visitors each year. In places, these popular paths in the National Parks have widened to 45 yards.

Too many climbers will also damage the parks. Some 250,000 people climb Mam Tor in Derbyshire every year, and in 1993 the summit had to be restored with an importation of 300 tons of rock and soil.

THE IMPACT OF WINTER SPORTS TOURISM

One fragile ecosystem in Europe is under particular threat. This is the Alps, and because the system is spread across no fewer than seven countries, collaboration to prevent the worst of the environmental effects of tourism is more difficult. The Alps receive over 50 million international visitors a year, and some 7 million passenger vehicles cross them each year, as they lie at the heart of Europe. To accommodate the huge increase in winter sports tourism that has occurred since World War II, some 41,000 ski runs have been built, capable of handling 1.5 million skiers an hour.

The region suffers in a number of ways. The proliferation of ski-lifts, chalets and concrete villages above 6,000 feet, and the substantial deforestation required to make way for pistes, have led to soil erosion, while acid rain caused partly by high volumes of traffic crossing the Alps is having a serious impact on the remaining forests, 60 per cent of which are now affected. Artificial snow-making machines have smothered alpine plants, reducing the vegetation, while wildlife has also declined as the animals' territories are reduced. A new danger is posed by the introduction of roller skiing on grass and four-wheel drive car racing in summer. Potential damage, both ecological and economic, to the region is now so great that an organisation, Alp Action, has been set up, with the support of the Aga Khan, to help preserve the Alps as a single ecosystem. It has to be added, however, that not all authorities welcome further control in this fashion; some Swiss cantons have expressed concern at the potential slowdown in the economic development of their region which results from this conservation movement.

Other authorities have already taken steps to control overuse. At Lech and Zuers in Austria, skiers are counted by computer through turnstiles which give them access to the pistes. Once 14,000, deemed capacity, have been admitted, tourists are diverted to other sites. Lillehammer in Norway, site of the 1994 Olympic Games, took account of the problems already occurring in the Alps when designing its new facilities. Apart from efforts to minimise tree clearance, the authorities also took steps to avoid visual pollution in an area where comparatively few buildings exist; ski jump runs were moulded into the mountainside to ensure they did not project above the tree line, and similar efforts were made to conceal bob and luge runs in the forests. The speed skating stadium was built twenty yards away from the water's edge to protect waterfowl, and leak-proof cooling systems were embedded underground in concrete containers. Private cars were excluded from the town during the period of the Games.

It is not only sports activities which can threaten a snowscape. Glaciers, whose ecosystems are invariably fragile, attract large numbers of sightseers when located in accessible regions. At the Columbia Icefield in Banff National Park, Canada, giant 'snowmobiles' are employed to bring tourists onto the glacier (see Figure 17.3). The inevitable consequence of too many vehicle trips will be damage to the surface of the site, unless careful control is exercised over the numbers carried.

EROSION OF BUILDINGS BY TOURISTS ON FOOT

Although man-made sites are less fragile, nonetheless they too can be affected by erosion in the long term. The Acropolis in Athens has had to be partially closed to tourists to avoid wear and tear on the floors of ancient buildings, while the wooden floors and staircases of popular attractions such as Shakespeare's birthplace in Stratford-upon-Avon or Beaulieu Palace in Hampshire also suffer from the countless footsteps to which they are subjected each year. Some sites have constructed artifical walkways above the level of the floor to preserve the original flooring. Nearly a million people visit

Figure 17.3 Snowmobiles in use on the Columbian Icefield, Alberta, Canada. *(Photographed by the author)*

Bath's Pump Room and Roman baths complex each year, and inevitably there will be fears for the original stone flooring in the baths; but it may put the problem into context when it is revealed that Roman visitors, wearing hob-nailed boots, did even more damage to the flooring than do contemporary visitors, though they were far fewer in numbers.

THE TOURISM DANGER TO FLORA AND FAUNA

Even souvenir-hunting can affect the ecological balance of a region. The removal of plants has long given cause for concern (the Swiss were expressing anxiety about tourists' habit of removing gentians and other alpine flowers before the mass tourism movement started), and in Arizona, visitors taking home cacti are affecting the ecology of the desert. The removal, either as souvenirs or for commercial sale by tourist enterprises, of coral and rare shells from regions in the Pacific is also giving cause for concern.

But perhaps of even greater concern is the threat to endangered animal species from tourism. There are many examples to cite, from the decline of some animals in the African game reserves due to lack of privacy to mate, as they are hunted down by tourist safari vehicles, to the threat to loggerhead turtles in Greece and Turkey, which are distracted from laying their eggs by the bright lights of tourist resorts, and even the use of search-

lights to observe their coming ashore to lay their eggs on the beach.

At Philip Island, near Melbourne in Australia, 500,000 people a year come to sit and watch the evening 'penguin parade' of fairy penguins coming ashore to their nests. This event has become highly commercialised, and the large crowds are proving hard to control – although ropes are placed to prevent them from getting too close to the penguins, and sanctions are in force regarding the use of flash photography, noise, or standing up, all of which disturb and alarm the penguins; however, in practice the public frequently ignore these strictures.

Animal behaviour can change from prolonged exposure to tourists. In some countries, food lures are used to attract wildlife to a particular locality; for example, in Samburu National Park, Kenya, goats are slaughtered and hung up for crocodiles or leopards. This modifies hunting behaviour, and may encourage dependency upon human feeding. In some wildlife parks, hyenas are known to watch for assemblies of four-wheel drive vehicles in order to take the prey from cheetahs' hunts. 'Bearjams' are created in Yellowstone National Park, USA, as bears trade photo opportunities in exchange for offerings of food.

The desire to bring back souvenirs of animals seen abroad poses another form of threat to endangered species. The Convention on International Trade in Endangered Species (CITES) imposes worldwide restrictions on the importation of certain animals and animal products from countries visited by tourists. Some 34,000 endangered species have been identified, and the importation of many of these is banned, including ivory, sea turtle products, spotted cat furs, coral, reptile skins and sea shells, as well as certain rare plants. Concern is also expressed about the ill-treatment of animals which are kept in captivity for the amusement of tourists. Even EU countries are at fault here, and UK groups are taking action to protect and free, for example, chimpanzees or other monkeys used for tourist photographs in Spain.

OTHER ENVIRONMENTAL CONSEQUENCES OF MASS TOURISM

Narrow roads in heavily visited towns lead not only to problems of traffic congestion if not controlled, but to potential damage to buildings, as coaches try to navigate. Increasingly, cars and particularly coaches are restricted from access to such towns, with park and ride schemes or other strategies introduced to reduce traffic. However, impeding coaches from picking up and setting down passengers in the centre of a town such as Bath or Oxford can make it very difficult for coach companies to operate, as many are on short stopover visits as part of a day trip.

Many Third World countries face similar problems of congestion and erosion, as tourists turn to long-haul travel. Goa in India was hailed by many operators as an 'unspoilt paradise', but its sudden appeal in the early 1990s has caused environmental lobbies such as Tourism Concern to draw attention to the dangers the region faces. Water shortages in the area are made worse by the tourist consumption (one five-star hotel uses as much water as five villages), and sand dunes have been flattened. Apart from the environmental impact, there is also a social cost, with private beaches denying access to the locals, and a 'Westernisation' of the local carnival which dilutes the traditional identity and culture of the region. With projections of as many as 2.3 million visitors a year by the turn of the century, this 'unspoilt paradise' may soon be completely destroyed by tourism.

Sometimes, well-meaning attempts by tourist officials to 'improve' an attraction can have the opposite effect. Historic rock carvings over 3,000 years old in Scandinavia were painted to make them stand out for visitors. When the paint eventually flakes off, a process that has speeded up with the effect of acid rain, it takes part of the rock surface with it.

Tourism development will invariably require the sacrifice of natural landscape to make way for tourist facilities. An example of this is to be found in the construction of golf courses. The demand by Japanese tourists in particular for golfing has led to a huge expansion of courses in the Pacific region; for example, the island of Oahu in Hawaii, which had already constructed twenty-seven courses by 1985, received a further thirty applications after the Hawaii legislature agreed to allow them to be built on agricultural land. Apart from the loss of natural scenery, golf courses also require huge amounts of fresh water, which in

some areas of low rainfall imposes a severe burden on local resources.

Planning for control and conservation

We have now given plenty of illustrations of the environmental impact of tourism, and a few illustrations of how this might be managed. Some argue that it is not enough for individual authorities to tackle the situation; that it should be tackled on a global scale. Unfortunately, governments so far have appeared unwilling to tackle the issue on this scale. International designation of an attraction as a 'World Heritage Site' by UNESCO, the United Nations Educational, Scientific and Cultural Organisation, undoubtedly helps, but Stonehenge, arguably Britain's greatest heritage attraction, is so designated and yet the site has been called a 'national disgrace' by the Public Accounts Committee of the House of Commons, financial support from the Millennium fund has been refused, and arguments continue about how best the site should be developed and protected. The Earth Summit held at Rio de Janeiro in 1992, called in order for all the leading nations to tackle threats to the environment, failed even to place tourism on the agenda. However, leads have been given by the World Tourism Organisation (WTO) and the World Travel and Tourism Council (WTTC), both of which support the concept of sustainable tourism, designed to minimise damage to the environment, wildlife and local indigenous populations. They have particularly recommended the use of local building materials for tourist sites, the recycling of waste and water and the recruitment of locals for jobs within tourism. Together with the Earth Council, these two bodies have published a report, *Agenda 21 for the Travel and Tourism Industry: Towards Environmentally Sustainable Development*, which encourages the industry to take the lead in preserving the environment in the areas they develop.

The European Union has taken an active role in recent years to attempt to control the worst effects of environmental pollution, with Blue Flags awarded to beaches reaching the required standards. Where this affects the cleanliness of sea water, it will, of course, affect the tourism industry. In Britain, a large proportion of the popular beaches fail to achieve EU-approved standards of cleanliness, including notable sites such as Blackpool. Although Britain's record is not high in comparison with other EU countries, some of these countries actually fail to carry out all the required tests at their beaches, so figures may not be comparable.

At a national level, the concept of managing and protecting tourism sites of scenic beauty is by no means a new one. As early as 1872, the United States established its first National Park at Yellowstone, while Europe's Abisco National Park in Sweden dates from 1909.

PROTECTION IN THE UK

In Britain, growing concern over possible despoliation of the Lake District led to the formation of a Defence Society in 1883 to protect the region from commercial exploitation. The National Trust was created in 1894 to safeguard places of 'historic interest and natural beauty', and promptly bought four and a half acres of clifftop in Cardigan Bay.

The National Parks and Access to the Countryside Act, 1949, led to the formation of ten National Parks in England and Wales, each administered by a National Park Authority. The Broads achieved virtual National Park status under the Norfolk and Suffolk Broads Act of 1988, and the New Forest in Hampshire is also a national park in all but name (see Figure 17.4). In 1997 it was announced that Loch Lomond would become the first National Park in Scotland, following devolution and the formation of a Scottish parliament. Other parks are likely to follow soon after, with the Cairngorms already high on the list.

The National Parks Act also led to the designation of thirty-seven areas (nearly 8 per cent of the area of England and Wales) as 'Areas of Outstanding Natural Beauty' (AONB) meriting protection against exploitation; the first of these, the Quantock Hills in Somerset, was designated in 1957, and the most recent, the Tamar Valley in England's West Country in 1995. Since this date, there have been numerous moves to protect

Figure 17.4 National Parks of England and Wales (including other parks of similar status)

features of historical or architectural interest, or areas of scenic beauty, from overdevelopment, whether from tourism or other commercial interests. Notable among these are some 150 designated nature reserves and a large number of Sites of Special Scientific Interest (SSSI) which contain rare flora or fauna.

The UK government has also recognised the growing threat posed by tourism, and more generally by leisure. The Government Task Force report, *Tourism and the Environment: Maintaining the Balance*, which is discussed later in this chapter, stressed the need for harmony between the visitor, the place and the host community; and a further report from the House of Commons Environment Committee, *The Environmental Impact of Leisure Activities*, appeared in 1995.

MANAGING SUSTAINABLE TOURISM

Planning controls, whether executed centrally or regionally, are essential to avoid the inevitable conflicts of interest that arise between the public and private sectors. Private enterprise, unrestricted, will seek to maximise profits, often in the short term, and this can be best achieved by concentrating marketing effort on the most popular attractions and destinations, rather than seeking to develop new destinations. Airlines will find it more profitable to focus on the routes already producing the most traffic, while hotels in a boom resort will build large and relatively cheap properties, if this can be shown to produce the best level of profits. Of course, it would be wrong to suggest that this always occurs – other organisations will see the market gaps left for better-quality development – but without some form of central control to ensure good design and careful restoration of old buildings, the original attraction of a traditional resort can be lost.

Local authorities can also be a partner to this despoliation, putting commercial advantage before aesthetic considerations. Spain experienced a sudden boom in tourism during the 1960s, but the resulting massive overdevelopment along its east coast and in the Balearics nearly destroyed its success. Failure to maintain the quality of the environment in other directions can also lead to a massive loss of tourist business, as the popular Spanish resort of Salou found, following a drinking water scare in 1989. However, the widespread fall-off in visitors to Spain as a whole in the 1980s and 1990s caused a reversal of policy and much greater control over speculative tourism development. A good example of this can be found in the Balearics, whose parliament passed legislation in 1991 to nominate large tracts of land in Majorca, Ibiza and Formentera as restricted zones for further development. In Majorca, only four- and five-star hotels were permitted to be constructed, with a minimum of 120 square metres of land per bed, in an effort to drive tourism up-market, while badly run-down resorts like Magalluf were given an injection of capital to widen pavements, introduce traffic-free zones, plant trees and shrubs and install new litter bins and graffiti-free seating. In all, Spain spent over £300 million in the five years prior to 1993 in improving tourism facilities along its coasts. However, once a resort has gone down-market, the evidence suggests that it is very hard to bring back a higher quality of tourist, and there

is a very real danger that the high-price hotels that are permitted to be built will remain empty.

A general awareness of the problems which tourism creates has led in recent years to a new movement to curtail its excesses. This movement calls for a new tourism – variously described as 'sustainable tourism', 'eco-tourism', 'green tourism', 'soft tourism' or 'responsible tourism', arguing that tourism must be developed as part of a properly thought-out management strategy, with collaboration between the private and public sectors, to prevent irreparable damage to the environment before it is too late.

The World Tourism Organisation and the United Nations Environment Programme, sensitive to this growing lobby, issued a joint declaration in 1982, which called for the rational management of tourism to protect, enhance and improve the environment. In the following year these bodies suggested employing zoning strategies to concentrate tourists in those regions which can absorb them and to disperse them where environments are too fragile to sustain mass tourism.

We must recognise, however, that tourists are not all seeking the same forms of tourism, just as the terms used above to describe the new tourism are not necessarily synonymous. Eco-tourism has been described (by the environmentalist Hector Ceballos-Lascurain) as, 'travelling to relatively undisturbed or uncontaminated natural areas with the specific objective of studying, admiring and enjoying the scenery and its wild plants and animals, as well as any existing cultural manifestations ... found in these areas'.

This is clearly not a description of the activities of the vast masses of tourists who go on holiday each year. However, it is appropriate to argue that all forms of tourism should be 'sustainable', that they should not destroy the destination to which the tourist is attracted. The growth of tourism must be environmentally compatible, as the World Travel and Tourism Council proposes in its ten-point guideline (see Figure 17.6).

In Britain, a government Task Force issued a report in 1991 giving a British view on the problem. The report, *Tourism and the Environment: Maintaining the Balance*, offers similar homilies, but one fears that without sanctions, the degree of

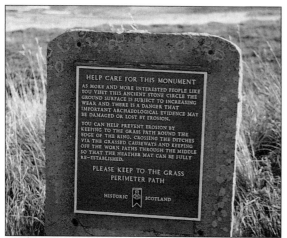

Figure 17.5 Sustainable tourism: signs can play a role in directing tourists towards good practice. *(Photographed by the author)*

1 Identify and minimise product and operational environmental problems, paying particular attention to new projects.
2 Pay due regard to environmental concerns in design, planning, construction and implementation.
3 Be sensitive to conservation of environmentally protected or threatened areas, species or scenic aesthetics, achieving landscape enhancement where possible.
4 Practise energy conservation, reduce and recycle waste, practise fresh-water management and control sewage disposal.
5 Control and diminish air emissions and pollutants.
6 Monitor, control and reduce noise levels.
7 Control, reduce and eliminate environmentally unfriendly products, such as asbestos, CFCs, pesticides and toxic, corrosive, infectious, explosive or flammable material.
8 Respect and support historic or religious objects and sites.
9 Exercise due regard for the interests of local populations, including their history, traditions and culture and future development.
10 Consider environmental issues as a key factor in the overall development of travel and tourism destinations.

Figure 17.6 A guideline for sustainable tourism. *(Source: World Travel and Tourism Council)*

sensitivity to the environment exercised by tour operators or developers will be limited.

Where the public sector has introduced legislation prohibiting development, or controlling tourism, sustainable tourism shows promise of being achieved. There are also now a growing number of examples of private companies, as we shall see below, introducing their own initiatives to ensure tourism is sustainable. Actions undertaken by public or private bodies have included:

- closing sites, either permanently (in cases such as Stonehenge or Lascaux caves) or temporarily (as in the examples at Lech and Zuers given above)
- reducing publicity, e.g. by limiting road signs. Local authorities have dropped reference to 'Constable Country' in their marketing of Dedham Vale (on the Essex–Suffolk border) due to congestion in the area caused by the popularity of visiting landscapes made famous by one of England's most renowned painters
- requiring advance bookings, or admitting those with tickets bearing specific admission times
- promoting alternative attractions
- introducing campaigns, such as the 'Keep Britain Tidy' campaign, to create greater public awareness of the problem, or providing awards, such as the 'Tourism for Tomorrow' award, to reward organisations making the best efforts to market sustainable tourism products
- pricing mechanisms to reduce or manage demand. Road pricing has been proposed for the North York Moors, coupled with the banning of cars on peak days of the year. Highland councillors have proposed a £1 fee for ramblers climbing Ben Nevis, Britain's highest mountain, as a means of paying for toilet facilities, litter collection, car parks and repairs to the mountain paths damaged by thousands of walkers each year.

There are many examples of successful control drawing on variations of these techniques. Highly fragile Third World destinations such as the Galapagos Islands restrict the total numbers of tourists that will be admitted each year, as well as imposing an entry tax, receipts from which go towards the conservation of the territory; the islands are divided into three zones, of which only two are open to visitors. However, even here control has been inadequate; the original carrying capacity of the islands was judged to be 12,000, but increasing demand led this to be 'reinterpreted' as 36,000. There is evidence that this figure is exceeded, especially taking into account the visits of private yachts, which are difficult to monitor and some of which have been known to throw refuse overboard, littering the shores. Nevertheless, the tight control over tourists visiting the island, all of whom must be accompanied by rangers, is an exemplary model for sustainable tourism: rules of conduct while ashore are given to each visitor (see Figure 17.7) Belize has also introduced very tight legislation drawing on a number of these techniques to avoid the destruction of its ecosystem, both in its rain forests and in the tropical waters of its shores.

Tourism, can of course, also be controlled simply by failing to provide the infrastructure it demands. Several of the most attractive Greek islands remain relatively unspoiled by tourism simply because they are accessible only by ferry or jetfoil craft; the failure to construct airports is a major factor in limiting tourism growth.

Government policies to attract large numbers of tourists have given way to policies designed to attract particular tourist markets. While this has in most cases meant trying to attract wealthy, 'high-spend' visitors, it has sometimes led to a move to encourage visits by those who will have the least impact on local populations, i.e. those who will integrate and accept local customs rather than seeking to impose their own standards on locals. In contrast, the local authority at Alassio, Italy, took rather extreme action in 1994, in an effort to discourage daytrippers and 'sacopelisti' (sleeping-baggers), who slept on the beaches and brought little income into the town, by asking the railways to provide fewer trains to the resort on weekends. Tourists were also to be accosted and asked to show that they were carrying at least 50,000 lire as spending money.

One question which concerns governments is whether to opt for a policy of dispersing tourists, or concentrating them. Mass charter movements of tourists are naturally easier to contain in one area, while the independent tourist will be less satisfied to be accommodated in one area along with countless other tourists. The simple belief that the independent traveller is in some ways 'greener' than the mass tourist cannot necessarily be sustained, however. Certainly, in terms of energy consumption, a full charter aircraft of package tourists does less damage to the environment than the same number of independent travellers spread across several half-empty scheduled flights. Similarly, it can be argued that maintaining tourists in one area – the 'ghetto' principle of tourism planning – rather than dispersing them across the country has the effect of limiting the damage to one relatively small area, and avoids possible confrontations between hosts and tourists, although admittedly it reduces opportunities to 'meet the natives'. Public sector bodies have taken different directions on this issue, with Senegal and Indonesia attempting to disperse their tourists and to avoid the development of tourism enclaves, to provide tourists with better contacts with the locals; while countries such as Tunisia have developed resorts well away from populated areas to reduce the impact of tourism on the local population. Neither solution is the perfect answer. While the ghetto approach has advantages in conserving the environment away from the tourists, it alienates the tourist from the culture and life of the community and also impacts on the local economy, reducing the spend in local shops and enhancing it within the (often foreign-owned) hotels.

INDUSTRY'S CONTRIBUTION TO SUSTAINABLE TOURISM

The public sector can impose controls, but without the cooperation of the tourism industry, sustainable tourism cannot be truly achieved. There is now evidence that many companies in Britain and elsewhere have come to understand the importance of sustainable tourism, not simply as a gimmick to get public goodwill, but as a long-term strategy for survival and growth. In this, Britain's Green Flag International, a small lobby of concerned environmental interests, has been influential in persuading travel companies to adopt a more responsible approach in their marketing and operations. The company awards a Green Flag to those organisations it deems to have

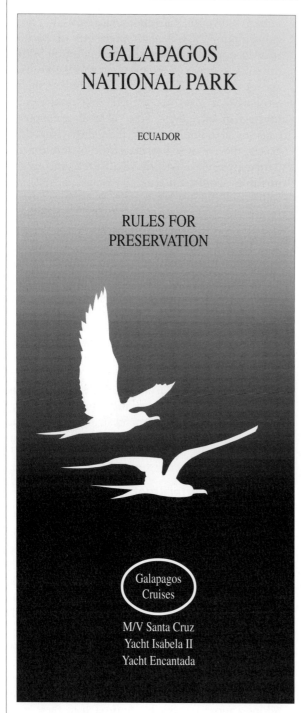

GALAPAGOS NATIONAL PARK

ECUADOR

RULES FOR PRESERVATION

Galapagos
Cruises

M/V Santa Cruz
Yacht Isabela II
Yacht Encantada

RULES TO BE OBSERVED WHILE IN GALAPAGOS NATIONAL PARK

Galapagos is yours to enjoy. Will your grandchildren still have the chance to see it as you do? Your help is needed to protect it. Please help the National Park to conserve Galapagos by following and helping to enforce these rules:

1. NO PLANT, ANIMAL, OR REMAINS OF THEM (SHELLS, BONES, PIECES OF WOOD), OR OTHER NATURAL OBJECTS, SHOULD BE RE-MOVED OR DISTURBED.
   Actions such as these are illegal and cause serious harm to the island's ecological conditions.

2. BE CAREFUL NOT TO TRANSPORT ANY LIVE MATERIAL TO THE ISLANDS, OR FROM ISLAND TO ISLAND. Check your clothing before landing on any of the islands for seeds or insects and destroy them or keep them on your vessel for disposal later on. Check your boot or shoe soles for dried mud before you leave your boat. This material will frequently contain seed and spores of plants and animals. Inadvertant transport of these materials represents a special danger to Galapagos. Each island has its own unique fauna and flora, and introduced plants and animals can quickly destroy this uniqueness. These rules also apply to pets and other animals and plants. DO NOT BRING THEM TO THE ISLANDS. One of the most destructive forces in Galapagos are ferel organisms (domesticated species gone wild) which have been brought to Galapagos by man.

3. For the same reasons expressed in No. 2 DO NOT TAKE ANY FOOD TO THE UNINHABITED ISLANDS. It is easy to introduce, together with the food, insects or other organisms which might be dangerous to the fragile island ecosystems. Fresh fruits and vegetables are especially dangerous. The orange seed that you drop may become a tree.

4. ANIMALS MAY NOT BE TOUCHED OR HAND-LED. All wild animals dislike this and will quickly lose their remarkable tameness if thus treated by human invaders.

5. ANIMALS MAY NOT BE FED. Not only can it be dangerous to your own person but in the long run it can destroy the animal's social structure and affect their reproduction. You came here to see a completely natural situation. Do not interfere with it.

6. DO NOT STARTLE OR CHASE ANY ANIMAL FROM ITS RESTING OR NESTING SPOT. Exercise extreme care among the breeding colonies of sea birds. Be especially careful not to drive boobies, cormorants, gulls, or frigate birds from their nests. These birds will fly from their nests if startled, often knocking the egg or chick to the ground or leaving it exposed to the sun. (A recently hatched booby chick will die in 20 to 30 minutes if exposed to the sun; frigate birds will also eat any unguarded chick.)

7. DO NOT LEAVE THE AREAS WHICH ARE DESIGNATED AS VISITING SITES. In the more heavily used visitor sites there are trails or areas marked with wooden stakes within which the visitor should remain. The trails are designed to guide the visitor to all of the points of interest within a given visitor site, and at the same time to protect the resource.

8. LITTER OF ALL TYPES MUST BE KEPT OFF THE ISLANDS. DISPOSAL AT SEA MUST BE LIMITED TO CERTAIN TYPES OF GARBAGE, ONLY TO BE THROWN OVERBOARD IN SELECTED AREAS. Keep all rubbish (film wrappers, cigarette butts, chewing gum, tin cans, bottles, etc.) in a bag or pocket, to be disposed of on your boat. The crew of your vessel is responsible to the National Park for proper trash disposal. You should never throw anything overboard. A few examples of the damage that can be caused:
   – Sea lions will pick a tin off the bottom and play with it, cutting their highly sensitive muzzles.
   – Sea turtles will eat plastic thrown overboard and die, for it blocks their digestive tracts.
   – Rubbish thrown overboard near an island will usually be carried to shore where, as it accumulates, will convert a once beautiful area into a rubbish pile, in addition to causing problems for the native plants and animals.

9. DO NOT BUY SOUVENIRS OR OBJECTS MADE FROM PLANTS OR ANIMALS OF THE ISLANDS, with the exception of articles made from wood. The best way to discourage this trade is to simply not buy any of these articles. If anyone offers you any of these souvenirs, please advise the National Park.

10. CAMPING ANYWHERE IN GALAPAGOS WITHOUT A PERMIT IS AGAINST THE LAW.

Camping is permitted only in certain sites designated by the National Park. Consult with the central office of the National Park in Sta. Cruz for further information.

11. WHEN CAMPING, DO NOT BUILD CAMPFIRES. Use a gasoline or kerosene stove. Fire scars are ugly and the fire itself may easily cause a brushfire in this dry climate. Dead trees which one would use for fuel, play their own role in the island's ecosystem and are better left alone.

12. DO NOT PAINT NAMES OR GRAFFITI ON ROCKS. It is against the law and it is extremely ugly to look at. Immortality can't be more important than the Island's natural beauty.

13. ALL GROUPS WHICH VISIT THE NATIONAL PARK MUST BE ACCOMPANIED BY A QUALIFIED GUIDE APPROVED BY THE NATIONAL PARK. The visitor has the responsibility to follow the instructions of the guide of his group in any situation, since it is the guide who is responsible for assuring that the regulations of the National Park related to the conservation of the flora and fauna are complied with.

14. THE NATIONAL PARK IS DIVIDED INTO DIFFERENT ZONES TO FACILITATE ITS MANAGEMENT AND ADMINISTRATION. There are certain sites where tourist activities are permitted, and others where the public is restricted or prohibited. The boat captains and guides know which are the visitor sites and will be responsible for obtaining the proper permits. Nevertheless, the personnel in the office of the National Park are available to answer any questions you may have.

15. DO NOT HESITATE TO SHOW YOUR CONSERVATIONIST ATTITUDE. Explain these rules to others, and help to enforce them. Notify the National Park Service if you see any serious damage being done. You may be a decisive factor in the Island's preservation.

Always feel free to visit the National Park Service's offices and the Charles Darwin Research Station if you have any questions. Your understanding of the Islands is important to their conservation. Enjoy yourself fully, but never at the expense of what you came here to see.

GALAPAGOS NATIONAL PARK

Figure 17.7 Rules to be observed while in Galapagos National Park reached an acceptable standard in this respect. It has particularly pressed for companies to recycle brochures, claiming some ten tons are wasted every year in Britain. While some companies have switched to using recycled paper in their brochure production, few have yet been willing to shoulder the cost burden of collecting and recycling brochures at the end of each year. The Association of Independent Tour Operators (AITO), composed of smaller companies, many of which carry tourists to environmentally sensitive areas of the globe, encourages its members to adopt a policy of sustainable tourism. Individually, some companies such as British Airways have undertaken an 'environmental audit' of their operations, and the Countryside Commission sells a Green Audit Kit which alerts companies as to how they can 'green' their tourism business. Eurocamp, the package holiday camping company, introduced an extensive policy to 'green' their product, appointing a green 'monitor' within their management structure to oversee its implementation. Activities ranged from monitoring their supply of household cleaners to ensure they were environmentally friendly, to donating older tents to charities at the end of the season, rather than destroying them as had been previous practice. The Intercontinental Hotels chain undertook its own worldwide environmental audit in 1991, leading to a policy of recycling its waste and introducing cruelty-free (not tested on animals) toiletries in the guest rooms; while some hotels in Hawaii have installed flow regulators on showers and taps to control wastage. Walt Disney Enterprises recycle oils, paints and cleaning materials used on their sites. Thomson Holidays has shown a keen interest in sustainable tourism, and among other activities has sponsored new litter bins in resorts in the Mediterranean. Center Parcs have made their resorts in the UK car-free zones, and offer visitors the use of bicycles during their stay. The specialist operator Turkish Delight Holidays, with the support of the environmentalist David Bellamy, launched a campaign to prevent further destruction by tourism of turtle nesting areas. The German airline Lufthansa introduced snacks at departure gates to avoid wastage resulting from serving in-flight meals (as well as being sustainable, this is also highly cost-efficient!).

There is still some scepticism as to the extent to which these activities are a genuine response to the threat to our environment, as opposed to a public relations exercise to win public favour. Nevertheless, what did start out for many companies as a marketing ploy has later turned to a genuine commitment to improve the environment. Perhaps the example of Cox and Kings, the oldest British tour operator, best demonstrates a commitment to sustainable tourism; the company promises that for every customer buying one of their 'environmental journey' holidays, they will buy one acre of rainforest in Belize, to be kept in its natural state in perpetuity. The relatively high cost of these package tours allows for some discretionary spending of this sort; the challenge will be to encourage down-market operators to increase their own prices to allow for a more sustainable product to be delivered. So far, however, the evidence in Britain suggests that while the public are keen on the concept, they are reluctant in practice to fund it through higher prices.

The socio-cultural effects of tourism

The cultural and social impact on a host country of large numbers of people, sharing different value systems and away from the constraints of their own environment, is a subject increasingly drawing the attention of social scientists and planners, especially those responsible for developing tourism in the Third World. The impact of mass tourism is most noticeable in less developed countries, but is by no means restricted to these; tourism has contributed to an increase in crime and other social problems in New York and London, in Hawaii and Miami, in Florence and Corfu.

Any influx of tourism, however small, will make some impact on a region, but the extent of the impact is dependent not just upon numbers but also on the kind of tourists which the region attracts. The mass tourist is less likely to adapt to the local cultures, and will seek amenities and standards found in the home country, while the independent traveller or backpacker will adapt more readily to an alien environment. This has been exemplified in a model devised by Valene Smith (see Figure 17.8).

Explorers, or tourists whose main interest is to meet and understand people from different cultures and backgrounds, will fully accept and acclimatise to the foreign culture. These travellers will generally travel independently, and be as little visible as possible. However, as increasingly remote areas of the world are 'packaged' for wealthy tourists, and as ever-larger numbers of tourists travel farther afield to find relaxation or adventure, these tourists bring with them their own value systems, either expecting or demanding the lifestyle and facilities to which they are accustomed in their own country.

At its simplest and most direct, this flow of comparatively wealthy tourists to a region will attract petty criminals, as evidenced by increases in thefts or muggings – a problem that has become serious in some areas of the Mediterranean, in Florida, Latin America, the Caribbean and even in Russia. Tourists may be seen as easy prey to be overcharged for purchases, a widespread problem even in London, where street vendors exploit the tourist in sales of ice-cream or other commodities. Where gambling is a cornerstone of tourism growth, prostitution and organised crime often follow. Certain countries which have more relaxed laws on sexual behaviour than those in the West, attract tourists for sexual encounters, and some countries, including Germany and Japan, have tour operators which will organise package tours to destinations such as the Philippines and Thailand for this specific purpose. This public promotion of commercial sex, especially where it involves sex with minors, has come under increasing criticism in the Western world from organisations such as the World Council of Churches and Tourism Concern. Britain, following the example of other Western countries, recently passed legislation to enable those who had indulged in paedophile tourism (sex with minors) to be prosecuted in their home country.

There are a number of less direct, and perhaps less visible, effects on tourist localities, known as 'relative deprivation'. The comparative wealth of tourists may be resented or envied by

Type of tourist	Numbers of tourists	Adaptation to local norms
Explorer	very limited	adapts fully
Elite	rarely seen	adapts fully
Off-beat	uncommon, but seen	adapts well
Unusual	occasional	adapts somewhat
Incipient mass	steady flow	seeks western amenities
Mass	continuous influx	expects western amenities
Charter	massive arrivals	demands western amenities

Figure 17.8 Adaptation of tourists to local norms. (*Source: Valene Smith, Hosts and Guests, 1992, Blackwell*)

the locals, particularly where the influx is seen by the latter as a form of neocolonialism, as in the Caribbean or some African countries. Locals come to experience dissatisfaction with their own standards of living or way of life, and seek to emulate that of the tourists. In some cases, the effect of this is marginal, as in the adoption of the tourists' dress or fashions, but in others the desire to emulate the tourists can threaten deep-seated traditions in the community, as well as leading to aspirations which are impossible to meet.

Job opportunities and the higher salaries paid to workers in the tourist industry will attract workers from agricultural and rural communities who, freed from the restrictions of their families and the home environments, may abandon their traditional values. This can result in an increase in promiscuity, and the breakdown of marriages.

The problem of interaction between the host and tourist is that any relationships which develop are fleeting, and superficial, and are often conducted for commercial ends. A report by UNESCO in 1976 identified four characteristics of host–guest relations in tourism:

1 Relations are transitory and superficial.
2 They are undertaken under constraints of time and space with visitors compacting sights into as limited amount of time as possible.
3 There is a lack of spontaneity in relations; meetings tend to be prearranged to fit tour schedules, and involve mainly financial transactions.
4 Relations are unequal and unbalanced, due to

disparities in wealth and status of the participants.

Most tourists visiting a new country for the first time, who may be spending no more than a week in that country and do not expect to return, will be concerned to condense their experiences, to a point where each tends to be brief and superficial. Add to this an initial fear of contact with locals, and tourists' comparative isolation – hotels often being dispersed away from centres of local activity – and opportunities for any meaningful relationship become very limited. Few relationships are spontaneous; contact is generally with locals who work within the tourism industry, or else it is mediated by couriers. Language may form an impenetrable barrier to genuine local contact, and this limitation can lead to mutual misunderstanding. The relationship is further unbalanced by the status of the visitor, not only in terms of wealth but the fact that the tourist is on holiday while the local is likely to be at work, often being paid to serve the needs of the tourist.

Sometimes, locals are exploited as 'tourist objects'. In British villages, local residents can be annoyed by coachloads of tourists emerging from their buses to peer through their windows. A more extreme example is to be found in Thailand, where in Chiang Mai Burmese refugee 'long neck' women are displayed to visiting tourists at an exorbitant charge which allows the tourist to enter a specially constructed commune. However, the Burmese exploited in this way have admitted to enjoying seeing the tourists' strange hair and eye colours!

Exploitation of this kind can result in both sides seeing contacts in purely commercial terms. In Kenya's Maasai Mara, the Maasai extract payment for photographs, of themselves or of a 'real' (but specially constructed) village. Charging for photographs has become a norm in many parts of the world. In exchange, feeling themselves exploited, tourists feel that it becomes acceptable to steal the towels from their hotel; the host–guest relationship has changed to one of supplier and client.

In this situation, the role of the courier or representative as a 'culture broker' becomes vital. These members of the industry enjoy local knowledge (and are often from the local community), help to avoid misunderstandings, can interpret the local culture for visitors and explain what is appropriate and inappropriate behaviour for the guests.

The breakdown in host–guest relationships can be largely ascribed to the volume of visitors. Doxey (1975) developed an 'Irridex' model of the relationship between tourism growth and community stress (see Figure 17.9). In the early stages of tourism development, the locals are euphoric, pleased to see investment and improved job prospects for local people. The comparatively small numbers, and the fact that most tourists will belong to the 'explorer' category and accept the norms and values of the hosts, means that tourists are welcomed, and even cultivated as 'friends'. As locals become used to the benefits they receive from tourism, and become aware of the problems which tourism generates as it grows, so they come to accept it, and their meetings with tourists become more common and more commercial. Further growth leads to a general feeling among locals that tourists are an irritant rather than a benefit, with the recognition of the way in which tourism is changing their community and their cultural norms. Finally, locals show open antagonism towards the steady stream of visitors, many of whom will have the attitude that locals are there to meet the tourists' needs and will insist on Western standards.

Naturally, this is a simplified model of the fairly complex relationships which actually develop between tourists and locals. Other factors that must be taken into account are the length of

Figure 17.9 Irridex model of stress relative to tourism development. *(Source: G. V. Doxey 'A Causation Theory of Visitor-Resident Irritants', 1975)*

Stages	Characteristics	Symptoms
Stage 1	EUPHORIA	visitors welcomed, little formal development
Stage 2	APATHY	visitors taken for granted, contacts become commercial
Stage 3	IRRITATION	locals concerned about tourism, efforts made to improve infrastructure
Stage 4	ANTAGONISM	open hostility from locals, attempts to limit damage and tourism flows

time a tourist stays in the community (longer-stay tourists will accommodate better and be seen as making a more effective contribution to the local economy), and the cultural gap between locals and tourists (domestic tourists sharing the values of the locals will be less resented).

Examples abound of the antagonism engendered between locals and tourists, even within Britain. An attitude change among locals can be detected by change in the vocabulary of tourism – for example, in Cornwall, the term 'grockles' is used, and locals may carry bumper stickers on their cars saying 'I'm not a tourist: I live here'. More open hostility can be detected already in Bath, where hoses have been turned on open-top touring coaches which use megaphones to provide a commentary. Breaking cultural taboos can produce a backlash: Alassio banned bikinis in the streets, and in the Alto Adige region of the Italian Dolomites in 1993, a local movement erupted spontaneously to prevent the spread of topless bathing in the lakes – while other residents expressed their concern that the publicity accorded this might dissuade some tourists from visiting! In Greece, what has become known as the 'Shirley Valentine factor' – British women escaping a humdrum life at home to find romance in Greece – has led to a reaction from women in Corfu and Crete, who resent the attention paid to foreign females, and feel that Greek women are now undervalued. However, it is also true to say that some Greek women have welcomed the increasing liberation from male dominance which tourism has brought.

A lack of understanding of local cultural traditions is common where these traditions appear to be contrary to what we view as tasteful and appropriate. British tourists in Tokyo may be surprised to see signs outside some nightspots declaring 'Japanese only here', reflecting a nineteenth-century imperialist tradition which has long died out in the Western world. Following the crash of a Pakistani Airlines plane over Nepal in 1992, it was reported that 'British Embassy officials were appalled by the public display of the bodies for relatives' of the English victims, which they described as a 'grotesque peepshow'. In Nepal, however, viewing the remains of the dead is an important part of the act of grieving, and the Nepalese were merely extending this courtesy to the foreign mourners.

While a considerable amount of research has now been undertaken into the effect of tourists on locals, rather less is available to tell us how locals in turn influence the tourists. We can undoubtedly ascribe our widening acceptance of foreign food and fashions in Britain to the influence, in part, of overseas travel, and the quality of foreign food, service, transport and hotel facilities have encouraged us to become more demanding in the provision of these in Britain. Research (Gullahorn and Gullahorn, 1963) also suggests that tourists go through three stages in adapting to the local culture of their holiday environment. In the first stage, the tourists are excited by the environment and the novelty of the situation; later, a second stage is reached in which the tourists become disillusioned, and more critical of the environment, as they become accustomed to the situation. Finally, in what may be a slow process, they learn to adapt to the new setting, and in doing so may experience 're-entry crisis', where it becomes difficult to readapt to their home environment when they return.

Other studies have examined the extent to which pre-travel attitudes affect adaptability, and whether travel broadens understanding or reinforces stereotypes (see, for example, Sutton, 1967). The evidence suggests that the self-fulfilling prophesy is at work here; that if we travel with the expectation of positive experiences, we will experience them. However, much more work is needed to explore the relationship between the tourist and the host from the former's perspective.

STAGED AUTHENTICITY

Given the constraints of time and place, the tourist demands *instant culture,* an opportunity to sample, even if superficially, the 'foreignness' of the destination. This gives rise to what Dean MacCannell (1989) has referred to as *staged authenticity,* in which a search by tourists for authentic experiences of another culture leads to locals of that culture either providing those experiences, or staging them to appear as realistic as possible. Culture in this way is in danger of becoming commercialised and trivialised, as when 'authentic' folk dances are staged for the package tourists as a form of cabaret in hotels, or traditional tribal dances are arranged, often in an artificially shortened form, as performances for groups of tourists. Such trivialisation has been suggested in Britain, with a proposal that the traditional ceremony of Changing the Guard should be mounted more frequently each day, in order to give tourists more opportunities to view it. Similarly, it has been suggested that Stonehenge, which for reasons already discussed can no longer be viewed close up, should be replicated in fibreglass near the actual site, to give the tourist an 'authentic' experience of seeing the stones more closely.

Tourists will seek out local restaurants not frequented by other tourists in order to enjoy the 'authentic' cuisine and environment of the locals, but the very fact of their discovering such restaurants makes them tourist attractions in their turn, and ultimately the 'tourist traps' tourists sought to avoid. Meanwhile, the locals move on to find somewhere else to eat.

The downgrading of traditional hospitality towards the tourist in Hawaii is exemplified by the artifical welcome to which tourists are subjected on their arrival in the islands. Traditionally, welcoming natives would place a *lei* of flowers around the neck of each tourist, but the cost of this courtesy and the huge volume of tourists has now forced the *lei* to be replaced by a plastic garland, which reinforces the commercial nature of the interplay which this has now become.

Tourists seek local artefacts as souvenirs or investments. In cases where genuine works are purchased, this can lead to loss of cultural treasures from a country, and many countries now impose strict bans on exports of such items. However, tourists are often satisfied to purchase what they believe to be an authentic example of local art; this has led to the mass production of poorly crafted works (sometimes referred to as *airport art*), common among African nations and the Pacific islands. Alternately, it encourages the freezing of art styles in pseudo-traditional form, as in the case of the apparently 'medieval' painted wooden religious statuary produced in Oberammergau and other villages of southern

Figure 17.10 Traditional dance: Ramayana Ballet performing in Bali, Indonesia. *(Courtesy Garuda International)*

Germany. In turn, artists and craftsmen are subtley encouraged to change their traditional styles, by making their works in the colours that are found to be most attractive to the tourists, or by reducing the size of their works to make them more readily transportable for the tourists.

It is perhaps too easy to take a purist stance in criticising these developments. One must point to the evident benefits which tourism has brought to the culture of many tourist destinations – indeed in many cases it has helped to regenerate an awareness and pride in local culture and traditions. But for the advent of tourism, many of these traditions would have died out long ago. It is easy to ascribe cultural decline to the impact of tourism, whereas it is as likely to be the result of mass communication and technological development. Since Western culture is the dominant influence around the world, it will inevitably undermine other cultures, particularly those of the Third World. However, it is equally clear that tourism from the Western nations has led to a revival of interest in local customs in other countries (and not just in Third World countries; the revival of morris dancing in English communities is a direct result of the impact of tourism). Traditional local cuisines in Britain have been regenerated, with the support of the national tourist boards, in the 'taste of England', 'taste of Wales' and 'taste of Scotland' schemes. Dying local arts and crafts have been revived through cottage industries in rural areas which have benefited economically from the impact of tourism.

Managing the social impact of tourism

Sustainable tourism, in terms of the social impact of tourism on indigenous populations, needs to be managed in two ways. Firstly, it is important that good relations are established between locals and guests, so that guests are welcomed to the region or country and social interaction benefits both parties. As we will have seen earlier in this text, there are different approaches to ensuring this. The choice is between two diametrically opposed management methods. Responsible officials can attempt to integrate the guest into the local community, and to control the overall number of visitors so that the local population does not become swamped by tourists. This is really only practical where demand for the destination is limited to comparatively small numbers, and the market attracted shows empathy for, and sensitivity towards, local culture; specialist tourism will allow for this solution to be adopted, but mass tourism will not. Alternatively, officials can aim to concentrate the visitors in particular districts, sometimes referred to as tourist 'ghettoes', often some distance away from residential neighbourhoods, so that any damage is limited to the few locals who will have contact with these guests, usually involving commercial transactions. In this way, most locals and visitors will not come into direct contact with each other,

though this may also reduce the economic benefit of tourism to the local community. The integrated resort complex is becoming increasingly common, examples being found in Cancun, Mexico, Nusa Dua in Bali, Indonesia, Puerto Plata in the Dominican Republic and Langkawi development in Malaysia.

The other issue is the need to ensure that locals benefit economically from in-coming tourism, through the provision of employment at all levels, and through ownership of facilities. However, this requires a measure of sophistication among the local population, requiring education and training, as well as assistance in raising finance for investment in local tourist businesses. The solution cannot be achieved merely by putting businesses into the hands of local residents. To illustrate this, the example can be given of a tour operating company in Arnhem Land, Australia, which was originally managed by foreign nationals, but was eventually handed over to local Aboriginal administration. While the new Aboriginal owners were fully capable of handling the operational aspects of the programme, they had little knowledge of, and no contacts with, the overseas markets they existed to serve, and in consequence they found it difficult to attract new business.

The future of tourism

We have seen in these chapters how tourism has developed to a level where it has become a major industry, a major force for social change and a major power for good, or if uncontrolled, for evil. We have also speculated upon the future of tourism, and the possible consequences of a five-fold or tenfold increase in tourists in the early part of the twenty-first century. Some understanding of the magnitude of the problem can be seen in the rapid development of tourism to the former Eastern European countries following the collapse of the Communist system in these countries. Soon after the fall of Communism in Czechoslovakia, Prague was estimated to have been receiving some *83 million* visitors a year (admittedly, many of these were taking short trips across the border, and as few as 10 million were thought to be staying visitors). Similar huge numbers thronged to see the other new states, with their journeys made easy by the eradication of visa requirements. This sort of expansion, however, cannot be sustained on a worldwide scale, and global growth will not be on the scale of the 1950–80 period.

Nevertheless, the world is in a period of rapid transition; the traditional tourist-generating countries are moving from an industrial stage to becoming post-industrial societies. With this change, lifestyles and values are also changing; the old desire to accumulate material possessions shows signs of abating; leisure forecasters are now trying to determine whether this will result in a new desire, as prophesied by Alvin Toffler (1970), to accumulate experiences as avidly as we formerly collected possessions. The concern of the tourism industry will be to ascertain how this will affect the consumers' demand for travel.

Technical developments, although not advancing at the same speed as a few years ago, will still provide new opportunities for travel. While aviation experts agree that the development of jet aircraft has reached a plateau where productivity and efficiency are unlikely to be substantially improved, and the real costs of travel will not decline until some radical breakthrough in air travel occurs, there is promise of such innovation early in the twenty-first century. Although the British government has failed to support British Aerospace's proposal to develop an experimental aircraft capable of leaving and re-entering the Earth's atmosphere (the so-called HOTOL concept), the US aircraft industry has shown more interest in the plans. Such an aircraft would be capable of flights into space, carrying its own supplies of liquid oxygen to burn when beyond Earth's atmosphere, but using oxygen from the air, as does a normal airliner, when flying within the atmosphere. Orbiting the globe up to 185 miles above the Earth's surface, the aircraft would be capable of flying between London and Sydney, Australia, in a little over one hour.

Meanwhile, research continues in other areas of advanced transport. In shipping, work is continuing on designs for more fuel-efficient craft. Successful sea trials have taken place with vessels that complement the use of their engines with metal sails, increasing the overall speed while reducing costs. The appeal of cruise ships that resemble floating hotels with a full range of leisure facilities is leading to the construction of ever-larger vessels. Proposals have been advanced for much larger catamarans and trimarans (twin-hulled and triple-hulled vessels) capable of transporting large numbers of passengers at high speed and at far more comfort, without the customary problems of motion sickness experienced in single-hulled ships. Such vessels might be constructed to cross the Atlantic in under 48 hours. An even more exciting venture has already been developed by the Russians beyond the prototype stage; a surface-skimming hydrobus known as the ekranoplane, used by the Russians as a military transport, has potential for development as a civilian vehicle capable of carrying 400 passengers at a cruising speed of over 300 mph, with a range of up to 10,000 miles. Fuel efficiency is far greater than in normal aircraft, offering the very real prospect of low fares for long-haul travel. This would make possible transatlantic journeys overnight, and at comparatively cheap fares, reaching an entirely new market. British ferry companies have expressed an interest, as have the Americans.

Meanwhile, Japan is working on the use of electromagnetic thrusters for ships. Toshiba has designed a 150-ton vessel which is pushed through water by the effect of counteracting magnets; this could again lead to the development of vessels of much larger size.

On land, as we have seen, railway development is making great strides. Japan's Linear Express, capable of cruising at speeds up to 300 mph, has already reached the prototype stage. This vehicle has the advantage of superspeed and super quietness; the track consists of a metal trough generating a magnetic field which repels magnets in the train, causing the vehicle to ride 10 cm above the track. There is therefore little wear and tear, and in consequence, much reduced maintenance cost. If the technology proves successful, rail services could certainly pose a major threat to air routes of distances overland up to 1,000 miles.

Some futurologists have prophesied that there will be little need to travel away from home in the twenty-first century. Holographs are capable of reproducing any environment artificially, so that we will be able to recreate in the home any environment of our choosing in order to 'experience' foreign travel. This could include activity holidays such as simulated white water canoe and raft rides, winter sports or the piloting of an aircraft. BT announced in 1997 that it was working on the production of a machine which can reproduce some of the world's biggest attractions, not only on computer screens but also on wraparound screens or as holograms. Using the device, called 'Head', one can, in BT's words, 'visit Times Square or take a walk into a pyramid without leaving the room'. Whether this form of entertainment replaces travel, or only serves to whet the appetite of most of those viewing such destinations remains to be seen. What is certain is that those who cannot now travel – the very poor, the severely disabled – will for the first time be able to experience something akin to real world travel.

Other forecasters predict that underwater leisure cities will be built on the seabeds adjoining our coasts, where a controlled climate will make the annual exodus to the sun no longer necessary. Some of these predictions take us into the realms of science-fiction. We can be safer in forecasting those short-term changes which expand on current trends, and which we can expect to take place before the turn of the century.

Holidays abroad have now become a habit for millions of people living in the developed countries. The fast-developing nations such as Malaysia, South Korea and Taiwan also show signs of equal commitment to the annual holiday abroad, while the emerging nations of the former Soviet Bloc, in spite of their limited disposable income of many of their citizens, are producing large numbers of newly wealthy businesspeople who are choosing to head for Mediterranean destinations in their millions, anxious to experience the classic sun, sea, sand holidays which Westerners have enjoyed since the 1960s. This new market has already proved to be the saviour of some down-market Spanish resorts which had seen declining numbers of Western tourists for several years.

For Western Europeans, while the traditional sun, sea, sand holiday will remain a strong attraction, consumers will expect and demand more

from it. The demand for activity and special interest holidays is growing rapidly among all sectors of the travel market, and passive beach holidays may become a thing of the past. This change may be hastened by the growing body of medical evidence linking sunbathing with skin cancer, which is a particular threat to fair-skinned Anglo-Saxons. In the short term, this fear is more likely to affect older travellers than the young, who have so far shown little desire to change their holiday habits; as with smoking, many youngsters feel that the risk is too remote for it to concern them. In the longer term, the message may get home, but tourists' reaction is more likely to be to cover up and to engage in different activities, rather than to shun the traditional sunshine holiday resorts of the Mediterranean or Caribbean.

Whether the more traditional British seaside resorts can survive in an age where almost every Briton has holidayed abroad at least once is debatable. Global warming may nudge up the average temperatures of our south coast resorts and improve their appeal, but in the short term only massive investment in facilities, particularly indoor entertainment, is likely to retain the domestic market. The success of Center Parcs' holiday centres in Britain has shown that if all-weather facilities are provided and the product offers value for money, the domestic market is attracted. The way forward may be epitomised in Japan's 'Seagaia Ocean Dome' on the island of Kyushu, which is based at the seaside but offers a covered beach with a volcano effect occurring every 15 minutes, and wave machines creating artificial *tsunami* wave effects to instil real excitement into the traditional pastime of sea bathing. This coupling of adventure and sea bathing has proved to be enormously popular with the Japanese domestic market. However, the British consumer continues to demonstrate a nostalgic commitment to tradition and the past, with respect to their choice of holidays as much as other products; and this has been to the benefit of heritage sites, steam railways and other attractions which emphasise their links with the past.

Changes in lifestyle will affect the traditional forms of holiday accommodation. The desire for greater flexibility, coupled with advances in 'convenience' food and more adventurous eating habits, suggest that the swing to self-catering, with more meals out for 'special occasions', will continue, and hotels and guesthouses will have to consider how they can adapt their product to win back this market.

The move up-market, evident in the early 1990s, is also likely to continue. Value for money will play a more important role, counteracting the industry's own emphasis on low price. Long-haul holidays can be expected to continue to outpace short-haul in rate of growth. British tourists will take more frequent holidays and more short breaks.

Advances in computer reservations will allow individual holidaymakers to select their destinations, accommodation and flights, put together their own packages, book and pay for the booking by direct debit to their bank account, all without leaving their armchair. Already experimental programmes of 'computerised shopping' along these lines are available on the Internet. The ability to book from home would suggest a rise in impulse booking, and demand for even more 'late availability' products, coupled with a decline in traditional patterns of advance booking. Indeed, if consumers can package their own holidays at home at the push of a button, conjuring up on their home TV screen all the images of the resorts they wish to choose from, it is possible that this could make the present tasks of operator and travel agent redundant. This is likely to be the case unless both can provide a level of service far exceeding what they offer at present. Agency counter staff must be sufficiently skilled and knowledgeable to be able to offer a genuine counselling service; one attempt to do this was demonstrated by Thomas Cook in 1993, when 'neural computing' was introduced as an aid in analysing the characteristics of their prospective travellers and matching them to the preferred holiday destination. This would allow pinpoint marketing and greatly enhanced prospects of satisfying the customer.

QUESTIONS AND DISCUSSION TOPICS

1 Static caravan sites are frequently criticised for the 'visual pollution' they bring to a scenic region. Discuss current legislation to control this, and discuss what other steps could be taken to improve the situation.

2 Is there an inevitable conflict between conservation and tourism development? Examine examples of such conflict in any country of your choice, and discuss how harmony could be achieved.

3 Argue the case for a policy of concentrating tourists rather than dispersing them, using examples from both Third World and developed countries.

4 How do you see your own holidays changing over the next few years? Discuss the factors that would account for these changes, such as age, family composition, income and changes within the tourism industry itself.

1 You are a freelance journalist for one of the travel trade papers in Britain, and your editor has asked you to produce a short article for the paper which is designed to persuade tour operators to take a more responsible attitude to developing new destinations. Write an article, not to exceed 600 words, with this objective.

2 Undertake an 'environmental audit' of any nearby town or destination which receives a significant number of tourists. Look at features such as litter, graffiti, visual pollution, parking, etc. and produce a report (maximum 1,000 words) for the Director of Tourism for the location, identifying the major weaknesses you have found and making recommendations for action.

3 You have recently been appointed resort representative for a tour operating company which offers 'cheap and cheerful' package holidays in a downmarket resort on the island of Corfu, Greece. There has been a good deal of friction lately between English tourists and Greek locals, and you have been asked by your company to try to help improve the relationship. Prepare notes for a talk you will give your next group of in-coming tourists, designed to effect this.

Bibliography

A note on this bibliography

The following is a selection of texts deemed of particular value to students following *post-A level* programmes of study in the field of tourism, whether as a core subject or as an option within wider fields of study, up to degree level. Books earlier than the 1980s are included only where they are seminal, or relevant for the study of the history of tourism. Publications other than books are largely excluded, again except where they are deemed vital to the contemporary study of the subject.

Adamson S H, *Seaside Piers*, Batsford 1977

Addison W, *English Spas*, Batsford 1951

Alderson F, *The Inland Resorts and Spas of Britain*, David and Charles 1973

Allcock J B, *Tourism in Centrally Planned Economies*, Pergamon 1990

Allcock J B, Bruner E M and Lanfant M-F (eds), *International Tourism: Identity and Change*, Sage Publications 1993

Apostolopoulos Y, Leivadi S and Yiannakis A (eds), *The Sociology of Tourism*, Routledge 1996

Ashford N, Martin Stanton H P and Moore C A, *Airport Operations*, Pitman 1991

Ashworth G J, *Heritage Planning*, Geo Pers 1991

Ashworth G J and Dietvorst A G J, *Tourism and Spatial Transformations: Implications for Policy and Planning*, CAB International 1995

Ashworth G J and Goodall B, *Marketing Tourism Places*, Routledge 1990

Ashworth G J and Larkham P J, *Building a New Heritage: Tourism, Culture and Identity in the New Europe*, Routledge 1994

Ashworth G J and Tunbridge J, *The Tourist-Historic City*, Belhaven Press, 1990

Ashworth G J and Voogd H, *Selling the City: the Use of Publicity and Public Relations to Sell Cities and Regions*, Belhaven Press 1990

Audit Commission, *The Road to Wigan Pier? Managing Local Authority Museums and Art Galleries*, HMSO 1991

Bachmann P, *Tourism in Kenya: A Basic Need for Whom?*, Peter Lang 1988

Badger A, *Trading Places: Tourism as Trade*, Tourism Concern 1996

Barke M, Towner J and Newton M, *Tourism in Spain*, CAB International 1995

Barlay S, *Cleared for Take-off: Behind the Scenes of Air Travel*, Kyle Cathie 1994

Baum T (ed.), *Manpower in Tourism*, Butterworth Heinemann 1991

Baum T (ed.), *Human Resource Issues in International Tourism*, Butterworth Heinemann 1993

Baum T, *Managing Resources in the European Tourism and Hospitality Industry: A Strategic Approach*, Chapman and Hall 1995

Bell G, Bowen P and Fawcett P, *The Business of Transport*, M&E 1984

Bennett T, *The Birth of the Museum: History, Theory, Politics*, Routledge 1995

Benson D and Whitehead G, *Transport and Distribution*, Longman 1985

Binney M, *Our Vanishing Heritage*, Arlington 1985

Binney M and Hanna M, *Preservation Pays: Tourism and the Economic Benefits of Conserving Historic Buildings*, SAVE Britain's Heritage (n/d)

Blackshaw C, *Aviation Law and Regulation*, Pitman 1991

Boissevain J (ed.), *Revitalising European Rituals*, Routledge 1992

Boissevain J (ed.), *Coping with Tourists: European Reactions to Mass Tourism*, Berghan 1997

Boniface P, *Managing Quality Cultural Tourism*, Routledge 1995

Boniface B and Cooper C, *The Geography of Travel and Tourism*, Heinemann, 2nd edn 1994

Boniface P and Fowler P, *Heritage and Tourism in the 'Global Village'*, Routledge 1993

Boo E, *Eco-Tourism: The Potentials and the Pitfalls*, World Wildlife Fund 1990

Boorstin D J, *The Image: a Guide to Pseudo-Events in America*, Penguin 1962

Böröcz J, *Leisure Migration: A Sociological Study on Tourism*, Pergamon 1996

Borrett N, *Leisure and Tourism Services*, Macmillan 1991

Bottomley Renshaw M, *The Travel Agent*, Business Education Publishers, 2nd edn 1997

Bouquet M and Winter M, *Who from their Labours Rest? Conflict and Practice in Rural Tourism*, Avebury 1987

Bramwell H, Henry I, Jackson G, Goytia Prat A, Richards G and van der Straaten J (eds), *Sustainable Tourism Management: Principles and Practice*, Tilburg University Press 1996

Bramwell B and Lane B (eds), *Rural Tourism and Sustainable Rural Development*, Channel View Promotions 1993

Brendon P, *Thomas Cook: 150 Years of Popular Tourism*, Secker 1991

Briggs S, *Successful Tourism Marketing: a Practical Handbook*, Kogan Page 1997

Briguglio L, Archer B, Jafari J and Wall G (eds), *Sustainable Tourism in Islands and Small States: Issues and Policies*, Frances Pinter 1996

Brunt P, *Market Research in Travel and Tourism*, Butterworth Heinemann 1997

Bryden J M, *Tourism Development: A Case Study of the Commonwealth Caribbean*, CUP 1973

Bull A, *The Economics of Travel and Tourism*, Longman, 2nd edn 1995

Burkart A J and Medlik S, *Tourism: Past Present and Future*, Heinemann 1981

Burns P and Holden A, *Tourism: A New Perspective*, Prentice Hall 1995

Burton A and P, *The Green Bag Travellers: Britain's First Tourists*, Deutsch 1978

Burton J and L, *Interpersonal Skills for Travel and Tourism*, Longman 1994

Burton R, *Travel Geography*, Pitman, 2nd edn 1994

Butler R W and Hinch T (eds), *Tourism and Indigenous Peoples*, International Thomson Business Press 1996

Butler R W and Pearce D (eds), *Change in Tourism: People, Places, Processes*, Routledge 1995

Button K (ed.), *Airline Deregulation*, David Fulton 1990

Buzzard J, *The Beaten Track: European Tourism, Literature and the Ways to Culture, 1800–1918*, Clarendon Press 1993

CAB International, *Fashionable Resort Regions: Their Evolution and Transformation*, CAB International 1993

CAB International, *Leisure Policies in Europe*, CAB International 1993

CAB International, *Tourism in Europe: Structures and Development*, CAB International 1993

Cabinet Office Enterprise Unit, *Pleasure, Leisure and Jobs: The Business of Tourism* (the Young Report), HMSO 1985

Callaghan P (ed.), *Travel and Tourism*, Business Education Publishers 1989

Carmouche R and Kelly N, *Behavioural Studies in Hospitality Management*, Chapman and Hall 1995

Carter J, Goodey B and Binks G (eds), *Heritage Interpretation Management: Audience Characteristics, Evaluation and Impact*, Wiley 1997

Casson L, *Travel in the Ancient World*, George Allen and Unwin 1974

Cater E and Lowman G, *Ecotourism: a Sustainable Option?*, Wiley 1994

Clark M, *Interpersonal Skills for Tourism and Hospitality Management*, Chapman and Hall 1995

Clarke J and Critcher C, *The Devil Makes Work – Leisure in Capitalist Britain*, Macmillan 1985

Clarke M, Riley M and Wood R C, *Research Methods in Hospitality and Tourism*, International Thomson Business Press 1997

Clift S and Page S, *Health and the International Tourist*, Routledge 1995

Collins V and Griffith S, *Working in Tourism: the UK, Europe and Beyond*, Vacation Work Publications 1995

Conlin M V and Baum T, *Island Tourism: Management Principles and Practice*, Wiley 1995

Cooper C, *et al. Tourism Principles and Practice*, 2nd edn, Longman 1998

Cooper C and Go F, *Tourism Education and Training*, Belhaven Press 1994

Cooper C, Shepherd R and Westlake J, *Tourism and Hospitality Education*, University of Surrey 1994

Cooper C and Wanhill S R, *Tourism Development: Environmental and Community Issues*, Wiley 1997

Corbin A, *The Lure of the Sea: The Discovery of the Seaside in the Western World 1750–1840*, Polity Press 1994

Corke J, *Tourism Law*, Elm Publications, 2nd edn 1993

Corner J and Harvey S, *Enterprise and Heritage: Cross-Currents of National Culture*, Routledge 1991

Craig-Smith S and French C, *Learning to Live with Tourism*, Pitman 1994

Crick M, *Resplendent Sites, Discordant Voices: Sri Lankans and International Tourism*, Harwood Academic Publishers 1994

Croall J, *Preserve or Destroy: Tourism and the Environment*, Calouste Gulbenkian Foundation 1995

Crotts J L and van Raajj W F (eds), *Economic Psychology of Travel and Tourism*, Haworth Press 1994

Dandel S and Vialle G, *Yield Management: Applications to Air Transport and other Service Industries*, Institut de Transport Aérien 1994

Dann G M S, *The Language of Tourism: A Sociolinguistic Perspective*, CAB International 1996

Davidoff D M, *Contact: Customer Service in the Hospitality and Tourism Industry*, Prentice Hall 1994

Davidson R, *Tourism*, Pitman, 2nd edn 1993

Davidson R, *Business Travel*, Pitman 1994

Davidson R, *Travel and Tourism in Europe*, Longman, 2nd edn 1998

Davidson R and Maitland R, *Tourism Destinations*, Hodder and Stoughton 1997

Deegan J and Dineen D, *Tourism Policy and Performance*, International Thomson Business Press 1997

Delgado A, *The Annual Outing and Other Excursions*, George Allen and Unwin 1977

Dickinson R H and Vladimir A N, *Selling the Sea: An Inside Look at the Cruise Industry*, Wiley 1997

Dobson A, *Flying in the Face of Competition*, Avebury Aviation/Ashgate Publishing 1994

Doganis R, *Flying off Course: The Economics of International Airlines*, George Allen and Unwin 1985

Doganis R, *The Airport Business*, Routledge 1992

Doswell R, *Tourism: Understanding its Development and Management*, Butterworth Heinemann 1995

Doswell R, *Tourism: How Effective Management makes the Difference*, Butterworth Heinemann 1997

Douglas N, *They Came for Savages: 100 Years of Tourism in Melanesia*, Southern Cross University Press 1996

Downes J and Paton T, *Travel Agency Law*, Pitman 1993

Doxey G V, 'A Causation Theory of Visitor–Resident Irritants: Methodology and Research Inferences', Proceedings of the Travel Research Association Sixth Annual Conference, San Diego 1975

Drower J, *Good Clean Fun: The Story of Britain's First Holiday Camp*, Arcadia 1982

Dutton G, *Sun, Sea, Surf and Sand: The Myth of the Beach*, OUP 1985

Eaton A J, *The International Airline Business: Globalisation in Action*, Avebury Aviation/Ashgate Publishing 1995

Eaton B, *European Leisure Businesses: Strategies for the Future*, Elm Publications 1996

Eber S (ed.), *Beyond the Green Horizon: A Discussion Paper on Principles for Sustainable Tourism*, Tourism Concern/World Wildlife Fund 1992

Eco U, *Faith in Fakes*, Secker and Warburg 1986

Eco U, *Travels in Hyper-Reality*, Secker and Warburg 1987

Edgell D, *International Tourism Policy*, Van Nostrand Reinhold 1990

Edgerton R, *Alone Together: Social Order on an Urban Beach*, University of California Press 1979

Edington J and M A, *Ecology, Recreation and Tourism*, CUP 1986

Elkington J and Hailes J, *Holidays that Don't Cost the Earth*, Gollancz 1992

Evans N and Robinson M, *Issues in Travel and Tourism*, vol. 1, Centre for Travel and Tourism/Business Education Publishers 1995

Farrell B (ed.) *Tourism and the Physical Environment*, Pergamon 1987

Feifer M, *Going Places: The Ways of the Tourist from Imperial Rome to the Present Day*, Macmillan 1985

Fjellman S, *Vinyl Leaves: Walt Disney World and America*, Westview Press 1992

Foley M, *Doing your Dissertation: A Guide for Students in Tourism, Leisure and Hospitality Management*, Chapman and Hall 1995

Foley M, Lennon J and Maxwell G (eds), *Strategic Management in Hospitality, Tourism and Leisure*, Cassell 1996

Forsyth T, *Sustainable Tourism: Moving from Theory to Practice*, Tourism Concern/Worldwide Fund for Nature 1996

Foster D, *The Business of Travel Agency Operations*, McGraw-Hill 1991

Foster D, *First Class: An Introduction to Travel and Tourism*, Macmillan/McGraw-Hill, 2nd edn 1994

Foster D, *Sales and Marketing for the Travel Professional*, McGraw-Hill 1991

Fowler P J, *The Past in Contemporary Society: Then, Now*, Routledge 1992

France L (ed.), *The Earthscan Reader in Sustainable Tourism*, Kogan Page 1997

Frechtling D, *Practical Tourism Forecasting*, Butterworth Heinemann 1996

French Y, *The Handbook of Public Relations for Museums, Galleries, Historic Houses, the Visual Arts and Heritage Attractions*, Museum Development Co 1991

Fridgen J D, *Dimensions of Tourism*, Educational Institute of the American Hotel and Motel Assocation, 1991

Gayle D and Goodrich J (eds), *Tourism Marketing and Management in the Caribbean*, Routledge 1993

Gee C, Choy D and Makens J, *The Travel Industry*, van Nostrand Reinhold 1997

Gee G, *Calculations for the Leisure, Travel and Tourism Industries*, Hodder and Stoughton 1991

Getz D, *Festivals, Special Events and Tourism*, Van Nostrand Reinhold 1990

Getz D and Page S, *Business of Rural Tourism*, International Thomson Business Press 1997

Gialloreto L, *Strategic Airline Management: The Global War Begins*, Pitman 1988

Glasson J, Godfrey K and Goodey B, *Towards Visitor Management*, Anthony Rowe 1995

Go F and Pine R, *Globalization Strategy in the Hotel Industry*, International Thomson Business Press 1995

Gold J R and Ward S V (eds), *Place Promotion: The Use of Publicity and Marketing to Sell Towns and Regions*, Wiley 1994

Goldblatt J J, *Special Events: The Art and Science of Celebration*, van Nostrand Reinhold 1990

Goodall B and Ashworth G, *Marketing in the Tourism Industry: The Promotion of Destination Regions*, Routledge 1987

Goodey B (ed.), *The Handbook of Interpretive Practice at Heritage Sites*, Wiley 1997

Gordon S, *Holidays*, Batsford 1972

Graburn N H H (ed.), *Ethnic and Tourist Arts: Cultural Expressions From the Fourth World*, University of California Press 1976

Graham B, *Geography and Air Transport*, Wiley 1995

Grant D and Mason S, *The EC Directive on Package Travel, Package Holidays and Package Tours*, University of Northumbria 1993

Gregory A, *The Travel Agent – Dealer in Dreams*, Regents/Prentice Hall, 4th edn 1993

Gullahorn J E and Gullahorn J T, 'An Extension of the U-Curve Hypothesis', *Journal of Social Sciences*, vol 19, 1963, pp. 33–47

Gunn C, *Tourism Planning: Basic Concepts and Cases*, Taylor and Francis 1994

Gunn C, *Vacationscape: Designing Tourist Regions*, Van Nostrand Reinhold, 3rd edn 1994

Hall C, *Hallmark Tourist Events: Impacts, Management and Planning*, Wiley 1992

Hall C M, *Tourism in the Pacific: Development, Impacts and Markets*, Pitman 1994

Hall C M and Jenkins J M, *Tourism and Public Policy*, Routledge 1995

Hall C M and Johnston M, *Polar Tourism: Tourism in the Arctic and Antarctic Regions*, Wiley 1995

Hall C M, *Tourism and Politics: Policy, Power and Place*, Wiley 1996

Hall C M and Page S J (eds), *Tourism in the Pacific: Issues and Challenges*, International Thomson Business Press 1996

Hanlon J P, *Global Airlines: Competition in a Transnational Industry*, Butterworth Heinemann 1996

Harris G and Katz K, *Promoting International Tourism to the Year 2000 and Beyond*, The Americas Group, 2nd edn 1996

Harris R and Leiper N (eds), *Sustainable Tourism: An Australian Perspective*, Butterworth Heinemann 1995

Harrison D, *Tourism and the Less Developed Countries*, Wiley 1992

Harrison L and Husbands W, *Practising Responsible Tourism: International Case Studies in Tourism Planning, Policy and Development*, Wiley 1996

Harrison R, *Manual of Heritage Management*, Butterworth Heinemann 1994

van Harssel J, *Tourism: an Exploration*, Prentice Hall, 3rd edn 1993

Havins P J N, *The Spas of England*, Robert Hale 1976

Hayles J *et al.*, *Guide to Green Tourism*, Victor Gollancz 1991

Hayter R, *Careers in Training in Hotels, Catering and Tourism*, Butterworth Heinemann 1993

Heath E and Wall G, *Marketing Tourism Destinations: A Strategic Planning Approach*, John Wiley 1992

Hembry P, *The English Spa 1560–1815: A Social History*, Athlone Press 1990

Henley Centre, *Inbound Tourism: A Packaged Future?*, Tourism and Leisure Sector Group, NEDC 1993

Herbert D (ed.), *Heritage, Tourism and Society*, Mansell 1995

Hern A, *The Seaside Holiday: The History of the English Seaside Resort*, Cresset Press 1967

Hewison R, *The Heritage Industry: Britain in a Climate of Decline*, Methuen 1987

Hibbert C, *The Grand Tour*, Weidenfeld and Nicholson 1969

Hill J M M, *The Holiday*, Tavistock Institute of Human Relations 1965

Hindley G, *Tourists, Travellers and Pilgrims*, Hutchinson 1983

Hitchcock M, King V. and Parnwell M, *Tourism in South East Asia*, Routledge 1992

Hodgson A (ed.), *The Travel and Tourism Industry: Strategies for the Future*, Pergamon Press 1987

Hodgson G, *A New Grand Tour*, Viking 1995

Holloway J C and Robinson C, *Marketing for Tourism*, Longman, 3rd edn 1995

Horne D, *The Great Museum: The Representation of History*, Pluto Press 1984

Horner P, *The Travel Industry in Britain*, Stanley Thornes 1991

Horner P, *Travel Geography for Tourism*, Part 1
United Kingdom; Part 2, *Worldwide*, Stanley
Thornes 1993

Horner P, *Travel Agency Practice*, Longman 1996

Horner S and Swarbrooke J, *Marketing Tourism,
Hospitality and Leisure in Europe*, International
Thomson Business Press 1996

Hudman L and Hawkins D, *Tourism in Contemporary
Society: an Introductory Text*, Prentice Hall 1989

Hudson K, *Air Travel: A Social History*, Adams and
Dart 1972

Hudson K, *A Social History of Museums*, Macmillan
1975

Hudson K and Pettifer J, *Diamonds in the Sky: A
Social History of Air Travel*, BBC Publications 1979

Hunter C and Green H, *Tourism and the
Environment: A Sustainable Relationship?*,
Routledge 1995

Inkpen G, *Information Technology for Travel and
Tourism*, 2nd edn, Longman 1998

Inskeep E, *Tourism Planning: An Integrated and
Sustainable Development*, Van Nostrand Reinhold
1991

Inskeep E, *National and Regional Tourism Planning:
Methodologies and Case Studies*, Routledge 1994

Inskeep E and Kallenberger M, *An Integrated
Approach to Resort Development: Six Case Studies*,
World Tourism Organisation 1992

Jackson I, *An Introduction to Tourism*, Hospitality
Press 1994

Jakle J A, *The Tourist: Travel in 20th Century North
America*, University of Nebraska Press 1985

Jefferson A and Lickorish L J, *Marketing Tourism*,
Longman, 2nd edn 1991

Johnson P and Thomas B (eds), *Choice and Demand
in Tourism*, Mansell 1992

Johnson P and Thomas B (eds), *Perspectives on
Tourism Policy*, Mansell 1992

Johnson P and Thomas B, *Tourism, Museums and the
Local Economy*, Edward Elgar 1992

de Kadt E, *Tourism: Passport to Development?*, OUP
1979

Kearns G and Philo C, *Selling Places: The City as
Cultural Capital, Past and Present*, Pergamon Press
1993

Kaiser C and Helber L E, *Tourism Planning and
Development*, Heinemann 1978

Khan M A, Minish R and Khan M M, *Hospitality and
Tourism Management: The Profession of the 21st
Century*, Wiley 1997

Khan M A, Olsen M and Var T, *VNR's Encyclopaedia
of Hospitality and Tourism*, Van Nostrand Reinhold
1993

King B and Hyde G, *Tourism Marketing in Australia*,
Hospitality Press 1989

Kinnaird V H and Hall D, *Tourism Development: The
Gender Dimension*, Wiley 1994

Klugman K, Kuenz J, Waldrep S and Willis S, *Inside
the Mouse: Work and Play at Disneyworld*, Duke
University Press 1995

Kockel U (ed.), *Culture, Tourism and Development:
The Case of Ireland*, Liverpool University Press 1994

Kotler P, Bowen J and Makens J, *Marketing for
Hospitality and Tourism*, Prentice Hall 1996

Krippendorf J, *The Holiday Makers: Understanding
the Impact of Leisure and Travel*, Heinemann 1987

Landry J L and Fesmire A H, *The World is out there
Waiting: An Introduction to Travel and Tourism*,
Prentice Hall 1993

Lane B and Bramwell B, *Sustainable Tourism:
Principles and Practice*, Wiley 1997

Lanfant M-F, Allcock J and Bruner E, *International
Tourism: Identity and Change*, Sage 1995

Lavery P, *Travel and Tourism*, Elm Publications, 3rd
edn 1996

Lavery P and Van Doren C, *Travel and Tourism: A
North American–European Perspective*, Elm
Publications 1990

Law C M, *Urban Tourism: Attracting Visitors to
Large Cities*, Mansell 1993

Law, C M (ed.), *Tourism in Major Cities*,
International Thomson Business Press 1996

Laws E, *Tourism Marketing: Service and Quality
Management Perspectives*, Stanley Thornes 1991

Laws E, *Tourism Destination Management: Issues,
Analysis and Policies*, International Thomson
Business Press 1995

Laws E, *Managing Packaged Tourism*, International
Thomson Business Press 1996

Lawson F, *Hotels and Resorts: Planning, Design and
Refurbishment*, Butterworth Heinemann 1995

Lea J, *Tourism and Development in the Third World*,
Routledge 1988

Leed E J, *The Mind of the Traveller*, Basic Books 1991

Lewes F and Brady G, *Holidays in Britain*, Ginn and
Co 1970

Lewis R and Wild M, *French Ski Resorts and UK Ski
Tour Operators: An Industry Analysis*, Sheffield
Hallam University 1995

Lickorish L J, Bodlender J, Jefferson A and Jenkins
C L, *Developing Tourism Destinations: Policies and
Perspectives*, Longman 1991

Lickorish L and Jenkins K, *An Introduction to Tourism*, Butterworth Heinemann 1995

Lickorish L J and Kershaw A G, *The Travel Trade*, Practical Press 1958

Lino B (ed.), *Sustainable Tourism in Islands,* Vol. 1 *Issues and Policies;* Vol. 2, *Case Studies*, Mansell 1996

Lowenthal D, *The Past is a Foreign Country*, CUP 1985

Lowenthal D, *The Heritage Crusade and the Spoils of History*, Viking 1996

Lumley R (ed.), *The Museum Time Machine*, Routledge 1988

Lumsdon L, *Marketing for Tourism: Case Study Assignments*, Macmillan 1992

Lumsdon L, *Tourism Marketing*, International Thomson Business Press 1997

Lundberg D, *The Tourist Business*, Cahners, 4th edn 1980

Lundberg D and C, *International Travel and Tourism*, John Wiley, 2nd edn 1993

Lundberg D, Stavenga M H and Krishnamoorthy M, *Tourism Economics*, Wiley 1995

MacCannell D, *The Tourist: A New Theory of the Leisure Class*, Schocken (NY) 2nd edn 1989

MacCannell D, *Empty Meeting Grounds: The Tourist Papers*, Routledge 1992

McIntosh R, Goeldner C and Brent Richie J, *Tourism, Principles, Practices, Philosophies*, Wiley, 7th edn 1995

Mancini M, *Selling Destinations: Geography for the Travel Professional*, South West Publishing 1992

Mason P, *Tourism: Environment and Development Perspectives*, World Wildlife Fund 1990

Mayo E J and Jarvis L P, *The Psychology of Leisure Travel: Effective Marketing and Selling of Travel Services*, CBI 1981

Medlik S, *The Business of Hotels*, Heinemann, 3rd edn 1994

Medlik S, *Managing Tourism*, Butterworth Heinemann 1995

Medlik S, *Dictionary of Travel, Tourism and Hospitality*, Butterworth Heinemann, 2nd edn 1996

Mele A, *Polluting for Pleasure*, W W Norton 1993

Middleton V, *New Visions for Independent Museums in the UK*, Association of Independent Museums, Andover 1990

Middleton V, *Marketing in Travel and Tourism*, Heinemann, 2nd edn 1994

Middleton V (with Hawkins R) *Sustainable Tourism: A Marketing Perspective,* Butterworth Heinemann 1998

Mill R C, *Tourism: The International Business*, Prentice Hall 1990

Mill R C and Morrison A, *The Tourism System: An Introductory Text*, Prentice Hall, 2nd edn 1992

Mills E, *Design for Holidays and Tourism*, Butterworth 1983

Mills P, *Quality in the Leisure Industry*, Longman 1992

Minhinnick R, *A Postcard Home: Tourism in the Mid-1990s*, Gomer 1993

Moir E, *The Discovery of Britain: The English Tourists 1540–1840*, Routledge and Kegan Paul 1964

Montarani A and Williams A (eds), *European Tourism: Regions, Spaces and Restructuring*, Wiley 1995

Morgan M, *Marketing for Leisure and Tourism*, Prentice Hall 1996

Morinis E A (ed.), *Sacred Journeys: Anthropology of Pilgrimage*, Greenwood Press 1993

Munday S and Doolan C, *Information Technology in Leisure and Tourism*, Cassell 1996

Murphy P E, *Tourism: A Community Approach*, Methuen 1985

Murphy P E, *Quality Management in Urban Tourism*, Wiley 1996

Nash D, *Anthropology of Tourism*, Pergamon 1996

National Heritage, Department of, *Tourism: Competing with the Best*, HMSO 1995

Neale G (ed.), *The Green Travel Guide*, Kogan Page 1997

Nelson Jones J and Stewart P, *A Practical Guide to Package Holiday Law and Contracts*, Tolley Publishing, 3rd edn 1993

North R, *The Butlin Story*, Jarrolds 1962

Norval A J, *The Tourist Industry*, Pitman 1931

Ogilvie F W, *The Tourist Movement*, Staples Press 1933

Opperman M and Chon K-S, *Tourism in Developing Countries*, International Thomson Business Press 1997

Ousby I, *The Englishman's England: Taste, Travel and the Rise of Tourism*, CUP 1990

Owen G, *Accounting for Hospitality, Tourism and Leisure*, Pitman 1994

Page S J, *Transport for Tourism*, Routledge 1994

Page S J, *Urban Tourism*, Routledge 1995

Page S J and Getz D, *The Business of Rural Tourism:*

International Perspectives, International Thomson Business Press 1997

Pape R, 'Touristry – a Type of Occupational Mobility' in *Social Problems*, 2/4 Spring 1964

Pattullo P, *Last Resorts: The Cost of Tourism in the Caribbean*, Cassell 1996

Pearce D, *Tourism Today: A Geographical Analysis*, Longman 2nd edn 1995

Pearce D, *Tourist Development*, Longman, 2nd edn 1989

Pearce D, *Tourism Organisations*, Longman 1992

Pearce D and Butler R W (eds), *Tourism Research: Critiques and Challenges*, Routledge 1992

Pearce P L, *The Social Psychology of Tourist Behaviour*, Pergamon 1982

Pearce P L, Moscardo G M and Ross G F, *Tourism Community Relationships*, Elsevier Science 1997

Peters M, *International Tourism*, Hutchinson 1969

Phipps D, *The Management of Aviation Security*, Pitman 1991

Pimlott J A R, *The Englishman's Holiday*, Harvester Press 1976

Pizam A and Mansfield Y (eds), *Tourism, Crime and International Security Issues*, Wiley 1995

Plog S, *Leisure Travel: Making it a Growth Market Again!*, John Wiley 1991

Pompl W and Lavery P, *Tourism in Europe: Structures and Development*, CAB International 1993

Pond K L, *The Professional Guide: Dynamics of Tour Guiding*, van Nostrand Reinhold 1993

Poon A, *Tourism, Technology and Competitive Strategies*, CAB International 1993

Poustie M, Clarke A, Stewart W and Ross J, *Hospitality and Tourism Law*, International Thomson Business Press 1996

Powers T, *Marketing Hospitality*, Wiley 1990

Poynter J, *Foreign Independent Tours: Planning, Pricing and Processing*, Delmar 1989

Poynter J, *Tour Design, Marketing and Management*, Prentice Hall 1993

Poynter J M, *How to Research and Write a Thesis in Hospitality and Tourism: A Step by Step Guide for College Students*, Wiley 1993

Prentice R, *Tourism and Heritage Attractions*, Routledge 1993

Price M (ed.), *People and Tourism in Fragile Environments*, Wiley 1996

Priestley G K, Edwards J A and Coccossis H (eds), *Sustainable Tourism? European Experiences*, CAB International 1996

Quest M, *Horwath Book of Tourism*, Horwath Consulting 1990

Rafferty M D, *A Geography of World Tourism*, Prentice Hall 1993

Rapoport R and R N, 'Four Themes in the Sociology of Leisure', *British Journal of Sociology*, vol. XXV/2 June 1974

Reader I and Walter T (eds), *Pilgrimage in Popular Culture*, Macmillan 1993

Reason J, *Man in Motion: The Psychology of Travel*, George Weidenfeld and Nicolson 1974

Renshaw, M B, *The Travel Agent*, Business Education Publishers 1992

Richards B, *How to Market Tourism Attractions, Festivals and Special Events*, Longman 1992

Richards G, *Case Studies in Tourism Management*, PNL Press 1991

Richards G, *Cultural Tourism in Europe*, CAB International 1996

Ritchie J R Brent and Goeldner C (eds), *Travel, Tourism and Hospitality Research: A Handbook for Managers and Researchers*, John Wiley, 2nd edn 1994

Robinson M, Evans N and Callaghan P (eds), *Culture as the Tourist Product*, Business Education Publishers 1996

Robinson M, Evans N and Callaghan P (eds), *Managing Cultural Resources for the Tourist*, Business Education Publishers 1996

Robinson M, Evans N and Callaghan P (eds), *Tourism and Cultural Change*, Business Education Publishers 1996

Robinson M, Evans N and Callaghan P (eds), *Tourism and Culture: Image, Identity and Marketing*, Business Education Publishers 1996

Rogers H A and Slinn J, *Tourism: Management of Facilities*, Pitman 1993

Rojek C, *Ways of Escape: Modern Transformations in Leisure and Travel*, Macmillan 1993

Rojek C, *Decentring Leisure: Rethinking Leisure Theory*, Sage 1995

Rosenow J and Pulsipher G L, *Tourism: The Good, the Bad and the Ugly*, Century Three Press 1979

Ross G F, *The Psychology of Tourism: Australian Studies in Tourism No 1*, Hospitality Press 1994

Rutherford D, *Introduction to the Conventions, Expositions and Meetings Industry*, Van Nostrand Reinhold 1990

Ryan C, *Recreational Tourism: A Social Science Perspective*, Routledge 1991

Ryan C, *Tourism, Terrorism and Violence*, Research Institute for the Study of Conflict and Terrorism, London 1991

Ryan C, *Researching Tourist Satisfaction: Issues, Concepts, Problems*, Routledge 1995

Ryan C (ed.), *The Tourist Experience: a New Introduction*, Cassell 1997

Sampson A, *Empires of the Sky: The Politics, Contests and Cartels of World Airlines*, Hodder and Stoughton 1984

Searle M, *Bathing Machines and Bloomers*, Midas 1977

Seaton A V and Bennett M, *Marketing Tourism Products: Concepts, Issues, Cases*, International Thomson Business Press 1996

Seaton A V, Jenkins C L, Wood R C, Dieke P U C, Bennett M M, MacLellan L R and Smith R (eds), *Tourism: The State of the Art*, Wiley 1994

Seddon S, *Travel*, Alan Sutton/Thomas Cook 1991

Selwyn T, *The Tourism Image: Myths and Myth Making in Tourism*, Wiley 1996

Shackley M, *Wildlife Tourism*, International Thomson Business Press 1996

Shackley M (ed.), *Visitor Management: Case Studies from Cultural World Heritage Sites*, Butterworth Heinemann 1997

Sharpley R, *Tourism, Tourists and Society*, Elm Publications 1994

Sharpley R, *Tourism and Leisure in the Countryside*, Elm Publications, 2nd edn 1996

Sharpley R and J, *Rural Tourism: An Introduction*, International Thomson Business Press 1997

Shaw C and Chase M (eds), *The Imagined Past: History and Nostalgia*, Manchester University Press 1989

Shaw G and Williams A M, *Critical Issues in Tourism: A Geographical Perspective*, Blackwell 1994

Shaw G and Williams A M (eds), *The Rise and Fall of British Coastal Tourism: Cultural and Economic Perspectives*, Mansell 1997

Shaw S, *Air Transport: A Marketing Perspective*, Pitman 1981

Shaw S, *Airline Marketing and Management*, Pitman, 3rd edn 1990

Sigaux G, *History of Tourism*, Leisure Arts 1966

Sillitoe A, *Leading the Blind: A Century of Guide Book Travel 1815–1914*, Macmillan 1995

Sinclair M (ed.), *Gender, Work and Tourism*, Routledge 1997

Sinclair M and Stabler W (eds), *The Tourism Industry: An International Analysis*, CAB International 1991

Sixsmith M (ed.), *Touring Exhibitions: The Touring Exhibitions Group's Manual of Good Practice*, Butterworth Heinemann 1995

Smith S L J, *Tourism Analysis: A Practical Handbook for Students*, Longman, 2nd edn 1995

Smith V (ed.), *Hosts and Guests: An Anthropology of Tourism*, Blackwell 1992

Smith V L and Eadington W R, *Tourism Alternatives: Potentials and Problems in the Development of Tourism*, Wiley 1994

Soane J V N, *Fashionable Resort Regions: Their Evolution and Transformation*, CAB International 1993

Somerville C, *Britain beside the Sea*, Grafton 1990

Stokes H G, *The Very First History of the English Seaside*, Sylvan Press 1947

Studd R G, *The Holiday Story*, Percival Marshall 1948

Stutts A, *The Travel Safety Handbook*, Van Nostrand Reinhold 1990

Sutton W A, 'Travel and Understanding: Notes on the Social Structure of Touring', *International Journal of Comparative Sociology*, vol. 8/2, 1967

Swarbrooke J, *The Development and Management of Visitor Attractions*, Butterworth Heinemann 1995

Swinglehurst E, *The Romantic Journey: The Story of Thomas Cook and Victorian Travel*, Pica 1974

Swinglehurst E, *Cook's Tours: The Story of Popular Travel*, Blandford Press 1982

Syme G J, *The Planning and Evaluation of Hallmark Events*, Gower 1989

Syratt G, *Manual of Travel Agency Practice*, Butterworth Heinemann, 2nd edn 1995

Taylor D, *Fortune, Fame and Folly: British Hotels and Catering from 1878 to 1978*, Caterer and Hotelkeeper 1977

Taylor J, *A Dream of England: Landscape Photography and the Tourist Imagination*, OUP 1994

Teare R, Calver S and Costa J, *Hospitality and Tourism Marketing Management*, Cassell 1994

Teare R, Calver S, Mazanec J and Crawford Welch S, *Marketing in Hospitality and Tourism: A Consumer Focus*, Cassell 1994

Teare R and Ingram H, *Strategic Management: a Resource-based Approach for the Hospitality and Tourism Industries*, Cassell 1993

Theobald W (ed.), *Global Tourism: The Next Decade*, Butterworth Heinemann 1995

Thomas R (ed.), *The Hospitality Industry, Tourism and Europe: Perspectives on Policies*, Cassell 1996

Toffler A, *Future Shock*, Bodley Head 1970

Towner J, *An Historical Geography of Recreation and Tourism in the Western World 1540–1940*, John Wiley 1996

Tribe J, *The Economics of Leisure and Tourism: Environments, Markets and Impacts*, Butterworth Heinemann 1995

Tribe J, *Corporate Strategy for Tourism*, International Thomson Business Press 1997

Tunbridge J E and Ashworth G, *Dissonant Heritage*, Wiley 1995

Turner L and Ash J, *The Golden Hordes: International Tourism and the Pleasure Periphery*, Constable 1975

Urry J, *The Tourist Gaze: Leisure and Travel in Contemporary Societies*, Sage Publications 1990

Urry J, *Consuming Places*, Routledge 1995

Uysal M (ed.), *Global Tourist Behaviour*, International Business Press 1994

Uysal M and Fesenmaier D (eds), *Communication and Channel Systems in Tourism Marketing*, Haworth Press 1993

Uzzell D (ed.), *Heritage Interpretation*, Vol. 1, *The Natural and Built Environment*; Vol. 2, *The Visitor Experience*, Belhaven Press 1989

Vallois F, *International Tourism: An Economic Perspective*, Macmillan 1995

Veal A J, *Research Methods for Leisure and Tourism*, 2nd edn Longman 1997

Vellas F and Bécherel L, *International Tourism*, Macmillan 1995

Vergo P (ed.), *The New Museology*, Reaktion Books 1989

Vladimir A, *The Complete Travel Marketing Handbook*, NTC Business Books 1988

Voase R, *Tourism: The Human Perspective*, Hodder and Stoughton 1995

Vukonic B, *Tourism and Religion*, Elsevier Science 1997

Waldren J, *Insiders and Outsiders: Paradise and Reality in Majorca*, Berghan 1997

Wall G and Mathieson A, *Tourism: Change, Impacts and Opportunities*, Longman, 2nd edn 1997

Walsh K, *The Representation of the Past: Museums and Heritage in the Post-Modern World*, Routledge 1992

Walsh-Heron J and Stevens T, *The Management of Visitor Attractions and Events*, National Publishers 1990

Walton J K, *The English Seaside Resort: A Social History 1750–1914*, University of Leicester Press 1983

Walton J K and Walvin J, *Leisure in Britain 1780–1939*, Manchester University Press 1983

Walvin J, *Beside the Seaside: A Social History of the Popular Seaside Holiday*, Allen Lane 1978

Ward C and Hardy D, *Goodnight Campers! The History of the British Holiday Camps*, Mansell 1986

Watt D, *Leisure and Tourism Event Management and Organisation Manual*, Longman 1992

Weiler B and Hall C M (eds), *Special Interest Tourism*, Belhaven Press 1992

Wells A T, *A Casebook for Air Transportation*, Wadsworth 1990

Wells A T, *Air Transportation: A Management Perspective*, Wadsworth 3rd edn 1994

Weston S A, *Commercial Recreation and Tourism: An Introduction to Business Oriented Recreation*, Brown and Benchmark 1996

Wheatcroft S, *Aviation and Tourism Policies*, Routledge 1994

Williams A and Shaw G (eds), *Tourism and Economic Development: Western European Experiences*, Wiley, 2nd edn 1991

Williams G, The *Airline Industry and the Impact of Deregulation*, Avebury Aviation/Ashgate Publishing, 1994

Wilson A, *The Culture of Nature: North American Landscape from Disney to the Exxon Valdez*, Blackwell 1992

Witt S F, Brooke M Z and Buckley P J, *The Management of International Tourism*, Unwin Hyman, 2nd edn 1995

Witt S F and Moutinho L, *Tourism Marketing and Management Handbook*, Prentice Hall, 2nd edn 1994

Witt S F and Witt C A, *Modeling and Forecasting Demand in Tourism*, Academic Press 1992

Wood K and House S, *The Good Tourist*, Mandarin 1991

World Tourism Organisation, *Global Distribution Systems*, WTO 1996

Wright P, *On Living in an Old Country: The National Past in Contemporary Britain*, Verso 1985

Yale P, *From Tourist Attractions to Heritage Tourism*, Elm Publications 1991

Yale P, *Tourism in the UK: A Basic Textbook*, Elm Publications 1991

Yale P, *The Business of Tour Operations*, Longman 1995

Yaqub Z and Bedford B (eds), *European Travel Law*, Wiley 1996

Yeoman I and Ingold A (eds), *Yield Management: Strategies for the Service Industries*, Cassell 1997

Youell R, *Tourism: Introduction Frameworks*, International Thomson Business Press 1997

Young G, *Tourism: Blessing or Blight?*, Pelican 1973

Zurick D, *Errant Journeys: Adventure Travel in a Modern Age*, University of Texas Press, 1995

Key trade, professional and academic magazines and journals of relevance to travel and tourism

ABTA News	monthly	*Leisure, Recreation and Tourism Abstracts*	
AIEST Tourist Review (Revue de Tourisme)		(CAB International)	quarterly
(Switzerland)	quarterly	*Leisure Studies* (Leisure Studies Association)	quarterly
Airline World	weekly	*Motor Transport Weekly*	weekly
Annals of Tourism Research (USA)	quarterly	*Progress in Tourism and Hospitality*	
ASTA Travel News (USA)	monthly	*Research*	quarterly
British Travel Brief (BTA)	quarterly	*Revue de l'Academie Internationale du*	
British Traveller	monthly	*Tourisme*	3 per year
Buses	monthly	*Service Industries Journal*	Mar/Jul/Nov
Business Traveller	10 p a	*Tourism* (Bulletin of the Tourism Society)	quarterly
Business Travel World	monthly	*Tourism, Culture and Communication*	quarterly
Coaching Journal and Bus Review	monthly	*Tourism Enterprise* (ETB)	monthly
Countryside Commission News	monthly	*Tourism Intelligence Quarterly* (BTA)	quarterly
Executive Travel	monthly	*Tourism Management*	quarterly
Executive World (British Airways)	monthly	*Transport* (CIT)	bi-monthly
Flight International	weekly	*Transport Management* (ITA)	quarterly
Holiday Which? (Consumers Association)	quarterly	*Transport Reviews*	quarterly
ICAO Bulletin	monthly	*Travel Agency*	bi-monthly
In Britain (BTA)	monthly	*Travel and Tourism Analyst* (EIU)	quarterly
Insights (ETB)	monthly	*Travel Business Analyst*	10 p a
International Tourism Quarterly(EIU)	quarterly	*Travel GBI*	monthly
Journal of Air Transport Management	quarterly	*Travel Industry Monitor* (EIU)	quarterly
Journal of the ITT	quarterly	*Travel Research Journal*	quarterly
Journal of Leisure Research	quarterly	*Travel Trade Gazette*	weekly
Journal of Sustainable Tourism	quarterly	*Travel Trade Gazette Europa* (Continental	
Journal of Tourism Studies (Australia)	quarterly	edition)	weekly
Journal of Transport Economics and		*Travel Weekly*	weekly
Policy	Jan/May/Sept	*World Travel (Tourisme Mondiale)* (WTO)	bi-monthly
Journal of Travel Research (USA)	quarterly		

Index